THE KARJALA STORY

Revolution, War, and Wonder

The History of Karelia
As seen through my families eyes

ISBN
978-1-77370-180-6 (Hardcover)
978-1-77370-179-0 (Paperback)

This book is dedicated to:

My father for starting me on this journey
My mother and my uncles in gratitude for the sacrifices
they made and the joy they brought
My cousin Sirkka in remembrance of her unflagging love for Karjala
The soldiers of Finland for their valiant protection of Karjala and Finland
To my children and grandchildren, lest they forget

and

To all the people – current and past – of Karjala

Introduction

This book is the story of Karjala (Karelia) from prehistory to after World War II as seen through the eyes of my family. As Karjala was an integral part of Finland the book is also an outline of Finnish history. And as Karjala was the battleground between Finland and Russia, it is a military history. It is also a "cultural" history as the book looks at the epic, and enchanting, history of Karjala from a human perspective.

Few people outside of Finland know about Karjala, its' people and its' history. I have not been able to find a book in English on the history of Karjala – for that matter very few in Finnish. The story is as fascinating as it is little known.

Karjala (In English Karelia) is the part of Finland that was lost to Russia in World War II. Karjala stretches from St Petersburg to the White Sea on the eastern side of present day Finland. From pre historic times the Karjalainen people had been part of Finland – genetically, ethnically, and linguistically. For 800 years, from the time of the Vikings to the modern age, Karjala served as the battle ground between the West and the East - initially in wars between Sweden and Russia, and then in wars between Finland and Russia.

All nonetheless was not grief and sorrow. The Karjalaiset maintained a welcoming and joyous attitude to life. Their capital city of Viipuri was known as the Paris of the North – a vibrant merchant city of art and culture - the streets resounding with Finnish, Swedish, Russian and German.

While multi-lingual, Karjala and Viipuri was overwhelmingly Finnish. It is no longer. During the Winter War and Continuation War all the population fled when Karjala was lost to Russia in the peace settlement. The enchanting architectural gem of a city – Viipuri – was destroyed during the war. Over the last 70 years it has been slowly repopulated with people from throughout the Soviets. It still retains the scars of the war - new houses and derelict buildings side by side. But it still retains a special beauty.

While this book is about a "nations" history, I have woven that history around my families' stories. My family roots go back 500 years in Finland and Karjala. Both my parents were from Karjala, father from the city of Viipuri and mother from the nearby farming community of Kavantsaari. I have combined historical facts with family lore, family memoirs, original manuscripts, and excerpts from classical as well as less known Finnish books. I include many photos in an endeavor to bring the story to life - family photos, Finnish military photos, and images of classical Finnish art.

The first portion of the book covers the periods from Prehistory and the age of Kalevala, through 600 years of Swedish and Russian wars, the Finnish Civil War (during the Bolshevik Revolution), and the sunshine years before WW II. To bring life to the story, I draw upon the Kalevala epic poem, ancestral family ties from the 1500s, my fathers' written memoirs of life as a boy in Viipuri during the Revolution, the official state records of grandfathers' Civil War trial, as well as my family memories and many historical reference books. The renowned epic trilogy Under the

North Star by Vaino Linna provided me with a complement to, and validation of, my own familics' memories.

The second part of the book deals with the Winter War of 1939-1940 between Russia and Finland – from the viewpoint of both the men and the womenfolk. The battle front was our homeland in Karjala. I provide a historical overview of the military campaigns and politics; and trace my fathers and my five uncles' life on the battlefront; and, the flight of my grandparents, mother, aunts and children from our home. The four volume Talvisota Historia provided me with a definitive and detailed resource base on the war. My father and my uncles having lived the horror of the war never talked about it. I was however able to follow their lives on the front based on the official diaries of their units' officer (sota paiva kirja) and through books on their regiments. In recounting the flight of the womenfolk from home I was able to draw on my families' stories, my Uncle Erkki's letters home from the front, and the written memoirs of my cousin Sirkka. The Finnish classic, Kollaa Kestaa, by Lieutenant E Pololampi provided an eloquent first hand narrative of life on the front lines.

The last part of the book deals with the Continuation War of 1941 – 1944 between Finland and Russia and the subsequent short Lapland War against Germany. Again I provide a historical military and political framework - this time provided by the six volume Jatkosota Historia. As for the Winter War section, I trace the men's lives on the front through the war (including the epic battles of Ihantala and Ayrapaa, and the loss of Viipuri); and my families' flight ("evakkomatka") from Karjala. Here the classical novel Unkown Soldier by Vaino Linna was an inspiration. He served in the same regiment as Uncle Vilho. As well I am indebted to Lieutenant K Mietteinen's recounting of his combat engineer (Pioneeri) experiences during the war. Uncle Arvo served with Lieutenant Mietteinen in his platoon.

I wish to thank the Finnish National Archives (Kansallis Arkisto) and the Sota-Arkisto for usage of their photos (SA Kuva) and records. They have a vast repository of historical material - digitized no less, and available through the internet. I was able to retrieve my families genealogical records; the transcript of the Wiipuri Court of Crimes Against The State for my grandfather; and a vast number of Finnish military records. The military repository included the officers journals (sota paiva kirjat), the military records of my father and my uncles (kantakortti), and wartime photos (SA Kuva). Without the kantakortti I would not have had any way of knowing which units my uncles served with and when. It would have been only: "somewhere east of Lake Ladoga" and "on the Kannas".

I wish to thank my extended family for their stories– in particular cousin Sirkka with whom I conversed with at length, and who shared her memoirs of the war years and the flight from our cherished Karjala home.

While I have diligently endeavored to keep the history facts accurate, I have undoubtedly made some errors and omissions given the breadth of over 2000 years of history and the depth of the presentation on the Talvisota and Jatkosota. For any such errs and omissions, I apologize.

I intend to visit Karjala and Viipuri again. I hope you do as well. It is a beautiful and enchanting area. While drenched with blood and history, it also resounds with the joy of life and the echoes of culture and civilization.

I hope you enjoy this book on my Karjala.

Karl Armas Tuira
September, 2017
Oakville, Canada

KARJALA

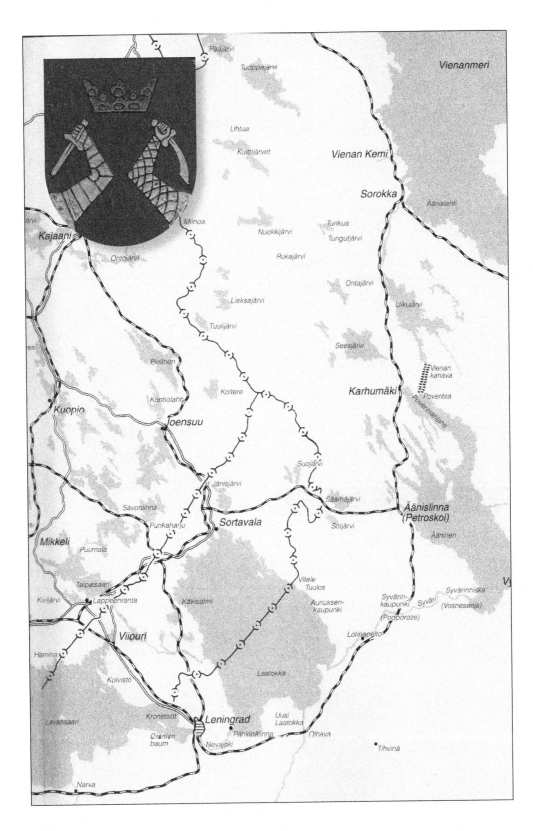

Table of Contents

PRELUDE
Going Home

BOOK I
Karjala - The Early Years

PART I: A Historical Interlude Suomi
and Karjala's Early Years

BOOK II
The Talvi Sota
"The Winter War"

PART IV: Talvisota, a Military Summary

BOOK III
"Jatkosota"
The Continuation War

PART VII: An Uneasy Peace

PART VIII: War Returns

PART IX: The Summer Assault 1941

PART XV: The Home Front during The Summer of '44

PART XVI: Peace

PART XVII: The Lapland War

PART XVIII: After the War

SEQUEL
Returning "Home" to Karjala

APPENDICES

PRELUDE
Going Home

Going Home

Ahh, thank god, finally across the border – three and a half hours in queues, passport control and customs leaving Finland and entering Russia– and that with my passport and Russian visa in perfect order ...

The old Mercedes purred quietly as Reima drove towards Viipuri – Arto and myself hanging out the windows...only 50 kilometres away my father had said – the signs in Cyrillic certainly didn't help any.

Nondescript fields mostly hidden by trees anxiously went by. Down an embankment edged by old cut stones, around a curve, and suddenly ...there it was – Viipuri !!my breath stopped, my heart melted...the ageless castle raising out of the bay, the church towers and old city buildings beckoning in the afternoon sun beyond the bridge.

The magical city of Viipuri - the home of my father and my mother – the subject of many emotional time shrouded stories of blood, battle and beauty. Viipuri and Karjala, Finland's bastion against the east. Viipuri and its' people melded together on the hearth of history. A thousand years of tears and joy - Swedish, then Russian, occasionally Hanseatic, today again Russian, but forever Finnish.

For a thousand years, the castle has glimmered and glowed on its' island – nurturing and protecting its' town folk and the land of Karjala. Karjala,

- The home of the Karelian people since time immemorial
- Swedens' bulwark against the east for four hundred years
- A bastion of Russian might for two hundred years
- The pride of Finland for fifty years
- The setting of Russian rule for seventy years – but this time with a difference.

If only the stone walls could speak, what stories would they tell ? Would they be as mystic, as magic, as memorable, as the stories of my mother and father ?

A Brief History of Viipuri

Viipuri's history is long and colourful.

Now where is that official brochure I found that the Viipuri town council published in 1933 – eighty years ago ? It has a nice short summary ...ahhh here it is:

The historical records and traditions of Viipuri go back very far indeed. Over a thousand years have elapsed since the founding of the first settlements in the locality. In those early days a port and trading centre arose at the mouth of the western branch of the River Vuoksi. This Old Viipuri is believed to have been situated where Monrepos Park now lies, a couple of kilometres north of present day Viipuri. In the ninth century it appears to have been protected by ramparts.

The castle was founded in 1293 by Torgils Knutsson, Constable of Sweden, who arrived at the head of a crusading fleet. As the fore post of Swedish power and western civilisation the settlement, which guarded an important trade route, had frequently to endure the hardships of war. In the Middle Ages it was besieged by the Russians in 1294, 1322, 1351, 1411 and 1495; the last mentioned year is the date of the Big Bang of Viipuri, an explosion engineered by the commander of the defending forces, Knut Posse, to scare away the attackers.

The town of Viipuri is mentioned in records of the fourteenth century, but it was not until 1403 that the settlement received its town charter, being then situated on the site of the present old town, the rocky point south of the castle. During the period 1457—81 the town was provided with walls dominated by numerous towers and pierced by gates. Other fortifications followed during the reigns of the Swedish kings Erik XIV (1560—68), Johan III (1568—92) and Karl IX (1599-1611). In the sixteen-fifties the first town plan was drawn up, turning the Viipuri of those days into a beautiful town with many fine buildings of stone.

Through the Middle Ages mighty feudal lords ruled over Viipuri much as they liked. They even waged wars on their own behalf, concluded peace treaties, and were otherwise actively engaged in high politics. "Wiborgswelde" or "Terra Viburgensisi" is often mentioned in records of those days on equal terms with the Swedish realm. It could even become necessary on occasion to send the Royal army to subdue a mutinous vassal holding Viipuri.

The early history of Viipuri does not, however, lack interest also from the point of view of peaceful interests. It was ruled at one time by the most learned man in the whole kingdom: Kaarle Ulfsson Sparre (1386—94 and 96—99), and during the reign of Krister Nilsson (1418—42) it was the centre where the leading political strivings of North Europe met and clashed, and where important peace councils were held. As early as the beginning of the sixteenth century, Erik Turesson Bjelke was already planning a canal from the Gulf of Finland to Lake Saimaa.

The lords of Viipuri castle did not neglect to reveal their high station in outward pomp, proof of which is the brilliant court life many of them knew how to maintain. Not for nothing were noble youths sent at one time from Sweden to Viipuri — to learn fine manners. Nor, doubtless, was Gustavus I misinformed in declaring that in no other Swedish or Finnish castle was life lived on such a grand scale as in Viipuri. The period of the greatest magnificence was reached during the rule of Karl Knutsson Bonde (1442 —48), who subsequently ascended the throne of Sweden, and Count Johan Hoya (1525—32).

Meanwhile the swords of the mighty lords of the castle were not allowed to rust. As we have mentioned, this important stronghold had frequently to be defended against attacking hordes, and time after time the enemy was driven off with sore losses. In the words of a medieval poet: "Moscorumbusta Viburgum" (Viipuri is the Muscovite's grave). From the very beginning commerce formed the chief means of livelihood of Viipuri's inhabitants, and many of the feudal lords did their best to develop trade with the town. In the Middle Ages, however, commerce in this quarter was mostly in the hands of German Hansa merchants, who traded chiefly with Tallin, but also with Danzig, Lubeck, and — eastward — with Novgorod.

Franciscan and Dominican monasteries kept alive and spread the influence of the Roman Catholic Church.

The period of Viipuri's history with which we have been dealing has been termed the feudal or Hansa period. It was followed, from the reign of Gustavus Vasa (1523—60) to the Peace of Stolbova (1617) by what has been called the period of crisis, during which the reigning kings broke the previously unrestricted might of the feudal lords, and the German merchants lost their dominating position to purely Finnish burghers. Trade flourished exceptionally well and great fleets of merchant vessels filled the harbour.

After the Reformation the town was made a Bishop's seat, the first Bishop of Viipuri being nominated in 1554.

After the hostilities between King Sigismund and the Duke Karl were at an end, the latter entered the town at the head of a large force and put a number of Sigismund's followers to death.

The period of crisis was succeeded by the Mercantile Period. Having secured the privileges of a staple town, Viipuri, now fairly far from the frontier after the Peace of Stolbova, soon developed into the biggest commercial centre in Finland.

Viipuri was not, however, allowed to flourish in peace for long. Already in 1676 the burghers were called upon to drive off enemy forces which had appeared before the town walls. In 1706, during the Great Northern War, the town was again besieged. On that occasion it still withstood the attack, but in 1710 it fell to Emperor Peter, a heap of ruins after the brave defence put up by the inhabitants.

So began the period of Russian rule. Viipuri became the capital of the areas ceded to Russia at the Peace of Uusikaupunki (Nystad).

Four different nationalities were represented among the burghers, the German element dominating after its new rise to power during the Mercantile Period. Friction and party conflicts between the different elements were common. In other respects too, uncertainty and despotism marked the early part of the Russian period, causing a decline in the trade done by the town. The population, which had increased to 3,500 by the middle of the seventeenth century, fell to 1,400.

Being once again an important fortification — this time against the West — the defences of Viipuri were considerably enlarged by the Russians. For these new works so much land was ruthlessly appropriated that two-thirds of the inhabitants had to seek new homes. In this way originated the extensive suburbs outside of the ramparts.

Private building did not revive until the reign of the Empress Catharine II (1762—97). At that time a number of two-storied stone buildings were erected along the two streets called Linnankatu and Karjaportinkatu. In those days the square called UusiRaatihuoneentori and the Parade Ground were given their present form, and around them were built a number of public buildings still in existence today. Elsewhere too in the old part of the town architectural remains from bygone centuries have been preserved in spite of the fact that great fires caused much destruction in the years 1627, 1628, 1652, 1672, 1676, 1682 and 1790, often destroying the finest buildings in the town.

The year 1812 inaugurated a new and happier phase in the history of Viipuri. The sorely tried province was again united to the rest of Finland and after its long isolation was able to develop parallel with the rest of Finland. Viipuri became the capital of the provincial administration. Its new development was rapid. In 1839 came the founding of the Viipuri Court of Appeal, in 1856 the opening of the Saimaa Canal, in 1870 the completion of the Riihimaki—St. Petersburg railway passing through Viipuri, and in 1894 the opening of the Carelian railway with its terminus at Viipuri. The town became an important railway junction, the administrative centre of East Finland and the seat of the cultural and commercial interests of the province.

Its area rapidly expanded. The walls and ramparts built in the Middle Ages and later by the Russians had to go. Only here and there was an historical relic of more than average value allowed to stand amid all the new that was rising. The old part of the town was left farther and farther from the main traffic routes. Wide main arteries were planned, land having in some cases to be reclaimed from the sea for these. Big business buildings arose where formerly the waters of the bay had rippled or on the site of former earthworks and kitchen gardens. The present business centre was laid out in 1861. The clearing of the main thoroughfare Torkkelinkatu was begun in 1871, the planting of the present magnificent Esplanade in 1862.

Viipuri had been born anew, and this latest curve of its development has continued, in spite of the prevailing depression, to this day. The rapid growth of the town imposed on the Town Fathers a number of serious municipal and economic problems, which had to be solved. After the state of stagnation brought about under Russian rule, Viipuri was compelled to undergo an enormous development within the space of a few decades. It was not really until Finland had become independent and the alien garrison was no more that the municipality was really free to handle its problems and bring the town on a level with the times.

As the biggest timber port in Europe the town had to set to work energetically to improve its harbours, 33,000,000 Finnmarks being spent on the outer harbour alone within two years. New municipal buildings representing the last word in modern hygiene and efficiency replaced the old. The new municipal hospital, tuberculosis sanatorium, abattoirs, the enormous technical school and other educational institutions, the poorhouse, mental asylum, child welfare centre, etc., are all buildings of which any town might be proud. The relaying of the streets to meet the demands of modern motor traffic and similar measures show the same spirit of municipal pride.

The heaviest burden on the municipal finances, however, has been the incorporation of the very extensive suburbs into the town area. This has been done by stages, the last areas being incorporated on January 1st 1933. The cost of these measures can be gauged from the fact that the immediate expenditure connected with the first stage nearly 43,000,000 Finnmarks and the annual burden on the municipal budget nearly 8,000,000 Finnmarks.

Once again, in the present century, Viipuri has been the scene of warfare. The first skirmishes in the Finnish War of Liberation took place here, but it was not until three months later, after a five-day siege, that the White Army, on April 29th 1918, finally captured the town.

In 1933 the Viipuri town council also talked proudly about the commerce in their city:

Present day Viipuri bears in its outward appearance traces of its varied and chequered history. It is a combination of old and new, delightful in its strangeness. Busy traffic in broad tree bordered streets and medieval perspectives of narrow old passages, splendour and homeliness, bold planning and small-scale intimacy. Historical memories everywhere, and beside these the newest manifestations of the modern spirit.

A feature peculiar to Viipuri, called into being by its centuries old, extensive business connections, is the liveliness and colourfulness of its atmosphere, a special character met with nowhere else in Finland. Commerce was the old life-nerve of the town. It is still that to-day. The routes of communication from the wide provinces of Carelia and Savo meet in Viipuri. And in the lively commerce of the town the Finnish element once again dominates. (Of the total population, 83 per cent are Finnish-speaking.)

Viipuri can with cause be called the capital of East Finland. The most varied strivings of this part of Finland all centre on Viipuri, through whose harbours the products of its wealth of forests reach the markets of the world and the greatest part of the imported goods needed arrive. In 1931 goods to a value of 784,200,000 marks were shipped abroad from Viipuri's harbours, including 386,900,000 marks for timber and wood goods and 365,900,000 marks for pulp and paper. The total trade passing through the town's harbours represented a value of 1,076,300,000 marks. Moreover, in these figures the effect of the world depression is visible. Two years earlier the total figure was 1,093,100,000 marks. In 1931 altogether 6,807 vessels passed through the Saimaa Canal, carrying goods to a weight of 597,184 tons. The corresponding figures for 1927 were 11,148 vessels and 997,185 tons.

In addition to its harbours Viipuri has an outer harbour at Uuras (Trangsund), widely known and with the biggest traffic of any harbour of its kind in Finland. It is situated about 12 kilometres from the town, along and around the Uuras Straits between the roads south-west of the town and the outer Viipuri Bay. Most of the timber exports are concentrated on this outer harbour, the largest export harbour in respect of size of traffic in all the Northern Countries. Here one meets with ships from all parts of the globe.

Imported goods are unloaded chiefly in the South Harbour, always a busy scene. Regular passenger routes connect Viipuri with the other South Finnish and Baltic ports. A few figures will show the dimensions of Viipuri's harbours. The total length of the quays is 6 1 / 2 kilometres at Uuras and 31/ 2 in the town proper. The harbours were visited in 1931 by 4,379 vessels, with an aggregate tonnage of 1,975,069 gross reg. tons. This was during the depression; for 1928 the figures are 7,205 vessels and 2,494,349 reg. tons. The total imports in 1931 weighed 293,207 tons, and exports were 377,348 tons and 975,732 cubic metres; in 1928 imports totalled 407,999 tons and exports 181,416 tons and 1,502,560 cubic metres.

Railways lead to Viipuri from five different directions. The great volume of traffic from the Saimaa Canal passes through the town harbours. Motorbuses, the new "highway trains", connect Viipuri with all parts of Carelia and lead out to the rest of Finland. In the town are a number of important banks, commercial houses and industrial institutions. The latter include sawmills, engineering works, tobacco, soap, candle, matches, margarine, meat canning, confectionery, clothing and leather factories, breweries, etc.

As the capital of the county the town naturally contains a number of public offices. The Governor resides here, and here are also the various county administration offices. The Court of Appeal will soon be able to celebrate its centenary. The Bishop's Seat and Council have again been transferred from Savonlinna (Nyslott) to Viipuri. Societies, associations, clubs, etc., are very numerous. Viipuri enjoys a high reputation as a centre of athletics and gymnastics, and is especially famous for its bandy team. Numerous clubs have their own training quarters. Educational institutions include ten schools leading to the University, a commercial school, an industrial school, schools for navigation, sawmill foremen, various trades and handiwork, a conservatoire and a college for church music, a school of music for the young and a People's Conservatoire, an art school, a workers' college, etc.

The town further owns an extensive lending library, an interesting museum and a fine new Art Museum splendidly situated on the old seaward ramparts.

A symphony orchestra gives concerts in the winter, when the Municipal Theatre also gives performances.

The hospitals are especially good and well worth visiting by specialists in this field. In general close attention has been paid to hygiene and health; the town's water-system is drawn from deep artesian wells yielding a crystal-clear pure water. The biggest sports ground is in the Papula Park. A plan exists for a modern Stadium, work on which has already been begun. Skating, skiing and the sleigh-run at Papula provide recreation in the winter.

From the military point of view Viipuri is one of the most important garrisons in the country. Soldiers are indeed in evidence everywhere, and there are barracks and other military buildings on every side of the town.

Four newspapers serve the town and province, viz., Karjala (every day including Sundays), Kansan Tyo (six days a week), Maakansa (six days a week) and Viborgs Nyheter (three times a week).

Tourists will find Viipuri a very pleasant place, especially in the summer. The site of the town, almost surrounded as it is by water, and the nature of the ground, together make for a pleasing general view. The old town with its pretty vistas and historical relics, and in contrast to these broad new thoroughfares and leafy esplanades, the fine parks with open-air music in various parts of the town, and the busy life of the market-places and harbours, guarantee the widest range of impressions. As, in addition, there is no lack of good hotels and restaurants, the tourist can be sure of finding everything necessary to his welfare.

The rosy world of the town fathers lasted only another 6 years before the relentless cycle of history once more battered Viipuri.

In November 1939 Viipuri and Karjala once more felt the tramp of soldiers' boots. Russia declared war (Known as the Talvisota, or Winter War) on Finland. Fierce fighting occurred throughout Karjala. Viipuri, although heavily bombed and shelled, did not surrender. But with the peace settlement Finland lost Karjala. The Finnish forces marched out of the city and Karjala – not just the troops - but the entire population of Karjala -400,000 people- left. Home, although priceless, was not worth the price of life long slavery under Stalin.

As in times of yore, after a short truce, in June 1941 Finland and Russia were at war again (This war was known as the Jatkosota or Continuation War). The Finns attacked aggressively and successfully to take back their homeland – marching into Viipuri once more in August 1941. Although the city had suffered extensive destruction, Viipuri castle was intact. The people of Karjala moved back home.

But in June 1944 they fled again, as the Russians advanced up the Isthmus. Finland and Russia signed a peace treaty – the terms of which included once more surrendering Karjala to Russia – back to the borders of Peter the Greats' peace treaty of 1721.

As all the population had fled, Stalin settled Viipuri and Karjala with peoples from far flung parts of his empire. People without the slightest ties to Karjala or Finland. The city was allowed to deteriorate – the bombed and burned out buildings remained – derelict and forlorn.

In 1990, Viipuri became part of the Leningrad district and slow restoration of the city started. Indeed Viipuri was declared a Russian Heritage City.

What would I, being of Viipuri heritage, think ?

A Town of Historical Landmarks

We drove across the bridge onto the cobble stone streets of the city. After driving in circles, meaninglessly comparing my 1935 Finnish map names with the Cyrillic street signs, we finally checked into our little hotel in the old town.

We wandered the old cobble stone streets – beautiful yet strangely empty. The Jungen buildings, the medieval church towers and churches. Interspersed with Soviet era concrete block buildings built in place of the structures destroyed in the bombing and artillery attacks of the Talvi and Jatkosota wars.

Viipuri was a multi-cultural and multi lingual city. The population of Viipuri always had a mix of Finnish, Swedish, German and Russian inhabitants. The population grew slowly after the castles establishment in 1293, reaching 3,500 in 1650, and the dropping down to 1,400 in the first decades of Russian rule. During these years the population figure did not include the military forces, which dependant on which war, and which campaign, swelled to over 20,000.

In 1812, shortly after Finland became a Russian Grand Duchy, 3,000 people lived in Vyborg - 42% Finnish, 28% Russian, 13% Swedish and 12.5% German. In 1850 the population of 8,500 was 32% Russian. By 1910 the population had exploded to 48,000 -a reflection of the work brought by the completion of the Saimaa canal. Finns now comprised 80% of the population, Russians 11%, Swedes 6.5%, and Germans 1%.

Yet the city remained fully multi-lingual. My dad had said that when one walked the streets one could hear Finnish, Swedish, German and Russian – and indeed he himself spoke all four languages – some of course better than others. Actually there was a Viipuri language which was an amalgamation of all the languages – depending on who you were conversing with, you used more or fewer loan words of a particular language. Linguistic purity was not something that was allowed to be a barrier in communicating.

Now, when I tried Finnish, English, French, or even a few words of German – "nyet"; and either a bright smile or a stolid stare. Except of course in the Market Hall where the shop keepers, as in the days of yore, spoke Finn and even a bit of English; or else we just managed to communicate with the universal language of commerce - shaking the head, pointing, nodding, and showing American $$ bills.

Viipuri was a medieval walled city – but where were the walls ? Certainly there are churches and church ruins in the old town which reflected Viipuri's multi-cultural heritage and the march of history.

- The ruins of the original Lutheran Church – its' KelloTorni tower still standing
- The Orthodox Cathedral of the Transfiguration of Christ in Raatihuoneen Tori
- The Finnish Tuomiokirkko Lutheran Cathedral – now just levelled stone and grass.
- The Swedish and German Lutheran church - Pietari-Paavalin Kirkko in Paraatikentta square
- The ruins of the old Catholic Dominican monastery (Luostari) with its' RaatiTorni tower
- The small Catholic Pyhan Hyacinthuksen kirkko – in 1403 the Franciscan monastery
- Even a synagogue at 31 Kalevankatu

Looking up Vodnaya Street in the old town, I catch sight of an old white tower on the crest of the hill at the end of the street. As I walk up the narrow cobble stoned street, the

tower beckons me onwards, as it has done for the people of Viipuri for centuries.

Scarred white tower standing firm, green copper roof, open belfry, old clock.

The KelloTorni, now just an architectural landmark, has borne witness to the story of Viipuri for the last 500 years.

Initially the tower was the belfry of the old Vyborg Catholic Pyhan Marian and Pyhan Olavin Church. The church and belfry were built with the funds of parishioners who in return were promised absolution for 7 years of sins (A much better return than today's tax deduction for charitable donations ... you think?).

When the Reformation took hold in Finland in 1554, the Roman Catholic vestments were discarded and the church magically became the Lutheran Church. Mikael Agricola, Vyborg schooled, student of Luther, founder of the Finnish written language, and prominent proponent of the Protestant Reformation was said to be buried under the church floor in 1557. Unfortunately the church and its' floor were destroyed and rebuilt many times in the following 400 years, so whether Agricola was buried there is still unconfirmed.

The high tower has a magnificent view of Viipuri. A view which was put to good use in the 1600s - the tower serving as a fire lookout. In the 1600s the tightly packed old city suffered many devastating fires.

And many bombardments, including that of Peter the Great. When Peter conquered the city in 1710, the old church had another change of heart – now becoming a devoted Greek Orthodox – but not before doing some penance. Before it became the Vyborg Orthodox church, the church served as the stables for Peters' cavalry horses for a few years.

With the advance of time, a clock was installed in 1753 below the tower bells. The bell tower became known as the Clock Tower, or KelloTorni.

As well as Peter the Great, Catherine the Great visited Vyborg. Catherine was in a more benevolent mood though, as Vyborg was now the capital of Russian Old Finland. She donated a set of new tower bells to the city in 1796. Although I did not hear them, the bells apparently toll still today...

Catherine the Great was however not content to worship in a small church, even one with wonderful bells. She commissioned a new Orthodox cathedral to be built. Upon the completion of the new Viipuri Orthodox Cathedral in Raatihuoneen Tori, the KelloTorni church fell into disuse. For the next 100 years the church became a mundane granary warehouse – the only worshippers being any rodents blessed enough to gain entrance.

By the time of the Finnish Civil War and the creation of the Finland as an independent country in December 1917, the population had increased and the Lutheran religion had again become the state religion. In 1919, the church was renovated and once more welcomed worshippers as the Lutheran Varuskunta Agricola Church.

I wonder if grandfather Georg's funeral in 1923 was held in this church ?

When the fierce Talvisota erupted in 1939 between Finland and Russia, the church became the Finnish army garrison's church.

It also served as the Viipuri field cemetery. The bodies of the slain soldiers lay in the depths of the church awaiting blessing and burial. A Russian bomb landed on the building destroying it and the bodies. A plaque placed there reads, " *In memory of the 108 fallen soldiers of the 1939-40 war who lie here.*" The memorial script is in Russian as well as Finnish.

From 1940 to today the church has remained in ruins.

But the KelloTorni still stands – a survivor of 500 years of battle, fire and religious fervour.

I continued down the slope towards the south harbour. There its' bronze green belfry glowing in the bright midsummer evening light, was the old RaatiTorni. Its' sturdy hexagon base cloaked in shadows reminded me that before it saw religion, the tower had been a defensive tower in the medieval town walls.

Soon, in 1481, it was put to multi-purpose use, serving both as a defensive tower and as the bell tower of the Dominican Monastery which was constructed beside it. The friars originally came to Vyborg in 1300. The first to come were the Franciscans, the grey brothers; followed by the Domincans, the black brothers.

Now nothing remains of the monastery except a roofless dilapidated shell surrounded by a car parking lot.

In the late 1500s, the Reformation transformed the monastery into the Swedish, Finnish, German Viipurin Maaseurakunta Lutheran Church. It was burnt and rebuilt many times. While remaining a Lutheran church, in 1799 the congregation became solely Finnish. In celebration in 1830 the church was refurbished and restored in a classical style.

The church and belfry stood in peace for a hundred years, until a Russian bomb hit and destroyed the church in 1939 during the Talvisota. The medieval tower remained intact but the church burnt to its' foundations. And in 1941 during the Jatkosota when Viipuri was recaptured, the belfry roof was destroyed.

The church was rebuilt and the belfry repaired by the Finns in 1942-43. This came to nought as with the loss of Karjala to Russia in the peace of 1944, Stalin's worshippers converted the church into an electrical devices factory. And in Viipuri tradition, it burnt once more in 1989.

Now there it stood, a sad, roofless, battered shell. But the old medieval tower still stood there -reaching for the last of the evening light - unperturbed, resolute, fully alive.

We walked in the light of mid summer evening rays back towards the centre of town. Only a block later we came upon a large cobble stoned square –the Raatihuoneen Tori - lined by old large well maintained five story buildings from the late 1700s. The square clean swept and empty, except for a white, onion domed cathedral.

Ahh, Catherine the Greats' Orthodox cathedral. In continuous use since it was commissioned by the Empress in 1793. The cloying heavy scented chant filled interior, graced by visits by Alexander I, Alexander II, Alexander III, and Nicholas I. Not a scratch nor a blister from the Talvi and Jatkosotas. The Russian bomb and artillery canon sights definitely had a Finnish focus.

Around the corner another cobbled square – the Paraatikentta - and a church – yellow and white with a solid bell cupola –the Swedish German Lutheran Church built in 1799 and initially called the Pietari – Paavali church after Tsar Peter the Great and Tsar Paulus I (1796-1801). By the 1800s each of Viipuri's linguistic groups had their own church – no need to check what time the Swedish, or Finnish, or German or Russian language service started. The Catholic church avoided the issue with a more universal solution – conducting all its' services in Latin.

To the side of the square was a statue – a bust of Mikael Agricola –the Vyborg son and reformist founder. Strangely unimposing – a mere token of the renowned statue that had once stood by the Tuomiokirkko Finnish Cathedral. Although it was made from a cast of the original bronze, without the worshippers at its' feet which were part of the original statue destroyed in the war, it would have been more appropriate inside the church.

In the centre of the empty square there was a rough rock encircled water fountain. No water now, just a couple of empty beer bottles. And a chiselled granite stone bear – why ?? ahh, it is one of the stone bears that graced the entrance of the Viipuri railway station !!! It is all that remained in the ruins after the railway station was destroyed by the Russians in 1941 when the Finns retook their city.

The Pietari-Paavali church itself suffered little damage during the war. The church bells did however disappear after the Talvisota – perhaps bells for a Russian church - or more probably copper for shell casings for Stalin's artillery.

As we wandered back a cobbled street to the hotel, we passed some young artists,easel and paint brushes in hand – hard at work beside an old church – a humble one this time. . . once the Pyhan Hyacinthuksen Church. Stuccoed white walls, tile roof, small over grown weed filled yard, wrought iron fence – picturesque poignancy beside the narrow street.

It was originally built in 1403 as the Franciscan "grey brothers" monastery school. With the expulsion of Catholicism, it gathered dust. In the 1650s the Viipuri nobility decided that they warranted their own "palace" and rebuilt the monastery into their assembly house. Thus it became known as the Knight house.

At the start of the 1800s with the advent of more liberal times, the building once more became a catholic church, a purpose it served for 150 years.

Damaged in 1944 at the end of the Jatkosota, the church building was restored in 1972 as the Knight House (as opposed to the St. Hyacinth Church). Today it serves as a gallery as well as a youth art school. I wish I had gone inside to see some of the old 17th century interiors – and of course, the works of its' current youthful artisans.

The next day, we walked down Torkkellikatu towards the castle. Only two blocks down the street was another legendary part of Viipuri - the old Kauppa Tori (Market Square) – and there on the inland side of the square leaned the iconic Pyorea Torni (Round Tower)–thick mortared stone walls, a few recessed windows, copper hat - standing slightly askew for five hundred years, witness to twenty five

generations of soldiers and merchants. It was originally built in 1550 as a standalone fort to guard the borders of the stone town – the ancient part of Vyborg. It was also known as Passinlinna (Ram Castle) as in its' early years it guarded the gate to the outlying meadows – usually the tower just watched the passing of town folk, livestock, sheep and rams – but definitely not always.

- In 1556, during the eternal Russo- Swedish wars – it was surrounded by a 20,000 strong Russian army which surprisingly withdrew without attacking. History is not clear whether they withdrew because of change in orders, poor discipline, disease; or, whether they, like visiting European soccer fans, withdrew after enjoying several days of pillaging and looting.
- In 1599 the heads of 15 supporters of the defeated King Sigimund bled from the gate spikes.
- In the 1600s the flames from the numerous town fires licked its walls
- In 1710 the shells of Peter the Great's army and navy pounded the Round Tower
- Attacks decreased once Viipuri was ceded to Russia, until during the Finnish Red White Civil War of 1918, it watched as the blood of its' brothers washed over its' cobblestone square
- In 1939 during the Talvisota, Russian bombs rained over the tower
- In August 1941 it saw the victorious Finnish troops conduct a march past in front of the viewing stand
- And in June 1944 after further Russian bombing, it brooded as Russian troops captured Vyborg

The difficult days of Pyorea Torni are hopefully over. Now it serves as a restaurant. We went in for lunch. The tower itself is a surprisingly spacious three story solid stone building. In the late 1700s, the more rash residents affectionately called it Paksu Katarina (or chunky Catherine) after Catherine the Great - for obvious reasons.

The restaurant advertises that, *"in the age old tower and its' restaurant one can forget today's problems and be transported to days long ago".* And indeed that was true. As we sat over a delicious meal and a few vodkas, the stone walls and the timbered ceiling did indeed cause one to reflect.

The window aperture I looked out of was the same as that the guards looked out of at the Russian army in 1556 and 1710. The fact that the tower walls are indeed thick – over 10 feet – I don't think made them feel totally safe.

In front of the Round Tower sits the Kauppa Tori – the oldest market square in Viipuri. When the town walls and fortifications were demolished in 1860, the area was a meadow – the population of Viipuri didn't start growing until the 1850s. When the ground was levelled and the current cobbled market square constructed, a 1500 era plague grave yard was revealed. Later bones and a wooden ark were found underneath the tower floor – which noble we don't know.

After the cobbled market square was constructed it became a vibrant market square – filled with farmers and merchants selling their wares. Grampa Juho was there hawking his fish, vegetables, eggs and butter. Great Uncle Hjalmar was there selling his bread and making business deals. Hjalmar had a large bakery business but he still kept a stall in Kauppa Tori. Dad and Uncle Yrjo were undoubtedly darting here and there on their boyhood escapades.

Looking at the large expanse of cobbles I notice raised numbers on some cobble stones – five, six,...twenty two. Ahh, numbered stones to mark each stall. I wonder which one Gramps Juho used when he brought produce in from his farm in Kavantsaari? ... and; which one was great uncle Hjalmar at when he died of a heart attack on the Kauppa Tori in 1933 ?

The market was a social meeting place as well as a food market. The kiosks sold not only healthy goods – liquor was sold as well, legally or illegally. Today the market is empty. I wonder if that is the case all week ?

Old buildings line one side of the square. On the other side a few buildings – and a broad cobbled walk way and park which beckons one to Viipuri Linna - re landscaping after the area was bombed and burnt flat during the war.

In the opposite corner from the PyoreaTorni is the Market Hall (Kauppahalli). A large low red building built in 1904 in the modern style of the period. The hall blends in gracefully with the surrounding buildings of other eras - a credit to the architect and to the town of Viipuri. All major buildings were designed by noted architects with an eye towards heightening the overall beauty of the town – not just the building itself.

Most of the market hall was destroyed in the Talvisota, but thankfully was rebuilt by the Russians afterwards.

Today the market hall is full of bustling stands and vocal shop keepers – food of all sorts, clothes, dishes, art work, and knick knacks.

We wander along the north harbour towards the castle. A short walk beside the shore brings us to the Torkkeli square - a wedge of land by the bridge leading to Viipurin

Linna – a wedge true, but the most valued bit of land in the city. At the back of the square is a large L shaped building – pastel pinks, reds, and yellows - it gracefully gazes at the castle - a courtesan viewing her rough-hewn warrior across the bridge.

Built in 1610 as the Weckroth mansion, it saw many galas but none as grand as when Catherine the Great slept over. Later the long part of the mansion became the town hall while the part at the end became the Hotelli Mellblom. When the town hall was moved to Raatitori, it became the Viipuri Museum.

Destroyed by a fire bomb at the end of the Talvisota, it was partially rebuilt by the Russians – until in Viipuri fashion it burnt again in 1989. Around 2000, the Russians fully rebuilt / restored the house – quite nicely I might say – at least from the outside. It is now a rental residence.

Standing in the centre of the square is the statue of Torkkeli Knuutinpoika. Torkkeli, the founder of Viipuri Linna, certainly deserved a statue. In 1888 the Swedes erected one in the square. Neither the Finns nor the Russians cared for a Swedish monument on Viipuri soil and it was removed and put into storage.

In 1907 Tsar Nicholas II finally agreed to its placement and there it stood until the end of the war in 1944. After the war the Russians removed the statue and once more Torkkeli languished in storage.

In 1993 upon the 700th anniversary of the founding of Viipuri it was once more placed in the square. A fine bronze, it looks strangely unimposing against the backdrop of the elegant Weckroth courtesan.

Now we should wait no longer – it was time to visit the castle. Only 100 yards across the bridge – or should we take the tunnel under the water?

While no one has traversed the tunnel for centuries, entry tunnels and old locked iron doors have been found in the castle and the Weckroth mansion. I wonder who last walked the tunnel of love between the courtesan and the warrior?

When the channel was being dredged in the 1920s work men came across part of the brick roof and walls of the tunnel. I wonder if one of the work men who came across the tunnel was great uncle Jarl? He was killed in an accident in 1926 while working on a dredge clearing the harbour.

Around the same time period the harbour master had to do some special harbour clearance – as the sailboat of dad and his boyhood buddies sank in the harbour!

We walked the short distance across the bridge to the castle island. The water glassy calm, the red rock castle walls imperturbable, the castle tower a solid white washed bastion topped with a green roof. No flag was flying from the top. But certainly many armies had tried to place their flag there. While the city and castle were besieged in 1294, 1322, 1351, 1411, 1495, 1706, 1710, 1918, and 1944, the castle was never breeched. It did surrender twice – to Peter the Great in 1710, and to Stalin's army in 1944.

- The early years saw the forces of Novogorod and Muscovy encamped periodically below the Swedish walls.
- In 1495 Ivan III sent Prince Daniil Shchenya to lay siege to Viborg.
- After a three month siege, the Russian invaders breeched the castle ramparts. With the invaders about to conquer the castle and the town, the Viborg commander Lord Knut Posse, triggered a massive explosion under one of the castle towers "scaring the Muscovites out of their wits" and precipitating their retreat.
- In 1710 Russia captured Vyborg. Peter upon deciding to build his capital St Petersburg in 1703 in the swamp by the Neva River determined that Sweden's mighty castle Vyborg, was too close for comfort. He attacked Vyborg with a large army, bombarding the castle from the shore and his war ships. After a

6 month assault with no help coming from Sweden and supplies running low, the castle surrendered.

- In 1856 as a result of celebrations during the opening of the Saimaa Canal, the castle was seriously damaged by fire. It started from candles that were not attended to properly during the raucous festivities. The castle was not restored until 1895.
- In 1918 during the Red White Civil War, the castle walls received more scars. The first skirmishes in the Finnish Civil War took place here, but it was not until three months later, after a five-day siege, that the White Army, on April 29th 1918, finally captured the Red town of Viipuri.
- At the end of the Jatkosota in 1944, Stalin's forces captured the town. The Finnish regiment protecting Viipuri uncharacteristically retreated from the city after only nominal fighting. The cheeks of Marshall Mannerheim, the legendary commander of the Finnish armed forces, are said to have flushed a rosy red upon hearing the news. The Colonel in charge was prosecuted by the Finnish government and imprisoned.

Unlike strangers of yore, we had no problems entering the castle through the white commandant's residence (built in 1606). The only thing we needed was a bit of patience and some roubles.

Immediately the rough red rock rampart towered above us. A small semi-circle tunnel of light – the inner gate beckoned us towards the inner court yard. Meandering around the outer court yard, lined by buildings, we arrived at the foot of the St. Olaf tower. The stout, square, lower part preserved almost unaltered since Torgil built it in 1293 – no wonder - the walls are 15 feet thick. The upper octagonal part, built in 1563, towered above our craning necks. So, join the queue and buy tickets for the tower. In we go and start to circle up to the top –one step, two steps ...two hundred and thirty nine steps. Out of the shadows through a small opening onto a narrow ledge. It took my breath away – not just the view but the low iron railing which was all that protected one from soaring unimpeded into the water below.

Yikes !! not for me to walk around the narrow viewing track. A few moments by the entrance admiring the spectacular view of the town and snapping pictures, and back into the tower with a sigh of relief.

The encircling ledge and railing is the same one as has been there for over a 100 years. I marvel at the Finnish soldier who climbed up to the flag pole at the top of the cupola. In August 1941 when Finland reclaimed Viipuri, the Soviet hammer and sickle was flying from the flag pole. The first squad into the abandoned castle of course wanted to take the flag down. An intrepid volunteer clambered to the top like a mountain goat and removed the Russian flag. Not having a Finnish flag with them, he took off his undershirt and attached it to the mast. There the soldiers undershirt flew for a couple of days until a Finnish flag with lion rampant on a blue cross arrived and was put in place.

When Viipuri was retaken in 1941, the city was heavily mined by the Russians. Some mines were placed in the castle itself. The mines were removed by the Finnish army combat engineers. My Uncle Arvo was one of the engineers. I wonder if he removed any from the castle itself? He like all front line soldiers never talked about the war. When he was in his 80s I asked uncle Arvo about the war. He said, *"I don't remember much anymore and that's the way I like it"*. And that was the case for my father and my five uncles. It is seldom that front line soldiers, as opposed to members of support units or safe senior officers, ever talked about the war. The memories are too horrible to talk about for those who were month after month, year after year, tasked with personally killing their fellow man, living ever day with the horror of quick or slow and painful deaths – pontificating officers, tedium, disease... terror.

I am sure the same applied to the armies of old. I wonder what the thoughts of the Viipuri castle defenders were in 1556, when they looked out from the top of Olaf's tower and saw the city surrounded by an army of 20,000 Russians.

The next time I am in Viipuri I will certainly make time for a tour of the castle interior and its' museum. Not only to see relics of war, but also to see golden goblets and finery; and to hear tales of the grand court life of pomp and pleasure of the medieval lords of Viipuri castle.

Viipuri Linna- the symbol of Vyborg, its' inalienable part and heart, the most ancient architectural monument in town, a witness to its entire history.

Back across the bridge and along the Southern Esplanade. The mid summer evening sun gently strokes the old buildings. Fine old buildings periodically rudely interrupted by a Soviet era apartment. The street winds by the rock strewn rubble of the old Munkkitori place. The Domincan monastery long gone and the surrounding buildings shattered by

the last war. But still standing nearby is the old Hanseatic guild hall; and of course the RaatiTorni tower.

The RaatiTorni was originally a tower on the town wall. And as we advance a hundred paces further our shoes are actually tredding on what remains of the old ramparts of the town of Viipuri (The walls were dismantled in 1860 to allow the town to grow). Whose footsteps from 300 years ago was I following?

The harbour on one side, and the town on the other – and straight ahead the Pantsarlahti bastion.

But I can't see the red bastion. Rather there bathed in the soft evening light, is a white Hellenistic structure – classical yet at the same time totally modern. It's the Viipuri Taidehalli – the Viipuri Art School and Museum designed in 1930 by Uno Ullberg. The V shaped building and the open see through courtyard makes me for a moment think of the Acropolis of Athens. The Viipuri Taidehalli is built on rock on top of the old Pantsarlahden Bastion. The 1600 fortifications and bastion remain, the Taidehalli built upon, and around, the old fortifications. The two fit together seamlessly, complementing one another.

There it miraculously stands. The building was damaged badly in the war but was restored and now houses a branch of the Hermitage Museum. It beckons me towards it. And I go willingly, for it is my father's school. Dad was accepted by the art school and went there for several years. He relished his time in the open creative learning environment where one was mentored as opposed to lectured at. Not to mention that the tuition was free for all who were accepted. In keeping with the spirit of Viiipuri, the art school was

funded by the merchants of Viipuri – indeed it was built by the merchants.

I walk up the old ramparts slope and the through the columns into the courtyard. It is tranquil and welcoming. The beauty and the memories soak in. I wonder what the hustle and bustle would have been like in my father's days ... and, was he jauntily dressed ... strolling around with brush, easel, and girlfriend under his arm ?

Advancing through the Taidehalli, I see the old red stone Pantsarlahti Bastion powder cellar and the remnants of the town ramparts – the town behind it. Now only flowers, not blood, flow over the stone crevices.

As we advance back to our hotel, we come upon a large, long park in the centre of town. Old trees and well kept paths parallel the main street running from Kauppatori Square to Punaisenlahti Square. Ohh, another of my fathers' memories come to life - TorkkelinPuisto.

Walking along the park boulevard, I suddenly come across a huge bronze statue of a majestic moose – my gosh, just like the faded photo in my dad's old newspapers. I had always thought it stood guard in a distant park - not the middle of the old town. The moose survived the war, receiving only a piece of shrapnel in its hoof. Its' legs shine dark gold from repeated stroking by children and adults. I give it a quick brush.

Behind the moose, I see a white modern building - the Alvar Aalto library. It was damaged during the war. Indeed a squad of Finnish soldiers who were trapped in Viipuri when the city fell to the Russians in July 1944, hid in the basement of the library. Soon captured, most thankfully

survived the war. We stuck our head into the library. Apparently the most striking impression is the original lighting of the reading hall - 57 cone shaped openings in the roof give mellow diffused light. The wooden ceiling in the lecture hall has an interesting wavelike construction which provides excellent acoustics (hmm, why in a library ?). We were not able to see much given that the library is still being restored – and effectively guarded by a robust Russian lady.

Wandering along the park we pass various kiosks. We buy some water, pointing out the bottles we want to the shop keeper behind the locked window. Than we pass the roubles through the money latch and receive water ... and change... in return. The park benches welcome our now tired feet.

A life size bronze statue catches my eyes – a young man and bear cub – the Metsänpoika. Not beauty and the beast; but rather the purity and strength of youth, the freedom of nature, and the love of a faithful bear cub.

The statue as well had survived the war.

There however was no sign of Georg Winter's ravishing bronze female nude – Naishahmo, or Torkkelin Tilta as it was known by the locals. It disappeared from the park during the period between the Finnish evacuation of Viipuri in March 1940 and it's recapture in August 1941.

I wonder which Russian Commissar's or General's estate it ended up in.

We continue up Torkelli park towards the battlements (Patterinmaki). Shortly we arrive at Punaisenlahti Square.

The Punaisenlahti (red) market square is the largest square in Viipuri and dates from the mid 1800s. It was used as a busy market and as a gathering point throughout the centuries.

The square is bordered on three sides by large building and at one end by Torkkeli Park. A statue of Lenin was placed at the north end of the square in 1957.

From 1300 to 1500 it was called the munkilahde as the monks got their water from the then clear spring in the Salakkalahti woods.

In 1599 Duke Kaarle (He became King Kaarle IX of Sweden) conquered Viipuri from King Sigismund's supporters. Kaarle was a hardened fanatic and a fervent Protestant, opposed to the Catholic Sigismund - King of Poland & Sweden. Kaarle executed 15 of the defenders at

Munkkiilahde. The blood flowed into the spring turning the waters red. The heads were mounted on stakes and placed at the Karjaportti by the Pyorea Torni. Decades later the spring turned rust red for other reasons. Thus the spring became known as red spring –Punaisenlahde.

Nearly 300 years later, in 1900, the bottom of the spring was covered with fill, trees, and branches. It was levelled and soon became a market known as the Punaisenlahteen tori.

Now Lenins statue is in the middle of it, adding further to its' redness.

But certainly the square had seen Red Communists before. Dad "took part in" a major Bolshevik rally there in 1917.

> *"The square was so full of soldiers and revolutionaries, that there was no room to squeeze any more people in. We boys nonetheless managed to find ourselves a spot immediately before the speaker platform. The speaker was a fervent emotional orator – like a wild whirling devil – (never before, nor after, even to this day, have I heard a more impassioned and inspirational speaker). The crowd was whipped into a frenzy, shouting "bravo !!! daa, daa !! hurray, hurray !!!." I, caught in the moment, shouted as fervently as I could. A huge soldier, who was standing beside me, patted me on the head and said "yell louder, louder !!"*

The speaker may have been Lenin himself as he lived in Viipuri during Sept/Oct 1917, finalizing his plans for the Bolshevik Revolution before going to St Petersburg. But most probably it was Trotsky. Trotsky was noted as a great orator.

Today the square was empty.

But not as empty as the site at the Torkkeli park end of the square where the Finnish Tuomiokirkko cathedral used to stand. The Tuomiokirkko was an impressive gothic church with a high steeple and room for 1,800 faithful.

Only forty-seven years after it was built, in February 1940, the altar portion was badly damaged by bombs during the Talvisota. Instead of repairing or abandoning the church during the year they held the city, the Russians managed to dismantle the church tower, the roof and the upper walls, and to remove all church vestments. Czar Nicholas II's gift of the main chandelier also found a new owner.

During the Jatkosota the Finns did not have time to reconstruct the church. Today nothing remains except some anonymous open space.

Beside the church there was a Sankari Hautausmaa (Military Cemetery. In Finland during the wars the bodies of the fallen soldiers were transported back and buried in their home parish). As well as the Sankarihauta, there was a memorial for the fallen Whites of the bitter Red White Civil war - The Reds had to make their memorial to their fallen on the outskirts of town.

The Sankarihauta continued in use until the end of the Jatkosota. About 700 sons of Viipuri are buried there. The Sankari monument and the soldier's head stones have disappeared. A new memorial was placed there in 1993 – a flat granite stone block and benches. An inscription in Finnish, Russian, Swedish and German reads, *"In memory of all those buried in Viipuri".*

At the end of the old town past "Red Square", there is a large rocky hilltop – Patterinmaki; and, beyond it the newer (1900) part of Viipuri.

My great grandmothers' home was on the other side of the hilltop. The area was totally demolished during the war, so we only did a quick drive by.

But we did climb Patterinmaki (Battery Hill). It contains extensive fortifications built by Alexander II in the 1860s. Bastions, old walls, ramparts and deep trenches abound.

The fortifications did not see any activity until 1918. Then it was the site of bloody battles between the Reds and Whites during the Finnish Civil War. Further battles occurred there in March 1940 during the Talvisota, when the Finnish forces halted Russia's advance into Viipuri – and sadly on June 20, 1944 when Viipuri fell to theRussian army.

What drew me to the battlements however, was not the fortifications, nor the military history; but rather, the fact that it was the boyhood playground of my father, my uncle and their chums.

While I had wandered with admiration and rapt interest through all of old Viipuri; it was only here in Patterinmaki that I suddenly felt my spirits lift and felt a strong attachment to the surroundings. Perhaps it was the clean air as opposed to the slightly mouldy old town ... or, maybe it was something else.

Today the battlements are the M. Kalinin municipal park; and, I am sure, still a boyhood playground.

We walked back to our hotel, through a mix of Soviet era, Medieval, Renaissance, Jugend, and 1930s Finnish architecture.

After a quick shot of vodka at the hotel bar and a brief rest at the hotel, we departed once more. This time I was drawn across the north harbour towards ships on the other side. Not just any ships – Viking ships !! I strolled along a pleasant harbour side walkway to the two Viking boats.

Their fiercesome prows challenged me to come closer. Knowing they were merely replicas, I walked up to them. Built to full scale, the ships are impressive - surprisingly large – about 18 feet across and 60 feet long.

While the Vikings were ancient adversaries of the Russians, they also were the founding kings of Russia. From 800 A.D. the Vikings raided up the rivers from Viipuri and Lake Ladoga to Novgorod, Kiev and Constantinople. They actually were known as the "Rus" from which the name Russia is derived. In 862 Rurik became "Tsar" of Russia in Novgorod, followed by Oleg of Novgorod and Igor of Kiev. The Rurik dynasty ruled Russia until the death of Ivan the Terrible in 1547.

The Viking ships provided yet more food for thought.

With food in mind, we departed post haste to the Kamelot restaurant near the Kauppa Tori. As we sat in the restaurant enjoying an excellent dinner and some fine vodka, my thoughts turned towards Viipuri. So this was my fathers' home and the lost mystical land of Karjala. Was it as magic, as memorable, as the stories of my mother and father ?

And, yes, for me, it was.

In Memory of Grandfather Georg

The next day we left for Kavantsaari, my mother's home 20 kilometers north of Viipuri. But first before departing for her homestead we drove a short kilometre and a half along Kannaksentie to the old Ristimaki cemetery. As Reima drove, I looked to the right as we approached 45 Kannaksentie the site of my fathers' boyhood home .... nothing except some Soviet apartment blocks. Well, I knew that the whole area had been levelled by Stalin's bombs and artillery, and there would be nothing to see ... yet still ...

Almost immediately we arrived at the Ristimaki Cemetery – the site of my grandfather Georg's grave. No one in the family had returned since we fled Viipuri in June 1944. The cemeteries were damaged and desecrated during the war. Old gravestones were removed for building materials and the enclosed cemeteries used as pig pens.

But this cemetery seemed to be in good condition. I walked through a heavy rain down pour, by the small Orthodox chapel, through the main gate, into the cemetery. Now what was it that dad had said ?

> " Father died in 1923. His grave is to the left about 30 metres in after you go through the main gate."

I walked down the well kept stone walk way trying to estimate 30 meters in the pelting rain. The cemetery on both sides of the path was well kept; albeit, few grave stones could be seen among the grown trees. Looking straight ahead I realized that this was a special entrance, as 100 yards ahead of me on the right I could see a long line of polished granite slabs inscribed with endless names... and beyond a statue surrounded by glorious flower wreaths. It was a Russian memorial to the soldiers killed in the Talvi and Jatkosota wars with Finland.

I searched briefly on the right for gramps gravestone but gave up quickly given that most of the head stones were embedded in the soil and tree roots. Arto said,

"Karl, given the condition of the cemetery and this heavy rain, why don't you leave your memorial stone from Canada by this tree. I'm sure you are near where your gramps bones are resting."

I laid my Canada stone by the tree, saying,

"Gramps here I am – your grandson Karl. All is well with us in Canada. You would be proud of your large group of grandchildren and great grandchildren. Rest in peace. We have not forgotten you."

We walked back to the car. While Reima and Arto got in out of the rain, I crossed the street to a large treed over-grown neglected patch of land. It was the abandoned old Viipuri Swedish – German cemetery. I clambered over a muddy ditch and through the derelict brick gateway. Now where had dad said great grandmother Maria Christina was buried ?

"She is buried in the Ristimaki Swedish cemetery there. When you go in through the gates, the grave is directly to the right about 20 metres. "

Here there was no finely cobbled road, only a narrow overgrown dirt path. I followed it in for 50 feet but there was nothing to see except a few leaning grave stones, a vault or two, and large holes in the ground. I wasn't sure whether the holes were bomb craters or sunken burial vaults. I quietly set down my small Canada stone for great grandmother and left. I was a bit too shook to say any words.

To the Ancestral Kavantsaari Home

Back in the car we headed back through Viipuri towards Kavantsaari, or so we thought. The roads that seemed so clear on the 75 year old Finnish map was difficult to follow as Cryillic road signs flashed by behind the wind shield wipers. We reached a fork in the road and stopped. There was a huge rock with a small plaque with Finnish writing ("Tienhaaran Taistelu").

"Ohh, we're on the road heading for Finland. We have to turn back. That is a memorial for the fallen of the battle of Tien Haara during July 1944."

Back into Viipuri and turn left towards the train station. We glance at the train station as we drive by. It looks very Russian. And so it should. The magnificent classical Finnish railway station designed by Saarinen in 1913 was blown up by the Soviet forces in 1941 as they retreated out of Viipuri.

After several forks in the road and stops to jabber and point at the map with kindly service station attendants, we rolled on down the road. Why oh why hadn't I written down the new Russian name of Kavantsaari – and needless to say written it down in Cyrillic. There were clear road signs posted on the highway, but only clear for Russians. For all the good they did us they could have been beer bottle advertisements.

We carried on through the rain. At the junction of a small road we saw a parking lot with a large monument opposite it. It was memorial to the Russian soldiers who fell during the battle of Tali Ihantala. This time it was a large square bordered by a low row of polished granite stone simply inscribed with the names of the fallen. At the front a large pillar with the legend 1941-1944 and a limp wet flag on a flagpole. At the back a grouping of large flower wreaths. We were on the right road – the war road.

We drove straight ahead. We came to a Y intersection clearly marked with arrows and bold Cryillic letters ...Ok, we should be at the Ihantala turn off to Kavantsaari, mother's home. But where is Ihantala, the village where the family church was ? I had a small stone from my cousin to put at her fathers' grave, and one from myself for my mothers' grandmothers grave. I knew that Ihantala had been the site of a horrific multi week battle between Finland and Russia. Finland had stopped the Russian armies drive into Finland here. The losses had been so huge that Stalin decided that Finland was not worth the sacrifice it would take to conquer her. Yes, I heard the church and the village had been levelled, but where was the large Finnish memorial that was supposed to be at Ihantala ?.

We drove back to a muddy lot just before the Y intersection. Looking to the right I saw a passenger bus about 200 yards in the field by a little knoll. We drove up the muddy gravel road to it. As we approached I noticed Finnish words on the bus – and a huge boulder with people clustered around it. It was the Ihantala memorial. The people departed shortly and we were left alone in the drizzle by the boulder. Some Finnish words chiselled into the whitish gray boulder, some flowers stuck into shell casings from the battle. Nothing magnificent here to commemorate a pivotal point in Finland's existence, and to remember the lives of the 2,500 Finnish soldiers who died here. But the soldiers would not have wanted it any other way. True they fought and died for

" Uskonnon, kodin, ja isanmaa poulesta – for god, home, and country"

but not for fame and glory. To them war was not something to be glorified and embellished.

We spent a few moments in quiet reflection looking down across the field that the Russian tanks had tried to cross.

After, I walked behind the monument looking for some sign of the cemetery that used to be there. The cemetery where my uncle Erkki and my great grandmother Henrika had been buried. True, I knew there was probably nothing left as the grave yard had been shelled and bombed into oblivion. Indeed in their desperate defence the Finnish soldiers had actually dug defensive trenches through the coffins. I paid my respects and gently tossed my Canadian stone mementos among the rocks and pine trees.

Across the road, was the Ihantala church where my folks worshipped. No trace was to be seen. We crossed the road and I started to tramp through the underbrush up a small over grown hill top. I returned dispirited to the car - no success. Arto however found the church further down the road.

But there was not much to be found. All that remained was the concrete church steps. The rest of the large church had been dismantled by the Russians between the wars. And even the small interim church the parishioners had built between the wars was nowhere to be seen. Close by, the entrance pillars to the old church yard cemetery still

stood. After the devastation of the battle, all that was left of the actual grave yard was mowed grass.

In the centre of it stood an upright marker for the sons of Ihantala who had fallen during the war. Needless to say it had been erected after the war. In the 1980s the Russian state allowed Finland to erect simple memorials and to clean up those old Finnish cemeteries that still existed. I initially thought this was a humane gesture by Russia– and it is a humane gesture – but one mandated by international law.

While the experience had been sobering, I felt a thrilling and a warm connection to my roots. I was only the second person in our entire extended family who had been able to visit.

But this was only our church village, what awaited me at our homestead ?

I knew mothers family farm was just seven kilometres down the right hand side road from the Ihantala battle. I looked for the little hamlet of Kaipola, as the farm was shortly after it. But before we knew it we were in Kavantsaari. The hamlet of Kaiploa had disappeared.

Not too much to Kavantsaari either. Run down, but still inhabited houses. A well maintained and large rail way track running across the highway. A mockery of the fine tidy village my mother had described.

The old railway station still stood there. The station where grandma, persistently late, ran daily with her milk cans to deliver the milk to market. Where my Aunt Hilda as

a17 year old had been led through by the Whites, chained with other alleged Reds en route to be executed (thankfully not). Where Uncle Kauko had boarded the train to return to the front again. In such a hurry he wasn't able to go home to get his military carbine. Where gramps and Uncle Erkki disembarked tipsy and happy after a successful day at the Viipuri market.

The store by the railway crossing seemed busy. We went in to pick up water and something to eat. About ¼ of the shelves were reserved for liquor. One of the bottles of vodka was calling to me. I didn't resist. Roubles offered. Vodka bottle received.

We drove back through the now heavy rain towards the farm. This time I noticed the small overgrown road leading off the highway. We stopped the car. While Reima stayed watching the car, Arto and I walked up the road through the weeds and puddles towards the farm. We could see the family fields in the distance.

As my cousin Sirkka had told me there were no longer any buildings left. All had been dismantled and taken away after the war. In the Soviet, independent farms did not exist. All farming was done by large collectives. But the collective was not as large as the Thesleff estate had been during Gramps day. The estate had been the largest one in Karjala. A fiefdom land holding it was first granted by King Kustaa Vasa in the 1530s to the Steward of Viipuri castle. Afterwards it passed through various families at the whim of the monarch until it was sold in 1848 to the Governor of Viipuri, Major General Alexander Thesleff. Thence it passed to his son Nikloai; and, in 1909 to his grandson Nikolai J. Thesleff. While well regarded by the establishment, Nikolai was the bane of independent crofters such as Gramps Juho.

The rain continued to pour down and a large squadron of mosquitoes descended upon us, oblivious to the rain. After taking a photo or two, Arto and I toasted Gramps Juho with a couple of quick slugs of vodka. I picked up two stones from the road as a reminder of my roots, and retreated to the car.

While there was nothing remaining of the farm except for somewhat over grown fields, I wish we had gone further

in to where the house and farm had originally stood. It had been a prosperous farm, one where Grandma Hilda and Grandpa Juho had successfully raised four daughters and six sons.

I have seen the fields of my mothers' joyous childhood, and walked in my fathers' footsteps in Viipuri; but, there is yet a little empty spot in my soul. I must return again someday - soon.

Karjala and Viipuri still calls.

BOOK I
Karjala - The Early Years

Albert Edelfelt: Silmapouli Karjalainen

So the ancient Vainamoinen
There, himself, these words he uttered:
"Give to us, Lord and Creator,
Happiness throughout our lifetime,
Always let us live with goodness
Finally to die with honour
In our Suomi, so beloved
In our beautiful Karjala
The Kalevala, Rune 43

PART I

A Historical Interlude
Suomi and Karjala's Early Years

E. Tanttu: Seppa

A Historical Interlude Suomi and Karjala's Early Years

Karjala was a land of lively social people who had a deep love for nature, and a fierce determination to protect their independence.

The first people moved into Karjala about 10,000 years ago, at the end of the last ice age. For many thousands of years the land was sparsely inhabited by hunter gatherers. Indeed until about 5,000 years ago most of Finland remained under water. With the Bronze Age small settlements began to be established by the sea side – an era immortalized in the Finnish epic Kalevala.

Finland and Karjala remained a pagan hunter gatherer society well into the second millenium. A loose Karelian tribe emerged which warred with the western Hame tribe of Finland.

From the 750s to 1050 Vikings traversed through Karjala enroute to raid and trade in Russia and Constantinople.

Swedish crusades began in 1155 to bring Christianity to pagan Finns and Karelians – and the Greek Orthodox Christians of Russia. Karjala was not greatly touched by this until the Swedish Marshall Torgils Knutson established a fortress in Viipuri – the Viipurin Linna.

From that point on Sweden and Russia embarked on 600 years of war – fought primarily on the battleground of Karjala.

In 1710 Peter the Great captured Viipuri and made Karjala part of Russia. In 1810 Alexander I conquered Finland, combining it with Karjala into the Grand Duchy of Finland.

CHAPTER 1

Laulumaa

Artist Unknown in Aleksis Kivi book, Nummijuutarit

CHAPTER 1

Laulumaa

I have delved at some length in the previous chapter into the storied Karelian city of Viipuri. But Karjala consisted of much more than just that city.

Karelia, or Karjala as it is known to the Finns, of course borders Russia. It stretches from just north of St Petersburg to the White (Viena) Sea and east from the Finnish border to Lake Onega (Ääninen).

Karjala has been the home of the Karelian people for a millennium before the birth of Christ. While the Karelians were a Finno Ugric people like those in Finland, they formed a separate tribe within "Finland", led by their own chieftains.

The Karelians spoke Finnish, but with a distinctive dialect. They are descended primarily from peoples who migrated from the eastern end of the Baltic. There was minimal Swedish / West European genetic impact. This changed at the end of the 19th century when many Finnish families (including my parents' families) migrated to Viipuri and the Karelian Isthmus.

Karjala is traditionally divided into six areas.

- Karjalan Isthmus / Kannas (Wiburg) ;
- Ladoga/Laatokan Karjala (Kexholm- Käkisalmi);
- South Karjala / Etelä Karjala (Kotka-Savolinna);
- North Karjala / Phojois Karjala; (Joensuu)
- Olonets Karjala /Aunuksen Karjala; and,
- White Karjala / Vienan Karjala

Not all of this area became part of Finland when it became an independent country in 1918. Olonets Karjala

and White Karjala remained part of Russia. During the late 1800s through to the end of the Jatkosota a political movement arose to merge these areas into Finland (The Greater Finland or Suuri Suomi movement). This would have made all Karelians part of Finland.

Both South Karjala (Kotka and the Savonlinna area) and North Karjala (Joensuu, Lieksa and Lake Pielinen surroundings) remain part of Finland today.

The section from Lake Ladoga (Laatoka) to Lake Onega (Äänien) was more Orthodox and Russian, while that west of Lake Ladoga was Lutheran and more Finnish.

The most inhabited and prosperous portion of Karjala was the Karjalan Kannas, the section between the Gulf and Lake Ladoga stretching three hundred kilometres northwards from St Petersburg.

Only small portions of Karjala were urban. The major city of Karjala was the celebrated city of Viipuri. The capital of Karjala since times immemorial, Viipuri had a way of life and culture of its' own which I have tried to capture earlier in this book – and to which I will add to later.

Other small cities /large towns were Kakisalmi, on the west shore of Lake Laatoka near the northern end of the Vuoksi River; Sortavala at the north end of Lake Laatoka; and, Karhumaki, Poventsa and Petroksi – all on the western shore of Lake Oinen. The largest of these places, Sortavala, had a population of 9,000.

The heart of Karjala was the countryside - the land of the tales of Kalevala, rune singers and kantales. Villages and hamlets with larger parish towns dominated by impressive Lutheran parish churches – and, an occasional onion domed orthodox "cathedral" in the eastern parts of Karjala. Rich farm land in the Karjalan Isthmus; elsewhere a beautiful, sparsely populated wilderness of forests and lakes.

Karjala was known as the land of song (Laulumaa). It was populated by a spirited, cheerful, and hospitable people who had a deep attachment to their land and an unwavering resolve to defend it.

"Always joy, laughter, and humour, irrespective of even the most burdensome conditions - carrying food in two hands to visitors even if the cupboard would be bare for the next week. "

And as Marshall Mannerheim comments in his Memoirs:

The Karelian Isthmus was not unknown to me, but I was to come to know and love it more than before. The more I saw of the Karelians, the more I admired this wonderful people, who from generation to generation had weathered the storm from the East, without losing their happy disposition or their unbroken will to defend themselves.

Today Finns are usually characterized as being quiet, serious, diligent, hard working, and unassuming, in other words Hämäläinen and Pohjalainen (Osthrobothnia) Finns. The joy and laughter of Karelia or the chatter and conviviality of Savo are no longer part of the Finnish self-image. Why this is the case when these people still exist, I assume reflects the impact of the current "ruling class" and media. The Karelians lost much of their influence and visibility when they lost their homeland.

Journalists Ilkka Malmberg and Tapio Vanhatalo collected popular conceptions of the Finnish tribes in their book *Heimoerot Esiin ja Härnäämään*.

The Karelian is often described with such adjectives as 'lively', 'sociable' and 'unreserved'. The above saying illustrates that the Karelian tribe thinks that it is the most cheerful, light-hearted and optimistic of all the tribes. The Karelian and the Savolainen tribes together form the group of the eastern tribes.

The Karelian tribe is extroverted, which means that Karelians are talkative and genuinely, and actively interested in other people. They are warm, open-hearted and unpretentious. Nevertheless, they are often perceived as being untrustworthy, especially in the west, because of their talkative nature. The Karelian tribe is also impulsive. Unlike the Hämäläinen tribe and the typical Finn, Karelians act upon their urges and do not worry about what others might think. The Karelian tribe is also tolerant of different people, ideas and ways of life. They are emotional and passionate. They are always ready for a good time, laughter and joy.

Spiritually, the Karelian tribe are somewhere between Finland and Russia; after all, they have lived on the border zone of two cultures, the east and the west, for centuries. Their position between Russia and Sweden and the sufferings this location has brought upon the tribe over the centuries has refined the Karelian nature to be unyielding. They will bend but they will not break.

Certainly the Karelians have recognized that while Finnish, they are different from their western brethren, as exemplified by the traditional Karelian saying that:

"An Ostrobothnian wedding is drearier than a Karelian funeral."

Hmm, although I left Finland when I was only a small boy, the Lively Karjalainen description seems to fit. Even my second cousin in Finland calls me the "Iloinen Karjalan Poika – cheerful Karjala boy". I guess I inherited it undiluted from my parents. It is not a matter of my genes (as I will relate later on), rather one of the culture and outlook on life which nature and history imbued into all Karjalainens.

The Karjalainen people enjoyed the natural beauty surrounding them, and longed for what was lost, as is captured in a traditional Karjala song:

Already in the Karjala countryside is a leafy tree,
Already Karjala's birch forests burst forth.
A cuckoo sings there, and it is spring.
Take my eternal yearning there.

I know your tree covered hills and mountain ridges
and the burnt over area's smoky slumbering nights
and primeval trees among dark forests
and dimly seen straits and inlets of bays
where often my wandering journey
went, through forests and rugged shores,
and standing still, bareheaded on top of the hill
I saw in front of me
magnificent Karjala..
Or, when I went to see the village men
where they lived up high,
I saw the honest and joyful workmen
And there I saw where beat Karjala's heart.

Already in the Karjala countryside is a leafy tree,
Already Karjala's birch forests burst forth.
A cuckoo sings there, and it is spring.
Take my eternal longing there.

And indeed my mother always pined for her Karjala home, commenting on the beauty of the summer nights - often softly, happily, singing in Finnish,

"Jo Karjalan kunnailla lehti puu, jo Karjalan koivikot tuuhettuu. Käki kukkuu siellä ja kevät on. Vie sinne mun kaihoni pohjaton" ...

When my mother talked about Karjala, she glowed with joy.

Beauty and gratitude for the land bursts forth in the poem from a 1914 Antrea Church Youth Group booklet:

Beautiful, flowing, voluble are you Vuoksi, beautiful Karjala's most mighty river.

I have seen you in winter when snow blankets you, covering the spry waters with a deathly shroud, the snow dusted trees sparkling like jewels in the moons glow on the rivers' edge.

I have seen you in the spring when awakening from your winter dreams, brawny and free, you shatter the ice into shards.

I have seen you in the summer, when your shores flush green and the light wind ripples the sun baked waters and the night moon throws shimmering silver upon your surface.

I have seen you in the autumn when raging fall storms whirl forward your lacquered waves with reckless speed.

I have seen you, Vuoksi, through all the seasons and always I have admired you, never quite knowing myself when you are the most beautiful

The Karjala countryside may be beautiful it is true, but it is not spectacular. It is mostly flat countryside interspersed with rocky knolls, lakes, ponds, swamps and rivers.

In fact when I visited my mothers' Kavantsaari home in 2012, the main impression was that of scrub bush interspersed with periodic small lakes and rivers.

The book Antrea describes my mothers' area of Kavantsaari before the war in more generous terms:

Nature had granted Kavantsaari with unusual richness. The lands were among Finland's finest farmland and the lakes were full of fish...

The Kavantsaari manor forests were particularly worth seeing. Many parts reminded one of primeval forests. The large variety of species, ever old trees, and the wildness of the forest made one feel like one was in an earlier time. One who desired solitude and peace could find it in the Torogi backwoods where ones only companions were the pine trees reaching for the clouds.

Among the large number of plant life unique to the area were red water lilies. There were small fish which are found nowhere else. Bird life was profuse. Nightingales were abundantly represented; and also such rarities as bitterns whose species one met more than once.

Mother certainly loved her home in Kavantsaari exclaiming often on its' charm and beauty. Even the local mega wealthy manor lord – Nikolai J Thesleff – is quoted as saying:

"I have been to Italy and Rome, but nowhere is it as good and as beautiful as in Kavantsaari".

And when I look at old photos I see a different country-side from that of today – one of gently rolling fields and inviting well kept homesteads. And its' beauty becomes self evident when this is combined with its' joyous sociable people and healthy prosperous life style – one in harmony with nature.

Pre History

Akseli Gallen-Kallela: Hiiden Hirvi

Vipunen the great rune singer,
Ancient bard of ageless wisdom
In whose mouth is mighty knowledge
In whose breast is powerful prowess
Raised the lid of his word casket
Spread the chest of verses open
So to bring forth all its treasures
So to sing his peerless wisdom
Sang the legends of creation
Sang the spells for time's beginning
Runes not sung by any children
Nor perceived by many stalwarts
In these evil hopeless ages
In this fleeting life of sorrow

THE KALEVALA – RUNE 17

CHAPTER 2

Pre History

A millennium before the Viipuri castle walls rose, Karjala and Viipuri was inhabited by the Finno Ugric Karelian tribe – and even before that by early hunter gatherers. 10,000 year old fishing nets were found in Antrea – only twenty kilometres from my mother's Kavantsaari home.

Perhaps those fishermen were my mother's ancient ancestors...they were from Karjala

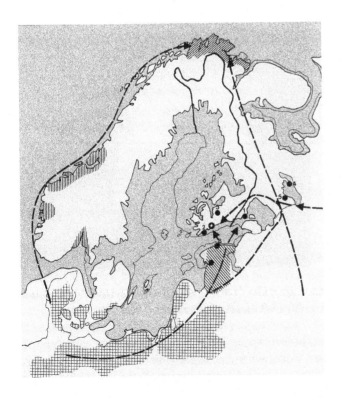

Ancient Inhabitation

While "central Finland" was populated from the Baltic and Scandinavia, Karjala was primarily populated from Volga in the east - although it did have later migrations from across the Baltic.

Finland pre history can be separated into different eras:

- 8,000 to 6,500 B.C. – Askola culture (late Holcene)
- 6,500 to 4,000 B.C. – Suomusjarvi culture (early Neolithic)
- 4,000 to 2,500 B.C. – Comb Ware culture
- 2,500 to 2,000 B.C. – Battle Axe, Bell Becker cultures & Asbestos Ceramics
- 2,000 to 1,500 B.C. – Kiukaisten & Asbestos Ceramics
- 1,500 to 500 B.C. – Bronze Age
- 500 B.C. to 600 A.D. – Roman Iron Age
- 600 A.D. to 800 A.D. - Merovingian Age (Clovis to Charlemagne)
- 800 A.D. to 1050 A.D. – Viking Age
- 1050 A.D. to 1300 A.D. – Northern Crusades

The first people came to Karjala around 8,000- 7,000 B.C. as the ice was retreating. Stone Age hunter gatherers, they arrived from the east - part of the Askola culture. Before that the Komsa people came but they moved to the northern Finland and the Arctic Sea.

In 7,000 B.C. most of Finland, except for Karjala was under water. The map on the next page shows almost all of Finland as a sea. As the earth recovered from the ice pressure Finland arose out of the sea at the rate of 100 metres every 100 years. Even today Finland is rising 30 to 40 centimetres every 100 years.

Population was sparse – located close to the sea. It survived primarily through fishing, seal hunting, and some game hunting.

By 5,000 B.C. much of Finland was inhabitable. While still a hunter gatherer culture, it was now established and is known as the Suomijarvi culture. As well as stone, bone, wood, and ceramics were in use.

The era from 3,000 B.C. to the beginning of the Bronze Age brought a new influx of peoples primarily from the Volga, but also from the Baltic and Sweden/Denmark. Among these were the Baltic Battle Axe peoples who settled around the Viipuri Gulf area just before the Bronze Age. (While the axes were periodically used for battle, their prime purpose was to fell trees and clear fields).

Many cliff drawings from the 2,000 B.C. era have been found in Karjala. These depict people and animals, shaman type forms, fishing and hunting scenes, and celestial stars and seasons. Also among these drawings are images which are part of Kalevala mythology such as men skiing behind elks and men netting giant fish.

The Kalevala

Ahh, now might be the appropriate time to talk about the Finnish epic Kalevala.

Kalevala is an epic poetic saga of Finnish mythology and folklore. It consists of 50 poems/songs - a total of 22,795 lines of poetry. The Kalevala describes the creation of the world, the ancient gods, the pagan animistic religion, and ancient wars, as well as the foibles of love, life, and death. As is the Finnish custom it celebrates the life of the peasants as well as warriors and magicians.

The book was written by Elias Lonnrot in 1835, and further expanded by him into the definitive 1849 edition. Elias wrote it based on stories he gathered while travelling throughout Karjala. The book was instrumental in the development of the Finnish identity, and the solidification of Finnish as the official language of the country. .

In the Kalevala, Finland arises out of a great sea, the Earth created by the goddess Imatra from the shards of a duck egg.

Suddenly she shook her knee,
Twitched her limbs,
The eggs tumbled into the water,
Into the sea waves propelled;
Cracking the eggs into bits,
Into small shards cut.
The eggs were not muddled in the mire,
The bits not jumbled through the water;
Splendidly did the fragments turn out,
The pieces transformed into things of beauty:
The eggs lower portion
Into Mother Earth below,
The eggs upper portion
Into the Heavens above,
The top half of the yolk
To glow as the Sun,
The egg white
To gleam palely as the Moon,
Any speckles on the eggs,
Those became Stars in Heaven,
Any black spots on the eggs
Those indeed became the Clouds in the Sky.

....

Now in the ninth year,
In the tenth summer
She raised her head from the sea,
Lifts up her head completely,
Begins to perform her acts of creation,
To carry out her works
On the wide ocean expanses,
On the broad open sea.
Where she swung her hand,
There she arranged headlands;
Where she touched the bottom with her foot,
Pools for fish she hollowed;
Where air bubbled in the water,
Eddies there she deepened.
Her hip against the land she rolled:
There fashioning smooth shorelines;
Her feet against the land she turned:

There creating salmon weirs;
Her head against the land she pressed:
There fashioning bays.
Then she swam farther out from land,
Lingered on the ocean deeps.
Formed little islands on the sea,
Produced hidden reefs
For a ship to run aground on,
Seamen to destroy.
Now the islands were arranged,
Little islands created in the sea,
The pillars of the sky erected,
Lands and continents sung into being,
Patterns marbled in rocks,
Designs drawn on crags.
Vainamoinen is not yet born,
The eternal singer has not appeared.

THE KALEVALA- RUNE 1, VERSES 213-288

Vainamoinen was the first man. Born to the goddess Ilmatra, he created the forests, birds and animals. He is the principal character in the Kalevala epic.

Central to the Kalevala epic are many tales of love, envy, revenge and loss - birth, death, resurrection and escape from hell. – shamans, gods, goddesses, sun, moon, fire - magic monstrous fish, eagles and bears. Trees, boulders, birds, animals and fish are endowed with magical powers. Wars of survival are waged by the people of Karjala with the northern tribe of Pohjola. A magic ark which provides endless wealth and power is forged and then lost forever as the two tribes battle. The kantele (a lap harp) is created by Vainamoinen to bring music to the people.

Throughout, many songs describe and celebrate peasant life in the primeval wilderness and itemize magic charms for curing life's ills and worries and ensuring happiness and successful hunting.

The stories of The Kalevala are much in keeping with the actual pre history of Finland which rose from the sea; the southern Askola culture warred with the northern Komsa culture; pagan animistic religion ruled; and all of nature - from rocks and trees to animals, fish and birds - was respected and endowed with life and magic powers; the

common people lived in the wilderness in tune with nature, while "Viking" era warriors fought on horses and ships.

I wonder what ancient event one of the central stories of the book, the creation and loss of the magic ark of plenty, is based on ? Perhaps it is just an echo of the Christian era Ark of the Covenant.

Origins of the Finnish People

The Kalevala while providing intriguing insights into mythological Finland, does not identify where today's Finnish and Karjalainen people came from.

There are two schools of thought on the origin of today's Finnish people.

1.) They are descendants of the new Indo European settlers who crossed over the eastern part of the Baltic Sea around 600 – 500 B.C. during the early Iron Age era; or,

2.) They are descendants of the original settlers who came thousands of years earlier during the Bronze and even the Stone Age; and who assimulated the new 600 B.C. wave of settlers.

Certainly the older Finno Ugric peoples and culture survived in the eastern parts of Karjala; and among the Saami of northern Finland.

Resolution of the origin of the Finnish people will have to rely on future advances in DNA collection and analysis. Unfortunately the availability of the traditional indicators of earlier inhabitants (burials, buildings, bones) is minimal due to the climate, the quick deterioration of bones and artifacts, and the low population density.

While the DNA of the people may have changed, certainly the old language remained. The Finnish language is Finno Ugric, not Indo European like the rest of Europe. Even Russian is an Indo European language. Finno Ugric is a North West Asian language which today survives in north western Russia, Siberia and in Finland, Estonia, and Hungary – but not elsewhere. The Saami branch of the language separated from the Ugric language base around 3,500 B.C., while the Finnish branch separated a thousand years later.

How a European descent people ended up speaking an Asian language is a mystery to me; and, a subject of ongoing scholarly research. One theory is that the conquering "Indo

European" migrants took Finno Ugric wives who raised their children to speak Finnish. Suffice it to say I speak Finnish as does over 95% of the Finnish population. And yes, it is very different from English, French, Portuguese, or German - just ask my children.

My "Pre History"

Now while my children are only fifty percent Finnish (Their mother is Canadian of British origin), my prehistory is one hundred percent Finnish. I have deep maternal and paternal roots in Finland, both from a genetic and written history perspective.

While I cannot guarantee when my ancestors came to Finland, I have been able to trace my ancestors back over 500 years through family folk lore and the Lutheran Black Books. (The Swedish King made the Lutheran clergy his official record keepers. They recorded every birth, marriage, death, and move in or move out of the parish into official parish ledgers which became known as the Black Books).

So, according to the Black Books I can confirm that my pedigree is, with the exception of one black sheep, pure Finnish; and indeed at least one quarter ancient Karjalainen.

While certainly Finnish, based on my Y chromosome DNA tests, a small part (6%) of my deep heritage is Saami – the original ice age inhabitants of Finland who were pushed north by the Finnic tribes and the early Swedish colonizers of Finland.

My father ancestors, the Tuiras, were "Western Finns" from the west coast of Finland.

My father's DNA haplotype is the Z180-L1198 subclade of I2A2A (I-M223). My father's ancestors originally migrated over the western part of the Baltic Sea into Denmark and Sweden around 1,000 B.C., and thence to the west coast of Finland. When specifically my ancestors came to Finland I do not know. They may have been part of the Bronze Age settlement of Sammallahdenmäki in Satakunta which was inhabited from 1500 to 500 B.C.; or perhaps they came in 750 A.D. during the Viking era; or during the 1100s when King Erik of Sweden and Bishop Henry were expanding Roman Catholicism to the Finnish heathens.

Dad's paternal ancestors' were the Ruickas (My great, great grandfather changed his name to Tuira in 1830 when he moved to Oulu). The Ruicka home in 1550 was in Simo in northern Finland on the northern coast of the Gulf of Osthrobothina (The Baltic Sea between Finland and Sweden). They moved to Simo from Kokemäki in Satakunta. Satakunta is one of the initial inhabited areas of Finland near Tampere. Here my earliest known ancestor was Lauri Larens Ryika. There are references to him in the Kokemäki law books of 1469.

Father's maternal ancestors, the Hellman/ Carréns, were from the Swedish settlements of Uusikaarlepyy/ Kristiinankaupunki on the Osthrobothnian coast half way up the west coast of Finland. Written records show they resided there from at least 1750.

My mother's ancestors, the Öhmans, were "Eastern Finns" – and indeed, partly from Karjala itself.

My mother's MtDNA deep ancestry haplotype is H1f1, a common Finnish haplotype. While not the original settlers, the H1f1 peoples came to Finland in the early Bronze Age about 4,000 years ago as part of the Bell Becker Culture.

Mother's paternal ancestors, the Öhman/ Eiskonens were from Viitasaari in central Finland (since the 1720s) and from Joutseno in Karjala (since the 1750s). Joutseno is about 100 kilometers north of Viipuri.

Mother's maternal ancestors, the Tiainen / ??s , were from the lake area of Sääminki parish south of Savonlinna Karjala. They had resided there since at least the 1720s. My ?? paternal maternal ancestor (my great grandfather) is a matter of conjecture as grandmother was born out of wedlock.

So over a quarter of my early heritage is Karelian – the rest is western and central Finnish.

And, for the last century my ancestry is entirely Karelian as all my ancestors migrated to the Viipuri area of Karjala in search of a better life. All of my grandparents were in the Viipuri area by the beginning of the 1900s during the Tsar's reign. Both my father and mother were born there.

My paternal grandparents were city folks and settled in Viipuri. My father's parents, Georg and Valencia Tuira, along with great grandmother Maria, and most of the siblings from both sides of the family, moved from Oulu to Viipuri in 1900, drawn by the work opportunities provided by St Petersburg's booming economy. The industry of Oulu, building and retrofitting sailing ships had vanished with the advent of steam ships.

My maternal grandparents settled on a farm in Kavantsaari, in the countryside twenty-two kilometres north east of Viipuri. My mother's grandfather Erkki Öhman moved to the Viipuri countryside in 1872 from Viitasaari in central Finland. The fifth son of a farmer, he had little future there as primogeniture gave the family homestead to the oldest son, and little to anyone else. The Viipuri countryside provided the potential to own land and to find work.

I have included a list of my family in Appendix E, "My Karjala Family" at the back of this book to help keep track of individuals as they emerge in the book.

CHAPTER 3

A Millennium of Swedish and Russian Wars

Akseli Galleen-Kallela: Kullervon Sotaanlahto

Protect him, mighty Creator,
Guard him, fair God,
Lest the boy be lost,
The mother's child not fall in battle,
Not vanish from among the
creations of the Great Maker,
Those formed by God !
Ukko, reknowned God,
Heavenly Father !

Bring me a fiery cloak,
A flaming shirt to put on,
Under which protection I may wage war
Behind which I may fight,
That my head not come to grief,
My hair not be slashed
In the bright blades whirl,
During a grim swords' reaping !

THE KALEVALA – RUNE 43

A Millennium of Swedish and Russian Wars

Karjala and Viipuri since the earliest times was the battleground between east and west.

Even before the birth of Christ, east and west were in conflict. The Karelians were constantly at war with the other Finnish tribes of western Finland - the Finns "Proper", and the Hämäläiset / Tavastians.

In the 800s this conflict transformed into another age old conflict – one between Sweden and Russia.

Through out the period of Swedish rule continuous wars were waged primarily in Karjala with Russia.

Viking Forays (780-1050 A.D.)

Vikings began the initial Swedish forays into Finland by the late 700s. The Vikings did not colonize Finland, only setting up outposts and trading centres. A large number of these sites were located on the western shores of Lake Ladoga in Karjala.

Starting around 780 the Swedes in the form of the Vikings (also known as Varanagthans, Rus) from Gotland sailed to the Viipuri Gulf, and then raided up the Neva River to Lake Ladoga, up the Olhava River to Novgorod, and from thence, over a 100 years, pillaged along the Dneiper, Don and Volga watersheds to Kiev and Moscow, arriving in Constantinople around 860.

While the Vikings were ancient adversaries of the Russians, they also became the founding tsars of Russia. While the Rus (or Vikings) never populated Russia, in 862

the warring Novgorod tribes requested Rurik, a Viking chieftain, to become their king. (Novgorod was the area of Russia south of Lake Ladoga and St Petersburg). Rurik's descendants expanded the empire to Kiev.

Cooperation and dynastic marriages between Novgorodian and Swedish royal families continued for 150 years. Viking inter marriage with the Karelians themselves was minimal. The Karelians however maintained friendly relations with the Novgorodian merchants and traders.

During this time the Viipuri area itself remained a quiet fishing outpost. The first known settlement in the Viipuri area is from the 9th century, on the site of the present-day Monrepos Park. Its residents made their living hunting, fishing, farming and trading with the Baltic countries.

The First Crusades (1155 – 1250)

Finland and Karjala remained paganistic Hame and Karelian societies until the mid 1100s. In the 12th century Sweden converted fully to the Catholic Church. The Catholic Church issued Papal decrees for crusades against the Novgorod lands controlled by the Orthodox church.

Sweden and Russia drifted into hostilities that could not be permanently settled ever again – such is the healing power of religion...

The Swedish-Novgorodian Wars: 1150--1323

Wars, known as the Swedish-Novgorodian Wars, commenced between the Russians and the Swedes, with raids and wars continuing for 150 years until 1323 - the First Crusade (1155) - the Second Crusade (1249) - and the Third Crusade (1293).

In 1155 Sweden, under King Erik and Bishop Henry, arrived in Finland – the purpose being to expand the Swedish domain and to convert Finland from paganism to Catholicism. Settlement began first in south west Finland around Turku (Indeed around my cousins home in the hamlet of Nousiainen just outside Turku). Not many Swedes actually moved to settle in Finland. The Swedes who came were bishops and priests and Swedish nobility (and their entourage and troops) who were granted estates in return for ruling the area on behalf of the Swedish monarch. Along with them came burghers and retainers.

While south western Finland came under Sweden's sway Karjala itself did not come under Swedish rule until 1293 when the castle of Viipuri was established.

Indeed before 1293 the Karelian tribe supported Novgorod, raiding together with them along the Baltic Coast of Finland. Sweden and the Hame tribes reciprocated with periodic raids to Lake Ladoga.

This changed in the Third Crusade.

The Swedish Marshall Torgils Knutson led the Third Swedish Crusade against Novgorod (Russia). In 1293, upon arriving in Viipuri, he ordered a castle to be built on the small island.

While the Swedes raided into Russia, the Russians responded in kind with their own forays into Finland. One of the Novgorod raids into Vanaja Finland is recorded in the Novgorod Chronicles. (Vanaja is an old iron age town near Hämeenlinna in central Finland. I visited Vanaja quite often as my Uncle Yrjö lived in Hämeenlinna after the war and is buried in the old Vanaja church yard).

"In 1311 the men of Novgorod went in war over sea to the country of the Swedes, against the Finnish people, with Prince Dmitri Romanovich and having crossed the sea they first occupied the Kupets River. They burned villages and captured people and destroyed the cattle. And there Konstantin the son of Ilya Stanirmirovich was killed by a column that went in pursuit. They took the whole of the Black River and thus following the Black River they reached the town of Vanaja and they took the town and burned it.

And the Swedes fell back into the citadel. For the place was very strong and firm, on a high rock, not having access from any side. And they sent with greeting, asking for peace, but the men of Novgorod did not grant peace and they remained three days and three nights wasting the district. They burned the large villages, laid waste all the corn fields, and did not leave a single horn of cattle; and going hence, they took the Kavgola River and the Perna River and they came out to sea and returned all well to Novgorod"

The Treaty of Pähkinnäsaari/ Noteborg of 1323 ended the Swedish – Novgorodian wars. With it Finland, Karjala and Viipuri officially became Swedish territory. At that point no northern boundary was set as the area north of Savonlinna was inhabited only by nomadic Saami.

When the peace treaty of Noteborg was finalized in 1323, Magnus II created a special fief in Vyborg in recognition of its' importance as a bulwark against the east. From the 13th through the 15th century the castle commanders ruled Viipuri province as almost a separate state. The law of the land, they had the power to dispense justice, wage local war, and to collect taxes. They were entitled to spend the tax money as they saw fit – be that to improve fortifications and raise armies in defence of the realm's eastern border – or to increase their own wealth.

The Swedish monarch appointed the lord of the fief of Vyborg. Although the fief of Vyborg castle and its countryside was not formally hereditary, almost all appointees were related to the Bonde-Baat-Haak family. While they had a free hand, they were nonetheless Swedish nobility and usually returned to Sweden to embroil themselves in politics – often to be ultimately executed like Torgils Knutson - sometimes like Kaarle Bonde, to become King of Sweden – King Kaarle IX.

While quite autonomous on local matters, the Viborg ruler did follow the dictates of the crown on major wars.

Through the subsequent four hundred years the castle was the home of the ruler and military commander of Viipuri and Karjala. War and peace continued constantly through the centuries between Sweden and Russia.

During the second half of the 1400s, Russia while not advancing aggressively into Finland and Sweden, nonetheless continued to raid into Karjala. During this period the Viipuri commanders constructed further fortifications against Russia. In 1474 the defensive towers and medieval walls were built around the town of Viipuri to protect it against the marauders.

As well, in 1475 the Viborg commander established another castle, Olavinlinna, over a hundred kilometres north of Viborg in Savo. The Viipuri fief holders were responsible for holding the northern border as well as the southern one. Through the Middle Ages, the fortress remained under the command of Viborg.

The Russo-Swedish War: 1495-1497

A major war, The Russo-Swedish War, erupted in 1495 between the Swedish regent Sten Sture the Elder and Tsar Ivan III.

The Russo-Swedish war itself resulted from an alliance between Ivan III of Russia and Hans of Denmark against the Swedish Monarchs -the Sture family - rulers of the Norwegian, Swedish, Danish Union of Kalmar.

It was during this war that the much talked about Viipuri explosion (Viipurin Pamaus) occurred - an event that resounded throughout Europe. Ivan III sent Prince Daniil Shchenya to lay siege to Vyborg. The siege lasted for three months and ended when Knut Posse the Vyborg castle commander detonated a huge explosion which "scared the Muscovites out of their wits". On November 30, 1495 when the Russian invaders breeched the castle ramparts and were about to conquer the castle and the town, Lord Knut Posse, triggered a massive explosion under one of the castle towers.

Although what happened is shrouded in folklore, the attackers fled. The attackers left alive after the explosion escaped in great fear. The tremendous concussive waves, intense noise, dust and devastation had come totally unexpectedly. The explosion resulted in an intense light

phenomenon similar to a cross appearing in the sky. The date of the attack, November 30th, was the feast of St Andrew. The attacking Russian army full of religious adherents - both officers and peasants - thought the saint was protecting the town. They halted their attack and retreated from the town.

The Russo – Swedish War ended in 1497 without any major territory changes.

Peace reigned for sixty years. Bitter internal religious conflict however arose as a result of King Kustaa Vaasa's conversion to Lutheranism in 1523. Roman Catholic churches became Lutheran, and the Catholic clergy, such as the Franciscan and Dominican monks of Viipuri, were banished. In 1554 Viipuri became a Lutheran diocese with its' own bishop.

King Kustaa Vaasa's religious fervour, and his aggressive expansionary policies, garnered victims throughout Finland, not just in Viipuri. It claimed my forebears Olli and Bridgetta Ruicka in Simo in northern Finland.

In 1566 Olli and Bridgetta were burned at the stake as witches by the Swedish government and the Lutheran clergy. The formal charge was practicing the old animistic religion. And while this may have been some truth to this, the prime reason was that he was a wealthy influential man who was seen as a threat to the newly expansionary Swedes and to the success of the Lutheran clergy's campaign of religious purification. (Prior to the reformation period the Roman Catholics had been less sanguine).

The Livonian War: 1554-1595

The next major war, The Livonian War, was fought from 1554 to 1595 during the reigns of King Johan III and Tsar Ivan IV the Terrible.

War commenced between Sweden and Russia in 1554 fuelled by personal animosity between Gustaf I and Ivan IV the Terrible; and, by the collapse of the Teutonic Order . The Teutonic Order had ruled the south eastern Baltic coast from Prussia to Estonia for three centuries. Sweden wanted to acquire Livonia, the Estonian and Latvian portion of the empire rather than having it fall into the Russian sphere of influence.

During March 1555, Russia mounted an organized attack into Finland. After initial success they were beaten back when Sweden sent reinforcements to Finland. In turn the Swedish-Finnish troops attacked the Noteborg fortress (Pähkinälinna) east of present day St Petersburg; but, without success.

In 1556, Russia attacked Viborg with a 20,000 strong army. However, after a few days of pillaging in the area around Vyborg, the Russian forces left. The reason for this is not clear. Conceivable reasons might be bad discipline or a raging disease among the Russian soldiers. Perhaps it was never the aim to conquer Viborg, only to ravage the areas surrounding the town as a demonstration of power.

Relative peace reigned until 1590, broken by the famine of 1586-87. The Viborg commander writes,

"God grant that the poor people stay alive until we get grain in the spring".

In those days "relative peace" had a somewhat different meaning. In 1581,

The Russians pillaged the North Country, burning all the houses in Simo, including my paternal ancestral home. Simo is located between Oulu and Sweden on the coast of the Gulf of Osthrobothnia.

In 1590 concentrated fighting began again in Estonia. Concurrent with this, Russia ravaged the coast of Finland from Viipuri to Helsinki.

Fighting also occurred in 1590 in Eastern Karelia, where the Swedes together with Finnish peasants sacked Russian settlements bordering the White Sea. Russia gradually overcame these setbacks, pacifying Karelia.

Swedish losses were so great and the situation so difficult, that in 1594 Swedish King Kaarle IX granted Vyborg commoners freedom from taxes in return for fighting the Russians – promising worthy horses and good swords.

Sweden emerged victorious at the end of the war.

The peace treaty, The Treaty of Täyssinä (Kakisalmi) of 1595, as well as providing Livonia to Sweden, expanded Finland north to Murmansk by the Barents Sea.

The Ingrian War (Inkerinsota): 1610-1617

Fifteen years later in 1610, The Ingrian War flared up between King Gustaf II Adolph and Tsar Michael I.

The 1617 Treaty of Stolbovo which ended the war, added Ingria (the area just south west of St Petersburg) and the west coast of Lake Ladoga (Kexholm/Käkisalmi) to Karjala.

Anders Munck, an ancestor of my great grandmother (rakas mummo) commanded a cavalry regiment stationed in Ingria after the peace. The family had come from Denmark around 1611 as mercenary knights.

The Finnish boundaries set by this peace, with the exception of Ingria, formed the boundary of Finland when it became an independent country three hundred years later in 1918.

While the Stolbavan Peace increased the commercial importance of Viborg, it temporarily reduced Viipuri's military importance as the border moved further east and further south.

The Ruptuuri War (Ruptuurisota)- Sweden's Second Northern War: 1650- 1658

Forty years later, in 1650, The Ruptuuri War, part of Sweden's Second Northern War started.

The Russo – Swedish portion of the war ended in a stale mate.

During the war my ancestor Anders Munck, was the Colonel in charge of the Karjalan Cavalry Regiment,
fighting in Latvia and Poland. I can not image what that was like.

The Treaty of Kardis, signed in 1658 between King Karl X Gustav and Tsar Alexis I, maintained the territorial accords of the Treaty of Stolbovo of 1617.

Religious boundaries however changed. Karjala's Orthodox Christians fled to Russia, rather than being forced to convert to Lutheranism.

Less than fifty years later The Great Northern War started. This started the end of Sweden's rule of Finland, and the transition of the country to Russia.

CHAPTER 4

Karjala and Suomi Under the Tsars

E Tanttu: Isho Viha

CHAPTER 4

Karjala and Suomi Under the Tsars

Tsar Peter the Great conquered Karjala and placed it under his rule in 1710. Wars, known as the Great Hate and the Lesser Hate, ravaged Karjala.

In 1721 as part of Treaty of Nystad / Uuusikaupunki, Karjala became a part of Russia known as Old Finland.

In 1810 in the Suomen Sota, Tsar Alexander I wrested all of Finland from Swedish rule. Karjala was once more joined with the rest of Finland, now the Grand Russian Duchy of Finland.

The Great Northern War (The Great Hate): 1700-1721

The Great Northern War (or the Great Hate – *"Iso viha"* as the Finns knew it) started in 1700 with Russia and its' allies attacking Sweden. Russia's allies included Poland, Prussia, Germany, Lithuania, and surprisingly, Denmark and Norway. Sweden by comparison was allied with the Cossacks of the Ukraine and the Ottoman empire.

The war was driven by Sweden's desire to found a great Swedish Empire - the obsession of Sweden's young warrior king, Kaarle XII. The war engulfed all of Northern Europe. Troops of course were levied throughout Finland. Indeed Kaarle XII's personal regiment was largely Finnish.

Over twenty years, fighting occurred in Ingria, Estonia, Poland, Ukraine and Germany. After many victories in the initial years of the war, Kaarle XII's main army was destroyed in 1709 by a much larger Russian force at the Battle of Poltava in the Ukraine. After the disaster of Poltava in 1709, Finland was left largely to fend for itself.

In 1710 Peter the Great captured Vyborg. Russian forces had attacked the city already in 1703 but without success. Peter the Great attacked Vyborg with a large army, bombarding the castle from the shore and from his war ships. After a six month assault with no help coming from Sweden and supplies running low, the castle surrendered with a promise that they could leave safely...and not for the first, nor the last time in world history... the promise was not kept. Peter marched the majority of them into slavery in Russia to build the city of St. Petersburg.

With the loss of Vyborg, the Swedes lost an important naval and land base, and their activities in the Gulf of Finland were restricted. Russia's occupation of Vyborg allowed the creation of a base to supply troops and build ships, and expanded the zone of action of the Baltic Fleet (At this point St. Petersburg did not exist).

Vyborg demonstrated this importance as a key military base from 1712 to 1714, when full-scale Russian land operations began in Finland. Thus, in effect, the capture of Vyborg and Karjala served to determine the outcome of the Great Northern War by establishing a staging area for further military actions.

In 1712 Russia started its' first campaign to capture Finland. It ended in failure. A better organized campaign in 1713 managed to capture Helsinki and drive the defending Swedes away from the coast. In February 1714 the Swedish army in Finland was decisively defeated at Isokyrön near

Vaasa. Sweden continued to try to hinder Russia's advance into the Gulf of Bothnia by blockading the coastal sea routes. The Swedish fleet was however defeated by the Russian flotilla at the Battle of Gangut in August 1714 near Hanko.

The remaining Swedish fleet and army abandoned Finland in late 1714.

After the loss at Storkyro, the Finns began waging partisan warfare against the Russians. As retaliation, the Finnish peasants were forced to pay large contributions to the occupying Russians (as was the custom in that time). Plundering was widespread. Churches were looted and towns burned to the ground. A scorched earth zone several hundred kilometres wide was burned to hinder Swedish counter offensives. Thousands of Finnish civilians were killed and many more were taken away as slaves. Peter the Great wanted to create an empty buffer zone between Sweden and Russia, and ordered everything there destroyed, including the people.

> *The Russians raided through my Simo ancestral home again. Peter the Greats forces pillaged and plundered burning down the houses and the church. I wonder if some of my family was killed or enslaved ? Several caches of buried Swedish plootu coins unique to that era have been found in the area. Obviously the owners did not survive to dig them up again.*

Thousands, especially officials, fled to the safety of Sweden. The poorer peasants hid in the woods to avoid the ravages of the occupiers and their press gangs. Atrocities were at their worst between 1714–1717 when the infamous former Swedish Count Gustaf Douglas was in charge of the Russian occupation.

When Kaarle XII was killed in a battle at Fredriksten Norway in 1718, the Great Northern War ended. Peace treaties were signed with Prussia and Saxony in 1719, Norway and Denmark in 1720, and finally Russia in 1721.

The war ended the Swedish empire, leaving Russia as the new major power in the Baltic Sea and an important new player in European politics.

With the Treaty of Nystad / Uusikaupunki of 1721, Sweden lost its' territories in Ingria, Estonia and Latvia.

Viipuri and Karjala became part of Russia, known as Old Finland. The borders of modern day Finland reflect those drawn up in the Treaty of Nystad / Uusikaupunki.

A new age commenced in Viipuri's multicultural history with Russian influences mixing even further with the city's Swedish, Finnish and German cultures.

It took several decades for the Finnish population and economy to recover after the devastation of the war and the subsequent Northern European black plague. Just in time for the Second Northern War.

The Second Northern War (The Lesser Hate): 1740-1743

The Second Northern War, known as The Hats War in Sweden; and in Finland as The Lesser Hate (Pikku Viha), commenced in 1740 between King Frederik I Hessen and Tsarina Elizabeth I.

At the start of the war Russia successfully marched from Vyborg into Finland conquering the Hamina fortress near Kotka. A major battle was also fought in Lappeenranta between four Finnish regiments and the Russian forces. Both sides suffered over 2,000 casualties in the ½ day battle. The Finnish forces lost. The Russian forces pillaged and burnt the town - but did not advance further into Finland . An armistice was agreed to with Russia in early December 1741. Nonetheless during the winter Russian Cossacks and Hussars raided the Finnish side of the border but were often repulsed by local Finns.

Lappeenranta is an old town near my Hyva Mummo's home. While just 70 kilometers north of Viipuri, it is still part of Finland. When I visited the city in 2016 I was impressed by the old fortress on the hill overlooking the Lake Saima harbour. I stopped to read the plaque on a monument outside the fortress gates to the battle of 1741. The inscription ends with the words:

> *Carefully guard this soil. It has been bought with the blood and sweat of your ancestors.*

A message that has been repeated too often throughout the centuries of Finland's history.

In the spring of 1742 the Swedish commander organized an attack against Vyborg, but the Swedish navy refused to support the assault.

The Russians again seized the initiative and moved onto the offensive. With the support of the Russian galley fleet, a 30,000 man strong Russian army under the command of Field-Marshal Lacy marched from Vyborg. In June after crossing the border, it once more took Hamina.

Russia continued its' advance into Finland, supported by its fleet, taking Pori without encountering effective Swedish resistance. With inept Swedish military command, and no support from the Swedish fleet, Helsinki fell in August.

All the Swedish forces retreated to Sweden in early September 1742, leaving Finland occupied by the Russians – a period known as the Lesser Hate due to the pillage, occupation and devastation of the countryside.

The war came formally to an end with the Treaty of Turku (Abo) in 1743. The border was moved 65 kilometres further west to the Kymi River – providing Russia with control of the stretch from Kotka to Savonlinna. This placed the old fortresses of Hamina and Olavinlinna in Russia.

The area acquired by Russia became known as Old Finland. Neither Olonets Karjala - stretching north from the Svväri River between Lake Ladoga and Lake Onega – nor White Russia - the large area north of Lake Ladoga/Onega between Finland and the White Sea – became part of Old Finland. Although populated by the Karelian tribe, they had never been part of the Swedish territory. They had always been part of Russia.

Initially Old Finland was part of the St. Petersburg Governate. After the Treaty of Turku and the addition of Käkisälmi and Kymi, Karjala became a separate governate called the Governate of Wiborg managed by an appointed Governor General. Located in Viipuri, the Governor General administered the area on behalf of the Tsar. The Wiborg Governance consisted of three areas which reflected when the area became a Russia territory; namely Wiburg, Kexholm and Kymi. Today those areas of Karjala are known as Karjalan Kannas; Laatokan Karjala; and South Karjala. All became part of Finland when Finland became a country in 1918. The Kannas and Laatokan Karjala were lost to Russia in the Talvisota and Jatkosota wars, but Kymi (Kotka and Savo areas) remained part of Finland.

During the Old Finland period, life changed little from the Swedish era; other than Karjala became part of the Russian empire instead of the Swedish one. Existing customs, both religious and cultural, were allowed to continue. Serfdom was not imposed.

Peace reigned until the Napoleonic Wars with Old Finland prospering under Russian rule. While the Tsar now ruled Karjala, Russia wanted yet a further buffer with their ancient enemies.

The Suomen Sota (Finland's War):

In 1808 Sweden and Russia were at war again - the Suomen Sota (Finland's War) – as Russia endeavoured to gain control of the Baltic Sea during the Napoleonic wars. Finland again was the battleground.

One of the major battles of the Suomi War occurred in Juthas in 1808 – on "gramps' Hellman's farm. Family folklore has our ancestor:

"Ranting and raving during the battle, complaining about the Swedish/Finnish and Russian soldiers tramping through his rye and oat fields – and why couldn't they go fight elsewhere."

In the Battle of Juthas the Swedish/Finnish forces defeated the Russians. The battle of Juthas has become legendary as a result of Johan Ludvig Runeberg's epic poem Doeblin at Jutas. In the subsequent battle of Oravainen, Sweden lost Finland, the eastern province of their kingdom. All of Finland became part of Russia.

The losing Swedish army retreated from Finland back to Sweden along the road that ran by the front steps of my great, great grandfather Johannes Tuira' home in Simo. I wonder what impression it left on him as a 10 year old boy ?

In 1809, after a victorious Russian campaign, peace was signed between Sweden and Russia. Sweden ceded Finland to Russia thereby ending over 600 years of Swedish rule of Finland.

Finland became a Grand Duchy of Russia, reporting directly to the Tsar. As such it had substantial autonomy over its own domestic affairs.

One of my ancestors from central Finland had a bayonet with a medal affixed to it. The Cyrillic enscription on the medal reads "For excellent marksmanship". Based on the type of musket the medal appears to be 1800 vintage – so from the Suomen Sota period. Why one of my Finnish ancestors would have an "1809" Russian marksmanship medal is a mystery.

Life in Tsarist Finland

The next century of Russian rule was overall a period of prosperity for Finland. During this time peace reigned and Russia invested significant monies in modernizing Finland.

But of course even during this period there was war. In this case the Crimean War of 1853 – 1856 between Russia and France, England, and the Ottoman Empire.

During this period British navy ships bombarded the Åland archipelago and the west coast of Finland, including the seafaring town of Kristiinankaupunki, home of my father's mother's mother Maria.

"Maria Christiana recounted, that when I was a little girl and England was bombarding us, we had to flee from the shelling of the town into the forest. It was hard as grandmother was quite old and kept crying. My mother had to take care of both myself and grandma"

The population of Finland quadrupled. With it, a large class of industrial workers and tenant farmers emerged, altering the social profile from one consisting purely of an upper class of nobility, clergy and educated gentry; and a lower class of rural uneducated farm workers.

The upper class was primarily Swedish while the workers were Finnish. Finland had always been a Finnish speaking country. At the start of the 19th century 85% of the population's mother tongue was Finnish and only 15 % Swedish. Today 5% of the population is Swedish speaking.

The Russian language never took a major hold in Finland even though Finland was a Grand Duchy of Russia. The Russian speaking inhabitants were comprised mostly of Russian officials and the Russian army. The exception to this was Karjala, the eastern area of Finland, where Russian was more common.

While Finnish was the language of the people, the language of government and of the upper class remained Swedish. During the 1850s the Fennoman movement arose. Its' goal was to make Finnish an official language and to lift Finnish culture to be on a par with Swedish culture.

With Finland no longer ruled by Sweden, the Finnish language and culture increased in importance. Together with this, Finnish nationalism increased.

While Russia allowed Finland considerable independence and governance over its' domestic affairs, Finland continued to be governed by the age old Swedish upper class, in government, religion and commerce.

With the industrialization and population growth, the working class began to push for social equality – votes, better pay and working conditions, collective bargaining, more equitable sharing of the country's wealth, and ownership of land. While Finland was not a feudal society and rural Finns had never been serfs, the majority of the land was owned by local landed gentry and the clergy. The ordinary Finns were tenant farmers, cottagers, or hired workers.

The rural peasants were free to leave and go work wherever they wished in Finland. Movement outside the parish however was minimal as long as work was available from the local land owners, and famine did not force one to leave in search of food.

During the reigns of Alexander I, Nicholas I, Alexander II, and Alexander III, the Grand Duchy of Finland prospered in relative calm.

The exception to this was a disastrous climate induced famine from 1866 to 1868 which killed 15% of the population, affecting Karjala and all of Finland. Among those who suffered were great grandfather Henrik Hellman of Juthas. As my second cousin Elina recounts;

"Henrik and Caisa and their children left their home in Juthas. Probably they moved due to the need for food, and the fact that Caisa's four younger sisters also lived on their mothers small tenant farm.

During the years 1858 through 1870, the family wandered throughout Ostrobothnia. Based on the records of the birth of their children they were living in Kyrkoby in 1858; in Urjala in 1862; and in Helsinki in 1868.

The period was a time of famine in Finland. The hardest years began already in 1862 and it struck worst in Bothnia. The years 1865-66 gave poor crops, but the most horrible was 1867, when the winter continued even to the Midsummer. Tens of thousands perished during their beggar wanderings from hunger and diseases. 270,000 died in 1866-68 - 15% of the entire Finnish population of 1,747,000. As in some other regions in Urjala, there was organized building of railways as emergency work in return for little more than bread as payment.

All of Henrik and Caisa's children except for Karl August died within one year of their birth.

Caisa herself died in 1868 in Helsinki due to complications of child birth only a few days after the birth and death of her 4th child.

During the reign of Alexander I, the capital of Finland was moved from Turku to Helsinki in order to negate the influence of the old ruling class located in Turku. Under the direction of the architect C.L. Engel, the small military and commercial city was transformed into an impressive new capital city.

The liberal reign of Alexander II (1855-1881) was especially positive for Finland. In 1863 Finnish was proclaimed an official language. In 1865 Finland was allowed to establish its' own currency, the markka. And, in 1878, Finland was permitted to establish its' own small army.

In 1899 with the ascent of Nicholas II, this changed. Nicholas II began a program to Russify Finland and to place it under the rule of the Russian government, as opposed to leaving Finland to rule its' own domestic affairs. With this also came a reversal to a more autocratic class system as opposed to increased democratization.

Nicholas II's Russification policy, together with the growth of Finnish nationalism, and the raising social unrest in Finland, augmented by shortages caused by World War I and continuous upheaval in Russia, led to a decade and a half of conflict, culminating in the Finnish Civil War.

But first a few words about the parishes and feudal manors of the Karjala countryside before delving into that bitter and contentious subject - the Finnish Civil War.

CHAPTER 5

Parishes and Feudal Manors

Akseli Galleen-Kallela

Whence the sound box for the kantele ?
From the jaw bone of a huge pike
Whence the pegs for the kantele ?
From the teeth of giant pike fish
Whence the strings come from the kantele ?
From the mane of Demon's gelding

THE KALEVALA - RUNE 40

Parishes and Feudal Manors

Parishes

Karjala was organized into administrative districts based on the original church parishes. The churches were about thirty kilometres apart, centered so that it was no longer than an hour and a half horse and carriage ride to church. In the most populated portion of Karjala, the Kannas / Isthmus there were 30 parishes.

Kavantsaari, my mothers' home was part of the Parish of Antrea. Antrea in many respects was representative of the Karjalan Kannas countryside (Other than for the manor holding which was the oldest and by far the largest in Karjala).

Antrea (St. Andrew) by the Vuoksi River was inhabited since the Stone Age. Indeed the earliest inhabitants were there in the Mesolithic Stone Age as 10,000 year old fishing nets were discovered near Antrea. Kavantsaari itself was inhabited early in Finland's history. A bears' head stone axe from about 1800 B.C. as well as Bronze Age ornaments were discovered in Kavantsaari. By the 1300s a small hamlet existed. The "center of civilization", the Kavantsaari manor, was established in 1523.

Antrea did not become a centre of note until a church was established there in 1724. Before Antrea got its own church it was part of the Jääski home parish of St Peters. It was when its' own church was established, that Antrea officially got its' name. The name is variously attributed to being by the Vuoksi River which in earlier times was known as the Andrea River; and, being named in honour of Peter the Greats' brother, Andreas.

The parish/district of Antrea was 35 kilometers by 31 kilometers in size. Within it there were twenty "school districts" of which Kavantsaari was one. Kavantsaari did not become part of the Andrea parish until 1862. Prior to that it was part of the Viipuri countryside parish - Viipuri Maaseurakunta.

The Feudal Manor of Kavantsaari

There were many estates in Karjala, especially on the Kannas. Before the Civil War, life in the parishes revolved around the manor (Hovi as it was known by my parents).

Kavantsaari had the largest and oldest estate in Karjala.

Before the Kavantsaari land became an estate, the land was part of the Fief of Viipuri. From 1320 to 1534 Viipuri and Karjala was an independent fiefdom of Sweden. In 1320, Viipuri castle and its' dominions were obtained by Lord Peter Jonsson (Haak). As a fiefdom, the lord owned all the land and associated monies and taxes. Finland did not have serfdom, so the fief holder did not own the people. The lord was however, needless to say, the law of the land. In return he was responsible on behalf of the king for the military protection of the area. And in the case of Viipuri this responsibility was significant.

When King Gustav Vaasa abolished independent fiefdoms in 1534, he established the Kavantsaari estate – granting it to Maunu Niilonpoika Stiernfors, the Steward of Viipurin Linna, in consideration of his protection of Sweden's eastern border.

Stiernfors however had a disagreement with the king in 1555 and was called back to Sweden. The land reverted back to the crown. The estate then exchanged hands at the will of the Swedish monarch. In 1562 King Erik XIV granted it to Bertil Goraninpoika Mjohundi who was also the Steward of Viipurin Linna, and then to the Sklam family. The Sklam family abandoned it by 1600 –partly as a result of the estate being burned down by the Russians in the 1570-1595 war (ended by the Täyssinä/ Käkisalmi peace) .

After being forsaken for several decades, Queen Kristiina of Sweden (1632-1654) granted the Kavantsaari estate to Lieutenant Colonel Bernard Taube. It remained in the Taube family until the late 1600s. Around 1655 Taube's brother in law, Henrik Rehbinder, bought it. Rehbinder was the Commander in Chief of Sweden's army in Finland.

Upon Rehbinders death in 1680, his, and Taubens' heirs, were unable to retain the holding and it reverted to the Swedish crown.

It languished once more until 1710, when, after Peter the Greats' conquest of Karjala, it became the property of the Russian crown. For some years it served as the colonel's headquarters and administrative centre. In 1726, Catharine the Great granted the estate to Major General Ivan Schuwaloff, the commander of Viipuri. The estate remained with the Schuwaloff family until 1803.

In 1803 it became part of the holdings of the Olchi merchant family. In 1846 Count Carl Gustaf Mannerheim (the grandfather of Marshall C.G. Mannerheim) bought it. However it was sold within two years to Viipuri's governor, Major General Alexander Thesleff. It remained with the Thesleffs until Finland lost Karjala in 1944.

The history of the Kavantsaari estate exhibits the power of the monarch and the importance of the military. All the owners of the estate were military leaders of Viipuri and Karjala - the land bestowed to them at the whim of the reigning Swedish or Russian monarch.

The estate was the largest landholding in Karjala, covering an area of about fifteen square miles.

The size of the landholding was even larger initially. During King Gustaf Vaasa's reign it was six mantals.

In that era an estate of one mantal had to provide one mounted warrior with horse and equipment. One mantal was around 500 to1,000 hectares dependant on the fertility of the region. Based on this, the original Kavantsaari estate would have been 3,000 to 6,000 ha. – twenty square miles. So very large for Finland, as an estate of even one mantal was considered a large manor.

The manor was located on the shores of Kavantjärvi lake in the shade of hundred year old trees. Its garden's oak trees were 600 years old. As well, giant sequoia, so large that two grown men could not get their outstretched arms around them, towered along the shore.

The estate had thirty six tenant farmers plus an additional 2,500 hectares of forest, lake and field.

The classic styled manor house was modest for such an old esteemed land holding. Two stories, it consisted of eighteen rooms filled with old furniture and valuable paintings. Dependent on the room, it was furnished in Late Empire, Biedermeier or Jugend style. East-Indian or Wedgewood porcelain, and wonderful 1700 era silver graced the tables during parties.

The house itself was built in 1720s by its' first Russian owner – Major General Schuwaloff.

Not only the manor lords made the house their home. It was the headquarters of the Red commanders during the Civil War; the site of a field hospital and headquarters of the 1st Division during the Talvisota; and, the headquarters of Lieutenant General T. Laatikainen during the epic Tali-Ihantala battle of the Jatkosota. Kavantsaari being on both an important rail link and a road junction into Finland, was a much fought over military gateway.

But the purpose of the Kavantsaari estate was agriculture. Its' farm buildings were considerably more impressive then the house. The stone cattle barn held 300 cows and 10 bulls, while the separate stables sheltered 40 horses.

The manor employed a large full time work force – estate manager, foremen, cow herds, milk maids, hired hands, drivers, cooks, parlour maids. This work force was supplemented by part time assistance of the tenant farmers as part of their land agreement.

Concerning Land
Ownership & Crofters

Most of the land in Karjala as elsewhere in Finland was seized by the Swedish crown in 1300. The monarchs in turn granted it as huge independent fiefdoms to various Swedish nobility / military leaders. As well the clergy received large tracts of land. In 1534 King Gustaf Vaasa disbanded the fiefdoms, taking them back for the crown. In return the monarch granted various estates based on services rendered or family relationships.

Small independent farms (talo/ itsenäinen tila) did arise: either residual lands of early tribal chiefdoms, land purchased from the crown, or land granted in return for some particular service.

But the vast majority of arable land was owned by the manor lords (hovis) – except of course for the expansive Finnish wilderness, which remained unclaimed. These holdings were either kartanos (large estates but still paying tax), säteri (owned and tax free) or rälssitalo (owned, tax free, and with hereditary rights). While the ultimate was the rälssitalo, in reality the nature of the land holding changed with the either the thrust of the sword, or the stroke of the pen – be it of either the monarch, or in later years, the government. The Kavantsaari estate was a rälssitalo.

A requirement through most of the years of Swedish rule of all small and large farm owners, irrespective of type, was to provide soldiers to the Crown.

Unless it was a large estate, generally three or more farms had to get together in order to be able to source and support one soldier. For example from 1682 to 1810 my Ruicka "witch" ancestors living in Simo in northern Finland had to meet the military levy. As outlined in Simonkylän Vanhojen Talojen Historiaa by Tariina Heikkilä:

The soldier levy was established by Kaarle XI. In 1682 he established a dependence of land holding on compulsory military service, leading to the birth of the army. The state reached an agreement with the countryside, which tied land ownership to an agreed number of military conscripts. Every two to four houses jointly raised the required conscripts,

dividing the cost equitably based on relative land size and wealth.

The soldiers got paid. They received a torppa farm and food. If away on training or service the farm was taken care of for them. As recompense for a full conscript complement, the landowners got relief from taxes or paid less taxes. If the conscripts place became open they had to find a new man within three months. If it was a cavalryman this was six weeks. The soldiers' annual compensation was thirty taalaris on top of the torppa. The torppa had to have a nine forearms long and wide house, a six forearms long and wide storage house, a small barn and hayloft, a silage/cabbage building, half a barrel of grain, eight pecks of summer fodder, and two winter loads of hay.

This conscription was ended in 1810 when Finland became an autonomous Grand Duchy of Russia. Instead of conscripts Finland had to pay Russia compensation monies. Of course this resulted in higher taxes.

The vast portion of the country people did not own land, being rather "peasants" of two types:

- Landless workers, and
- Land renters

The landless workers were villagers and farm hands. Most worked as farm hands (renki) and maids (piika), living on the farm and being paid in room and board and minimal wages. Others worked either in the village as craftsmen or as day workers on farms. Irrespective of where they worked, they were free men, not serfs. They were able to leave whenever they wished, subject to any debts they may have incurred.

The land renters were either tenant farmers (torppari) or cottagers (mäkitupa). The land renters grew in numbers starting in the early 1800s. As the ravages of constant wars and famines abetted, the population numbers began to grow. This led to clearing and settling of the forests and swamps of the land owners in return for day work.

The mäkitupa or cottagers rented small landholdings generally of five hectares or less. While they farmed their land, the land was not their primary source of living. They worked as independent hired hands for larger landholdings or as carpenters or other village workers in order to make a living.

The torppari or tenant farmers "leased" a large enough landholding (usually thirty to fifty hectares) to make a living. The torppa was granted by the large hovi land owner, or sometimes the clergy. The torppari in return was obliged to work a set number of days of work on the hovi in payment. Sometimes payment was made in goods such as grain, hay, even money, as well as in day work. The torppari became a very powerful and militant group in rural Finland.

The torparri never owned the land. There was no guarantee that they could remain on the land forever. "Rental" was agreed to for specified time periods, and while usually renewed could be arbitrarily terminated by the lord. Any houses and barns that were built and clearing of land / improvements reverted back to the manor.

Vaino Linna in his epic book Under the North Star, vividly captures the nature of the relationship, as his central character Jussi Koskela struggles to wrestle a productive tenant farm from the parsonage swamp land holding.

> In the beginning, Jussi approaches the old pastor on whose estate he had been working and living since he was an orphaned little boy about creating a tenant farm.

"I've been thinking, being a hired man when you're married is not much of a life. If you, Mr. Pastor, would let me have the swamp...

My good boy, don't talk nonsense ...a farm in that raw swamp ? And what's wrong with your staying here ?

> A year and a half later Jussi endeavours to obtain a formal agreement for the land.

"No actual contract had been drawn up, and the pastor would answer Jussi's anxious questions only by saying he would come and take a look first. When the spring weather turned warmer, he did come...he was amazed at what he saw...

The pastor initially hesitates as the swamp is turning into a much bigger farm than he envisioned. But the old parson agrees to a formal contract with agreed upon terms:

"The work in lieu of rent would not begin until a year from that autumn. First a day a week on foot, the following year a day a week with a horse, the year after that a day a week with a horse and one on foot, and finally, two days with a horse and one on foot. The rent would not exceed that amount, at least while he ruled the parsonage. And a proper document would be drawn up that would apply until his death."

> Five years later when the old pastor died, the agreement expired. The new pastor visited the farm with his parish council to appraise the land and to determine whether Koskela should keep it, and under what terms. The new pastor discussed the matter with Toyry an influential independent land owner on the council.

That Koskela wants a contract now. How does one deal with tenants here ? How long do the contracts last ?

It varies a lot. Some can be cancelled with a years' notice, others with five or ten years. There are even lifelong contracts ... but for church property the last law says you can make a contract for fifty years ... but not longer...and the tenant farm must be well run, and the tenant not convicted of any crime in a court of law...as a rule I don't favour long term contracts myself. I'm not talking about the Koskela case, just in general terms. It's like this: give a tenant a long term contract, and he lives like an animal in the fields. The threat of eviction is the only thing that keeps them a bit in line... there is no benefit from those tenancies anyway – it s better to take them over yourself. .. I myself am on my 4th tenant.

> The pastor dithered for a week or so until finally informing Jussi that:

"You can have the tenancy while I am the incumbent, but not for longer, since I can't bind my successor. That clause of the contract gives you assurance that you need not fear eviction." ...

> Then ten years later the parson and the parish council, short on funds, decide that the Koskela land holding is a solution.

"How is Koskela's health ?

*It gives me enough to think about. The back is so-so
and the stomach keeps acting up.*

*... the church council has voiced the opinion that the
parsonage should get back a little of the Koskela land,
not much, just part...about four hectares, no more
than that.*

*That's a full one third of the land. And half the best
land !!...*

*Well...what has to be done...I suppose we have to
renew the agreement.*

*That won't be necessary. Look we're not renewing
the agreement, just returning a part of the land.
Its boundaries weren't clearly defined in the
contract anyway."*

So irrespective of any contract between the land owner
and his tenant farmer, the land owner could evict his tenant
farmer without cause.

Indeed the Kavantsaari manor lord Nicholas Thesleff
did just that. In 1906 he evicted some tenant farmers on
his estate. Why I do not know, but the fact that it resulted
in a strike by the estate workers that lasted for a month,
signals that it was not just a matter of evicting some negligent torpparis...

Yikes, I wonder if my grandfather took over the farm of
one of the torpparis that was evicted !!! – gramps a picket
line breaker ?! Gramps and his young family had moved to
the Syvälahti area of Kavantsaari in May 1904. His occupation is listed as being a "lampuoti/arrendator" - renter
of an independent cottage land holding . However in the
September 1906 he is a "torppari" in Kavantsaari itself. Old
maps show the land that gramps settled on as belonging to
a different family, the Ukkolas – so certainly gramps did
not hew it out the wilderness. Many of the tenant farms had
been established fifty to a hundred years earlier – during
the ownership of the Olchin family.

Hmm, somewhat ironic given gramps' later antagonistic
relationship with the Thesleff manor lord. While grandfather farmed the land for many years after he obtained it in
1906, he nonetheless did not own the land until twenty-two
years later..... ten years after the Revolution.

Revolution

PART II

Revolution

In 1918 Finland underwent a violent civil war. The destruction and cruelty of the war, and the unresolved class differences, however resulted in hatred and bitterness that lingers to this day.

But it also brought pride and happiness, as it was through the throes of the war that Finland became an independent non communist country. A capitalist, hard working republic, true, but ultimately an egalitarian one with effective social programs and strong sense of social equality and individual worth and freedom. In actual fact Finland declared its' independence on December 6, 1917 in the lead up to the civil war, but it was the war that secured it.

The war started on January 27, 1918 and lasted until May 15, 1918. The fighting was triggered by the working classes desire for a say in the government of the land; better working conditions; the ability to own land; and more equitable distribution of power and wealth.

The war pitted the primarily Swedish establishment, clergy, and bourgeois (known as the Whites) against the factory workers and country peasants (known as the Reds).

The war was a Civil War pitting brother against brother, and neighbour against neighbour.

The White army led by Mannerheim defeated the Red forces. The White militia was augmented by a full division of the German army. The Reds received armaments from Bolshevik Russia, but minimal troops.

The Whites defeated the Reds in major battles at Tampere, Helsinki, Lahti and Viipuri. Only about 5,000 were killed on each side during the fighting. However in the aftermath, the Whites imprisoned all the Red forces, arbitrarily executing many. Almost 20% (over 23,000) of the Reds died in the White prison camps, either executed or dying from hunger and disease.

In Karjala major fighting occurred in Viipuri and on front lines in Ahvola just north of my grandparents Kaavantsaari home. My grandfather was imprisoned by the Whites.

A Synopsis of
Finland's Civil War

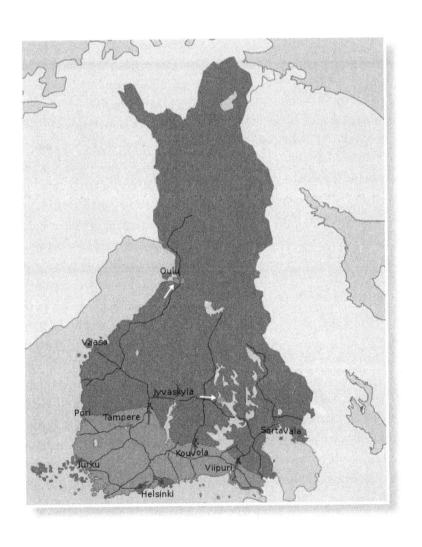

CHAPTER 6

A Synopsis of Finland's Civil War

Perspectives

The revolution remained for many decades a subject that was not discussed. Those aspects that were discussed centered on the victory of capitalism and the defeat of communism – echoing the truism that *"It is the victors who write the history "*.

The war became a hazy subject without even a common name. Official circles called the war variously The Finnish Civil War *Sisällis sota*, or The Independence War *Itsenaisyys sota*. Others knew it as The People's War *Kansalais sota*, and occasionally The Class War *Luokka sota*. Sporadically it is called the *Veljensan sota* (Brothers War), and rarely, The Revolutionary War - *Vallankunouksellisen sota*. To the common people it was known simply as the Red–White War - *Punaisten -Valkoisten sota*.

The war was not a religious war, nor a race war. It was a war of neighbour against neighbour, brother against brother - and sister (On the Red side Finnish women took part in the conflict, fighting in the skirmishes and battles). It was a class war with the Reds being primarily the small farmers and factory workers, while the Whites were the entrenched establishment – landed gentry, factory owners, clergy, the educated civil service, and the urban bourgeoisie plus conscripted peasants. The north wasWhite territory and the more industrialized south Red territory (Map opposite).

The formal war only lasted four months, starting January 27, 1918 and ending May 15, 1918. Both sides in the war had an army of approximately 90,000 men. At the start of the war the Reds controlled the more industrialized southern Finland, and the Whites rural northern Finland and Ostrobothnia.

Fierce battles occurred in Tampere, Helsinki, Lahti and Viipuri between the Reds and the Whites. Deaths during the battles were actually low – about 5,000 on the Red side and 3,500 on the White side.

Terror campaigns were waged in the local parishes – with innocent parishioners killed arbitrarily by whichever faction controlled the parish. Individuals were killed by both sides by official "military" flying cavalry detachments, and by local "councils" pursuing personal vendettas. These deaths were relatively few during the war with approximately 1,500 Whites and 1,500 Reds executed.

The horror of the war was the aftermath. The victorious Whites undertook upon themselves to do some "cleansing". Although the Reds formally surrendered to the Whites, 9,000 Reds were arbitrarily executed by the Whites – either immediately beside the battlefield; in their local parishes; or in official White prison camps.

In addition to those who were executed, over 12,000 Reds died of hunger and disease in the appalling conditions of the White prison camps. 75,000 to 80,000 Reds were imprisoned by the Whites after the war.

There were prison camps throughout Finland. My grandfather Juho Öhman was arrested and placed in the Viipuri prison camp, narrowly escaping death. All of Suomi Linna - the island fortress opposite Helsinki - was turned into a prison. My great uncle on my fathers' side – Jonne Starck was imprisoned there.

My father always commented that,

"When Mannerheim took command in Viipuri, the killing and imprisonment stopped, quoting Mannerheim as saying; "Although we have differences, we will not have Finns murdering Finns".

But I couldn't understand how this could be given Mannerheim was the Commander-In-Chief of the White army until I read his memoirs. To quote

Nor did my attitude with regard to the judicial sequel to the rebellion or my personal contribution to the solution of this question seem to be generally known. The humanitarian policy I had pursued as commander-in-chief in the spring of 1918, when I opposed the incarceration of all the rebels without distinction in prison camps, I was determined to maintain as Regent.

On April 1st, 1919 a decree was issued terminating the work of the high treason courts, followed by another in June granting a general amnesty. Thus all who had taken part in the rebellion were set at liberty, with the exception of such as had been found guilty of murder, incendiarism, and similar grave crimes.

However Mannerheim's negation of his designation as the *"lahtari - butcher"* and *"murha Kustaa –murderer Gustaf"* is not entirely valid. During the war itself, the Commander in Chief was known, *"to quietly sanction even the most whole-hearted illegal executions".* Indeed there is one official order dispatch that he did send out in February, 1918 which does order executions. It reads:

Mannerheim: Commander in Chiefs 25.2.1918 order:

Notice to be strictly adhered to:Individuals who are found behind the army lines destroying roads, bridges, vehicles, telegraph services, and phone lines are to be shot on the spot. The same as well applies to individuals who are in armed resistance against the countries legal army, such as snipers and arsonists.

Anyone, who 8 days after this notice is read in the area parish church, is found with stored weapons

for which they do not have the relevant permission, or whom we apprehend armed behind the back of the army, shall be shot on the spot.

While not adhering to the Geneva Convention on Prisoners of War, the announcement is not all that shocking a war time notice. However for those Whites who chose to interpret it loosely, it officially sanctioned executions.

It was not until the late 1960s that the war started to be discussed. Indeed for many decades after 1918, the winning Whites would not allow the families of the executed Reds to even place crosses or flowers at the local parish execution pits, never mind moving the bodies to the local cemetery. By contrast the fallen Whites were buried in the parish cemetery and memorials to the fallen Whites were erected by the church door. It was only after the second world war when all Finns irrespective of Red or White disposition, gave their lives for "God, Home and Country", that small commemorative monuments to the Reds began to be placed in the church yards – needless to say a bit to the side, not in the full glory of god's church entrance.

To this day it is difficult to find a history book which presents the war objectively and in detail. Examination of the war finally began after 1960 when Vaino Linna, Finland's pre-eminent author, published a trilogy called Under the North Star. The second volume dealt in detail with the plight of the common man during the civil war. Although fictional it was based on extensive factual data.

An Overview of the Revolution

While the Revolution can be attributed to the quest for social equality, it was precipitated by the power vacuum created by Russia's withdrawal from Finland as a result of the Bolshevik Revolution.

The eighteen year road to revolution was marked by numerous major events.

In 1899 in reaction to Tsar Nicholas II's regressive measures the Finnish workers' movement founded the Finnish Social Democratic Party. [Note as I mentioned in the previous chapter, Finland was actually a semi autonomous grand duchy of Russia *"Suomen suuriruhtinakunta"* and the Tsar was actually the grand duke. But for simplicity purposes I refer to them as tsars].

In 1902 the Tsar, in contradiction to the terms of the Finnish constitution, started conscripting Finnish men into the Russian army

In 1903 Tsar Nicholas II appointed Nikolai Bobrikov as Governor of Finland. Bobrikov initiated a harsh campaign of Russification and autocratic rule. He was assassinated in 1904 by a young Finnish nationalist – Eugen Schauman. Afterwards he was replaced by a more moderate governor.

In 1905 in concert with the upheaval in Russia, the Finnish workers called a general strike in support of better working wages and conditions, and the vote for all Finnish citizens. The strike was supported by the rural agricultural workers as well as the urban factory workers.

In 1906 in order to quell the general unrest, the Tsar introduced universal suffrage and replaced the parliamentary estate system with an elected unicameral parliament. Promises were also made to allow tenant farmers to own their land.

The universal suffrage provided the vote to all adult Finns including women. The number of voters increased tenfold.

In the subsequent election in 1906, the workers' Social Democratic Party gained a substantial number of seats.

Parliament however had little success over the next decade. The elected right and left factions seldom agreed. More importantly Nicholas II continuously intervened in Finnish politics, among other things calling for new elections almost annually. In practical terms he ruled as an autocrat.

In February 1917 the Russian workers revolted. During this time the Finnish workers in Helsinki also went on strike demanding food, better social conditions and the transference of legislative power from the Russian government to the Finnish parliament.

On 15 March 1917 Tsar Nicholas II was disposed. The tsar's power was transferred to the Russian Duma and the provisional government of Kerensky, which at that time had a bourgeois conservative majority.

Concurrent with the disposing of the Tsar, the institutions operated by the Russians in Finland were dissolved. One of these was the police. In response, both the upper class and the workers formed independent security groups for their own protection – the White Guards and the Red Guards. These groups had already been forming for a decade as in 1905 Tsar Nicholas II had withdrawn the right given by Tsar Alexander II in 1878 for Finland to have its' own army. At first, the militia groups were local and largely unarmed. Many Whites were voluntary fire brigades while the Reds were members of the Workers' Union. Dependent on the geographical area, one group or the other prevailed. By autumn 1917, the forces began assuming a more military character.

In July 1917 the Finnish Social Democrats had an absolute majority in the Parliament and a slight dominance in the Senate. In the fall the work day for the tenant farmers and farm hands was set at eight hours. Before this they had to work from sunrise to sunset. Any work on their own property was done, *"By the light of the torppari's sun – the moon"*.

As well the Finnish parliament passed the Tokoi Senate bill, called the "Power Act". The "Power Act" incorporated a plan to substantially increase and concentrate the power of Parliament, as a reaction to the non-parliamentary and conservative leadership of the Finnish Senate. The bill also furthered Finnish independence, restricting Russia's influence on domestic Finnish affairs - limiting the Russian Provisional Government to determining the foreign and military policies of Finland.

The Russian Provisional Government refused to accept the "Power Act" and sent more Russian troops to Finland. In July 1917 with the co-operation and support of Finnish conservatives, Parliament was dissolved and new elections announced.

In the subsequent 1917 elections, the Social Democrats lost their absolute majority. The Social Democrats considered that new elections should not have been called. As parliamentary means did not seem to work, the labour movement became more radicalized.

In October, Lenin and the Bolsheviks revolted and on November 7, 1918 seized control of Russia.

In November 1917 the Finnish labour unions called a general strike. During the strike thirty four Whites were killed by radical components of the Red Guards, heightening tensions.

While the political parties had diametrically differing objectives, they both agreed on Finnish sovereignty. On December 4, 1917 the Finnish government put forward a statement of independence. This was endorsed by Lenin and the Russian government. While supporting the social revolution in Finland, Lenin also believed in the self determination of nations. In conjunction with this he wanted to end the war with Germany. During the talks Germany strongly pushed for Finland's independence as they wanted access to Finland's mineral resources.

The joint initiative to achieve Finland's independence was the sole success of Finland's Parliamentary system. While moderate elements on both political sides tried to reach compromise on governing the country, positions polarized, and the more extreme elements took control as a decade of democratic efforts had bore no fruit.

Effectively the country split into two, ruled by two different armies and political factions as illustrated in the map at the start of this chapter.

The southern more industrialized part of Finland was controlled by the Reds. This encompassed the major urban centres of Turku, Tampere, Helsinki, Lahti, and Viipuri.

The northern and western part of Finland, especially Ostrobothnia (except for the city of Oulu), was controlled by the Whites. While Ostrobothnia was rural, the extent of discontent of the landless farmers was less than elsewhere in Finland as the manor land holdings were smaller and less contentious. In addition much of the population was of Swedish heritage, the same as the White leadership.

Both armies had approximately 90,000 men.

The Red army / Red Guard was primarily comprised of volunteers recruited through the labour unions and the local worker's farm cooperatives. These were supplemented by some former Russian army forces (about 9,000 Russians). The Reds were armed by the Russians. While the Red army was nominally led by Ali Aaltonen, in practise each area was led by its' own commander. While the Reds were armed by Russia, Lenin, although fully supporting the Finnish Reds and sending 10,000 rifles and other armaments to them, did not commit any Russian troops to the conflict.

The White Guards were organized by local men of influence, usually bourgeois, academics, industrialists and major landowners. While the clergy did not overtly belong to the White Guards, the Lutheran church strongly endorsed the Whites. Not only would the clergy not consecrate any fallen Reds; in Helsinki they would not even marry Red couples.

The White militia consisted of a small core of volunteers led by a fully trained war hardened regiment of Finnish Jaegers (Jääkärit) who had returned from Germany. The bulk of the White army consisted of men conscripted from the Ostrobothian population. When war started the White government enacted conscription in the parts of Finland it controlled. The White army was armed by the Germans. And, while the army commander in chief was the former Finnish Russian General Carl Gustaf Mannerheim, close to fifteen percent of the forces in fact consisted of a fully equipped German army division. This operated under the independent command of the German General Rudiger von der Goltz.

The White Guards were in fact the official army of Finland. On January 12, 1918 before the start of the conflict, the conservative led White Senate voted to create a strong police authority compromised primarily of the White Guards. Shortly thereafter they appointed Carl Gustaf Mannerheim as the supreme commander of the White Guards. Mannerheim was a Swedish Finnish former Russian general who today is venerated as Finland's most legendary warrior and statesman, primarily as a result of his leadership during World War II. The White Guards were designated as Finland's official army, head quartered in Vaasa.

The Red Guards refused to recognise these actions, and established a military authority of their own, led by Ali Aaltonen, located in Helsinki. Aaltonen had been trained as a Lieutenant in the Russian army.

Preliminary battles occurred in southern Finland and Viipuri from January 9th to the 21st as both sides jockeyed for weapons and for control of Viipuri. The Reds succeeded in making Viipuri a Red controlled city.

The inevitable Civil War commenced on January 27, 1918 with the Whites declaring war on the 25th of January, and the Reds reciprocating the next day.

An initial bloody battle occurred on February 3rd in my ancestral home, Oulu, with the Whites defeating the Reds.

I wonder what my 66 year old great grandmother Johanna Tuira thought as the battle raged across the inlet from her Pikkisaari home ? I guess she would have been a White as her parents owned a factory in town. Now, I think her deceased husband, great gramps Karl, would have been another matter.

The first major battle occurred in Tampere. The Whites led by Mannerheim attacked the Reds in Tampere on April 3rd. A fierce battle raged throughout the city for two days. The Whites emerged victorious. Surrendering Reds were executed forthwith against the factory walls and 11,000 were taken prisoner. The remnants of Tampere's Red forces retreated east.

On April 11th, the White German army invaded Helsinki, taking it from the Reds two days later on April 13th. 9,000 Reds including my Great Uncle Jonne Starck were imprisoned on Suomenlinna.

The defeated Red forces retreated towards Viipuri.

The German troops together with White forces attacked Lahti on April 19th. The Reds in Lahti held out until May 2nd before they were overcome. 22,000 Reds were taken prisoner and incarcerated in the Fellman Fields concentration camp.

On April 24th Mannerheim with his White army attacked Viipuri. By April 29th the 18,000 strong White army had defeated the 7,000 strong Red army. 6,000 Reds were taken prisoner.

While Viipuri had been a Red stronghold, the rest of Karjala was held by the Whites throughout the war. The headquarters of the White Karjala army was in Antrea, fifty kilometers north east of Viipuri and only fifteen kilometers from Kavantsaari, my mother's home. Trench warfare continued near there in Ahvola from February to April. The number of recorded war dead in Karjala was 6,958, the 3rd largest of any of Finland's province.

The war ended on May 15, 1918.

A White reign of terror began as soon as they had won. Close to 9,000 Reds were executed either through speedy "trails" in the hours and days after the battles; or, in local purges. Today Finland is covered by small memorials in over 175 parishes, mostly throughout southern Finland - finally bearing witness to "Reds" executed by local White vigilantes in swamps, gravel pits and road sides (The Finnish Labour Museum in Tampere "Tyovaenmuseo Werstas" has photographs of most of the memorials together with a brief description of the number killed and imprisoned).

75,000 Reds – basically the entire Red army (2 ½ out of every 100 Finns) - were imprisoned in concentration camps in Tampere, Suomenlinna, Tammisaari, Lahti, Riihimaki, Hameenlinna, and Viipuri. 12,000 Reds died of starvation and disease in the appalling conditions of the brutal White prison camps.

Several months after the end of the war a formal court marshal process was initiated by the Finnish government due to Western pressure. This greatly slowed the rate of executions. The majority of the prisoners were paroled or pardoned by the end of 1918 (albeit without civil rights for some years). Only 1,000 were still imprisoned in February 1920.

After the war the Whites governed Finland. They endeavoured to turn Finland into a monarchy. Actions were taken to make Prince Friedrich Karl Ludwig Konstantin von Hessen- Kassel, Kaiser Wilhelm's son-in-law, Finland's king. He in fact "ruled" Finland from October 9th 1918 to December 14th 1918 but did not enter the country. The initiative however faltered when Germany lost WW I. Finland instead established itself as a Republic. Finland was officially recognized as a nation in May 1919 by the UK and the USA. An official peace treaty with Russia, the Treaty of Tartu, was signed in October 1920.

Major differences endured between the workers and the establishment, but both sides, scared by the violence of the civil war, endeavoured to work together. Elections were held again in March 1919 and many socialists were elected. Acts were passed to provide tenant farmers and cottagers ownership of land.

Famine still was pervasive, as it had been since 1917, when Russian military spending and grain assistance disappeared. The USA government under President Hoover stepped in to help Finland, sending much needed grain and supplies.

Partly driven by the shock of the Finnish people at the appalling post war White terror campaign, moderates gained ascendancy in the government. Finland slowly evolved to normalcy... but the destruction and cruelty of the war, and the unresolved class differences, resulted in hatred and bitterness that lingers to this day.

Both my father and mother lived the reality of The Finnish Civil War. Their true stories, as well as those of other Karjalaiset, follow, along with more detailed information on the war in Karjala.

CHAPTER 7

Viipuri
During the Revolution

E Tanttu: Vaupauden Tiella

CHAPTER 7

Viipuri during the Revolution

Viipuri, the second largest city in Finland, was a Red city from the start of the war – not surprising given its' industrialization and its' proximity to St. Petersburg. There were nonetheless a large number of White supporters as well.

Boyhood Memories

Dad in his twilight years wrote his recollections of that time. They provide a riveting, first person picture, of a 10 year old boys' first hand view of Viipuri before, and during, the Russian and Finnish revolutions. I am presenting them here verbatim with the occasional comment interspersed with an explanation of the historical events.

In the fall of 1917, the Reds began to mobilize in Viipuri.

... But then came 1917 – certainly a chaotic year. The Russian Revolution started a cataclysmic uproar. Finland, while a separate Russian grand duchy was very much part of the revolution.

A huge Red (Bolshevik) rally was organized outside the Viipuri railway station to greet some Bolshevik leaders coming in from St Petersburg.

We boys of course went to watch. The square was so full of soldiers and revolutionaries,

that there was no room to squeeze any more people in. We boys nonetheless managed to find ourselves a spot immediately before the speaker platform. The speaker was a fervent emotional orator – like a wild whirling

devil – never before, nor after, even to this day, have I heard a more impassioned and inspirational speaker. The crowd was whipped into a frenzy shouting "Bravo !!! daa, daa !! hurray, hurray !!!." I, caught in the moment, shouted as fervently as I could. A huge soldier, who was standing beside me, patted me on the head and said "Yell louder, louder !!"

[At the first stage of his return from Europe, Lenin lived in Viipuri during September/October 1917, finalizing his plans for the Bolshevik Revolution before going to St Petersburg. Perhaps the orator was Lenin himself. Or more probably it was Trotsky. Trotsky was renowned for his speaking skills.]

The next event that I remember, occurred at the railway yard. There, the soldiers loaded themselves into cattle cars. It struck us as strange that both the older and younger soldiers, all made the sign of the cross. They went, I heard, to help over throw the St Petersburg government.

War came to Karjala . Skirmishes were already underway in Viipuri before the civil war started on January 27th 1918. The majority of the fighting occurred north of Viipuri in Ahvola and Hannila south of the White head quarters of Antrea. Trench warfare settled in from January through March.

Viipuri was the key railway connection to St. Petersburg with Russian armaments being shipped through Viipuri to the Reds in central Finland. One such rail shipment of rifles to Mikkeli was blown up by the Whites on Jan 17th. Explosives and armaments were also being secretly manufactured by the Whites in Viipuri's Pietsen Factory. The Reds upon discovering this, attacked the factory on January 19th and shut it down. The Russian soldiers separated the two sides before blood was shed. (Viipuri at this point before the war still had a Russian military detachment of 1,500 men.)

As well as the Russian unit there was a White "Home" Guard detachment of 500 men and a slightly larger Red Guard force. On January 23th the White home guard detachment under Woldemar Hägglund endeavoured to take over the town but were thrown back and forced to flee over the ice of ViipurinLahti to Venäjänsaari, three kilometres south of the city. From thence they retreated to Antrea, the White head quarters for Karjala.

The Reds, under Oskari Rantala, held the city throughout the war. Relations were quite cordial until the White attack on Viipuri on April 24th.

While there was no fighting in Viipuri a three month long battle was underway in Ahvola near Antrea. Both Red and White sons of Viipuri were returned home with both sides burying their fallen with appropriate honours.

During the war Viipuri was the Red head quarters for Karjala. (The total Red complement in Karjala was around 10,000 men). The Reds air base was in Viipuri. Panzer trains were built in the town's machine shops. In addition to the existing hospitals, the Red Cross ran a hospital in Viipuri.

Life in the city during the revolution was not easy:

In the winter they fought – in places such as Hannila and Ahvola. Martta, my wife's home was also underfoot.

Of the neighbourhood's older boys, some went to Russia, others to Germany to be Jaeger soldiers, some escaped to the Whites side. Many joined the Reds, others were forced to join, many died.

I went with my boyhood companions to the general hospital's temporary mortuary shed in the yard, to see who had died.

It was difficult to own a house during the time the Reds were in power. You could not live in your own home just by yourself. Although we owned our own home at 45 Kannaksentie, we were given only one small room – truly a very small room for 4 people. The rest of the house was allocated by the Reds to other people.

We lived there until our home was burnt during the war.

During the Red Party (Bolshevik) period in Viipuri, of course the bread stopped first, and with it everything else.

I remember one winter morning. Snow had fallen. It was hard to walk. In the morning mother gave me a milk can and money, and told me that milk was going to come that morning to the store on Repola St. I knew the store and started off for it. The morning was quite dark. I got to the store, but there was a long line at the door. I thought "I won't be able to get any milk – it will surely be gone by the time I get inside". Being small, I slipped up near the door. There, they lifted me up asking "Where did this boy come from. He was not here this morning." They would have surely thrown me aside, but just then the door opened. I realized soon that I had not hit the ground, but was in front of the counter. I got two litres of milk. I was happy.

They doled out food at the railway station yard. Food for living was in short supply. There we had to wait in line many times. A man was always standing at the entrance. The same person watched, a rifle always hanging ready. I guess he was managing on behalf of the rationing committee. In later years I saw the same person many times in town.

In time, I also got to work for the railway, working as a supervisor. Then, I had to many times manage the dispensing of equipment from the store room. I remembered, how as a boy, I stood in lines here or stood there, waiting for bread. I never mentioned my trials as a boy to anyone else. I just marvelled to myself.

The Battle of Viipuri

After Helsinki fell on April 13th , the Red government under Kullervo Manner moved to Viipuri The Red forces in Viipuri were reinforced by Reds retreating from the battles at Taipalsaari and Joutseno, as well as from Ahvola.

On April 24th the main White attack on Viipuri commenced with 18,000 men and 82 artillery guns. The White forces under the German Colonel Ullrich von Cole attacked from the north, and German Lieutenant Colonel Erik Jernström from the south east. Captain Sihvo's forces arrived from the Ahvola front via Naatali and Kilpeenjoki near the end of the battle and effectively stopped the Red retreat to the west. The Red force of approximately 7,000 men led by Oskari Rantala and Mihael Svetsnikov, fought back fiercely for five days.

After heavy artillery bombardment by the Whites, and intense combat, Viipuri fell to the Whites on April 29[th.]

The following extract from the book Sisallissodan Pikku Jaattliainen by P. Haapala, T. Hoppu, provides a concise outline on the attack on Karjala and the battle of Viipuri and surroundings.

The attack on Karjala was under the command of Major General Ernst Loftstrom. Under his command were 18,400 men and 82 artillery guns – the largest battle force of the civil war. Under Lofstrom's command in the north was Captain Aarne Sihvo, in the middle Colonel Karl Wilkman and in the south the German Colonel Eduard Ausfeld. Against the Whites was a Red force estimated at 15,000. The command of the Red forces had been transferred to Kullervo Manner but in reality the Red units were led by Oskari Rantala, assisted by Mihail Svetsnikov.

The operation started on April 19th with Ausfeld advancing to cut the Viipuri to St. Peterburg railway line at Raivola. Ausfeld's forces arrived at Kivennapa on April 21st . From there part of his force continued towards Terijoki and Kuokkala. By April 24th, Raivola, Terijoki and Kuokkala were under White control. The Red commander of Terijoki, succeeded in escaping on a panzer train to St Petersburg together with several hundred of his men.

With Ausfeld's success, the main attack on Viipuri could start the night of April 23rd. The intent was to avoid fighting in the city itself, and rather to blockade the Red town from the north. The German colonel Ullrich von Cole's group conquered Tali on the morning of April 24th but then turned – despite his orders – towards a surprised Viipuri. The attacked town's strong Red defense resulted in von Cole having to stop his direct attack on the town.

Further south the Whites attacked Kamara and afterwards Sainio, both by the morning of April 24th ending up in White hands. The Reds in the vicinity of Viipuri had several panzer trains but their effectiveness was quickly diminished by artillery fire and the initiatives of White combat engineers...

On the evening of April 23rd Kullervo Manner ordered the Reds on the middle battleground to begin drawing back to Viipuri and onwards to Russia – connecting with their northern and southern forces was too risky.

Already during the night of April 25th, the Red government abandoned Viipuri via boat. Only Edvard Gylling remained in Viipuri to fight.

On April 25th the Reds managed to stop an uprising as the dormant Viipuri White Home Guards endeavored to reclaim key areas of the town.

On April 24th -25th the Red forces at Antrea and Joutseno began withdrawing towards Viipuri. On the morning of April 25th Captain Aarne Sihvo's group moved towards Joutseno and its' empty battle front. Sihvo started back towards Viipuri but the main Red front forces managed to slip through an opening between Sihvo's and von Cole's forces into Viipuri. The Whites plan to isolate the northern Reds miscarried but the expected motti between the town and its western side was formed. The Reds succeeded in throwing back the first attacks against Viipuri on April 25-26. Because of the heavy losses Mannerheim ordered the attack to cease.

The remaining Red government leader in Viipuri, Edvard Gylling, tried to negotiate a surrender with von Cole, but the rejection of the offer left the Reds no choice but to fight onwards. Escape was only possible for smaller groups, and on the evening of April 27th about 1,000 Reds broke out from the east shore of Viipuri Lahti towards Koivisto. The next day another Red group moved southwards.

During this outbreak the Reds captured twenty members of the 2nd company 17th Jaakari battalion. These prisoners were taken from Uura by boat to St Peterburg where they were first put in prison. The prisoners later were put to work among other things, loading logs. At the end of May / beginning of June they were sent back via Rajajoki to Finland. Only one prisoner died - Mikko Kotka of penumonia - while imprisoned in St Petersburg [Quite a difference from the horrendous number of deaths of White prisoners]

The White's heaviest attack began in the middle of the night on April 28th. The Red resistance lasted a full day. By the morning of April 29th the Whites had captured Viipuri. [The Whites attacked the city after an extensive artillery barrage. Von Cole attacked from Papula in the north while Jaakari Lieutenant Colonel Erik Jernstorm attacked from the south east (Having arrived south east of Viipuri on April 25th after heavy fighting in Kamara and Sainio). The Whites overran the Reds southern defenses. The Reds withdrew to the protection of the Patterimaki battlements built by Alexander II in 1860. Bitter street fighting lasted throughout the day.

A large group of the Red forces retreated westwards. At least part of the Reds hoped to get to Russia via the Kymenlaakso harbor [near Hamina]. Sihvo's forces however stopped the escapees at TienHaara and Naulasaari where on the morning of April 29th 5,000 to 6,000 Reds surrendered. "

My father wrote a more vibrant first hand account of the battle of Viipuri ...

Winter went by somehow or other. When spring came, the Whites began their attack. They surrounded Viipuri, taking a week to complete the

full encirclement. The Whites wanted to take the battlement grounds.

Then the fighting started. We boys were there as well, hiding from view behind the mounds, as the Red Guard women soldiers fired and crawled. We gathered up shells. The soldiers asked us to go home, but we didn't - the shelling was exciting.

The women soldiers were tough. I remember they went towards the front in a single line down Saima St, so that the Whites could see them from Loikka.

During the major periods of fighting, we stayed in the cellar. Dad made some wood sleeping bunks for the cellar. Once, the White's made a full hit on the nearby gun battery bunker. Our cellar shook as well !! so strongly that the bunk shelves were thrown to the other side.

That spring, the Red's conscripted all the men for the front lines. They came to the machine shop, and said: "Everyone must come to the front, otherwise the Whites will break through". Dad would have had to go, but the railway shop engineer arrived just in time, yelling, "Tuira here!! A panzer railway train has come in and needs to be fixed!"

Nothing of the sort was the case. It was a brave deed that the engineer did.

During the battle, the Reds set up a machine gun nest in the railway yard water tower. The White's fired a canon shell through the centre of the tower puncturing it. The Reds took flight.

During the spring of 1918, the fighting continued behind the Viipuri race track. From there they brought the wounded back in two wheeled carts. The horses raced frequently back and forth carrying the wounded.

Around this time, a big man showed up at our place. He had red ribbons on his hat and sleeves. I remember what he looked like. He was Herman Laakso, the brother of Uncle Jaakko's wife. He belonged to the Red (Bolshevik) Party leadership. I heard, as he told dad, that "Now the game is over, all is lost". He left via ship for St. Petersburg. All the big shots left. They succeeded in going, leaving on passenger ships from the pier beside Viipuri Linna. The ordinary people were left to fight – as is always the case.

During this sad time everything was bedlam. A large company of Red soldiers escaped east along Karema Street towards Koivisto, and from there to Inoo, and onwards to Russia.

Another group tried to go west to Hamina, thinking that it was still held by the Reds. The Whites however advanced against them on Naula Island. The fighting ended there.

With the ceasefire, the clean up started - with the guilty and the not guilty being killed, as is always the case.

The Whites continued the attack after their victory, shooting incendiary shells into Loikka, setting the area on fire. Our house burned as well. We lost everything when the Whites burnt our house. We sat on the road on the brushes and litter, and watched as our house burned down.

A large part of Rosu burned, as well as the adjoining part of Koilikko - a big area. The White's burnt the town down on purpose.

That first night we slept in a wood working factory beside the railway tracks. The next morning I was sore and stiff. We then moved to live at grandmother Maria Hellman's place at 5 Virasto Street. It was now owned by Uncle Hjalmar as grandma Hellman had died several years earlier.

There, in the next days, we ran in our bare feet to look at the fallen and killed men. They were in a lot of places. At the corner of Suuri St and Kirves St. there was a dead man with his brain's spilling out. Us bare foot boys dared one another as to who would be the first to prod the brains.

All sorts of war material had been thrown into many places. We gathered some gun powder, which we placed into long narrow ribbons. It was fun to watch

them burn. There were canon shells as well, and rifle shells. We took the lead out of the shells and then hit the shells on top of the rock, and watched as the gunpowder exploded. Brother Yrjo particularly liked doing this.

We found a machine gun hidden in the underbrush, but we could not keep it. The army men came and took it away with horses – which was for the best.

The White Terror

This ended the White military conquest of Viipuri – but started the White's horrific imprisonment and execution of their Viipuri Red "brothers".

During this time, out of the blue, Uncle Jaakko showed up at our place with his family. They came from Russia from just north of St Petersburg where they had been living. Before he left, Herman, his wife's' brother who was a Bolshevik party leader, came to their house and told them not to leave. Nonetheless, they walked on the ice, over the mouth of the river at the border, to the Finnish side. When they arrived, they were quarantined for a couple of weeks in Terijoki , as disease was prevalent during this period, and the authorities were concerned about it spreading. I heard afterwards that Uncle Jaakko and family went to Turku.

Uncle Georg Hellman was with the Red Guards – due to the goading of his wife Maiju. Georg's wife convinced him to join the Reds. Georg got a rifle but never did anything. He just put it into the wood shed. When the White's arrived, they found the rifle, interrogated Georg and imprisoned him.

Uncle Hjalmar Hellman saved his brother – among others- at the final hearings. As mentioned earlier, Hjalmar was a pervasive individual with many influential friends. He owned a large bakery in town and had connections with the Tsar's army. Georg got off with just a reprimand as the original factory packing grease was still in the rifle barrel.

Uncle Hjalmar was at heart a son of Viipuri, neither Red nor White. Hjalmar's son, and dad's cousin and boyhood buddy, Veikko, recounted some revolutionary years experiences in his memoirs "The Hellman Bakery":

During the rebellion winter the house was frequently visited by Red patrols to search for foodstuffs, weapons, and men, without finding anything. However, there was a secret crawling tunnel under the building that after several turns ended up in a dry and warm cabin under the ovens. Many a man even with his gun was hiding there, a White one during the period of the Reds, and a Red one during the time of the Whites. All of them survived and later got back to their own troops.

From those hard times I remember the name of an older friend of mine, Eino Tyni, son of a divorced widow. This young lad showed off nearly every day in the dress of an officer of the Red Guards, swords, daggers, and pistols on the belt, and red roses on the cap. Perhaps he sometimes helped us and warned of coming patrols. In the morning after the fighting at Naulasaari he came running. "Dear master, help me now! "And he disappeared in no time. A year or two later a greeting came from Russia.

It is difficult to obtain accurate figures of the Reds that were executed and imprisoned as the White victors did not want the Finnish people to know the extent of their inhumanity. But 5,000 to 6,000 Reds were imprisoned in Viipuri. This rose to approximately 10,000 by May. Approximately 1,200 Reds were summarily executed during the first week after the conquest. Hundreds of innocent Russians were executed.

One of the catalysts for the executions during the initial days was the Reds' murder of thirty Whites imprisoned in the Viipuri district jail during the night of April 27th . As well as common criminals, the jail held White businessmen and leaders. A Red terrorist unit from the Taiplasaari front commanded by Hjalmar Kaipianen took over the prison. Initially they only killed four White leaders, but fuelled by vodka, by five in the morning they had killed thirty. Among the murdered was not only the original prison commander,

but also the commander the Reds had appointed. Obviously he took exception to the executions.

The Finnish National Archives have many documents from the year 1918. These include the transcripts of prison and criminal proceeding for almost every Red imprisoned by the Whites.

In addition there are various documents of oral history. I am including various excerpts of these first hand memories that Outi Fingerroos included in her paper Places of Memory in the Red Vyborg of 1918. They illustrate the terror Viipuri experienced after the city was conquered.

Vyborg was a Red city throughout the Civil War...nonetheless during this period all of Vyborg's inhabitants were treated with civility. During the war both White and Red casualties from the Karelian front were transported to Vyborg to be buried there. All were treated with equal respect. Civility disappeared when the Whites captured the city.

I will never forget the image, when the last soldiers and the tormented Reds were taken from Tienhaara to Vyborg. Everyone has seen the bedlam when a large group of cattle is moved ruthlessly by numerous cowherds. The transportation of those animals occurred more humanely than the transportation of these prisoners. The winners knew their position well. (TMT 68: 61.TA)

Reds were arrested, homes were searched and terror reigned. The Reds were then either marched through the city to the prison camp in Aleksanterinkatu; or, were executed on the banks of the Hiekka, or in the mass grave behind the Ristimäki.graveyard

My mother told me: Many Reds were killed between the banks of Hiekka. Many "old women" went to see it and to look for their husband, brothers or sons among the corpses. The bodies were piled up like logs into a load to be taken to the graveyard." (SKS, KRA. "1918"/39: 118)

Russian prisoners were executed in the hundreds.

When the Whites came to the town, in the morning of the 29 April, I saw how an old couple was hustled with the butt of a rifle in the street (Torkkelinkatu)

*towards the castle bridge. I heard that the couple
did not understand a word of Finnish – they were
Russians. One of the soldiers kicked them in the
buttocks now and then [...]. In this case as in many
others, they were sentenced to death only because
they were Russians (although innocent). (SKS, KRA.
"1918"/48: 191)*

The Whites made sure that the Reds were unworthy of
human respect. They were terrorized and executed, their
bodies were exhumed and dishonored.

*The Whites had a real drinking party, and for many
days. In those days the life of
a working man was worth nothing. In the morning
between five and six, machine gun
fire could be heard from the graveyard of dogs. That
was the end of journey for
several hundreds of workmen and women. (TMT 68:
61. TA)*

*The Reds were originally buried on the hill of
Papula and prisoners had to go there and dig their
own friends up, although the bodies were already
decaying, and they were
taken to a marsh. Many prisoners got a lethal disease,
then lingered on and finally
died, they were too weak and could not live with the
smell. (6B: LI. KA)*

*Every morning around five o'clock, we could hear the
familiar sound of the rapid firing
of bullets, which usually came from the dog grave.
(SKS, KRA. "1918"/52: 52)*

The dog grave referred to is the mass graveyard for the
Reds located close to Ristimäki cemetery, off the central
area of the city on the road to St. Petersburg. Indeed the
grave yard was less than a kilometer from my fathers' home.
Undoubtedly as a ten year old he heard the early morning
sound of the machine guns; and knew about the desecration
of the Red bodies. While dad was unendingly positive and
upbeat irrespective of the situation, I think the memory
was one that even in his later years he did not want to
vocalize; merely stating that:

*"With the ceasefire, the clean up started - with the
guilty and the not guilty being killed, as is always
the case."*

The people of Viipuri made an effort to remember
their lost Red comrades, unsuccessfully trying to set up
a monument. A memorial foundation was built but even
this was violently broken with sledge hammers during the
Lapua movement.

Many of the Viipuri people were traumatized by the
events. Teija Sutinen in an article in the Helsingin Sanomat
newspaper recounts the experiences of her grandfather who
was imprisoned in Vyborg. He was charged with treason
because he joined the Red Guards. In this case not a rifle
carrying member, rather according to the official Criminal
Court Interrogation Records, a potato peeler:

*"Time and place involved in battle, involved in what
other action, what weapons carried, and location of
weapons now:*

*"Peeled and boiled potatoes, washed cabbage,
heated and cleaned barracks. In last weeks, worked
as receptionist in soup kitchen. Never carried a
weapon, and committed no crime. Finally escaped.
Had no weapon."*

Court Decision

*"Red Guard volunteer, although apparently a
harmless person. Propose that he be kept under arrest
for time being."*

Teija's grandfathers' "time being" turned out to be six
months. After being released in a general amnesty he lived
to carry out a long life in Finland. During which,

Juho stayed away from politics after the war, but he
did pull one radical stunt. In Suonenjoki he went to the
vicar›s office and removed his family from the books of
the Lutheran church.

*The involvement of clergy on the side of the Whites
had offended him deeply.*

*[I wonder if part of my Oulu Tuira family were Reds.
The church book page on which they should be listed
is missing].*

Only Whites were God's children to the Lutheran clergy.

Parishes and Imprisonment

CHAPTER 8

Parishes and Imprisonment

The War in the Karjala Countryside

Viipuri was Red territory. And so was my mother's home in Kavantsaari in the countryside about twenty kilometres north of Viipuri.

As mentioned earlier while Viipuri had been a Red stronghold, the entire area of Karjala north east of Antrea was held by the Whites throughout the war. Antrea itself was the headquarters of the White Karjala army.

Karjala was basically separated between the Reds and Whites by a line running from the west in Joutseno, to Antrea, and thence south to Muolaa and Rautu. The area west of the line was under Red control while to the east and north it was White territory.

Battles occurred in Joutseno/Imatra, Jaaski, Ahvola, and in Rautu. The major battleground was in Ahvola/ Hannila just fifteen kilometers north of my mother's home in Kavantsaari on the railway line from Viipuri to Antrea. Antrea itself of course was only twenty kilometres north east of moms home.

Antrea at the beginning of the war was occupied by a 250 man strong Russian garrison. On January 26th a White Guard unit took control of the town. The strength of the White forces was augmented to 950 men when Woldemar Hagglund retreated from Viipuri and Venanjansaari to Antrea. On February 3, Mannerheim appointed Jaakari Captain Aarne Sihvo as commander of the Karjala forces. By mid April the White forces numbered 7,000.

The Whites had a fully equipped head quarters in Antrea complete with a military barracks, combat engineering unit, field hospital, airfield, newspaper - even a military band.

The Red headquarters for Karjala was of course in Viipuri.

The Red headquarters for the Ahvola/Antrea front was in Kavantsaari – actually in Thesleff's manor.

At the beginning of February, the Red forces began to advance towards Antrea. Antrea was important because it was the White head quarters and was on an important railway link into Finland. The Reds captured Ahvola but had to retreat before an onslaught by the Whites and their panzer train. On February 13th the Reds launched another attack with 400 men to capture Ahvola but were stopped. The front line became the nearby Kilpeenjoki.

The area settled into trench war fare. Initially battle was a day job. It was accepted by both sides that at night the only action was sleeping or guard duty. This however changed as further offensives were launched. On February 22nd the Whites attacked Pullila but were repulsed. The next day they captured a slice of territory in adjoining Kilpeenjoki and Syvalahti only to be forced back by the Reds on February 25th . Fighting continued for a month. An intensive attack was launched by the Reds, with counter attacks by the Whites, from March 16th through 26th. No longer was the battle an amateur affair. Ahvola became known as the Verdun of Finland. When Marshall Mannerheim visited the devastation in Ahvola in the mid April he exclaimed: *"But this looks just like the front lines in Western Europe".*

During the March attack on Ahvola, the Reds launched a major offensive all along the Karjala front – from Imatra through Jaaski, Ahvola, Salmenkaita and Rautu. However minimal territory changed hands.

A major battle occurred in Rautu. There the small Finnish Red force of 350 men was augmented by 1,450 Russian troops led by General Jeremejev. In initial battles on March 25th and 26th the Reds won. However the Whites received reinforcements and in the battle of April 4th succeeded in defeating the Reds. Casualties on both sides were high – the Whites suffering 600 dead and wounded while the Reds lost 800. After the battles the Russian general withdrew his forces, leaving the theatre to the Finnish Reds and Whites.

While the casualties at Rautu were significant, the losses on the Ahvola front throughout the war were considerably more. Continuous casualties were incurred by on both sides. During the week of March 16th , 165 Whites were killed.

By late April the Whites were beginning to gain an advantage on the Ahvola front. However before an attack was launched the Reds retreated to protect Viipuri.

A View of Karjala Parish Life during the Civil War

The community next to mother's home was Ihantala. Indeed Ihantala was where our family went to church.

I have been fortunate to obtain a copy of a book written in 1990 by the community expatriates remembering life in Ihantala from 1900 to 1944 when their homes were lost to Russia. The book, Ihantala Rauhan ja Sodan Aikana, is 424 pages. Only 2 pages refer to the Civil War. Such is the silence regarding the Civil War.

The section on the Civil War is called Kipeat Vuodet – The Bitter Years. I'm including almost the entire two pages as it provides an insight into life in a small Red parish in Karjala during the Civil War.

> "The Ihantala, Vakkila and Ylivesi area was not a particularly remarkable site during the Civil War, one that warrants special notice of its' events; but, the community residents still have personal memories of those painful years...

> ... during the weekly women's coffee party it was noted that "Finland as well is trying for its' independence". The matter however was not discussed any further as no one really knew what this independence was and how one could use it.

> Jaeger regiment recruiters travelled the Karjalan Kannas villages but no one in our school district signed up to be trained as a Jaeger.

> In the fall of 1917 Red Guard forces also moved through the village. They set up a command centre in the Yliveden workers house, from which they forcefully recruited men into the Red Guard ranks.

> In the fall as an outcome of their shooting, they took over the Ihantala manor as their head quarters, which at that point was being leased by the agronomist Lofgren. Lofgren himself had already left. The manor holdings/grounds then as well were vandalised.

> During the 1917-1918 year end they took grain from the largest farms but left the smaller farms alone, although Red Guards did stay in them when they were on leave from the front.

> The front line was formed in a strange way. East of the Ahvola Pullila line, men were called up into the White militia. West of the line the men became part of the Red Guards. Men from the smaller farms were recruited without being formally called up. And about 10% of the crofters went to one side or the other dependent on who summoned them first.......

> The village did not escape some incidents. Intense gun fire erupted on the Ihantala hill when a forty to fifty man Red Guard unit sought to enter the Ihantala manor grounds which at the same time were being occupied by a small White reconnaissance patrol. One White died.

> The lack of food worsened. One Ihantala villager recalls that: "Mother finally had flour on Feb 18th and was making dough, which had almost completed rising. At the same time a notice came that we should flee the house due to the danger of an explosion/

shelling. While the others left, mother stayed behind. The dough was too precious to leave to spoil. Nothing happened after all. When the family returned warm rye bread was waiting for the children. Nothing could have been better as we had been without bread since the previous summer."

During this time boys from the small farms were being constantly commandeered into the Red Guard whose head quarters now were in the Ihantala manor house.

A lot of fighting happened on the front in March and April. The Ihantala men did not become enamoured with the war, despite what you may have heard. In April the front rapidly advanced towards Viipuri. Shortly afterwards the Red Guard abandoned Viipuri. The men of many of the Ihantala households who had been forcefully recruited, or had volunteered, returned home not expecting any reprisals. During this time the Ihantala manor changed into the Whites possession.

The former Red Guards, even if they had not fought, were brought to the Ihantala manor to stand before a Whites only kangaroo court. The trial, such as it was, was swift, and the judgement harsh. Quick, reckless decisions were made and carried out. Personal differences, covetousness, petty slights– and occasionally real felonies - became cause for execution. The harshness of the sentences may have been influenced by the manor trial location. The manor barn had been burnt and the work force badly frightened by the Red Guards. Men who had been totally innocent of any involvement in this action were nonetheless executed because of this. The White mob outside the courtyard made sure of this.

Before the Talvisota, behind the Vakkarara sauna, there was still a grave site surrounded by stone posts and chains, mute testament to the executions which had been carried out. This small memorial was much better than that afforded to most Reds who were executed.

Most shocking was the fate of three 14 to 16 year old boys. They had been picked up on the road one Sunday by Red Guards and dragooned into the Red forces. After the surrender of Viipuri, they were murdered as they were returning home on the very road from which they had been taken. The boys were buried in Viipuri and a combined funeral service held for them in Ihantala. While there was much commiserating in the village, the murderers were never brought to trial.

The older members among the expatriates, those who at that time were themselves small children, still remembered those sorrowful times. "

Such was life in Ihantala seven kilometres down the road from mothers' home in Kavantsaari.

Life in Kavantsaari was no less harsh.

Kavantsaari and Grandpa's Imprisonment

Kavantsaari was Red territory throughout the war. Indeed the Red army headquarters for the Antrea front was in the Thesleff manor house.

In April the Reds retreated to reinforce Viipuri. Some weeks thereafter grandpa was arrested and incarcerated in the Viipuri prison. Mother would have been ten years old then.

My mother recounted that;

Father was arrested by the Whites and put into prison camp during the civil war.

There was another farm house directly across from us– not as prosperous and productive as ours. The neighbours (The Harkönens) across the road were envious. During the Red / White conflict the neighbour (apparently the neighbor's wife was the instigator) accused grandfather Öhman of being a Red in the hope of being able to take over the farm.

In 1918, the Whites along with the manor lord Nikki Thesleff came to our tenant farm and took dad away. While we had little of value in the house, they decided to take a beautiful home-made comforter.

My grandmother "Hyva mummo" Öhman however peered from behind a corner and cried out, "You scoundrels, don't take that!! It's my wedding gift to them!" Ashamed, they left it.

Life in the prison camp was dire.

There was little food. My older brother Erkki (who was 16 at the time) initially stayed for three weeks just outside the prison enclosure. Every morning Erkki handed food to father through the barb wire barricade. One had to be discrete, as officially, giving food packages was prohibited. As the days went by, Erkki being the oldest son, had to leave to work the farm. Then my mother Hilda brought food whenever she could. When he was given the food, father immediately tried to conceal it and surreptitiously eat it, as most of the other prisoners had nothing except the starvation prison rations. And indeed, father ate grass like many of the other prisoners. Many inmates died of starvation.

Every morning, the camp commandant lined up the men, arbitrarily selected ten, and shot them. Father said he tried to remain inconspicuous in order to avoid being selected.

Father survived for many months in the prison camp before being released.

I had always wondered why grandpa was actually arrested. Recently I learned that the Finnish National Archives had documents on the court proceedings for most of the Red Civil War prisoners. I enquired and was astounded to receive a document in the mail several weeks later. I continue to be amazed by the depth of the Finnish Archives and the helpfulness of its' staff.

I, eagerly, but nonetheless with a bit a trepidation, opened the package. Twenty pages !! The transcripts covered his entire record. After the Reds surrendered, grandfather Juho Öhman was arrested by Baron Thesleff and the local White Guard in mid May; interrogated in Antrea by a local tribunal on May 18, 1918; and sent to the Wiipuri prison camp. He was released on parole by the Wiipuri Court on August 2, 1918.

The transcripts record that:

On May 18, 1918 the Antrea tribunal of Toivo Tapanainen & Antti Henttonen determined that our grandfather:

"assisted the rebellious Red Guard and has made himself guilty of robbery and other crimes. He is sent to Wiipuri prison camp to be judged as a II group prisoner of war in the court."

On August 2, 1918 Judge Eduard Hallsfors and his tribunal of the Wiipuri Court of Crimes against the State heard the case against gramps for treason and ruled that:

"Juhana Öhman has, after the rebels had robbed certain movable property, without himself participating in the robbery, taken some of that property, and therefore the Court considers it proper according to CL (criminal law) 32 § to sentence Juhana Öhman to captivity for six months. However, Juhana Öhman is released according to laws for paroled captivity, from taking his punishment, and the period of probation is three years."

Grandfather was fortunate that the local police chief Otto Strandman contradicted the Antrea Home/White Guard headquarters accusations, submitting three appeals to the Wiipuri Judge stating that Juho Öhman was innocent of theft and was not a member of the Red Guard.

"To the Highly Respected Investigating Judge of the administration of the prisoners in Wiipuri.

I beg most humbly that the Respected Judge would take into consideration the attached records of the police investigation, in which appear the criminalities of Juho Öhman, tenant farmer in relation to the Red rebellion, so I therefore dare to appeal to the respected judges with the petition that on the grounds of the guarantees left on the 5th of current July that he could be released, also keeping in mind that the mentioned J. Öhman has a big and poor family, and he is the only worker on the tenant farm.

The undersigned will take him under my watch.

Hannila 12. July, 1918
Otto Strandman
Local police"

The specific case against grandfather outlined in the court proceeding was that:

> "at the request of Red Guard has during the war time: driven all accumulated night soil from the Kavantsaari station to his fields without any salary; once they compelled the informant to haul cannon balls from one side of the railway to the other at the Kavantsaari station; has sold milk to Red Guard, and one time when he was transporting milk to the manor the Red Guard were distributing items of the manor. He too took a pile of china plates, about twenty, wrapped them into an old cloth and brought them home; that one time Samuli Kala ordered him to give the Red Guard a cow, which was compensated for with a cow from the Kavantsaari manor; the given cow was farrow; he was not at home when the exchange of cows took place, but he talked about the matter later on with Kala; altogether the Red Guard took four cows from the informant.
>
> Recording, that the rural police chief of Antrea has stated that when he was carrying out investigations it has appeared the accused has performed very criminally and has threatened for example to kill the police chief and the owners of the Kavantsaari manor and has also urged other people to do likewise, if an opportunity appears."

After the rebellion, when the manor lord returned, grandfather took the china, and the cow, back to the manor. He got no compensation for the four cows of his that the Red Guard had taken, nor for his work emptying the Kavantsaari station lavatories – rather internment in the Viipuri prison camp.

The next door neighbours – the Harkonen's, as well as the neighbour Riihimaki across the lake, are recorded as accusing Juho Öhman of being a member of the Red Guard, promoting revolution, and menacing supporters of the legal government.

The testimony of local workmen officially taken by Otto Strandman, the local police officer, contradicts this however. As per the testimony of one worker:

> Antti Juhonpoika Suikkari, a worker, told, that he was all the war time at Kavantsaari and sometimes at Kaipola, and he was well aware of the actions of the above mentioned Juho Öhman in relation to the Red Guard, which he can on oath confirm, that the mentioned Öhman did not join the Red Guard, and neither took part in armed robbery, but during the war he was urged to serve at the front, but the mentioned J.Öhman strictly refused, so later the Red Guard proposed him transportation of manure, which he accepted as he was allowed to take the manure to his own fields from Kavantsaari station and its outhouse; there was no collaboration with the Red Guard, only when the headquarters of the Reds demanded milk for the headquarters...

My grandfather was not the only member of our family who almost lost their life. My cousin Anna Liisa, recounted her mother (my Aunt Hilda who was seventeen at the time) saying in later years that,

> "I am so happy to be alive, and that they did not shoot me at the Kavantsaari Railroad Station in 1918. White Guard matrons burnishing pistols and guns, took myself and six other neighbourhood girls, and led us roped together by our necks to the Kavantsaari station. They were going to shoot us but we were let free when another battle / skirmish started in the area."

The Finnish Civil War brought out the worst in many people such as the covetous Harkonens and the miserly manor lord, Thesleff.

That gramps lived, is however due to the fact that the war also brought out the best of others such as the courageous local policeman Otto Strandman. Indeed even the State Crimes Judge, Eduard Hallsfors, reviewed the case objectively.

So, from the Öhmans of today:

> "Kiitos Otto - you were a true man – a man of courage and compassion. "

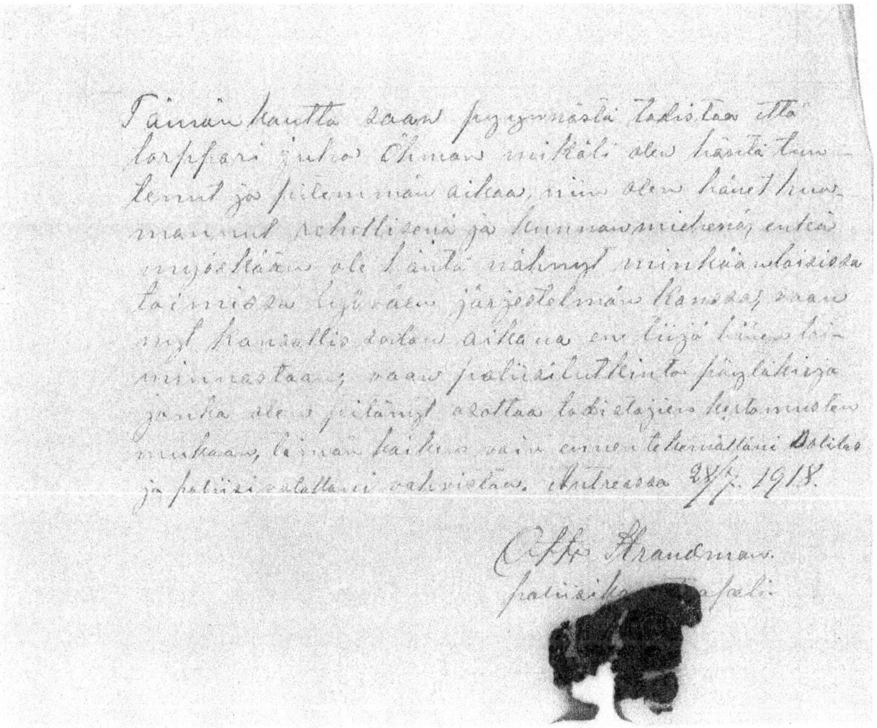

PART III

Karjala Sunshine Years

Karjala Sunshine Years

The period after the Revolution and before the Winter War were years of prosperity and happiness.

The crofters got to own their own farms; Thesleff manor life thrived; my mother and grandparents prospered on their tenant farm; village life bustled.

In the Paris of the North – Viipuri - my father grew from boyhood to manhood.... and married mother.

CHAPTER 9

Country Life

E Tanttu: Tseremissien "Valkoista Kansa"

CHAPTER 9

Country Life

Land Holding

As noted earlier, the inability to own your farm even after settling and working on it, became an increasingly contentious issue.

Although the victorious Whites were primarily the nobility and bourgeoisie / professional class, the government changed the land tenancy structure soon after the end of the Civil War. Partly to acknowledge support for the Ostrobothnian conscript peasant soldiers who had made up the Finnish White Army; but, primarily to defuse an explosive social issue.

With the Crofters Law of 1918, tenant farmers obtained ownership of their land if they had worked it for five years. The State bought and held the land until the farmer was able to pay the mortgage off. As the valuation was in 1914 prices, with post war inflation the price became significantly less. With the Lex Kallio in 1922, the government further enhanced land ownership particularly for smaller land holders such as the cottagers. Thus even though losing the war, the Reds did achieve one revolutionary change; namely, the ability of the common people to own land.

Even though ownership was decreed by the Finnish government, the Kavantsaari tenant farmers were not able to own their land until over a decade later. Most of Karjala's land owners had already given independence to their workers at the turn of the century before the Civil War. In the neighboring Ihantala parish this had occurred in 1910.

However Nikolia Julius Thesleff, the owner of Kavantsaari estate had of course not done so, and now declined to adhere to the law. The issue dragged through the courts and political lobbyists for a decade and a half. The issue illustrated the influence of the Thesleff family who had been a power not only in Viipuri but also in Finland for a hundred years.

Nikolai Thesleff offered to give the twenty-four Kavantsaari tenant farmers land in the Vehkeenniity meadows as opposed to the land they were cultivating. The tenant farmers naturally strongly objected as these were not the homesteads and fields that they had so laboriously cleared and improved. It was not until 1928 that grandfather and the other crofters were able to get their own lands. Even then another ten torpparis in Vehkee did not get their own land until 1937.

After the crofters finally received independent lands, relationships between Niki and the villagers became positive. Niki is quoted as saying:

"Hatred shall NOT remain".

Expedient and benevolent, but meaningless given that he did not have to pay any penalties.

The Kavantsaari manor estate originally approximated 4,000 hectares. Even with forfeiting 1,300 hectares of land, Nikolai still had 2,532 hectares.

The land of course was all lost to Russia after the Jatkosota – all the land – the land of the topparis, the cottagers, the villagers, and the manor lord.

The Finnish government gave some compensation to the Karelians in the early 1950s. Not much, as my cousin who owned a cottage land site of two hectares without any buildings, said;

> *"Mother received barely enough to buy a restaurant meal for the family."*

For those who had livestock and buildings the compensation was more.

The story is that after the war, Nikki Thesleff applied for compensation for more land then he had. This was noticed and he was cautioned and almost jailed.

This was not unusual. Paraphrasing the comments of a member of the extended family, Marianne Thesleff:

> *This was not the first time Nikki had demurred paying taxes. Even after 1918, he continued living like in the good old Russian times, not paying any taxes, never voluntarily. Every year it was the same procedure! Taxes were not paid, and when the bailiff came he was impolitely asked to go away. Then an article appeared in the Viipurin Sanomat newspaper stating that the Kavantsaari cattle would be auctioned off in the Viipuri marketplace for the unpaid taxes. All the manor was upset, but just before the first bid the taxes were paid and everyone could breathe freely once more !*

So Nikki was definitely a business man who parted grudgingly with his property. But that is a characteristic of many entrepreneurs. The robber barons of America such as the Rockefellers, Kennedys and Carnegies built their fortunes with dubious practices. Even today fortunes are built with little regard for social justice.

Another land owning characteristic was primogeniture – namely that the first born son inherited the farm. The accepted tradition was for the oldest son to get the farm. In return he agreed to take care of his parents in their old age. Dependent on the benevolence of the son, he gave some compensation to his brothers – but none to his sisters.

Even into the mid 20th century, land primogeniture was practiced. I remember my mother breaking down in tears when she learned her brothers had divided the money that they received as compensation for the family Kavantsaari homestead among themselves. They did not give any of the money to their sisters who had worked just as hard as they had, if not harder, on the homestead. Indeed, after the war mother and dad had given grandfather a home and taken care of him until he died a few years later.

From the brothers – nothing...and although the sum they divided was not necessarily magnificent, thoughtfulness and consideration would have been wonderful. My father was incensed. In his family everything was split evenly. Mother just cried...and forgave her brothers.

Manor Life

Now who were these Thesleffs and why refer to them so often ?

Firstly, the Thesleff estate was the largest one in Karjala. The owner controlled the life of Kavantsaari, including that of my mother and her parents. The Thesleff's were a powerful family in Karjala – indeed in Finland.

The Thesleff family were Hanseatic merchants from Lubeck who came to Viipurii in the late 1500s. Through the years they became very influential citizens, marrying well and amassing great wealth.

During the 1800s they served with distinction in the Russian army, and became extremely powerful and wealthy Finnish representatives of Tsar Nicholas I. General Alexander Amatus Thesleff was the acting Governor of the Duchy of Finland from 1833 until his death in 1847.

Alexander Amatus' nephew, Major General Alexander Adam Thesleff, was the Governor of Mikkeli and of Viipuri province from 1847 until his death in 1856. During the Crimean War Thesleff commanded the Russian forces on the Gulf of Finland protecting Viipuri and St. Petersburg from the attacks of the British and French fleet.

The families' military service continued into the 1900s. During the Finnish Civil War Major General Gosta Thesleff was Marshall Mannerheim's Chief of Staff. Vilhelm Thesleff served as the defense minister.

The Thesleff's had extensive landholdings - the Ventela sateri tila near Vaasa Finland, and several in Karjala near Viipuri - the Juustila kartano, Liimato kartano, and Kavantsaari ralssi In Viipuri, the Thesleff mansion covered three quarters of a block by the Pyroea Tori in the heart of Old Viipuri.

So, a family to be reckoned with.

...and secondly, one of the Thesleff twins was probably my great grandfather.

My grandmother Hilda Öhman was born out of wedlock to great grandmother Henrika, "Rakas mummo" Tianinen. This was a matter, as dad said, that was never spoken about. Indeed, I did not become aware of this aspect until after my mother died. When I asked my uncles and older cousins about the matter, nobody knew who the father might be.

Major General Alexander Adam Thesleff and Eugenia Amalie had twin sons Petter and Nikkolai who were about the same age as my great grandmother "Rakas Mummo".

Great grandmother worked on the Thesleff manor as a milk maid. Apparently great grandmother was not only a delightful person, but also a stunningly beautiful woman – a tall porcelain blond. Once my mother said something that struck me as odd and which stuck in my memory. When I was a young'un tom catting around she admonished me to remain celibate. At the same point, she commented that,

> "Mistakes have happened in the hot summer nights as they happened to your great grandmother. However what could one do, if you were young and beautiful and were approached by the charming and powerful son of the local hovi. One can't be blamed entirely".

The photo of one of the twins, Petter, bears an uncanny resemblance to one of my male cousins; as does that of Eugenia Amalie to one of my female cousins.

I was recently finally able to find a birth record for grandmother. She was not born in Kavantsaari; rather she was born in Ahvionsaari in Saaminkii parish to Henrika Tiain . No father is listed.

Saaminki is a parish just south of Sulkava and Savolinna - about a hundred kilometers from Kavantsaari. It appears that great grandmother went home to have her daughter. Young love is one thing, marrying into powerful "nobility" is an entirely different matter.

Circumstantial evidence of parentage to be sure, but intriguing ...

So for both local influence and hereditary reasons, a bit more information on the Thesleff family of the 1850 to 1950 era is in order.

The first owners of the estate were Major General Alexander Adam Thesleff and Eugenie Amalia Thesleff, parents of the twins.

Major General Thesleff bought the Kavantsaari estate in 1848, but died soon thereafter in 1856 at the age of forty two. Even though ensconced in governing the province and leading the army in fending off the British and French fleet during the Crimean War, he took an interest in the estate. He adopted modern agricultural practices and imported purebred Ayshire cattle.

His wife Eugenie Amalia Thesleff prior to her marriage served as a lady in waiting to the Empress. She was a first cousin of her husband as her father was General Alexander Amatus Thesleff, the acting ruler of the Duchy of Finland. Eugenie (known as Jenny) lived on the estate until she died there in 1899 at the age of sixty two.

After her husband died she ran the estate for a decade and a half until her son Nikolai came of age. Jenny was much loved by the people of Kavantsaari. Jenny founded a school for the workers which she funded, and taught in.

Jenny as well was the local "doctor" given the absence of any local medical professionals. As the book Antrea comments,

> "I am not sure whether the generals' wife had received medical training in her youth, but certainly she had a lot of medical knowledge. People even came from parishes far away, in their sickness to ask her help. And she cheerfully dispensed both advice and drugs free of charge. My grandmother who died in 1937, aged over ninety years, explained often how she and her husband were cured with the countess's drugs."

The Major General and Jenny had six children: Alexander; Jenny Anna; Olga Maria; Petter; Nikolai; and Jenny

Surprisingly the eldest, Alexander, did not take over the Kavantsaari estate, rather Nikolai did. Whether Nikolai was born earlier then his twin brother Petter I do not know. Perhaps neither Petter nor Alexander wanted to take over the estate. There certainly was enough wealth in the family for them to do whatever they wished.

Petter, my probable grandfather, left the estate to become an academic in Helsinki. He married Emmy Elisabet

Cajander in 1885. They had one daughter – Wally Ester but she never married.

Nikolai the second owner of the estate remained in Kavantsaari running the land holding until his death in 1909 in Kavantsaari. He married Mathilda Johanna Iverson in 1886 in St Petersburg.

Mathilda was born in 1862 in Viipuri and died in March 1939 in Kavantsaari before the start of the Talvi sota. Her father was from Tallin Estonia while her mother was a Thesleff – another of General Alexander Amatus' daughters !! While certainly not in the league of the Pharaohs of Egypt nor of kissing cousins in the American Appalachians; the Thesleffs seem to have had a bit of a habit of marrying within the family.

Nikolai and Mathilda had three sons (Leo, Nikolai, and Kurt) and a daughter (Jenny).

Leo was the oldest in the family. Born in 1887 in Viipuri, he enrolled in engineering school but did not complete his degree. He returned to live in Kavantsaari, residing in the Uusi hovi across the road from the main manor. It was quite nice but burnt down during Leo's time. Leo, known within the community as Lelo, was eccentric. My cousin remembers him walking skulking around carrying a walking stick, peering here and there. She and the other children made sure they remained well away.

Jenny, the daughter, was born in 1889 in Viipuri, dying there in 1935. She married Viktor Thesleff, the grandson of General Alexander Amatus Thesleff. Ahh, shades of Egypt once more.

Kurt, the youngest son, born in 1895 in Kavantsaari became an agronomist. He never married, dying in Kavantsaari in 1936, a few years before the Talvisota.

The force in the family, the second oldest son, Nikolia Julius, inherited the estate in 1909 at the age of 18 when his father died. He operated the estate in my grand parents time.

His married Agnes Julie Marie Reinberg in November 1920 in Antrea. When he married, his mother Mathilda moved to live in the nearby Rinta hovi, as had his grandmother, Eugenie, the Major Generals wife. Agnes Reinberg was born in 1895 in St Petersburg. She died in 1944 after the war – I believe in Janakkala Finland. Nikolai himself died in Janakkala in 1959. Agnes was from a German family from Riga Latvia, her father being the architect Jakob Reinberg. Agnes and Nikolai were married in St. Petersburg in 1893. They did not have any children.

As well as my families' memories, two books Antrea and Kotiiseutemme Antrea, include some comments on Nikolai Julius Thesleff and the manor. Extracts follow:

As there were a lot of lakes, fishing was a popular income source. Nikki Thesleff forbade fishing on his lands except for old man Lonni who always snuck some fish to the workers. For the others, catching fish in the forbidden waters made them even more delicious. The truly keen fishermen took their catch into Viipuri secretly on the 6 a.m. train, sold it, and returned by 9 a.m. on the return train to their other work.

While fishing was a good source of additional earnings, one could make the same money on the railroad; nonetheless the larger families went to the manor for a couple of weeks of work at the end of the summer .

The manor was always trying to improve the quality of the cattle herd. Nikki only wanted to see black muzzles at the cow trough. When a calf was born with a pale muzzle, no matter how fine a calf, it was sold to the village. This improved the level of cattle in the village as well as the manor.

Nikki had a large stable of horses. He was a keen horse breeder. His stallion Marjus won many sulky races.

The manor lord loved animals and would not have the horses driven to sweat and therefore some field work could not proceed - which the day laborers had nothing against. If it was raining the men had to go work in the woods. Even if the day cleared the men were not assigned to other work.

While the manor wealth was immense, Nikki was stingy. He once baked a crow, to find out if one could eat crow. He seems to have inherited this trait from his mother Mathilde. She was very "economical". Food was not thrown away; rather food which was going bad was served to visitors.

When the workers asked for more pay Nikki said, "The pay won't increase, steal more". This happened with lamb skins and other material disappearing, whereupon he brought in the village constable. It became clear that his own work force was stealing. He became angry and said, "No matter how much you steal, the poor house doorstep won't loom in front of me."

When his brand new car was destroyed in a freak mishap in 1928, he hurried off immediately to buy a new car from the dealership. Money was not a problem.

When planning was underway in 1921 to build a new church in Ihantala near Kavantsaari, the intent was to make Kavantsaari part of the parish as the existing Antrea church used by the village was much further away. Kavantsaari however remained part of the Antrea parish, as Nikki Thesleff would not approve the change. Thesleff had even more influence then the church ...

Similarly when the Kavantsaari workers organization decided to build themselves a hall, they had to build it outside the Kavantsaari parish borders as Nikki would not give them any land to build it on.

Together with his actions during the civil war and the crofter land holding, the above paints a portrait of a hard and conservative man, one who loved husbandry and animals. Not a despot but definitely not a person beloved within the community.

Nikki's unbending, hard personality was at odds with that of his wife. This was the case for the wives of his parents and grandparents as well. All the Thesleff wives were compassionate and much loved.

Nikki's wife Agnes was no exception. Agnes by schooling was a nurse. She frequently helped cure and tend to the locals free of charge. During the war the mansion house served as a war hospital. Agnes herself helped tend to the wounded soldiers. The warm, compassionate and musical Agnes also volunteered with the local Woman's Institute.

So, the Thesleffs and manor life. Somewhat different from village life and the life of my family, the Öhman tenant farmers.

Village Life

Before the war the Kavantsaari village had a railway station, school, two stores, a dairy, a wheat mill, a saw mill, and some houses. The land lords' manor house was by Kavantjarvi lake, three quarters of a kilometer away from the village.

A major road, built in 1860, ran through Kavantsaari connecting Viipuri to Antrea and Sortavala.

But the major transportation link was the railway line built in 1892 that ran through the village. It connected Viipuri to Antrea, and thence via links to Sortavala further east, Savolinna in the north and Helsinki in the west. Of course the line from Viipuri ran to St Peterburg and Russia. Thus the trains contained all sorts of materials. From Kavantsaari itself, the trains carried garden and farm produce, planks, timber and granite. At one point Kavantsaari had thriving granite and chalk quarries, shipping granite as far as Moscow.

The village had two stores, a shoemaker, tailor, dressmaker, carpenter, stone mason, smithy, tannery, policeman, and a masseuse / cupper.

Itinerant vendors were a main stay. Cobblers travelled the countryside house to house. They stayed in the house until their work was done. By contrast pot and pan vendors just came and went.

Grandfather Juho himself liked to travel here and there. Whenever the gypsies were passing through, they stopped and visited at the farm. Gramps liked to catch up on the "world" news with them; and, of course, to trade horses.

Kavantsaari folks, like those in all the parishes of the era, were very appreciative of, and dependent on horses.

With respect to horses, grandfather was an expert – both as a horse trader and a horse doctor. The neighbors brought their horses to him whenever their horse was ailing. Gramps was good at diagnosing the problem and providing remedies, often of a herbal nature.

Kavantsaari did not have a doctor of its' own – the closest doctor being in Antrea or Viipuri. Agnese Thesleff, the manor mistress, often provided much needed nursing expertise. Mid wives or grandparents delivered the children. Folk medicine was used to cure less critical illnesses. Traditional services such as massage and cupping were used. (With cupping a local suction is created on the skin; practitioners believe this mobilizes blood flow in order to promote healing). Leeches as well were used to draw out bad "blood".

Grandfather Juho was a folk medicine practitioner. He served as the family doctor, determining what the problem was, and applying bandages and herbal remedies. I remember mom when we were children looking for this or that plant to take care of our minor cuts, rashes, bruises and tummy aches.

Kavantsaari did not have a church. One had to go twenty kilometers east to the parish church in Antrea, or twenty kilometers south to Viipuri. Thus until the nearby town of Ihantala built a church in 1927 our family only went to church for major life events such as christenings, marriages and deaths. Even then thanks to Nikki Thesleff, Kavantsaari was still officially part of Antrea's parish. The Ihantala church was built on the little hilltop by the Antrea / Jaaski road junction. The same hilltop the battle of Ihantala was fought on. The church was big and beautiful with a bell tower, and a beautiful altar painting by Urpo Lehtinen.

Grandmother was religious, particularly later in life. She was a member of the "Laestadian" religious movement – an evangelical conservative Lutheran sect founded in Lapland. As a result she always wore a scarf around her head. Grandmother always made sure her scarf was ironed and perfectly in place.

Even grandfather Juho was a Laestadian member for a short period, but lapsed to the point where in jest he said:

"There is no point in bothering me. I am too deep into sin now, so it is too late for me to return."

Laestadianism's central teaching is the forgiveness of sins – but it is a very conservative religion – outlawing alcohol and parties – hmm, not a surprise grandfather lapsed.

Now grandfather as well was a bit of a pagan, believing in various facets of the old Finnish animistic religion. He was also somewhat of a clairvoyant. Family stories relate various prognostications of his such as:

Hitler was going to lose the war (true)

A final Argammendon war would come from the east. It would be so severe that the men from seven villages could sit on one fence rail (not yet ...)

Water would become so precious that it would be sold by the spoonful (hopefully not)

He was superstitious but so were all Kareilians. When we were growing up, mother would make superstitious remarks when a specific event occurred.

When someone dropped a spoon, it meant that visitors were coming

If a woodpecker was pecking on the house wall there would be a death

If a crow flew directly over the house it was bad news

If you wiped the kitchen table with paper towels it would bring poverty to the house

Likewise if you swept the dirt from the floor over the door jam it would also bring poverty

Every New Years' Eve, we would melt tin and fill up a wooden bucket with cold water and snow. Then each person in turn would pour a cup of melted tin into the bucket. By looking at the shape that would be formed we would determine our fortune for the coming year.

Fortune tellers were common in that day. Mother on at least one of her trips to Viipuri as a young woman visited a fortune teller. When I was a youth, she relayed that the fortune teller told her that:

She would have five children, all of whom would do well in the world, but the youngest of them, he would be someone special.

Now, it is true that she had five children. My sisters and my brother have done well. Now myself, the youngest in the family, have yet to accomplish anything exceptional...

The Kavantsaari school was in mid town opposite the manor road junction. In the beginning the school was in a room at the manor. The school was actually established by Jenny Thesleff, the Major General's wife. Not only did she establish the school, she taught as well. Classes were held one day a week. All the books were provided by the manor. When Jenny died her daughter Olga took over the teaching.

When a separate school house was built in 1901 Mrs Miljaroi became the teacher – and continued to be the teacher for thirty six years.

One did not attend school every day, rather a couple of days a week in the winter and one day a week in the spring (In later years everyone went to school for more days). The school itself was open Monday through Saturday but the children were sorted into three groups. Only one group was taught per day. The class rooms included both girls and boys. School was closed from June through October during the sowing and harvesting season. The curriculum emphasized the 3 Rs, reading, writing and arithmetic, but included Finnish and Russian history, religion, geography, music, athletics and art. And of course an appreciation of both patriotism and religion was a given. School began with prayer. The one below, recited after the Lord's Prayer, encouraged the young generation of Kavantsaari to live a righteous and giving life.

> *Jesus send industry and diligence into my*
> *young heart.*
>
> *And give me the ability and wisdom to live righteously*
> *and virtuously.*
>
> *Pour into my heart reason and understanding of the*
> *good path of life,*
>
> *so that my parents can take pleasure in me.*
>
> *And be like a young tree near the waters' edge,*
>
> *which bears fine fruit and brings people delight.*

Mother only had basic schooling. Enough so that she could read, write and do math easily. The school was a four kilometer walk from the farm. It appears to have been a normal one room school environment with learning occurring on the play ground as well as in the school room. Mother ended up protecting her older, smaller sister – Ester – in the school yard. Mother was a big strong youngster, known as the Öhman karhu – Öhman bear.

All the children received schooling (indeed schooling was compulsory in Finland). None became scholars though. Grandfather could read and write – as his civil war transcript notes. Grandmother never knew how to read and write – that is until she was in her late sixties. Then she finally had some free time – and at that age taught herself to write as well as read !!

The village pulsated with groups and clubs. They usually met in the school as this was the only community facility.

There was a women's organization (Marttas), youth group, workers group, temperance group, agricultural cooperative, 4h club, children's aid, and of course the civil guard and Lottas.

The workers building on the outskirts of the parish hosted theatre, dances and bands.

The boys went to the dances to drink and to socialize with the area girls. The socialization was not restricted to the dances however as one of my uncles had an illegitimate child with the hired milk maid on the farm. There was some dispute among two of the brothers as to which of them was the father of the child. Sadly neither brother took responsibility and married the girl. Much like in Vaino Linnas' trilogy, the girl went back to her home village and ended up bringing up the child by herself.

Also just as depicted in Vaino Linna's book, socialization resulted in fights among the boys. Pekka, a family cousin who lived in the nearby hamlet of Kaipola, got into a serious knife fight. He and his opponent survived and the item was hushed up. However in private Pekka was thenceforth known as Puukko Pekka "Knife Pekka". Karjala boys, like those elsewhere in Finland all carried knives. Knives in those days were almost as much of a religious symbol to Finnish men as a kirpa is to a Gurhka today.

More healthy past times were encouraged though. Formal athletic groups fostered skiing, running and athletics.

> *Mother was a good athlete – particularly at cross country skiing. She won medals in the local races in her youth. She always took dad to task regarding his skiing ability. Mom was a keen skier even in old age.*
>
> *Her younger brothers Vilho and Arvo availed themselves of the local Esa Club Athletic association in Antrea and became known athletes.*
>
> *Vilho was an excellent runner, even beating the noted Finnish runner T. Liimatta in a cross country race. Vilho was groomed for Finland's Olympic team, the*

*association even sending a live in masseuse to the
farm one summer to take care of him. This came to
naught with the start of the war. I must say Finland
provided amazing support for its' athletes.*

*Arvo was the best athlete in the family. He was a
world class cross country skier. He dominated the
local Esa Club races before the war, and afterwards
medaled in Finnish championships. Later he
represented Canada in the World championships.*

Other social events were marriages. These ended up in
multi day festivities. In the early days of Karjala, even up to
early 1900s, marriages were arranged at community gatherings (Much like the Lughnas gatherings of old Ireland). At
the community gatherings in midsummer, the marriage
age girls and boys met on the church grounds to appraise
one another. When the boy had decided on his betrothal he
gave her a ring. The next Sunday the parents on both sides
came to the church to finalize the union. Afterwards there
were many ceremonies at the girls' home. The wedding was
a bit before Christmas. There was much feasting drinking
and eating

One key assumption was that the girl accepted the ring...
While these older customs were no longer in effect during
my mother's time, her sister Tyyne's ring acceptance made
an impression on my older cousins Sirkka and Anna Liisa.

*While in her twenties, Aunt Tyyne was living at
the farm. She was a much sought after beauty.
One wealthy merchant proffered her a diamond
engagement ring as they were sitting by the sauna.
Tyyne was hot blooded as well as beautiful. She
dramatically rejected it, throwing it among the rocks.
We children looked long and hard for the sparkly
jewel but with no success.*

The other more somber social occasion was funerals.
These occasions were fairly similar to current day practices.

One difference was that old women were employed as
official lamenters *"itkija naiset"*. They cried, wailed, and
recited traditional funeral verses (Bit of a change from Irish
wakes). The itkija naiset were also hired for weddings – the
verses and tempo being quite different in this case.

Another unique funeral custom was stopping at the
local centuries old risti petaja tree while en route to the

cemetery. One either carved a cross in the tree, or affixed
a wooden plaque to the tree – the purpose being to assist
the soul of the deceased to return to god. It was an old
tradition based on the ancient Finnish animistic religion.
The modern city relatives looked on bemused at this quaint
custom. To the country folk it was not belief in magic,
but rather an acknowledgement of tradition, and of the
existence of the spirits of nature.

Our Tenant Farm Life

The family farm was located three kilometers west of
the village on the south side of the road between Ihantala
and Kavantsaari. Just a kilometer or so further west of the
farm, there was a hamlet named Kaipola. It only had a few
houses. Later in the 1930s it had a small school. Ihantala,
about seven kilometers west of the farm, was a larger town
with a church, cemetery and school.

My mother's home in Kavantsaari was a traditional
Karjala Isthmus homestead. The farm was forty four
hectares in size. Initially grandfather was a tenant farmer
renting the land from the local manor lord Thesleff. As
related earlier, when land ownership laws were passed
after the Civil War, grandfather was able to actually own
the land.

My grandparents moved from Viipuri to the property in
1904. Grandfather had been a baker in Viipuri.

They had a family of ten children – four girls and six boys.

The two oldest children were born in Viipuri and the
remaining eight on the farm in Kavantsaari. A goodly
number, but not uncommon in the countryside. That all
ten children were healthy is however a testament to good
genes, good food, good fortune, and good care.

The good care was provided by two grandmothers. My
maternal great grandmother Henrika Tiainen (Or rakas
muumo [beloved grandmother] as she was known); and
my paternal great grandmother Maria Eiskonen (Or hyvaa
mummo [good grandmother]). Rakas mummo came in
1904 when the farm was acquired, living there until she
died seventeen years later in 1921. Hyvaa mummo moved
to live with her son when her husband, Erkki Öhman died
in 1911, living with the family until her own death thirteen
years later in 1924.

The grandmothers were indispensable to the farm. They freed both parents to work in the barn and the fields. It was they who took care of the children, prepared the food and made the clothes. In return they had a home to live in. Multi generation farm households were typical in Finland and throughout the world at this time – and indeed necessary for all.

When I asked mother about her mother, mom did not have much to say other then;

"I never saw much of my mother as she was always on the run with farm work. It was my grandmothers who brought me up. They were both wonderful. Rakas mummo in particular was delightful. "

In later years they had hired hands ...milk maids, cow-herds, and field workers. Without automation, farming was a labor intensive endeavor. Hay and oats were cut with scythes and sickles, and raked and stacked by hand. Later horse drawn mowers and rakes reduced the amount of manual labor.

For many years the family lived in a little old log farm house on a small hill in from the road. The house only had two rooms. It must have been very cozy for a family with ten children, especially in the winter. In the summer the older children slept in store sheds (aittas) in the yard. The house was typical for a tenant farmer or cottager of the period. Also usual for the period was that their neighbors homestead buildings were right beside them (The not so nice Harkonens of Civil War infamy). Clustering houses together was the norm for Karjala. Not quite sure why – perhaps for support; or perhaps just sociability.

Through the families unending hard toil and gramps business acumen, the families' fortunes slowly improved. In the mid 1930s, once the local landlord Thesleff finally stopped stone walling the Crofters Law, they at last owned the land. Finally secure in their property, they moved about ½ a kilometer down the field towards the lake and built a fine new house.

The farm land was typical for the Karjala Kannas. Basically flat with a couple of rocky knolls and marshy sections. The land continued to the shore of a lake (Helkalanjarvi) and indeed included a small island (Vuotsaari) in the middle of it. The lake was shallow and grassy but had a good beach for swimming.

The area to the west of the farm was reedy lake and swamp. Cousin George recalls that:

"When the neighbors on the other side of the swamp went hunting ducks, the ducks would come winging over to the Öhman side of the marsh – right to where my dad Erkki was standing ready with his shot gun. As he was a very good shot this always resulted in duck for dinner."

The new house was by a big rock. It was a large two story house with a third floor attic. Part of the first floor was underground in order to conserve heat during the cold winters. Both floors had a large fireplace / stove for both cooking and heating the house.

The barn was to the left down the hill. The sauna was to the right.

The sauna was the centre for the traditional Saturday night soaking and socializing. It also was used to wash clothes. And very importantly, it was the hospital - children were born there and the dead laid out there. Mother along with her brothers and sisters were born in the sauna. The sauna had hot water, was draft free and warm, and could be easily cleaned and sanitized.

Nothing now remains of the homestead.

When Finland lost Karjala to Russia for the final time after the Jatkosota, freehold farms were replaced by farm collectives and all the old farmstead houses, barns and outbuildings dismantled.

The farm was a prosperous one. Just before the start of the Winter War the family had:

- 12 cows plus heifers and calves
- 3 horses
- sheep and lambs
- pigs
- hens

The family made money by selling produce in the Viipuri market. Twice a week they took a twenty kilometer train ride to the city to sell milk, butter, eggs, meat, fish, vegetables and baked goods.

Grandfather according to mom was an excellent baker. My mother herself, in everyone's opinion, was a baker par excellence. For her to say her father was even a better baker makes one marvel. Grandfather actually worked in a bakery in the Talikkala area of Viipuri before they purchased the farm.

While a no nonsense workaholic, he also liked his alcohol when he went to Viipuri. Cousin Sirkka remembers him and her father Erkki returning in the dusk after a successful day at the Viipuri market, singing away. Unfortunately sometimes gramps would beat grandma when he returned home after having a jug too many. Dad took him to task when he saw this occurring (I'm sure because mom would have been very upset), admonishing him not to do that (Dad, a non drinker, was a big athletic man). It did not occur again when mom or dad was around. Dad and gramps respected each other after that.

Grandmother took milk daily to the local town. Apparently she was often late – running frantically with her milk cans to catch the train. This became such a regular event that the train usually waited a while for her if she was not in sight.

While money was made by selling milk and produce to Viipuri, the key to raising and feeding ten children was that not too much needed to be purchased. Rather the land provided almost all that was needed.

- Cows provided milk for both home and commercial consumption
- Butter was churned from the milk
- Sheep, pigs and occassionally cattle were butchered for meat
- Hens, ducks, and geese provided both eggs and meat
- Fish was harvested from the lake with nets - eels as well
- Wheat and rye was taken to the mill and refined into flour and baked into all manner of delicious goods.
- Mushrooms were gathered in the woods.
- Berries were picked in the wild and in the garden
- Vegetables, turnips, cabbages and potatoes were grown in the garden along with apples and other fruit.
- Produce was preserved for the winter
- Clothes were made from wool and flax. The women carded the sheep wool on spindles and weaved cloth on the looms. Indeed mother mentioned that the

big Karjala dogs they had, were also sheared for wool. Flax grown in the fields was also used to make clothes.

The Öhman Children

The ten Öhman children grew up healthy and happy on the Kavantsaari farm, slowly dispersing as they became adults.

Hilda, the oldest in the family, was born in 1900. As mentioned she was almost executed by the Whites in 1918. Some years later she moved to Viipuri and married Aatu a Viipuri boy. She often came back to the farm to visit and help out. They had two daughters, one of whom, Anna Liisa, has recounted many stories from that era to me.

Erkki, the first born son, of course inherited the farm. He married Saima one of the parlor maids at the manor. I wonder how he was treated by the manor lord, as

The village boys were not allowed to go to the maid servant house. Many had married the maids taking

away the work force. Thus Nikki started to fine the boy visitors/suitors a markka an evening and took it off their pay.

Mind you Nikki was not as harsh as his brother Lelo. Lelo, who lived in a separate manor, would lock the maids in at night and would not let them leave. The maids were needless to say terrified. When my mother Saima was a parlor maid in the main manor she came to visit the Uussi hovi. She told Lelo's maids to leave if they wished. She would leave the door open as she was departing. One maid did - with Lelo shouting and screaming after her as she ran away."

Erkki and Saima had two sons and two daughters. They settled in the homestead and progressively by the mid 1930s were operating the farm. Sirkka their oldest daughter wrote her memoirs on Karjala and the wars. I refer to these at length in the next books.

Armas, the second oldest son, left the farm and moved to Canada in 1928 when he was in his early twenties. Armas lived a comfortable life in America – but not initially. During the Depression he lived a hobo life, riding the rails looking for work. He was a card carrying Communist – not surprising given the manner in which the Whites had treated the family, and the harshness of the Depression years.

Esther, the second oldest daughter likewise departed for America the same year. In the case of Esther a large going away party was held for her. In those days if one left for overseas, it was almost similar to a funeral (mind you much more upbeat) as there was a good probability that the family would never see her again. I don't know why a party was not held for Armas. Perhaps because it was not that unusual that men left to wander the world in order to earn a livelihood. After all, none except the first son would inherit the scarce farm land. Women by contrast did not wander far afield, usually marrying one of the men in the parish.

My mother Martta was the next oldest daughter. Mother as well departed for Canada when she was twenty two. She however returned to the farm in December 1932, staying there for a couple of years until she and dad got married in June 1935.

Tyyne, the next child, also departed for Canada at the behest of Armas and Esther. She however as well returned to the farm. In the 1950s she returned to live in the USA. Married several times, she had no children. Both Armas and Tyyne had outgoing effervescent personalities. While hard working and helpful, they were Olympic partiers.

Armas returned briefly once before going back to Canada permanently, marrying and raising a family of two boys. Esther moved to the United States, marrying and raising one daughter. Both Armas and Esther married transplanted Finns. While they were "Americans", integration had not yet reached the stage where marriages were with other nationalities.

My grandparents had four sons after their last daughter Tyyne was born; namely:

- Kauko
- Toivo
- Vilho, and
- Arvo

I talk at length about their lives in the next books on the wars.

All of the boys worked on the farm until they were called up for a year of military service shortly after they turned eighteen – Kauko in 1932, Toivo in 1936, Vilho in 1938, and Arvo in 1939. Previously the older brothers had done their service. The family photos show them booted and spurred, cavalry sword in hand.

The family survived the depression years relatively unscathed as they had always relied on the farm for their food and livelihood.

No one was swept up in the Lapua fascist movement of 1932. Not surprising given that the roots of the Viipuri area of Karjala was grounded in many centuries of socialism, multi-culturalism and liberalization.

The younger boys did get caught up in the Finlandization which was sweeping the country in the late 1930s. In 1938 they all changed their surname from the Swedish Öhman to a more Finnish sounding one. In that period many people changed their names. An individual could choose whatever name they wished as long as it was not already taken. Changing names was not that reprehensible given that less than fifty years before most individuals did not have a surname, but nonetheless... The two older sons Erkki and Armas declined to discard their heritage, remaining Öhmans. A decision which served them well when they came to America. Unlike their younger brothers they did not need to continuously spell their surname.

Vaino Linna, once more captures the issue vividly in his book, Under the North Star

> *The new enlightened vicar's wife is talking to the crofter:*
>
> *"Your name was Koskela ?" (Koskela means by the brook)*
>
> *"It is ...It's my extra name."*
>
> *"Extra name ? What do you mean ?"*
>
> *"Well, it's like a place name. In the church records I'm just Anttisson." (Antti's son)*
>
> *"Lauri, you'll have to enter Koskela as this man's family name immediately"*
>
> *"Yes, of course my little Fennophile." said Vicar Lauri*

Life is Karjala Food

Before talking about the my fathers' boyhood life in Viipuri – The Paris of the North – I can not resist saying a few words about Karelian food.

For Karelians food was not just subsistence. It was central to making one happy purely by itself, and for socializing with ones' family and friends. Food was the centre of any gathering and was joyously shared. All Karelians had known famine, so to keep food only to oneself was "tribally" unacceptable.

Karjala food is quite simple but delicious (I freely acknowledge that Finland is not the gastronomic centre of the world). The food is definitely not spicy...and always well cooked. In the early days the Karelians were self sufficient. All of the food was local – harvested from the land, the forest, and the water. Except for that staple of Finnish life - coffee !!!

I experienced Karjala cooking in person. Indeed I grew up eating almost solely Karjala food.

Karjala is noted for two signature dishes – karjalanpaisti (a "pot roast" made of beef, pork, and lamb meat); and piirakka (small open faced rye pastries filled with rice or other foods). And yes a third – mushroom soup. Mushrooms were a sought after delicacy. Of course there were many other fish, poultry, meat, vegetable and dairy dishes. Bread, baked goods and porridge were staples. Domestic and wild berries formed a key part of the diet.

Most of the main courses were cooked in the oven. Needless to say given the time period, food was not frozen. It was eaten fresh, or preserved by drying or by pickling and preserving. Generally little was smoked. Even bread was preserved as hard tack or as dried rye bread. The rye bread had a hole made into it so it could be inserted on a pole placed near the ceiling. Fresh bread as opposed to hard tack however was the norm.

Mother was a Karelian chef extraordinaire – creating authentic, traditional dishes passed down to her at the cooking stove by her mother and grandmother. Our enjoyment was even more genuine as our environment in northern Ontario approximated that of the Karjala days. We had access to the same foods as we lived on a backwoods farm close to nature. And, we still had a wood stove on which mother cooked. Ahh, the warmth and the wafting aroma of baking bread or simmering stew !!

For major Sunday family meals or holidays, mom excelled with Karjalan paisti. Prime cut roast beef with some lamb and pork added - slow roasted in a pot, moistened and softened so it fell apart. The aroma wafted through the house all day. It always had a simple tasty sauce to which carrots were added. Sometimes potatoes were added but usually mashed potatoes were served on the side (Of course liberally smothered with the delicious sauce). As the beef was from our own cattle, the meat was exceptional. I remember when Uncle Armas passed through with a friend en route to Alaska. The friend said it was the best food he had ever had. And yes it was.

Another Karjala dish - cabbage rolls – was an additional signature dish of mothers. They were filled with a magic ground beef and rice mixture and carefully wrapped in the best cabbage leaves. I remember mother wrapping each meat/rice ball with the cabbage leaf and then deftly tying it with thread so that it would not fall apart as it succulently baked away. No extra tomatoes, peppers, or spices, just the basic ingredients with some salt and pepper added. I don't know whether it was the quality and freshness of the ingredients or the slow cooking, but somehow the flavors were sublime. Probably both the ingredients and the oven; but, most certainly the magic touch of a master chef.

Day to day dishes included chicken and pork – all baked slowly in the oven of the wood stove or in the case of chicken breasts, pork chops etc. fried on top of the wood stove in an iron frying pan. Also fabulous meat balls served with a sauce. After frying the meat balls, mother just seemed to throw water and flour into the frying pan – and voila marvelous gravy to mash the potatoes into.

Another periodic plate was liver coated in flour and fried with onions. That did not become a favorite of mine until late in life. Generally other offal such as heart, lungs etc did not make it to our table. Now head cheese did. Again made by mother into an inimitable and tasty morsel.

Potatoes were a dinner time staple - any which way - boiled, baked, mashed, even made into soup and casseroles.

For some reason it was not the Karjala habit to have steaks. And whatever chops we had were always well done – a Finnish must. I remember when we were immigrating to

Canada dad took us into a restaurant in Copenhagen as we were awaiting our next ship. He ordered steak. The steak arrived bloody. We all sat aghast looking at the food. Not only was the meal far more expensive then we could afford, but most of it was left on the plate. Such are eating habits.

Now fish, that we had no problem eating raw. Pickled herring was a must. In Karjala there was pike, perch, whitefish, trout, salmon, sturgeon, smelts, even eels. Occasionally our fish was pan fried, but usually it ended up in fish soup. Smelt was a special delicacy. Mother rolled the fish in flour, added salt and pepper and threw them into a hot buttered skillet. Being a small fish we ate it head, tail and all. Usually the entrails were removed. Another delicacy which was served at Christmas - lipca kala I did not care for at all. Lipea kala was dried cod or haddock, soaked in a lipea acid solution for a couple of days so it would rehydrate and then cooked in a casserole with milk, onions etc. It had a very strong, to me, unpleasant bouquet and mushy taste.

With all the meals we had mom's bread. Her light rye bread was sought after by our relatives and neighbors. Mom just kneaded it, threw in this and that, into the oven, and voila. I guess there was a recipe as mom gave it to my sisters. None of them could reproduce the magic though. There was nothing quite as good as arriving home from school to bread fresh out of the oven - still warm. You added our home made butter. Let it melt momentarily, and – mmm. Occasionally mother made dark sweet rye bread which had molasses in it.

Now she never made the signature treat of Viipuri - the Viipuri rinkelli. The rinkelli is a large soft pretzel made with wheat flour, eggs, sugar, butter, yeast, cardamon, and nutmeg, brushed with an egg and butter mixture once baked. The recipe was originally brought to Viipuri by the Franciscan monks in 1500. In the early years it was considered a delicacy for nobility and was enjoyed over the centuries by such aristocrats as Pehr Brahe the Commander of Viipuri in 1640 and Tsar Alexander III in 1880. In due course it became available to the populace – becoming a symbol of Viipuri itself, just like Viipuri Linna.

At home for the meals of course we had our own vegetables. In the summer this was freshly pulled out of the garden just before dinner. Carrots, peas, beans, beets, turnips, onion, lettuce, cucumber, tomatoes. And of course, our fresh potatoes. Mom had a magic cucumber recipe where she added salt, sugar, and new dill to thin cut cucumbers. She then just tossed this between two soup plates – ahhh. I've tried to do the very same thing but haven't been able to attain the ahhh.

In the early summer mom made "spring" vegetable soup. Now I was not the biggest fan of this. I was always astonished as dad demolished his bowl and asked for more. Dad had a well founded reputation for never eating raw vegetables such as peas, tomatoes, etc. But into the dish went peas, onion, peas, beans, cabbage, carrots, other … whatever was fresh in the garden.

I was a great fan of mom's baked mashed turnips though. There were a lot of casserole dishes ranging from turnips to potatoes in Karjala cooking.

In the winter although there were no fresh vegetables, we still had our own vegetables from the root cellar – potatoes, turnips, carrots, beets. And apples – both as jam and as crunchable teeth cleaners. In Karjala plums and cherries as well as apples were cultivated.

And we had preserves – pickles, beets et al, but also berries. Most especially berries. In the summer we went and picked strawberries which mom preserved. Raspberries as well. And especially blue berries. Many were the expeditions we took on the bluffs to gather blueberries.

In Karjala there were also lingon berries, red and black currant, gooseberries, cloudberries, and cranberries. Most of the berries were picked in the wild as opposed to being cultivated in the garden.

Wild strawberries were especially esteemed. And I agree they are special. Mother tried to get us to pick the wild strawberries just as she did in her youth. And we did, once or twice, but discovered that it took forever to fill just a mug (partly because we were doing a lot of quality control sampling). So we reverted back to the Canadian standard – filling the basket with big cultivated strawberries.

Another Karjala delicacy mother tried to gather were wild mushrooms. The problem was that mushrooms did not grow as bountifully in northern Ontario as in Karjala. Mother took us with her mushroom hunting once. We did not have much success. The only thing I remember from searching through the damp underbrush, was mother musing;

"Can't see any of those Karjala mushrooms. I wonder if those growing on that stump are tasty ? edible ? or at least non poisonous ?"

Mother abandoned mushroom hunting after one or two failed expeditions. So we never did have taste bud exploding Karjala mushroom soup.

Mother made great dessert pastry – be it oatmeal, peanut butter or raisin cookies, cakes, cinnamon rolls, or her legendary pulla. Pulla is a traditional Karjala sweet coffee bread made from wheat flour. Dough is mixed and left to rise, kneaded and rolled, braided, baked and at the end brushed with a sugar based butter and egg coating. Sometimes cardamom was added. Again non replicable. Recipes yes, but the flavor and lightness of mothers' baking – no. Sometimes even mothers' pulla was not demolished within a couple of days, in which case mother added a bit of sugar and cinnamon and baked it in the oven resulting in crunchy pulla or korpo. Great to soak in your coffee.

And I must not forget munkki - deep fried pulla dough coated in butter. Doughnuts in other words. But what doughnuts !!! Fresh out of the kettle dusted with sugar and flour with centers of homemade jam. All the more desirable as we had to convince mother to make them as it involved a lot of additional work to get a kettle of oil bubbling.

Now piirakka is another "known for" Karjala food that mother made. It is an open faced rye pastry that looks like a moccasin with no top, which is filled with rice, buttered, and baked. The filling differed dependent on whether you wanted it as part of the main course or as dessert – for dessert strawberry, blueberry, apple, rhubarb, rice – as a main course potato, cheese, mushrooms or even ground beef.

A key ingredient of all baking was butter. We made our own butter. When the milk was ready after brewing for a couple of days, it was my job to churn it. This required sitting there turning, and turning, and turning the crank that moved paddles in the butter churn (upright wooden churns with a paddle plunger in the early days). On a good day – hallelujah!! only 20 minutes and the butter started to congeal. On bad days, an hour of butter churn elbow and spinning boredom. This usually happened on days with pending thunder storms.

But the resulting butter was truly special, tasty and salted just right. And true butter milk resulted as well. It actually had globs of butter in it. Delicious, soothing, thirst quenching.

Dessert other then coffee bread or fruit was not always provided. Certainly there was dessert on holidays and family gatherings with cookies and cake; or usually a traditional Karjala dessert such as: luumukiisseli (plum and fruit soup with whipped cream); rhubarb and strawberry soup, vispipuuro (a sweet pink dessert porridge with lingonberries served with milk and sugar); rice pudding; yogurt; cloudberry jam with leipa justo (a squeaky baked cheese made from cow's milk); and piirakka.

Neither wine nor beer were usually served with dinner. A beer or a shot of vodka before dinner, yes; and lakka or mesimarja liquer with coffee after dinner. However, drinking was a separate occasion onto itself. A hallowed tradition which was enjoyed perhaps too often and to too great excess.

Mother did make some non alcoholic beverages - kalja and sima. Kalja was made from molasses while sima was a type of mead. Both were provided during the summer to quench the thirst of workers in the fields.

Now there was always coffee. Indeed coffee was served throughout the day to combat the long dark days of winter. Coffee was close to a religion. Being allowed to drink coffee was a "coming of age". Until you were six or seven, you were not offered coffee – rather as the others drank coffee you were offered "hopea teeta' – silver tea. This was hot water with milk and sugar.

Speaking of sugar, the old ladies drank their coffee in a distinctive manner. They poured the hot coffee onto their cup saucer, blew onto it momentarily to cool it, and then slurped it in through a sugar cube.

One Christmas mom outdid herself cooking a twelve day Christmas extravaganza. Every day we had something special for dinner – be it the main course or dessert. She made all sorts of special pulla, cookies, and pirrakkas. This peaked with the Christmas day feast itself – turkey with all the trimmings and that Finnish Christmas standard that I never really tuned into - lippea kalla.

The New Years standard I adored however. Mother made a fresh leg of ham. The ham was soaked in salt and magic herbs for a couple of days. Then it was covered in dough and cooked slowly in the wood oven for what seemed like days. The ham was delicious. The baked salted dough covering was addictive. There was enough to chew and salivate on for four or five days – assuming I managed to keep ahead of my brother.

Ahh, I have forgotten breakfast. Although there was eggs and bacon, porridge was the staple here. I was not like the three little bears. I did not like my porridge.

I also did not like the many fermented milk and milk curd dishes that were also a Karjala standard.

Most of the food I loved though !

Mind you not everything was fine dining. There was pea soup. Excellent !!! Not so excellent was mulligan wiener soup and laski sauce and potatoes. Especially laski sauce and potatoes – a concoction of bacon fat and rinds in a flour sauce with potato. Not too tasty but stuck to the ribs. When I complained mother would say,

> "In the lean years that was all we had to eat. We ate it and were thankful. Now you better finish what is on your plate and be thankful as well".

As you can tell, my Karjala roots show through in my joy of food.

Food was also central to life in the city of Viipuri. Life there however was different from country life.

CHAPTER 10

Viipuri City Life

CHAPTER 10

Viipuri City Life

While mother was working in the fields, dad was living the unfettered life of a city boy in Viipuri.

The Whites had devastated and burnt a considerable part of the town, and imprisoned its' populance; but as in days of yore, Viipuri recovered. By the early 1920s prosperity returned. By 1939 Viipuri had almost doubled in size, growing to 78,000.

The harbor was the cities commercial heart. It served as the port for exporting the vast timber reserves of the interior, particularly via the Saima Canal. In 1928 about 7,200 vessels from around the globe sailed into the harbor. From the cities railway hub, railway lines fanned out into five different directions – including of course the link between Helsinki and St Petersburg. Today Viipuri still serves as the gateway from Russia to the West. Much of the traffic today is via transport trucks. I was astounded when we drove to Viipuri to see the trucks lined up for twenty kilometers from the border. It takes them up to a week to cross !!

Important banks and commercial houses supported the trade transactions.

Factories and commercial enterprises including sawmills, engineering works, tobacco, soap, candle, match, margarine, meat canning, confectionery, clothing and leather factories, breweries, etc. employed additional people.

As the capital of the Province of Viipuri, and de facto centre of Eastern Finland, it contained various public offices. Even the Bishop's Seat and Council was once more in Viipuri, transferred from Savonlinna.

The city was still a major military centre, with garrisons located throughout.

Educational institutes abounded - high schools, industrial colleges, trade schools, music conservatories, an art school.

An extensive library, a historical museum, an art gallery, a symphony orchestra and a theatre ensured that culture retained its' important role in the city.

Numerous societies, associations, and athletic clubs, etc. provided further social and athletic outlets.

Four newspapers served the town and province: Kansan Tyo, Karjala, Maakansa, and Viborgs Nyheter.

New hospitals were built, the municipal water and sewage infrastructure renovated, and roads expanded.

Throughout all the construction the city architect ensured that the buildings themselves contributed to the renown and beauty of the city.

As the 1933 Viipuri city brochure proudly notes:

> Present day Viipuri bears in its outward appearance traces of its varied and chequered history.
>
> It is a combination of old and new, delightful in its strangeness. Busy traffic in broad tree bordered streets and medieval perspectives of narrow old passages, splendor and homeliness, bold planning and small-scale intimacy.
>
> Historical memories everywhere, and beside these the newest manifestations of the modern spirit.

While by 1933 the population of close to 80,000 was now 83% Finnish, the multi-lingual and multi-cultural heritage of Viipuri still vibrated in the culture and in day to day life. As the 1933 city fathers state:

> *A feature peculiar to Viipuri, called into being by its centuries old, extensive business connections, is the liveliness and colorfulness of its atmosphere, a special character met with nowhere else in Finland.*

A Viipuri Boyhood

In this milieu my father grew to manhood. As he recounts:

> *Times were still difficult in the initial years after the Civil War. We had lost our house and all our worldly belongings. Food was scarce. But we were all alive.*
>
> *I guess we lived for a couple of years in grandmother Maria Hellman's house at 5 Virasto Street.*
>
> *Bread was scarce, particularly during the early fall of 1918.*

On the other side from grandmother's house was Uncle Hjalmar's' bakery, in which he himself lived. Uncle Hjalmar had a large bakery, employing about twenty people in addition to the family– bakers, drivers and helpers. But during the rebellion year and for some time thereafter the bakery had to close. Dad's cousin Veikko, Uncle Hjalmar's son recounts:

> *During this time, shortage of flour and other food stuffs came first. The national food commission provided repeatedly smaller amount of flour of decreasing quality, and did not allow flour from the black market. When flour was nothing but husks and forage oats, Hellman ceased baking.*
>
> *The employees were, of course, let go nearly completely, except for few confidential personnel. Confidential, because Jallu Hellman did something else, He started with carrying "women's goods merchandise" - gloves, laces, underwear- to St Petersburg in suitcases, as there was a great shortage of these items in St Petersburg.*

> *He "quite legally" brought back normal foodstuffs, sugar, tea, candies, fruit - even full carriage loads by train. I accompanied him on one trip at the age of five years, as a camouflage. It was of no benefit, the custom-house officers caught him and the suitcases. I could not help crying bitterly as the train was leaving. However, my dad showed up with the suitcases. He had given some roubles to each man "for tea"; and caught, but barely, the last coach of the train.*
>
> *That kind of business came to its natural end with time, but it was followed by a period of completely illegal wartime profiteering. Meat, butter other supplies were brought from as far away as unravaged White Finland, and sold to those who were in need.*

By the early 1920s prosperity returned. Viipuri almost doubled in size by 1939, growing to 80,000 by 1939. Dad recounts:

> *After all the turmoil settled, I had to go to the public school. About that time dad got the Spanish influenza. I did as well. We both recovered. [Despite the cities continued efforts at health and hygiene, global epidemics and contaminated water resulted in disease].*
>
> *A few years later the parents bought a large house at 9 Ilmari St, on the corner of Ilmari St and Hirvi St. There we had two rooms, a kitchen, and a good porch. The house again was a tall building. Part of the roof was tile.*
>
> *On the first floor, there were three rooms and a long hallway. There, dad, together with Uncle Jonne Starck, set up a machine shop called "Ilmarinen". The first room was a saw sharpening room, the second had a big welding machine, a drill machine and a blade honing stone. In the long hallway there were electric motors which provided the power for all the equipment. In the third room there was a welder who did whatever he did under his own name.*
>
> *There certainly was a lot of activity. Dad and Jonne went to the Varkaus factory and bought used/broken equipment at their auction. They were big machines. They fixed up the machinery and then sold them.*

We lived on top of the machine shop.

On the rest of the floor, there was first the Tarvaiset, then the Koskeltiinit. The next name I don't remember, but the final one was the Honkaset. As well there was another bigger room.

The house was made of logs with a solid stone foundation. However there was no water. We had to get it from a house at the bend of Kivi St. They had a well.

[It certainly seems that people in those days did not require a lot of space. Many families lived in the same house. Indeed home ownership was less than 20% in Viipuri. Most people rented.]

When we were living there Yrjo started school near Havin. In the fall I started in the Reali school, in second grade as it turned out.

Some years later the parents got reparation for the burning of our house in Rosu. At that point they discontinued the machine shop business and held an auction. Dad went to Terijoki. There he bought an old log cabin and moved it to Viipuri. They put it up themselves on our old property on 45 Kannaksentie in Rosu.

It was a big house. They had eight renters. They themselves still had two rooms and a kitchen. The house had a full length basement. Two renters lived there. There was a wood shed for everyone to use, a big washing room where there was a water pump. They had their own well with good clear water. New dirty waste water pipes went through the Bari's yard joining up with their sewage system.

The new house drawings were done by Kaljuna. The house was built by Kantasa together with his sons Paavo and Huukko. Huukko ended up in the army in the Karjala Guards regiment during the TalviSota. He was killed soon after. He was a good person. We travelled together a lot .A laughing face - a joyful companion.

And speaking of joyful outings, father seemed to have had many of them. As the preceding writings of dads' illustrate,

his life in Viipuri was not easy, particularly during the Red/White Revolution years.

However dad always emphasized the many care free aspects of his child hood. He periodically regaled us with stories of his boy hood escapades. He never complained about his lot in life.

Dad's boyhood escapades were fueled by the fact that neither his mother nor father kept a close rein on him or his brother. They happily wandered and cavorted throughout the city in their copious spare time. The boyhood troop usually consisted of dad, his brother Yrjo and his cousins – Veikko Hellman and Walter and Risto Starck.

I've included the stories of some of the "Huck Finn worthy" escapades below. Boyhood is boyhood ...

Smooth ... Sailing in Viipuri Harbor: The boys were avid sailors. One evening when they were sailing in Viipuri harbor their boat sank. Only the mast remained visible. They got to shore quickly and furtively snuck back home. The major issue was not drowning, but rather trying not to be noticed. While the boat was not too valuable, it sank in one of the shipping lanes. While the harbor master could see the mast, it took some effort to move the sunken boat and reopen that harbor area.

Ski Tall: The boys, like all Finns, liked to ski. They often skied on a trail in the country which they knew quite well. One day an unknown older skier came up behind them shouting "latu, latu – or trail, trail" – the common instruction for get off the trail and let me by. The boys did not heed him and took off down the track. While the older skier would have undoubtedly beat them, he unfortunately broke a leg when the younger boys scooted down a hill on the tight course. The hill ended suddenly by a wood fence. Being small, the boys ducked down and whizzed through a hole under the fence. An opening far too low for the taller older skier, in hot pursuit, to fit through.

Football Too Valuable ... The boys were playing football near the army barracks. They kicked the ball inadvertently over the perimeter fence into the parade ground. The guard however would not let them in to recover the ball. The ball was hard to replace, so a couple of the boys taunted the guard so that he started chasing them. During the commotion, one of the other boys slipped in from the other side of the barracks, retrieved the ball, and slipped back out through a hole in the fence.

Two Bullets, One Rabbit: "Lively was the day, when we went to the Papilla point. The first snow was on the ground. There was Veikko (Veikko had the gun), Yrjo and a couple of the Starck boys. In the bushes a rabbit hopped . Right beside us, Veikko shot. But the bullet did not come out – only a strong hissing – the poor rabbit was sitting nearby. I shouted shoot !! shoot !! after it !!. Veikko fired. There were certainly two bullets in the barrel - there was a huge bang, sparks and smoke. No one talked anymore, about the rabbit, about the gun, nor about the explosion. Nor ever after that, did we hear about the rabbit or the gun."

Wild Pig, You Say ? "Another time during the summer, we were hunting ducks on Salo lake with the shot gun. We did not get anything.

We were marching back along the forest trails going home. Hanne was leading, followed by myself, Veikko, and brother Yrjo. Yrjo was carrying the shot gun. Suddenly Hanne stopped, spread his arms and motioned "Give me the gun - there is a wild boar". He shot !! and there was a great commotion in the bushes... Out came the Antilla's pig – a pregnant mother sow. She ran squealing down the hill !!

We wondered, what do we do now ? Together, we decided that we would go home, but that we would go around the Antilla place. We went a long way around it on a forest trail. We heard nothing further.

Here, in Canada, while I was working in the lumber camps, I got into an argument with the Antilla grandson who was also in the camp. I said "Don't disagree with me about the matter young man, I was dancing at your mother and father's wedding." Antilla, however responded – "Yes, but I also know that you shot our pig." I was astounded. How did they know? Apparently they saw us when we went on the lake, but no one dared to come after us as we still

had the guns [and heaven knows what the hooligans would shoot if they shot our pig]."

A Fish Story Hard to Believe ... "We were in Kaipola a couple of summers at Tuntallas. During one of the summers Veikko came along. We went fishing. We sank a long baited fishing line with many hooks, lowering it into the depths of Salo Lake. The next day we pulled it out. There was work to do, as we lifted out a lot of salmon. We brought them into the camp. The old householder Tuomas muttered to himself wondering whose line we had emptied. I said it was our own line. However, I never did any line fishing again."

Summer Outings: "During my boyhood years when we lived on Ilmari St., we were always out with the Starck boys and Veikko Hellman. This was especially the case during the summer. We went on many outings.

We went to Havilla often to go swimming. It had a good sand beach and docks from which one could jump in. We watched as on the horse platform, the horsemen swam and washed their horses. The bluffs were high. We lounged on them sun bathing. Only hunger brought us home.

At Karema, behind Viro, were hills where we often went swimming. Longer trips took us to the Lintimuksi, Lastukka and Papilla inlets. Sometimes we stayed overnight in Lintu.

Uncle Georg Hellman had a row boat. We rowed with it to Latukka and Pitkasaari. But Georg's boys did not associate much with us. For a while, they stayed away from the Starck boys as well (Walter and Risto). They were somewhat younger then we were.

When we were older, we went on enjoyable trips. It was nice to go through the Juustila locks with the boat. We were often at the Huus inlet. There was a restaurant there where we had coffee. We drank it outside on the park bench. It tasted good.

Our older boyhood years were blessed. We were content - life was easy. They were great times."

Father's great times stopped when his father died in 1923 when dad was fourteen. My grandfather Georg died in the fall of 1923 at the age of forty-four at home on 45 Kannastie shortly after the home was finished. He died of some type of fever.

Dad has related to me many times that on his death bed grandfather told him,

> *"That he would be waiting to greet him on the other side when dad himself died."*

As mentioned, grandfather Georg was buried in the Finnish Riistimaki cemetery in Viipuri. Due to the Russians desecration of the cemetery after WW II, no monuments remain. The Russians used the cemetery as a pig enclosure. Head stones were used as foundations for buildings. Not that Finns are entirely blameless themselves. During the Civil War the Whites executed several hundred Reds and buried them in a mass grave. They then set up a pig enclosure on top of the grave.

Life after grandfather died was difficult:

> *"Of course mother had a great shortage of money. I did not want to go to school. I did not want to be thrust into classical school [Reaalikoulu school – This is general high school which teaches Latin etc. as opposed to a technical school].*
>
> *Instead, I went to work for the city many a time, courtesy of Kaljunen who was the responsible manager. I think my earnings helped a lot.*
>
> *The house at 45 Kannastie was left to us. It had fourteen rooms. Mother soon made a living renting out apartments.*
>
> *It burnt down again in the last war in 1944. Those wars will continue to come. We lost everything. We were lucky to escape with our lives. "*

Dad, along with some of his friends, joined the wrestling and boxing club. [As noted earlier Viipuri had many athletic associations]. Dad enjoyed the wrestling and the camaraderie. Dad did also mention that the other reason he enjoyed the club is that the members got into dances for free, and, were able to meet a lot of pretty girls.

In typical dad fashion, not all was work and worry.

A Soldier's, Artist's, Engineer's Life

Like all Finnish men dad had to serve in the army when he turned eighteen.

> *"When it was my time, I had to join the military in the transport battalion at Tervaniemi. During my time in the army, I managed somehow or other. I was unhappy however that they put me in the quarter masters transport supply battalion. For fifteen months I thought that Finland had too large an army as there was never enough clothes nor food to distribute.*
>
> *During the summer of 1928, I was in the Karjalan Isthmus with the cavalry in Commander Iissakson's Karjala Regiment. I rode with Major Heinrichsen (he was OK) and his unit [Heinrichs rose to command the Kannas Army in the Talvisota].*
>
> *Actual combat and military training was limited. There was a lot of attention paid however to the chain of command and showing appropriate respect for ones superiors. There seemed to be scores of generals and officers. Officers during this time were*

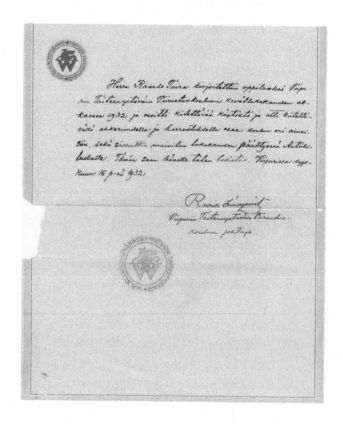

a privileged lot. We occasionally saw them pop into the office, but only to collect their salary, and a good one at that. The men themselves however were the very best.

I got discharged in December of 1929 with a rank of Corporal. The army wanted me to stay and enlist in officer school. However, I did not like military service.

I was a civilian again. There wasn't work anywhere – it was during the Depression Years. They were tough years but they passed. During that time I went to art school and subsequently to the civil engineering school. "

Dad was an accomplished artist:

"One winter I was in the Viipuri art school.

Valpe Valeniukse, my friend, was there, indeed he suggested I enroll. I submitted a wood relief of a horse as an example of my art work. The school accepted me. The school was entirely funded by the businesses and merchants of Viipuri. There was no set class curriculum. Rather one learned by doing and being mentored through the process.

It was the best school I've ever been in."

Dad received his artist certificate in 1932 when he was 24 (A photo of his original diploma from the Wiipurin Taiteen Ystavat Piirustos Koulu is on the previous page).

Mother said dad was a very good artist [and mother was not one to give praise lightly]. The principal of the school thought he had potential. When he learned that dad was related to Werner Astrom a noted Finnish artist, he said, "ahh now I understand where the talent comes from".

Of course, making a living as an artist was not very promising. So he went to engineering school.

"Valpe said to me that we should go to the civil engineering school. I was hesitant, but Valpe convinced my mother, and away we went [Dad said that Valpe asked his mother for a loan to go to school. Mother said she would give him one if dad went].

We went there for three years – 1932, 33 and 34 –I worked here and there. Sometimes there was work, sometimes not – you could never tell. The

Engineering school saved me. For the first time, it forced me to work hard. Finally I got my head together. Most of the subjects did not mean a thing in the real world, but you had to struggle through them anyway. I got out in the spring of 1935.

Work was hard to get even at that time. I tried to get myself a job at the railroad. It was the only company that had jobs in the whole town. Viipuri was a port city and a trading centre. There was a large logging center, the countries' largest. It served a large hinterland - all of Karjala and Laatokka, and most of Savo."

Dad after graduating did get a job with the Finnish Railway. Grandmother Valencia convinced dad to not only join the railway, but to remain there as it provided a stable reliable work place.

When we came to Canada dad brought along his original official art and engineering transcripts/ diplomas as he hoped to get work in these fields. As well, he brought over a twenty volume set of fine leather bound engineering books.

Life for people with credentials from foreign countries was the same than as it is today. He ended up going to work as a lumber jack in northern Ontario.

Quite a change, as our mother said, from walking around with his hands behind his back directing people. Dad lost his engineering ring while opening the passenger car window during our train trip from Halifax to Toronto. Dad said it was an early indication that he would not be doing any more engineering work. Dad never complained about his new "career."

Married Life

Our mother was in Canada for three years – from late 1929 to November 1932.

Dad had known her before she went to Canada. Indeed he met her as a younger girl - initially, when he accompanied his father delivering goods from his store to Kaipola – a hamlet near mom.

While mother was in Canada dad wrote her many letters - letters which influenced mother to come back to Finland.

Mother and dad got married on June 6, 1935 after dad graduated. Their wedding was held in Viipuri, but they had the wedding party at mothers' home in Kavantsaari. The marriage lasted for over fifty years – surviving WW II and the move to Canada.

While they formally got married in Viipuri on the 9th they also had a large wedding party on the farm later in June. Cousin Sirkka remembers the wedding as a five year old:

"It was a beautiful wedding on Mid Summer Nights Eve at the farm. Your mother and dad walked down a long rug to a beautiful bower of birch branches and flowers. Your mom was in a lovely white wedding dress and veil and your dad in his tux.

My mother Saima and Aunt Hilda worked for several days baking the wedding cake and the various pastries. Everyone ate at the farm and then went to the nearby neighbors – the Harkkanens - for dancing. There was a lot of room at that house as there was only the Harkkanen son and his wife. [His mother (and father) were the ones who had gotten grandfather put into prison. Those mutual feelings of distrust had obviously not been passed on to the next generation].

The people went back and forth between the two houses – dancing and eating. I really wanted to be a flower girl but they did not have any flower girls or a wedding party"

Dad's mother Valencia, while cordially supporting the marriage, was not totally enamored with the union - perhaps because she was losing her son - perhaps because mom was a country girl, and dad a city boy. But possibly I am over stating the case, as most certainly the major factor was that they left Finland in 1951, leaving her without her son and her only grand children.

Mom and dad settled near Viipuri in the village of Liimatta. It is five kilometers south of the central Viipuri rail way station, at a junction of two railroads. Dad at that time was working with the railroad. Both my oldest sisters Terttu and Tellervo were born there. Terttu Tuulikki on July 5, 1936 and Tellervo on September 26, 1937.

The home in Liimatta was part of a long building which had several families living in it. [A version of a row house].

Terttu remembers the Liimatta Viipuri home as being a very nice place.

Life was very promising; but then life exploded. Their home became a battlefield.

BOOK II
The Talvi Sota
"The Winter War"

Albert Edelfelt: Poltettu Kyla

*The Finnins have continual warres with the
Muscovites in the bosome of the sea Finnonicus;
using in Sommer the ayde of Shyppes, and
in Winter they combat upon the ice.
George North, 16th century traveler*

For God, Home and Country
For Freedom

Talvisota, a Military Summary

Talvisota, a Military Summary

The Talvisota lasted 105 days. Russian attacked Finland on November 30, 1939. Peace was signed on March 13, 1940.

In October Stalin pressured Finland to become part of its' " sphere of influence" as agreed upon by Stalin and Hitler in the Molotov-Ribbentrop Treaty. Although carrying on talks, Finland did not accede to Russia's demands, knowing that the Russian end objective was to take over Finland.

During the war Finland stubbornly fought back against the overwhelming force of Russia. She was alone as none of the Western Powers came to her aid – not even Sweden her weak next door neighbor.

Finland succeeded in stopping the Russian attack in Northern Finland. On the Kannas where the brunt of the attack came, Finland successfully held the Russians at bay at the Mannerheim Line for 2 ½ months, before having to withdraw to the Intermediate Line and subsequently to the Back Line.

When peace was signed, Viipuri was still in Finnish hands.

The war was fought on land. Naval encounters were minimal given the frozen seas and the relatively small size of the Russian navy. In the air Russia bombed the front lines and the Finnish cities at will. Russia had 10 times as many planes as Finland.

On land Russia mobilized an army over a million – Finland 340,000 – every able bodied Finnish man.

Finland was "outgunned" 10 to 1 by Russia's artillery. Russia had 3,000 tanks – Finland only a few outdated useless WW I vintage Vicker tanks.

Finland nonetheless was able to stop Russia on the front. The front as through times immemorable once more was Karjala.

Finland succeeded due to its' defensive lines, military tactics, and most importantly, the will of its' army to sacrifice all for their countries freedom and independence.

CHAPTER 1

Politcal Prelude

CHAPTER 1

Political Prelude

War in Europe started on Sept 3, 1939 between Germany and the Allied forces of Britain and France.

Germany had already conquered Poland. And according to the secret Molotov-Ribbentrop non aggression Pact of August 23rd 1939 Germany and Russia had each taken their designated part of Poland. (Molotov with Stalin in the photo opposite)

Russia forthwith gathered the Baltic countries under its' iron fist, signing "security agreements" with Estonia September 2, 1939, Latvia October 5th, and Lithuania on October 11. Or in other words took over the countries.

The Molotov-Ribbentrop Pact had also secretly allocated Finland to Russia.

Finland however was not about to become a vassal once more of its ancestral enemy.

Finland had cut back its' expenditures on defence during the Prime Minister Cajander years, despite feverish requests for more funding for armaments and defensive lines from Mannerheim among others. After all Finland and Russia had signed a mutual non aggression pact in 1934 that was good until 1944 ...

Now alarmed by the emerging threat of war in Europe, the Finnish government finally realized that it needed to prepare her defences.

During the summer of 1939 she embarked on a hectic course of updating its' defensive line on the Karjalan Kannas. Workers and students, lawyers and professors volunteered for two weeks of physical labour to help upgrade the Kannas defensive works.

In October, having enveloped Estonia, Latvia and Lithuania, Russia turned its' attention to Finland.

On October 5th Russia requested that Finland come to Moscow to discuss Russia's plans for "security agreements" with Finland.

On October 7th Finland began calling up its' reserves living in Karjala. Among them were my uncles.When Finland first heard Stalin's "security agreement terms" on October 12th , it declared full mobilization of all its' reserves under the guise of supplementary reserve training. It became known in Finland as *A 51 day blessing*, as it allowed the country to prepare for the upcoming inferno.

From October 12th to the 14th initial negotiations were held in Moscow between Russia and Finland. Russia demanded Finland move its border to thirty kilometres south of Viipuri, destroy the Mannerheim Defensive Line, cede islands in the Gulf of Viipuri, provide Hanko to Russia as a military base (Hanko is only thirty kilometres from Helsinki and at a strategic narrowing of the Gulf of Finland), and cede Petsamo and the Rybachi Penninsula on the Arctic Ocean (the location of a major nickel deposit and Finland's only access to the Arctic Ocean).

The Finnish Parliament rejected the request, seeing it for what it was, the first step in the annexation of all Finland.

Negotiations continued in Moscow from November 8th through the 13th. But both sides knew that they were over on November 9th. That morning the Finnish delegates J.K. Passikivi and Vaino Tanner went for their final meeting with Stalin and Molotov. After an hour of discussion it became clear that no agreement could be reached. When the groups parted Molotov waved and said *"Au revoir"*. Stalin shook hands all around and wished the Finns, *"All the best"*.

Kruschev in his memoirs comments on arriving at a meeting on "November 24th" in Stalin's apartment with Stalin, Molotov, Zhdanov and Otto W. Kuusinen (Kuusinen was a Red Finn from the 1918 Finnish Revolution who had fled to Russia and became a member of the Cominterm. Stalin named him the head of his puppet People's Republic of Finland)

> *The consensus of the group was that the Finns should be given one last chance to accept the territorial demands that they had already rejected during the unsuccessful negotiations. If they didn't yield to our ultimatum, we would take military action. This was Stalin's idea. Naturally I didn't oppose him. Besides, in this case I agreed that it was the right thing to do. All we had to do was raise our voice a little bit, and the Finns would obey. If that didn't work we would fire one shot and the Finns would put up their hands and surrender. Or so we thought. When I arrived at the apartment Stalin was saying, 'Let's get started today".*

Nonetheless the Finnish government felt that it should show some flexibility and on November 24 1939 stopped arms manufacturing, lifted the black outs, and encouraged people to return to their homes in the cities.

On November 26th, the crisis escalated. Russia staged an artillery attack on their own town of Mainila on the border between Finland and Russia and accused Finland of the attack.

> *After the prescribed time had elapsed, Artillery Marshall Kulik was dispatched to supervise the bombardment of the Finnish border. We waited to see what would happen. Stalin was confident. None of us thought there would be a war. We were sure that the Finns would accept our demands without forcing us to go to war … Suddenly there was a telephone call. We had fired our salvo, and the Finns had replied with artillery fire of their own. De facto, the war had begun.*

On the morning of November 30, 1939 Russia initiated an unprovoked attack on Finland. At 06:50 Russia started an artillery barrage and crossed the border. At 09:00 Russia began bombing the Finnish cities of Viipuri, Helsinki and Lahti. The Finnish Parliament declared war and the Winter War began.

Mannerheim had been serving as Minister of Defense in the Finnish Government, albeit considerably frustrated by his inability to obtain adequate funding. President Kyosti Kallio had been entreating him to take over the armed forces but Mannerheim had declined, and indeed was about to resign as Minister of Defense. On November 30th, he accepted a final request, and at the age of 72 was appointed Commander in Chief of the Armed Forces (replacing Hugo Osterman). A fortuitous and timely appointment despite Mannerheim's advanced age. Mannerheim was a seasoned military leader having commanded armies in three wars – The Russo Japanese War, World War I (Commanding the Russian army in the Ukraine), and the Finnish Civil War. A former President of Finland, and head of the Finnish Red Cross, he was known and respected in the West. Even in Russia, Stalin had grudging respect for him despite Mannerheim's support of the Tsar. Mannerheim knew war, and knew Russia.

On December 1st Risto Ryti, the Minister of Finance, replaced A.K. Cajander as Prime Minister, and Vaino Tanner became Foreign Minister in place of E. Erkko.

Russia invaded with an army of 630,000 men. They increased this number to well over a 1,000,000. Finland mobilized an army of 250,000 men. This included former Civil War communists and Reds. They, to Stalin's surprise, supported Finland as opposed to Russia.

The Western world, while making comforting noises, did not come to Finland's aid. While they expelled Russia from The League of Nations on December 14, 1939, the only sincerely supportive leader was the French Premier Eduardo Daladier. He strongly advocated that the West send troops but his proposal was rejected by the Western Supreme War Council and Great Britain. Daladier continued to pressure for military aid for Finland through to March, indeed promising troops on March 8, 1940. Unable to get the Allies to deliver troops he resigned – a sad end for a man of conviction and principle.

Finland's historical ruler and neighbor, Sweden, became the Switzerland of the North. With the luxury of having Finland protecting her from Russia as it had in days of yore, Sweden espoused a policy of neutrality. The Swedish Prime Minister Albin Hansson blithely declared on September 1, 1939:

> *Friendly with all other nations and strongly linked to our neighbors, we look on no one as our enemy. There is no place in the thoughts of our people for aggression against any other country, and we note with gratitude, the assurances from others that they have no wish to disturb our peace, our freedom, or our independence. The strengthening of our defense preparations serves merely to underline our fixed determination to keep our country outside the conflicts that may erupt amongst others and, during such conflicts, to safeguard the existence of our people.*

While Sweden gave Germany access to her iron ore, she would not allow Western forces to cross Sweden to aid Finland. 8,000 Swedish men contradicted their nations' orders and volunteered to fight with Finland, arriving in the closing weeks of the war. One of them was the father of Sten, a good colleague of mine at my local gym – small world.

Volunteers also came from Demark (1,010), Norway (695), Hungary (346) and America (372). Few arrived in time to take part in the war.

One Canadian who did make it into the conflict was a neighbor of ours – Oscar Pylkkanen. A wealthy farmer, he was visiting his former homeland. Although already in his 40s, he volunteered. He ended up driving a soup kitchen on the front lines. Oscar was known to keep close watch over his money. Dad in one of his few comments about the war, jested that;

> *"Oscar would have been the perfect army cook. I'm sure he made the food provisions go a long way. Oscar definitely wouldn't have dished out a single additional sprat to the men."*

Jesting aside, Oscar was a good man and a valued friend of the family. I wish I had asked him about his experiences during the war. But probably like all the veterans he would not have had anything to say.

Many Western nations did give aid in food and military materials – among them South Africa which provided 25 Gloster planes. In America, the former USA President, Herbert Hoover, was a firm friend, strongly supporting fund raising events for Finland.

So began the battle between David and Goliath – Finland a nation of 3 ½ million fighting for its' life against the might of the 170 million strong Russian empire.

CHAPTER 2

Armaments & Forces

CHAPTER 2

Armaments & Forces

The war was fought solely in Karjala. With the exception of some guerilla patrols in the north, no Russian forces were able to cross the historical Uusikaupunki /Nystad border into current day Finland (The border defined by Peter the Great when he annexed Karjala in 1721).

However all of Karjala, from the Arctic Ocean to St Petersburg, became an inferno of fire and blood; suffering and courage.

Military Manpower

At the outbreak of the war Finland had a regular standing army of 33,000 men plus frontier troops. There were nine Frontier companies (Rajakomppania) on the Kannas, one in Petsamo, and six detached battalions north of Lake Ladoga. The Rajakomppania, while separate from the army, were a full military organization whose job was to guard the border. Lieutenat Palolampi's in his classic book Kolla Kesta describes them as:

> " a combination of real soldier and wilderness gentleman. They were calm, assured and understated, open and straightforward as well as good natured. In them was imprinted the silence of the districts vast forests, and the obligation to serve."

While the size of the existing military organization was limited, the number of available trained military men was over 350,000. All Finnish men had to serve at least twelve months in the army after they turned eighteen. Of the additional men:

- 127,000 men were members of the provincial armies. Each Finnish "province" had an infantry division.
- 100,000 were army reserves.
- 120,000 were members of the Civil Guard (Suojeluskunta). The Civil Guard was a legacy of the White forces of the civil war. After the war they formed paramilitary units to protect Finland from the scourge of communism.
- The Civil Guard promoted patriotism and military preparedness. Its' members kept themselves ready for active duty, maintaining their own rifles and equipment, and participating in military exercises. The organization ran general civic awareness functions; and indeed military training and military

manoeuvres on behalf of the army. It had a large youth organization for which it ran youth programs promoting patriotism, fitness, and military skills.

- 65,000 members of the Civil Guard saw service in the army during the Talvisota. The remaining 55,000 were either too young or old, or had reserved occupations. The Civil Guard provided some of the best soldiers in the army – both officers and men.

- Another important organization was the Lotta Svard, the women's version of the Civil Guard. 100,000 strong, they performed support roles ranging from staffing air raid observation platforms, to providing medical assistance, preparing food, repairing uniforms, manning telephone exchanges, and providing various administrative aid. As well they were instrumental in fund raising. Their assistance released men for the front. Some Lottas were located near the front, where their presence greatly improved morale.

The 33,000 regular standing army was augmented in October before the start of the war by the formation and mobilization of a separate force of 21,000 men, the Suojajoukot (Protective Forces). With the outbreak of World War II in Europe the Finnish government of Cajander finally agreed to Mannerheim's requests to bolster Finland's defenses.

The Suojajoukot units were positioned along the border to bolster the existing frontier guards. Their purpose was to delay Russia's first attack across the border. The 33,000 strong regular army was positioned in central Finland, and required time to fully mobilize and move to the border.

The Suojajouko units were composed of reservists from the areas along the border – namely Karjalaiset. They were familiar with the locale in which they would be fighting; and, were fiercely determined to protect their homes. Both Uncle Erkki and Uncle Aatu became members of these units.

By the end of the war Finland had an army of 340,000 – close to 10% of its' population of 3,700,000. Russia had an army of over 1,000,000, or less than 1% of its' 180,000,000 population.

Battling on the Sea & in the Air

In addition to the army Finland had a small navy and air force.

While Russia fielded triple the troops that Finland had, the deciding factor was Russia's overwhelming superiority in artillery (10 to 1), tanks (27 to1), and planes (16 to1). As well Russia had naval superiority.

Finnish Naval Forces

The Finnish sea forces were minimal, consisting of only 2 armored ships, 4 gun boats, 7 torpedo boats, 14 patrol boats, 1 submarine, 6 minesweepers and 1 minelayer. The Russian Baltic fleet, albeit not a global leader, had 200 vessels. No naval battles occurred.

Finland, although not having anywhere near as meaningful a sea force, did have strong coastal batteries and fortifications protecting the Finnish shores.

The prime objective of the Russian navy was to destroy the coastal fortifications and make landings in the rear of the Finnish armed forces. While the Russians did seize the islands of Suursaari, Lavansaari, Tytarsaari and Seiskari in Viipuri Gulf, the Finnish coastal batteries could not be silenced. On the Kannas, the Finnish coastal fortresses at Kovisto on the west side of the Kannas, and Kaarnajoki on the east played a particularly effective role in protecting the Finnish army.

The Russian navy abandoned their efforts in late December with the advent of winter. Russia lost one submarine and Finland one escort vessel. Four Finnish merchant vessels were sunk but the sea lanes were kept open with Sweden, although Sweden did nothing to help.

Finnish Air Force

The Finnish air force was somewhat larger than the Finnish navy and did play a strong role, albeit not a central one, in the war. The Finnish air force commanded, by Major General Lundquist, was a separate arm of the Finnish armed forces reporting directly to Mannerheim.

From the beginning of the war Russia had undisputed aerial superiority. When the war started, the Russian Air Force had concentrated about 1,500 military aircraft on the northwest border. In addition the Baltic Fleet and the Northern Fleet had 487 aircraft.

When the war began Finland had 235 mostly outdated military aircraft of which 121 were combat aircraft.

The air force consisted primarily of fighter planes and dive bombers.

What bombing the Finns did, they did with the English Bristol Blenheim bomber of which they only had 14. The bomber regiment (Lentorykmentti) LeR 4 was located in Luonetjarvi in central Finland near Jyvaskyla. The plane had a 3 man crew – pilot, navigator/bomber, and gunner/telegrapher. It had front and rear 7.7mm machine guns and carried a quite light bomb payload of 450 kg. They could be outfitted with skis for winter. The Blenheim bomber was faster than the Russian bombers and was suited for long range night bombing runs. The planes carried out 423 missions.

The primary Finnish fighter and dive bomber planes were the Dutch Fokkers.

- Of these, 36 were Fokker D-21 fighter planes. The Fokker D-21 was rugged and manoeuvrable, but a somewhat slow at 420 kilometers per hour. This was only 37 kilometers faster than the Tupalov SB-2 bombers they were pursuing. It had four 7.92 mm guns but could only carry a bomb load of 300 kg. While effective initially, by the end of the war it was too lightly gunned for the new Russian planes.
- 27 were Fokker C10s. These were used as dive bombers on the front. Although agile it was too slow to be a fighter plane. A bi-plane, with a pilot and an observer, it had a speed of 320 kilometers per hour, had three machine guns, and carried a bomb load.

On the Kannas the Fokkers were flown by:

- The LeR 2 regiment located near Imatra had Finlands sole fighter force, the LLv 24 squadron (Lentolaivue). Located in Immola, Lappenranta, and Suur-Merijoki, it had 36 Fokker D.21 fighters.
- The regiments' other squadron LLv 26 had 10 Bristol Bulldogs. The Bulldogs were dated but managed to down a few Russian aircraft. They had two 7.7 mm Vickers machine guns.
- The LeR1 flight regiment located south of Viipuri and at Lappeenranta.
- It had two squadrons –LLv 10 and LLv 12, who together had 24 Fokker C.10 dive bombers.
- A third squadron – LLv 14 was located at Kakisalmi. It had 4 Fokker D 10s and seven even older Fokker FO planes which were only effective as reconnaissance planes.

While the focus of the air force was the Kannas, some fighter forces operated with AK IV north of Lake Ladoga. The LLv.16 squadron located north of Lake Ladoga had 9 Ripon II F planes and 5 Junker K-43s. Both of these were aged and very slow and were used as float and ski planes.

The LLv.36 squadron in Kallvik near Helsinki had 6 Ripon planes.

Bombs were attached to all the fighter planes dependent on the type of mission – for example the Bristol Bulldog could carry four 9 kg bombs.

By the end of the war the aged Finnish fleet was being slowly updated with modern Fiat, Morane Sauliner and Gloster Gladiators war planes (as well as captured Russian planes). Twenty – seven Morane Saulnier planes arrived in time from France to be used during the Viipuri Lahti battle in the last weeks of the war.

The primary Russian planes were:

- The Polikarpov I-15, I-153, I-16 fighters
- The Tupalov SB-2 fast bomber and the Iliushin DB-3 long range bomber
- The Tupalov R-5 reconnaissance plane

From the beginning of the war Russia had undisputed aerial superiority. It was difficult for the Finns to use the roads and railways in the eastern part of Finland during daylight.

On the front, the Finnish air force, usually in patrols of of two or three planes, attempted to attack Russian bombers which were protected by the Russian Polikarpov fighters. Early in the war, in the month of December, Finland's fighter force had great success downing fifty four Russian planes at the cost of only one of their own.

In February Russia started even more aggressive bombing to support its' attack on the Kannas. From February 1940 the Finnish fighter force focused its operations on the Kannas. Owing to the enemy's evident aerial superiority the Finns bombing raids and reconnaissance flights were mainly restricted to dawn and dusk and to night raids.

While the Finnish fighter force was flying as many as eighty eight sorties a day, the frontline troops had to fight without much fighter cover except on the Viipurilahti front during the last days of the war.

During the war Russia was able to transfer aircraft to the area of Finland much faster and to a greater extent than Finland succeeded in getting aircraft from abroad. When military ops stopped the Red army had 3,885 aircraft in the theatre. Finland had 164 combat aircraft.

During the 105 days the Finns flew 5,800 sorties, an average of 55 sorties a day. Of these 3,900 were defensive sorties; lauched to counter Russian attacks.

During the Winter War the Finnish air force lost 62 aircraft, 47 of these in military operations. The Russian air force lost 740 aircraft, at least 490 of which were lost in military operations.101 were lost in aerial combat and about 390 to ground anti aircraft fire. The Finnish ace was Lieutenant Sarvanto, who shot down 17 Russian planes with his Fokker fighter (13 confirmed and 4 unconfirmed – 6 in one day).

Russian Air Raids

While strongly supporting its' armies' assault, the major objective of the Russian air arm was to bomb Finland into submission as per the High Command Order:

"Aerial bombing must direct systematic and powerful strikes at targets situated deep in the rear; enemy government and war industrial targets, railroad bridges, railroad junctions, harbors and cargo ships".

The first air raids began at 9:00 am on November 30th with heavy bombing of Finland's cities. Viipuri, Helsinki and Lahti in particular were hard hit.

Russia bombed Finland from their bases in Estonia, dropping bombs throughout Finland – in total 23,146 tonnes of bombs -55,000 explosive bombs and 41,000 incendiary bombs. The incendiary bombs did not have the immediate destructive force of the explosive bombs, but were more devastating. Incendiary bombs do not explode. They are filled with a sticky flammable liquid which instantaneously starts fires wherever they strike. A pre war enhancement was the development of a mechanism which permitted the release of one bomb which broke up in the air into many smaller incendiary bombs, thus greatly increasing the area impacted.

Dad had firsthand experience with these bombs. He was at a railway supply depot when it got hit by incendiary bombs. As the bombs came through the roof, dad grabbed a shovel and started tossing them out as fast as they came in and organized other people to do likewise. The depots were a particularly important target for the Russian bombers, as supplies were critical for the Finnish army.

The main cities that were bombed were Viipuri, Sortavala, Lappenranta, Turku, Rihimaki, Lahti, Kouvola, Hanko, Tampere, and Elisenvaara. After the first attack, Helsinki did not suffer many bombing runs. As the West had many journalists in Helsinki, Russia did not want to publicize the extent of their attacks against the Finnish people:

Mind you, when I was in Helsinki I was struck by the statue in front of the Finnish National Archives building. Unlike the many other pristine monuments in Helsinki, it was quite pitted ...the result of night time vodka fuelled hooliganism ?? no, rather bullet scars from the strafing runs of Russian fighter planes.

Viipuri was the most heavily bombed city. 4,700 bombs fell on Viipuri from attacks by 1,400 Russian bombers. Sunday February 18th 1940, the beginning of Russia's assault on the Kannas, was one of the worst days. Even though the temperature was minus 15 C, the frozen snow covered Viipuri streets turned to water due to the fires and explosions started by 700 bombs from 350 planes. But the Finnish flag waving over Viipuri Linna never came down.

Indeed the bombings, rather than destroying Finland's morale and resistance, increased Finland's resolve. A thousand civilians were killed. The number was minimized by Finland's air raid warning system, bomb shelters and anti aircraft gun emplacements.

Canons, Tanks & Rifles

The armaments and manpower of the Finnish army were significantly less then those of Russia.

Canons

The Finnish army had a dearth of artillery. They were "outgunned" 10 to 1 by the Russians. The Finnish artillery guns were not only far fewer, but consisted primarily of dated WWI, and even earlier models. Added to this was that there was such a shortage of shells that usage had to be rationed.

During the Russian attacks the Finnish infantry could rely on little covering artillery fire.

The artillery, under the command of Lieutenant General Nenonen, was organized into:

- Five heavy artillery battalions (i.e. Rask.Psto 4) each with twelve guns - 105-107 mm guns and 150-152 mm howitzers. These however were under the direct command of GHQ who deployed them as they saw fit to the most important sectors of the war. At the start of the war three battalions were stationed on the Kannas.
- In addition nine divisions had a field artillery regiment (i.e. KTR 4) consisting of three battalions. Each battalion had three batteries - two batteries were equipped with 76 mm guns, and one with 122 mm howitzers.
- Six detached light artillery batteries (i.e 1. Er.Ptri) with four to six 76mm guns (a couple only had 87mm canons). These units were in the northern wilderness theatres.
- Five Suojajouko (i.e. Psto/1.Pr) artillery battalions, usually with eight 76mm guns and four 122mm howitzers.

The total number of guns in the entire armed forces was 420 – three hundred and six 75/76 mm light guns, seventy two 122mm howitzers, ten 107 mm heavy canons and thirty two 150/152 mm heavy canons.

By contrast the Russians had 3,500 artillery guns at the start of the war, and 5,500 at the end.

And just as critical, Finland had a lack of ammunition.

Tanks

Finland had no tanks – or rather only a few ancient Vickers which were useless.

Russia had seven armored brigades plus 26 tank battalions – a total of 2,200 tanks at the start of the war and 3,000 at the end. These tanks included the T-26, T-28, T-35, T 37 and BT-5.

The T-35 was particularly terrifying. Weighing 45 tons and 30 feet long, it had a crew of 10. It had a one 76 mm howitzer, two 45mm canons, five 7.62 calibre machine guns, and front and rear turrets. For the T-35s, even the tank trenches and the multi ton granite stone boulder obstacles were too small to be a deterrent.

Finland did not have any anti tank guns until the end of the war with which to stop the metallic death spewing monsters.

Without anti tank weapons, or air and artillery support, the Finnish rifleman had to rely on crawling up to the tank and stopping the tanks by jamming a log in its' treads – or by throwing a satchel bomb or a Molotov cocktail.

The Molotov cocktail became the weapon of choice. While having many variations, the Molotov cocktail was basically a glass bottle filled with a mixture of petrol and napalm with an attached kerosene soaked match and cord fuse. To use it, one had to get within throwing distance of the tank, light the fuse and throw the bottle. It was very effective as immediately upon shattering it exploded into a raging fireball. But usage required Finnish sisu - courage, desperation, self sacrifice. Getting within throwing distance of a tank armed with a canon and several machine guns, protected by infantry rifle squads, and returning alive, was problematic.

The Molotov cocktail was not invented by the Finns, but they made it into an effective weapon of last choice. They also named it. They called it the Molotov cocktail in derisive reference to the Russian Minister of Foreign Affairs who negotiated the Molotov-Ribbentrop Pact giving Finland to Russia. The Finnish soldier wryly stated that no Finnish vodka should be wasted - the Molotov cocktail bottle was provided by the Finnish Alcohol Commission.

Surprisingly desperation had its own reward as the Finns had destroyed an amazing 2,268 Russian tanks by the end of the war through sisu – be it Molotov cocktails, mines, air strikes or artillery barrages.

Rifles & Machine Guns

While there was a dearth of planes, artillery guns, tanks and anti tank weapons, Finland did have a good supply of the basics: rifles, submachine guns and machine guns.

- The army used Russian Mosin-Nagant M1891 rifles. Finland had a large stock pile of these after the Civil War. They standardized on these, altered the design somewhat and began manufacturing more in Finnish factories.
- Lahti-Saloranta light machine guns. These were refined to too exact tolerances and had a tendency to jam in action in the harsh winter. The soldiers replaced these wherever possible with captured Russian "Emma" light machine guns.
- Maxim heavy machine guns. These were slightly altered in 1932 from the original Russian Maxim gun
- Suomi sub machine guns designed and manufactured in Finland. These came to have a reputation as being the best in the world. The Russian soldiers called it the White Death.

In most cases the ammunition caliber was the same as it was for the Russians weapons. So the Finn soldiers freely appropriated and used captured Russian weapons and ammunition.

The Army Corps

Finland had 340,000 soldiers by the end of the war (Compared to over a million for Russia).

Infantry

The Finnish army was structured into:

- army corps (60,000 men),
- divisions (14,200),
- regiments (3,500),
- battalions (800),
- companies (200)

The Division, of 14,200 men had 11,000 rifles, 250 small machine guns, 250 light machine guns, 116 heavy machine guns, 18 mortars, 54 field artillery guns (37mm to 152 mm).

The Russian division was slightly larger at 18,000 plus soldiers. A major difference was a much larger artillery force (126 guns) and most importantly 50 tanks plus 10 armoured cars. The Russian division also had an anti-aircraft company and 45 anti tank guns (45mm). Neither of these two units was in much need given Finland's lack of tanks and limited number of planes. The division also had 427 automobiles/trucks and tractors to supplement its' 5,393 horses.

Usually commanded by a Colonel, or Major General, the Finnish Division consisted of;

- Headquarters
- Supply column,
- 2 pioneer (combat engineering) companies
- 2 signal companies,
- A light detachment with a Jaeger company,
- A small cavalry troop,
- A machine gun platoon
- A field artillery regiment
- 3 infantry regiments (JR)

Each infantry regiment of consisted of about 3,600 men

- Headquarters command (13)

- Headquarters Company (169)
  - Head office company (41)
  - Field kitchen (27)
  - Signal platoon (55)
  - Combat engineering platoon (45)
- Regimental column (155)
  - Munitions (59)
  - Food (96)
- Housing company (83)
- 3 infantry battalions

Each infantry battalion consisted of 845 men

- A headquarters of 6,
- Jaeger platoon
- Supply company of 118 men,
- Machine gun company of 154 men with 12 heavy machine guns,
- Mortar company of 83 men with four 81mm or 82 mm mortars;
- 3 infantry companies of 191 men with
  - Company head quarters,
  - Battle messengers - 1 officer, 1 corporal, 4 men;
  - Signals unit - 1corporal and 3 men;
  - Gas protection unit - 1corporal and 3 men,
  - 4 rifle platoons
    - Platoon HQ -1officer, 1 NCO, 2 messengers
    - 2 rifle sections with 1 NCO and 9 men with one sub machine gun and 2 light machine guns;
    - 1 rifle section with 1 NCO and 6 men with 1 light machine gun and 5 rifles

Within the standard army units there were two specialized forces:

- Jaegers, and
- Sissi

Jaegers (Jääkärit)

The Jaeger companies and battalions were elite, schock troops. They were light infantry units with bikes or skis, well equipped for quick movement. Using bikes sounds "unwarlike" but troops on bicycles could move ten times faster then those on foot. Unlike horses they required no upkeep, were inexpensive, and easily disposable.

The Jaeger troops were the younger and fitter and more select soldiers. They were the best trained and equipped with the best weapons. The heritage, reputation and philosophy of the units was founded on that of the Finnish Jaeger soldiers who served in Germany during WWI prior to returning to Finland to lead the White forces in the Finnish Civil War. At the beginning of the war the Jaeger battalions were part of the Suojusjouko forces on the Kannas.

Lieutenant Palolampi in his Kolla Kesta book captures the reputation of the Jaegers. He comments on a company of Jaeger Battalion I (JPI) that had been called up to retake a Russian break through of the Kolla defenses.

A company of JPI arrived to reinforce our troops. The company was composed of energetic upbeat conscripts who had drive and the traditional Terijoki Jaeger spirit.The boys were told in Loimalla that they had to take back the positions that the Russians had over run. The company captain Honkanen responded on behalf of his men:

"We are Jaegers and if we die, we die as Jaegers; our reputation shall not be sullied"

The next day the Jaegers attacked straight across the swamp wading through the heavy snow without skis. The Russians had placed several heavy machine guns and around twenty light machine guns on the small hill top. In the withering fire of the machine guns, twenty Jaegers fell. They could not advance rapidly over the swamp because of the deep snow, and the company called off its' attack. Our howitzers softened the hill top with heavy fire and in the evening dusk the Jaegers stormed forward once more. This time they gained the hill top. Hand to hand combat raged. With hand grenades, bayonets and knives they annihilated

the unfortunate bravely fighting Russian defenders to the last man. Part of the enemy force started to retreat back across the swamp but they were mowed down by our machine gun fire, falling among the bodies of their comrades who had died in their successful attack several days earlier. Two Russian infantry companies were oblitered.

There were four Jaeger battalions during the Talvi sota. As well, each Division had a Jaeger company as part of its' light detachment.

Sissi

During the Talvisota there were also Sissi companies and battalions in the northern wilderness. The units acted primarily as guerrilla units operating behind the enemy to cut supply lines and communications links. They harassed the Russian lines from the sides as they advanced. Attacking on skis they launched swift surprise forays before withdrawing just as quickly. They usually slept during the day and "worked" during the night. Some units also acted as standard infantry – particularly those with Phojois Suomi Ryhma.

There were five Sissi battalions during the Talvisota – SissiP1 (Phojois Suomi Ryhma); SissiP2 (Ryhma Taleva): Sissi P3 ( ); Sissi P4 (12.D); and SissiP5 (Kuhmo – Osasto Kari). In addition Sissi companies played an active role with Er P17 of Salla and with Osasto Petsamo. The Sissi soldiers were expert skiers. The members were usually reservists who volunteered for the unit. About 6,000 had received specialist training by early December.

The Sissi units were organized to be self sufficient as they usually ranged far from the main regimental forces. Structured to move quickly, they were not as heavily armed as the regular infantry battalions. They did not having machine gun, mortar, or combat engineer companies. Rather the battalion consisted of three self sufficient rifle companies.

Other specialized organizations were formed during the Winter War. Of these I am going to mention two:

- The Medical Corps; and
- The Home Guard

The Medical Corps

The medical corps was part of the army. The medical units were a key part of the Finnish forces, given that one in three soldiers was either killed or wounded (And many more than one third in the actual fighting force).

The Medical Corps was commanded by Colonel E Suolahti. There were nineteen medical companies. Ten of the companies were associated with specific divisions , nine were with either a brigade, regiment or independent battalion. Each company had eight doctors as well as supporting staff. Thus there were only 152 doctors at the front – one doctor for every 2,200 soldiers, or one doctor for 300 wounded soldiers. In addition to the front line doctors there were doctors in the military hospitals.

The wounded, dependent on the severity of their injuries, were treated at a:

1. Company bandaging site (JSp – Joukkosidon paikka).
2. Battalion bandaging site (PSp – Paasidon paikka).
3. Field hospital (KS – Kentta sairaala)
4. Military hospital (SotaS – Sota sairaala).

The first place the wounded were taken by stretcher bearers / medics was the company bandaging site (JSp – Joukkosidon paikka). The wounded were triaged and bandaged here. The purpose was to stabilize the wounded sufficiently to move them further. In critical situations the doctors operated. The company medical sites were domiciled in temporary quarters ranging from bunkers, to tents, to tarps under trees, depending on the battle situation. From there the wounded were sent via horse and cart, or medical automobile/bus to either the battalion Head Bandaging site or to the division Field Hospital.

The second medical position was the battalion bandaging site (PSp – paasidon paikka). Here further triage was done, stabilization and critical operations performed. Here and at the Field and Sub Field Hospitals the doctors worked non stop during major battles.

From thence the soldier was moved to the Field Hospital (KS – kentta sairaala) or Sub Field Hospital (KSO). Operations were performed here and short term convolesence taken care of. There were 28 army field hospitals, one in each division. As well the Kannas army, the IV AK, and some brigades and regiments also had field hospitals. In addition there were 8 field hospitals run by the Red Cross and the Lotta Svard. During major battles the doctors in the Field Hospitals, and Sub Hospitals were known to work for weeks at a time with next to no sleep.

The final destination for the seriously wounded soldier was the military hospital (SotaS – sota sairaala). There were 51 military hospitals located through out Finland. Some were used for civilians as well as military personnel. The hospital in Viipuri was closed early in the war due to the danger from Russian artillery and bombing. The wounded were transported to the military hospitals by hospital trains (SotaJ)or hospital buses (SAutoK).

35,000 hospital beds were in place by the end of the war. Certainly war wounds formed the majority of the problems, but general disease, and particularly frost bite resulted in many soldiers being hospitalized. Most of the farm boys had no problems with frost bite as they wore their own felt boots (houpa tossut). Those who wore rubber boots, particularly if they were a bit small, experienced more cases of frost bite.

Medical warehouses and laboratories were located through out Finland and near the battle front. Morphine and chloroform were the scarcest drugs – and the most needed.

There were units in place to handle the dead as well. The dead were taken from the front to each army corps' KEK unit (Kotiseiden Evakusoisti Keskushoito). Here they were washed and placed in caskets for the journey to their home parish for burial.

The Home Guard

Another important large organization was the Home Guard (The Suojeluskunta mentioned earlier)

The home front was under the control of the Home Guard, commanded by Lieutenant General Lauri Malmberg. The organization was instrumental in keeping the home front operational.

The organization ensured that troops were raised and trained, anti aircraft batteries were in place and manned; air raid shelters were functional; weapons and material manufacture continued; rationing was in place; rail and road transportation worked; and the prisoner of war camps were operational.

Both my father and his brother, my Uncle Yrjo, were in the Home Guard, as their jobs with the railroad were a reserved occupation. Father was responsible for operation of part of the rail system leading to the Kannas, as well as commanding a panzer train (more on these later).

While Uncle Yrjo was with the railroad he as well had a second job:

> Uncle Yrjo's day time job was with the railroad, but he also spent a great deal of time manning an anti air craft battery. He was a good mathematician and had the task of manually calculating the correct firing trajectory.
>
> Uncle Yrjo had gotten married before the war. Much of his time was spent away from his new bride. This entailed a lot of night work protecting the home front from Russian night bombing sorties. His wife also had a lot of night sorties. She found a new par amour to warm her cold winter nights. Patriotism only goes so far I guess. They separated at the end of the war.

CHAPTER 3

The Northern Military Theatres

CHAPTER 3

The Northern Military Theatres

The war was fought on five fronts:

1. Lapland (Petsamo and Salla)
2. Mid North (Ilomansti – Tolvajarvi) – "North Karjala"
3. Northern Finland (Kuusamo - Suomussalmi – Kuhmo) – "White Karjala"
4. Northern Lake Ladoga (Kitela - Kolla- Suojarvi) – "Ladoga Karjala"
5. The Karjalan Isthmus (the Kannas)

All of my family, with the exception of Uncle Kauko (Ladoga Karjala) and my father (Finnish railroads), fought on the Karjalan Isthmus, within 100 kilometers of their ancestral homes. As such I will be focusing on that Karjalan Isthmus theatre.

While the majority of the fighting occurred on the critical Karjalan Isthmus, surprisingly the Russians also attacked in force on four northern fronts. Each of these provided a bridge from the impassable Karjala wilderness to the Finnish road and railway network, and thus into central Finland. Major battles swirled on these fronts as well as on the Kannas. A brief summary of the campaigns on these fronts (from north to south) follows.

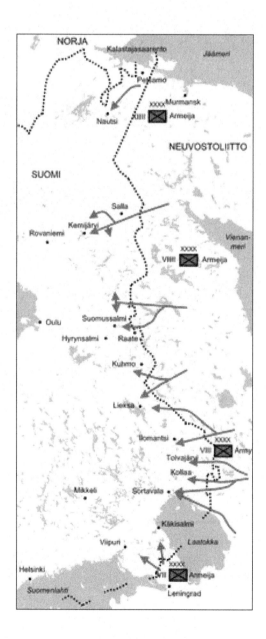

I - Lapland (Petsamo and Salla)

This theatre was under the command of Major General Kurt Wallenius, an old compatriot of Mannerheim's from the Finnish Revolution. Wallenius had a dubious background, having in 1932 led the "Fascist" Lapua forces effort to overthrow the Finnish government.

Lieutenant General Ernst Linder, the leader of the Swedish volunteer brigade, took command of the Lapland forces when Wallenius was seconded to the Karjalan Kannas front on February 28th 1940. Linder had commanded some of Mannerheim's White forces during the Revolution.

The Russians attacked Lapland on two fronts: Petsamo and Salla.

Petsamo

The Russian 14th Army Corps attacked Pertsamo. The 14th AK consisted of 3 divisions – the 104th, 14th, and 52nd. The 14th and 52nd divisions attacked Finland. The 14th division remained protecting Murmansk.

The Russians attacked Petsamo in order to close Finland's access to the Arctic Ocean and to capture the rich nickel deposits. As well the front provided a route, albeit a rudimentary one, to Tornio and the Swedish border; and to Oulu in "mainland Finland".

The Russians force of 40,000 men took Petsamo at the start of December. Before the Finns retreated they destroyed the ships and the harbor equipment. After taking Petsamo the Russians deployed the 104th Division to protect the shoreline while much of the 52nd division was deployed along the Norway's northern border. One regiment – the 205th consisting of over 3,000 men, tanks and specialized ski patrol troops attacked the Finnish forces. On December 18th the Finnish forces stopped the Russian advance at Hoyhenjarvi.

By March 13th the Russians had advanced a bit further south to Nautsia, but had not been able to break onto the Arctic highway.

The Finnish force of 800 men, along with their reindeer provision teams, and the winter nights of -50 degrees Celsius, had proved too strong a barrier.

I wonder what Aunt Tyyne's first husband Kalle Lehtimaki thought of it all. He was with the Finnish forces at Petsamo.

Salla

The other attack Russia made in Lapland, was along the Salla road to Kemijarvi and Rovanniemi. From Rovanniemi there was a good road and railway link south to Tornio and Oulu. A successful attack would of course have also cut off the Finnish forces withdrawing from Petsamo.

The Russian force of two army divisions, the 88th and the 122nd attacked from Alahurtti on the border, taking Salla on December 8th. The Finn forces consisted of 3 battalions - Er P17, Er P25 and Er P26; and one regiment JR40. A complement of 6,000 as opposed to the Russian force of 18,000.

By December 16 the Russians were advancing towards Kemijarvi from Pelkosniemi in the north and Joutsijarvi in the south. The Finns counter attacked in January pushing the Russians back to Saija and Markajarvi near Salla by the wars' end. By March the battle had settled into a holding pattern.

A Swedish volunteer force of 8,400 men under Lieutenant General Linder arrived at the beginning of March to relieve the Finnish forces. Two Finnish battalions remained with Lieutenant General Linder while the remainder were moved south to help stop the Russian advance on the Kannas. The Swedish volunteers only saw limited action before the war ended.

In 2012 I visited Kemijarvi to see the theatre where my father was during the Jatkosota. In the church yard there is a large sankarihauta. Many of the Finns who died during the Salla campaign are buried there. A large statue of a soldier protecting his wife and children and looking defiantly towards the east, stands guard over the simple stone markers of the graves of his comrades. The markers list the soldiers' name, date of birth, and when and where they died. The place names where the soldiers fell – Mantyvaara, Joutsijarvi, Markajarvi and Salla predominate. But there are many with no place name other then the sorrowful,

"Jaanyt kentalle -left on the field of battle"; or the almost equally sad "Vammoihinsa – died of his wounds".

Together, including the Petsamo front, 828 Finns were killed and 1,401 wounded. The Russians lost many more.

II - Northern Finland (Suomussalmi/Raate Road –Kuhmo/Repola) – "White Karjala"

The area along the eastern Karjala border from Kuusamo south of the Salla theatre to Suomussalmi - 300 kilometers of wild forests, swamps and lakes - was protected by the Pohjois Suomen Ryhma commanded by Major General W. E. Tuompo.

Within this area the Russian 9th Army Corps launched major attacks at:

- Suomussalmi/Raate road,
- Kuhmo/Repola

In addition separate smaller attacks were launched against Kuusamo, north of Suomussalmi; and, Lieska, south of Kuhmo/Repola. These attacks were turned back by the Finnish forces. All four locations provided gateways to the railroads and roads that led to Oulu on the Gulf of Osthrobothnia and to junctions leading into southern Finland.

Kuusamo

Kuusamo, the most northerly sector, was protected by one battalion – Er P16 and one independent company under Lieutenant V Seppala (Er K Seppla). Kuussamo protected the southern flank of Salla and the northern reaches of Suomussalmi.

The Russian forces did not launch major offensives against Kuusamo, rather sending feinting attacks across the border. Battles did take place at Pistojoki-Kiimasvaari and Piispajarvi. After the first part of December defense

of the sector was left to the Er K Seppla company as the Er P16 battalion was transferred to aid Suomussalmi.

Suomussalmi

The Suomussalmi sector was the site of heavy fighting with the Russian 9th army commanded by General Ivan Dashitev. The sector was the site of the Raate Road motti battle. The Russians had two fully equipped divisions - the 44th and the 163rd - and a tank brigade – a complement of approximately 40,000 men. Finland initially only had one battalion but this was quickly reinforced with the Finnish 9th Division.

On November 30th the 163rd division attacked Suomussalmi from the northeast. The magnitude of the attack came as a surprise to Finland. Finland only had one battalion Er P 15 protecting Suomussalmi. Suomussalmi was taken easily by the Russians. The Finns retreated to Niskanselka and Haukipera, destroying the town of Suomussalmi as they withdrew.

Fighting raged from December 8th to January 8th with attacks and counter attacks.

On December 8th Mannerheim placed the theatre under the command of Colonel Siilasvuo of the 9th Division and changed its' reporting so that it reported directly to GHQ.

Initial units from the 9th division - Er P16 and JR27 - arrived quickly to reinforce the front. Christmas Eve brought another strong Russian attack but they failed to break through the Finnish lines.

Shortly thereafter the Finnish forces were reinforced with two additional 9th division regiments – the 64th (Fagernas) and the 65th (Mandelin). The Finns attacked forcing the Russian 163rd division to retreat over the frozen lakes to Kiantajarvi, destroying two of the Russian regiments. Group Susi (primarily JR65 and Er. P16) commanded by Lieutenant Colonel P Susitaival completed pushing the 163rd to near the border at Juntusranta, destroying the remaining regiment by Christmas.

While the Russian 163rd division had been attacking from the north east, the 44th division had started towards Sumoussalmi along the southern Raate Road.

Colonel Siilasvuo moved JR27 and JR64 of his force to stop this attack, counter attacking on New Year's Day 1940. While the Russian division was 18,000 strong and heavily armored, it could only advance in single file along the narrow wilderness road. The Finnish forces effectively began separating the strung out division into isolated groups – or mottis. Motti means a cord of stacked wood. The cords were stacked separately, hence the name some unbeknownst Finn ascribed to the separated, relatively helpless, blocks of Russian troops.

The mottis stretched for 45 kilometers from Raate to Suomussalmi. Finnish ski troops would suddenly emerge from the frozen wilderness and destroy the Russians – white avenging ghosts on skis. The cold and cloudy weather limited the amount of Russian air support. By January 7th the entire division had surrendered. Russian losses approximated 8,000 men, many killed by the infantry fire, but many also dying from exposure and lack of food.

A large amount of military supplies, tanks, guns and vehicles were captured. These were put to good use by the Finnish army.

Throughout the entire conflict, the Finns suffered 1,000 dead and 1,000 wounded. The Russians lost 13,000 to 27,000 dead and missing. The Russian troops fought bitterly and to the end – only 2,100 Russians were taken prisoner.

Finland's success provided a strong morale boost to the country and its' troops. It also became a classical military case study of how with proper tactics and leadership a small force can take advantage of the geographical terrain and defeat a much larger enemy force.

After successfully destroying both Russian divisions, Colonel Siilasuvo moved the bulk of the 9th division to help stop the Russian advance at Kuhmo. Detachment Kari (Er. P15 plus) remained on the Raate road blockading the border.

Kuhmo/Repola

The Red Army's 54th division, an over 17,000 strong force, attacked from Repola inside Russia towards Kuhmo. It fought its way forward towards Kuhoniemi in the north and Korpisalmi in the south. On December 6th it reached the Raate Road junction – an important Finnish north – south supply route.

To repel the Russians, the Finns established the independent Vuokko Brigade (five infantry battalions and an artillery battalion). They succeeded in stopping the enemy.

When the battles of Suomossalmi and Raate ended, Siilisvuo moved the main parts of his 9th division south to support Kuhmo.

By the end of January the main part of the Russian 54th division was hemmed in – split into many mottis over a 45 kilometer stretch of the Repola to Kuhmo Road (from Riihivaara just west of the border to the Raati Road junction).

On February 8th three elite battalions of special Russian ski troops (Dolins Ski Bridgade) tried to make contact with the 54th attacking from the Ahvenvarra over the wilderness terrain. But by February 16th the Finns had stopped the Russians at Kisseli - completely destroying the Dolins Ski Brigade. I wonder if the Dolins Ski Brigade was the force Kruschev was referring to in his book when he commented that:

> In the winter it was decided to bypass the Karelian Isthmus and to strike a blow from Lake Ladoga to the north where there were no fortifications. But when we decided to strike from the rear, we found ourselves in an even more difficult situation than before. The Finns, who are people of the North, and very athletic, can ski almost before they can walk. Our army encountered very mobile ski troops armed with automatic high velocity rifles.

We tried our own troops on skis too, but it wasn't easy for ordinary, untrained Red Army soldiers to fight on skis.

We started intensively to recruit professional sportsmen. We had to bring them from Moscow and the Ukraine as well as from Leningrad. We gave them a splendid send-off. Everyone was confident that our sportsmen would return victorious, and they left in high spirits. Poor fellows, they were ripped to shreds. I don't know how many came back alive.

At the beginning of February the Russians set up a special relief operation in Repola to provide the encircled 54th on the Repola Kuhmo Road with supplies and air cover, as well as trying to attack from Repola with another regiment of troops. Without artillery support the Finns made slow progress in destroying the Russian forces in the mottis. On March 3 they successfully eliminated the Russian forces in the great Luelahti encirclement and on March 8th in the eastern Luelahti encirclement.

The other parts of the 54th however succeeded in defending themselves in difficult conditions until peace came.

Lieska

Further south, part of the Russian 155th Division (7,000 men from JR529 plus other units), attacked along the road from Inari towards the Lieska railway station.

The Finnish force of two detached battalions – Er P12 and 13 stopped them at Nurmijarvi on December 8th . With the support of the three company strong Kev Os 9, the Finns counter attacked forcing the Russian troops back over the border at Kiivivaara by the day after Christmas.

The Finns as well defeated the Russians in two secondary battles at Savijarvi in the north and Inari in the south.

III - Mid North (Suojarvi - Ilomansti – Korpiselka/Tolvajarvi) – "North Karjala"

In the Mid North the Russian 1st Army Corps attacked from Suojarvi on the border along two routes – along the northern road through Kallioniemi and Oinaansalmi towards Ilomantsi; and along the south road through Algajarvi and Aittojoki towards Tolvajarvi and Korpiselka.

If either route was breeched it would provide access to the north south railway and road network and the key transportation junction of Joensuu. The railway line was the Finnish supply route to the whole Ladoga front as well as being one of the connections to the Kannas.

At the beginning of the war the entire area from northern Lake Ladoga north to Suojarvi was part of the IV Army Corps commanded by General Hagglund,

However, Mannerheim, given the sudden broad attack by the Russians in Suojarvi, as well as along the shores of Lake Ladoga, formed a separate force for Suojarvi, the Talvela Group. The Group, under Colonel P. Talvela, reported directly to Mannerheim as opposed to General Hagglund of the IV Army Corps. The area by Lake Ladoga remained under the command of the IV Army Corps.

Ilomantsi

Colonel Talvela placed the troops of the Ilomantsi area under the command of Colonel P.O. Ekholm. The Ekholm Detachment consisted of one regiment (JR41), the Er. P11 detached battalion, and an artillery brigade KT-Pr – in total approximately 5,000 men

Attacking them were the Russian JR786, JR659, and JR436 regiments of the 155th Division – over 10,000 troops.

The Ekholm Detachment stopped the enemy forces that were advancing towards Ilomantsi at Oinaansalmi in the southern area of the offensive; and in the northern area, at the Kallioniemi ferry.

The detachment suffered minimal losses of 147 dead and 275 wounded; while the Russian losses were in the 1,000s.

Korpiselka (Tolvajarvi)

In the southern Korpiselka area, the Russians attacked with two divisions – the 139th (JR718, 609, 384, 34) and the 75th (JR28, 115, 28 and part of 364)– about 45,000 men plus tanks and artillery.

Major General Talvela placed the Korpiselka area under Colonel A. Pajari. The Pajari Group had over 11,000 men. It consisted of one regiment (JR16); three detached battalions (Er. P9, 10 and 112); a bicycle battalion – PPP7; two plus Sissi battalions (SissiP2 and SissiP3 and one company of SissiK); and an artillery battalion and a Pioneer battalion.

The Talvela Group gained the first important victory of the Winter War by striking the Russian 139th Division at Tolvajarvi in the southern part of the Korpiselka area.

On December 12th the Talvela Group began a counter attack in the area of Tolvajarvi. By December 14th , after fierce battles, it had beat the Soviet 139th division which was facing it.

From Tolvajarvi the counter attack was continued through Aglajarvi to Aittojoki until December 23rd when the attack was ordered stopped on the orders of GHQ. The Soviet 75th division which was facing the Finnish troops was forced to withdraw.

The Finnish forces captured a large amount of armaments as well as inflicting major losses on the Russian forces. The Finns confiscated 31 artillery pieces, 59 tanks, 220 machine guns, 142 light machine guns and over 3,000 rifles in addition to large numbers of trucks and horses. The Finnish army quickly repositioned the weaponary for its own use, particularly the Emma light machine guns.

In January 21-28 the Russians attacked but were turned back at Aglajarvi and Aittojoki. Later in February the Russians attacked once more – but unsuccessfully.

The Finns suffered losses of 1,546 dead and lost and 2,328 wounded. The Russian dead were in excess of 4,000.

IV. Northern Lake Ladoga (Kitela - Kolla) – "Ladoga Karjala"

The Russian 56th Army Corps attacked towards Kitela from Kasnaselka in the north and Manssila in the south; while the 56th Division of the 1st Army Corps attacked towards Kolla from Hysrsyla and Naistenjarvi in the north.

The Finnish IV Army Corps, consisting of the 12th and 13th Divisions, the Rasanen Detachment and the 11th Detached Battalion, was responsible for protecting the area north of Lake Ladoga (The area of the road leading northwest to Loimala and the areas of the Tulemajarvi-Kiltela and Sami-Kitela roads.)

The 12th Division (with the Rasanen Detachment and the 11th Detached battalion), was responsible for the northern area south of Suojarvi (The Naistenjarvi/Hysrsyla to Loimala railway line); while 13th Division was responsible for the area around the northeast shore of Lake Ladoga.

The IV Army Corps used delaying tactics until December 11th finally stopping the Russian attack along a line connecting Kolla, Syskyjarvi and Kitela.

Kolla

In the Hyrsyla and Loimantsi area the 12th Division under Colonel L Tiainen stopped the enemy at Kollanjoki and managed to maintain its position there until the end of the war. The Kolla battle became a Finnish classic; not only because of the heroic Finnish resistance, but also because one of the Lieutenants E. Palolampi published his first hand account of the fighting in a book Kolla Kestaa shortly after the Winter War ended. The book became a Finnish masterpiece.

I found a copy of the book among my father's effects after he died. Dad had many books - but none on the wars. Perhaps he got it because he commanded an armored train car during the war.

Whether he was with the train at Kolla or elsewhere in Finland I have not been able to determine. Like all my families veterans of the war, he would not talk about the war. I only found out that he commanded an armored train when my uncle took me to see the armored tanks and trains at the Parolan Panssarimuseo near Hameenlinna when I visited in the 1970s. Dad afterwards did say yes this was the case.

Now looking at the worn book I see that my uncle Yrjo bought it in 1940 and gave it to my dad in 1973.

Syskela- Kitela Road (Kitela,Uumo, Lemetti mottis)

West of Kasnaselka and Salmi, the 13th Division, commanded by Colonel H Hannuksela, used delaying tactics to stop the enemy attack along the Syskela-Kitela line.

On December 12th the Finnish army corps began its attempt to counter attack in order to cut communications between the Russian flanks. A third counter attack begun on December 26th led to the Kasnaselka Road being cut at Uomaa. The fourth attack begun on January 6th led to the Ladoga lakeside road being cut and the creation of the great encirclement at Kitela. The Karjalian encirclement battles continued to the end of the war.

By January the Finns succeeded in dividing the Russian 18th Division into several separate mottis. Some ten encirclements were formed on the Kasnaselka – Kitela Road.

The Russians stubbornly defended themselves. The Finns were able to destroy some of the encirclements, including Lansi-Lemetti (February 4), Pikitsamaki (February 18th) and Ita-Lemetti (February 29). However the mottis at Siira and Uomaa held their ground until the end of the war as did the great encirclement at Kitela.

The entire 168th Division was trapped in the great Kitela encirclement. The Russians air dropped supplies and fought desperately. They formed their encirclement into an armed fortress burying their tanks into defensive positions. Without artillery or air support, the Finnish units could not make rapid progress. While inflicting large casualties, the Finns could not destroy the encirclement before the war ended.

The Finnish 12th division suffered 1,326 dead and lost and 3,101 wounded. The 13th division suffered 1,329 dead and lost and 3,155 wounded. Russian losses in both men and weaponary were horrendous.

Finland was successful in stopping the advance of the Russian armies in all sections of Karjala north of the Kannas. At the end of the war Finland had about 90,000 soldiers in the area, while Russia had over 240,000.

But while successful in decisively defeating the sudden strong, but secondary, Russian advance in the northern wilderness, the Karjala Kannas, our families home, was another matter.

The Karjalan Kannas

CHAPTER 4

The Karjalan Kannas

The Karjalian Isthmus, as since time immemorial, was the primary battleground during the Talvisota. Major attacks came in the west at Summa and in the east at Taipale on the shores of Lake Ladoga.

The Isthmus, a 135 kilometer stretch south of Viipuri between the Gulf of Finland and Lake Ladoga, is an amalgam of marshes, rivers and lakes interspaced with stretches of fields and rocky outcrops. The eastern part is separated from the western isthmus by a large river – the Vuoksi.

Defensive Lines

Starting in 1918, soon after its' independence, Finland began designing a defensive line across the isthmus as a protective bulwark against its' historical enemy Russia. The line, which became known as the Mannerheim Line, was located about 35 kilometers south of Viipuri, running across the Isthmus from the Gulf of Finland to Lake Ladoga.

Construction began in 1920 based on the plans of German Colonel O. von Bradenstein with revisions by French Major J. Gros-Coissy and the Finnish Lieutenant Colonel Johan Fabrius. Construction stopped in 1924 due to lack of funds and stabilization of European politics. Construction did not begin again for almost twenty years. In 1932 construction commenced, once more under the direction of Fabrius, but moved ahead slowly due to minimal monies. From mid 1938 to 1939 building sped up significantly due to the worsening European situation. During the summer of 1939, construction became a national priority. The entire nation got involved with students, professors and workers voluntarily working many weeks during the summer strengthening the defensive works. The line was however far from complete when war began on November 30th.

Finland has always valued its' military services, albeit being limited by its' financial resources.

I remember in the 1980s when glasnost occurred, and the Western world was swooning with happiness and love for the new Russia, that Finland was busy buying armaments now that prices were exceptionally good. My father laughed at the West's naivety commenting at that time,

"Russia will always be a ravenous and distempered grizzly bear, not a teddy bear. It is good that

Finland is buying armaments now that the prices are low".

Certainly prescient given today's reality of a sabre rattling Putin once more aggressively pushing Russia west.

Finland as well as investing in armaments has invested in troops. As well as maintaining a standing army, Finland is one of the few modern countries that still has conscription. Every male over the age of 18 must serve in the military forces for six to twelve months (the time is dependent on which service/ specialization they join). Periodically afterwards they can be called up for maneuvers.

Innovation has stretched the military dollars. When visiting Finland in 2012 I was surprised at special markings and signs on the freeway between Mikkeli and Helsinki. My cousin explained. The highway served as a special landing strip for fighter planes.

The Mannerheim Line was not the only defensive line across the isthmus. In fact there were four lines:

1. The primary one, the Mannerheim Line (from the west coast through Summa to Taipale on Lake Ladoga)
2. An intermediate line,
3. The back line and indeed
4. A deep back line, the Salpa Line

The Mannerheim Line (Paalinja)

The Mannerheim Line (Paalinja), the primary and most southern line, ran eastwards from Kyrönniemi on the Gulf of Finland through Kuolemajärvi, Summa, Muolajärvi, Yskjarvi, and Punnus to Pasuri and across the Vuoksi River to Vuoksela and thence along the Vuoksi River through Suovanto to Taipale on the shores of Lake Laadoga.

The area around Summa and Muolaa was the most heavily fortified as the main road and railroad between Viipuri and St Petersburg ran through it. The Gulf of Finland coast was guarded by Fort Saarenpää, and the Lake Ladoga side by Fort Järisevä. These coastal artilleries had 5 inch, 6 inch and 10 inch guns.

The line consisted of defensive bunkers, pill boxes, trenches, tank barriers, mine fields and barbed wire barriers. Maximum use was made of the natural terrain full of bogs, rivers, lakes, interspersed with periodic farm fields. The Mannerheim Line had 157 machine gun positions and eight artillery positions. The line while a significant deterrent was not of the same caliber as the Maginot Line. Its' reputation was inflated by Finland's initial success in turning back the Russian assault. The foreign journalists covering the war dubbed it the Mannerheim Line despite Commander in Chief Mannerheim's objections.

The Intermediate Line

The Intermediate Line ran north of the Mannerheim Line, from Somme (ten kilometers south of Viipuri on the Gulf of Finland) through Leipasuo/Pienpero, Ayrapaajarvi and Salmenkaita to the Vuoksi River. Once across the Vuoksi it ran somewhat north of the river through Haitermaa and Pyhajarvi to just north of Fort Jariseva on Lake Ladoga.

The key western section crossed the St Petersburg-Viipuri railroad just north of Kamara. This section of the line was only ten kilometers north of the Mannerheim Line. The line was not as heavily fortified as the Mannerheim Line nor the Back Line; serving primarily as a delaying line..

The Back Line

The Back Line was about twenty kilometers north of the Interrmediate Line.

It ran from Viipuri through Tali and Kuparsaari across the Vuoksi River and thence north east to Kakisalmi on the shores of Lake Ladoga about fifty kilometers north of Taipale. It did not go south east to Taipale.

Specifically it ran from Karemalahti (on the Viipuri Gulf), through Viipuri, Tammisuo, Karstelanjarvi, Tali, Lyyklanjarvi, Naatala, Noskuanselka, Kuuparsaari, and across the Vuoksi to Vuoksenranta, Raisala, and Kakisalmi.

The Deep Back Line, or Salpa Line

The Deep Back Line, or Salpa Line was located further back, about 40 kilometers north of the Back Line. It did not see action in either war as the Russians were never able to breech the Back Line.

It was located in current day Finland, running north of Viipuri from Sakkijarvi on the Viipuri Gulf through Simola, Lappeenranta, Saimaan Kaakkoisranta, and Vuoksenniska, to Hiitola on the shores of Lake Ladoga.

Kannaksen Forces

Mannerheim placed the protection of the Kannas under one army - the Kannaksen Army (Army of the Isthmus).

The force was placed under the command of Lieutenant General Hugo Ostermann, the former commander in chief of the armed forces. Ostermann resigned in mid February, impacted by the serious injury of his wife in a Russian bombing raid; by the Russian breeching of the Mannerheim line; and by battle fatigue. He was replaced by Lieutenant General A.E. Heinrichs.

The army headquarters was in Imatra in the Valtio Hotel.

Land Units

At the start of the war the Kannasken Army consisted of 132,000 men organized into two army corps:

- The II AK (65,000 men under Lieutenant General Harald Ohquist) was the primary force. It was responsible for protecting the western gateway to Finland, a large section from the Gulf of Viipuri to Valkjarvi (south of the Vuoksi River, 35 kilometres east Taipale). It included the primary Russian railway and road attack corridor from St Petersburg to Viipuri. Within it were the critical battlegrounds of Summa, Muolaa, Ayrapaa/Vuosalmi and Viipuri itself.
- Initially headquatered in Viipuri, it moved in the first weeks to six kilometres north of Viipuri in the Ihantala Parish – our families' home parish. The headquarters itself was in the Saarela Kartano, but

the general slept across the lake in the Konkkala Kartano.

- At end of war on March 13th the front lines were in front of Saarela Kartano. Konkkala was in the actual battle zone east of Tali.
- At the start of the war the army had three divisions:
  - 4. D at Johannes protecting the west coast of the Kannas. It was composed of JR10 (From Helsinki), JR11 (Helsinki), JR12 (Helsinki – Uudenmaa)
  - 5. D at Leipasuo protecting the main road and railway route from St Petersburg. It consisted of JR14 (Turku), and JR15 (Turku- Turunmaa)
  - 11.D at Heinjoiki/Ayrapaa protecing middle eastern Kannas. It was composed of JR31 (Lappeenranta), JR32 (Kouvola),and JR33 (Lahti – Kymenlaakso)
- The III AK (47,000 men under Major General Erik Heinrichs). It was responsible for the battleground of Taipale and the area from east of the Vuoksi to Lake Ladoga.
- It had two divisions
  - 8.D at Inkila/Sakkola. It consisted of JR23 (Seinajoki), JR24 (Kokkola) , and JR26 (Oulu – Etela Phojanmaa)
  - 10.D at Phyajarvi. It consisted of JR28 (Jyvaskyla), JR29 (Jyvaskyla), JR30 (Jyvaskyla – Keski Suomi)
- Added to this was the Suojusjouko (Protective Forces) of 21,000 men, and nine Frontier Guard companies.

- It was the task of the Suojusjouko to delay the Russian advance into Finland in order to allow the IIAK and IIIAK to position themselves on the Mannerheim Line.
- The Suojusjouko consisted of four groups. These were positioned across the Isthmus from Viipuri Lahti in the west to Lake Ladoga in the West. The groups from West to East were:
  - The Uussikirkko Group (U Group) – Er P3, JP1, Hame Cavalry Regiment (HRR), Uudenmaa Dragoon Regiment (URR) versus the Russian 70th Division
  - The Muolaa Group (M group) – Er. P1, Er P4, JP3, 5 Raja K versus the Russian 24th and 43rd Divisions
  - The Lipola Group (L Group) – Er P5, JP2 versus the Russian 90th and 43rd Divisions
  - The Raudu Group (R Group) – Er P6, JP4, 8. Raja K, 9.Raja K versus the 142nd Division

Uncle Aatu was a member of the Muolaa Group and Uncle Erkki of the Lipola Group.

After December 7th, the Soujusjoukot became part of the Kannas Army – the Eastern Raudu Group became part of AK I, while the remainder became part of AK II.

Three months later at the end of February, when under heavy assault by the Russian forces, Mannerheim split part of II AK into a new army corps – the I AK under Major General Taavetti Laatikainen. The I AK was made responsible for the central Kannas area east of the II AK from Tali (10 kilometers north east of Viipuri) to Kuuparsaari on the Vuoksi River.

Also at the end of February, just prior to the March Russian attack across the frozen Viipuri Gulf west of Viipuri, Mannerheim established a separate Rannikko Ryhma (Coast Group). It was made up of sections of IIAK plus a few reinforcements.

He initially placed it under the command of Major General Kurt Wallenius, the former head of the successful Lapland defense of Petsamo and Salla. While effective in the smaller hinterland battles, Wallenius was overwhelmed by the force of the major Russian offensive across the Gulf of Finland. Upon taking command on February 28th, he immediately started to drink heavily, and stayed drunk in his head quarters for three days until Mannerheim relieved him of his command and of his position in the Finnish army.

Mannerheim's head of staff, Lieutenant General Karl L Oesch, took command on March 3rd.

As well as the army, the Finnish sea and air forces took part in the fighting on the Kannas. Neither group was large.

The sea forces did not play a material role on the Kannas. Its' coastal batteries fortresses at Saarenpaa and Jariseva did however effectively thwart any amphibious Russian landings at Summa or Taipale.

Fighting in the Air

The air force, albeit small, was heavily involved on the Kannas.

The air force focused its bomber and fighter operations on the Kannas.

The main, and only, fighter squadron, LLv.24 led by Kaptain Magnusson, flew out of Immola, Laapeenranta, and Suuri Merijoki (near Viipuri). Part of LeR2, it remained under the command of the Air Force.

By the end of the war three dive bomber squadrons of the LeR1 flight regiment reported directly to the Kannas Army command.

- One unit under the Kannas GHQ command, the LLV.10, had 12 Fokker dive bombers in Lappeenranta. It was commanded by Major K Janarmo until January 14th 1940, and then Kaptain K Gabrielsson.
- Another unit, under the command of the II AK, the LLV.12, flew 13 Fokker D.10 dive bombers out of the Raulami, Rompoli and Paakola air fields located south of Viipuri. It was commanded by Major A Nisonen until January 14th 1940, and then by Kaptain O Holm.
- On the III AK's eastern side of the Kannas, the LLV.14 flew 4 Fokker C.10s and 7 even older Fokker C.5s out of Ilmi and Kakisalmi. They were commanded by Major J. Moilanen

The Finnish air force was vastly outnumbered by the Russian air force, and as such could only provide limited support.

This they generally provided at night in order to try to avoid engaging the Russian air force. The Finnish fighter patrols, consisting usually of only two or three Fokker planes, did attack the waves of Russian bombers with success. However as the Russian bomber numbers were vast, they did little to thwart Russia's air attack. By February the Finnish air support dwindled further as their numbers had been decimated while the Russian air cover and fighter technology had improved along with their tactics. Now the bombers were protected by swarms of 30 to 40 Russian fighter planes.

Almost always, the Finnish frontline troops had to fight without fighter cover except for the last days of the war on Viipuri Lahti. That was due to paucity of Finnish fighter planes – only 36 at the start of the war and 22 at the end of February. They were effective. LLv.24, the only fighter squadron, had 120 kills at the cost of only 11 of its' own planes. They were brave. Several received the Mannerheim cross.

In March when the Russians troops began the attacks across the ice of the Gulf of Viipuri, the air force took part in repelling them. In this case they effectively used their new French Morane-Sauliner fighters, bombing and strafing the advancing Russian forces – destroying the ice upon which they advanced - sending many Russian units to a watery grave.

The Kannas Battles

The war on the Kannas lasted 105 days. Except for a trench warfare "lull" in January, battle raged throughout. During January Russia, while trying to determine how to win the war, constrained itself to bombing and shelling the Finnish positions, interspersed with isolated surveillance attacks.

Phases of the War

The war on the Kannas went through stages:

- November 30 – December 5: Delaying action of the Suojusjoukot and withdrawal to the Mannerheim Line
- December 6 – December 22: Initial Russian assaults against the Mannerheim Line
- December 23 -24: A brief unsuccessful Finnish counter attack
- December 25 – Jan 31: Trench warfare
- February 1 – February: Russian assault on the Mannerheim Line

- February 17 – February 27: Russian breakthrough and Finnish withdrawal to the Intermediate Line
- February 28 - March 7: Withdrawal to the Back Line
- March 8 – March 13: Viipurin Lahti battles & Tali, Viipuri and Taipale battles
- March 13: Peace

The primary thrust of the Russian army came north from St Petersburg over the Western portion of the Kannas west of the Vuoksi River. A major battle also raged almost continuously in the eastern portion of the Kannas at Taipale by Lake Ladoga. My uncles served on the Western Kannas. As such I will not be dealing extensively with the Taipale conflict. Rather I am summarizing the action below.

The Taipale Front

The major battlefront for the III AK was Taipale, although in the last weeks of war battles were fought at Ayrapaa and Vuosalmi as well. (Taipale was where the Vuoksi River emptied into Lake Ladoga).

The III AK had two divisions – the 8th and the 10th. The III AK was commanded by Major General A.E.Heinrichs until he was made commander of The Kannas Army on February 19th 1940. Now, Heinrichs almost had his military career cut short many years earlier. As dad recounted:

When I was doing my conscript service in 1928, I was part of Heinrichs' unit. Heinrichs was a Major then. During one outing I was with him when he was reconnoitering the Russian border. I noticed that the red border marker was on our left. We were on the Russian side of the border. I yelled out. The horses jumped quickly to our side. The major was relieved that we had not been inadvertently captured. He asked me not to tell anyone. I didn't.

The 8th Division was responsible for the western section by the Vuoksi River. At the start of the war it consisted of JR23, JR24, and JR26, Kev 8, and JP4. Major battles occurred at Suvanto, and at the end of the war at Ayrapaa/Vuosalmi.

The 10th Division was responsible for the eastern area by Lake Ladoga. Within it was the legendary, and bloody, Taipale sector. The 10th consisted of JR28, JR29, JR30, ER P6, and Kev Os 10. As well the 13th, 14th, 31st and 32nd Pioneer companies provided invaluable support on the front lines. KTR10, Er Psto 2, and Rask.Psto 4 provided artillery fire. In addition the coastal batteries at Kaarnajoki and Jariseva were able to bring their heavy 6 inch guns to bear on the battle field.

On January 1, 1940 the Army renumbered the 10th Division to the 7th Division in an attempt to briefly confuse Russian intelligence. The infantry regiments were also renumbered: JR28 was changed to 19, JR29 to 20, JR30 to 21, and Kev Os 10 to 7.

The Russian 49th and 150th Divisions together with the 39.Hv.Pr tank brigade launched fierce attacks at Taipale throughout the war. By Christmas Russia had four divisions on the front – and 111 artillery batteries vs Finland's 9 batteries. The attacks began on the first day of the war and continued to its' end. The Russians pounded the Finnish trenches with artillery barrage after artillery barrage, followed by endless battalion strength attacks led by tens of tanks.

On December 6th Russian troops began their attack. They managed to cross the Taipale River and dug themselves in at Koukunniemi. JR28 met the first assault on the 6th but the Russian forces were able to cross the river taking the open fields on the Koukunniemi River. JR30 led by Lieutenant Colonel A. Kemppi lauched a counter attack constraining the Russian advance across the river to only the small isthmus. Fierce battles continued to December 11th. The Finnish forces held.

On December 15th the Russians attacked both Kirvesmaki at Koukunniemi and Terentilla, breaking through the Finnish lines.

On December 17th the Finns counter attacked taking back their lines. The Russian troops however were able to hold their earlier position at Koukunniemi.

December 25th through the 27th brought another major attack.

Russian attacks continued through 1940, although at a lessened intensity. During the major Russian offensive in February they inflicted heavy casualities on the Finns but the Finnish defenses at Taipale held.

In March the Russians turned to concentrate their attack at Vuosalmi / Ayrapaa. In the last week of the war attacks accelerated at Taipale once more.

JR30 had 2,954 men. 538 of them were killed (almost 1 of every 4 soldiers). Of the dead soldiers, 65 or 12% were lost, or in other words their body was not recovered – a reflection on the furious back and forth fighting, and the destructive power of artillery and tank fire. Three quarters of the soldiers in the regiment were killed or wounded. Eleven soldiers took their own lives.

Sadly the other regiments fighting at Taipale lost even more men – 809 of JR28's men were killed, 781 of JR23.

The battles and life on the Taipale front are vividly presented in the novel Talvisota by Antti Tuuri; and in the associated movie – Talvisota. While the book is a novel, it is based on the real events and experiences at Taipale. The excerpt below describes the carnage on Christmas day

Those Russians started coming across our field. When all that mass came rolling towards us we hoped that our artillery would fire again into the middle of the field. But no artillery fire came, and we had to start shooting Russians with every weapon we had; with

machine guns and rifles, and automatic rifles and tommy guns.

Our anti tank guns succeeded in setting fire to two tanks that came tight up to our position. That scared the other tanks. They drew back some distance and started firing their canons at us. We shot the infantrymen when they came out from behind the tanks, shouting their spine-chilling attack shout as they came. It seemed to mean nothing, but came from deep within, from depths one could not believe in a human being. The Russians had even brought a rapid fire cannon into their positions and were firing with that; shell bursts showered earth from the edges of our trenches and we kept losing men all the time, but not as many as the Russians, since we could lie in our positions in a shelter of sorts and they were under fire in the open with no protection but that afforded by the snow and shell holes.

By midday there was nothing they could do but try to get back to the banks of the Taipale River. It looked as if the officers and politruks were shooting their own men to keep them from running, but the officers could not contain such a mass of men. They ran once they had taken a notion to do so. They forgot all about us, just turned their backs and ran as fast as they could. Many of them died there.

The tanks turned back and drove noisily at high speed across the field, crushing the infantrymen with their treads. The officers and politruks shot them and we shot them. Many boys from the steppes reached their journey's end that day at Terenttila. Afterwards we wondered if the men had been drunk when they attacked. They must have fortified their courage with vodka. They came with such stupid bravery, running upright and counting on their numbers. It made no sense to count on numbers when we were in the trenches and could fire all our weapons calmy and accurately at those trying to get into them. It was slaughter of human beings, that Christmas morning attack there at Terenttila.

While the novel high lights the Russian losses, Finnish losses were significant as well. Major Jaakko Sohlo the commander of JR30's 1st battalion was killed that day, along with 72 other Finnish soldiers. As well 131 were wounded – 42 seriously. In the next two days the Finns suffered another 173 casualties.

What the actual number of Russian casualties were, we'll never know. One typical attack lasting an hour resulted in 1,000 Russian dead and 27 destroyed tanks. Taipale was a slaughter house for the Russians.

PART II
My Families' Talvisota

My Families' Talvisota

My family was in the vortex of the war.

The womenfolk and the children had to flee our homes in Karjala.

My father and all of my uncles served in the military.

Viipuri was heavily bombed and shelled throughout the war. My mother and father's home just outside Viipuri was hit by a bomb and burnt to the ground. In the last days of the war the Russian army was in the suburbs of the city. Viipuri did not fall, but it ended up as a shattered burned ruin – a shadow of its' former self.

Our family farm in Kavantsaari never felt the tramp of the Russian army. The Russian army was stopped just ten kilometers south of it at Portinhoikka and Tali.

Our family however had to flee from our beloved homestead at the start of the war, except for Grandpa Juho who remained, taking care of the herd and the homestead until the last weeks of the war.

The Women and the Men

CHAPTER 5

The Women and the Men

The Women Homefolk

Not only were my uncles fighting on the Kannas but our homes were in the path of the war. All of my family had to flee from Karjala.

- Mother and my sisters from our home just south of Viipuri;
- My Aunt Hilda and her two daughters from Viipuri;
- My grandmother, grandfather and my Aunt Saima and her four young children from the beloved family farm in Kavantsaari. Aunt Saima shared with me the letters her husband Uncle Erkki sent from the front. Their daughter Sirkka shared with me her many memories, and her memoirs, of the time.

The Men at War –

My uncles and my father had left their homes already in October to fight for:

> " Uskonnon, Kodin, ja Isanmaa puolesta – For God, Home and Country"

Five of my uncles served on the Kannas. None of them kept any records identifying where they served nor did they volunteer any information. By the time I started looking for specific information, only one of my uncles was still bright and alive. He, my uncle Arvo, who was in his late 80s, answered my question on where he served and with what units, with:

> I don't remember much anymore and that's the way I like it."

Fortunately I was able to acquire a copy of their military records (kantakortti) from The Finnish National Archives. This, along with exhaustive research of both Finnish military history books on the war, and the actual journals of the unit officer (sota paiva kirjas) has allowed me to piece together each of their wars.

In this I was greatly aided by the Finnish militaries' excellent four volume Talvisodan Historia ... and by Finland's digitization of its' manuscripts.

> When visiting Finland in 2012 I reserved part of a week to visit the National Archives to read at least a few of the applicable sota paiva kirjas. Imagine my surprise when upon asking the front desk how I could access the manuscripts (perhaps on microfiche if I was lucky), to be told that; "Yes we can get them for you, but you know they are accessible online via internet." A most fortunate turn of events as it has taken me months and months to read and decipher all the applicable journals.

What I found was that:

Uncle Erkki

Uncle Erkki was food driver in the supply column of Er Psto 4, the detached artillery battalion of the 4th brigade of the Suojusjouko on the Karjalan Isthmus.

Uncle Erkki's unit was on the section of the Mannerheim Line between Muolajarvi, Valkjarvi and Punnus. At the start of the war his artillery units were part of the Lipola Delaying Group.

He took part in the battles of Valkjarvi, Pasurinkangas, Kyyrola, Parkkila, Sikniemi, Kuparsaari, and Nisalahti.

- In first days of the war they were at the border supporting the Lipola Delaying Group south of Valkjarvi.
- They then drew back behind the Mannerheim Line to the Pasurinkangas north of Valkjarvi.
- In mid December they moved to Oinala and Kyyrola near Aunt Saima's Muolaa home (The sector was just east of the Leipasuo sector where Erkki's brother Toivo was fighting).
- In mid February they retreated back through Koprala and Riistseppala/Sikniemi to the Intermediate Line defenses.
- At the end of February they moved back to Kuparsaari on the Back Line.

- On March 8th they marched through Antrea and Ihantala to the Viipiuri Lahti to support the Rannikko Ryhma force in the Viipurinlahti battles.

Uncle Aatu

Uncle Aatu was a messenger with 3./Er P4 - the 3rd company of the 4th detached infantry battalion of the Muolaa Delaying Group on the Karjalan Kannas.

Uncle Aatu was located between Muolaa and Yskjarvi. In the first month of the war, Uncle Aatu was west of Uncle Erkki. By January both were in the same area, indeed part of the same Division.

He was in the battles of Siiranmaki, Klymaoja, Ahijarvi, Oinala, Kyyrola, Ilves and Revonkyla.

- On November 30, 1939, at the start of the war, Er P4 was on front line by the border just north of Mainila;
- It withdrew, fighting battles as it moved through Siiranmaki, Kylmaoja and Ahijarvi, arriving on December 7th behind the Mannerheim Line at Oinala/Kyyrola (near Muolaa).
- On December 23rd the Finnish army undertook a major offensive against the Russians. Er P4 attacked north east of Parkkilanlammi.
- The offensive failed and the war settled into trench warfare from Christmas 1939 until mid February 1940. Er P4 was responsible for Kyyrola sector of

the Mannerheim Line east of Muolaa and west of Yskjarvi.

- With heavy airplane and artillery bombardments, massive tank attacks, and vastly greater numbers, the Russians were able to breach the Mannerheim Line on February 18th 1940. The Finnish Army retreated to the Back Defensive Line.
- Er P4 retreated through Ilves (south of Koprala and Ristseppalai) to Revonkyla on the Back Line just south of Kuparsaari, holding their positions from February 27th until peace was announced March 13, 1940.

Uncle Toivo

Uncle Toivo was a rifleman with 1/1.Pr – the 1st company of the 1st infantry Brigade. Twenty-five years old, he was in the front lines for most of the 105 days of the Winter War. His unit fought on the Mannerheim Line at Leipasuo just east of Summa (and just west of Uncle Aatu and Uncle Erkki), before fighting fierce rearguard battles at Pien Pero and Lyykyla as it withdrew. In the last weeks the unit was moved to Nisalahti to blunt the Russian assault across the Viipuri Lahti.

The battles of Leipasuo, Pien Pero, Lyykyla and Nisalahti (Sakkijarvi) are noted in his kantakortti.

- Until December 19th he was being trained, awaiting assignment.

- Once assigned to 1/1.Pr, he was positioned on the Mannerheim line at Leipasuo - just east of Summa. For the next six weeks until mid February the unit thwarted Russian attacks on the Mannerheim Line.
- When the Russians launched their major assault and broke through the Mannerheim Line, the unit fought rearguard battles at Lyykyla and Pien Pero.
- With the ferocious Russian attack across the ice of Viipuri Lahti, the 1st battalion was transferred on March 8th to the Ranniko Ryhma at Nisalahti to counter the Russian assault.

As Uncle Arvo said,

"Toivo was in the worst places with the fiercest fighting through both wars."

Uncle Arvo

Uncle Arvo received his draft notice in September 1939. There is no official entry as to when he started training. The first entry was February 15, 1940. According to Uncle Erkki's letters he definately reported for training before that.

And he was at the front before the end of the war. The Kannas battles of Nuijamaa, Kuparsaari and Kuolumajarvi are noted in his Kantakortti.

Uncle Vilho

Uncle Vilho was a medic with I/21 Kev It Ptri. This was the 1st unit of 21st light anti aircraft battery located in Antrea. While located on the edge of the combat zone, Vilho did not see much action

Uncle Kauko

Uncle Kauko was a driver with Rak P4, the 4th construction battalion of the IV AK north of Lake Ladoga.

Father

Father was in the Home Guard responsible for keeping sections of the railway line from Helsinki to Viipuri operational; and at some point, acted as one of the commanders on one of the panzer trains (The Home Guard records are minimal, as were dads' comments).

The stories of their wars, and that of their families, follows.

October and November
"A 51 day blessing"

CHAPTER 6

October and November
"A 51 day blessing" Call to Arms

On October 7th 1939 Mannerheim called up all the reserves on the Kannas for extraordinary training.

Uncles Erkki, Aatu, Kauko, and Vilho each received a knock on their door and were handed the following note from their local Suojeluskunta (Civil Guard) officer or policeman. The order was brief and to the point.

ORDER

Extraordinary Training Call Up

"Erkki Johannes Öhman, soldier

Kavantsaari, Antrea Parish"

As per the Compulsory Military Service xxx section and the application of yyy section, the Minister of Defense orders You to partake in extraordinary training. You are to leave, at the latest 5 hours after you have received this request, via the shortest route to

.... where you are to report in to ....

Signed Per Military District Commander ......

Reservists are requested to bring with them their military passport and everything possible of the following kit: proper outdoor boots, two pairs of underwear, two pairs of socks, sweater, packsack, towel, military uniform or other outside apparel, knife, needle and thread, metallic food dish and water container, skis and poles; and rifle, pistol ,binoculars and compass. Civil Guard Reservists are to arrive with their full military kit.

Reservists who have not arrived on time at the designated maneuvers will be punished as stated in criminal law

The order was direct and to the point: one had to leave within five hours, or else be subject to criminal prosecution.

The order as well was explicit in what the men were to bring with them. The Finnish Army was short of supplies. Most reservists ended up fighting in the clothes they came in, distinguished as a member of the Finnish Army by a cockade for their hat, a belt and army ammunition pouches. This outfit became known as the "Cajandar model" uniform – a wry reference to the pre war Prime Minister of Finland, Cajandar, who had left the army bereft of funding.

While perhaps not totally unexpected, the order must have raised chaos in the homes in the brief five hours before departure'

- As Uncle Erkki departed, he left behind his wife Saima and his four children Martti (11), Sirkka (9), Yrjo (6) and Irja (3); and his sixty year old parents - grandmother Hilda and grandfather Juho. Left them behind to take care of the large family farm in Kavantsaari.

- Uncle Aatu said goodbye to his wife Hilda and his two daughters Anna Liisa (12) and Maija (11) in their home in Viipuri.

- Uncle Kauko parted with his wife Margit in Oripaa in central Finland.

- Uncle Vilho parted with I do not know whom, nor from where. He was a freewheeling bachelor living here and there.

Neither Uncle Toivo, Uncle Arvo, nor Dad was called up on October 7th.

- Uncle Toivo was called up three weeks later on October 28th. I don't know why he was not mobilized immediately. He was living in Kallislahti at that point with his wife Alina.

- Uncle Arvo was working in Viipuri awaiting his notice to report to military training camp.

- Father had already been "mobilized". In July he had done three weeks of training on the operation of panzer trains at the Perkjarvi heavy artillery training centre. As operation of the railways was critical to Finlands' defense, his vocation was a reserved one and as such he was not called up to the army. Instead he was made responsible for operation of a section of the Finnish railway.
- Mother and my sisters Terttu (3 ½ years old) and Tellervo (2 ½) were left in our row home by the Liimatti railway station just south of Viipuri.

Trying, turbulent times awaited everyone.

On the Front Lines – Rapid Moblization

Uncle Erkki

Uncle Erkki's unit was Er Psto 4, the artillery battalion associated with the 4th detached infantry brigade (4. Pr commanded by Colonel J. Sihvo). Erkki's Er Psto 4 unit itself was commanded by Major Lauri Wahe.

The artillery battalion had 3 batteries. Each battery had close to 200 men. In the case of Er Psto 4 they did not have a howitzer battery.

Each battery was equipped with four of the 76 mm LK shortened guns. Although 1913 vintage, the 76 mm guns fired a 600 kg shell 6.9 kilometers. While the infantry appreciated having the support of the 76 mm guns, the guns were nonetheless known by the soldiers as *"hernepssy"*, or peashooters ...

The gun was horse-towed. Each battery had 18 drivers and 8 horse riders; and, indeed a vet and horseshoer/farrier. Horses were the logistical heart of the army.

Uncle Erkki was a horse man, but of a different type. He was assigned as a food supply driver in the battalion supply column (Kev kol / Er Psto 4, commanded by Lieutenant Selim Rantala). The supply of food was of course critical – *"every army travels on its' stomach"* . The one supply column supported all three artillery batteries.

Er Psto 4 was closely associated with 4.Pr – the 4th detached brigade of the Suojajouko. The unit operated in the 25 kilometer sector between Muolajarvi and Valkjarvi. The unit primarily supported the 2nd Division, except for the end of the war when it was moved to help defend Viipuri Lahti.

Uncle Erkki along with his fellow reservists arrived at his Suojajouko base in Pollakka at 03:30 a.m on October 8th . The train ride from the familiar Kavantsaari station, through Viipuri to Pollakka (just south of Ayrapaa) had been short and uneventful. Sleep probably evaded everyone as they wondered about what was to come ...and what they had left behind.

After arriving, the reservists remained only two days in Pollakka.

On October 10th the 800 strong battalion departed west for Sainio 15 kilometers south of Viipuri. This time Uncle Erkki was driving his horse and supply wagon. While an expert horseman, it must have been a bit chaotic with newly formed horse and driver teams jostling among each other.

Departing at 07:00 on the 11th they covered the 50 kilometers (as the crow flies) to Huumola near Summa in 11 ½ hours arriving there at 18:30. The horses handled the journey well. The men – well I guess it depended on their background and whether they had to march. But most were farm boys like Erkki. For them it probably felt like an easy day.

At 18:00 the next day they moved 10 kilometers to Sainio, the entire battalion arriving by 22:00.

For the next month and a half they remained in Sainio area building defensive lines and receiving training.

On November 27th the battalion moved 55 kilometers eastwards again to Valkjarvi. They took over Jaeger Battalion 2's (JP2) barracks. JP2 had already been dispatched to the border.

Erkki turned 37 on November 28th . I don't believe he gave much thought to his birthday, given that everyone knew war was eminent.

November 30th found them supporting the Lipola Delaying Group and the 5.RajaK frontier company at Kivennapa and Lipola close to the border with Russia. The Er Psto batteries were located several kilometers behind the infantry units - ErP 5, ErP2, and JP2. The Jaeger battalion and the frontier company were located directly at the border.

Uncle Aatu

When Uncle Aatu was called up on October 7th, he like Uncle Erkki was assigned to the Suojajoukko. In his case he was assigned to Er P4 (Detached Battalion 4) of the Muolaa Group.

After the war started Er P4 spent the entire 105 days integrally enmeshed in the battles on the Kannas – initially as part of the Muolaa Soujajouko - and later just like Uncle Erkki, as part of the 2nd Division.

On October 8th, upon arriving at the units' base in Kyyrola, Uncle Aatu was assigned as a messenger/dispatch rider for the 3rd company. In his case he rode a horse, not a motorcycle, relaying messages from the company commander to its' various platoons, to other companies, and to battalion head quarters. Although a city boy, he like all men of the era knew how to ride a horse. Or if he hadn't, he had had to learn during his military service.

On October 11th Er P4 left for Kekrola about a 80 kilometers away, marching from 19:00 to 00:45 from Kyyrola to Pamppala (20 kilometers) before bivoacing there overnight. At dusk on the 12th they departed at 18:00 arriving

at Ahijarvi at 23:30 (10 kilometers), only to depart an hour later for Kekrola. The long 18 hour march from Pamppala got them to Kekrola at 12:30.

But there had really been no need to hurry, as the battalion spent the next month and a half until the outbreak of the war upgrading the defenses at Kekrola.

- Laying barbed wire barriers
- Digging firing trenches
- Setting up firing pits and machine gun placements
- Building dug outs
- Clearing supply roads

While the defenses were not part of the industrial strength Mannerheim Line, they were important as they provided the unit some protection from Russia's first assault across the border.

Uncle Toivo

Uncle Toivo was not called up until October 28th.

For all of November he was part of the Karjala reserves – not assigned to any specific unit – fate pending.

In the six weeks between when he was called up on October 28th and mid December, he received refresher training with other reservists - and waited. Any rest during the initial six weeks was more than made up for in the ferocity of the following nine weeks.

Fate was not kind to Uncle Toivo, as on December 19 he was assigned as a rifleman with the 1st company of 1.Pr, one of the replacements for the casualties the unit had already encurred. The 1st Brigade was part of the 1st Division of the II AK. He spent the remainder of the war in front line battles on the Kannas.

Uncle Arvo

Uncle Arvo was in Viipuri, working and waiting.

Uncle Kauko

Uncle Kauko was called up on October 7th leaving his wife Margit in their home in Oripaa north of Turku for the Karjalan Kaartin Regiment. He was assigned as an automobile driver for the headquarters unit.

On November 11th he was assigned as an auto driver with construction battalion 4 of the IV AK (Rakennuspataljoona – Rak.P4). The unit spent a hard but relatively uneventful winter building and upgrading the defensive works at the north end of Lake Ladoga.

Uncle Vilho

Uncle Vilho as well was called up on October 7th. In his case he didn't need to go far – just twenty kilometers.

He was assigned as a medic for the 21st light anti aircraft battery (I/21 Kev It Ptri) located at Antrea.

The I/21 Kev It Ptri was part of AK II. The unit had 20mm Oerliko and BSW guns and 40 mm Bofors anti aircraft guns. The Oerliko was effective to a height of 1,200 meters and the Bofors guns to 3,000 meters. The Russian bombers usually flew at a height of 2,000 to 5,000 meters.

While the unit certainly spent a great deal of time shooting at Russian bombers passing overhead, it fortunately only suffered one casualty in the war – so the medic workload was negligible. I am sure Uncle Vilho had other responsibilities as well.

I am not sure how such an athletic and competent young man was assigned to a back line job located only twenty kilometers from home. He spent the war in relative comfort and security.

Father

October found father in the Home Guard managing the track operations for a portion of the Finnish Railway.

On the Home Front – Wary Preparations

On the Karjala home front life proceeded ahead, albeit somewhat differently after the men had all left. Everyone was apprehensive as the news was grave and progressively got worse.

Mother and My Sisters

Mother and my sisters Terttu and Tellervo remained in Liimata on the southern outskirts of Viipuri, in their row house by the railroad. Father was not home as he was railroading ...

Aunt Hilda and Her Daughters

Aunt Hilda and her daughters Anna Liisa (age 12) and Maija (age 11) remained in Viipuri anxiously monitoring the wars progress, awaiting news from their father Aatu.

Aunt Hilda continued working as a tailor of men's vests and pants while the girls went to school.

At one point Aatu and Hilda discussed sending the girls to Sweden for protection but Aunt Hilda was adamantly against it. Many of the Finnish city residents, particularly the wealthy ones, or those with relatives in Sweden, did send their children to Sweden for the war. During the Talvisota around 7,000 children left for Sweden. Some left with their mothers, many left alone.

The Kavantsaari Homestead

At the Kavantsaari homestead everyone had to work a bit harder due to the absence of Uncle Erkki. Luckily October and November are quiet months in the agricultural calendar. Gramps once more took active control of the farm while the women and children pitched in even more than usual. This along with the help of the hired hands (mostly women and older men now) resulted in the farm running on a relatively even keel.

In early November after Uncle Toivo had been called up, Aunt Alina came to join the family at the farm.

Beloved Horses

On the farm the only other event that stood out was the receipt of a requisition notice from the Minister of Defense:

Minister of Defense Notice

Horse and Vehicle transfer /surrender for the Needs of the Armed Forces

The horses must be well shoed and equipped with strong harness, horse blanket and belt, drinking pail and cleaning brush. Each horse should have with it 50 kg of oats and 100kg of hay

They had to give up one of their horses to the army.

Grandfather gave them their oldest horse, Veikko. While this was the practical thing to do, grandmother was disturbed that the horse that had worked for them so long and faithfully, now had met such a sad fate. While the army kept thorough records and promised to return all the horses, they never saw Veikko again.

While cavalry units were a thing of the past, the Finnish army relied totally on horses for moving their supplies and artillery (In Lapland reindeer were used). The horses were better suited than automobiles for the rough Finnish terrain in which the fighting occurred. 71,805 horses were in the army at the end of the war as opposed to the 4,500 at the start. Finland had 173,297 fit for "conscription", so over 40% of the countries healthy horses were enlisted in the army.

Each Division had 3,539 horses – or one horse for about five men as opposed to only 46 vehicles. Each infantry regiment had 494 horses - 1 vehicle and 2 motorcycles. The artillery regiments had more then double the number of horses at 1,164. The horses were used to move food, clothes, ammunition and other goods as well as heavy materials and artillery guns. Even the heavy artillery guns were moved by horses, as opposed to tractors.

The army, as well as the men, valued its horses. Each battalion had a veterinarian and farriers. Three quarters of the countries vets were conscripted to take care of the horses. There were hospitals for horses as well as men. Often Lottas helped in the horse hospitals. The Finnish horses were a hardy breed, but even though the soldiers built them stables of logs and spruce boughs whenever possible, and vets and horse hospitals tended to them, war and winter took its toll. 34,945 horses were wounded or became sick, and 7,204 died - like our horse Veikko.

CHAPTER 7

December
War Begins

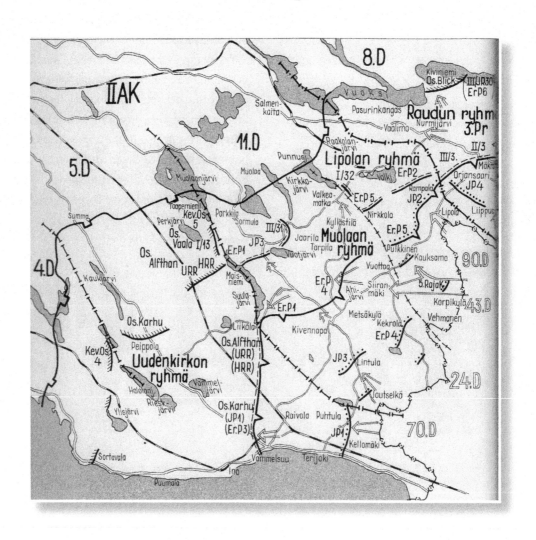

CHAPTER 7

December - War Begins

On November 27th, the small Russian village of Mainila across the border on the Isthmus was destroyed by a shell barrage. The Russians claimed that the Finns had fired the shots. This was explicitly proven to not be the case. Rather the Russians had destroyed their own village as a pretext to initiating a war with Finland.

For the next few days Finland continued communications with Russia regarding a possible peace even though it knew that it was for naught.

Indeed it was for naught. At 06:50 on the morning of November 30th 1939, Russia started an artillery barrage and crossed the border. At 08:52 the air raid warning sounded in Viipuri. At 09:15 it went on in Helsinki. The first bombs hit Viipuri at 09:00. War had begun.

The Finnish parliament declared a state of war.

Prime Minister Risto Ryti took over as Prime Minister from Cajander on December 1st.

Already on November 30th Mannerheim had taken over from Hugo Osterman as commander in chief of the Finnish armed forces. For some weeks President Kyosti Kallio had been trying to convince a reluctant 72 year old Mannerheim to accept the position.

Once war started he answered the call. His first communiqué to his men read:

Commander-in-Chief's Order of the Day # 1

The President of the Republic has appointed me on 30 November 1939 as Commander-in-Chief of the armed forces of the country.

Brave soldiers of Finland !

I enter on this task at a time when our hereditary enemy is once again attacking our country. Confidence in one's commander is the first condition for success. You know me and I know you, and know that everyone in the ranks is ready to do his duty even to death.

This war is nothing other than the continuation and final act of our War of Independence.

We are fighting for our homes, our god, and our country.

> *Field Marshall C.G. Mannerheim*

Finland's soldiers answered his call.

On The Home Front - Bombs & Loss

On November 30th the women and children in our family were most certainly aware that war had started.

Mother and My Sisters

For mother and my sisters, that first day left them homeless.

One of that day's bombs fell on our house in Liimatta. The house was at a railway junction. The house and everything in it was destroyed. Nothing was left – all the furniture, family photographs, dads' paintings and other valuables were destroyed.

Mom and dad kept some valuables in a small metal box. While it was recovered, it had gotten so hot that the contents were singed. I have mother's partially charred passport from that period. It had been in the box.

Mother had taken the girls with her to the bomb shelter. My sister Terttu remembers that mother had a hard time getting her to leave right away. Terttu told mom;

"I won't go until I finish eating my porridge."

She was 3 years old at the time. Luckily, mother prevailed.

Aunt Hilda and Her Children

The day was a memorable one for cousin Anna Liisa as well. She remembers that:

When the bombing started we were in school and departed quickly for the bomb shelter. From the shelter we could hear the bombs exploding all around us.

Sirkka and the Homestead Womenfolk

The day had no impact directly on the homestead, but it did affect Aunt Saima and Aunt Alina:

Aunt Saima and Aunt Alina were in Viipuri shopping. When the bombs started falling on the city, they were actually having morning coffee with Aunt Hilda. They ran to a shelter. After the all clear, they hastily left Viipuri for the farm - but not via train. They had to walk the entire 20 kilometers back to the farm. The rail road to Kavantsaari had been damaged and no trains were running.

On The Front Lines
Fighting a Delaying Action

While the war had been expected, Finland had not mobilized its' full army, nor positioned it on the front, in order not to escalate the situation further.

It was the task of the 21,000 strong Suojajouko which had been mobilized on the frontier to delay the Russian advance. From November 30th to December 5th the Suojajouko fought a delaying action at the border against the advancing Russian army. By December 6th they had withdrawn to just south of the Mannerheim Line.

Uncle Erkki's artillery battalion and Uncle Aatu's infantry company were in the heart of the conflict.

Uncle Erkki

The start of the war found Uncle Erkki's Er Psto 4 unit south of Valkjarvi near the border supporting the Lipola Delaying Group. The Raudu Delaying Group was on their right and the Muolaa Delaying Group on their left. The Lipola Delaying Group consisted of the JP2 Jaeger battalion and the Er P2 and Er P5 independent battalions- a force of about 3,000 troops. Opposite them was the over 30,000 strong 90th and 43rd Russian divisions.

On November 30th the Er Psto 4 battalion headquarters was in Valkjarvi. The 1st and 3rd artillery batteries were further south near Lipola supporting the Er P5 and JP2 infantry units. The 2nd battery was in the Muolaa Delaying Group sector supporting JP3.

Over the next week the Lipola Group fought rearguard battles as it retreated 30 kilometers to the Mannerheim Line. By December 7th the Lipola Group, was positioned just south of the Mannerheim Line on a section stretching from the Pasurinkangas by the Vuoksi River to Oinala on the east side of Muolaajarvi.

The start of the war is captured by the commander of Er Psto 4's 1st battery – Lieutenant Poso. The 1st batteries

view of the war on November 30th was not exactly what they expected.

At 3:40 on Nov 30th I and part of the 1st battery unit left Nirkkola by sleigh to go talk with the 5th battery of 2.Pr at Keisarimaki. We arrived via the road through the village of Lipola. We went to 5th commanders' bivovac in a house in the village. It was 200 to 300 meters downhill from the front line defensive positions. The road to the village went through barbed wire barricades and stone tank barriers.

We arrived at the house. The men unharnessed the horses and unloaded the load. The little house was full of civilians – women, children and a few men. We were astonished. There were civilians still in our previous location in Nirkalla 10 kilometers behind the lines - but here beyond the defensive trenches and barricades !

We hardly had time to exchange greetings with the 2. Pr 5th battery commander and joke that " no white man should get up before the cock crows" when the Russian artillery barrage started.

At 7:05 it started with a huge howitzer explosion and further hellish firing. It was still dark. The opening to the west of the village was a sea of red. A shell hit the nearby group of houses, including the neighbors' yard. Fragments flew over us up the slope towards the battery position. The cottage was suddenly empty. The soldiers had departed immediately for their defensive positions. The household had also disappeared – starting on their long sad refugee road.

The first infantry and tank attack came at 9:30. The Russian barrage continued. Soon the village caught fire - burning - shrouded in smoke.

....

Later in the day an unusual event occurred to the 2nd company of the 2nd Jaakari Battalion. A well known local household master drove a sleigh full of wheat, bread, butter, meat and eggs to Lieutenant Lindholm's command post. The others in the household had left several days earlier and he had remained. Now that the Russian artillery fire had started he wanted to give the remaining food provisions to the Finnish company. He offered the help of himself and his sleigh, "if the aid of a man such as himself was of use".

Of course civilians and old men were not suited for front line combat locations, but the company commander advised him to talk with the doctor of the medical unit. A position was found for him during the battle driving wounded to the road side for evacuation. That is until during the withdrawal he himself met his end from artillery fire. The doctor heard the wounded man's last words. Thus was lost another of the fatherland's guardians.

The 2nd Jaakari Battalion lost 22 men on that first day – the most of any Finnish unit.

The fighting continued as the Lipola Group retreated. Battles occurred at Valkajarvi, and then further north east on the Pasurinkangas. Uncle Erkki's supply column withdrew with the battalion headquarters unit from Valkjarvi to Vehkalahti south of the Mannerheim Line's Salmenkaita defenses.

By December 6th all the Lipola Group had successfully withdrawn behind the Mannerheim Line.

While casualties in the infantry units had been significant, losses for the Er Psto 4 artillery battalion had fortunately been negligible – only one casualty from friendly fire and one from shrapnel. Artillery units, being positioned kilometers behind the battle lines, were much safer places than the infantry units who were only a bayonet thrust away from the enemy.

Throughout the battles, Uncle Erkki drove food supplies to the battalions' three artillery batteries. He undoubtedly experienced some harrowing moments as he drove his horse and sleigh under the Russian artillery fire and strafing fighter planes. His military record notes that he took part in the battle of Valkjarvi. I wonder what his thoughts were

as he drove by his wife Aunt Saima's childhood farmstead near the Muolaa church.

As the Delaying Groups retreated, the rearguard frontier guards and Jaeger companies burnt the villages and farms behind them. The Finnish farmers took the loss of their ancestral homes and livelihood with toughness and patriotism – and pride:

In one village a detachment of border guards sadly informed an aged peasant woman that she must prepare to leave her home the next morning with only the belongings she could carry on her back and could load into the horse drawn sled tethered to the cabin. In the morning when they returned they were startled to see that the entire dwelling had been scrubbed and washed until it sparkled. Kindling, matches and kerosene had been placed near the door. When the soldiers asked her why she had gone to so much trouble she pulled herself upright with all the dignity she could summon, looked them in the eye, and replied, "When one gives a gift to the fatherland it should be like new."

Another old farmer was finally convinced to leave his home. The soldiers torched it, only to see the old man back the next day prodding the ashes. When asked what he was doing, the farmers gnarled features twisted into a grim smile and he said, "This farm has been burned down twice because of the god damned Russians – once by my grandfather, and once by my father, but I'll be damned if I could drive away without first making sure you had done a proper job of it."

Toughness, patriotism and pride, yes; but also a deep attachment to the soil and their roots.

Uncle Aatu

Uncle Aatu and his infantry unit, part of the Muolaa Delaying Unit, was only ten kilometers west of Uncle Erkki.

On November 30, 1939, Uncle Aatu was with the 3rd company of the Er P4 on the front line in Kekrola by the border just north of the village of Mainila. Indeed they had already been there on November 26th. I wonder if he heard the Russian artillery firing in the early morning on their own village of Mainila, and their own people ?

In the next days, it retreated, fighting battles as it withdrew through Siiranmaki, Kylmaoja and Ahijarvi, arriving on December 7th behind the Mannerheim Line at Oinala/Kyyrola (near Muolaa).

The 3rd companies' military diary (Sota Paiva kirja) chronicles the events from November 30th to December 6th :

30.11.39

07:00 The Russians opened up with an intense artillery fire at the companies locations in Kylii, Velsmaa, Soppikyla, the Kanalan school, and the surrounding countryside. The 1st platoon was posted in Velsmaa, the 3rd at Soppikyla, and the 4th at the Siltaisa bend, the 2nd as reserve at the Kanalan school. The admin group moved away through the artillery fire, based on an order earlier in the morning, to the Eskola area of Vuotta.

21:30 The company drew back first to Siiranmaki and then to Kylmaoja in Vuotta. The 3rd platoon withdrew through enemy forces to Kylmaoja. No casualties have been incurred up to now. Soldier Rytkonen disappeared.

1.12.39:

01:30 Company began pulling back to Ahajarvi to prepare to draw back along the road. There the Russian tanks pushed aggressively in direction of the Kylmaoja-Vuotta road. Between Vuotta and Kaukolammo an explosion killed soldier Sevola. Likewise on the same road – Vuotta to Riihisyrja – a Russian tank company followed our company's withdrawal route. We could hear the rumbling of tanks. Soldier Vuronen fell.

06:00 Russians arrived in front of our Ahajarvi lines and started an intense fight. The Russians drove two trucks full of men to right in front of the barbed wire. The men jumped out and started to cut the obstacle. The trucks ended up in front of the tanks but we couldn't destroy them as we had no "poltta pulloja" Molotov cocktails.

3.13.39:

17:00 30 men marched to Jaarila where the 5th companies' supply depot was. Lieutenant Ripatu and medical doctor Captain Bjorklund joined the company as well as the machine gun company's field kitchen and part of 1st companies 2nd platoon.

22:00 We marched with this group to Lehtokyla

4.12.39

11:20 Left Lehtokyla for Parkkila passing by the Muolaa church.

5.12.39

The company marshaled in Parkkila and checked for battle readiness. The lost soldier Kol, and probably Leskonen, became captives of the Russians.

6.12.39

17:00 Marched to Kangaspelto via Indaoja

03:00 The company took part in an extra, battalion organized reconnaissance attack and advanced to Oinala via Rintala without encountering enemy forces en route. The enemy forces harassed us in the morning, forcing us to draw back to Kangaspelto.

As is case for all the sota paiva kirjas, the account is cryptic and detached.

The reality was far more personal and intense – the fighting at Siiranmaki on November 30th ; at Kylmaoja on the 30th and the 1st ; and at Ahijarvi on December 1st and 2nd are noted as actual battles in Uncle Atu's military record.

By December 7th all the Finnish units on the Kannas from Taipale in the east to Terijoki in the west had retreated back to just south of the Mannerheim Line.

The 21,000 strong Suojajouko had done its' job of slowing the attack of the 500,000 strong Russian army until Finland's regular army forces arrived.

On The Home Front - Flight

The home front also retreated – or rather fled for their lives in the days after the start of the bombing.

Mother and My Sisters

With her home in ashes, mother gathered the children, packed the one suitcase allowed per person, got on a train and fled from their home south of Viipuri.

But then it would not have been that simple.

- *I wonder where they stayed initially after they emerged from the air raid bunker to find their home gone ? Grandmother was living in Viipuri, as well as mother's sister Hilda, and several of dad's uncles. Although both grandmother's and Hilda's homes were destroyed in the war they weren't destroyed in the first days. Probably they stayed at her sister Hilda's.*
- *And during that cold early winter day what did they pack in that one suitcase each was allowed? Everything including their clothes had gone up in flames. Aunt Hilda must have given them what old clothes she had from her girls' younger days, or ...?*
- *How did they get hold of dad who was somewhere in Finland ? Dad must have been frantic with worry when the bombing started. Phones did exist but it would have been difficult to make contact. Probably mother and dad had agreed in advance what to do if the war started. I*

am sure father drew some comfort from knowing that with the large extended family in Viipuri, and in nearby Kavantsaari, that they would take care of each other
- *How was it arranged that they go stay with dad's Aunt Brita in Kuopio ? While direct family, the relationship was not a close one.*

Grandmother Valencia also left Viipuri, suitcase in hand for Hameenlinna where her younger son, our Uncle Yrjo, lived.

What a frightening, uncertain, frenzied time it must have been. What it was truly like I can only surmise as mother was not one to talk about those days, and I never asked.

Aunt Hilda and Her Daughters

Aunt Hilda and the girls left Viipuri within a few days as the bombing continued, going to the family farm in nearby Kavantsaari.

Their home was destroyed later in the war by the continuous Russian bombing.

Sirkka and the Homestead Womenfolk

My cousin Sirkka was as a 9 year old girl when the war started. She was living on the family farm with her mother Aunt Saima, and her siblings - Martti, George and Irja- and Grandmother Hilda and Grandfather Juho.

In the first week of December Aunt Hilda together with her daughters Anna Liisa and Maija arrived at the farm.

Shortly thereafter in early December 1939, spurred by a government order to evacuate, the family fled their farm and home in Karjala for central Finland. Grandfather Juho remained to take care of the herd and the farm.

They left for Forsaa in central Finland near Hameenlinna. While everyone was free to go where ever they wished when they fled Karjala, the Finnish government identified specific communities where people from each parish could go – trying to keep the evacuees together with their original neighbors. That is why the Öhmans arrived in Forsaa, along with others from the Kavantsaari area.

Cousin Sirkka not only shared her stories, but also actually wrote down her memoirs. The excerpt covering those initial days follows:

I remember when on the morning in early December we left with bundles under our arms walking to the railway station where we were loaded into the railway car (cattle car). Aunt Hilda and the girls were with us.

After two days we arrived in Forsaa. We ended up staying in some parish building. Aunt Hilda tended to things. Irja and George ended up in another place for the night. Of course mother got upset, but in the morning we found each other. Shortly thereafter mother noticed that George had escaped. We found him under some tables.

The journey continued on the back of a truck towards Tammela parish's Sukula village. We arrived at Sukula's public school. There the "beauty contest" started when the home owners came to pick their winners.

My sweet grandmother caught the attention of a teacher. He went home at lunch and brought his mother-in-law, Jaakkola's old mistress, to meet us. And she liked everything she saw. She said that between them, from her side it was an acceptable fit. There were nine of us. God led us to a good person.

Even today I appreciate and remember that kindness, although then I was only a 9 year old.

Grandpa Juho and the Farm

While everyone else left, grandfather Juho remained on the farm, running it with the help of two hired hands (women). I have to admire his physical strength and mental toughness. At age 61 he was an old man – but definitely a tough one. Doing heavy physical work all day while envisioning the loss of their home, must have been draining.

But he was not about to abandon the home that he had built up with over forty years of toil just because some Russians were coming.

Uncle Erkki muses in his first letter to his wife Saima:

I wonder how my dad is managing at home with the cattle. Maybe we should have got another hired hand. I guess the herd was still together when you fled, wasn't that so? I don't think the livestock needs to be moved from the homestead yet.

Somewhere Out Here

Aunt Saima saved the letters that Uncle Erkki sent home from the front. She shared them with me. When I read the yellowed thin sheets I felt close to him. His commitment to his family and country, his courage, and his positive outlook, springs clearly from his pen ... to me.

His letter of December 22nd from Somewhere Out Here speaks for itself:

Somewhere Out Here 22/12/1939

Dearest Saima

Thank you for your letter, I got it.

It is sad that the home affairs became so mixed up that you and the children had to leave and move so far away. Our home has ended up suffering because of this war. There are so many households that have been emptied across the land and moved to another parish. But there is no point in sorrowing about the event and the great loss.

On this battleground we will still win. Then we can once again organize our home life in our own parish.

I have been healthy and well, as have the other boys from our area.

You don't need to send money as you can't do anything with it here. They take good care of us. There is enough food, and everything we need we can get. We also get a bit of money to buy whatever little we need.

I haven't got the parcel you sent yet, but I'm sure it will arrive in good time. It is certainly welcome, especially the warmer socks and that underwear.

I wonder how my dad is managing at home with the cattle. Maybe we should have got another hired hand. I guess the herd was still together when you fled, wasn't that so? I don't think the livestock needs to be moved from the homestead yet.

To end, don't worry about us, we are well. I'm a bit lonely without yourself and the children, but nothing comes from complaining. Here we are alive and fighting together for an important cause.

Say hello to whomever may be there from our area.

Martti wrote that there is still not enough snow there to go sledding. That would be a nice diversion for the children.

I can't think of anything more to say other then greetings to you my dear wife and beloved children. Give mother a big hello from me, and remember to write.

Erkki

On The Front Lines
Initial Russian assaults against the Mannerheim Line

After the Delaying groups had withdrawn by December 6th to near the Mannerheim Line, the Russian forces continued to attack until December 22nd in an unsuccessful effort to break through.

The assault came across the entire Kannas – in Uncle Erkki's Lipola Sector; Uncle Aatu's Muolaa Sector; and Uncle Toivo's Leipasuo Sector.

Uncle Erkki

Uncle Erkki's Er Psto 4 artillery battalion was near Uncle Aatu's Er P4 unit. Indeed they were providing artillery support for Uncle Aatu's Er P4.

- From the 6th to the 17th Er Psto 4 supported the Finnish forces as battle continued on the Pasurinkangas. Now a week into the war both JR33 and JR32 along with Kev Os 11 had arrived in Pasurinkangas to bolster the ErP2, ErP5 and JP2 battalions.
- From the 18th to the 22nd the battle moved further south west along the Mannerheim Line to Oinala near Muolaa.

Lieutenant Poso commander of Er Psto 4's 1st battery notes:

- *On December 6th the Russians launched a fierce attack against III/ JR33. At 05:30 the darkness resounded with the shouts of " 'Taliini, 'Taliini'. As the battle exploded some of the companies panicked. In places the Russians were able to gain the trenches. The seasoned Er P5 unit attacked quickly from their reserve position stopping the flight of the JR33 men and pushing the Russians out of the Finnish defensive lines.*
- *JP2 as well arrived to bolster the defenses. On December 7th JP2 counter attacked to regain some of the area in front of the Mannerheim Line. They were however thrown back.*
- *On December 8th Er P5 re-attacked towards Valkjarvi and by evening was 7 kilometers south of the headquarters. They returned at night.*
- *On December 11th a weak Russian attack was turned back. JR33 successfully counterattacked towards Valkjarvi. The Russian forces fled, leaving a significant amount of equipment behind.*
- *JP2 was on reserve at Ala Kuusa and Kev Os 11 at Yla Kuusa .*
- *The Pasurinkangas front remained quiet thereafter.*

In mid December Er P5 moved further south west on the Mannerheim Line to positions between Yksjarvi and Kirkkojarvi. There from December 18th to 22nd , supported by Er Psto 4 1st artillery battery, it fought to hold the line. Just to the west of them Uncle Aatu's Er P4 was fighting between Muolaajarvi and Yskjarvi.

On the 22nd of December Uncle Erkki and the Er Psto 4 supply column moved to to Ala Kuusa on the northern part of the Pasurinkangas.

It was from Ala Kuusa just 7 kilometers east of the Punnus railway station and just 10 kilometers north east of his wife's childhood Muolaa home, that Uncle Erkki wrote home from Somewhere Out Here on December 22nd, 1939.

Uncle Aatu

The period from December 6th to December 22nd brought little relief for Er P4. They continued in action protecting the Muolaajarvi to Yksijarvi section, fighting rearguard battles at Oinala and Kyyrola, back and forth with the Russians:

- On December 14th the Er P4 defenses collapsed at Oinala. JR31 was however able to recapture the positions.
- On December 18th the Russians retook Oinala with a strong attacks supported with heavy artillery
- On December 19th the Finnish forces (I&II /JR31, II/ JR 32 and 2./JP2) counter attacked but failed to take Oinala back.
- From December 20 to 21, JR32 once more tried unsuccessfully to take the positions back

Uncle Aatu's 3rd company's military diary records:

6.12.39

17:00 Marched to Kangaspelto on the northern outskirts of Oinala

03:00 The company took part in an extra battalion organized reconnaissance attack and advanced to Oinala via Rintala without encountering enemy forces en route. The enemy forces harassed us in the morning, forcing us to draw back to Kangaspelto

7.12.39

05:00 We marched to the Tervola area and set up as reserves

8.12.- 9.12.39

Reserve in Tervola

10.12.39

06:00 Marched to front line taking over the 5th companies' position

11.12-12.12.39

Manned front line positions

13.12.39

Patrol sent out to Valola. Accidentally stepped on own mines. Soldiers Pelto and Nuoa seriously injured

14.12.39

09:00 Heavy Russian artillery bombardment of our position

15:00 Russian tanks supported by infantry attack. Attack thrown back. Two Russian tanks destroyed. Soldiers Malkkonen and Nielossa wounded. Jarvilinen went insane. Sokura killed.

15.12.39

03:00 Company moved back behind Mannerheim Line

Morning Tried to fix barbed wire barricades in front of us but driven back by enemy fire. Corporal Lassila wounded

16.12.39

19:00 Company moved to reserve in the 2nd battalion along the Kyyrola- Oinala road. Reserve Lieutenant Taina placed in command

22:00 III platoon tried to lay mine fields between Oinala – Valola. Driven back by enemy fire

17.12.39

19:00 Moved from Er P4 sector to battalion reserve at the junction of a road branching south from of the Kyyrola- Oinala road. Former 7th company bivouac location

18:12.39

Company II, III, IV platoons dispatched to Oinala to lay mines. They did not succeed. The enemy and our men got tangled together

19.12.39

Hasty withdrawal from Oinala

20.12.39

09:00 Company's I platoon and half of the II platoon shielding themselves in Olkkola from enemy armed column fire. Koskilainen wounded, Silvola killed.

21.12.39

I platoon on front lines in the 2nd company's position

II and IV platoons tried to build barbed wire barricades on the Yskjarvi but had to abandon it due to enemy artillery fire

IV platoon on guard duty on Yksijarvi shore

22.12.39

II and IV platoons continued setting up barbed wire barricades on Yskjarvi shore

Uncle Aatu's military record notes that he took part in the Oinala Kyyrola battle from the 9th to 14th of December, and the Kyyrola battle from the 15th to the 17th.

I wonder if it was during these battles that he was almost killed. Cousin Anna Liisa related that:

During the war dad had his horse shot out from under him as he rode with a dispatch. It remained a vivid memory for him forever: the Russian bullets whistling through the air; the horse suddenly collapsing; the desperate roll away from the falling steed; crawling frantically through the bullets to a protective tree clump – dispatch bag still hanging from his shoulder.

Uncle Toivo

At the start of December Uncle Toivo had still not been assigned to a unit. On December 1st he had spent his 25th birthday training with 4./VVK.

But on December 19th, 1939 he was assigned to 1st company, 1st battalion, 1st Brigade, 1st Division, II Army Corps. He spent the remainder of the war with them.

The 1st Division, commanded by Major General Tavetti Laatikainen, was responsible for Leipasuo sector of Mannerheim Line. The division had 14,000 men. The division consisted of three infantry brigades: 1.Pr, 2.Pr, and 3.Pr; and the JR14 infantry regiment.

The 1st Brigade itself, was commanded by Colonel Einar Vihma until December 17th; and then by Colonel U Sihvo. The brigade had an artillery battalion, as well as three infantry battalions.

In November the brigade was in the Pollakkala – Malokola area. The brigade was held in reserve until December 10th when it was moved to the front lines to man the Leipasuo sector of the Mannerheim Line together with JR14 and Kev Os 5 and I/KTR 10. The Leipasuo sector was just east of Summa. It was fifteen kilometers wide stretching from Munasuo just west of theViipuri – St Petersberg railway line to the western shore of Lake Muolaa.

On December 10th the 1st Battalion was on the Munasuo – Tassianlammi front line –a 5 kilometer stretch just east of the Summa sector. Just east of them, on the eastern shore of Lake Muolaa was Er P4 and Uncle Aatu.

On December 12th, the 2nd battalion together with the 1st and 4th companies of the 1st battalion and a JR14 company attacked to take back positions south west of the Leipasuo

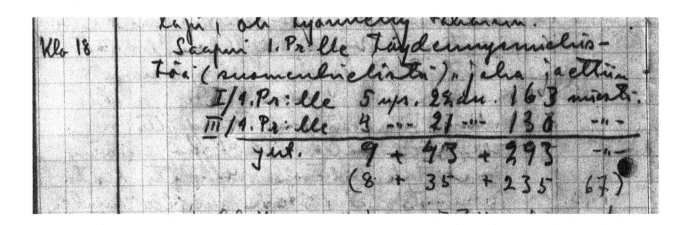

station. The attack failed due to heavy Russian artillery fire and resistance – and almost non-existent Finnish artillery support. The Finnish artillery fired all of 10 shells before the infantry had to attack across open ground. 1.Pr suffered heavy losses - 120 killed and wounded.

On December 18th the Russians launched a major attack across the Western Kannas. The 1.Pr forces in the Leipasuo sector were subjected to heavy artillery barrage, but fortunately only small ground attacks.

On December 19th the Russian attack continued.

And on that day at 18:00 Uncle Toivo arrived at the Leipasuo railway station. As the brigade journal notes, he along with 5 officers, 22 NCOs, and 163 men were assigned to the 1st battalion. They were greeted with artillery fire and bombing.

At 12:45 on the next day the 1st battalion left to man the eastern defensive positions of their sector.

December 23rd Failed Finnish Attack

On December 23rd the Kannas Army launched an attack across the Isthmus. Lieutenant General Osterhuis, the Kannas Army commander, felt that while the Russian army was still in disarray that a pre-emptive strike could succeed in Finland regaining its' border. Mannerheim was not that sure.

Mannerheim was right. The command structure was not able coordinate an advance of so large a magnitude. Miscommunication and lack of artillery support resulted in the attack being called off by the end of the day.

The army withdrew back to their positions on the Mannerheim Line.

Uncle Toivo

During the assault Uncle Toivo's 1.Pr brigade attacked southwards from the Leipasuo sector on the west side of Perkjarvi.

1.Pr began taking down their tents at 01:00 on December 23rd preparing for the attack. However due to poor HQ coordination and communications the order to attack did not come until 15:45. The 2nd and 3rd battalions of Pr 1 attacked towards Perkjarvi. They encountered little resistance for 2 kilometers until they came across the Russian defenses at the Perijoki River. The Russians were too heavily dug in to be able to breech their defenses without Finnish

artillery. That did not come. The Finnish artillery fired a sad total of 187 shells during the whole attack on the Leipasuo sector. The artillery support was to have been provided by the 2nd and 3rd battalions of KTR 1, the 2nd battalion of KTR 5, and Rask Psto 3.

Some units however got to just north of Perkjarvi.

At 18:00 the Kannas command cancelled the Kannas attack. The situation was the same in all the sectors. The Finnish artillery could not provide meaningful support and poor communications among the units resulted in an uncoordinated and confused assault.

By 22:00 1. Pr was back behind the lines setting up their tents.

Fortunately Uncle Toivo's 1st battalion did not take part in the attack, having remained on reserve on the Mannerheim Line. Fortunately, as the one day attack resulted in 440 Finnish casualties in Uncle Toivo's Division.

Through the full month 1.Pr estimated that they caused 500 Russian casualties, and destroyed 14 tanks.

For the period from the start of the war to before the December 23rd assault, the Finnish IInd Army Corps suffered 2,082 casualties – 744 killed and 1,225 wounded and 113 lost.

Uncle Erkki and Uncle Aatu

On Uncle Erkki and Uncle Aatu's front, just east of Uncle Toivo, the 4.Pr attacked south from Parkkila. After some initial success, the attack was stopped by the Russian 43rd Division.

During the attack Uncle Erkki's Er Psto 4 provided artillery support for 4.Pr. I assume that their artillery support, like that of 1.Pr's batteries, was not optimum. But hopefully much better than the woeful 187 shells 1.Pr's batteries fired.

Uncle Aatu's Er P4 was part of the 4.Pr attack. Er P4 was ordered to the front lines at 11:30 - but as reserve only.

Fortunately, as 4.Pr suffered significant casualties – 124; as opposed to only one soldier being killed in Er P4.

Christmas & New Years

The rest of December after the aborted Finnish attack of December 23rd, was disrupted only by periodic Russian artillery barrages and bombing runs.

Uncle Erkki

For Uncle Erkki, Christmas Eve was relatively quiet. Every member of the unit got an Unkown Soldier Christmas Package. This was much appreciated by everyone. Mail delivery was still haphazard, and packages dispatched from home took time to arrive.

Christmas Day brought a heavy Russian artillery blessing. Perhaps the Russians, being Orthodox Christians felt the birth of Christ should be celebrated in January ...irrespective, peace and joy was not the message of the day.

The rest of December was spent setting up shelters for the horses and building dug outs.

New Years Eve was uneventful. Some men gathered together and sang "God is My Shelter" and the officer gave God's Blessing.

Uncle Aatu

For Uncle Aatu as well, Christmas was markedly different from what he was accustomed to.

At 18:00 on Christmas Eve the 3rd company was building barbed wire barricades on the shore of Yskjarvi.

03:00 Christmas morning brought a heavy artillery barrage in the encampment area – soldiers Suuroni and Touturi were wounded.

Earlier, at 20:30, soldier Valkari had run away – the situation being too much.

The rest of December was spent building barricades or manning the front line trenches.

Soldier Halkenahi was wounded New Years Eve.

Uncle Toivo

For Uncle Toivo, Christmas Eve brought artillery fire. Christmas Day artillery fire once more; and, a sunny sky filled with Russian bombers.

For the next four days until New Years Eve, there was only light artillery fire and sporadic bombing.

On the Home Front
An Anxious Christmas

Christmas on the home front, like on the battleground, had been different.

There were no fathers or men around the Christmas table. Indeed fare at the table was sparse given the shortage of food and money. While the women folk of course made some gifts for their children, a jolly Santa Claus did not arrive at the door step.

I am sure however that Aunt Saima, Aunt Hilda, Grandmother Hilda, Sirkka and the other children went to the midnight mass at the Forssa church on Christmas Eve even though it was a nine kilometer sleigh ride away. The Forsaa church was a large red brick building with a fine bell tower, a beautiful altar, and stained glass windows depicting the birth, crucifixion, and rise to heaven of Christ.

Certainly there was no Twelve Days of Christmas celebration, where starting 12 days before Christmas, a different delicacy is served at the dinner table on each day.

I wonder how mother and my sisters celebrated Christmas ?

And what about grandfather ? I doubt that he went and cut down the traditional Christmas tree

On Uncle Toivo's sector at 23:00 on New Year's Eve, the Russians fired a few artillery rounds to wish the Finns a Happy 1940.

That it would not be.

January
Trench Warfare
&
Family Warmth

CHAPTER 8

January - Trench Warfare & Family Warmth

January was bleak and cold – both from a weather and life perspective. But the whole country pulled together, bolstered by the fact that all knew that their nationhood and their personal freedom was at stake.

At home everyone's daily life was affected by the war - coping with new interim homes; worrying about their men folk on the front lines - and Russian bombers over the home front; and working filling the jobs that their men had vacated, be that running the farm, working in armaments factories, or indeed serving as home front Lottas.

At the front the fighting had settled into trench warfare. The Finnish soldiers manned the Mannerheim Line, sheltering from Russian bombing and artillery barrages and occasionally rebuffing small Russian attacks.

On the Home Front – Family Warmth

Our family pulled together.

My sister remembers that mom tried to make herself useful cleaning the house and scrubbing the floors.

Mother and My Sisters

Mother and my sisters were doing the best they could, living with dad's Aunt Brita in Kuopio.

While having lodging and care, the relationship was a bit strained as they all lived together in the same small house. My sisters being two and three undoubtedly unsettled the household equilibrium. In this case it was not a matter of leaving in three days as the old adage recommends; "Visitors are like fish, you need throw them out after three days as they go bad."

Sirkka and the Homestead Womenfolk

The Öhman family was together in Sukula. Aunt Saima and her children Martti, Sirkka, George and Irja; Aunt Hilda with Anna Liisa and Maija; grandmother Hilda. Together, they drew comfort and warmth from each other.

As Sirkka relates, other members of the family soon joined them.

One winter day Aunt Alina showed up in the Jaakola yard. When Uncle Tovio was called up to the reserves, she had gone to live in Kavantsaari. They had been living in Kallislahti before. She had brought mothers sewing machine with her. We thanked her for that. With it we were able to get much needed work.

Aunt Tyyne also showed up in Sukula. (Aunt Tyyne had been in Petsamo/Murmansk at the start of the war where her husband was stationed).

Alina and Tyyne got a room to live in at the neighbors.

At the Jaakola house there were also their relatives from Helsinki who were escaping the Helsinki bombings. Their daughter became a good friend of the entire Öhman family, particularly Aunt Tyyne.

Grandpa Juho at the Farm

On the family farmstead grandpa Juho was keeping the farm operating. As Uncle Erkki states in his January 18th letter home;

> *I got a letter from dad. There at home he said it was going well. I am writing to him as well.*

While the farm may have been more or less the same, the Kavantsaari neighborhood had changed. Not only had the women and children left, the army had moved in.

The II Army Corps headquarters of Lieutenant General Harald Ohquist was located in the Saarela manor near the families' church village of Ihantala. While working in the Saarela command centre, Lieutenant General Harald Ohquist slept in the Konkkala manor across the lake.

Kavantsaari itself had received an influx of 1st Division army support units. Kavantsaari was on a railway line just eleven kilometers north of the Back Defense Line, and close to Viipuri. As such it was well located to provide support.

The 1st and 2nd supply units (Tp1 and Tp2) were located in the village itself. Nearby there was a horse hospital, the 2K.HevS – I believe in the Thesleff stables.

The Tesleff manor itself became a field hospital (KS 1). A field hospital company KS Os.15 was nearby.

I am sure Grandpa Juho did well selling milk and produce to the army.

Somewhere Out Here

On January 18th Uncle Erkki was Somewhere Out Here in Kyyrola near Aunt Saima's childhood home, 40 kilometers (a mere marathon distance) south east of Kavantsaari.

His spirit and his conviction that Finland would win was strong – as was his concern for the well being of his family.

Somewhere out here 18/1/1940

Hello to all the family in Sukula

Thank you sister Tyyne for the letter. It is nice that you wrote. It is good to hear how my sisters and brothers are doing. Were you thinking of going to live in the Lehtimaki home? It is good that you were all able to live together. It would be more comforting for Saima and the children if you stayed but you can't do anything about it if there isn't room.

I'm now continuing for mother – Do you want to stay there with Saima and the children or what would you prefer? With Hilda and the girls time must go by happily. There in the middle of the children there must be a lot of activity as they are probably not going to school.

Saima have you received the letter where I thanked you for the parcel you sent with Hilda sister? I wrote yesterday when I received your last letter. In it I heard Aatu was worrying about me, but as they say in the songs, "I will for sure return if God so wishes".

I have been healthy. Tell him we will meet someday when we get the enemy out of our land. Everyone is fighting here with the belief that we will still win and our country will live free.

I trust the children know that father thinks of them every day. Little Irja will sing father home when father comes ...

There is little hope at this time that I will get leave but perhaps later I will be able to come.

I'm asking that Martti and the other children read my letter together.

I got a letter from dad. There at home he said it was going well. I am writing to him as well.

Hello to all you friends, dear wife and children, sisters and mom.

I am keeping well.

Erkki

On the Front Lines
Trench Warfare

January was a quiet month all across the Mannerheim Line. The Russians continued with periodic small attacks, intermittent artillery fire and periodic bombing runs. The Finns held fast, occasionally dispatching reconnaissance patrols into the Russian sector.

Enemy planes continued to fly all day over the front and Finland – bombing and strafing.

Uncle Vilho and Russian Air Attacks

The intensity of the Russian air attack is vividly illustrated in the January 5th sota paiva kirja for Uncle Vilho's anti aircraft battery in Antrea.

January 5th   -24C and clear,

- *9:30 Air alert*
- *10:12   Air attack, 9 enemy planes from east*
- *10:15   Planes above battery*
- *10:16   Battery fires 85 shells without a hit. Planes continue flying towards Imatra*
- *10:22   9 enemy planes approaching from Viipuri towards Antrea*
- *10:26   Planes over Antrea. Battery fires 68 shells without a hit. Planes continue at 2,900-3,000m further up the Vuoksi River*
- *10:35   3 enemy planes approaching from north*
- *10:39   6 enemy planes from Ayrapaa*
- *10:50   9 enemy planes above Antrea from Vuoksi iver*
- *10:53   4 enemy planes approaching from Ayrapaa*
- *10:54   17 enemy planes approaching from Ayrapaa*

- *11:13   Enemy planes expected from west*
- *11:22   Enemy planes expected from the south over Antrea*
- *11:27   Warning 3 enemy planes approaching from west side of Antrea*
- *11:28   3 enemy planes approached from the south-west and turned on the west side of the Vuoksi directly east. Battery fired 37 shells upon which planes fled*
- *11:32   8 enemy planes circling over west side of Antrea*
- *11:38   Warning, 9 enemy bombers approaching south from Imatra*
- *11:40   Warning, 11 enemy planes approaching from the direction of Jaaski*
- *11:45   7 enemy planes over the battery. Battery fired 35 shells. Planes diverted southwards along the Vuoksi*
- *11:47   Warning, 9 enemy planes*
- *11:57   Warning, 4 enemy planes approaching south from the direction of Imatra*
- *12:03   Several enemy planes approaching from Viipuri at 2,600 elevation*
- *12:45   Air alert over*
- *12:50   Air alert, awaiting 5 enemy planes from the north*
- *12:56   Aforementioned planes approaching westwards from Jaaski*
- *13:02   Planes turned south (at 2,600 m height)*
- *13:22   Air alert over*

- 13:30   *Air alert, 3 enemy planes approaching Antrea from Ayrapaa. 3 enemy fighters approaching from west*
- 13:45   *3 enemy fighters now over the Vuoksi Bridge. Battery fired 20 shells. One hit a plane. Plane began to smoke and fell over the east side of Raisala. The sound of planes continued*
- 14:03   *3 enemy fighters approaching west side of Antrea*
- 14:27   *Air alert over*
- 14:34   *Air alert, 3 enemy fighters approaching from the south*
- 14:38   *Air attack 3 unknown planes approaching from the south*
- 15:18   *Air alert over*

Uncle Toivo

January found Uncle Toivo's company manning the Mannerheim Line trenches in the Leipasuo sector.

New Years Day brought rice pudding and plum soup. It also brought clear skies, artillery fire, and for the first time bombing runs over the Leipasuo sector.

The company's sota paiva kirja for January notes:

On January 8th the company sent out a small patrol at 18:30. It returned 3 days later at 10:30 – all members alive.

On January 11th Russian observation balloons were seen overhead for the first time. The observations must have been successful as January 12th brought heavy artillery fire, the most accurate to date.

The company was relieved from the trenches, and returned to the battalions reserve encampment for rest and saunas. An opportunity not only to get clean and warm, but also to get rid of lice.

I wonder if the sauna experience was the similar to the one that Lieutenant Palolampi describes on the Kolla front trenches?

"The small two person earthen sauna with tin sauna grate was fiery hot. We threw our clothes and felt boots out onto the door step and got up on the sauna bench. Steam hissed angrily against the low ceiling whose logs dripped pitch. Occassionally a howitzer shell hit the hill and the sauna shook slightly. Steam hummed, and over the sputtering and sizzling of the sauna stones, one could hear the rat a tat tat of the machine guns and the bark of the artillery guns. We bathed to our hearts content, washing each others back, in between even going outside to massage our skin on the gun powder greyed snow.

The return home on the dark path was lite by a fine Russian night time artillery barrage, as was the norm. The machine guns and canons fired tracer shells which criss crossed like fire flies over the front line trenches. The heavy artillery fired large impressive flares which exploded like celebratory fire works, and by Juutila's sector a search light moved quickly back and forth."

January 17th was extremely cold – 38C and clear. Irrespective it brought heavy artillery fire and bombing and strafing runs. The battalion had finally received some antiaircraft canons two days before but they proved to be relatively ineffective. They did succeed in downing one Russian bomber with the result that the Russians became a bit more cautious. Nonetheless the next day brought bombing runs all day

On January 20th at 05:30 we left for the trenches. Two to three tanks appeared but departed at 14:10 when our artillery started. At 20:00 we sent out a patrol of 11 men. They returned at 01:00. The next day we noticed a new Russian machine gun position only 50 meters away. We heard the noise of rumbling tanks. The following day we stopped a Russian attack, destroying three tanks.

The following week brought light artillery fire. We sent out two successful patrols. Unfortunately one of our men was killed by friendly light machine gun fire.

January 28 brought heavy Russian artillery fire. We sent out a patrol but they could not find an exit through the Russian positions. Heavy artillery fire continued the next two days, along with bombing.

On the last day of month we sent out a 20 man patrol at 20:00. They were successful but suffered 2 killed and 1 wounded.

As the journal notes frequent patrols were sent out to gain intelligence and to get Russian captives.

According to my cousins Uncle Toivo was often part of the patrols that were sent out. He was a fit, brave country boy who knew the Kannas terrain of lakes, rocky knolls, swamps, meadows and fields. Indeed Uncle Toivo was recognized as being one of Finland's best orienteers before the war.

But it must have been a different matter when losing your way, making too much noise, or being too slow to react to a slight disturbance resulted in death, not the loss of championship points.

The Russians as well as the Finns were stalking for prey. Advance or retreat, kill or be killed ... quietly.

1.Pr remained positioned on the front lines at Leipasuo at the end of the month. The brigade command estimated they had killed 800 Russians in January.

Uncle Aatu

January found Uncle Aatu and his Er P4 unit on the Oinala Kyyrola sector of the Mannerheim Line, just east of Uncle Toivo.

January was quieter then on the Leipasuo sector – only light artillery fire and periodic bombing. Reconnaissance patrols however were frequent on both sides.

During the month two of the company were killed and five wounded. One of the wounded was a 2nd lieutenant who shot himself in his foot while he was cleaning his pistol. Another was wounded while on a food run to Kyyrola village.

Uncle Erkki

Uncle Erkki's artillery battalion was now part of the 2nd Division. At the start of the month the Kannas Army command changed the division unit number from 11 to 2 in an attempt to confuse Russian intelligence. At the same time the numbers of the infantry regiments in the division were changed; JR31 became JR4, JR32 became JR5 and JR33 became JR6. The 4.Pr brigade which Uncle Erkki's Er Psto 4 was associated with did not change its' designation - nor did Uncle Aatu's Er P4 battalion.

Throughout January the battalion batteries supported the infantry along the Oinala-Kyyrola sector. The sector was a 7 kilometer wide expanse of the Mannerheim Line stretching from Lake Muolajarvi in the west to Lake Yskjarvi in the east (Valkjarvi where the battalion had been fighting earlier was on the other side of Yskjarvi).

The 3rd battery was located on the west side just north of Oinala; the 2nd near Kyyrola on the shores of Yskjarvi and the 1st in the middle at Sudenjoki. The gun emplacement positions were located about 3 ½ kilometers behind the front line defenses. The fire command location was much closer to the lines. It was connected to the gun emplacement by physical phone wires – a situation that became problematic under conditions of heavy Russian bombing and artillery fire.

Among the infantry units Uncle Erkki's artillery supported was Uncle Aatu's Er P4.

Their 76 mm canons fired at the Russian positions almost every day, destroying various pillboxes, mortar stations and columns. The Russians of course fired in reply but the only major Russian barrage was on January 19th.

The other barrage that occurred was the propaganda barrage. On January 21st the Russian planes dropped the first leaflets exhorting the Finnish soldiers to overthrow their capitalist officers and join the great proletariat dream.

The Finns however knew that the dream was a nightmare despite the leaflets:

They did however look forward to the Russian loud speaker programs from the Russian embankments. The broadcasts gave the men a chance to relax as they knew they did not have to worry about bombing runs nor artillery fire while the broadcast was on.

There was music and exhortations from a honey tongued woman, and enticements from O. Kussinen the leader of the Finnish puppet government Stalin had set up in Terijoki.

Among the promises was; "A collective hut, a cow, and ½ hectare of land".

This prompted one of the Finnish soldiers to shout back that: "That is not good enough. I already have my own cottage, two cows, and a larger piece of land".

The Finnish army also had a propaganda campaign but it as well was ineffective. The hold of the Russian Politruk officers was such that the Russian soldiers would kill themselves rather than surrender (if the Politruk had not already shot them for not attacking). They had been assured that they would be tortured and killed by the Finns if they were captured; and that there was no place in Russia for those who did not give their all for Mother Russia.

On the Food Front

Uncle Erkki's job was to keep the troops supplied with food.

Food rations were critical to keeping the soldiers healthy and strong. The army published a list outlining the recommended daily consumption per soldier (below).

Soldiers Daily Food Ration
Average Calories 4,150

Normal Serving	Daily grams	Alternative Foods
Dry rye bread	500	Fresh bread 600
Butter/cheese	60	
Sausage	60	Pork stew 60, or beef stew 80
Sugar	50	
Tea	2	Coffee 20 or cocoa 5
Barleycorn	125	Flour
Potatoes	600	Cabbage 600 or fresh greens 800,
		or dry greens 100, or peas 175, or
		macaroni 100, or barleycorn 100
Beef	200	Pork 150, or pork stew 100, or
		beef stew 150, or sausage 175, or
		fresh fish 250, or herring 150
Salt	15	
Flour	25	
Tobacco	5 smokes	

The only thing missing from today's balanced diet is fruit. The high calorie count exhibits the vast amount of energy the soldiers needed. But none of the men were fat. In all the photos I have seen of the war, the only fat ones seem to be of higher ranking officers. Indeed it is easy to determine which photos are real, and which ones are staged or come from later movies. All of the real front line soldiers look raw boned, intense, preoccupied.

During the January lull Uncle Toivo's signal's company noted the daily breakfast and evening meal (lunch was also noted but the nature of the food was not specified – undoubtedly it was not a hot meal). As well each day's weather is noted. I have included an extract for part of January to provide a flavor of their food. Military activity was also logged in the log but I have not included that in the extract below.

January 1st : Cloudy -1C; 06:20 rice pudding and plum soup; 17:20 potato soup

Janury 2nd: Snow -3C; 06:00 oatmeal porridge; 17:20 potato soup

January 3rd: Cloudy -5C; 06:00 oatmeal porridge; 17:20 potato soup

January 4th: Clear -15C; 06:00 oatmeal porridge; 17:20 potato soup

January 5th: Clear -18C; 06:00 barley gruel; 17:20 potato soup

January 6th: Clear -16C; 06:00 barley gruel; 17:30 potato soup

January 7th: Clear -22C; 06:00 barley gruel; 17:30 pea soup

January 8th: Cloudy -6C; 06:00 barley gruel; 17:30 potato soup

January 9th: Partly cloudy -19C; 06:00 barley gruel; 17:30 potato soup

January 10th: Cloudy - 6C; 06:00 barley gruel; 17:20 potato soup

January 11th: Cloudy -4C; 06:00 barley gruel; 17:30 potato soup

January 12th: Cloudy +1C; 06:00 barley gruel; 17:30 potato soup

January 13th: Cloudy -1C; 06:00 rice gruel; 17:00 pea soup

January 14th: Clear -8C; 06:00 barley gruel; 17:30 potato soup

January 15th: Clear -34C; 06:00 rice gruel; 17:30 potato soup

The hot meal is almost always potato soup in the evening ; with oat, wheat, or barley porridge in the morning. Meat is only on the menu about once a week. But the meals were hot and filling. Hot rations were particularly critical during the bitterly cold winter days.

The food was brought to the front line positions by horse drawn field kitchens, driven by field cooks such as our Canadian neighbor Oscar Pylkannen. During February the bombing was so heavy that the food could only be delivered at night, if at all.

I remember once as a youngster seeing Uncle Toivo come rushing into the house shouting for food. He must have seen me looking askance at him as he said, " I have to eat frequently. I have stomach problems as during the war we sometimes went without food for many days."

Food was critical fuel – not necessarily an appetizing repast. The officers did eat better however. Lieutenant

Palolampi, recounting his Kolla days, notes that each of the company commanders had their own cook. While the food was usually basic occasionally special feasts appeared:

Then Elo, the cook, put his saved delicacies "on the move" and the table groaned with the repast. There was cold cuts, herring, sardines, liver, dessert pudding, cheese, coffee with pastry - followed by King George or Capstan cigarettes or else cheroot cigars.

.....

Once when some regimental officers and correspondents visited he even had milk – real milk from where I do not know. I had not had milk for almost three months !

While the field kitchens were driven by soldiers / cooks to the front lines, the Lottas often prepared meals behind the trenches. And, on the home front in Central Finland, they baked bread to send to the battle theatres – an average of 100,000 kilos a day ! The bread was primarily dark rye along with some hard tack. True Finnish rye bread is heavy and dense.

My father laughingly commented one day when mother baked dark rye bread as opposed to the sumptuous light rye she usually made, that it reminded him of the army bread. That bread he said was sometimes so hard that it was bullet and bomb proof.

On the front the Lotta's cooking was greatly appreciated. The beef soup was delicious but it did not start out that way as one Lotta recalls:

The food took a week to arrive from Central Finland. The beef was skinned carcasses. The beef was of course from old cows not young ones. The meat was somewhat decayed when it arrived. The only way to make it safe was by boiling it. First we soaked it in vinegar for 6 hours, to remove the horrible smell and sanitize it. We cooked it for many hours to soften it. We added potatoes and turnip. With hardtack and a pat of butter beside the bowl of soup – a delicious repast.

February
A Frozen Hell on the Front-
New Friends at Home

SA-Kuva

CHAPTER 9

February -
A Frozen Hell on the Front -
New Friends at Home

In February war erupted with full fury. At the start of the February Stalin replaced Marshall Voroshilov with Marshall Timoshenko as the People's Commissar of Defense.

Timoshenko now launched a massive attack across the entire Kannas. The first half of the month brought intensive artillery fire and bombing of the Finnish positions on the Mannerheim Line. The second half a massive tank led infantry attack. The Mannerheim Line broke at Lahde/Summa. The Finnish forces retreated to the Intermediate Line and then to the Back Line.

The attack targeted the Finnish home front as well as the front lines. Kruschev comments:

I remember Stalin saying, very typically, "Our air force has been called into action. The assignment is to demolish the Finn supply lines to the front, knock the railroads out of commission, bomb the bridges, and strafe the locomotives. Many bridges have been destroyed. Many trains have been crippled. The Finns have only their skis left. Finns can never be without their skis. Their supply of skis never runs out."

On the Home Front
New Friends

By February life had settled into a routine on the home front.

Mother and my Sisters

Mother and my sisters took life day by day at Great Aunt Birta's home in Kuopio. While there was food and a warm roof over their head, the atmosphere was chilly.

My sister Tellervo remembers that:

Great Aunt had a lovely radio. Unfortunately she would not let us listen to it.

Tellervo however did constantly listen for planes. When she heard any overhead she ran into the house and hide under the table. Apparently mother found this humorous.

When the air raid siren did come on they ran into the woods for protection – not under the table.

Sirkka and the Homestead Womenfolk

The Öhman family relations with their hosts were friendly and warm. As Sirkka recounts:

We had a cabin where we lived. The cabin had four beds, a table, benches and a rocking chair. We cooked on the big house stove.

In the evening we killed off the hours, musing about those cattle cars we travelled in when the home life changed and we fled.

The teacher (Aino Jaakola) came just about every day to sit in the rocking chair and talk.

We were invited into the house's living room to listen to the evening news.

Little Irja got the place of honor on old man Jaakola's lap. Once while the old gentleman was talking Irja said don't babble; and, of course Irja had to ask his forgiveness. The old man said quietly that we understand each other.

In the house their son's son taught my brother Martti all sorts of things – carpentry, trapping beaver, hunting.

Irja missed her father and her home. At night she would cry and sob: "Father come home, and we'll go to Tatataarelle, we'll go upstairs". By Tatataarelle Irja meant Kavantsaari. Irja was not quite three and had problems pronouncing big words.

Grandpa Juho and the Farm

Life in Kavantsaari continued. Uncle Erkki comments in his February 9th letter that:

I've received letters from my brothers now and then and a letter from dad and a package and he hopes that I get a chance to come home.

Arvo was home on leave. He drove wood home as dad is old and it is heavy going for him carry on in his old way; but otherwise I hear things are moving ahead.

Dad is working busily taking care of the home chores with the hired hands.

While just a small village, Kavantsaari was being bombed. The February 20th military journal of Uncle Vilho's nearby anti aircraft unit notes:

- 8:52   *8 enemy planes coming from Kuparsaari*
- 8:54   *Battery fires*
- 9:21   *4 own fighters west of battery (approaching from Kavantsaari)*
- 9:24   *8 own fighters west of battery*
- 10:11   *Airplane noise*
- 10:25   *14 enemy planes from Vuoksi direction*
- 10:30   *Previous planes skirted the battery on the west side after bombing and machine gunning Kavantsaari*

Undoubtedly one of the reasons Kavantsaari was being bombed was the railway and the supply depots. In addition Major General T. Laatikainen had established the new headquarters of his I AK in February in Ahvola just north of Kavantsaari; while Colonel Armas Martola had set up the 1st Division headquarters in the Kavantsaari Thesleff manor.

Some Where Out Here

On February 9th Uncle Erkki was no closer to his beloved home. He was still Somewhere Out There - now near Kyyrola – positive, but pining for his family.

Somewhere Out Here 9/2 1940

My Good Saima

Thank you for the letters. It would be nice if I even got a letter from you every day. I was very worried as it was almost 2 weeks since I had heard anything more from you. I had written 3 letters one after another and have waited for a reply from you.

I've received letters from my brothers now and then and a letter from dad and a package and he hopes that I get a chance to come home.

Arvo was home on leave. He drove wood home. As dad is old it is heavy going for him to carry on in his old way, but otherwise I hear things are moving ahead. Dad is working busily taking care of the home chores with the hired hands.

A shame that Martti had an accident - breaking the neighbors skis. It was sad that he couldn't take his own ones from home so he could ski to his hearts' content. It is good that you paid the houses man for the broken skis so that it's not their loss.

You wrote that the people were friendly towards you and that the house you are living in is good. It is reassuring to know that you are staying in a strangers' place that is hospitable. All of you my kin are in my mind each day. It would be great if one day I was able to come and see you. Perhaps that day will come if we just wait. It would be great if I got a chance to visit. I wonder if little Irja will recognize me.

I got a letter from Aatu. He is doing well. He asked me to come and visit him at his tent. He said he would boil us some coffee – some very hot coffee. But it would be tricky to go looking for him as I don't know for sure where he is located.

I don't have much more to write this time. But receiving a letter from you even one with just a few lines is wonderful when you get it often.

Best wishes to Hilda and girls and Alina, and to Tyyne if she is there. Warm greetings to you and the children, and mother.

Erkki

February on the Front Lines

Life on the front lines in February was anything but routine. It brought an overwhelming Russian bomb and artillery barrage, followed by a massive tank and infantry attack.

The Mannerheim Line was broken through. The Finnish forces retreated to the Intermediate Line.

Russian Artillery and Air Attack

At the start of February the Russians started intensive artillery barrages and bombing of the Mannerheim Line.

Marshall Timoshenko assembled 2,800 canons ranging from 76.2 mm to 280 mm behind the front. ...Mammoth railroad weapons heaved gigantic 12 inch projectiles into Viipuri ... On the average each mile was supported by 80 cannon.... When Timoshenko opened his offensive, 300,000 shells crashed into the Viipuri gateway in the first 24 hours of bombardment. The sound of that opening salvo was felt a100 miles away in Helsinki.

The artillery fire storm continued unrelentingly for the entire month across the entire front in an effort to destroy the Mannerheim Line physically and to pound the Finnish soldiers into a stupor.

In mid February they launched massive tank and infantry assaults against the Finnish defenses.

On February 13th they broke through the Mannerheim Line defenses at Lahde on the Summa sector, but the advance was contained from spreading. At 16:00 on February 15th Mannerheim authorized a withdrawal to the Intermediate Line. The Finns retreated, fighting bitter rear guard battles as they withdrew.

Bombing and Uncle Vilho

Intensive carpet bombing pulverized the front.

The February 2nd military journal for the 2nd battery of Uncle Vilho's anti aircraft unit in Antrea captures the scale of the Russian air attack.

- The Russian air activity is non stop for the entire day light hours during the freezing minus 35C degree day;
- The continuous flights of bombers with their fighter escorts come from all directions – from the east, the south, the north, and even the west.
- Over 200 Russian bombers and fighters fly over during the day - in flights ranging from 6 to 45 planes;
- Periodically 4 Finnish Fokker fighters skirmish among the Russian planes;
- A Russian observation plane flies over.

Uncle Vilho's anti aircraft battery only fires a couple of futile salvos in an endeavour to protect the Antrea town church.

February 2 -35C

- *8:54 Air alert, several bombers over Ayrapaa*
- *9:05 8 enemy planes coming north*
- *9:10 the 8 planes flying towards Raisala now*
- *9:18 Warning over but alert remains*
- *9:35 Air alert, 10 enemy planes coming from the east, 4 of our own fighter planes are circling north of our battery*
- *10:15   Air alert over but warning remains*
- *10:47   One of our Fokkers flying from the north towards the east*
- *11:35   Air alert, 9 enemy planes coming from the direction of Heinajoki*
- *11:40   45 enemy planes flying northward from Heinjoki*

- 11:42   *1 enemy plane flying towards Antrea from the west*
- 11:45   *At least 36 enemy planes between Antrea and Imatra, heading towards Imatra*
- 11:51   *9 enemy planes coming from the north*
- 11:54   *9 enemy planes flew by the battery, about 5km to the east*
- 12:04   *Over 10 enemy planes coming from Ayrapaa*
- 12:11   *Own planes on the move*
- 12:35   *Air alert over, warning remains*
- 12:49   *Air warning over*
- 13:12   *Air warning*
- 13:20   *Air alert*
- 13:30   *4 of our own fighters coming from north*
- 13:40   *Air alert over, warning remains*
- 14:22   *Air alert, 6 enemy planes coming north from Ayrapaa*
- 14:37   *Air alert over, warning remains*

- 14:50   *Air alert, several enemy aircraft coming from Heinjoki*
- 14:35   *6 enemy fighters coming from Vuoksi, turning towards us*
- 15:09   *11 enemy planes circling Enso, own fighter is among them*
- 15:35   *9 enemy planes coming from Heinjoki*
- 15:38   *15 enemy planes coming from Ayrapaa*
- 15:40   *6 enemy planes above Antrea church centre move towards the battery, 9 others move towards east. 1 enemy survey plane coming from east*
- 15:45   *Battery fires 7 rounds*
- 16:02   *Air alert over*
- 21:33   *Air alert*
- 22:05   *Air alert over*
- 23:20   *Battery on the move*
- 05:30   *Battery arrives in Myllypelto*

Defense of the Mannerheim Line

The key western section of The Mannerheim Line stretched for approximately 75 kilometers from Kyroniemi, just opposite Finland's Saarenpaa Naval Fortress, to the Vuoksi River near Pasuri.

Defending it were the 4th, 3rd, 1st and 2nd Finnish Divisions.

- The 4th Division of Colonel Kaila was responsible for the 25 kilometer stretch beside Viipuri Gulf at Kyroniemi, north through Kuolemajarvi, and Hopila to Karhula. On February 1st the Finnish units JR12, Kev Os 4, JR11, Er.7 and JR10 were in the front lines. PPP 5 was in reserve.

- The Russian 43rd, 70th and 113rd divisions were south of them.

- The 3rd Division of Colonel Heiskanen was responsible for the 12 kilometres from Karhula through Summa to Leipasuo. It was defended by JR7, Kev 3, JR8 and JR9. The area was targeted by Russia as the prime point to breakthrough. While the

Mannerheim Line bunkers were quite strong at this point, the area was flat with many large fields and few lakes or rivers. As well the main road from Leningrad to Viipuri ran through it. Thus the effectiveness of the Russian armoured divisions was more similar to operating on the open steppes. The IIAK command of Lieutenant General Ohquist recognized this and had the 5th Division on reserve behind the line.

- South of the line were the Russian 100th, 138th and 123rd divisions.

- Just east of the 3rd Division, the 1st Division of Major General T Laatikinen, protected an 8 kilometer stretch from Leipasuo, just beside Summa, eastwards to Muolajarvi.

- The 1st Division was Uncle Toivo's division.

- The 2nd Division of Colonel E Koskimies manned a longer 30 kilometer stretch from Muolaajarvi through Yskjarvi, Kirkkojarvi, and Punnusjarvi to the Vuoksi River.

- The sector from Oinala, on the eastern shore of Muolaajarvi, to Kyyrola, on the banks of Yskjarvi, was where both Uncle Aatu and Uncle Erkki were fighting.

Opposite the Finnish forces of approximately 60,000 men, guns, and no tanks, were twelve Russian divisions – over 240,000 men supported by innumerable tanks and artillery guns.

Uncle Toivo

On February 1st Uncle Toivo's 1st battalion of the 1st brigade I./1.Pr along with 2.Pr and Kev 5 were positioned in the bunkers and trenches on the Mannerheim Line. 3.Pr and Os B were behind, held in reserve.

The 1st brigade was from Helsinki, the 2nd brigade from Viipuri, and the 3rd brigade from Mikkeli. I do not know how Uncle Toivo, ended up with a Helsinki based unit. But certainly while initially the majority of the men in each brigade were from the area where the unit was founded, as the war progressed they were replenished with those men who were available to be deployed.

In this sector, like in Summa, the geography was more conducive to tank warfare. The railroad between Leningrad and Viipuri ran through the sector, with the Perkjarvi station being just south of the line on the Russian side, and the Leipasuo and Kamara stations just north of the line on the Finnish side.

Opposite the Finnish forces were the Russian 90th and 24th divisions.

Uncle Toivo and his 1st company were in the trenches and bunkers just west of Leipasuo.

February 1st brought the start of mind numbing artillery fire and bombing. On Uncle Toivo's sector the heavy artillery fire and bombing actually started on January 31st, continuing through February. Periodically the Russian tanks probed the defenses, occasionally attacking with infantry platoons.

On February 11th at 12:15 the Russians launched a major attack against Leipasuo at Rave with over 20 tanks and

infantry regiments after over a day of very heavy bombing and artillery fire. The Russians overran the Finnish forward positions, but the Finns were able to take back their positions the next day, only to regroup to their back positions the next day.

On the 15th they withdrew to Perojoki. There the Russians broke through their defenses once more with large tank formations. The 1st battalion counter attacked and took back their positions – for once there was some Finnish artillery support. However at 23:00 the next day the last units withdrew destroying their own bunkers before leaving. They arrived in Kamara at 01:00.

I wonder what Uncle Toivo thoughts were during the trench warfare and hectic battles. Was it like Lieutenant Palolampi's thoughts at Kolla:

The naturally calm and strong nerved men survived somehow, but sleep disappeared for the weaker and more nervous.

One must guard the line for 12 hours in a trench fox hole somewhere on the ridge where it was dangerous to move during the daylight hours.

Then when he got back to rest, his sub conscious nonetheless knew that he had to return.

Back 12 hours later along the same path where the Russian howitzers fired, into the same fox hole where bullets whistled around ones ears, and in front of whom the enemy was digging trenches and moving steadily closer each the night.

Afterwards one had to freeze there for 12 hours and if it happened to be a double shift, another 12 hours more. One could not get food during this time. Adding to this was the numbing cold −minus 40C; 12 hours, and 12 hours...Night ... draw the barbed wire in front of your stations... the enemy firing wildly once again.

Although it was quiet period now at Kolla, the exchange weighed heavily each day on the men. The distance between the foxholes became increasingly longer. The men manned their stations ever more alone. When will my time come?

The mens nerves were strung tight. The perpetual waiting tormented ones mind. Many could no longer sleep at night. They staggered, pale, shaking as they went to their stations and back. Stomachs disorders irritated - ones' nerves continuously strained to their utmost.

Uncle Toivo's defensive trenches were more robust than those at Kolla. On the Mannerheim Line the defenses were concrete and steel pill boxes and bunkers in no man's land as opposed to just trenches buttressed with sand and logs. But after the bombers, artillery, and tanks had pulverized the defenses, protection became only sand trenches and flesh and blood. Even the steel and concrete bunkers did not protect the soldiers. Although the bunkers were not destroyed by the intensive barrage and bombing, it did destroy the Finnish soldiers inside. In many of the bunkers the Russians found the Finns dead inside – untouched except for blood trickling from their eyes. The concussions had been so severe they had killed the soldiers in their places.

Russian Breakthrough at Summa

There are few written narratives by front line soldiers that describe the inferno. Those front line soldiers that survived did not want to revisit the horrible memories.

I did however discover a recounting of the Russian break through of the Mannerheim Line at Lahde in the Nousiaisten Sotaveteraainen Matrikkeli (In the late 1990s each parish published a book written to honour the soldiers from the parish who served in the Talvi and Jatko Sotas. The books provide articles and reminisces of the wars as well as identifying each soldier from the parish who fought in the war). My cousin gave me copy of the Nousiainen book. Although Uncle Toivo did not serve with the Nousiainen unit he settled in Nousiainen after the war and is therefore included in the book – his parish of Antrea no longer exists – lost to Russia in the war.

The Nousiainen men together with men from the neighboring Mietoisten parish made up the 2nd company of JR13. The article describes the reality of the front lines during Russia's break through of the Mannerheim Line.

February 12th: In the small hours of the night the company arrived at the regiments head quarters, which was on the right side of the main road, less then ½ kilometer behind the companies back trenches. In the early morning the company manned the trenches on the side of the main road where the company had constructed stations during earlier duty at the front.

It became clear that it was here that the enemy had broken through the main defenses and was now between the front and back defenses. The only defenses between the men and the enemy infantry and tanks were trenches in the flat sandy soil which the company had themselves dug earlier and a few machine gun pits, in front of which were only quite weak barbed wire barricades. But in the fox holes and trenches there were the Nousiaisten and Meitoisten men. We believed we would force the enemy back, as the Finns had done up to now.

The enemy attack began at 7:00. It pushed more tanks and infantry through the broken crumbled main defenses and at 9:00 the back line became the front line. The battle lasted until late evening. Between 15:00 and 16:00 a tank company rumbled along the roads east side to the front of the company's positions. On the tanks and behind them came infantry. After 16:00 when it could advance no further, the enemy infantry hidden behind the tanks finally jumped into the shell craters. Our company did not have any anti-tank guns available. This days' battle was a gun fight at 300 meters, at times seared by fierce enemy mortar and tank fire.

On February 13th in the dark small hours the enemy easily got its teeth into the tank obstacles located 300 meters away, and began at 6:00 to blow up the sides of the barriers so that the tanks could move through. In the gray dawn, when the enemy began preparing for their artillery barrage, all the men were called up to their positions in the trenches. At 9:30 unbelievably severe canon and mortar fire started. From behind the front barricades, the hated tank canons and machine guns added additional fire. From the trenches began to flow the blood of the Nousiaisten and Meitoisten men and that of their comrades. The medics tried as best as they could to get the wounded back to the back dugout. It now became the wounded shelter and first aid post. From thence they pulled the wounded back with sleds to the company dressing station, the more lightly wounded moving by their own strength.

The company commander asked for artillery fire but none came. The signals/communications men had been trying since the start of the day to keep the phone lines working, but the artillery fire had cut the phone cables, and as a result the artillery spotter could not get his request to the fire commander. As well, the scarcity of shells was such that it was a matter of when the artillery unit got shells, and when they did get them it was usually only a few mortar shells.

At 10:00 numerous tank companies began to roll over the tank barriers firing with all their weapons into our stations.

At 11:30 the horrendous enemy artillery and mortar barrage moved to elsewhere and tens of tanks rumbled forward again firing with all their weapons. No one could count the number of tanks, in any phalanx it consisted of tens of tanks. They formed up in front of our company, as the ground there was smooth sandy soil. Our stations were slightly sloping towards the enemy. The open trenches were not sufficiently deep. Direct shell hits had broken and lowered them, and the snow banks hastily thrown up in front could not provide protection against the tanks fire power.

Casualties grew horrendously. Our bullets klinked off the front of the infantry's ski equipped tank sleds and the machine guns as they moved behind the protection of the tanks.

Our anti tank guns, of which three were to have been brought up front for us, were now far behind. In our defenses, where they were so sorely needed, there were none, only satchel bombs and Molotov cocktails. They, in the absence of better weapons, were good tools in the war, but now they were ineffective as the tanks stood too far away. To get from the trenches to

within attacking distance of the tanks was impossible. Not one of the men who tried got near them alive. An unwarily raised head lost many lives.

At 12:00 our own artillery fired one volley, but it for the most part, sadly went over the tanks. Despite our requests, we did not get another salvo. Our company was in a terrible spot in the trenches with respect to being able to destroy the enemy tanks.

Around 14:00 the tanks got an opening between us and the 6th company on our left. The situation began to become completely unbearable. The company commander sent a notice to the battalion commander: the remaining members of the company can no longer hold back the tide.

It has been said that between 12:00 and 13:00 permission came to pull back. It is impossible to confirm after the fact whether such permission or order came from the battalion commander. At this moment one can picture the conflict that tore at the young and brave company commanders' soul. Withdrawing felt awful, but leaving what was left of the company to destruction by the overpowering all encompassing the tanks, was too heavy a burden. The only thing that could have saved the situation would have been to quickly receive artillery and anti-tank help before the enemy avalanche started.

When help did not come, as heavy as it was to give the command, at 15:00 the remnants of the company began to withdraw from the trenches. Withdrawing from the trenches in front of the rattling and powerful fire and steel breathing tanks was extremely difficult and resulted in more casualties. There were no proper connecting trenches backwards and the ground sloped evenly upwards.

Some of the tanks drove over the trenches immediately when they emptied, while the others remained firing from the sides. The enemy infantry company followed the tanks during this exchange suffering heavy casualties from their own machine gun fire. The enemy company on the right followed immediately *after, and also probably the company on the left side did likewise.*

The previous days breakthrough of the main line, whose spearhead was at the companies back defensive position, had now deepened to behind the back line. The break through of the Mannerheim Line had now truly happened. The break through by the tank spearhead had crushed the Nousiaisten and Meitoisten companys' ability to fight back.

It was not the fault of these men, nor of their commanders. Everyone did their duty without complaint, even in their weakened state after nearly two days without food. The cause was the terrible overpowering force of the enemy; and, on our side, our inability to provide artillery and anti-tank gun fire before the enemy was able to finally plunge into the back trenches.

Some type of terror overcame the distressed, hungry, and tired men's minds. Everyone's heart convulsed with the understanding of what their situation was. It brought a foreboding of how far reaching the consequences of today's battle could be, as today's happening at the Lahde sector back line was the culmination of the enemies huge attack begun in February.

Company casualties during the battle, when one considers both days, were 25 killed, 26 wounded (of whom 2 two died in the hospital); and 9 wounded and ill who were left in the bunkers to become captives. All together the casualties were 60 officers, NCOs and men. In them were the brave young company commander, 2 platoon leaders and 11 squad leaders.

On that one February 13th day, three men from one Nousianen family died – two sons and their adopted son. Their obituary is below:

The poignant verse added by each man's family read:

Mauri Haahti

Mauri is not coming home any more,
He lies dead on the field of honor
Departed hero, powerful, young, truthful,
Died protecting our home
Always will we bless and remember you

Mauno Haahti

Great is our sorrow
Bitter is our longing
A hero's death took you in its hands
In the middle of your flowering youth
With thanks we remember you

Otto Hunsa

We know that with valor you went
Where the battle hotly raged
And under Karjala's stars
There in the frosty snow you remain
Bless oh lord, our loved ones in their unkown resting place

They are honoured with marker stones in the military cemetery in the old Nousiaisen church yard. Neither Otto's, Mauno's or Mauri's bodies were returned. The battle had been so desperate that the unit had to even leave their wounded behind.

Nousiaisen is a small rural community north of Turku. It has one of the oldest churches in Finland built in the 1200s. The first Catholic bishop of Finland, Bishop Henriks was originally buried there...and today is the home of Uncle Toivo's descendants.

Uncle Erkki and Uncle Aatu

Uncle Erkki and Uncle Aatu 's units, were now under the command of the 4.Pr of the 2nd Division. The 2nd Division of Colonel E Koskimies manned a long 30 kilometer stretch from Muolaajarvi through Yskjarvi, Kirkkojarvi, and Punnusjarvi to the Vuoksi River. The line was protected by Er. P1, JP2, Er.P4, 4.Pr, JR4, JR5, JR6 and Er.P5. Kev Os 2 and Er 2 were on reserve.

Opposite them were the 136th, 17th and 142nd Russian divisions.

The sector from Oinala, on the shores of Muolaajarvi, to Kyyrola, on the banks of Yskjarvi, was where both Uncle Aatu and Uncle Erkki were fighting.

Uncle Erkki's Er Psto 4 artillery batteries were providing artillery cover for 4.Pr and JR26. On the 1st of February the 2nd battery was in Kyyrola, the 1st and 3rd batteries were located on the Oinala portion .Indeed the 3rd battery of Er Psto 4 set up their radio and observation post in the Muolajarvi church tower - the family church of Aunt Saima's youth. Now doing Lord's work of a different kind.

Activity on the Oinala sector was intense from February 2nd to the 7th as the journal of the 26th regiment's 1st battalion reflects

> *2.2 06.00 About a battalion – at least 2 companies attacked Tervolaa. Our artillery and soldiers fire stopped the attack. A considerable number of the enemy were killed*

> *3.2 The attack continued. At 18.00 we were beaten back out of our positions by artillery fire. Er P2 and the battalion reserve counter attacked. 8 prisoners were taken. Our own casualties were 5 dead and 12 wounded.*

> *An observation blimp was overhead Taaperniemi all day.*

> *In Rantalla about 150 Russians were killed and wounded – 35 to 40 during the counter attack. They suffered further casualties in the back from our artillery fire*

> *4-6.2 The Russians tried to clear our barricades. Artillery continued on both sides. The battalion continued building barbed wire barricades on the Muolajarvi side*

> *7.2 12.00-15.30 Our artillery fire stopped enemy movement on the Taaperniemi Road*

On February 9th when Uncle Erkki wrote home he was located at Kyyrola just west of Oinala. Uncle Aatu was at Oinala, 15 kilometers away. Given theconfusion of the intense Russian attacks and Finnish counter attacks it is little wonder that he felt he wouldn't be able to find Aatu to have that very hot cup of coffee with him. Although from the tone of his letter the family at home would think that nothing was amiss.

On February 11th the fighting ramped up across the entire 2nd Division front. The 2nd Division report to the 2nd Army Corps on February 11th at 17:30 records:

> " *enemy are attacking after a heavy artillery barrage on the whole front. Pressure highest on the Muolaa and Punnus sectors, and Oinala.*

> *Tanks on sectors from west to east as follows:*

> *Kyyrola 50 ; Muolaa c 50; Punnus c 30; Pasuri 2. Tanks which broke through: at Oinala 1, Muolaa church 10, Punnus right side 14. Destroyed 9 (not confirmed)...*

> *Situation at 17:15*

1. Oinala attacked – enemy broke through. Counterattack underway as of 16:50. At Parkkila there is a small insert, not dangerous

2. At Pallila tanks broke through, likewise at Muolaa but their infantry could not break through with the tanks. The main defensive line is holding

3. On the right 11 tanks are through and are now in front of the rock tank barriers. Two battalions are attacking. In Muolaa church area they broke through. Counter attack underway

4. Attack continuing from Sarkola direction. Communications connection broken since 17:00

5. Airplane activity not too intense, but observation balloons are directing the artillery fire. The anti-aircraft battery shot down 2 bombers – one came down on our side and the other behind their lines

Uncle Erkki's 4th brigade notes the Oinala battle activity.

11.2 Heavy fire enemy reached the line positions. Er P2 threw back an enemy attack. Individual trench fights continued all night. 4. Pr Reserve Battalion 2 on ready but not needed. 1 of the Russian tank group of 11-22 tanks were destroyed.

Our casualties consisted of 139 dead and wounded. Russian casualties were in the multiple 100s.

Our artillery was able to silence the enemy battery. But due to lack of shells they were unable to damage the tank group.

The Russians succeeded in breaking Er P1 at Oinala but together with Er P2 reserve, we retook the positions in the afternoon.

Kaptain E Tirrosen's I/KTR4 and Major L Vahe's Er Psto 4 artillery effectively supported this recapture.

While the above entry highlights the contribution of Uncle Erkki's Er Psto 4's artillery unit, the Finnish artillery's ability to support its' infantry during the war was a problem. Even Lieutenant Poso, the commander of the 1st battery of Er Psto 4, recounts in his book that:

We helped stop the Russian attacks with our artillery fire. But truly more of it was required. Often the infantry was placed in very desperate situations as we were not able to give them artillery support. Not only did we not have enough guns, but there was a huge shortage of shells. We moved the guns around as best we could from where the pressure was the least to where it was the greatest.

Our infantry valued artillery support. The Russian attacks were difficult to stop as their infantry was always supported by tank squads. I remember one company lieutenant pleading with us, " to fire at least a couple of howitzer shells to throw up a few craters. We will take care of the rest with our rifles ."

Unfortunately often we could not even do that.

From the 13th to the 16th attacks continued across the entire 2nd Division part of the Mannerheim Line. While the line held the Russian pressure was such that on the 16th the 2nd Division headquarters received an order to draw back to the Intermediate Line.

The JR26th regiment 1st battalions' journal cryptically notes the activity for February 12th to 16th in Uncle Aatu's and Uncle Erkki's Oinala sector:

12.2

04.00 Artillery fire started

06.40 Enemy attacked overcoming one battery position.

Er P2 Got another company as reserve.

18.30 Enemy withdrew to Rantala where their own artillery fire hit them.

84 enemy killed and wounded, and 6 tanks destroyed.

13.2-14.2

Threw back several tank attacks.

Enemy artillery fire unbelievable.

15.2

Stopped a Russian effort to break through the line.

During the night received an order to prepare to withdraw from Oinala.

16.2

18.00 began withdrawing from Oinala. The Russians did not follow

The 4.Pr command estimated that the Russians suffered 1,500 to 2,000 casualties and lost 7 tanks over the four days of February 11th through the 14th . There is no note on what the brigade's own losses were.

Holding the Intermediate Line

The first half of February had been bright and very cold – minus 20 to over 30 C. The weather warmed on the night of February 21st , starting a heavy snow storm which lasted for a couple of days. At the end of February the snow was a meter deep.

The II Finnish army corps had retreated to the Intermediate Line. Except for a narrow section along the Gulf of Viipuri, the forces moved back about 30 kilometers to a line about 10 kilometers south of Viipuri.

- The command of the Western section of the line was separated into two.
- A Viipuri Lohko running from Humalajoki/Kovisto to Makslahti was placed under JR12 and Kev Os 4.
- To their east the 4th Division had its hands full protecting the stretch from Makslathi through Kaisalahti to YlaSommee.
- Opposite them were still the 43rd, 70th and 143rd Russian divisions.

- The former Summa defensive position had moved back 30 kilometers to YlaSommee and Kamara. The front line was now manned by the 5th Division, the 3rd Division having now moved back to reserve. Two new regiments – JR61 and JR62 had been added as well as the Er 20 battalion.
- In addition, a new 23rd Division under Colonel G Heinrichs consisting of JR67 and JR68 were on reserve north of the 3rd Division.

- Opposite them was were now not only the 100th, 138th,and 123rd Russian Divisions, but also three more – the 84th, 7th and 90th a total of six divisions

Uncle Toivo

The 1st Division to which Uncle Toivo's 1st brigade belonged, was now further north – protecting the line from Kamara, through northern Leipasuo east to the northern end of Muolaajarvi.

VI-KT, X-KT, and XI-KT had been added as battalion size reinforcements. They operated as the Osasto Berg group. The KT units were Kenttataydennys units – or new units put together expressly to provide new troops in company and battalion sized units. These units were normal infantry units but ones that had had limited training, were less well equipped, and consisted normally of old and younger troops. Even with the limited training they had the advantage of having been operating as units. They were commanded by seasoned regular army officers.

The addition of new units was a result of the significant loss of men in the 1st Division and the increase in the size of the Russian assault force. The Russians had added another division, the 80th , to supplement the existing 2 divisions.

Intense fighting occurred all along the 1st division's defensive line.

From the 17th to the 19th heavy fighting occurred on Uncle Toivo's sector. Uncle Toivo's battalion was not in the trenches, being held in reserve.

The night of the 20th brought intensive fighting for Uncle Toivo:

The II/1.Pr confirmed that the Russians were continuously moving more troops towards Mustalampi. On the north east side of Kamara station (now held by the Russians) it was estimated that there were 100 tanks.

On the evening of the 20th 1.D commander T Laatikainen ordered the 1/Pr positioned on reserve south of Kamarajarvi. This in order to be positioned to launch a counter attack westwards over Perijoki through the Mustalampi line to counter the Russian advance. The brigade began immediately marching towards its attack start area.

The attack of Colonel Sihvosen's 1.Pr began at 23:30 on the 20th. The 1st battalion attacked on the left and the 3rd battalion on the right. XI/KT was held in reserve. The assault reached ... and the battalions got to the start of the path to Mustalampi Pien Pero The 1st battalion manned the Mustalampi line and threw back a weak enemy attack from the south.

The northern turning 3rd battalion ended up in a Russian attack in the morning. With day break the battalion fled from the heavy enemy fire, returning in the morning to their start position.

1.Pr afterwards manned the west side of Perijoki with the 1st battalion coming to the Hamalaisenn area, XI/KT to Pien Pero, and the 3rd battalion remained as a reserve on the west side of Kamara village. The defensive positioning was ready at 13:00 on the 21st.

From the 21st to the 24th the Russians attacked the 1.D sector continuously, but all attacks were rebuffed with intense fighting and counter attacks. The 1.Pr together with its' JP2 battalion held the Mustolampi line until the small hours of Feb 24. On the 23rd they suffered heavy losses from Russian tank, artillery and mortar fire.

On the 27th of February at 05:00 they received an order to withdraw. Prior to withdrawing the 1st battalion

counter attacked one last time. At 03:00 February 28th the brigade withdrew from Salonahovi along the Lyykyla to Heinjoki Road.

Uncle Toivo's company fought a rearguard action. This was probably when Uncle Toivo almost got killed. His daughter Paivi recounted to me that at some point during the Talvisota,

Father was withdrawing with his squad across a field. Being winter, he was on skis, pulling a sleigh loaded with ammunition and guns. The pursuing Russians fired a hail storm of bullets at them as they fled over the open snow. Luckily father was not hit.

How his heart must have pounded from exertion- and in anticipation of the searing impact of a bullet −of being killed, or worse still, wounded and left to die on the battlefield.

I wonder what his thoughts were during those difficult February days. Were they like those of Lieutenant Palolampi at Kolla ?

The hell of a major battle is devilish, ones body goes numb from the combination of torrents of rocks, wood pieces, metal splinters, explosives shattering the air, flying bloody human parts; continuous roar , rumble and crackle, torturing the ground which constantly changes shape - and death, everywhere death ...

This is inanimate matter battling against man, war material against life, where ones spirit is shown - is it unconquerable or will the massive force overwhelm it. Man against raging war material and its'crushing storm is weak and small, his connection with the living world immeasurably thin.

Under the roller coaster of aching nerves and battles' numbing drugging, one from moment to moment feels deaths' hand on his shoulder and waits for it to squeeze him tighter. Ones brain beats out only one thought: Hold ones position, do your job, be ready to die at any moment, but do not give way. Against this thought fights another which says: One can not stay alive here, this destruction and devastation of everything is madness, leave this insane place, save yourself, one can not fight against machines and a million horse power explosive force, as one is human .

This is deaths kingdom, where there is only one heartening feeling and knowledge: Brothers in arms, suffering together.

Uncle Erkki & Uncle Aatu

The 2nd Division now stretched from the north end of Muolaajarvi to Ayrapaajarvi and Sikniemi and from thence to south of Pollakka on the Vuoksi River. Upon withdrawing on February 16th to the Muolajarvi – Ayrapaajarvi – Salmenkaita portion of the Intermediate Line, there were some quiet days. The men spent the time resting and refurbishing their equipment.

Both Uncle Erkki's and Uncle Aatu's units were positioned on the front line between Muolaajarvi and Ayrapaajarvi. Uncle Erkki's artillery batteries were a kilometer behind the front lines at Koprala. Uncle Aatu's Er P4 were in the trenches on the western shore of Lake Muolaajarvi.

The Russian 136rd and 8th divisions were opposite them south of Muolaajarvi.

In the morning of the 18th the Russians engaged 4.Pr at Kangaspelto to get a first feel for the new line. That day Uncle Aatu's Er P4 infantry battalion was relieved from their positions on the Muolaajarvi shore and moved to reserve.

On the 19th enemy scouting continued as they tried to determine the best points on the line to attack. While the Russian attack was muted, some fierce fighting occurred. Russian bombing and artillery fire was intense. The tired units not at the bunkers initially slept in houses in the Koprala village. This small comfort during the bitter cold came to a sudden end when on the night of the 19th a Russian bomb hit one of the houses, killing 15 of the resting Finnish soldiers. Thereafter any rest was taken in tents.

On the 20th the Russians attacked Ayrapaajarvi, and the next night Salmenkaita. In both cases the attacks were rebuffed. On the evening of the 20th Uncle Erkki's Kev Kol moved from near Korpala to Linkerinlammi near Riistseppala.

On the 21st the Russians attacked the 4.Pr s Koprala sector. Uncle Aatu's Er P4 was pulled out of reserve to help. The attack was stopped. During the attack Uncle Erkki's artillery units were under heavy Russian shelling. Two of the 2nd batteries horses were hit. Artilleryman Nyberg of the 3rd battery shot himself.

On the 23rd the Russians continued the attack with battalion and regiment strength forces, breaking through the 4.Pr line. The fiercest fighting occurred at Kaenneimi on the west side of Ayrapaajarvi. With the help of JR5's 2nd battalion 4.Pr was able to recapture their positions and reclaim the line by nightfall from Russian 136rd division. During that day Uncle Erkki's artillery battalion drew back its' 2nd battery from Koprala to Pilkapaa, and its' 3rd battery from Yksjarvi to Riistseppala. The 1st battery remained in its' position in Koprola.

On the 24th the Russian attacked from both directions. 2nd Division was able to hold the lines, although a battalion strong Russian force broke through at Kaenniemi before being rebuffed by a counter attack. On JR4s sector nine Russian tanks drove into the defensive line but withdrew when their infantry did not follow them.At Salmenkaita the enemy artillery fire was so intense that the fortifications began to collapse and six of the bunkers domes were shot through.

During this inferno Uncle Erkki's Kev Kol withdrew from Liemajarvi to Risteseppala.

On the 25th Mannerheim reorganized the Kannas Army to provide quicker responsiveness. A new army corps – the I AK was established under T Laatikainen. IAKE took command of 1.D and 2.D. 4.Pr and Er P4 became part of 1D. Now Uncle Erkki, Uncle Aatu and Uncle Toivo were all part of the same division - 1.D, commanded by Colonel A Martola. With the realignment, the 1.D eastern line now ran north from Ayrapaajarvi to Heinjoki, while the western border ran from Pien Pero north to Lyykyla.

The change in Finnish command had little effect on the Russians as they continued to attack in force across all sectors on February 25th and 26th . They gained small break throughs which the Finnish forces were unable to retake. In the 4.Pr sector - the east side of Muolaajarvi - the enemy succeeded in breaking through with tanks at Kaenmaa. The brigade was unable to dislodge them.

On the 26th and the 27th the Russians could not make any further inroads. All the Russian attacks were rebuffed.

Nonetheless at 12:40 on the 27th orders were received from IAKE to withdraw from the Intermediate Line to the Back Line. Withdrawal began at 22:00.

The1st battery withdrew from its' position behind the Intermediate front lines at Koprala where it was supporting JR4's 1st battalion. A major concern as they withdrew was the Russian bombers hitting one of the wagons loaded with canon shells. Prior to withdrawing the infantry battalion set fire to what was left of the village of Koprala. The villagers' worries about their homes were at an end. The scene as the soldiers left must have been similar to that described by another soldier tasked with setting fire to his own village.

A buzzing hum came from the burning village buildings and the crackling of the burning houses was terrible, covering all the other sounds. The glow of fire balls made the entire sea side so bright that we instinctly skied closer to the shore of the island, where we rose up to the land.

We stood there on our skis looking at the panorama to the south east – the sky and the snow drifts glowing red as the entire village burned in the background, and in front of us the future rose as gloomy as the darkest night. I turned my skis towards the forest and told the boys that we must leave. And we never looked backwards.

Concerning the Other Men of the Family

Uncle Arvo

During this period Uncle Arvo as well joined the front lines. His Kantakortti (military record) for this frenzied period is incomplete and sparse so I do not know where he served. The first entry in his records for the Talvisota is that he was with the 3./Pion Koulu K on February 15, 1940. The records note that he took part in the battles of Nuijamaa, Kuparsaari, and Mannikkala.

The start of his draft service is not noted. But he had been called up sometime after September 9, 1939 for his conscription service, probably on the first day of the war - November 30th. Much like a soldier in Kemijarvi comments sixty years later in the Kemijarvi Veterans Memorial book:

> " I went to my draft registration in September '39. I was left waiting for when I would be called up. According to traditional practise I expected that to be December 20, 1939. Finland's situation demanded otherwise. War erupted. Russia attacked Finland. Immediately on the first day of the war I received the command to gather at Kemijarvi from whence we left right away for Salla to be outfitted.
>
> ... after two weeks of training we departed for Loytovaara where the Russians were fighting fiercely to extract themselves from a motti. Prior to departing the company commander addressed us saying, "Tonight you are getting into a train. Gather any extra clothes and send them home. You are now leaving for there where you will be forced to look death eye to eye."
>
> Those words remained in my mind, and live there still today.

Now I never did get a chance to ask Uncle Arvo when he actually was called up. But despite the lack of any entries in his kantakortti he was in the army far before the February 15, 1940 entry in his record. According to Uncle Erkki's February 9th letter:

> Arvo had been home on leave.

And in his March 3rd letter he comments that:

> Arvo I believe came to visit you there before he went for his noncom schooling. He wrote that at the same time that he might be able to come to your village.

Although he appears to have been slated to receive some NCO training at the Pioneer school February 15th, he was sent to the battlefield, - probably along with all the other members of 3./Pion Koulu K.

At this point, the Finnish military situation was dire and all available manpower was sent to the front lines – young recruits and old men with minimal training.

The Pioneers were the Finnish Combat Engineer Corps. They supported the front line troops constructing and demolishing minefields, entrenchments, pontoon bridges, roads, etc. Some Pioneer companies focused on road and bridge repair and maintenance (even plowing the winter roads), not combat engineering.

I, in my very first days of trying to understand the war, was under the misconception that the Pioneer units did not see direct action. When I was talking with Uncle Arvo in 2008, I mentioned that he was probably constructing fortifications. He however said:

> "No, no. We were not just involved in construction, we were also directly involved in the fighting".

And that Uncle Arvo certainly was. The battles of Nuijamaa, Mannikkala, and Kuparsaari are noted in his kantakortti for the short four week period he was in the field. In addition there is a note for Kuolemajarven Os "Misuri". I have not been able to determine what this means. It doubtless refers to the operations of a special unit (Os means group), as by the time Uncle Arvo was in the battlefield, the Kuolemajarvi sector had already fallen to the Russians.

I have not been able to determine precisely where 3./Pion served. However it was part of the I AK, and appears to have been dispatched where most needed. The battles noted in Uncle Arvo's kantakortti are all in the 1st army corps area. Mannikkala is near Tali and was the location of fierce battles by 3.Pr at the end of the war, while Kuparsaari was in 4.Pr's sector. Both brigades were part of the I AK.

I was also confused about the reference to the Nuijamaa battle. Nuijamaa was behind the front, indeed it is at the current border with Russia. No battles occurred there. Nuijamaa is however on the Saimaa Canal. The Saimaa Canal has a major system of locks 10 kilometers from Tali. On March 2nd when the Russians were advancing against Tali, the Finnish engineers opened the gates to the Saimaa Canal flooding the low lying terrain to a depth of 3 feet, including the areas around Tali (and the Mannikkala battle refered to in Uncle Arvo's kantakortti) . This reduced the ability for the Russian tanks to maneuver. Tali, with low lying and sandy fields, otherwise was perfect country for the Russian tanks.

Uncle Arvo was a strong, courageous, and able man, with a fierce will to persevere. His character was undoubtedly taxed during the bitter February and March weather as he laid mines and repaired barbed wire barricades in no man's land during lulls in the battle; frantically set new mines while under enemy fire in an endeavor to blow up the attacking tanks; and under strafing fire from Russian fighter planes opened the Saimaa Canal locks in the freezing March weather.

Uncle Kauko

Uncle Kauko was a driver with Rak P4, the 4th construction battalion of the IV AK north of Lake Ladoga. He was 27 at the start of the war.

Prior to the start of the war the defensive lines at the northern end of Lake Ladoga were incomplete. Work was undertaken to upgrade the defenses from Salmi in the south through Kitela / Impilahti to Janisjarvi and from thence north east through Loimala to Suojarvi.

A major task was upgrading the main defensive line from the northern tip of Lake Ladoga to Janisjarvi (20 kilometers); and, later upgrading the Tolvajarvi defenses. The work primarily entailed building tank obstacles, barbed wire barriers, log barriers, and field defensive

stations. Not surprisingly little work was done constructing bunkers or pill boxes as the weather was too cold for concrete construction.

The Rak P4 battalion was established as a separate construction unit as the temporary army workforces that were initially used ended up being quickly returned to their primary task – fighting. The battalion was composed of civilian workers working under military direction and command. Led by Engineering Lieutenant K Kayhko, the military managed the work units and their distribution; oversaw the building and work methods; and provided the building material, housing, and food.

The workers were paid day labourers and paid volunteers. One group (the Korhonen group) was composed of conscientious objectors and disciplinary/social misfits. Some of the workers left the construction groups volunteering in December to serve as soldiers in Osastao Eloma; and in February in Osasto Wahlfors at Lemetti.

There were nine work groups, each associated with one of the following areas:

1. Salmi
2. Uuomaa
3. Kitila
4. Syskjarvi
5. Leppasyrja
6. Loimola
7. Suvilahti
8. Suojarvi
9. Tolvajarvi

In addition to the work companies the battalion included a separate truck company.

The central warehouse was in Harlu on the main defensive line, five kilometers south of Janisjarvi.

Uncle Kauko joined the battalion on November 11th from the Karjalan Kartti Regiment. He served as a head quarters driver. No battles are listed in his kantakortti. While the service was not life threatening, certainly it must have been taxing working in the bitter northern winter, sleeping in cardboard tents, avoiding periodic bombing runs.

Father

And where was father during all this time ? That dad never told me. All I remember as a youth was that he had a jam jar full of medals and a military compass and military wrist watch.

At the start of the war dad was 31, an engineer, working with the Finnish Railway responsible for track operations out of Viipuri.

Operation of the railroads was critical during the war, and as such dad was placed in the Home Guard with responsibility for the operation of portions of the Finnish Railroad. And, at some point he also was a civilian officer on one of the Panzer trains. But the details I do not actually know, as no entries were made in the kantakortti for Home Guard service, nor did the Home Guard keep military unit journals. No books seem to have been written about the railway operations during the war.

Regarding his Panzer train service:

Firstly, I had no idea dad had anything to do with Panzer trains until I was in my twenties visiting my Uncle Yrjo in Finland. Uncle Yrjo took me to the Panssarimuseo in Parola near Hameenlinna. He pointed out an armoured panzer railway car saying that dad had commanded one. Upon returning home I asked dad whether this was true. He said *"Yes"* but didn't offer any further information – and at that point in my life I didn't have any further questions myself.

The car and the associated locomotive looked like something out of Doctor Zihvago and the Bolshevik Revolution. And indeed it was. The first panzer trains came to Finland at the start of the Finnish Civil War. They were used by both the Reds and Whites – normal locomotives and freight cars which had been fortified and armed.

Before the Talvisota the army formed two panzer trains from the old revolutionary ones - Pansaarijuna 1 and 2 for use on the Kannas and north of Ladoga.

Dad's kanttakorti notes that he spent 25 days from July 20th 1939 to August 13th in Perkjarvi with the P7/KTR artillery unit receiving training for the panzer train.

The Talvisodan Historia notes that both 1.Pans.Juna and 2.Pans.Juna were part of the Suojajoukot of IIAK. The units were formally commissioned on October 9th 1939 in Sainio.

Each train actually consisted of two trains – the actual panzer train and a separate maintenance train. The latter

even had its' own sauna. The panzer train had a command car; an artillery car with a 76mm anti aircraft gun and 6 machine guns; a machine gun car with 8 to10 Maxim machine guns; an artillery car with 37mm Maxim guns; the engine; and a ballast wagon with gravel and coarse stone. The cars had 20 mm thick steel plating.

Panssarijuna 1 had 4 officers, 25 NCOs, 50 men, 1 railway ministry official, and an administrative Lotta. With the exception of Lotta and the railway official the entire complement consisted of military personnel. (The railway rep was responsible for helping with train movement. I am mystified as to why there was a Lotta on the train).

Panssarijuna 2 had a strength of 3 officers, 22 NCOs, 47 soldiers, 8 railwaymen, and 1 ministry official.

Probably father was with Panssarijuna 2. Or possibly there were armoured cars attached to regular trains carrying critical supplies to the front lines, in which case he would logically be in charge of the armoured car. Unfortunately while there is a sota paiva kirja journal available for Panssarijuna 1, the one for 2 has been lost. There is only one source I have found on panzer trains – a booklet by Jouni Sillanmaki entitled Panssarijuna Suomessa. The four pages on the Talvisota provide some insight into the usage of the trains during the war.

During the Talvisota Panssarijuna 2 operated primarily in the IV AK area at the north end of Lake Ladoga. However for the month of December it provided support for the II AK on the Kannas. It was primarily in the Valkjarvi area protecting the 2nd Division units including Uncle Erkki's 4.Pr. At Salmenkaita its' AA gunners downed four Russian planes. At the end of December it moved to Impilahti taking part in the Kittela motti. On January 23rd it was supporting the 13th Division at Lemiti.

From the beginning of the war Panssarijuna 1 was with the 12th division on the Loimalla front. Early in December it was quickly moved to support JR 36 during the Kolla battles. The train seized up and had to be moved to Kuopio for refitting on February 4th . It remained there being refitted until near the 2nd week of March. On March 11th the train came under heavy bomber attack. The engine was thrown off the track by one bomb while another bomb landed between the machine gun car and the artillery car damaging the artillery car.

Panssarijuna 2 moved to Kolla to replace train 1. Near the end of the war Panssarijuna 2 was moved to the vital Eisenvaara railway junction to provide it with anti aircraft protection against the Russian bombers and fighters.

The armoured trains had a dubious reputation for effectiveness. While they had anti aircraft guns they did not have a great deal of success. Once they accidentally shot down one of their own planes. The pilot was able to successfully eject. He angrily confronted the train crew, heatedly exclaiming;

" *Sure you bastards can hit your own plane, but not the enemy !! "*

The infantry officers did not like the Panzer trains, calling them " *Bad news birds"* because the trains always attracted heavy Russian air, tank and artillery fire. Indeed on February 4th apparently one hundred and sixty nine Russian fighter planes spent the day attacking Panssarijuna 1. One hundred and sixty nine fighters is a rather unbelievable number. Perhaps the Russian fighter command decided to attack the train for target practice and diversionary light entertainment. The train survived.

Erkki Palolampi in his book Kolla Kesta writes about the Panzer train during a December battle:

" *As we were defending against a fourth violent attack, at least some of our unit was moving forward at the same time. The Russian tanks drove clanking onto the road and simultaneously tried to move into the forest. Our panzer train moved towards them on the railroad. The men peered at it closely as it was a source of protection.*

The firing was fierce and then someone started to shout that the tanks were firing back !! They were unstoppable !! the men's eyes were wide open with horror, others saw their terror and a shout went out from the men that nothing could stand against them – the tanks were coming, the tanks were unstoppable !! The men started to wade through the snow and to ski backwards, unhearing of the officers shouting and swearing. The panic spread ...machine guns were left at their stations, tents were left standing, sleds were left behind with their supplies, everyone had but one objective – to get away from under the monstrous tanks. The belief that the panzer trains firing would destroy the tanks was unfounded, and a paralyzing fright took hold of other units.

This opinion of the effectiveness of the trains was shared by father. He mentioned to my brother that:

" *Our firing was not that effective, but the sight of the heavily armoured cars and the noise of the big guns made the men feel better.*"

Nonetheless the Panzer trains played their part both on the front and in protecting key railway junctions.

The Red Army itself had five Panzer trains on the front.

Railway operations:

When, where and for how long dad served on the Panzer train I can't confirm. But I do know that he was responsible for the operation of portions of the railway network. The rail lines were vital for Finland being able to supply ammunition, materials, and men to the front; and transporting wounded soldiers and fleeing civilians back from the front. A favorite target of the Russian aircraft was the Helsinki - Viipuri rail line, crowded with civilians fleeing west and military traffic moving east.

I can confirm that dad definitely saw action. He was awarded two medals for valour during the Winter War.

One medal is The Medal of Liberty "Vapaudenristi"– First class. It was the highest award a noncombatant (i.e. Home Guard) could get. It was presented to dad by Marshall Mannerheim himself in 1940 after the war.

Dad has another medal – the Medal of Merit for Civil Defense - for valor during the Winter War. Dad was awarded the medal, with ribbon on January 15, 1941, by Lieutenant General Sihvo, the commander of the Finnish Civil Guard. The medal shows a man with a shield protecting his family. It is the "Suomen Vaestonsuojelun II Luokan Ansiomitali". "Finnish Civil Guard 2nd Class Medal for Bravery".

Most of the medals for the Winter War were awarded in late 1940 or early 1941 as many of the actual medals had not been defined until after the Winter War; and, there was little time for awards ceremonies.

ISÄNMAAN NIMESSÄ

ja

SUOMEN PUOLUSTUSVOIMAIN YLIPÄÄLLIKKÖNÄ

olen minä

ansioistanne sodassa 1939-1940

antanut TEILLE

Kaarlo Henrik

Tuira

1 luokan VAPAUDENMITALIN

Sotamarsalkka *Mannerheim*

My brother George says he once asked Dad how he got all of these medals. Dad simply said,

"That he just happened to be around when they were being handed out."

He did however later recount why he received the medals:

The Mannerheim medal was for defusing a bomb dropped by the Russian bombers on a train. The bomb became wedged between two railway cars effectively paralyzing the train and blocking the railway line. Dad said he vividly remembers that it was still hot and sizzling. Dad lifted it out carefully and defused it. Was it on a supply train on the railway line from Helsinki to Viipuri – or shades of the Panssarijuna 1 incident of March 11th - was it actually on Panssarijuna 1 ?

Dad also said one of the medals was for saving a supply depot. A railway supply depot got hit by incendiary bombs dropped by the Russian Air force. As the bombs came through the roof, dad grabbed a shovel and started tossing them out as fast as

they came in and got the other people organized to do likewise. (According to my brother, incendiary bombs do not explode. They are filled with a sticky flammable liquid and are intended to instantaneously start fires wherever they strike I do not know what was being stored in the depot.)

My beloved brother George received dads' bravery and service medals (As behoves one who is the eldest son and is a former member of the Royal Canadian Mounted Police). He has the medals stored in a safe place – in a jam jar in a drawer just like dad did !!

So that is all I am able to relate about Panzer trains, railway operations and dad during the Talvisota.

...but not quite...

I was just rereading a fine old leather bound book of grandfather Georg's. Dad has enscribed the words "Toin muistoksi kodistamme Viipurista 14/3 – 40: Brought by myself from Viipiuri March 14, 1940 as a remembrance of my home".

Was dad actually at his childhood home in Viipuri the day after peace was declared ? The peace terms stated that the main forces of the Finnish army must withdraw 1 kilometer from their front lines immediately after 11:00 a.m., and at 10:00 a.m. on March 15 begin withdrawing back to the new border. However the rear guard did not have to withdraw until 06:00 on the morning of the 15th . The peace terms did not require the Finnish army to surrender its' arms.

Father being responsible for sections of the railroad must have gone with a train to Viipuri after the peace to bring back armaments / material for the Finnish government / military. Our grandparents' home was less than a kilometer from the Viipuri railway station (Dad and mom's own home had of course been destroyed by a Russian bomb on the first day of the war). At the end of the war Viipuri was still in Finnish hands. The Finnish front lines were at Patterimaki just south of dad's childhood home.

It must have been a heart rendering moment when he selected the book.

CHAPTER 10

March
Inferno before the Peace

March
Inferno before the Peace

March was a desparate month as Russia drove the Finnish forces back on the Kannas. Now they attacked in force across the frozen sea of Viipuri Lahti as well as on the land. The Finnish soldiers gave ground grudgingly as all knew that if the Russians broke through there would no longer be a home front. Finland would be no more.

On the Home Front
Waiting

On the home front, March was a period of anxious waiting. While news about the battles was minimal, the increase in bodies and the injured soldiers returning indicated that the war was not going well. Indeed they knew that the Finnish Army, although fighting courageously, had had to abandon the Mannerheim Line and was now retreating slowly towards Viipuri.

Mother and My Sisters

Life for mother and her sisters in Kuopiio had settled into a routine of living with father's aunt, fleeing from Russian bombing runs; and, anxiously awaiting further news about father and mother's brothers.

Sirkka and the Homestead Womenfolk

Life was "routine" for the Homestead Womenfolk as well. In their case they did not have to worry about bombing as they were in the countryside far from any city and the front. Aunt Saima and Uncle Erkki had been thinking of her and the older children returning to Kavantsaari. But on March 3rd he was no longer of that opinion:

I wrote before that if I got permission that you could go to our home but perhaps it is best that you stay there with the children.

I'm sure dad will manage somehow as there are the hired hands to take care of the cattle.

Grandpa Juho and the Farm

Grandpa Juho was being forced to finally to abandon his cherished home. Uncle Erkki notes in his March letter that:

> I heard that in the Antrea parish that any old folks and the children still there have to leave. Dad as well may have to leave and join you.

Indeed Grandfather Juho did leave, driving the cattle and horses with his herdswomen towards Forsaa. As cousin Sirkka recounted;

> Grandfather Juho did not leave until March 1940, bringing the cattle and horses. At that point grandfather had 2 hired hands (women) working on the farm helping him. Together they drove the 12 cows and the horses to Forsaa. The helpers drove the cows.
>
> Near the end of the trip grandfather separated from the herds women – off to visit old friends, leaving the cattle to the cowherds. Unfortunately the herdswomen were never seen again – nor was most of the herd. While the cows may have arrived in the Forsaa, we were only able to find 3 of them (This was a major loss). We don't know what happened to the rest of the herd. I saw one of the herdswomen afterwards in the town but she avoided me.

At the end of the war on March 13th the front lines were at the Saarela Kartano – less than 10 kilometers from the farm.

Somewhere Out Here

On March 3rd Uncle Erkki was in Kuparsaari on the Back Line. Irrespective of the situation, still positive about life and concerned about the welfare of the family.

Somewhere out here 3/3/1940

Dear Saima

Thanks for your letter. I got it today. I know that you wait as anxiously for my letters as I do for yours.

I haven't yet got the last parcel you sent. Brother Arvo also sent a parcel which I haven't gotten but perhaps they'll still come in time unless for some reason they've been lost.

I wrote before that if I got permission that you should go to our home but perhaps it is best that you stay there with the children.

I'm sure dad will manage somehow as there are the hired hands to take care of the cattle.

I heard that in the Antrea parish that any old folks and children still there have to leave. Dad as well may have to come there / leave. But don't worry, when peace returns to the land the home matters will get organized again.

Even I hear that payment / wages will be arranged so that the base family payment will be increased by 150 markkas for the first child and another 100 markkas for each additional child. The monies will be sent to the home somehow although I don't know how it'll be done.

I guess Hilda sister is there with her girls. I got a letter sometime back from Aatu. He said if he gets leave he'll arrange for his family to go to Sweden. I assume he's written to my sister (Hilda his wife) about that.

Arvo I believe came to visit you there before he went for his noncom schooling. He wrote that at the same time that he might be able to come to your village.

I have strongly hoped for leave so that I can come and see you there – perhaps someday.

Now I have nothing more to write other then dearest greetings to you and the children as well as mother and my sister and any other of our relatives who are still there.

Erkki

March
On the Front Lines - Inferno

The situation by February 27th was bleak. All units were in the process of retreating to the Back Line. The withdrawal from the Mannerheim line had affected the morale of men:

"The line was our strength – now we must believe only in own strength."

Finland had an army of 90,000 protecting the western Kannas. Russia was attacking fiercely with an overwhelmimg force of men, tanks, artillery and planes. On February 27th

- The 4th Division was holding a line from Uuras to Ylasommee. The unit composition had not changed.

- The 5th Division was defending a short 7 kilometre stretch from Ylasommee to Nakkijarvi. Its' primary force was JR15 and OS J. The 3rd Division was being held in reserve north of Viipuri.

- The 23rd Division, now under the command of Colonel V Oinonen, was holding the five kilometre section from Nakkijarvi to Pien Pero. It was here that the main Russian thrust was aimed. The division now had JP3, JR13, JR14 and part of JR61, as well as its original JR67 and JR68 regiments.

- The 2nd Division was now defending a shorter line from Ayrapaajarvi to the Vuoksi.

- The 1st Division under Colonel A Martola was still holding the stretch from Pien Pero through Muolaajarvi. It had also taken over the defenses from Muolaajarvi to Ayrapaajarvi. The former 2nd Division units of 4.Pr, Er 1, Er 2 and Er 4 were now under 1st Division command.
- X-KT had been disbanded. They had incurred heavy losses as a result of their position and inexperience. The X-KT troops still remaining were moved to other units to replace men they as well had lost.

- Opposite them were five Russian divisions.

- Now Uncles Toivo, Erkki and Aatu were all part of the 1st Division. Uncle Arvo, thrust into the battle just two weeks earlier, was part of the 1st Army Corps, to which the 1st Division belonged.

Uncle Toivo

All through the first week of March Uncle Toivo and his unit fought a fierce rear guard action as the brigade withdrew slowly to the Back Line Line. At the end of the week the exhausted 1st battalion was slated to go on reserve to get some rest at Ihantala. But this was not to happen. As soon as they arrived at Ihantala they were seconded to Lieutenant General Karl Oesch's Ranniko Ryhma to stop the Russian break through across the Viipuri Lahti.

A summary from the battalion's journal outlines the action during the 1st week of March.

- *On March 1st a patrol sent out was thrown back by the Russians after several hours of fierce fighting. The 1.Pr set up the Lyykyla defense line. The 1st battalion was on the front lines when the Russian attack came from the Heinjoki direction.*
- *On March 2nd the 1st brigade withdrew at 19:00 under a heavy Russian attack, arriving at their new positions at 23:45. About 400 to 500 Russians died. Finnish losses were relatively light. At night the Pioneer unit mined the Lyykyla-Naatala-Patakahja Road.*
- *On March 3rd the brigade withdrew to the east side of Lyykylajarvi under a fierce Russian attack supported by heavy artillery and howitzer shelling. About a 1000 Russians were killed. The 1st battalion withdrew to Leinola – Saunalahti- Kantimylly.*

- On March 4th the Russians attacked along the Lyykyla-Mannikkala Road which was being defended by the 1st and 2nd battalions.
- On March 5th the 1st battalion was ordered to continue to hold the line. The tent hospital was set up at Toronkilampi.
- On March 6th and 7th the 2nd battalion joined the 1st in defending the line from the Russian attack.
- From March 4th to the 7th there are no entries in Uncle Toivo's company's military diary. (Ones life and the life of ones men was too important to risk laying down ones rifle to take make even a few cryptic entries in any journal).
- On March 7th the 1.Pr was ordered to move to Ihantala - Uncle Toivo's childhood home - as reserve for the Kannas Army.
- On March 8th at 05:00 Kaptain E Palonheimo the commander of the 1st battalion along with his troops – exhausted from thirty days of continuous fighting - arrived at Ihantala to rest and be reserve for the AKI

I wonder if Uncle Toivo was able to make a quick visit to the family farm, just seven kilometers away; or, at a minimum visit his "Rakas mummo's" grave in the Ihantala cemetery. It must have been unsettling to be a battle scarred exhausted soldier marching through the land of ones ancestral home and joyous boyhood.

But Uncle Toivo was probably not able to visit home, as instead of resting, the 1st battalion was seconded to the command of the Rannikko Rhyma now commanded by Lieutenant General Karl Oesch.

At 15:00 on the March 8th just ten hours after arriving at Ihantala in an overnight march, the 1st battalion received the order to move to the Viipuri Lahti front.

The 1st battalion was placed under the command of Major Varko – Battle Group Varko (The rest of 1.PR was under Colonel Ruotsalo). Battle Group Varko was part of the 4th Division Tervajoki Lohko commanded by Colonel Johan Arajuuri. The Tervajoki sector stretched fifteen kilometers westwards from Tienhaara (outside Viipuri) to Nisalahti. Battle Group Varko was on the western end. Colonel Ruotsalo was located in the middle, while JR11 under Colonel Inkala held the eastern end.

To the west of Battle Group Varko was Rhyma Berg. Here on different sides of the Villajoki were the critical head lands of Villaniemi and Haranpaaniemi.

West of Haranpaaniemi, the coast was protected by the Hamina Ryhma of Major General Hanell. The Hamina Ryhma was not part of Lieutenant General Oesch's Rannikko Ryhma.

The winter of 1939 was extremely cold. Normally the ice would not have been sufficiently thick to support an attack, but unfortunately for Finland the winter had been the coldest in fifty years. The Russian army attacked over the frozen ice across the Viipuri Gulf. While there were Finnish defenses here, the sector was not as well defended as the Kannas.

The major Russian attack was along the coast between Tervajoki and Villajoki. The 28th Army Corps consisting of five divisions plus tanks and 2,000 planes started their attack on March 2nd.

On March 2nd the Russian forces attacked the islands in the Gulf of Viipuri. While fierce resistance from the small Finnish forces delayed the advance, on March 4th the Russian forces gained a small beachhead at Vilaniemi and Haranpaaniemi at Nisalahti. A Finnish counter attack recaptured them but had to withdraw due to the heavy Russian tank fire.

On March 4th another Russian force attacked further west against the Hamina Ryhma. Seven ski battalions of the Russian Baltic Fleet advanced across the ice between Kotka and Ristniemi. The attack was thwarted by the Finnish infantry regiments and by the Finnish coastal batteries and the 4th regiment of the Finnish air force (LV.4). The bombing and shelling opened huge chasms in the ice, swallowing the unfortunate attacking Russian forces – tanks, artillery guns, men and all.

By March 8th six divisions of the Russian 28AK were dug in for over twenty kilometers along the coast. On March 8th the Russian's were able to cut the highway between Viipuri and Helsinki at Karjaniemi. Later on the 10th they succeeded in cutting the highway further west at Villajoki between the orginal beach heads of Villaniemi and Haranpaa.

The advance in both cases was contained from widening by the Finnish forces. Since the start of the attack, reinforcements had been hurriedly brought in from other fronts to help the embattled units. Among these were Uncle Toivo's 1.Pr infantry brigade and Uncle Erkki's Er.Psto 4 artillery unit. JR 68 as well was moved from the Kannas, and units were brought from the Lapland (JR40) and the Lake Ladoga IV AK front (Er.P18 and Er.P22).

Fighting continued until March 13th without the Russian forces being able to break through further.

Finnish casualties were high – 1,600 killed and 2,600 wounded – or 8% of Finland's total war time losses. Russian casualties were enormous.

Kaptain Palonheimo, the commander of Uncle Toivo's 1st battalion wrote his report and observations on the battle on April 10, 1940 a month after the battle. During the chaos of battle there was no time for journals.

March 8

- *15:00 – Order to move from Ihantala to Vakkila, to Juustila, and be ready by 01:00 in Juustila*
- *22:30 – March*

March 9

- *03:30 Arrived Juustila –*
- *Observation: Told road was reserved for them but arrived late due to road traffic - II/Pr1 supply column and JR62 with canon & horses were coming in the opposite direction. Near Juustila more artillery going to Juustila*
- *06:00- 15:00 Moved via truck to Vanhakyla*
- *Observation: only 6-8 trucks versus promised 29. Moved in clear daylight. Lucky no one killed as Russian planes were attacking*
- *15:00 to 05:00 – Rested in Vanhakyla*
- *Observations: Shared barracks with JR11 – many slept sitting up as there was no space – little sleep for anyone*

March 10

- *08:00 March to Iso Leitjarvi*
- *12:00-13:00 Arrived. Heavy plane movement but no strafing or bombing*
- *Observations: none*
- *Placed under command of Major Varko – Battle Group Varko*
- *1.Pr order - Stay in place*

- *14:15 - Order to move to east side Nisalahtikyla. Enroute hit by 2 artillery barrages. 1 killed, 2 wounded.*
- *19:00 No further news, so moved in dark and cold to east side of IsoLietojarvi and PeinLietojarvi and bivouacked – periodic artillery & bombing*
- *21:15 As putting up tents question from Varko re bivouac. Order at 21:45 to provide him with a "moukku" at 21:30 but didn't know what moukku meant*
- *22:00 4.DE order to reinforce IsoLietojarvi – PienLietojarvi line-*
- *Observations: Communications problem. Orders from 3 different units -1.Pr, 4.DE , and Major Varko. Battalion nonetheless moved to front lines per small drawing.*

March 11

- *Peaceful night*
- *06:00 "Working" on the line*
- *09:00 Varko order to move to Nisalahti*
- *09:20 4DE.1 order from Colonel Inkala to move towards Repola. Continued to work awaiting clarification*
- *14:45 Order from 4DE to take position "19.1"*
- *1530 – Moved out. Heavy firing from both sides of the road north of IsoLieto Road. Company arrived at IsoLieto*
- *New 4DE order to move to Repola but couldn't extract ourselves as in midst of fighting Russians. Finally able to move along the west side of IsoLieto towards Repola. Met JR11 (Colonel Inkala) and told to set up to the right of another unit but couldn't find the unit*
- *22:00 Returned to original bivovac*
- *22:30 4DE order to move via Peltola to location "20.1" – impossible. 4DE then said stay in place as Russians had broken through at Kankaapaa*
- *Observations: Confusing orders from many sources at same time, and HQ had poor knowledge of enemy locations*
- *1killed, 2 wounded*

March 12

- *Quiet night – continued work*

- *11:45 Move to Lukko battalion and help stop retreat.*
- *Await artillery support*
- *16:00 We attacked even though poor artillery support*
- *18:30 Heavy losses. Russians too well dug in to push out. Heavy Russian artillery*
- *20:00 Gave up positions and withdrew – Order to leave delaying unit and withdraw rest*
- *2nd company – 20 dead, 52 wounded [1/3 of the unit]*
- *Casualties for rest of 1st battalion without the 2nd company - 16 dead, 37 wounded*
- *Russian dead estimated at 150*

March 13

- *Artillery fire from 10:00 until 11:00 am*
- *11:00 - PEACE*
- *Observations: Enemy strong and dug in. Without own artillery support can't dislodge. Men tired as well. Russians incurred about 30% casualties*

The 1st Pr suffered 187 casualties - 49 dead, 138 wounded – mostly in Uncle Toivo's battalion. Luckily Uncle Toivo was not one of them. The Russian dead were estimated at a thousand.

Uncle Erkki

Uncle Erkki and Er Psto 4 retreated on February 28th from Riistseppala to Kuukauppi eight kilometers north of Kuparsaari on the Back Line. The battalion remained at Kuukauppi until receiving orders on March 7th to move to the Viipuri Lahti to help Lieutenant General Karl Oesch and the Ranniko Ryhma stop the Russian advance across Viipuri Lahti.

At 18:00 on the night of Feb 27th due to heavy bombing, the battalion had moved forty kilometers north from Riistseppala through Kuuparsaari to Kuukauppa, arriving at Kuukauppa at 10:30 on the 28th. Kuukauppa is just across the bridge from Antrea. Uncle Erkki was on familiar home ground. Ground that I am sure he was happy to see even under these circumstances.

The headquarters and Uncle Erkki's supply column remained near Antrea until March 7th . The three batteries themselves moved back to the front line in order to provide support for the infantry against the attacking Russian Division.

On March 7th they received orders to move to Viipuri Lahti and march to Kilpeenjoki. Uncle Erkki and the Kev Kol departed at 23:00, arriving at 05:30 on the next day.

They marched either directly by Kavantsaari on the Antrea to Ihantala Road or possibly via a somewhat longer route from Antrea through Hannila and Syvalahti to Kilpeenjoki. Of course as usual they moved during the night in order to avoid Russian bombers. Despite marching at night, bombing left 1 soldier dead and 1 wounded, 7 horses killed and 1 gun destroyed.

My cousin Sirkka told me:

> Father stopped in at home. I am not sure whether it was while he was at Kuukaupaa or when they marched to Kilpeenjoki. If it was during the march the farm would have been right beside the road if they took the Antrea -Ihantala Road. If it was the other route the farm was only five kilometers down a small road from Syvalahti – a road that father had trod since he was a small boy.

> By this time gramps Juho and the herdswomen had left with the cattle. The oldest cow was still on the farm, being tended by a Finnish unit bivouacked on the farm. Gramps Juho had left it on the farm when they departed. The cow was too old to make the trek. Father told the soldiers to shoot it if they had to leave rather than leaving it to suffer.

It must have been a sad visit for Uncle Erkki. His beloved home still beautiful and untouched – but empty. Just as empty as I am sure his heart was.

The Kev Kol departed from Kilpeenjoki at 23:00 of the day they arrived. At 05:00 they arrived safely at Rautukyla. They left again at 23:00 that night arriving at Nurmi at 13:15 on March 10th. From there they marched twenty kilometers the next day to Nisalahti /Tervajoki, the heart of the battle – to join Osasto Varko's forces. The artillery batteries had already arrived on site at their firing stations at Peltola at 06:30 on the 11th. The need was urgent.

The situation seemed hopeless. A quarter of the Finnish infantry were youths and old men who had not seen action. The rest were exhausted veterans of the Kannas battles.

Uncle Erkki was now fighting for the life of Finland, unbeknownst to him, beside his brother Toivo. The situation may have seemed hopeless against the overwhelming numbers and weaponary of the Russians. "Hopeless" however is a word that has little or no meaning to the Finnish people. All of its' existence had been based on "Sisu"- the ability to presevere and fight against overwhelming odds – and to fight with bravado and a will to win.

Through the frantic days of March 11th and 12th the battle see sawed back and forth with the Russians breaking through the defenses only to be pushed back by Finnish counter attacks. The batteries shelled the Russian advances and supported the Finnish counter attacks.

The fighting was so close that the batteries did not have any margin for error. The positions of the respective forces changed constantly. Radio and phone communications was difficult. Accurate firing and the ability to reposition the batteries and the firing coordinates quickly was paramount. The artillery commander reassured some unbelievers stating;

> " The batteries are so moveable and the men so
> well trained and capable, that they can successfully
> reposition their guns from even under the very nose
> of the Russians."

At 10:40 on the morning of March 13th Er Psto 4 fired its' last volley.

The Russians had only been able to cut the Viipuri to Helsinki Road at one spot for a day. The Finnish army had retreated but had not been defeated.

Uncle Aatu

Uncle Aatu and his Er P4 battalion retreated to Revonkyla on the Back Line just south of Kuparsaari.

On February 27th they withdrew under heavy enemy attack at 17:00 from their positions at Ilves/ Kaenniemi.

On the 29th at 04:00 they arrived at Revonkyla on the Back Line at Kuparsaari. The first few days were quiet but action soon heated up.

From March 5th to the 13th the days work in the bunkers and trenches was a steady mixture of repelling Russian infantry and tank attacks, counter attacking to retake lost

positions, reconnaissance patrols, and of course enduring heavy artillery shelling and Russian bombing.

The Back Line held.

Viipuri and Uncle Arvo

Viipuri as well held. In the Viipuri area a massive Russian attack thrust to the west of Viipuri over the Viipuri Lahti; to the east of the city towards and Tali; and directly at the city itself.

The Finnish forces held their defensive positions retreating only a few kilometers in two weeks against the advancing 7th Army.

Outside of Viipuri, the Finnish 5th Division held the advance of the Russian 100th and 24th Divisions at Tammisuo, while the 23rd Division stopped the Russian 123rd and 84th Divisions north of Tali at Portin Hoikka.

Uncle Arvo

Uncle Arvo's combat engineering unit was north east of Viipuri, moving to various points - laying mines and flooding waterways in an endeavor to stop Russia's armoured tanks.

Immediately east of Tali the 3.Pr was in fierce battles with the Russian forces at Mannikkala. Uncle Arvo was there. And likewise at Kuparsaari near Uncle Aatu.

Uncle Arvo also took part in the defense of Tali. In this case as part of the Nuijamaa battle on the Saimaa Canal. On March 2nd when the Russians were advancing against Tali, the Finnish engineers opened the gates to the Saimaa Canal flooding the low lying terrain to a depth of three feet, including the areas around Tali. This reduced the ability for the Russian tanks to maneuver. Tali, with low lying and sandy fields, otherwise was perfect country for the Russian tanks

Viipuri

At Viipuri itself the 3rd Division, which had been held on reserve north of Viipuri, was moved to the front lines at the end of February. JR 8 commanded by Colonel Laaksonen held the western Karemaki Gulf side of Viipuri. JR7 commanded by Colonel Kaila, and Kev Os 3 commanded by Captain Viisteria, held the centre of Viipuri.

Less than one Finnish division against three Russian Divisions (the 7th, 91st, 94th plus tank and artillery brigades).

At the beginning of March, JR 8 was holding defensive lines on both sides of Hevossaari 2,000 metres south west of Viipuri, while JR7 was dug in only 500 metres south west of Viipuri.

On March 2nd JR8 had to withdraw from Hevossaari under a heavy Russian tank, artillery and infantry attack. The 2nd battalion counter attacked unsuccessfully on March 3rd before withdrawing to a reserve position on the west side of Kolikkomaki in Viipuri city. The 3rd battalion continued to hold the defensive line at Huhtiala on the western outskirts.

The period from March 4th to the 6th was quiet. From the 1st to the 7th the Russians continuously brought more troops to the Liimata train station - mom and dad's home - south of Viipuri

March 7th brought a heavy Russian artillery barrage and attack against the JR8 3rd battalions' positions. They fell back, counter attacking on March 8th but without success. The 3rd battalion went on reserve, Kev Os 3 taking over new defensive lines west of JR7 at Kangasranta, 500 metres southwest of the city.

JR7's defensive sector on the southern outskirts of Viipuri east of Huhtiala was quiet during the first week of March. On the March 11th Russian forces attacked JR7's positions breaking through. JR7's counterattack took them back. The morning of March 12th brought a bitter artillery barrage followed by a Russian attack at mid day. JR7 held.

On the night of the 12th JR8 withdrew north of Viipuri to Tienharra leaving the defense of Viipuri to JR7 and Kev Os 3. That night JR7 and Kev Os 3 withdrew to defensive lines at Patterimaki in Viipuri – the site of Tsar Alexander II's fortifications; the Red's defensive lines during the Civil War; and, dad's boyhood playground.

Peace arrived on the 13th with Viipuri in Finnish hands – devastated but undefeated - the Finnish flag still flying proudly over Viipuri Linna.

March 13, 1940
11:00 Peace

March 13 – 11:00 PEACE

Peace came at 11:00 on March 13th - a bitter peace, particularly for our family. As part of the peace terms Karjala was ceded to Russia. Our beloved home was lost.

Casualities were enormous for both the Finns and the Russians.

But other then admiring the pluck of the Finns, the world had little to say, as it was engrossed in its own battle for life.

Our family gathered its sorrows, and drew together to build a new life. No longer in beloved Karjala - but in a free Finland – and all miraculously alive.

CHAPTER 11

On Our Front

On Our Front

On the Home Front
A Bitter Peace

As Uncle Erkki writes in his letter home of March 22nd :

That peace communiqué was overall joyous but it brought us gloom as our home was left on the enemy's side and we have been left homeless. Irrespective things should improve in the future as long as peace endures. We were able to ensure that we have a free Finland and freedom for every Finnish family.

Erkki's daughter Sirkka writes in her memoirs:

There the days and weeks went by in Sukula. The interim peace came in March 13, 1940. The sacrifice was great, Karjala was lost. The good part was that dad, his brothers and brother in laws lived.

During the turmoil of the war, all the family endeavoured to stay in touch with one another. But where the men were, and how they were faring was a source of constant worry. Indeed even the men did not know where the others of them were; and whether they were alive or not. The concern and uncertainty is evident in Uncle Erkki's joyous comment in his letter:

I saw my brother Toivo by chance a couple of days ago as our bivouac areas happened to be near one another. Both of us were overjoyed to be reunited again after all this turmoil and chaos. Toivo is well and is in as good shape as of old.

What a heartwarming reunion that must have been.

In the March 22nd letter from Somewhere Out Here, now from Onkamaa well behind the front lines near Kotka, Uncle Erkki writes:

Somewhere out here 22/3 1940

Dear Wife

Thank you for the letter as well as the package you sent in February. I received it today as well as the letter you sent on the 7th of this month. Listen my wife if you haven't sent a package to me now packages are not needed, as I will get to see you as peace comes to the land.

That peace communiqué was overall joyous but it brought us gloom as our home was left on the enemy's side and we have been left homeless. Nonetheless things should improve in the future as long as peace endures. We nonetheless have a free Finland and freedom for every Finnish family.

Have you heard from the papers about the help the government will pay to us refugees. Certainly it would be striking if we received that payment which was agreed but I haven't received those monies yet. I believe that it would be best if we could reach our parish officials to get it explained.

I guess father has arrived and no accidents have happened to him on the trip. It was regretful that you forgot my clothes at home when you had to leave. I wonder if father noticed to take them when he left. Those clothes were the ones in the attic. It would be

nice to have them when they finally say I can pull on my civilian clothes- but one can get clothes as long as one remains healthy and can start peacetime work.

I saw my brother Toivo by chance a couple of days ago as our bivouac areas happened to be near one another. Both of us were overjoyed to be reunited again after all this turmoil and chaos. Toivo is well and is in as good shape as of old.

Greetings to both you my dear and the children. Say hello for me to mother and father and my sisters. And again saying good bye.

Erkki

On the Front Lines
Dispersal after the Peace

Immediately the day after the peace the men started to march back over the border (The old Peter the Great border – now the new Talvisota sorrow).

The peace terms stated that the main forces of the Finnish army must withdraw 1 kilometer from their front lines immediately after 11:00 a.m., and at 10:00 a.m. on March 15 begin withdrawing back to the new border. However the rear guard did not have to withdraw until 06:00 on the morning of the 15th. For the section on the Kannas from Suomilathi to Enso (just north of Antrea) the Finnish forces had to be across the new border by 20:00 on the 19th - on the Enso to Ryhajarvi section by 20:00 on the 25th.

The peace terms did not require the Finnish army to surrender its' arms.

The quiet and release of peace must have been a strange sensation after all the physical, physchological and emotional stress of living at the edge of death for 105 days. Lieutenant Poso of Uncle Erkki's artillery battalion comments:

All of us shaved a few days after peace had arrived. It was curious looking into the mirror. Looking back

were strange, worn, creased faces with sunken cheeks. As one of my companions remarked:

" Someone has most certainly, unknownst to me, run over my face with a push sled – I can see the tracks that have been left".

The Finnish soldiers marched back to their original regimental barracks, or in the case of the Karjala units, to newly identified barracks. After a month and a half they disbanded. The Finnish army was not in a hurry to disband before they had to. The Finns had learned from long experience that Russia's word was not necessarily a promise kept. Interestingly in all kantakorttis none of the men are let go from their unit, rather they are stated as being on leave.

The Öhman men returned slowly to join the family in Forsaa:

- Uncle Toivo was released on April 23, 1940.
- His unit crossed the new border at Saamalaa at 12:35 on March 15th. From there they marched to the 1st brigade's home barracks in Kontula in Helsinki, arriving

at 16:45 on March 27th. Uncle Toivo remained there until "going on leave" on April 23rd.

- Uncle Erkki remained with his unit until May 4th.
- The diary notes that the artillery battalion crossed the border at Saamala at 12:30 on the 16th. The supply column had met the 1st brigade on the previous day. The brothers Erkki and Toivo must have had their joyous reunion around this time. By March 20th the battalion was in Onkamaa near Hamina. However by the 29th the battalion had moved back east to Pihlajaa near Virolahti, just west of the new border. They remained there for a month reinforcing the fortifications in the area before marching twenty kilometers north to Miekikkala.
- On April 25th the artillerymen left. On May 4th Uncle Erkki left, and the battalion officers a day later.

- Uncle Aatu went home on April 30th
- Er P4 moved back from Revonkyla to Viskari across the Vuoksi River from Antrea and thence north through Rahikalla before following back woods roads (close to gramp Juho's childhood home of Orvala) to Pentilla where they crossed the border on March 15th. They continued northwest to Rasola just south of Lappeenranta.
- Uncle Aatu remained there until being disbanded April 30th.

- Uncle Kauko was disbanded on April 28th.
- I have not been able to determine where he withdrew to before being released.

- Uncle Vilho stayed with his anti aircraft unit until July 5th.
- The unit left Antrea on the 14th, arriving at their new position in Savonlinna on the 15th. Savonlinna was the national anti aircraft headquarters.
- No marching for those boys. They took the train. I wonder at the connections their commander had.
- The next four months consisted of a routine of training, sports events, spit and polish and manning their position.

- Uncle Arvo remained in the army as a combat engineer until the end of Jatkosota – indeed the end of the Lapin sota.
- He had to complete his conscription service and then the Jatkosota started. During the Lapin sota against Germany combat engineers were at a premium. Thus he was not released from the army until November 23, 1944. Five years in the crucible of war.

- Dad remained with the railroad after the war. I don't know when he was disbanded officially from the Home Guard.

While national patriotism helped, the character of the Finnish soldier, and of life in Finland, had a great affect on the soldiers' ability to adjust after the war. This aspect is vividly captured in the comments in the novel the "Unkown Soldier" - the seminal novel on the Jatkosota by Väinö Linna. Väinö himself served as an infantryman in JR8. The book begins with the disbanding of the Talvisota veterans.

> " In warm spring weather the veterans departed, wearing their fur caps, tattered sheep skin coats, knitted jerseys and felt boots. For them there were no "difficulties of readjustment". Finnish fashion they got dead drunk, sobered and then went to work. Had the nation's sacrifices been in vain ? That was a question for those who had no spring planting to attend to.
>
> They were, for the most part, of healthy peasant stock. So what extraordinary psychological complications could have attended their return to civilian life ? They couldn't afford to make a stumbling block out of it. And as for their souls, old men with time to think of repentance might possess them, but a soldier hasn't the slightest use for such things. The eyes peering out of deep sockets above chapped and bearded cheeks reflected only the fierce determination of any wild animal to cling to its miserable life."

It was not quite that easy however. I have heard that some of my uncles had difficulty sleeping, intermittently reliving the war in their nightmares.

CHAPTER 12

On the Political Front

CHAPTER 12

On the Political Front

The Human Cost

The peace terms were onerous.

Karjala was ceded to Russia, along with the Suursaari, Tytarsaari and Koivisto islands in the Gulf of Finland, and Finland's outlet to the Artic Ocean, the Rybachi Peninsula. The Hanko Peninsula was leased to Russia for thirty years.

Finland as well had to build a railway from Salla to connect to the existing Finnish railway from Rovaniemi to Tornio and Oulu. This would give Russia access to the Gulf of Osthrobothia from the Murmansk railway (Russia was bulding the connecting link from the east) . I am mentioning this relatively minor item here as my father was one of the men in charge of building the rail link during the Jatkosota.

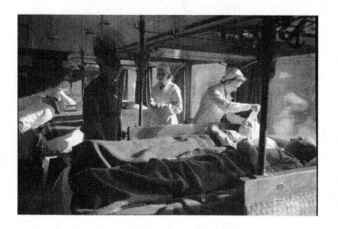

Finnish Casualties

Finland paid for the war in blood as well as land.

The Finnish army suffered 66,406 casualties – 24,531 or 35 % of these were men who were killed or lost; and 43,557 wounded. 16,437 of the wounded soldiers were badly wounded, and 27,120 lightly wounded.

Miraculously only 892 civilians were killed.

Of the Finnish casualties, almost two out every three casualties occured on the Kannas. The casualties by army group were:

- IAKT   10,828
- IIAK   17,007
- IIIAK   10,350
- IV AK + Talvela Group (RT)   15,082
- Pohjois Suomi Group (PSR)   6,641
- Lapland Group (LR)   2,229

While the casualty number pales in comparison to worldwide WW II losses, for a population of 3,695,000, the sacrifice is staggering. If the United States had suffered the same losses relative to its' 1940 population it would have resulted in 2,600,000 dead or wounded in 105 days.

The reserve officers (all were 2nd lieutenant or lieutenant rank) who served in the war made a major sacrifice – 972 died, by far the largest percentage. All were at the "coal face" leading their men. For example JR21 at Taipale had a 100 "junior officers" - 86 of whom were reservists.32 junior officers died. Only one senior officer – Major Jaako Sohlo - was killed.

Of Finland's total 24,531 dead, only 31 were above the rank of lieutenant (23 were captains and 8 were major and above). It perhaps explains why countries have historically gone to war. It is not the army's decision makers' lives that are at risk. And certainly there is no risk to the political decision makers.Wars entail no physical risk or deprivation at all for them.

Nor were the officers located in the cities at risk. Lieutenant Palolampi derisively comments on the officer dandies located in Helsinki:

Helsinki and other big cities were full of healthy, rosy cheeked young men who had grand uniforms, magnificent white fur coats, fine silk ribbons on their sleeves, big pistols on their belts and a self satisfied arrogant expression on their faces – sitting in front of tankards of ale pondering oh so important stratagems. The dirty and ragged front line soldiers were looked upon strangely by them.

These "swords men", also known as "cheese knife strategists", were as prevalent in Helsinki as cats at a fish mongers. Irrespective of what job they busied themselves with their officers pay came automatically; war was comfortable and safe.

The soldiers thought up an appropriate name for them but it can't be mentioned here as it would be disservice to the brave and decent Lottas.

Of course war requires some men in important positions on the homefront and at head quarters, but these rosy cheeked, fur coated ... !

Russian Casualties

Russia as well paid in blood.

The scantioned estimate is that Russia lost 230,000 to 270,000 killed and another 200,000 to 300,000 wounded.

However Kruschev states that:

I'd say we lost as many as a million lives

A soviet general looking at at the map of the territory Russia had acquired on the Kannas is said to have remarked;

"We have won just about enough ground to bury our dead"

What the number is we'll never know. But it was horrendous. A reflection on Russia's disregard for the life of its' soldiers, and a measure of the courage of its' soldiers.

Only 5,000 Russian soldiers were taken prisoner. All 5,000 Russian POWs were repatriated to Russia. Although no written confirmation has been found, reliable Russian sources have said that the prisoners were packed off to secret NKVD camps near the White Sea, interrogated, and shot.

Russia lost close to 1,000 aircraft, 2,300 tanks and armoured cars. It also lost an enormous amount of other war materials including munitions, trucks and horses. Material that Finland repurposed for its' own use in the Jatkosota, or already in the Talvisota.

Uncle Toivo's 1.Pr estimated that Russia lost 10,200 men and 73 tanks in its' battles with them. Not surprisingly 63% of the deaths occurred during the February assault on the Mannerheim Line and the Intermediate Line.

The Human Toll

The casualty numbers are dry and unfeeling – quite the opposite of real life. Despair at home, carnage at the front.

Finland was unique in that it sent all of the fallen soldiers by train to their home parish to be buried in the sankari-hauta within each churchyard.

Mother commented to me about the terrible smell that wafted from the cattle cars containing the dead bodies of the fallen soldiers as they went by on the railway track.

An average of 236 Finnish soldiers died each day. Usually all the soldiers whose bodies arrived at the parish on the same train were buried at the same time. The services were solemn, formal affairs with a Civil Guard honour troop, officiated by the Lutheran pastor in full vestments. They were attended by the entire church community as well as the fallen's grieving family and loved ones. The funerals bolstered patriotism and drew the nation together as well as providing what comfort possible to the fallen loved ones family.

The bodies were prepared near the front by the KEK units (Kotiseiden Evakusoisti Keskushoito) for their last journey home.

My second cousin Eeva's parents – Sylvia (Great Uncle Hjalmar's daughter) and her husband Vilho - worked in a KEK unit. Both were theologians. Vilho, while initially an artilleryman, opted out as a 'conscientious objector" from the killing fields. Sylvia joined him when he went to work in the 1st Army Corps KEK unit. Vilho put the dead in the caskets while Sylvia washed the bodies, collected the soldiers' belongings and sent them along with a letter to the family. The men needed to be unfrozen, unclothed, their hands and face washed, and the shrapnel torn places packed with with cotton wool.

Eeva's parents said little about the task other then saying the job was horrific.

The horror is captured in the words of a Lotta as she recounts her first day at a KEK units.

As I approached the drying barn I noticed a strange strong smell. Then I entered the actual sauna building.

I looked around the sauna benches. A soldier lay in an unnatural position, beside him another, on the upper bench a third ... the whole sauna was stacked full of fallen frozen men. One did not have a leg, another no head. They were my age if not younger.

My stomach turned upside down. It was the first time I had seen dead bodies and I frantically rushed outside. I sobbed and cried but wasn't able to throw up.

One can not ever imagine a feeling and image such as this... The sight remained engraved in my mind through the rest of my life.

To this day I do not understand how I was able to endure this work; but I had to - I had given my Lotta promise.

When peace came on March 13th and the unit had to withdraw behind the border, they were not able to take all the bodies. Of course the soldiers were not able to retrieve the bodies of all of their comrades – for some nothing was left – and others had to be left behind the enemy lines where they fell. The Finnish army identifies them in their records as "lost", as opposed to fallen. Only 5% of Finnish casualties were "lost". The almost hundred percent recovery of the bodies of their fallen comrades in arms is a testament to the soldiers and the medics.

The "lost"number did not include Prisoners Of War. Only 900 Finnish soldiers became POWs. 838 were exchanged at the end of the war.

On the World Front

In Finland, on March 13, 1940, World War II was a distant event in Poland, Germany and Russia having invaded and conquered Poland.

War had been declared on September 3, 1939 between the Allies (United Kingdom, France, Canada, Australia, New Zealand, and South Africa) and Germany. However Germany had not begun its' attack against Western Europe. Norway, Denmark, France, the Lowlands and Britain were untouched by war. The attack on Norway and Denmark did not begin until April 1940, and that against France and the Lowlands not until May.

While the West did not provide any help to Finland, the situation may have been different if Churchill had been prime minister of England. Churchill did not become Prime Minister until May 10, 1940 when Neville Chamberlain resigned as a result of Germany's invasion of France and the Lowlands of Belgium, Holland and Luxembourg.

Churchill commented upon the end of the Talvisota:

> "Finland alone – in danger of death, superb, sublime Finland – shows what free men can do. The service that Finland has rendered to humanity is magnificent ... We cannot say what Finland's fate will be, but nothing could be sadder to the rest of the civilized world than that this splendid northern race should at the end be destroyed and, in the face of incredible odds, should fall into slavery worse than death."

Russia, after signing the peace with Finland was not at war with anyone. Russia did not get into WW II until Hitler invaded Russia in June 1941. Russia then became an ally of the West.

Russia's inability to defeat Finland led to Germany believing Russia was not a major force; and to Russia reassessing its' military capabilities.

Kruschev in his memoirs comments:

> In our war against the Finns we had an opportunity to choose the time and the place. We outnumbered our enemy, and we had all the time in the world to prepare our operation. Yet even in these most favorable conditions, it was only after great difficulty and enormous losses that we were able to finally win. A victory at such cost was actually a moral defeat.
>
> And so the war with Finland ended. We started to analyze the reasons why we were so badly prepared and why the war had cost us so dearly.

Yes, Finland had fought valiantly and "successfully" – admired but alone.

Mannerheim's order of the day at the end of the war eloquently summarizes the successes, the sacrifices made, and the thanks due:

COMMANDER-IN- CHIEF'S
ORDER OF THE DAY
No 34

Soldiers of the army of Finland !!

Peace has been agreed between us and Russia, a harsh peace, in which we have ceded almost every battleground where you have bled blood to retain the ground, land which we hold dear and holy.

You did not want war, You loved peace, work and progress, but You were forced into battle, where You have done great work, work which in the coming hundreds of years will shine brightly in the annuals of history.

Over 15,000 of You who departed for the battleground will no longer see your home, and many more of You have lost your physical ability to work. But as well You have dealt hard blows, over several hundreds of thousands of the enemy lie in the snow or stare with sightless eyes at the stars in the heavens. The fault is not Yours. You did not hate or wish them harm, rather You followed wars' harsh law, kill or be killed.

Soldiers !

I have fought on many battlegrounds in the world, but I have not seen Your like as warriors. I am as proud of You as if you were my children, as proud of the men of the tundra of Pohjola as of the plains of Pohjanmaa, of Karjala's forests, of Hame and Satakunna's cultivated fields, of the boys of Uudenmaa and Varsinais-Suomi's mild groves. I am as proud of the sacrifice of each of You, which You offered equally – be You factory workers, poor country boys, or the rich.

I thank all of You, officers, NCOs and soldiers, but I want to offer special thanks to the reserve officers for their self sacrifice, their sense of duty, and the ingenuity with which they fulfilled their mission, one which originally had not been their responsibility. Accordingly the percentage of them that was lost was the highest, but that sacrifice was given freely and with an unshakeable sense of duty.

I thank the staff officers for their skillful and tireless work; and to conclude, I warmly thank my assistants, the headquarters officers, the army commanders, and the army group and division commanders, who made the impossible possible.

Thank you Finland's Army - a thank you to all of branches of its service, who from the very first days completed heroic deeds in their noble quest. Thank you for your courage with which you many times turned back overwhelming enemy forces who were equipped with hitherto unknown weaponry; and of your tenacity with which you have held unto each inch of your homeland's soil. The destruction of over 1,500 Russian tanks and over 700 airplanes attests to heroic deeds, often carried out by individual men.

With joy and pride I think of Finland's Lottas and their part in the war – their sacrifice and their untiring work in different areas which has freed thousands of men for the front lines. Their noble spirit has encouraged and strengthened the army, whose gratitude and esteem they have fully earned.

Also a place of honor is deserved by the thousands of workers during the wars difficult /severe times , who, often during the air attacks have voluntarily carried on work readying materials for the army, and also those, who under enemy fire have stayed at their factory stations preparing arms for the army. I thank them on behalf of the fatherland.

Despite all the bravery and sacrifice, parliament has been forced to agree to severe peace terms, which however can be explained.

The army was small and its reserve cadres were insufficient. We were not equipped against a large world power. Our valorous soldiers protecting our borders had to obtain by insuperable efforts that which was lacking. They had to build defensive fortifications where there were none, had to seek aid, which did not come. We had to search for equipment and materials on time, which all countries feverously gather against the storm which now swirls over the world . Your heroic work has awakened admiration around the world, but after over 3 ½ months of war we are still almost alone. We have received no foreign aid other then the equivalent of 2 battalions of tanks and planes for the front lines. Our own forces have fought day and night without relief, having to withstand continuous enemy attacks which have stretched the strength and life of their bodies to the brink.

When the history of this war is written, the world will come to understand Your accomplishment.

Without the ready help of the arms and materials which Sweden and the western world provided, it would have been impossible to battle against the enemies limitless artillery, tanks and planes.

Regrettably the valuable aid which the west offered could not be carried out, as our neighbor, protecting only herself, would not allow the reinforcement troops to pass through her borders.

After 16 weeks of bloody fighting without rest day or night our army still stands today in front of the victory less enemy, who despite horrific losses has grown yet more numerous; and the home front, where unending air attacks have spread death and terror among the women and children , has not wavered. Burnt towns and ruined villages far behind the front lines, even onto our western borders, bear witness to this nations suffering of the past months.

The circumstances are harsh, as we have been forced to leave land which for ages we have cultivated, to a foreign race which has a different world view and different values.

But we have to accept these hard results in order that with what we have left, we prepare a home for those who have become homeless and provide better opportunities for everyone; and, that we be as ready as before to protect our small fatherland with the same resolution and strength, with which we have defended our indivisible nation.

We have the proud knowledge that ours was a historic undertaking, which we have fulfilled, of protecting western civilization, which for hundreds of years has been our heritage; but, we know as well, that we have paid to the last penny that debt which we owed to the west.

MANNERHEIM

CHAPTER 13

Building a New Life

CHAPTER 13

Building a New Life

Our families began to slowly build a new life. Karjala and Viipuri were no more.

Mother and Dad settled in Iitti, dad continuing to work for the railroad.

Uncle Aatu and Aunt Hilda and the girls moved to Vaajakoski near Jyvaskyla. Uncle Aatu took up a job as a stone mason.

Uncle Toivo and Aunt Alina moved to their own place, as did Aunt Tyyne.

Uncle Kauko and Aunt Margit settled again into their home in Oripaa.

Uncle Vilho, still a bachelor, disappeared somewhere.

Uncle Arvo remained in the army.

Life for Sirkka and her parents and grandparents took a turn for the worst as Grandfather Juho lost the herd of cattle on the jouney to Sukula. You can tell in his letter home on March 30th that Uncle Erkki is dismayed despite putting his best face on .

Somewhere Out Here 30/3/1940

Good Saima

I am writing a few lines to thank you for your letter which I received last night. Don't worry about my clothes. For sure we will have time to take care of that when I am released to the civilian world. Here it seems I may receive permission soon but I can't be sure when I will get it.

Regarding mother's illness, tell her to go to the area's health centre, assuming you aren't so far from each other that you can't get to the place.

I wonder what will happen now that father came from home with only one horse. Our wealth has certainly decreased as we haven't been able to find a single cow and start a new herd - the state will compensate us if they had to butcher them. It would be good to know where the herd was moved ...

I don't have time now to write more as I have to go to work.

Best greetings to all the kin, and special greetings to you and the children.

Erkki

But Uncle Erkki, Aunt Saima and family along with Grandfather Juho and Grandmother Hilda started to build a life. As Sirkka recounts:

So grampa had to leave the Kavantsaari home for western Finland. The hired women started herding the cattle west. On that trip the cattle and the herdswomen disappeared.

Everyone moved to where they could find work. We and the grand parents stayed in place. Father went to work logging.

On the week ends mom and dad searched the area looking for the lost cattle, finding 3 of the 12 cows.

On April 30 1941 we left Sukula for Oitti, (100km eastwards towards Lahti). There according to the "evakko care" there was to be a place ready, but when we arrived there was no trace of a dwelling.

That night we slept in the Workers building. It was cold as I only had on a summer dress and a sweater – legs bare. No blankets or beds. The next day we found the dwelling. The owner was a Finnish Swede. He owned vegetable shops, and grew flowers and vegetables.

Those fields were my and my brothers' first work place. We got a small wage. (I don't remember how much per day. Dad took care of money matters. Then in August I was able to buy shoes with the money.

Life went on, but life was not the same

BOOK III
"Jatkosota"
The Continuation War

PART I

An Uneasy Peace

An Uneasy Peace

After the Moscow Treaty of March 13, 1940, Finland settled into an uneasy peace.

Global affairs were in disarray with World War II underway in Europe. Finland tried to form alliances with the West without success. Russia exerted its' influence of Finlands' affairs, but thankfully with little success.

Under threat from Russia and abandoned by the West, Finland drew closer to Germany.

Finland resettled its' 400,000 fellow Karjalainen Finns in Finland.

Our family, having lost everything except their lives, began to rebuild a new life.

But everyone knew that the future was uncertain.

CHAPTER 1

On the Political Stage

CHAPTER 1

On the Political Stage

After the March 13, 1940 peace ended the Winter War with Russia, Finland settled into a year of uneasy peace.

On the World Stage

On the world stage, World War II continued on the Western Front between Germany, France and the British Empire.

The Eastern Front settled into quiet after Germany and Russia had both taken over the eastern European countries as per their Ribbentrop- Molotov Agreement.

Finland had been able to keep its' armaments and a small armed force. To augment this they had increased the defense budget and expanded the length of conscription service from 1 year to 2 years (Ahh, I wondered why Uncle Arvo's conscription was longer then that of his brothers). In May 1940 they endeavored to form a Nordic Defensive Union with Sweden, Norway and Denmark but this was vetoed by Russia. After the German invasion of Denmark and Norway, Finland continued to try to form a defensive alliance with Sweden, but this was again stopped by Russia.

During the year between the Winter and Continuation Wars Germany began to pursue closer relations with Finland. However in response to questions from Stalin about the Ribbentrop-Molotov Agreement Hitler replied that he was only interested in trade with Finland for nickel, cellulose and lumber.

Finland, although independent, was within Russia's sphere of influence. Russia endeavored to influence Finlands' politics, proposing a long list of political and social demands, including who should be Finlands President, and which ministers should resign from the government.

They were unable to change Finland's government. Ryti remained President, Rangell Prime Minister, and Mannerhein Commander-In-Chief of Finland's armed forces. No elections were called so the members of Parliament did not change.

The Winter War had brought Finland closer together. The old civil war hatchets were buried. The focus was on a united independent country. Veterans all over the country formed veterans associations. Stalin in May 1940 started a counter movement – The Finnish-Soviet Union Peace and Friendship Society. It did not attract many members.

Germany had occupied Western Europe including Norway by June 1940. Thereafter in concert with Italy, it captured Northern Africa and the Balkans, effectively taking control of the Mediterranen by late summer 1940.

As Finland's overtures to the West for assistance were rebuffed, she had no choice but to turn to Germany for war materials, machinery and grain. Russia was continuing to pressure Finland for closer "relations" with Russia. Finland knew that Russia would never give up its' attempt to conquer Finland. The only western country that had showed some consideration towards Finland was the United States. This dissipated on December 11, 1941 when the United States joined the Allies in the war against Germany after Japan bombed Pearl Harbour on December 8th.

Resettlement

The terms of the peace of March 13, 1940 had been harsh. The most significant of these was Finland's loss of Karjala. All of the 400,000 inhabitants of Karjala fled to central Finland. Karjala comprised 12% of Finlands' population and 10% of its' land.

As part of the processs, the Finnish government designated a specific parish in Finland as the settlement area for each Karjala parish. Thus the communities could be kept together and some planning was possible for the resettlement of the Karjalaiset. However there was no requirement that anyone resettle in a specific area. All were Finnish citizens and could live wherever they chose in Finland.

I was surprised that during the recent 2016 refugee influx into Europe from the Middle East and North Africa that some misguided Finns said the Karjalaiset were similar refugees. The Karjalaiset were fellow citizens who were evacuees of war, much like evacuees of floods and fires - not refugees. Indeed the Finnish word for them was evakkot. Designating a citizen of your country, one who speaks the same language, and has the same shared history a refugee is incomprehensible. Never mind that almost all were families whose men had fought and often died for Finland; and whose land had served as a battleground buffer for the rest of the country. Certainly they had lost their homes and needed to find a new home and to start a new life. I don't know what word best describes them- yes perhaps refugee in the broadest definition of the word. But to equate them with unauthorized refugees from another country and culture leaves one speechless.The discussion initiated by some thankless ignorant pundits quickly died.

Resettlement of ten percent of its' population did put a strain on the country. Large swathes of private lands was nationalized and redistributed to the refugees. Public land as well was allocated. Mostly the land however was wilderness, not cultivated land. It took special grit to succeed.

While the resettlement put a strain of the country, it also ignited a surge of productivity, initiative, and creativity. None of the Karjalaiset became wards of the welfare state. They did not receive monthly cheques from the government. They built homes in the wilderness, found entry level jobs, and if qualified, well paying professional positions. The resettlement also triggered compassion. Most of the population readily helped (with exceptions as always) - be they relatives or strangers.

A "Home" Between the Wars

CHAPTER 2

A "Home" Between the Wars

After the peace my family started to build a new life. Everyone's happy home in Karjala was no more. The family dispersed, moving to various spots in Finland, to wherever they could find work.

Mother and my sisters left their temporary home with dad's aunt in Kuopio to join dad. Dad continued to work with the Finnish Railway as a construction engineer responsible for track operations and construction.

The family moved around various parts of Finland for the next year. I don't know where mom and dad lived from April 1940 until September 1941. Tellervo doesn't remember as she was only 3 years old, she only says: "many places"

Dad was able to get Uncle Kauko, Uncle Toivo and grandfather some interim work.

Dad's grandmother moved to Hammaslahti near Hameenlinna to be near her other son, our Uncle Yrjo who was living in Hameenlinna.

Aunt Hilda and her family moved to Vaajakoski near Jyvaskylaa in central Finland.

When Uncle Toivo came back he and Aunt Alina soon moved from Sukalakyla to Kallislahti near Sulkava/Savolinna. Kallislahti is near where rakas mummo Tiainen was born, so probably there were some distant relatives there.

Uncle Kauko and Aunt Margit went to Kallislahti for a time as well, before moving to Oripaa, a 100 kilometers north of Turku.

Aunt Tyyne moved to be with her husband Kalle Lehtinen in central Finland.

Uncle Vilho was still a bachelor and travelled here and there. His military file for the Jatkosota gives his call up contact as his father in Oitti.

Uncle Arvo remained in the army as he had not completed his full 2 years of service.

Uncle Armas and Aunt Ester were of course in Amerika.

Aunt Saima, Uncle Erkki, and their children along with Grampa and Gramma stayed in Sukula before moving to Oitti.

Uncle Erkki's letter in February 1941 to his sister Ester in Amerika encapsulates life. A true Karelian - still very positive but pining for the beloved Karjala home.

Sukula 20/2/1941

Dear Sister, Brother-in-law and Little Helen

Thanks for the letter which came today by airmail. Many thanks for the money you sent which came a few days ago.

Thanks as well for the packages you sent. They all arrived safely: 3 packages in dad's name; 2 packages in mom's name; and 1 package for Vilho and Arvo.

They asked me to convey how greatly they appreciated the packages.

For certain it is a great joy to receive the American offerings, but don't waste large sums of money on our behalf. You have to live yourselves, and if peace yet comes to this world, come here to see us. Assuredly that would be a joyous day !! Let's hope the day comes.

We are still here in the Hame area living in the same place we had come to when we had to leave beautiful Karjala and with it our beloved home. Here they are making new homes for us Karjalainens, but they won't become available for everyone at once. I don't know when the first people will get their new homes.

It would be marvelous to once more have a home where one could begin life again. But the greatest wish would be to some day be able to return to Karjala. But that is beginning to seem hopeless.

But we have all been healthy here. The older children are going to school, and little Irja is her mothers' helper. Martti has become an avid skier. Vilho, Kauko and Arvo got him new skis for Christmas. I then had to buy skis for Sirkka. We told Irja that next winter we would buy her nice skis. Irja is only 4 years old.

Now I will say again many thanks for the parcels and the money you sent. Many greetings to you from all the family and mom and dad. A special hello to little Helen from our children and her grandma and grandpa.

Goodbye Erkki

Cousin Sirkka further recounts:

Us and the grand parents stayed in place. Father went to work logging.

On the week ends mom and dad searched the area looking for the lost cattle, finding 3 of the 12 cows.

On April 30 1941 we left Sukula for Oitti (100 kilometers east towards Lahti). There according to the "refugee care" there was to be a place ready, but when we arrived there was no trace of a dwelling.

That night we slept in the Workers building. It was cold as I only had on a summer dress and a sweater – legs bare. No blankets or beds. The next day we found the dwelling. The owner was a Finnish Swede. He owned vegetable shops, and grew flowers and vegetables.

Those fields were my and my brothers' first work place. We got a small wage. (I don't remember how much per day). Dad took care of money matters. Then in August I was able to buy shoes with the money.

War Returns

PART II

War Returns

Inevitably war returned on June 25th, 1941.

Finland fielded an army of 530,000, along with a small air force and navy.

The Finnish Army fought on three major theatres –

- The Kannas;
- Ladoga/ Russian Karjala; and
- Mid Northern Finland.

Germany fought the war in Lapland. They fielded an army of 200,000 attacking Murmansk and the Murmansk Railway on two primary fronts – Murmansk and Salla.

The Continuation war went through three phases:

1. The Finnish assault of the summer of 1941
2. Trench warfare from the fall of 1941 until the start of summer 1944
3. The Russian assault of the summer of 1944

My father and all my uncles served in the war.

- Uncles Toivo, Arvo and Aatu on the Kannas
- Uncles Kauko and Vilho in Lake Ladoga and Karjalian Russia
- Father on the Salla front in Lapland.

Uncle Erkki was called up but did not serve as he was diagnosed with terminal cancer.

CHAPTER 3

The Road to War - Once More

SA- Kuva

CHAPTER 3

The Road to War - Once More

Russia continued to pressure Finland for closer "relations" with Russia. After all according to the Molotov-Ribbentrop Agreement, Germany and Russia had agreed that Finland was part of Russia's sphere. Furthermore the West was showing no interest in supporting Finland.

As Finland's overtures to the West for assistance were rebuffed, she had no choice but to turn to Germany for war materials, machinery and grain.

The alignment with Germany became closer when Germany declared war on Russia on June 22nd 1941. Hitler after having subdued Western Europe, turned to capture Russia, launching the Operation Barbarossa invasion of Russia.

Finland had had discussions with Germany regarding military cooperation for several months before the attack, and had allowed Germans troops to pass through its' territory in Lapland. It mobilized its' army on June 17th 1941. However it did not attack Russia.

On June 25th at 04:00 with no declaration of war Russia lauched a massive bombing campaign against civilian and manufacturing targets in Finland and opened fire on the border. Having no choice the Finnish Parliament declared war against Russia in the evening of June 25th, 1941.

Finland did not declare war against any other nations. The United Kingdom declared war against Finland on December 6th 1941 but did not participate in any military operations against Finland. The United States never declared war on Finland.

Finland adopted the concept of a "parallel war" whereby it sought to pursue its' own objectives in concert with, but separate of Nazi Germany. Historically there was a close relationship with Germany from the early Hanseatic merchant era to the Finnish Civil War period.

Finland operated as an independent republic. It had total control over its' own army, its' foreign policy, and political and civil institutions. Finland did not put any of her Jewish people into prisons, nor send them to Nazi Germany. Rather Finland was unique in that the Jews fought with their fellow Finns, and indeed there were some synagogues on the front.

Finland did separate the country into two military zones. Northern Finland / Lapland was placed under German military control. 200,000 German troops fought in Finland – almost all in Northern Finland / Lapland. The German troops in Northern Finland were under German command. At the beginning of the war there was one German Division on the Ladoga front. This was under Finnish command. When the Finns successfully reached the Syvari River, the German unit left to join the German forces besieging Leningrad.

Mannerheim explicitly made sure the war outside Lapland was under his control and was waged by Finnish troops. At the end of the war German fighter planes did play a significant role in the Battle of Tali – Ihantala. And throughout the war German provided Finland with armaments and food.

The primary objective of Finland from the commencement of the war was to recapture the part of Finland (Karjala) it had lost during the Winter War and to capture the Greater Finland portion of Russia in which the Karjalian people dwelled.

Indeed Mannerheim did not allow Finland to participate in the German attack on Leningrad, stopping the army just over The Old Finnish Border outside of Leningrad on September 9th, 1941. The Finnish army did advance substantially past The Old Finnish Border in Eastern Karjala to Petroksoi and Karhumaki on Lake Onega. Mannerheim however ordered the attack to stop before cutting the northern part of the Murmansk Railway.

Finland did not undertake the war lightly knowing the sacrifice it would have to make. But it also knew that without standing up for its' independence, that it would cease to exit.

CHAPTER 4

A Brief Military Overview
of the Jatkosota

SA-Kuva

The dog "Hupi" followed his master
through the Talvisota; Jatkosota, and Lappinsota

CHAPTER 4

A Brief Military Overview of the Jatkosota

After an interim peace of a year, Finland declared war on Russia after Russia bombed Helsinki. Finland wanted to reclaim the territory it lost during the Winter War and to prevent another attack by Russia on Finland. Some people wanted to build a Greater Finland based on romantic mythology and the German example.

Finland mobilized 530,000 troops. In addition in Lapland/Northern Finland, Germany fielded an army of 200,000.

The war was fought in Karjala from the Arctic to St Petersburg between the Finnish border and the railway line from Murmansk to St Petersburg.

Minimal fighting occurred in Finland outside of Karjala. The Russians did however bomb many parts of Finland. At the start of the war, the Russian air force launched a major attack against 18 Finnish cities, inflicting damage. Bombing continued throughout the war.

The Continuation War started on June 25, 1941 and ended on September 19, 1944 before the end of WW II.

The war went through 3 phases:

- The summer 1941 Finnish assault to recapture Karjala
  - Kannas – June 16 to August 31, 1941
  - Greater Finland – June 16 to December 1941
- Trench warfare – January 1942 to June 1944
- The Russian attack of summer 1944

The Finns attacked Russia in June 1941 in concert with the German Operation Barbarossa attack on Russia. As always, most of the fighting occurred on the Karelian Isthmus. Other attacks were made on Karelian Lake Ladoga, East Karelia and Northern Finland/Lapland.

The Finnish forces advanced through the Karelian Isthmus re-entering Viipuri on August 29, 1941. They continued to advance, halting on September 9th, at the Old Finnish Border 20 kilometers from Leningrad. Mannerheim would not participate in the German attack on Leningrad, perhaps saving Leningrad.

Mannerheim, likewise stopped the advances in Eastern Karjala on December 7th before entirely severing the Murmansk rail road. The Murmansk rail road was the Arctic supply route for delivering Allied and USA supplies to Russia.

Mannerheim, ever the astute politician, as well as an effective military commander, wanted to maintain the neutrality of the USA and Britain. As well, Finland had recovered the land she had lost in the Winter War. And, given her 500 years of war with Russia, Finland knew that being able to permanently defeat Russia was doubtful.

After early December 1941, no further advances were made during the Continuation War. Both sides settled down to 2 ½ years of trench warfare (asema sota) until Russia attacked Finland in the summer of 1944.

On June 9, 1944 Russia launched a major assault against Finland. The major thrust came on the Isthmus. Russia successfully forced Finland to retreat from its' lines at The Old Finnish Border. It captured Viipuri but was stopped in mid July by the Finnish forces in fierce battles at Tali-Ihantala and Ayrapaa/Vuosalmi. Peace was declared on September 17, 1944.

The Jatkosota was fought in 3 major theatres:

- The Karjala Kannas
- Ladoga Karjala
- Lapland and Northern Finland

The Kannas Theatre

The key battles of the war were fought in Karjala in south east Finland. Here, the Karjalan Kannas (Isthmus), as during the Winter War, was the main battleground. Controlling the Karelian Isthmus was the primary goal of both Finland and Russia. The Kannas is the area from: Viipuri on the Gulf of Finland east to Lake Ladoga; and, south from just north of Viipuri to St. Petersburg. This area was my mother's and my father's ancestral home.

Uncle Toivo, Uncle Arvo, and Uncle Aatu fought on this front.Uncle Vilho also fought on the Kannas for the first four months before being transferred to the Ladoga front in October.

On the Karjala Kannas, the Finnish army, in the first two months, recaptured Viipuri and pushed to the outskirts of St. Petersburg.

After September 1941, trench warfare continued on a defensive line between the Gulf of Finland and Lake Ladoga, until the Russian attack in June 1944.

In the summer of 1944, Russia began an attack on Finland (June 19, just after D day). This included bombing attacks on Helsinki, Oulu and Kotka. Finnish anti air craft defenses managed to repel the raids, limiting the damage.

The Finnish forces retreated up the Isthmus, one army corps stopping the Russians on the east side of the Isthmus at Vuosalmi. Uncle Toivo fought there.

Another corps however was unsuccessful, and Viipuri fell to the Russian ground forces on June 20, 1944. The loss of Viipuri is one of the few blights on Finland's stellar reputation as fierce defenders of their homeland. The Finnish forces abandoned Viipuri after only a token resistence.

Finland however was able to stop the Russian advance further north of Viipuri. This was in the ferocious bloody battle of Tali- Ihantala in the Viipuri country side – only a few kilometers from grandfathers' farm ...Finnish casualties were 1,000 a day – Russia's far more. The battle became part of Finnish war legend. Uncle Arvo was there.

The Ladoga Karjala Theatre

The other major theatre was Ladoga Karjala. This area of the war basically covered the area from Lake Ladoga east to Lake Onega; and north from the Syvari River to Karhumaki and Stalin's Canal. Specific battlegrounds were:

- Sortavala, at the northern end of Lake Ladoga
- The Aanus Isthmus, the area between Lake Ladoga (Laatokka) and Lake Onega (Ääninen) stretching from the northern end of Lake Ladoga south to the Syväri River (Svir Isthmus)
- The Maaselkä Isthmus between Lake Onega and Lake Seesjärvi (Segozero).

Uncle Kauko, and Uncle Vilho, fought in the Ladoga Karjala Theatre.

In the Ladoga theatre the Finnish goal was to reclaim Old Finland that had been lost during the Winter War; and, Greater Karjala, the area of Russia inhabited by the Karjala tribe of Finland of yore. However, irrespective of ancient tribal connections, the true Greater Karjala objectives were military ones:

- Cutting off the Syvari River connection from Lake Onega to Lake Ladoga and encircling Leningrad from the north east;
- Capturing Petroksoi the capital of Russian Finland located on the shores of Lake Onega;
- Severing the Murmansk railroad passing through the Maaselka Isthmus. Capturing the Maaselka Isthmus would cut Leningrad off from the Arctic Ocean, blocking Russia's receipt of war supplies from England. (The Salla thrust would have severed the rail road closer to Murmansk.). Indeed at the start of the war, the intent was to push 200

kilometers further north of the Maaselka Isthmus to Sorokka (Belomorsk) meeting with the Salla force and entirely cutting the Murmansk rail road (At Sorokka there was a junction where another track line separated off eastward to go to Moscow); and,

- Providing Finland with a more easily defendable eastern border.

As mentioned earlier, in September, Marshall Mannerheim halted the advance of the Finnish army towards St. Petersburg just north of the city. Some troops from the Karelian Isthmus front were moved to the Maaselka front in mid October to bolster the attack there. (Uncle Vilho's division was one of the units moved).

Sortavala and the Old Finland area was captured by mid August; the Syvari River by early September; Petroksoi on October 1st; and Karhumaki, the Murmansk railway, and Stalin's Canal in the first week of December.

After December 6, no further advances were made and the war entered into 2 ½ years of trench warfare, until the Russians began their attack into Finland in June 1944.

Defensive trench lines were set up:

- Along the Syväri River between Lake Ladoga and Lake Onega. (Uncle Vilho)
- On the Maaselkä Isthmus between Lake Onega and Lake Seesjärvi. (Uncle Kauko)

On both these fronts the Russians launched fierce but unsuccessful counter attacks in January / February 1942 before launching the final assault in June 1944.

The Lapland / Northern Finland Theatre

The war in Lapland and Northern Finland was waged by Germany. Mannerheim and the Finnish government ceded military control of the area from north of Oulu, Kajanni, and Raate to the Arctic Ocean to the German Army Command Norway (AOK Norwegen)- commanded by General von Furstenburg.

Germany wanted to capture Murmansk and severe the Murmansk to Leningrad / Moscow railway – the key Allied supply route to Russia. As well they wanted to protect the source of the steel they were receiving from northern Sweden.

Germany placed an initial force of 80,000 troops in the theatre. As well Finland allocated over two divisions. Facing them was a slightly larger force of seven Russian divisions. The Russian forces as well had major aerial and naval support – forces which Germany did not bring north.

The German command separated the attack (Operation Siberfuchs) into three separate fronts:

1. The Murmansk front whose objective was to capture Murmansk;
2. The Salla front whose objective was to severe the Murmansk railway at Kantalahti; and
3. The Finnish force "Kiestinki" front whose objective was to break through the Murmansk railway at Louhi and Vienan Kemi.

On the Murmansk Front the German attack (Platinfuchs) started on June 29th but stalled at the Kalastajasaarento peninsula east of Petsamo due to the difficult terrain and a strong and resilient Russian defense. A 2nd thrust made better progress but was stopped at the Litsajoki River on July 1st. The Germans made no futher progress towards their objective of capturing Murmansk, the Barents Sea port which was the Allied gateway from the Arctic Sea to Moscow and Leningrad.

On the Salla – Kantalahti Front the German XXXVI Army Corps supported by the Finnish 6th Division lauched an attack on July 1st towards the Kantalahti station on the Murmansk railway. They succeeded in advancing past The Old Finnish Border but stalled on August 19th at Vermajoki just 29 kilometers further. The two month and a half month attack only advanced 85 kilometres, 75 kilometres short of the Murmansk rail line before settling into trench warfare.

Father was on the Salla front.

On the "Uhtua/Kiestinki" Front the Finnish III army corps, led by Major General Siilasvuo, attacked towards the Vienan/Kemi and Louhi stations on the Murmansk Railway. The Finnish IIIAK, while under overall German command, was responsible for the 100 kilometers from Kuusamo south to Raate.

The Finnish attack towards Vienan Kemi ground to a stop outside Uhtua in the middle of August, 200 kilometers short of its objective.The Finnish attack towards Louhi successfully took Kietsinki by mid August.

Army Command Norway, given its' lack of success elsewhere, decided to focus its' entire Lapland attack on breaking past Kiestinki to capture the Murmansk railway junction at Louhi. It transferred SS Battle Group North to join the Finnish III AK of Siilasuvou. After limited success the joint attack was called off on November 17th at Mannerheim's request.

The Rukajarvi Front – Towards Sorokka on the Murmansk Railway

The Rukajarvi Front, just south of the Finnish III army corps, was manned by the Finnish 14th Division. Here the division was entirely under the Finnish High Command, not German Norway Command.

The divisions' objective was to cut through the wilderness to the Murmansk railway south of the Sorokka junction. It was able to advance to the Ontajoki River by September 17th.Mannerheim stopped the advance here – just 40 kilometers west of the Murmansk Kotskoma station south of Sorokka.

On October 26th the 8th Division linked with the 14th Division west of Seesjarvi, providing the Finnish command control of Karjala from the Syvari River to north of Rukajarvi.

No further advance was made. The division settled into trench warfare until pulling back out of Karjala in the summer of 1944.

Mannerheim did not want to severe the Murmansk Railway. In all cases, be they at the Louhi, Kotskoma/Sorokka, or Maaselka station, he stopped the advance.

One quarter of all Allied aid to Russia during WW II would reach it through the Murmansk railway – armaments, vehicles, steel, aluminum, and as importantly, food. The Murmansk railway split at Louhi; one line swinging east to Moscow, and the other continuing south to Lenigrad. Cutting the railway at Louhi would effectively cut off all Allied supplies from Murmansk to Russia.

Both Britain and the United States had told Mannerheim to stop the attack or risk the countries declaring war on Finland. Britain did declare war on Finland on December 6th but did not allocate any resources to Russia's attack on Finland. The United States never declared war against Finland.

The Finnish Air Force
&
Navy

SA-Kuva

CHAPTER 5

The Finnish Air Force & Navy

Finland's most important and major armed force by far was its' army.

Finland did have an air force and a navy. The air force was less then 10% the size of Russias' but did play a useful, albeit limited, role in the war. The navy was very small. Germanys' naval fleet controlled the Baltic Sea. Finlands' navy's role was protecting the coast outside Karjala, and conducting mining operations on the Gulf of Finland.

The Air Force

The Finnish Air Force was commanded by Major General Jarl Lundquist.

Finland did no have a large air force. Its' primary purpose was to support the ground troops with fighter cover. It had a bomber regiment which targeted Russian forces and supply depots. It did not bomb any civilian targets. Reconnaissance was a major task. This included aerial photography. As well the air force had several air ambulance planes.

The size of the Finnish air force was about 550 planes throughout the war. (Less than 10% of the air force Russia allocated against Finland). Downed and mechanically inoperable planes were replaced throughout the war by new planes from Germany or by retrofitting recovered Russian planes.

In June 1941 the air force had 344 air craft "available" for action - 240 fighter planes, 40 bombers, 55 reconaissance planes and 8 marine air craft. Usually about 70% of these planes were on front line duty. In addition to the 344 "action" aircraft, there were 218 training aircraft.

While Finland had a wide mixture of planes, the primary planes fighter planes were:

- Brewster B- 239 s
- Fiat G.50 s
- Morane-Saulnier 406 and 410 s
- Curtis Hawk 75A s
- Messerschmitt Bf 109 G-2 and G-6 s

The primary bombers were

- Bristol Blenheim Mk I and IV s
- Dornier Do 17 Z s
- Junker Ju 88 A-4 s

The Fokker C.X was the main reconnaissance plane.

Finland lost 389 planes during the war – 253 fighters, 88 bombers, 46 reconnaissance planes, and 2 others.

The Finnish Air Force downed 1,600 Russian planes – 265 bombers, 1,245 fighters, and 90 others. The anti-aircraft units downed another 1,031 planes. With 161 planes downed by other means, the total number of planes Russia lost was 2,792. The Finnish air force only brought down 2 German planes during the Lapland War. It did not lose any.

The primary periods that the air force was active, was during the Finnish summer assault of 1941 and the Russian summer assault of 1944. During 1942 through 1944, the air force played a role in helping counter act Russian Baltic Fleet movements and occasional bombing forays over Finland.

At the end of the war the The Finnish Air Force had five flight regiments.

- Flight Regiment 1 (LeR1) was a combined Fighter and Reconaissance regiment. It consisted of squadrons LeLv12 and LeLv32.
- Flight Regiment 2 (LeR2) was also a fighter and reconnaissance regiment. LeLv16 was reconnaissance, and LeLv28 fighters.
- Flight Regiment 3 (LeR3) was a fighter regiment. It consisted of squadrons LeLv24, LeLv26, and LeLv34.
- Flight Regiment 4 (LeR4) was a bomber regiment. It consisted of squadrons LeLv42, LeLv44, LeLv46, and LeLv48.
- Flight Regiment 5 (LeR5) had bombers, fighter and reconnaissance squadrons.It consisted of squadrons LeLV14 (recon), LeLV6 (bomber), and LeLV30

(fighter). The planes in this regiment were older more out dated ones.

In addition at the end of the war Germany provided a flight group (Detachment Kuhlmey) of 109 planes – Junker Stuka dive bombers, Focke Wulf fighters and fighter bombers, and Messerschmitt reconnaissance planes. This group was instrumental in the battles of Tali-Ihantala, Viipuri Gulf, and Ayrapaa-Vuosalmi during late June and early July 1944. Detachment Kuhlmey downed 126 Russian planes and lost 41 of their own.

In 1944 most of Finlands' air force was allocated to the Karjala Ladoga front. About 70 fighters (along with a few bombers and reconnaissance planes) were allocated to support the Finnish ground forces against Russia on the Kannas. In the1944 summer attack LeR4 conducted numerous bombing missions – supported by LeR3 fighters. In addition the LeR3 fighter planes countered the missions of the Russian bombers. The took part in the major battles of:

- Kuuterselka / Valkeasaari
- Siiranmaki
- Viipuri
- Ayrapaa- Vuosalmi
- Tali-Ihantala
- Viipuri Lahti

The battle of Tali-Ihantala was the largest air battle of the war.

The top two Finnish fighter aces were Warrant Officer Ilmari Juutilainen of 1/LeLv34 (94 kills) and Captain Hans Wind of 3/LeLv24 (75 kills). Nine members of the Finnish Air Force were awarded the Mannerheim Cross.

The Finnish Navy

The Finnish Navy was commanded by Major General Vaino Valve. It played a minor role in the war, with naval forces on the Gulf of Bothnia, the Gulf of Finland, and on Lake Ladoga and Lake Onega. As well as its' fleet of boats, the navy had shore batteries and several infantry brigades.

The Finnish fleet on the Baltic Sea was small consisting at the beginning of the war only of:

- Two coastal defence ships
- Five submarines
- Four gunboats

- Seven motor torpedo boats
- One minelayer
- Eight minesweepers

As well she had a training ship plus Coast Guard sloops, cutters, and patrol boats. During the war five additional torpedo boats were received from Italy. As well some vessels abandoned by the Russians on Lake Ladoga and Lake Onega were recommissioned.

The major navy in the Baltic Sea was the German Kriegmarine. Russia as well had a significant size fleet in Kronstadt outside Leningrad - 30 larger ships (battleships, destroyers and cruisers), 65 submarines, plus numerous gun boats and mine vessels.

As a result of the Winter War peace Russia had obtained the Island of Hanko at the entrance to the Gulf of Finland. They manned it with 35,000 troops. With its' fortress at Hanko supplemented by heavy mining of the Gulf of Finland, Russia effectively prevented German access. Germany in turn laid its' own mine fields at the mouth of the Gulf of Finland to prevent the exit of Russian submarines.

While Germany controlled the western Baltic Sea waters, the eastern side was left to the Finnish Navy as the German boats could not access the Gulf of Finland due to Hanko. Finlands' role in the eastern Baltic was primarily clearing Russian mines, laying Finnish mines and protecting Finland's own shores.

Russia was forced to abandon Hanko in December 1941 due to bombardment by German ships and Finnish coastal artillery. As a result of this Finland was able to get easier access to much needed bulk shipments – especially coal.

Minimal naval battles occurred even after Hanko was liberated as the Gulf of Finland was a mine field populated with almost 70,000 Russian, Finnish and German mines.

After the war it took ten years to clear the mines. Some mines still exist today.

The Finnish Navy only took part in a few campaigns:

- As part of Germany's Operation Nordwind in September 1941, it lost one of its' two coastal defense ships, the Ilmarinen, to a mine;
- In July 1942 the Finnish navy stopped Russia's attempt to capture the island of Sommers in the Gulf of Finland;
- During the Russian summer assault of 1944, the Finnish navy ships, infantry and shore batteries played a major role in preventing the Russian forces from crossing the Viipuri Lahti;
- During the Lapland War the Finnish navy was instructmental in preventing German forces from capturing Suursaari; and on October 1st, 1944 enabling the successful amphibious landing of the Finnish troops in Tornio.

The main focus of the Finnish Navy's efforts was successfully blocking the submarines of the Russian Navy from reaching the western part of the Baltic Sea. In conjunction with the German Navy they were able to contain the Russian Navy until the end of the Continuation War.

The Finnish Navy also conducted small operations on Lake Ladoga and Lake Onega. Here they used patrol boats, mine vessels, tugs and old captured Russian vessels. Here the main role was to securing the shoreline and transporting materials. In 1942 Germany dispatched a small flotilla to Lake Ladoga to patrol the lake with the Finnish gunboats, but withdrew it within a year. Among the German ships were armed ferries plus Italian patrol boats. Finland acquired two armed ferries from Germany when they left.

As well as the operations in Finland, the Finnish naval forces garrisoned the Ahvemaa Islands.

CHAPTER 6

My Father and My Uncles
& the Jatkosota

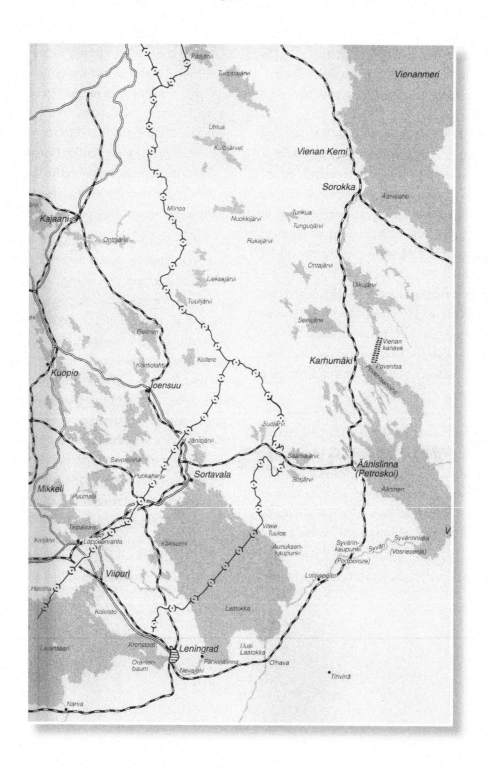

CHAPTER 6

My Father and My Uncles & the Jatkosota

My father and my uncles were once more in the depths of the conflict – on the Kannas, Lake Ladoga, and Lapland.

Father

Father was stationed from 1941 to 1943 on the Lapland frontier in northern Finland, between Salla and Kemijarvi. He was still with the railroad, initially located in Kelloselka near Salla and later at Kemijarvi. Initially he was overseeing the building of the railway in the Salla area, and later was responsible for building the bridge at Kemijarvi.

During 1941 – 1942 he once more had a dog tag. At night he rode the railway line guarding it from Russian guerillas intent on blowing up the track.

In November 1943 he was transferred to southern Finland with responsibility for the track from Kouvola to Riihimaki.

Uncle Erkki

Uncle Erkki, although already 39, was called up. During his medical he was diagnosed with terminal cancer. He was discharged and returned home to fight an opponent even fiercer then the Russians.

Uncle Toivo

Uncle Toivo once more fought on the Kannas never far from his beloved Kavantsaari home.

He was called up again on June 16, 1941. The military entry brusquely notes, *"Kivaari mies, taistelu lahetta – Rifle man, send to the front."*

Uncle Toivo was assigned to the 2nd company of the Kevyt Os 7 of the 18th Division. His unit attacked down the Karjala Kannas to the Old Finnish Border on the coast of the Gulf of Finland.

After October 27th 1941 his unit was transferred to Company 10 of the 3rd battalion of the legendary Tyrjän Regiment (2.D / JR7) of the Army of the Isthmus for most of the war. The exception to this was the period of January to October 1942 when Toivo was part of regiments 28 and 49. Both these regiments were located beside JR7.

During the trench warfare his unit held the notorious Ohta sector on the defensive line north of Leningrad.

When the Russian assault began in June 1943, his unit fought fierce rear guard battles at Siiranmaki, and Ayrapaa / Vuosalmi. These battles were of the same magnitude and ferocity as the Tali-Ihantala battle.

Toivo's regiment was part of the 2nd division. The 2nd Division suffered the highest number of casualties of any Finnish division. Over the 3 years of battle 17,168 or 143% of the divisions' complement was killed or was wounded. It is a miracle that Uncle Toivo survived unharmed.

Uncle Arvo

Uncle Arvo fought on the Karelian Isthmus (Kannas) from Viipuri south to St. Petersburg.

Uncle Arvo never left the army after the Winter War as he still had to complete his service.

During the Jatkosota he continued as a combat engineer with Company 3 of Pioneer Battalion 14 (3./Pion P14). PionP 14 was part of Army Corps IV. During the summer assault he was seconded to Os Kanerva, the elite Jaakari attack unit of the 12th Division which fought down the west central part of the Kannas to the Gulf just north of Leningrad.

During the trench warfare period he was in Viipuri defusing Russian bombs and on the Kannas building fortifications and mine fields. At the end of the war he fought a rearguard action back up the Kannas to Tali-Ihantala.

After the Jatkosota ended Uncle Arvo served in the Lapland War with the headquarters unit of Pion P14 in Kemi and Rovanniemi from September 1944 to the end of November 1944.

Uncle Vilho

Uncle Vilho was with Division 8. From the beginning of the war until March 1942 he served as a food supply column leader with Division 8. Division 8 was part of AK IV on the Viipuri front until October when it was transferred to the Maaselka front of the Ladoga Karjala theatre.

During the Maaselka campaign he remained with the divisional supply depot. In March 1942 he transferred over to Company 8 of JR45 of the 8th Division as an infantryman on the Syvari front. There he also did some combat engineering work – he had received some combat engineering training during his conscription service.

He was severely wounded on June 12, 1944 during the Russian assault across the Syvari River. He spent the next 4 months in Military Hospitals 66 on the Syvari front and 30 at Jyvaskyla. He never returned to his unit.

The 8th Division suffered 7,299 casualties, or 58% of its' strength.

Uncle Kauko

Uncle Kauko was with JR35 of the 1st Division. He served in the Ladoga Karjala Theatre.

From the start of the war until March 1942 he was a light machine gunner with the 5th Company of the 35th Regiment of the VI Army Corps. The VI Army Corps led the attack east to Petroksoi and from thence north to Karhumaki and Stalin's Canal.

In March 1942, after the war settled into the trenches, he was a assigned as a driver with the head quarters unit of the 2nd Battalion of JR35.

After going to the hospital for a month in October 1942 he returned to the JR35 1st battalions' headquarters unit as a transportation record clerk.

Then in October 1943 he was assigned to work in the Karhumaki Prison Camp 31 (SVL31) for 3 months. After this he served with IIAK headquarters forestry unit. From January 29th to June 1944 he was a foreman with the lumbering unit. In June 1944 when the Russian assault began he was assigned as a driver with Firewood Mill 5 until being disbanded on October 19 1944.

The casualties for the 1st Division were 9,401 or 78%.

Uncle Aatu

Uncle Aatu, although already 38 years old, served in the Continuation War. He served as a regimental messenger with the 48th infantry regiment (JR48).

JR48 was part of the 18th Division, of the II Army Corps. It attacked down the Karjala Isthmus from Enso towards Leningrad. The majority of its' fighting took place at the north western end of Lake Laadoga in July and August, as it pushed back the heavily entrenched Russian forces.

The battles of Vaskikumpu, Oinaanvaara, and Lahdenpohja are noted for Uncle Aatu.

By August 31st the regiment was at Korpikyla on The Old Border where it settled into a trench warfare holding pattern.

Uncle Aatu was demobilized on January 16, 1942 as the army no longer needed 39 year old soldiers. At this point JR48 was on the front line trenches at Valkesaari near the Gulf of Finland.

Uncle Yrjo

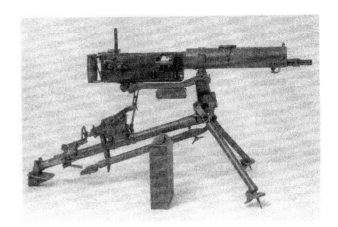

Uncle Yrjo, my dad's brother, was in the Home Guard as he was with the Finnish Railway working as a railroad dispatcher in the Hameenlinna area. As well he served with the local Civil Guard anti aircraft battery. An excellent mathematician, he was responsible for calculating the firing coordinates. He was disbanded on June 9, 1943.

PART III

The Summer Assault 1941

PÄÄMAJA.

YLIPÄÄLLIKÖN
PÄIVÄKÄSKY
N:o 1.

SUOMEN SOTILAAT!

Kunniakas talvisotamme päättyi katkeraan rauhaan. — Rauhanteosta huolimatta vihollisemme on pitänyt maatamme häikäilemättömien uhkailujensa ja jatkuvien kiristystensä kohteena, mikä yhdessä rikollisen kiihoitustyön kanssa yksimielisyytemme murskaamiseksi on osoittanut, että vihollinen ei ollut alunperin tarkoittanutkaan rauhaa pysyväiseksi. — Tehty rauha oli vain välirauha, joka nyt on päättynyt.

Te tunnette vihollisen. Te tiedätte sen jatkuvat tarkoitusperät kotiemme, uskontomme ja Isänmaamme hävittämiseksi ja kansamme orjuuttamiseksi. Tämä sama vihollinen ja sama uhka on nyt rajoillamme. Ilman aihetta se on röyhkeästi hyökännyt rauhassa elävän kansamme kimppuun ja pudottanut pommeja eri puolille maata. Isänmaan tu evaisuus vaatii Teiltä uusia tekoja.

Kutsun Teitä kanssani pyhään sotaan kansakuntamme vihollista vastaan. Sankarivainajat nousevat kesäisten kumpujen alta jälleen rinnallemme tänään, jolloin lähdemme Suomelle turvatun tulevaisuuden luodaksemme Saksan mahtavien sotavoimien rinnalla ja asetovereina vakain mielin ristiretkelle vihollistamme vastaan.

Aseveljet! — Seuratkaa minua vielä viimeisen kerran — nyt, kun Karjalan kansa jälleen nousee ja sarastaa Suomen uusi huomen.

Mannerheim

PART III

The Summer Assault 1941

The Continuation war between Finland and Russia began on June 25th, 1941. Prior to that Finland had mobilized its' army, recalling all the reserves to active duty on June 17th.

Mannerheim highlighted the cause to his armed forces in his first Commander-in-Chiefs Order of the Day:

Our glorious winter war ended with a bitter peace. Irrespective of the peace agreement the enemy have been issuing unwarranted threats and applying continuous pressure. Together with criminal acts, these actions have shattered our accord. From the beginning, the enemy has not meant the peace be a lasting one. The peace was only a temporary peace, one which has now ended.

You know our enemy. You know their goal is to destroy our homes, god, and country, and to enslave our people. This same enemy and threat is now at our borders. Without any reason they have brazenly attacked our peace living nation and dropped bombs all over our land. The future of our fatherland requires new deeds from YOU.

I call upon YOU to launch a holy war against our nations' enemy. Our fallen heroes are rising up from underneath the fresh green mounds of their graves to be beside us today, as we move forward to create a secure future for Finland beside the mighty forces of Germany - brothers in arms in the crusade against our enemy.

Brothers in arms – follow me yet this last time – now, as the nation of Karjala arises again and a new dawn breaks for Finland.

The summer assault began in July.

On the Kannas the full attack did not begin until July 31st, although initial unsuccessful forays across the border occurred on June 29th. By August 31st the Finnish forces were across the Old Finnish Border just 20 kilometers from the outskirts of Leningrad.

On the Ladoga Karjala front, the main attack began July 10th. By mid September the Finnish forces had recaptured all of Old Finland; and, had moved well into Russia crossing the Syvari River and penetrating one third of the way towards Petroksoi.

In Northern Finland / Lapland the German Army together with its' Finnish forces started their attack on July 1st. The German attack stalled by mid September without capturing Murmansk or reaching the Murmansk Railway.

CHAPTER 7

An Overview of
the War On the Kannas

SA-Kuva

An Overview of the War on the Kannas

The war on the Kannas lasted from June 25th to September 8th, 1941. Finland set up two armies in the theatre – AK IV and AK II (later also AK I).

Overall Military Organization

On the Kannas, Mannerheim organized his forces into two armies – AK IV and AK II.

The IVAK under Lieutenant General Karl Lennart Oesch, was responsible for the western section of the Kannas from the border near Hamina to Imatra. Its' objective was to liberate Viipuri. It consisted of the 8th, 4th and 12th divisions.

The IIAK, under Major General Taavetti Laatikainen, was responsible for a 105 kilometer section from Imatra to Pyhajarvi (50 kilometers northwest of Sortavala). Its' objective was to retake the area west of Lake Ladoga, and then cross the Vuoksi River near Antrea and advance south to the original border north of Leningrad. It consisted on the 18th, 10th, 15th, and 2nd divisions.

On August 13th after AK II encountered heavy fighting at Tyra, another army corps – AK I under Colonel Makinen - was formed. It took over from AK II in capturing the western shore of Lake Ladoga. This allowed AK II to allocate all its' efforts to breaking through the main Russian defenses on the central Kannas.

Mannerheim's strategy was to launch a two pronged attack.

1. The II AK would attack across the border from the north east portion of the Kannas. Their initial objective would be to overcome the Russian defensive line near the border and push south to Antrea. Once past Antrea, their objective was to cross the Vuoksi River, capture the western bank and from thence attack south west through Perkjarvi and Kivennapa to The Old Finnish Border by the Gulf of Finland.

2. Concurrent with this some of the forces would attack the Russian positions by Lake Ladoga – capturing Kakisalmi and Hiitola and Taipale and from thence push through Rautu to the Old Border.

3. As Viipuri and the western part of the Kannas was heavily defended, Mannerheim's plan was to wait until AK II had crossed the Vuoksi River and then attack Viipuri from the north - and from the south. Once AK II had crossed the Vuoksi, it could ensure

the Russian forces in Viipuri could neither receive reinforcements from the east nor retreat eastwards.

4. The southern attack entailed making a night time amphibious assault across the Gulf of Finland near Viipuri, and to then attacking north towards Viipuri thus encircling the Russian army in the Viipuri vicinity.

Opposing them on the Kannas, the Russians 50AK and 19AK of the 23rd Army put up a strong defense. The Russians construction of their main defensive line was partially complete. However along all the roads there were strong placements with bunkers, machine gun pill boxes, minefields and barbed wire.

The first Finnish forays across the border at the end of June proved that recapturing the Kannas would not be easy. An attack at Enso resulted in a bloody retreat, while one at Tyra resulted in a bloody stalemate.

As a result of this, and the uncertainty of Finland's attack east of Lake Ladoga, the II AK did not launch its' major assault until July 31st, and the IV AK not until August 21st.

The IIAK successfully crossed the Vuoksi River at Ayrapaa/ Vuosalmi on August 20th. From there they proceeded south gaining the Old Finnish Border on August 31st. The IVAK took Viipuri on August 29th. By Lake Ladoga, AKI reached the Old Finnish Border south of Rautu by the end of August.

The Units of My Uncles during the Summer of '41

Uncles Aatu, Toivo, Arvo and Vilho all took part in the summer '41 assault down the Kannas. Father was in Lapland and Uncle Toivo in Ladoga Russia. The roles and types of their units differed.

1. Uncle Arvo was a combat engineer with Pion P14. On July 7th he was a part of a platoon that was seconded to Osasto Kanerva an elite Jaakari attack force which was part of Kevyt Pr Tiianinen of the 12th Division of AK IV.

2. Uncle Toivo was a rifleman with Kevyt Osasto 7 - the elite light infantry group of the 18th Division of AK II.

3. Uncle Aatu was a messenger with the head quarters unit of the JR48th infantry regiment of the 2nd Division of AK II/ AK I.

4. Uncle Vilho was a leader of the food unit of the divisional supply column of the 8th Division of IVAK.

They were positioned on the Kannas from near the north western shore of Lake Ladoga to just east of Viipuri on the north shore of the Gulf of Viipuri. Uncle Aatu with the 2nd Division was on the eastern flank of the attack; Uncle Toivo with the 18th Division on the east side of the Vuoksi River;

Uncle Arvo on the west side of the Vuoksi; and Uncle Vilho east of Viipuri on the north shore.

Comrades in arms, as well as brothers, they were often only 20 kilometers from each other as they attacked down the Kannas towards Leningrad.

While all of them were soldiers, their responsibilities and units were unqiue.

Uncle Toivo

Uncle Toivo's unit, Kevyt Os 7 (Light Infantry Group 7), were the mobile shock troops of the 18th Division of AKII. Kevyt Os 7 consisted of:

- 2 Jaakari bicycle companies. While bicycles sound definitely non warrior kit, they were instrumental the units ability to move quickly during the summer from site to site on the countryside roads.
- 1 machine gun company
- An antitank artillery unit with light canons.
- A Headquarters unit
- A Supply unit
- A Pioneer platoon

On June 19th 1941 the units complement was 364 men. It was commanded by Major G Boisman and was part of Colonel A Pajaari's 18th Division. While operating under direct divisional command it was periodically seconded to the 49th, 6th, and 27th infantry regiments.

Casualties within the group were high. Over 50% of the original complement had been killed or wounded in the first month and a half. On August 16th when Uncle Toivo joined Kevyt Os 7, he was one of 198 new men.

Uncle Arvo

Uncle Arvo's unit was the Pion P14 combat engineering battalion. Pion P14, commanded by Captain V Tiainen, was not part of a specific infantry division, rather it was part of AK IV - to be assigned by Lieutenant General Oesch, and his Pioneer commandant Lieutenant Colonel N.M. Oinonen, to wherever special assistance was required.

Pion P14 was a combat engineering battalion - not a bridge construction engineering (SiltaK), road construction (TienHK), road maintenance / winter road clearance (Aur.K), temporary fortification construction (Lin.Rak.K), nor inland waters movement (Mt.Pont.K) company. When I talked with Uncle Arvo when he was already in his 90s, I was still unclear what military engineering forces did. I asked whether he actually saw action or was primarily behind the lines doing construction. He replied that, *"Yes we certainly were in the fighting."* – and, that was all he would say. The one other comment he did say now stands out in my mind even more.

Uncle Arvo commented that his brother Toivo – "Was in the midst of the worst of the fighting in both wars."

In Uncle Arvo's opinion what he himself saw and did during the wars was nothing compared to his brother Toivo.

Given what I now know about Uncle Arvo's own war, what Uncle Toivo must have experienced is beyond comprehension. But as I have learned about Uncle Toivo's war I now understand why Uncle Arvo made the comment.

As a combat engineer Uncle Arvo saw extensive action. He had responsibility for setting and clearing minefields, exploding bridges, breaching trenches and bunkers, setting and clearing tank traps – often in the midst of battle. And periodically when the circumstances were dire he was a rifleman and tank destroyer.

Not only was Uncle Arvo a combat engineer, he was a member one of its elite squadrons. On July 7th he was seconded to Osasto Kanerva as part of a special combat engineering platoon under Lieutenant Mietteinen. Osasto Kanerva was an elite Jaakari attack force that was part of Kevyt Pr Tianinen of the 12th Division of AK IV.

Given that the Kannas had been heavily mined by the Russians, the group needed an experienced and motivated group of combat engineers to help them deactivate the Russian minefields and defenses. Uncle Arvo, an intelligent resourceful individual, was definitely qualified – an exceptional athlete, a tough Kannas farm boy familiar with the countryside, and a seasoned Winter War combat engineer.

Os Kanerva was placed in the hardest fighting. The units' casualties were very high. Of a strength of 500 - over two months 40% or 200 - were wounded or killed - including the commanders of both companies.

Casualties with Light Brigade Tiianen (Kev Pr T) to which Os Kanerva belonged were high as well. At the start of the war the IV AK had formed units capable of quick attack. The most notable of these was Light Brigade Tiiainen (Kev Pr T) and Light JR 4. On July 7, 1941 Colonel Tiiainen, the commander of JR 3, was made the commander of Pr T from whence it got its' name. Light Brigade Tiiainen (Kev Pr T), had about 1,600 men. It was composed of two light infantry units (Kev Os 9 and Kev Os 14); two artillery companies (10 and 14.Tyk.K); a company of the Pion P 14 combat engineer battalion (1./Pion 14); the 121st light anti aircraft battery (121.Kev.It.Ptri); and the Kaptain A Kanerva led elite Osasto Kanerva infantry.

Uncle Aatu

Uncle Aatu's unit was the 48th infantry regiment. He was a messenger in the regiments' headquarters company.

JR48 was commanded until August 5th by Colonel Vartiovaara, and thereafter by Lieutenant Colonel Sora.

It was a typical infantry regiment.

- It had a complement of 3,600 men – 119 officers (3%), 543 NCOs (15%), and 2,954 men.
- These were organized into a head quarters unit, 3 infantry battalions, a Jaakari company, an artillery company, a howitzer company, a pioneer company, a communications company, a supply column, and a head quarters company (which Uncle Aatu was part of).
- Armaments consisted of 2,500 rifles, 400 sub machine guns, 144 light machine guns, 36 machine guns, 30 anti tank guns, 6 anti tank canons.
- The regiment had 415 horses and 344 bicycles. The bicycles were primarily for the Jaakari units. It only had 9 automobiles/trucks and 2 motor cycles.

Uncle Aatu as a regimental messenger delivered his dispatches by horse or bicycle. Being with the regimental head quarters, Uncle Aatu was not in face to face combat with the Russian tanks and soldiers like Uncles Toivo and Arvo. Nonetheless being a messenger he was near the mayhem and death as he delivered dispatches from the regiment to the company commanders.

Uncle Vilho

Uncle Vilho's unit was the divisional supply column of the 8th Division. The 8th Division led by Colonel Claes Winell was part of the IV AK. Stationed on the border of the IV AK's western flank the 8th Divisions objective was to cross the gulf west of Viipuri and to then attack north to free Viipuri.

The bulk of the Divisional Services units' duties was providing food for the men - and the horses. It also took care of medical, veterinary, housing, clothes and fuel supplies; as well as vehicle maintenance and operation of the field post office. The fuel supply for the autos and trucks was alcohol and charcoal. Gasoline, being scarce, was reserved for tanks and airplanes.

The artillery units took care of their own munitions and equipment needs as well as the ammunition for the infantry. The pioneer units likewise took care of their own supplies (explosives, land mines, tank mines, Molotov cocktails, et al). As well the communications, anti tank, and flamethrower units took care of their own specialized equipment and munitions. The pastoral office took care of the movement of the dead.

Uncle Vilho was one of the leaders of the food supply unit. The Divisions maintained 7 to 15 days food in a supply depot. The supplies were received primarily via rail either directly from Finland or from the Army Corps. Each Division had one auto / truck company as well as numerous horse transportation units. The Divisions distributed the food to the regiments, from where it was dispensed to the battalions and companies. Generally the Divisional supply units were located with the Divisional head quarters about 10 to 15 kilometers behind its' regiments. The divisional supply depots needed to be mobile during the summer assault to keep up with rapidly advancing infantry.

CHAPTER 8

My Uncles
Summer Days on
Their Kannas

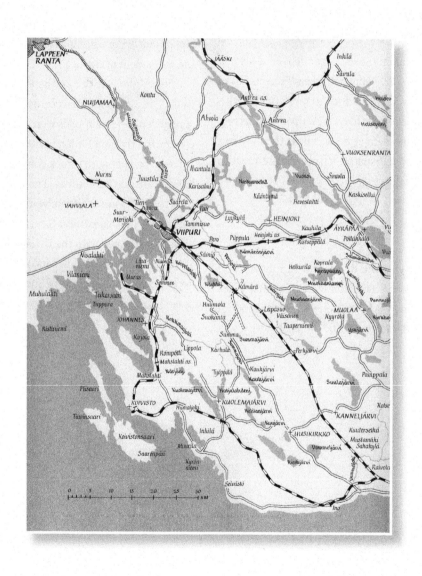

CHAPTER 8

My Uncles Summer Days on Their Kannas

The days of the summer assault on the Kannas for my uncles were:

- Quiet from June 16 to July 30, 1941 for all my uncles;
- July 30th to August 16th brought the attack by the IIAK and I AK to capture the north east portion of the Kannas north of Taipale east of the Vuoksi River; and, to cross the Vuoksi River at Vuosalmi / Ayrapaa.
- Uncle Aatu's regiment was in the heart of the attack through the entire two weeks.
- Uncle Toivo's unit was as well, but he did not join it until it reached the Vuoksi on August 16th.
- On August 22nd the IV AK launched its' attack to capture Viipuri; and, together with the II AK

to cross The Old Finnish Border just north of St Petersburg by early September.
- Now Uncle Arvo and Vilho's units joined the attack.

The map on the previous page illustrates the Kannas campaign.

In the remainder of this chapter I expand on my uncles campaigns day by day as taken from the sota paiva kirjas of their units. Many of the place names are for hamlets and small lakes which can only be found on the most detailed maps. While somewhat difficult to follow they illustrate the nature of the war in the countryside; the continuous characteristic of the fighting; and the numerous different attack routes taken by the many units.

June 16 to July 30, 1941

During the first month and a half of the war it was quiet for my uncles – and indeed it was quiet for all the army units on the Kannas.

The exception to this, were brief, bloody, unsuccessful forays across the border by the 18th and 2nd divisions.

Uncle Erkki

On June 20th Uncle Erkki received a summons to report for service. And he like all his brothers welcomed the call. None had any illusions about war being a heroic and painless endeavor. All however were ready and willing to sacrifice themselves for their country – especially as it would result in them recovering their home.

Uncle Erkki, now 39 years old, readily reported to the induction centre. Uncle Erkki did not serve however. During his induction medical on July 3rd, 1941 he was diagnosed with cancer and sent home to fight an even deadlier enemy then the Russian army.

Uncle Toivo

On June 22nd Uncle Toivo received his military call up summons at his home in Kallaslahti near Sullkava.

He was assigned to the 4th company at the troop mustering centre (4./HTK) north of the border. He waited and underwent refresher training. Obviously he was going to see action, but where ?

On August 16th he was assigned to Kevyt Os 7 (Light Infantry Group 7) of the 18th Division of AKII as a rifleman. As during the Winter War he was once more in the heart of the war's vortex.

Before Uncle Toivo joined the unit, it had crossed border at Ahola on June 29th in an endeavor to take Enso. They suffered major losses and retreated back across the border for the next month. When the summer assault started in earnest on July 31st Kevyt Os 7 was one of the lead attack units.

Uncle Arvo

The beginning of June found Uncle Arvo with the 6th company of the 14th combat engineering battalion (6./Pion P14). He had never left the army after the Winter War as he still needed to complete his service.

On June 16th when mobilization began, he was transferred to the 3rd company of Pion P14.

On July 7th Uncle Arvo was seconded to the special attack force Os Kanerva, located in Lappeenranta. On July 8th Lieutenant General Laatikainen reviewed the Os Kanerva force. Lieutenant Miettinen the leader of Uncle Arvo's Pioneer platoon remembered that:

The General stated that "The task that you are embarking on is both critical and dangerous. If things go well casualties will be low, but conversely if they go poorly casualties will be very large". After this the General gave the option for anyone to return to their original unit, but none in my Pioneer platoon retracted their promise to serve with the group. All were prepared to depart with Os Kanerva on its demanding and dangerous mission of provoking the enemy behind their lines. ...

In the following days the platoon moved with Os Kanerva to Lauritsala and from thence forward to the Joutseno area.

There Uncle Arvo waited with his unit until the middle of August.

Uncle Aatu

On June 18th, at his home in Vaajakoski near Jyvaskyla, Uncle Aatu received his call to join his regiment.

On June 28th he was with his unit, the headquarters company of the 48th infantry regiment of the 8th Division, north of the border just east of Pienen – Rautjarvi. Once more he was a messenger, this time with the regiment as opposed to the company.

On July 19th army high command switched JR48 from the 8th to the 2nd Division. To Uncle Aatu this of course did not mean anything.

Until the end of July, he and his regiment remained on reserve north of the border.

Uncle Vilho

Uncle Vilho was called up on June 19th. He was assigned to the 8th Division Supply Group as a food supply unit leader. I don't know why he was placed in a support organization while a healthy 24 year old, as opposed to becoming a front line soldier like his brothers.

In June, the 8th Division supply group was located in three depots north of Sakkijarvi.

July 30 to August 16th

On July 31st AK II started a full attack across the border with two of its' 4 divisions – 18.D north of Enso and the 2.D between Tyjra and Pyhajarvi.

AK II took Ilmee on August 5th after heavy fighting. It crossed the Vuoksi River initially on August 17th just south of Antrea at Hopesalmi. On August 21st the bulk of the forces crossed at Ayrapaa after both sides of the Vuoksi had been secured. This provided better roads for the armies attack west towards Viipuri and south west to the old border.

AKI to their east captured Tyra and Elisenvaara and then advanced towards Lahdenpohja and the Ladoga shore north of Kakisalmi.

The IV AK waited.

All of my uncles except Uncle Aatu also waited. Uncle Toivo waited to be assigned to his unit Kevyt Os 7. Uncle Arvo and Uncle Vilho waited as they were part of IV AK.

Uncle Aatu

Uncle Aatu most definitely took part in the assault. Uncle Aatu and his regiment were in the forefront of the attack on the north east Kannas.

- On July 31 the 2nd Division attacked with JR7 and JR48 to take Tyra and Oinaanvaara. JR48's objective was to capture Oinaanvaara.
- The Russian forces were heavily entrenched in the area and fought back fiercely.
- At 12:30 on July 31st JR48 attacked towards Vaskikummu but was stopped. After a day of fighting JR48 took Vaskikummu on August 1st. Uncle Aatu's military record notes the battle of Vaskikummu
- On August 3rd Aatu and his regiment were near Oinaanvaara. And like Uncle Aatu's military record notes, the battle here lasted five days – from August

3rd to August 7th . On August 3rd the unit had arrived at the town outskirts, the troops tired and worn out. On the following August 4th morning the regiment launched an attack against the heavily manned Russian defenses. The IIIrd JR48 battalion attacked from the north east and the Ist battalion from the east. The Russian regiments, JR181 and JR450 augmented by a battalion of JR461, launched many counter attacks. The Finnish attack stalled 5 kilometers north of the village. On August 5th the regimental commander Colonel Vartiovaara was replaced by Lieutenant Colonel Sora. Full day attacks began again on August 6th and 7th. By mid day the village of Oinaavaara was in Finnish hands.

- On August 8 and 9th JR48 was in Lotjakanka and Meria battling towards Pajasyra.

- From August 13th to the 17th Uncle Aatu was immersed in the Battle of Pajasyra. The regimental sota paiva kirja for August 13th is 4 ½ pages. The entries start with the commencement of the battle at 05:00 and end at 22:30. The entries illustrate the extensive coordination needed for the rapid deployment of the regiments companies during the battle. Uncle Aatu would have been busy that day delivering the many dispatches. The page below tracks the battle for 2 ½ hours from 09:10 to 11:40:

09:10 *The I Battalion reports that in the p80 area there are Russians, likewise in the south east part of p102 countryside.*

09:30 *The Likolammenmaki area has been cleared of the enemy.*

Order to gather the forces and march to Lapimaki, where prepare to move to the east and northeast. After preparations move forward to Kuokkaniemi, Niva - towards the west.

09:50   The II Battalion reports that Lapimaki has been captured – Order to seize the Heino-Aho-Tikka countryside and to send one company to seize the Niva railway station.

10:00   The regiments' doctor reported that, up until now, during the Pajasyra and Kukkalammi battle the regiment has suffered 155 wounded.

10:05   The Division headquarters reports that enemy air force action on other areas of the front has increased. The anti aircraft platoon must pay even more attention then before (information has been communicated to our own sub units)

10:30   Order to the II Battalion (change to earlier order): Send a company immediately to the Niva train station, but after eating.

11:40   Information from the Division:

"According to Russian captives: In Mensuvaara the artillery command post has been encircled. Also two weeks ago a 80-100 man guerrilla group, some disguised in Finnish uniforms and some in civilian clothes, left Uuksilta. To protect themselves on their return from being taken for Finnish soldiers, during the day they were to place white handkerchiefs on their rifles, and at night fire two light flares."

11:40   Bulletin from the Division (Captured message)

Message from Russian 2nd Army to the 168th Division at 14:00 on August 11th :

Order from the Russian Army command: Prepare the division and JR208 to move from the Hiitola area. At the time of the move only take the equipment necessary for fighting. That left behind will have to be recovered later. Immediately send the entire fleet to Rautalahti to evacuate the wounded and unnecessary goods.

- On August 17th JR48 was at Miinala, just east of Lahdenpohja near Lake Ladoga.

- As the regiment advanced they had captured a lot of war material. On August 20th in a motti at Maunojarvi – SuurKarilahti they captured: 10 tanks, 8 artillery guns, 300 autos and trucks, 10 motorcycles, and 750 horses, 200 cows, and 100 sheep. The horses of course were for moving goods and weapons – the cows and sheep I assume were for food.

The regiment suffered 770 casualties in the first two weeks of the war attack: 135 killed, 554 wounded and 80 sick. The 3rd, 4th and 11th companies had been down to half strength by August 10th. Given that the regiment complement seems to have had an average strength of 2,300, this means about every third man was a casualty. Casualties after August 17th were thankfully miminal as no major battles occurred.

Cold figures at the front – heartbreak at home.

	Esik.K	13.K	14.K	I P	II P	III P	KTR 15	Kev.Os. 6	Lin.K	Pion.K	LK 23	
Rykm:n JSp:iden kautta evakuoidut 1. – 15.7.41.												
Haav.	9	8	14	183	117	167	49	1	1	4	1	=554
Sair.		2	2	39	15	22	1					= 80
Kaat.			50	40	43	2						=135
										Yht.		770

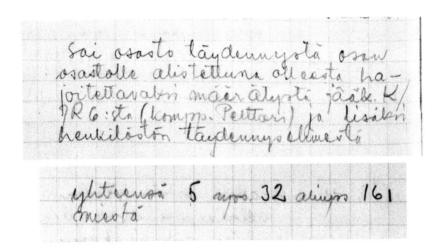

Note the figure is from the August 18th Paiva kirja. The heading says 15.7.41 but it is an error and should have been 15.8.41. JR48 was not in any battles before the attack started July 31st.

Uncle Toivo

During the period Uncle Aatu's 2nd Division was advancing towards Lake Ladoga and Taipale, Uncle Toivo's 18th Division was attacking south west towards Antrea and Ayrapaa on the Vuoksi River.

Kevyt Os 7 was one of the lead units in the 18th Division's attack. The unit moved continuously at a moments' notice to the next hot spot. There were many forays behind enemy lines, skirmishes, and battles. A great deal of material was captured and many Russians were killed and captured. But this was all at the cost of a large number of casualties. When taking the Russian lines at Ahola Kevyt Os 7 suffered 38 casualties. In the August 8 battle near Karjalaisenkyla/Kirvu the unit suffered 102 casualties.

- On August 5th the unit took Ilmee. On the 9th they were at Kirvu and Inkila.

- From thence Kevyt Os 7 led the attack past Inkila to Hiitola and the Ladoga shore. By August 10th they were near Vuokenranta. On August 11th they captured Hiitola.

- The 18th Division then turned its' attack towards Antrea. By August 14th the division had forced the Russian forces back over the Vuoksi River at Antrea.

- On August 14th Kevyt Os 7 was ordered to Sintola half way between Antrea and Pollakkala to prepare for the crossing of the Vuoksi River at the Hopesalmi narrows near Hevossaari.

- On August 16th, the day before JR27 crossed the Vuoksi River at Hopesalmi, Kevyt Os 7 was ordered to clear the countryside on the eastern side of the Vuoksi River from Hopesalmi to Vuosalmi.

- It was here at Rehuselka north of Orvaniemi that on August 16th Uncle Toivo joined the depleted ranks of Kevy Os 7. Uncle Toivo was one of 198 replacements – the remains of the Jaakari company from JR6, and seasoned Winter War veterans such as Uncle Toivo.

All together 5 officers, 32 NCOs and 161 infantry men joined the ranks of Kevyt Os 7.

Uncle Arvo

Uncle Arvo was waiting with attack group Os Kanerva, north of the border near Joutseno.

The IV AK had not started its' attack yet, waiting for the eastern flank on the Vuoksi River to be secured

Uncle Vilho

Uncle Vilho was with the divisional supply depot still north of Sakkijarvi near the border.

August 16 to August 31, 1941

The Finnish forces assault intensified in the middle of August. By Sept 8th Russian forces had had to retreat to just north of St. Petersburg. The I AK captured the western shore of Lake Ladoga all the way south to The Old Finnish Border. The II AK advanced across the middle of the Kannas to the Gulf of Finland just north of St Peterburg while the AK IV captured Viipuri. Unlike during the Winter War, the Finnish artillery was able to play a major role.

The II AK advanced aggressively.

- After crossing the Vuoksi AK II's 18th Division continued its' attack from Ayrapaa south through Muolaa and Perkjarvi to Kivennapa north of The Old Finnish Border. It crossed the border on August 31st.
- The 10th and 15th divisions continued liberating the western Ladoga shore. On August 18th the 10th division took Raisala, and on the 21st the 15th division took Kakislami. The two divisions then moved south westwards crossing the Vuoksi and arriving at The Old Finnish Border between Rautu and Lipola.
- The newly formed AKI attacked south beside Lake Ladoga with the 7th, 19th and 2nd Divisions, across the Vuoksi at Oravanniemi and Taipale, and onwards east of Rautu to The Old Finnish Border at Tappari and Raisala. On August 23rd the 2nd Division was returned to the IIAK, joining the 18th Division's attack.

While AK II and AK I had been advancing, AK IV had remained at its' positions on the border north of Viipuri. On August 22nd after AKII had successfully crossed the Vuoksi River, thus protecting AK IV's eastern flank, AK IV launched its' attack on Viipuri.

- The 12th Division, attacked on the eastward flank from the border north of Enso southwards beside the Vuoksi River through Ihantala and Kavantsaari, and onwards to the south east side of Viipuri at Lyykyla.

- During the advance our home in Kavantsaari was once more in wars path. The Russians on August 21st decided to cede Jaaski rather then being encircled, and retreated south. JR26 and Kev Os 1 pursued them southward. On the 22nd they advanced through Ahvola. After midnight Kev Os 1 struck the enemy forces in Hannila with a sudden attack. From there the unit moved to Pullila and Kavantsaari, arriving in Kavantsaari early in the morning of the 23rd . As victory on the Kannas was not yet a sure thing, they were ordered to sever the Antrea to Viipuri rail line and the major road junction. The unit then continued onwards from Kavantsaari towards Karisalmi and by night fall of the 24th caught up with Kevyt Pr T.

  I wonder if the Finnish units were the ones that destroyed the small bridge just west of Kavantssaari leading to Ihantala and grandpas' farm ?

- The 4th Division attacked Viipuri from the north - from Nuijamaa south of Joutseno through Juustila and Tienharra.The 8th Division attacked on the west flank. It launched an amphibious night time assault over the Gulf of Finland just west of Viipuri; and upon successful land fall pushed northwards towards Viipuri.
- Viipuri fell to the Finnish forces on August 29th. The Russian forces were caught in a motti at Porlampi south of Viipuri, as the retreat route to Leningrad was blocked by the 8th and 12th divisions, and AK II forces.
- By September 1st the Russian 4th Division was destroyed. Along with the surrendering troops, including their commander Major General Vladimir Kirpichnikov, the Finnish army captured a major arsenal of weapons -55 tanks, 300 tractors, 700 trucks, and over 550 howitzers and canons. Along

with the heavy weaponary, they captured millions of rounds of ammunition and thousands of rifles. All were put to good use by the Finnish army.

By the first week of September the Finnish forces were positioned across the entire length of The Old Finnish Border from Lake Ladoga to the Gulf of Finland. Here on September 9th Mannerheim stopped the attack– just 25 kilometers north of Leningrad.

The Finnish army set up its' lines and settled into almost 3 years of trench warfare.

Uncle Toivo

Uncle Toivo's 2nd Company of Kevyt Osasto 7 of the 18th Division crossed the Vuoksi River and attacked south west through Muolaa and Kivennapa arriving on September 3rd over The Old Finnish Border at Aleksandrovka on the Gulf of Finland.

On August 16th Uncle Toivo and his unit were at Rehuselka on the east bank of Vuoksi ready to cross the Vuoksi with JR27. The unit however was ordered to secure the land on the east shore of the Vuoksi from Hopesalmi south to Vuosalmi.

At 23:00 on the night of August 17th JR27 crossed over the Vuoksi at Hopesalmi. Fortunately they encountered little resistence. The Vuoksi was a large river. The Finnish forces crossed on pontoon boats under the cover of darkness. If Russia had had a larger contingent of troops and artillery located in the area the crossover would have been problematic.

The 23rd Pioneer Battalion (Pion P23) and the 5th Bridge Company (5.Silta.K) organized the cross over. In the early phases of the cross over of Hopesalmi they used 35 punts, 18 assault boats, 5 rubber boats, and 4 pontoon rafts.

Soon the Finnish forces had a 1 kilometer deep and 4 kilometer wide bridge head.

The bulk of the II AK forces however did not cross over at Hopesalmi. Uncle Toivo's Kevyt Os 7 had cleared out the eastern bank of the Vuoksi to Vuosalmi/Ayrapaa. Once both banks of the Vuoksi had been secured at Vuosalmi, the II AK started the crossover on August 20th at Vuosalmi / Ayrapaa. There they had access to a bigger road leading to both Viipuri and the border. Here JR 27 crossed on pontoon boats, supplementing the forces already on the west bank. The pioneer forces soon built a bridge. By August 24th trucks and artillery guns were moving across.

The boats and rafts from the Hopesalmi crossover were also used at Vuosalmi for moving the infantry. The heavy equipment such as the artillery was ferried over with rafts, a motor pontoon, and a motor boat. On the morning of August 24th at 8:20 they began to build a pontoon bridge over the Vuoksi River by the Ayrapaa church. By 13:25 it was complete. It required 57 pontoons, was 160 metres long, and would support 7 tons. The bridge was not dismantled until October.

Beside the pontoon bridge at the Ayrapaa church a 40 metre field bridge was constructed between Vasikkasaari and the north shore of the Vuoksi River which would carry a 12 ton load. It was ready at 10:00 on the 24th.

Meanwhile Kevyt Os 7 was protecting the back of the Finnish advance from Russian forces who were continuing to attack from the east. On August 21st Kevyt Os 7 was ordered to replace JR4 and take the town of Vuokse while JR4 crossed over the river at Vuosalmi.

On August 24th Uncle Toivo crossed the Vuoksi with his unit at Ayrapaa. I am sure that Uncle Toivo did not have any precognition that in 3 years he would be at the very same location fighting for his own life and the life of Finland.

From August 25th to the 29th they moved through Yla Kuusa, Kyyrola, and Oinala to Kivennapa fighting a battle and some skirmishes en route.

25.8.41 Monday

07:30 In the countryside between Ayrapaajarvi and Muolaajarvi our own artillery killed and wounded over 20 of our men. Three were from our group: 2 from 1K and 1 from headquarters

09:30 Commander ordered companies to move to the northwestern Koprala countryside

11:00 Division order arrived.

Group to break off immediately and move with bicycles through Siikniemi and through Kankkila-Malkola-Peippola to Yla Kuusa, where the job is to move quickly on the northwestern side of the Sudenoja – Kyyrola road and continue onwards with most of the force towards Kyyrola-Parkkila and with part of the force towards Oinala- Lavola.

13:00 Lieutenant Colonel Jarvinen arrived.

13:15 Gave order to move to Yla Kuusa.

1K and 2K moved out on bicycles via Siikniemi. Group signals unit followed 1K. Group battle provisions vehicles moved out via Kaukila – Malkola. 2nd Lieutenant Elsma's anti tank squad followed the provisions vehicles. Commander moved via car to the Yla Kuusa public school countryside. Supplies and aid post moved to north of Peippola

14:05 Commander left via Kaukila- Malkola for the Yla Kuusa school.

15:15 Commander arrived at destination.

15:30 Joined up with Lieutenant Colonel Jarvinen and Battalion Vahla.

16:00 Commander gave orders to:

1K (Lieutenant Tero) to get to Yla Kuusa from the south along the left side of the battalion from the direction of the Sudenoja road.

2K to swing around on the west side of the enemy via the Paakoli village road to the Sudenjoki road.

23:00 Lieutenant Peipari sent a message that :

2K had arrived at 21:00 at the Yla Kuusa – Sudenoja road Suursuo brook line. Prepared company positions on the north side of the brook line facing all directions. Attack on enemy on the road came as a complete surprise. During the skirmish took 24 captives.

Weather chilly and cloudy

26.8.41 Tuesday

07:00 1st company and most of Vahla's battalion was positioned about 1 kilometer south of Yla Kussa. One company of Vahla's group had circled around the right side to arrive at Luha's fields. The 2nd company was 700 metres north east along the brook line on the edge of swamp on the eastern leading road. In the middle was the motti.

10:30 The motti was finally cleared out. We obtained various armaments: 3 trucks, 1 tank, 3 canons, many machine guns and 1 armored car.

We suffered 10 killed and wounded and 2 lost.

About a 100 Russians were killed and over a 100 captured.

12:15 We continued onwards towards Sudenjoki on our bicycles.

14:00 Village of Sudenoja secured

16:00 Division headquarters unit arrived at our command post and directly thereafter the commander moved 1 kilometer towards Kyyrola from the Parkilla Sudenjoki Road junction.

At the same time we continued forward towards Oinola through the forest. 2K in the front with 1K following.

16:20 Sent order for 1K to return and move via Kyyrola to the Oinola road with the units heavy weapons.

16:40 2K upon arriving at the Oinola Kyyrola road got into a fire fight with the enemy.

17:30 Supply unit and aid station got order to move at dusk to the bush countryside on the north side of Kyyrola.

18:30 Oinola was captured with no further resistance. Moved the command post to Kyyrola and ordered:

1 K to continue moving to Lavola where they arrived as it was becoming dark

2 K to prepare to move towards Kangaspelto as well as Sudenoja and Kyyrola

Machine gun squads allocated to both companies. As well allocated 2 anti tank guns to both 1K and 2K. Remainder placed on reserve.

20:30 1K arrived at Lavola and took it without any incidents.

23:10 Lieutenant Tero reported that his reconnaissance mission 2 kilometers towards Perkjarve and Parkkila did not encounter anything.

Weather quite cloudy, no enemy possible overhead

27.8.41 Wednesday

At night a small attack from the Kangaspelto direct which we stopped. 4 captives

07:00 Got notice from Lieutenant Tero that at 5:05 that there were 50 Russians moving along the road from Parkkila whom they scattered - 1 captive

04:00 Strong enemy patrol group scattered by 2K - about a 200 man Russian rabble

07:15 Messenger brought order from Division command. Part of the group ordered to secure Oinola and Lavola countryside.

11:00 Commander of JR6 (Colonel Ekman) arrived at the command post. Group placed under the command of JR6.

11:40 Lieutenant Tero relayed via phone that they had nabbed 2 mounted messengers who were coming from Taapenniemi direction. Killed the horses and the messengers. They read their dispatches to us.

15:30 Lieutenant Tero announced that they captured a tank (amphibian) - but fully drivable and operable. A Russian squad attacked, but we drove back. At commanders direction drove tank to the command post by the Muolajarvi shore north east of Oinola.

18:00 Commander relayed to company commanders Colonel Ekmans order that the group was being moved to reserve in the Lavola Pankkarnkuhma countryside.

Left for the use of JR6s I battalion was Lieutenants Teros' heavy weaponry – 3 anti tank guns, 6 machine guns, and 2 mortars.

2K left 1 platoon to secure the direction towards Oinola Kangaspelto. Allocated 2 machine guns and an anti tank gun.

21:00 Commander gave group order to overnight in Oinola except for 1 K which already was in the Lavola Paakari

20:30 2nd Lieutenant Ivako brought prisoners captured earlier, marching them in columns to the place instructed by Adjutant Mikko - 17 Russians

Own casualties during the day – 1 lost

Russians killed – about 20

Weather clear and lovely – wind from north east - no enemy planes

28.8.41 Thursday

During the night took a dozen captives

10:40 Order to move to Putikko

15:20 Arrived at Pamppala and Putikko swamp cross roads.

18:00 Order to secure Putikko swamp and JR6s' border line Voipiala-Lukpola-Liekola

Weather rained all day wind from north north east

29.8.41 Friday

During the night JR6 and Border Guard battalion Avela cleared out 100 mines at the road crossing.

Russians fired at us throughout the day from the Kylmaoja direction which we communicated to our artillery. ......

On August 31st they were over The Old Finnish Border at Manila – where the Winter War had started. From September 3rd to the 9th they advanced through Ollila, captured the Russian town of Aleksandrovka near the coast, and then turned back towards the east.

During their push from the Vuoksi River, Kevyt Os 7 had suffered several casualties every day. Relative to their casualties from earlier days, and days yet to come, the number was minimal.

Uncle Aatu

On August 17th Uncle Aatu's JR48 unit was between Ristilahti-Lievajarvi. From there they attacked onwards towards the Ladoga shore. By the 20th they had pushed out the Russian 168 D who were extracted from the shore by the Russian Lake Ladoga navy.

They then turned back west towards the central Kannas.

- Between the 25th and the 27th JR48 crossed over the Vuoksi at Ayrapaa and moved through Yla Kuusa, advancing down the centre of the Kannas to arrive at Korpikyla on August 31st. While skirmishes occurred, Uncle Aatu's military record does not note any other battles after Pajasyra.
- From the 28th to the 29th they advanced south east of Muolaa/Parkilla at Lautsilta – Tarpia
- On August 30th JR48 was at Vuotta beside Siiranmaki. There they stopped a Russian attack on the Salokyla to Vuotta road.

By September 2nd JR48 was 10 kilometers further south of Siiranmaki at Korpikyla and Riihio just east of Kekrola at the old border.

Uncle Arvo

Kev Pr T and Os Kanerva were part of 12th Division of the IV AK.

Os Kanerva's two Border Jaakari companies and Uncle Arvo's Pioneer platoon crossed the Vuoksi River at Hopesalmi on August 20th . From there they advanced south west together fighting major battles at Natala/Lyykyla and Kuolemajarvi. They arrived eleven days later on August 31st at Muurila on the shores of the Gulf of Finland just north of The Old Finnish Border. In the initial days they cleared mines and built bridges over the swamps and streams. When they reached the railroad, they blew up the train tracks at Kuolemajarvi. Throughout they conducted reconnaissance patrols and skirmished with the enemy, as well as fighting in two major battles.

The commander of Uncle Arvo's Pioneer platoon, Lieutenant Kaarlo Miettinen wrote a recount of their campaign down the Kannas in the summer of 1941 ("Osasto Kanerva pioneerit Karjalan kannasksen taisteluissa kesalla 1941" in the book Pion P 14: IV AK Pioneeripataljoona). I have included the majority of his recount below. It provides a firsthand view of Uncle Arvo's experience. At the end there is a large section on the fighting around Kuolemajarvi.

When many years ago I asked Uncle Arvo (age 90) where he fought, the only place he mentioned was Koulemajarvi. At that point I had no idea where Kuolemajarvi was. I think

he mentioned it because he still remembered what happened there. I wonder what occurred there specifically to him ? Was Uncle Arvo the messenger that Lieutenant Miettinen refers to at Kuolemajarvi ? (He was Lieutenant Miettinen's messenger in 1944).

20/21.8.41 On the 20th and 21st in the Kaltovesi area we were involved in clearing mines, building bridges and paths over the swamps and streams and doing some reconnaissance work. We then moved towards Kuparsaari arriving at Naatala- Lyykyla area on the 22nd.

22.8.41 In the morning at Naatala, the Pioneer platoon served as the lead unit moving towards Karisalmi.

When we arrived at Karisalmi we surprised an enemy group in the oat field. As we did not know the size of the Russian unit, we decided to try a small trick. There was a Pioneer with us who spoke Russian. He took a megaphone and shouted: "Russian soldiers you are surrounded. For your own life stand up and put your weapons down by the big boulder by the field and move in fours to the spruce trees by the field". After the announcement was complete, about a platoon of men rose up from the field and moved as we had directed. But there was a political officer (politrukki) who did not get up. Instead he began to fire at us, luckily not hitting anyone. One of our boys directed a couple of bursts of his sub machine gun at him, lightly wounding him. He now followed our orders. We did not allow the politrukki to be with the others. The medics bandaged him and we conducted a brief interrogation. He was an indomitable man, spitting at me during the interrogation …

We tried in the evening dusk to cross over from Mannikkala to a field on the shores of Lyykyla Lake. When the lead scouts –Pioneers Vaanen and Laurila arrived at an opening to the field the enemy opened fire with machine gun and rifles. We had no choice but to crawl towards the firing and fire back ourselves. During the exchange Vaanen got hit. He was the first of our platoon to give his life for the Fatherland. As our Pioneer platoon had as directed now made contact with the enemy, I shouted to all the boys to pull back to the large ditch we had crossed over earlier. It was only here that I learned that Vaanen had fallen. In the dark it was impossible to retrieve his body from in front of the enemy machine gun nest. We moved 300 meters back into the protection of the forest and drew around the base of the dark tree roots and the tired men tried get some type of sleep. ....

After having receiving orders we left without delay westwards on the Heinjoki-Tali Road. En route we were caught in a howitzer barrage, having to dive down onto the ground several times as we ran forward. We escaped without casualties to our defensive line where I immediately had the men dig defensive positions in the field beside the SuurPero Road. We started first by digging firing stations. In the appropriate spots we dug fox holes for the light machine gun men and for the anti-tank men (who had the satchel explosives).

The enemy tried the strength and effectiveness of the defensive lines with several attacks. Each time they had to draw their forces back, unable to break through our lines. The hand to hand combat was effective and vicious. The roadside location was a difficult spot for the Border Jaakari to protect throughout the whole day.

Once during the fighting, the Border Jaakarit got into serious difficulties and had to retreat 200 meters and were unable to remain connected with us. Then we were in the same front line as the enemy, with only the road separating us. After the Jaakaris launched a counter attack our force got back into our stations. Once when the enemy attacked they fired a howitzer strike at our stations hitting a nearby tree. It exploded spraying shrapnel around. Two of our pioneers were lightly wounded and another one seriously. I ended up bandaging their wounds. The two lightly wounded men were able to withdraw on their own strength. The other one had to be carried out on a stretcher to the company bandaging site. At that point the end was truly near as the defensive stations shrunk by five men as two men were

needed to take the wounded while the enemy attack was underway...

Our artillery spotter came to ask me if I knew what the enemies movements were so that he could give firing coordinates to our own artillery. I told him the observations I had made while lying on the edge of the field and climbing look out spruce trees.

For sure the enemy received a series of artillery volleys. However the communication between the Os Kanerva command post and the company was not successful. When I sent a messenger to group head quarters, he got caught in an artillery barrage and was wounded. He had to go to the company bandaging site and from there on to the hospital. When we had not heard back from the messenger I sent another man on the same mission, but the same thing happened to him. In the evening when the battle quieted I told the company platoon leaders that I was going myself to the command post.

The platoon leaders during this time took care of the defense with Serjeant Raaskan acting as lead. I took a Pioneer with me whose job was to get more ammunition and food. At the command post I saw in the doctors' ledger that the earlier messengers had been wounded. At the command post I also learned that as the left side stations had collapsed, we had been hemmed in. The enemy had penetrated into the countryside behind our lines as far as Karisalmi and had succeeded in blocking in the Brigade (Kev Pr T)

Returning from the command post we got a little lost in the dark. We ended up a couple of meters in front of an enemy machine gun post. The machine gunner opened fire – the bullets whizzing by us. We jumped away so hurriedly that the alder bushes crackled. We never even had time to throw hand grenades, we were so overwhelmed by everything. Nonetheless nothing happened to either of us. During the dark the enemy had jumped in close to our stations without our men noticing it.

23.8.41 The enemy attacked with a strong force from Tammisuo-Sainio over the open Pero countryside towards the east and south east. At the same time Kev Pr Tiiainen's attack had to stop and in the evening the brigade was forced to settle into defensive mode.

24.8.41 In the early morning the enemy canon and howitzer fire boomed in full rage at the brigade's location between Mannikkala and SuurPero. The brigade's defense began to falter and our Jaakari companies and Pioneer platoon were forced into the hardest fighting and suffered a substantial loss of men. Our groups nonetheless remained in our positions even though we were surrounded for a period. At the same time on the south side of Mannikkala a couple of enemy companies broke through the lines with the help of tanks. We stopped the Karisalmi attack with the help of artillery fire, the enemy falling apart. In the Lyykyla direction enemy units forced their way through all the way to the Finnish artillery stations, but a counter assault led by Colonel Tiiainen stopped the enemy advance. ....

The men's nerves were stretched tight as during day, as during the night, the men could not sleep in their pits as the enemy was constantly harassing us. One had to smoke in order to remain awake and alert. When one saw or heard any movement in front of one volleys were fired as a deterrent - from more than one rifle. The movements of our own men were kept to a minimum for our own safety. At night we went to one another to confirm our own orders and to listen to the moves of the enemy tanks. Luckily during the defense we did not have to destroy any tanks. The enemy had undoubtedly found an easier break through point in the stations on our left. The enemy artillery fire was so heavy that no trees in the forest remained intact.

The notice that the group could leave the enclave was like a kiss of life to the men. JR26 took over the defensive positions and we went back to rest and replenish our supplies. We had been marching and fighting non-stop for four days and nights...

25.8.41 The enemy continued its heavy pressure on the Perojoki lines. Kev Pr Tiianinen remained defending the right side on the Mannikkala-Kyttala line. In the evening during the battle, there was a

direct hit on Kev Pr Tiianinen's command post. Colonel Tiianinen was critically injured. At the end of the day JR26 arrived to help, replacing the tired Brigade companies. After this the Brigade was subordinated to 12th Division and was moved to the countryside north of Lyykyla to be reorganized.

26.8.41 We did not have a chance to rest for long as already on the 26th we were en route to the Pilppula rail station south of Kamara and thence onwards via Villikkala towards the Munasuo and Summa countryside. Here the enemy had set up defensive positions.

28.8.41 On the 28th we bypassed Villikkala, partaking in only a few skirmishes.

29.8.41 After on the 29th, we moved along the east side of Kuolemajarvi lake to the Kuolemajarvi station. Before we arrived at the station we heard a train whistling and hooting. The commander ordered the platoon to cut the rail tracks by the brook on the east side of the station to prevent the train from escaping. The undertaking was not as easy as the commander thought. We located the right spot but then enemy units started coming east. Our first thought was, now what is going to happen as we saw that the train as well was approaching. We started doing the job as we had planned. We opened fire at the enemy on the tracks, driving them to the railway banks, and tried to keep the track clear long enough to attach the explosives to the rails and ignite them. The train approached too fast and we were only able to put explosives on one rail and connect it with only a short ignition wire - a danger to our own lives. The explosives did not damage the locomotive, exploding only under the cars. The train moved on slowly dragging the jumping cars behind it and on passing us gave a long hoot. As the train passed we fired several volleys at the enclosed cars so that at least they received holes in them from our visit. At the same time we blew up a couple of telegraph poles and were able to break the communications lines. When we started our trip back they fired after us from the side of the track.

Upon arriving at the Kuolemajarvi station, which our force had taken over, the commander gave us another undertaking on the western side of Kuolemajarvi. As we were expecting more trains from the west our mission was to put explosives under the bridge on the track and at the same time push our fire base further northwest but within sight of the enemy. We located a site in a field opening about 300 meters from the station. There, there happened to be a strong stone barn which provided good protection from the blast, and a good spot within eye sight to shoot at the enemy. When the enemy squads started to come across the open field on the lakes west side we had to fire a heavy volley for our own protection. Then many a boy truly feared that we would be encircled if the route we arrived on was closed. We nonetheless did not have time to grow older in this spot, as the way ahead was cleared and an order was received to move ahead.

During the Kuolemajarvi station conquest period a women enemy soldier fell and a couple of our own men were wounded. They were brought beside the road to be taken to the company aid post. During the battle the enemy succeeded momentarily taking the spot where our wounded were waiting When we recaptured the spot we found them shot dead. Thereafter we continued on towards Muurila. On the route we got into a fire fight with retreating Russians. During this time 2nd Lieutenant Martti Rinne arrived and took over 2nd Lieutenant Erosens' position as the platoons supplies leader.

Arriving at the field opening at the cross roads before Karjaisten village we discovered that the enemy was hiding in the field. As we had to move forward I asked if there was anyone who was ready to clear the enemy out of the field. Squad leader Ake Leskinen answered immediately that he was ready to lead his squad. Karlssons, Raaska's and Antillas' squads did likewise. After this we considered how to do it. As there was no motion in the alder underbrush leading to the next field opening, we decided that there wasn't a larger number of the enemy. After I had given the squad

leaders directions to enclose the field we moved ahead. We stepped over the road ditch to the field where there was a small field opening beside the road where an enemy soldier was hidden. A hand grenade exploded about 4 to 5 meters ahead. He had blown himself up. I wondered why he had not thrown the grenade at me. After this we heard them surrendering and rising from the field leaving their weapons behind. If I remember we got seven captives. We took them to the prison camp.

30.8.41 The forward march of Os Kanerva continued. We moved southwest fighting against large groups of Russians fleeing on the west side of the Karjalaisten village road. Some distance past the road junction one squad of the platoon went into the bunker behind the trenches. There Heimonen, who excelled in grenade throwing, threw back the grenades the Russians directed at us before they exploded. We did not suffer any casualties.

From here the unit struck south west towards Muurila and the nearby Gulf of Finland shore, fighting against the fleeing Russians as we went. In this battle a couple of our Pioneers were wounded. Both got a bullet through their heel. In these cases where a submachine gunner or light machine gunner got wounded the closest man usually jumped up to help his comrade and took him to the first aid post. Thus in these cases the sharp shooter would double the loss of manpower with his hit....

31.8.41 On August 31st Os Kanerva had to patrol between Kuolemajarvi and Muurila in order to enclose and capture the scattered enemy groups that remained. I had to intermingle my men into the groups located here and there along the road, protecting the supply columns.

After I had separated my platoon into squads, as dark was falling I went with my messenger a short distance past the Karjalaisten road junction to rest in a Russian bunker beside the forest. I left a squad to guard the road junction. When in the morning we went to back to the road junction, our boys at the guard post were surprised that we were still alive.

They related that they had heard and seen enemy soldiers moving in the early morning in the direction of Karjalaisten village. We followed the tracks of the Russians back to a bunker. Truly, as the boys had said, the enemy had eaten and rested in the bunker beside us and left in the early morning. Someone was looking over us as the enemy had not selected the bunker that we had slept in, and we were still alive.

I then went with my messenger to the next guard position which was in the shrubs in a ditch by a small swamp beside the road. They as well recounted that in the nighttime and morning they had fought with a small enemy group, killing about half a dozen. The rest had fled to the protection of the forest.

Upon receiving an emergency message we had to move quickly to the third guard post. I took the 4th squad, which had been resting, with me. The third squad and three Border Jaakari squads were at the roadside on the road leading southeast from Muurila village. They were positioned in a good defensive trench. An enemy communications unit column came along the road. Our group opened fire at the column. The column fled along the road leaving the horses unattended beside the road. In the first vehicle there were four action ready machine guns, along with other weaponry.

Once the enemy got over their initial surprise, they started to gather men together to launch a counter attack. During this time I alerted my 4th squad to move in to provide help. In the ensuing fighting the Border Jaakari Sergeant was killed. Our own group did not suffer any casualties. After things cleared we took the harnesses off the horses that were still alive. We took them into the forest and made a corral with branches to contain the herd of 60 horses. We drove the remaining wagons to the side of the road. The surviving enemy fled somewhere.

The commander came to give his thanks to our group for the good work we had done that day. That thanks was the first and only one that we received during two months of hard work. ...

1.9.41 *The pressure on the containment lessened after the 31st. Our platoon got a new task clearing the Inoa area countryside of any scattered enemy groups. On the evening of the 2nd we crossed the Old Border at Rajajoki.*

7.9.41 *By the end of the week the expulsion of the Russian forces from the Kannas was complete. On September 7th we were disbanded from Os Kanerva and returned to Viipuri.*

Os Kanerva met the objectives General Laatikainen had set out, but at high cost .Its' casualties were very high – of a strength of 500, 40% were wounded or killed, including the commanders of both the Jaakari companies.

Uncle Vilho

On August 26th Uncle Vilho's 8th Division attacked across Viipuri Bay to cut off the road on the coast leading south out of Viipuri.

The cross over of Viipuri Lahti was made with the help of Company 3 of Pion P 24 - Uncle Arvo's pioneer company. Uncle Arvo however was not with them, having been seconded to the special Jaakari attack group Os Kanerva of Kevyt Pr T.

The cross over is outlined in Pion P 24's book "Pion P 24: IV AK:n Pioneeripataljoona 1941-1944:

" Company 3 arrived late August 25th at the loading area on the sound between Turkisaari and Piispasaari [Two companies of PionP 22 were also moving troops from another near by site].

The job of the pioneer company was to build pontoon rafts and ferry the infantry forces across the gulf. The pontoon raft material arrived a ½ day late on the morning of August 26. The Pioneers started building the rafts at the same time as they were unloading the materials.

By 14:00 everything was ready but the unit rested until darkness at 21:00, when they started the crossing, taking materials to the other side and beginning to build the unloading site.

At 22:00 the movement of the troops started. [The set up was far more primitive than the Allies landing crafts. The Finnish "landing craft" consisted of a rudimentary open pontoon raft manned with machine guns that was pushed / pulled by a small boat with a large outboard motor manned by a couple of Pioneers].

But the element of surprise was totally in the Finnish troops favor and by 03:00 they had successfully moved 850 men, 78 horses and carts, 35 bikes plus equipment.

The only incident occurred at 2 am when two Russian patrol boats arrived and shot and rammed one raft before they were driven away by the Finnish troops fire.

All together with PionP 22, Pion P 24 moved 3,279 men, 9 cars, 344 horses & drivers, 192 bikes and 19,500 kg equipment without major losses. (There were clashes with small Russians units on the shore and some artillery barrages and fighter bombings, but luck and the Russians preoccupation with the Viipuri battle prevailed).

Once they were across the gulf, the 8th Division successfully attacked the Russian forces from south of Viipuri. Together with the Finnish forces attacking from north of Viipuri they were able to surround the Russian forces in a motti at Porlammi south of Viipuri.

The 4th division of the IVth Army Corps had advanced on Viipuri, taking the deserted city on August 29th. The Russians had decided to abandon the city but left too late and were encircled in the "Porlammi motti - pocket" between the 4th Division on the north, the 12th Division to the east, and the 8th Division on the south. Most of the force surrendered. Extensive armaments were captured. The armaments were retrofitted and placed back into use with the Finnish army. The captured soldiers were placed in prison camps. Included among them was Major General Vladimir Kirpichnikov, the commander of the Russian forces.

Once the Russian surrendered, the 8th Division pursued the remaining Russians forces southwards to Koivisto and the islands on the coast. They did not advance down the isthmus to Leningrad with the 12th Division.

Uncle Vilho's food supplies column followed behind with the division headquarters unit across Viipuri Lahti and south to Kovisto.

On The Ladoga Front – Uncle Kauko

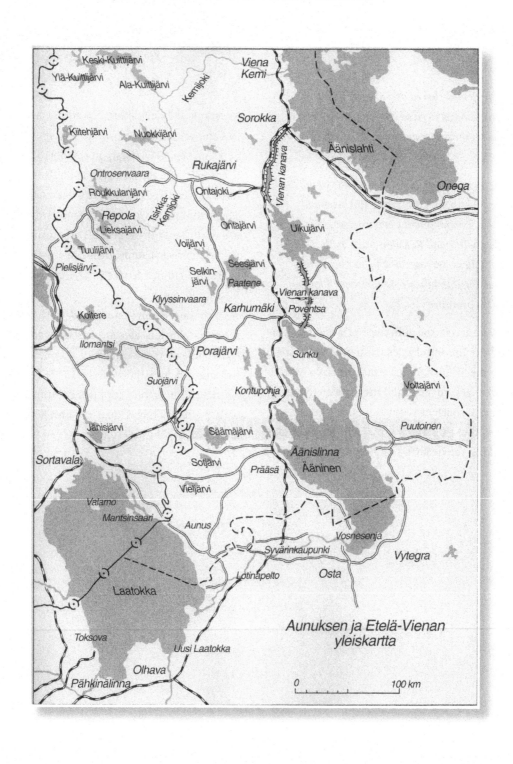

Aunuksen ja Etelä-Vienan
yleiskartta

CHAPTER 9

On The Ladoga Front – Uncle Kauko

The other major front the Finnish army attacked was on what was called the Karjalainen Front. This encompassed the area from the north end of Lake Ladoga eastwards to Lake Onega/Aanus – southwards on the Aunuksen isthmus to the Syvari River; and northwards to the Maaselan peninsula and Stalin's Canal connection to the White Sea.

The initial western part was Old Finland – the area ceded after the Winter War. The rest of it had always been part of Russia. It however had always been populated by the Karjalian tribe and as such was considered as Greater Finland. Mannerheim at the end of the Finnish Civil War had supported initiatives to conquer it from Russia and make it part of Finland. This however had not been realized.

The Karjalan Army assault had three major phases

1. First retake the north end of Lake Ladoga and free the old Finnish city of Sortavala.
2. Then proceed down the Aunus Peninsula and cross the Syvari River; concurrent with this capture the capital of Russian Karjala - the city of Petroskoi on the shores of Lake Onega.
3. Finally take Karhumaki and the Maaselka peninsula, thereby cutting off both the Murmansk railroad at a more northern point, and the Stalin Canal link to the White Sea.

All of the campaigns were difficult. The Russian army had built defenses in key locations throughout; and the countryside was difficult to traverse as it was full of swamps, rivers, and lakes. Most importantly it was defended by significant Russian ground forces who had been ordered to hold their positions at all costs. Blostering this was a large tank contingent and an active Russian air force. In this case though, the Finnish army had a numerical advantage as Stalin had redirected some of the Russian divisions to the protection of Leningrad.

The initial goals were to retake Sortavala at the northern end of Lake Ladoga, and the part of Old Finland along the eastern shore of Lake Ladoga. Sortavala was not taken until August 15th. Vitele on the Old Finnish Border on the the eastern shore of Lake Ladoga by the Tuulos River was taken by July 24th.

Subsequent to this the Finnish forces moved south and east. Syvari was reached on September 12th and Petroksoi was taken on October 1st. The assault then turned northwards to Karhumaki and the Maaselka kannas. Karhumaki was taken on December 5th and Poventsa and Stalins' Canal on December 7th. The Murmansk railway was cut at the Maaselka Station north of Karhumaki but progress was stopped here by Mannerheim on December 8th.

The Finnish Ladoga - Karelian Army

The Finnish Karelian Army led by Lieutenant General Heinrichs consisted of the VI and VII AKs and Ryhma Oinonen. After the assault on the Kannas was completed the Karjalan Army was re-inforced with divisions of the IIAK.

A key part of the army was the artillery. Finland had been able to build up a large and well provisioned artillery force in the year since the end of the Winter War. Although the terrain was difficult, the artillery units were able to keep moving and ably supported the infantry.

Finland had one tank battalion. Led by Lieutenant Colonel Bjorkmann, it was part of Colonel Lagus's Os Lagus. It had 40 Vickers tanks. While not overwhelmimg in either numbers or size they were a definite asset.

A German division was also part of the army - the 163rd Division of Lieutenant General Engelbrecht. It took part in the early August assault on Aittojoki, and afterwards in the attack down the eastern side of Lake Ladoga. Some months after the army had successfully crossed over the Syvari River the division left Finland and returned back to the German forces to take part in the capture of Leningrad. Mannerheim did not want any German units within Karjala or part of the Finnish armed forces.

While the VI and VII AKs led the main south and eastwards assaults, Ryhma Oinosen attacked east to the Winter War battlegrounds of Ilomantsi and Tolvajarvi

June 15 to September 15
"South" and "East" to the Old Border

The Karjalan Army started its' assault on July 10th, 1941.

Recapturing Sortavala

The VII AK attacked across the border on July 10th at the northwest corner of Lake Ladoga with the objective of capturing Sortavala and the surrounding area. The 7th Division crossed near Matkaselka, and the 19th Division at Kaalamo near Pyhaniemi.

The 19th Division encountered heavily fortified, fully manned Russian positions and had to slow down its' assault. The Finnish artillery was focusing all its efforts at supporting the rest of VII AK's advance and was not available to pulverize the bunkers and defensive trenches. On July 22nd Kaalamo was taken.

The 7th Division also encountered heavy fighting but on July 17th it took the Hamekoski area.

It then began an assault to take Sortavala together with the 19th Division. By July 27th they were within five kilometers of Sortavala. Here however the Russian forces stopped the attack for almost a month by the Tolmajoki River. On August 15th Sortvala was finally once more in Finnish hands. The city proper was secured with small

street to street battles rather than destructive artillery barrages in order to preserve the buildings.

Advancing to the Old Border
South and East of Lake Ladoga

The VI AK consisted of the 5th and 11th divisions. As well Uncle Kauko's 1st Division, which had been held in reserve by Lieutenant General Heinrichs, was seconded to the VI AK on July 17th. The German 163rd Division as well was part of the VI AK. In addition on July 16th Mannerheim transferred the 17th Division from the Hanko naval base to the Karjalan Army.

On July 10th the 5th and 11th divisions launched an attack towards the north eastern end of Lake Ladoga. On July 11th the 5th division together with the 1st Jaeger Brigade of Lagus took Korpiselka.The 11th division took Vartsila on July 11, and on July 15th Soanlahti at the north end of Janisjarvi.

The 5th Division and the 1st Jaakari brigade were placed under the command of Colonel Lagus. The Os Lagus group formed a quick attack force consisting of tanks and quick moving bicycle Jaakari companies and mobile artillery units. Os Lagus attacked down the eastern side of Lake Ladoga – taking Korinoja south of Impilahti on July 16th.

Impilahti had been my Uncle Toivo's home before the winter war – a pretty old church town serving a countryside parish of 15,000.

By July 18th one part of the force had crossed the old border in the interior at Kasnaselka 30 kilometres east of Impilahti.

On July 24th, further south by the eastern shore of Lake Ladoga, the Lagus group advanced over the Old Border at Vitele just north of the Tuulosjoki River. There the Karjalian Army command stopped the attack until August 13th as other portions of the army were still fighting well behind it in the north east by Sotjarvi – Saamajarvi and Suojarvi.

After Mannerheim gave the order to advance once more, the 5th and 17th divisions along with Os Lagus of the VI AK continued towards the Syvari River.

The 17th division swung inland. Fighting numerous battles, on September 12th they took the Syvari railway bridge near Podporoze.

Beside Lake Ladoga, Os Lagus and the 5th Division advanced southwards, arriving at the Syvari River by September 7th, despite strong Russian resistance. On September 15th Os Lagus took the Lotinanpelto power plant on south side of the Syvari River.

The German 163rd Division of Lieutenant General Engelbrecht took part in the advance along the Ladoga shore south of Vitele taking Kuuttilahti at the mouth of the Syvari River before rejoining the German forces east of Leningrad.

During this time the 1st Division and Uncle Kauko were clearing the area east of Os Lagus, and advancing slowly towards Petroksoi.

Uncle Kauko and the Advance over the Old Eastern Finnish Border

Uncle Kauko was with the 5th company of JR35. It was part of the 1st Division of the VII AK for most of the war. The 35th Regiment was from area north east of Turku. The regiment commander was Colonel Lauri Ruotsalo.

Kauko's unit – the 1st Division under Colonel Paavo Paalu, did not catch up with the fast moving VI Army Corps until July 16, 1941. At that point they were already beyond Vitele at the mouth of the Tuulosjoki River halfway down the east side of Lake Ladoga. Division 1's orders were to clear the area inland north east of Vitele in preparation for the attack east to Petroksoi. Roads in this area led east to Petroksoi and south east to the Syvari Railway Bridge.

The battles of Telgi, Ivas, and Hiisijarvi- Kirvesjarvi are recorded in Uncle Kauko's kantakortti.

The Sota Paiva Kirja for the II Battalion JR35 chronicles Uncle Kauko's war. The military journal kept by the II battalion, records the movement of the battalion in a fair bit of detail - and the writing is legible ! Although almost

entirely about troop movements, it does provide a bit of colour and perspective to Uncle Kauko's war.

- Uncle Kauko was living in Oripaa when he got his call up notice on June 17th to report to the enlisting location at Kyroo. The home district of the 35th regiment was the countryside north east of Turku in which Uncle Kauko's Oripaa home was located.
- According to the sota paiva Uncle Kauko along with his fellow reserves started arriving at Kyroo at 20:00 on the 17th with the majority arriving on the 18th. For the next few days they went through their medicals, were outfitted with clothes and weapons, and allocated to their units in the 35th infantry regiment.
- I wonder if Uncle Kauko was surprised that he was assigned as a light machine gunner to the 5th infantry company of the II battalion. While he had

not seen front line combat duty during the Winter War he was a strong and healthy 25 year old. He had had special firearm training during his conscription service in 1933/34. He had also been an active member of the Suojeluskunta from January 1936 to September 1938 when he was a bachelor working in Ahtari.

- The unit left via train from Kyroo at 16:00 on the 23rd of June, arriving in Lahti at the Likola barracks at 00:35 on the 25th .The regiment remained there for 10 days before departing on the 3rd of July via train to the east. They arrived two days later at Kontolahti north of Joensuu. It is surprising that the train took that long to get there. Traffic towards the border was heavy and the Russian air force was bombing the railroads relentlessly. From there they marched 58 kilometers over the next two days to Tuupavaara / Lastujarvi southeast of Joensuu.
- On July 14th they marched across the border to Korpiselka. Over the next 3 days they marched over 6 hours a day arriving at Korpjarvi on the 18th .

- The next day they got a taste of what war had in store for them. They suffered 11 casualties – 3 killed and 8 wounded due to artillery fire from Russian ships near Ikonen. That night at 20:55 they crossed the beloved Old Border near Tulmajarvi.

- From July 19th to August 1st they proceeded southwards along a route 50 kilometers inland from the Lake Ladoga shore incurring continuing enemy artillery fire, bombing and occasional Russian attacks. A major battle occurred on July 25th / 26th as the battalion attacked Russian defensive positions at Kuukojarvi.

25.7.41 "At 19:55 we came up to Enemy defensive line fortifications between the Kuukojarvi village and the lake east of it. The enemy tanks opened fire with their canons and machine guns as did the infantry with them. Our companies men tried to destroy the tanks with satchel bombs "kasapanoksilla" but only a few of them detonated and we were unable to stop the tanks.

26.7.41 The battle just ended, and the I battalion's 3rd company took over to secure the area and clear it of any enemy soldiers. Our own companies were able to go and rest about 1kilometer south of the village. The Jaakari platoon took up positions as the front guard posts.

The battle ended at 13:30

About a hundred enemy soldiers were killed and fifteen captured. We captured ten tanks as well as a large amount of other weaponry and vehicles.

We lost 6 killed – 2nd Lieutenant Lepisto, Under Serjeants Alakakko and Kouvo, Corporal Selkama, and soldiers Koskinen and Arlund. 6 of our officers/ NCOs and 23 of our men were wounded. "

> The II battalion remained in the Kuukojarvi and the nearby Sissoila village area until 21:00 on August 1st. During that time they endured Russian bombing and artillery fire and various skirmishes, but suffered only 1 casualty - a communications unit soldier who was killed during a Russian bombing run while he was laying phone cables.

- From the 1st to the 7th of August the unit continued slowly towards the Hiisijarvi / Ivas area. On the 8th the 5th company was involved in a major battle.

8.8 At 3:00 the 5th Company crossed over Lake Hiisijarvi using two boats. The cross over took about 5 hours. Major Jansson ordered the 5th Company to attack the village of Ivas. The 5th company and several machinegun squads gathered together at 10:30, attacking at 11:00 after a Finnish artillery and howitzer barrage. The Russians had dug out machinegun emplacements and defensive positions under the houses. The attack was made over a burnt over open field. The 5th company came under heavy Russian cross fire. Suffering major losses, it had to retreat.

After this two men from Serjeant Helttula's 8th squad succeeded in crawling up to a house, and setting it on fire. Soon the whole village was on fire and at 22:00 a new assault was launched from the other side of the village through the exploding fire balls. We took the village. Part of the Russian forces were able to flee. The majority were killed and a few were taken captive.

The casualties from the morning attack were 1 officer +2 NCOs+3 soldiers killed; and 5 officers, 4 NCOs, 9 soldiers wounded.

Killed

- *2nd Lieutenant Maentausi*
- *Under Serjeants Anttila and Toikka,*
- *Corporal Varho, Soldiers Makila, Pienjoki*

Wounded seriously

- *Soldiers Kelkki, Virtanen, Poyra, Kosiken, Eloranta*

Wounded slightly

- *Lieutenant Kotila, 2nd Lieutenant Mikitalo, Serjeant Major Rusnas, Master Serjeant Mathila, Serjeant Koivula,*
- *Under Serjeants Herra and Varpio,*
- *Corporal Kuhanen, Soldiers Kuhrala, Kivimaki, Lehtila*

After the battle the 5th company, the machine gun squads and the mortar unit moved back to the village of Pannila arriving at 01:00.

- From the 8th to the 20th of August the battalion was involved in ongoing battles, bombing and artillery barrages in the heavily defended Hiisijarvi area. The II battalion incurred several casualties most days. The Russian losses however were 7 to 8 times as severe.
- Occasionally the Finnish fighter planes arrived, upon which the Russian bombers dispersed.
- On the 12th Russian artillery and howitzer fire was particularly heavy; and was combined with bombing and strafing runs. Colonel Hagelberg of the nearby JR13 regiment was killed.
- After the 20th the fighting and bombing subsided. The battalion even had a chance to have a sauna and was entertained by a musical show.

- On the August 29th the battalion diary notes that replacements have arrived – and that Viipuri has been freed.
- On September 1st the battalion advanced through heavily mined and defended positions at Nuosjarvi (noted in Uncle Kauko's records) about 30 kilometers north east of Hiisijarvi.
- On September 2nd the regiment was seconded to the 4th Division who were attacking along the Suojarvi Finland to Petroksoi railroad south of Lake Saamajarvi. The rest of the 1st Division attacked north east towards Petroksoi on a more southern route along the Topasjarvi, Nirkko, Pyhajarvi, Paarsa road.
- The battalion was loaded onto trucks at 20:00 on September 2nd, and driven 127 kilometers north to Sammajarvi, arriving at 05:00 on September 3rd. Sammajarvi was about 60 kilometers east of Petroksoi on the Suojarvi Finland to Petroksoi Russia railroad. Running beside the railroad was a major road (by Annus Karjala standards).
- September 3rd was a rest day. The men took time to wash in the lake and clean their clothes. The battalion diary notes that the lake was beautiful and the water clear. (Being September, the water must have been brisk.)

- While the countryside was beautiful, the route to Petroksoi was not. The terrain was difficult and was defended by Russian units embedded in fortifications, supported by tanks, artillery and air force.
- On the 4th, the battalion left their beachfront bivouack and marched east to take part in a motti set up by JR 8. By the afternoon of the 6th they had cleared out the motti.
- From the 7th to the 15th they did not advance much further, rather setting up their own dug outs and sending out reconnaissance patrols. Throughout the week they were subject to Russian artillery barrages and bombing runs.

- On September 18th they began to advance east again.

The Lapland Front
And
My Father

CHAPTER 10

The Lapland Front and My Father

In the Lapland theatre Colonel General Nicholaus von Falkenhorst, the commander of German Army Command Norway, separated the attack into three separate fronts:

1. The Murmansk front whose objective was to capture Murmansk;
2. The "Salla" front whose objective was to severe the Murmansk railway at Kantalahti; and
3. The Finnish force "Kiestinki" front whose objective was to break through to the Murmansk railway at Louhi and Vienan Kemi

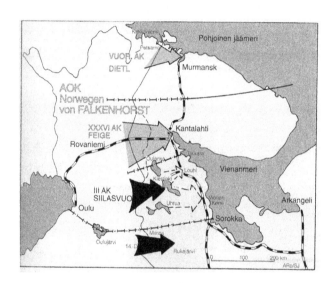

The Murmansk Attack

The attack on Murmansk, dubbed Platinfuchs, was led by Colonel General Eduard Dietl's Mountain Corps Norway (Gebirgskorp Norwegen). It consisted of the 2 and 3rd mountain divisions and the Finnish battalion strength Osasto Petsamo (Er.Os. P) and the Finnish 36th Jaakari Border Company (36.RajaJK).

Facing them was the Russian 14 AK under Major General V. Frolov with the 14th, 52nd and 86th divisions and bomber and fighter forces. As well Russia had a good railway connection with which to move and supply its' troops.

The Mountain Corps Norway's 37,500 troops crossed over the border over from Norway on June 22nd the day Operation Barbarossa began. Colonel General Dietl started a two pronged attack on Murmansk.

- One trust led by the 3rd division stalled at the Kalastajasaarento peninsula east of Petsamo due to the difficult terrain and the strong and resilient Russian defense. No further progress was made as the German 3rd Division was called back by Hitler to Germany. The Finnish JR14 regiment was brought up from the Aland Islands in southern Finland on July 12th to hold the peninsula.

- The other thrust led by the 2nd division made better progress but was stopped at the Litsajoki River on July 1st . No further advance was made against the two Russian divisions, as in this case, Hitler recalled a third of the German complement back to Norway.

The Germans had only been able to advance 24 kilometres of the 90 kilometre distance to Murmansk - this at the heavy cost of 10,290 German casualties. Russian casualties exceeded those of Germany.

The Salla – Kantalahti Attack

The second German force was on the "Salla" front. Its' objective was to cut the Murmansk railway at Kantalahti. Salla is only a few kilometers east of Kelloselka where dad was stationed.

The attack on Kantalahti was made through Salla by the German XXXVI Army Corps commanded by General Hans Feige. It consisted of the German 169th infantry division, and the German division strength SS-Div Nord group.

Part of the army was the Finnish 6th Division and three Border Jaakari companies (RajaJK).The Finnish 6th Division of Colonel Verner Viikala buttressed the German attack from the south. It consisted of 12th, 33rd, and 54th infantry regiments plus Kev Os 3.

Facing them were the Russian 122nd and 104th rifle divisions (plus JR242 near Kiestinki) of the 42 AK of Panin. As well the 1st Russian Armored Division participated until mid July.

The German 169th Division and SS Nord started their attack towards Salla on July 1st. Russian resistance and counter attacks at the Kuola River resulted in the SS Nord forces stopping and fleeing on the first day. Salla was finally captured on July 6th with the assistance of the Finnish 6th Division. The advance was stopped again at the Kairala Narrows on July 28th. The German forces made slow progress until September 19th when they were stopped beyond Alakurtti at Vermajoki, just over the Old Finnish Border. The assault stopped here settling into trench warfare until the end of the war.

The two month and a half month attack had only advanced 85 kilometres, 75 kilometres short of the Murmansk rail line.

The Finnish 6th Division had played a major role in the advance that the German XXXVI Army Corps had been able to make. In late September the Finnish division stopped supporting the advance – and so did the advance. Colonel Vikala, although reporting to the German XXXVI Army

Corps, independently ordered his division to quit attacking and move to the defence. It seemed that his decision was influenced by the pressure the USA was putting on Finland to stop its attack on the Murmansk line. He took his regiments "defeat" and his decision so personally he committed suicide at his command post in Karmalampi on 18 December. He did not know that he had been recommended for promotion to Major General and receipt of the Mannerheim Cross.

The "Uhtua/Kiestinki" Front - towards Louhi and Vienan Kemi on the Murmansk Railway

The 3rd prong of Major General von Falkenhorsts' attack was made by the Finnish III army corps commanded by Major General Siilasvuo.The IIIAK was responsible for the 100 kilometers from Kuusamo south to Raate.

Their objective was to break through to the Murmansk railway at Louhi and Vienan Kemi.

The Finnish IIIAK consisted of the 3rd Division. The division was comprised of the 11th, 32nd and 53rd infantry regiments, plus the 25th and 35th Border Jaakari companies and the 3rd Sissi battalion. The units were primarily from the Oulu district. The JR53rd regiment was from Ii/ Simo – my ancestral witch home.

Opposite them was the 54th Division of the Russian 7th army corps.

Siilasuvo split his forces into two:

- Osasto Fagernas under Colonel Frans Fagernas which was to attack on the southern portion from Suomussalmi to Uhtua; and
- Osasto J under Lieutenant Colonel Johannes Turtola which was to attack from Kuusamo to Kiestinki

Osasto F captured Vuokkiniemi on July 3 and Vuonninen on July 7th . Progress slowed thereafter, until the advance was ground to a halt by the Russian 54th Rifle Division outside Uhtua on August 10th .

Osasto J by July 11th was able to advance to the Sohjana River where the Russian 242nd division stopped them at defenses on the narrows between lakes Paajarvi and

Tuoppajarvi. On July 31st with German reinforcements Osasto J was able to break through and to take Kiestinki on August 8th. The Russians added the 88th Rifle Division and stopped Osasto J just east of Kiestinki.

Given its' lack of progress on its' other fronts, Army Command Norway decided to focus its' entire Lapland attack on breaking past Kiestinki to capture the Murmansk railway junction at Louhi. The Murmansk railway split at Louhi; one line swinging east to Moscow, and the other continuing south to Lenigrad. Cutting the railway at Louhi would effectively cut off all Allied supplies from Murmansk from Russia.

Army Command Norway transferred the entire dubious SS Battle Group North from the German XXXIII army to Osasto J. It now became Osasto DJ under Colonel Vaino Palojarvi. Once more SS Nord was ineffective, proving incapable of fighting in the Finnish wilderness. When the Russian's counterattacked on August 20th they were able to stop Osasto DJ. The Russian counter attack caught the Finnish JR53 of Colonel Turtola as well as 600 other wounded Osasto DJ soldiers, in a motti at the eastern railway line. The Finnish forces were only able to break out of the motti in early September – at the cost of 1,683 Finnish casualties including the death of Colonel Turtola. The Russian force lost 3,400 men in the counter attack.

The Russians continued their attack retaking Kiestinki on September 4th.

Despite orders to the contrary from Hitler and Mannerheim, von Falkenhorst and Siilasvuo decided to attempt one more assault to Louhi. Siilasuvou's III AK received an additional regiment while the German SS Nord division was also reinforced. The attack began on November 1st. Siilasuvou's Finnish forces were able to break through but once more SS Nord was not able to advance in their sector. Siilasvou called off the entire attack on November 17th due to the lack of German success, the improbability of getting any more troops, and Mannerheim's desire that the attack be stopped.

The Rukajarvi Front – Towards Sorokka on the Murmansk Railway

Mannerheim positioned the 14th Division under Colonel Erkki Raappanen between the German command and the Finnish Karelian Army. The area was entirely under the Finnish High Command, not German Norway Command.

The divisions' objective was to cut the Murmansk railway south of the Sorokka junction.

The 14th Division of approximately 14,500 men (JR10, JR31, JR52 and Kev Os 2) was able to defeat the Russian 54th rifle division. On July 8th they captured Repola. At Omelia they surrounded the Russian 337th rifle regiment in a motti. The regiment was decimated and armaments captured. On September 6th they captured Rukajarvi, and on September 17th were at the Ontajoki River.

Mannerheim stopped the advance here – 40 kilometers west of the Murmansk Railway.

The division then turned its' attention southwards. On October 26th the 14th division linked with the 8th Division west of Seesjarvi, providing the Finnish command control of Karjala from the Syvari River to north of Rukjarvi.

While Russia suffered a much greater number of losses then even the German Northern Army - the Finns also sacrificed. On my visits to ancestral homes in northern Finland in Kemijarvi, Simo, and Oulu, I walked around the sankari hautas in the cemeteries. I often noticed the names of Alakurtti, Kiestinki, Uhtua, Repola, Aglajarvi beside the head stones... strange places then. Now I know more about the sacrifice made that day... JR 12 was from Kemijarvi, JR54 from Simo and JR32 from Oulu.

War Begins Again for Father

During the war father was in Lapland, in Kelloselka and Kemijarvi building the Kemijarvi to Salla railroad.

Kelloselka was near the border 15 kilometers east of Salla. Salla had originally been part of Finland but by the Winter War peace terms it became part of Russia. Indeed, Finland had stretched fifty kilometers beyond Salla to Alakurtti.

The Winter War peace terms specified that a railway link be built from Salla on the border to Kemijarvi. A Finnish railroad already existed from Kemijarvi through Rovaniemi to Tornio on the Swedish border and to Oulu in the south. Before the Continuation War started Russia had completed building a railway connection to the Finnish border at Salla from the Rutji station (south of the Kantalahti) on the Murmansk railroad. The Russian objective was to have a rail connection that would allow them to access the West from the Murmansk line – for purposes of commerce ... and of course, war.

While Finland had started building the 80 kilometer railroad from Salla to Kemijarvi, it was not yet complete when the Continuation War started. As well as portions of the railroad not being ready, the major bridge at Kemijarvi still needed to be built.

Father was a construction engineer with the Finnish Railway. Father was in charge of work crews building the 80 kilometer rail link and the bridge at Kelloselka. He reported to the Finnish Railway's Chief Engineer for the area.

While working on the railroad, father was close to the Salla battle front. Father got to know many soldiers in the German 169th infantry division of the German XXXVI Army Corps and associate first hand with the attack towards Kantalahti.

Father was in Kelloselka when the war began.

He must have heard the news that the German forces had arrived in Rovaniemi. The S.S. Nord Group had arrived via truck from Norway on June 10th. The 169th Infantry Division arrived a couple days later, having travelled from Germany via boat to Tornio, and from thence via train to Rovaniemi. By the June 15th there were 40,000 German troops in Rovaniemi.

I am sure father knew that war was about to start. I wonder what his thoughts were ...

And war did commence. The first precursor of the challenges to come occurred on June 25th when the Russian airforce bombed Kelloselka. Although only a hamlet, Kelloselka was a provisioning point as it was the last point in Finland on the road to Kantalahti. Father would have been there in some improvised bomb shelter or bunker.

Probably a large German military presence was there as well as the German 169th Division and SS Nord started their attack towards Salla on July 1st. The might of the huge German attack force, complete with tanks, artillery and armoured cars must have been impressive.

While the German forces were impressive, so were the Russian defences. Russian resistance and counter attacks at the Kuola River resulted in the SS Nord forces stopping and fleeing on the first day. The SS Nord Group had been formed from the SS members occupying Norway. While German propaganda had promoted the SS Nord Group *'for their high willingness to fight and their deep determination'*, they were found wanting when they encountered real war.

The SS Nord Group fled past the Corps headquarters. Father probably watched them going past.

The 169th Division and the regrouped SS Nord forces were able to finally capture Salla on July 6th, primarily because the Finnish 6th Division was able to break through from the south. The advance past Salla was stopped by Russian counter attacks at the Kairala Narrows on July 28th . The Russian infantry was provided strong support by Russian bombers, fighter planes and tanks. The tank support only remained until July 17th. It was withdrawn to help protect Leningrad.

A letter below from the Kemijarvi Veterans book provides a sense of daily life on the front.

Somewhere Out Here 9/7 -41

Dearest Homefolks:

I am writing now for the second time after the war truly started. We have roamed through the forests and Finland's territory has grown greater with every step we have taken. We crossed the interim border at 02:30 on July 1ˢᵗ. We shall see when we will cross the Old Border and when the conquest of Karjala will begin.

Otherwise we have held up to our situation. Continuously there is haste. We cannot always have a campfire, dependent on how close the Russians are. Right now it is truly a bit difficult as it is cold and rainy, and due to the proximity of the Russian artillery we cannot light a campfire. But our situation is clear. The Russians have a small motti on a dangerous hillside, otherwise everything is good. The food is good. There is not quite enough tea and coffee, and of course there is little tobacco. I am doing right stoutly, I hope you likewise. How is Olavi and Aunt Fanni ? I guess you are still displaced from our home ("evakko"). Regarding the other members from Kemijarvi I don't know much other than that Eero Hulko was killed on the first day.

I cannot organize it for Mauri to come here, as we don't take volunteers into this regiment, probably because the hardship and dangers are great. For example last night from 02:00 to 07:00 we moved forward about 20 kilometers with 30-40 kilogram packs on our backs while at the same time keeping a lookout for Russians. This wilderness war is tough.

Otherwise I have nothing more to say other than many greetings and stay well.

Pauli

Pauli was killed 10 days later at Kelsinka. He was a 2ⁿᵈ Lieutenant in the Finnish 6ᵗʰ Division. He was twenty years old.

The advance continued slowly from Kelsinki, stalling at the Nairala Narrows and Alakurtti until being stopped in the mountainous terrain just over the Old Finnish Border at Vermajoki. The two month and a half month attack had only advanced 85 kilometres, 75 kilometres short of the Murmansk rail line.

As the assault progressed father must have watched as materials, troops, and casualties moved through Kelloselka. It was a priority to have the heavily used Kemijarvi-Kelloselka railroad fully operational as soon as possible.

Father was successful in completing the railroad from Kemijarvi to Kelloselka. It is in operation still today. The track however ends in Kelloselka. As the Russians retreated they demolished the railway they had built behind them. Even today no railway exists.

PART IV

September '41 – December '41
The Fall Assault into Russian Karjala

...

Elsewhere, Settling into
Trench Warfare

December 31, 1941 Ylipaallikon Paivakaskysta

The road to victory has been harsh, full of deprivation, and incessant danger of death.
Comrades by ones side have been killed or wounded,
but YOUR will to win has been indestructible
and your faith as unyielding as the most rugged mountain.

FIELD MARSHALL MANNERHEIM

September '41 – December '41 The Fall Assault into Russian Karjala; Elsewhere Settling Into Trench Warfare

By mid September fighting on all the fronts except for Lake Ladoga had settled into trench warfare.

On the Kannas, the front line was set about 20 kilometers north of Leningrad, just a couple of kilometers south of the Old Finnish Border.

In Lapland, the assault on Murmansk stalled. And in the Salla sector as well. In the Salla sector the front line trenches were set about 20 kilometers past the Old Finnish Border at Vermajoki.

In Northern Finland one attempt was made to break through Kiestinki to reach the Murmansk railway at Louhi in November. The assault failed. Another attack by the Finnish 14th Division through Rukajarvi to the Sorokka Murmansk railway junction was called off by Mannerheim despite Finnish success. Both locations settled into trench warefare.

On the Ladoga front the assault continued towards the Syvari River, Petroksoi and Karhumaki.

CHAPTER 11

Trench Warfare on the Kannas and in Lapland

Uncles Vilho & Toivo home on leave

CHAPTER 11

Trench Warfare on the Kannas and in Lapland

By mid September 1941 the Kannas had settled into the "asema sota" trench warfare period. It continued for almost three years until June 1944. Finland set up their front lines just south of The Old Finnish Border from Toppari by Lake Ladoga to Rajajoki on the Gulf of Finland - 144 kilometers of fortifications. The line was organized into sectors, the responsibility of a specific division. The sectors west of Riihio were organized into the Riihio, Ohta, Vaskisavotta, Valkesaari, Rajajoki and Coastal sectors.

Uncle Aatu

On September 9th when the Kannas attack was called off, Uncle Aatu and JR48 were at Kekrola –Siiranmaki. For the next four months they manned the front lines – initially on the Ohta sector, then Valkeasaari, and finally at Vaskisavotta.

- The middle of September found Uncle Aatu and the 48th regiment in the Ohta sector. Uncle Aatu himself was about 5 kilometers behind the lines at the regiment headquarters at Termola.
- On October 2nd JR48 was withdrawn and replaced by JR28 and JR7. JR48s headquarters unit moved to Siiranmaki.
- On the 19th of October JR48 was moved from the 2nd Division to the 18th, and JR49 was moved to the 2nd Division.

- Two days later on October 21st JR48 took over defense of the Valkeasaari sector front lines from JR49. The line ran west from Valkeasaari through Mottori to Aleksankrovka. JR48 set up headquarters in Uusi Alakyla about 5 kilometers behind the trenches. They manned the lines for a month until being relieved by Colonel Haanterra's JR27.

- On the 28th of November one week after moving off the front line most of the 3rd battalion was demobilized and sent home. The rest of JR48 went on reserve until the 18th of December, when they were sent to take over the Vaskisavotta (Kiven) sector south of Kivennapa, just west of the Valkeasaari sector.

- Four weeks later in January 1942, JR6 took over the Vaskisavotta sector and JR48 was placed on reserve.

Uncle Aatu did not have to worry about the calibre of the reserve accommodation. On the 15th of January Uncle Aatu boarded the train at Raivola station just north of Terijoki and went home. He was demobilized. The army no longer needed the help of 39 year old soldiers.

During the four months Uncle Aatu was in the asema sota, his unit endured periodic Russian raids and artillery fire. But it was not comparable to the turmoil and danger they had gone through during the summer assault. While there were casualties, they were miniscule compared to those the regiment had suffered when they attacked down the Kannas. The regiment had suffered 1,111 casualties (191 killed, 920 wounded) during the three weeks from July 31, 1941 to August 20th – a 34% casualty rate - 1 out of every 3 men.

Undoubtedly given the inter division transfers and the movement of the regiment from front line to front line, Uncle Aatu as a headquarters messenger, would have been frequently on the move. In between the work they found time for sauna and rest, – and befriending orphan calves left in the wars' wake.

On January 15th, 1942 when the army no longer needed him, I am sure Uncle Aatu felt he did not need the army anymore either.

Uncle Toivo

After arriving at the border by the sea in the southwest corner of the Kannas at Aleksankrov, Kevyt Osasto 7 settled with JR6 into the trenches in the Kuokkala / Valkeasaari area near Aleksandrov.

The period from then until Kevyt Os 7 was disbanded was quiet. The soldiers spent their time going to sauna, resting, replenishing supplies, and refurbishing equipment. Occasionally they built fortifications and even for a few days dug up potatoes. Once they chased a Russian reconnaissance patrol. There was no Russian artillery or bombing activity

Three Lottas arrived to run a canteen, a musical troupe from Tampere entertained, and on one occasion an opera and ballet group put on a show.

Promotions were handed out on September 31st – one was the promotion of Uncle Toivo to corporal.

On October 19th the commanding officer handed out medals before the group was partitioned. Uncle Kauko

19.10.41	9.oo	Suoritti komentaja osaston katselmuksen ja hyvästeli pois siirtyneitä miehiä.
		Suoritettiin kunniamerkkien jako pois siirtyville miehille ja os. upseereille.
		Välittömästi katselmuksen jälkeen suoritettiin siirto autokuljetuksella.
	21.3o	tuli D puh.san. jossa määrättiin 2 D ja 18 D uudelleen järjestelyn takia vaihtaa kev.osastojaan.

was awarded a VM medal second class – earned sometime during the last month – or indeed perhaps many times.

On October 23rd the regiments of the 18th (Pajuri) and 2nd (Martola) Divisions were shuffled. Kevyt Osasto 7 as well as JR49 were transferred to the 2nd Division. Before on the 19th Colonel Pajuri thanked Kevyt Osasto 7 and said he was sorry to lose them.

On the 27th of October Uncle Toivo was transferred from Kevyt Os 7 to the 10th company of JR7 as part of the process of realigning the units once the war had settled into trench warfare. All the soldiers younger than 28 years old were transferred over to JR7 en bulk. This included 34 officers/NCOs and 144 men. The 29 year olds were transferred over a couple of days later. The remainder of Kevyt Osasto 7 only remained active until March 1942. At that point the whole unit was disbanded.

The company got a new commander and underwent all types of training for the next month.

On November 24th the battalion was seconded from JR7 to JR49. They moved to Riihimaki where they spent 2 weeks building bunkers and battlements. A week later on December 14th they were sent to the Riihio sector front lines. The 10th company manned the Lehto area of the trenches. The Lehto trenches were on the eastern border of the Riihio sector.

The next month brought constant gun fire exchanges and ongoing shelling. Christmas Day brought special delivery Christmas candles from the Russian artillery.

And so began the dangerous, uncomfortable hardship of the asema sota.

Uncle Arvo

On September 7th 1941 Uncle Arvo's squad was released from Osasto Kanerva. He went back to his original unit, the 3rd company of Pion P14 in Viipuri.

During September and October the 3rd company was in Viipuri disarming mines that the Russian forces had left on the streets and in the buildings. These mines included radio mines.

The Russians had placed many radio bombs in the city – that is large bombs that could be activated by a remote radio signal.

The Finns determined that the bombs were triggered by a radio signal with 3 high pitches. They also discovered that if they played the quick "Sakkijarvi

Polka" that the Russians could not send the 3 high pitches required to trigger their bombs. Although the radio mines were progressively found and disarmed, apparently the polka was played continuously on Finnish Radio until 1942.

The work disarming mines was needless to say dangerous – their locations were hidden in doorways, stairwells and side streets, and were tripped by inadvertent contact. In the two months I am sure Uncle Arvo got to know the buildings and streets of Viipuri all too well – and got to love the Sakkijarvi Polka.

On October 29, 1941 Company 3 left Viipuri to build bridges over Santajoki and Sakkijarvi on the Kannas.

Father in Lapland

On the Salla Front the war had settled into trench warfare at Vermajoki just past the Old Finnish Border – about 60 kilometers east of Salla.

Father was in Kelloselka building the railway connection from Kelloselka back to Kemijarvi.

While his day job was building the railroad, Dad's war records for 1941-42 state that his night job was guarding the railway from Kemijarvi to Salla.

During the fall and winter of '41 father went out at night in Kelloselka, riding the track in his rail way hand car with rifle in hand, searching for any Russians partisans who might be sabotaging the track. While being on the Finnish / German controlled side of the front, Russian guerilla groups often struck the area in order to cut the German supply rail and road route from Kemijarvi. It was very, very cold outside during the winter – at least once reaching minus 52 C.

Ladoga - The Fall Assault into Greater Finland

CHAPTER 12

Ladoga - The Fall Assault into Greater Finland

While the fall brought an end to the Finnish advance on the Kannas and Lapland, the assault continued in Ladoga Karjala. Mannerheim continued the advance in order to capture:

- Petroksoi, the capital of Russian Karjala;
- Karhumaki at the north end of Lake Onega; and
- The Maaselka isthmus and the Murmansk railway by the White Sea

By reaching these objectives, Finland would control the area between Lake Ladoga and Lake Onega from the Syvari River to the White Sea. This would repatriate the ancient Kareilian tribal area, making Greater Finland a reality. More importantly it would cut off Moscow and Leningrad from the Murmansk railway and the White Sea.

Attack east to Petroksoi and Eastern Syvari:

While the VI AK had advanced south to the Syvari River, the VII AK attacked eastwards towards Petroksoi.

The 1st Division attacked directly east, advancing through heavy fighting and defenses at Topasjarvi, Nirkko and Pyhajarvi. On September 29th they captured Lohijarvi. On September 30th they were within 7 kilometers of the centre of Petroksoi. The advance had not been easy much of it being through the wilderness along poor roads.

The 11th Division along with the 4th Division, attacked on the northern flank of the 1st Division through Sotjari, Saamajarvi, Praasa, Villavaara and Viitana. On September 22nd they took Matrossa. This opened the roads towards Petroksoi allowing easy movement of artillery and tanks. On September 24th they were 15 kilometers south of Petroksoi. On September 26th the division moved north cutting off the road and rail network from Petroksoi to the north. They took Vikga on September 28th and on September 30th the Suolusmaa road junction and Murmansk rail line.

Lieutenant General Heinrichs had given the 7th Division to the VI AK on September 6th. It attacked eastwards south of the 1st Division through Kaskana towards Lake Onega. At the Tarvespol – Latva railway station it swung north, battling through Petajaselka to the south side of Petroksoi. Concurrent with this Os Lagus advanced up from the Syvari River.

On September 30th Petroksoi was surrounded. The 11th Division was on the north side, the 1st on the southwest and west side, and Os Lagus and the 7th Division on the south side.

On October 1st the 1st Division captured Petroksoi. A large portion of the Russian forces were able to escape via boat to the east side of Lake Onega. Others moved north to bolster the defense of Karhumaki. A large number were killed or captured.

A portion of the 7th Division pursued the Russian forces south along the Onega shore. By October 23rd they had crossed the Syvari River at Voznesinia and moved 25 kilometers further south to Kimjarvi and Osta. Here the Finnish forces set up their front lines.

Attack North to Karhumaki

On October 1st Mannerheim ordered the Karjala Army to take Karhumaki and the Murmansk railway stations in the Maaselka peninsula north of Karhumaki.

The VII AK attacked 150 kilometers northwards from Petroksoi towards Karhumaki.

They were joined by Major General Laatikainen and the II AK who attacked along the south side of Seesjarvi towards the Maaselka Peninsula north of Karhumaki. On October 7th Mannerheim had transferred Major General Laatikainen and his headquarters unit and the 8th Division of AK IV from the Kannas to the Onega front. By late October Ryhma Oinonen and the 4th Division became part of Major General Laatikainen's group.

The entire campaign from October 4th to December 8th was fought in the wet snowy fall conditions through a swampy wilderness of lakes and bogs. While the Murmansk railroad did traverse the area from Petroskoi to Karhumaki, roads were few and rudimentary. As such during much of the campaign the Finnish army had difficulty bringing its' artillery into the battle.

The 1st and 4th Divisions attacked north from Petroksoi – the 1st Division beside Lake Onega and the 4th Division further inland. The 2.JPr attacked eastwards from the Tsalkki inland area to join 4th Divisions' northward assault. Russian defensive fortifications were scattered in strategic bottlenecks throughout the area. Battles occurred at Lake Lohmajarvi, Gromovskojenniemi, Kontupohja, the Suunun River, Pyhaniemi, Juustjarvi, and Kappaselka.

By November 29th the Finnish forces were on the out-skirts of Karhumaki – the 1st Division, the 2nd Jaakari Brigade, and the 45th Regiment of the 8th Division in the south west; and the 4th Division and 1st Jaakari Brigade in the north west. A major part of the battle occurred on the western outskirts of the city on both sides of the Kumsajoki River. The Finnish artillery provided exten-sive support – unfortunately not always effectively. As the various Finnish armies were very close together, and

the command structure of the Finnish forces fragmented, delays resulted as the Finnish forces neared Karhumaki. And sadly, casualties from friendly fire also resulted.

On December 5th 1st Division forces captured Karhumaki.

Attack to the Maaselka Isthmus and the Murmansk railway by the White Sea

After the city was captured the 1st JPr and portions of the 1st Division continued on to take Poventsa and Stalin's Canal.

Stalin's Canal provided a low draft ship / raft route from the White Sea to Leningard via the Canal, Lake Onega, the Syvari River, Lake Ladoga and the Niva River. It was called a canal because Stalin had it dug out of the swamps from Karhumaki/ Poventsa to the White Sea. Over 200 kilometers of swamps, creeks and lakes, it was dug by hand by a 100,000 convict and political prisoner labor force. Constructed between 1931 and 1933 under brutal working conditions, it was a key component of Stalin's first 5 Year Plan. The political prisoners included Finnish Canadian socialists who had been enticed to go back to Karjala in 1930/1931 to fulfill the socialist dream. The dream turned into a nightmare. Stalin arrested them and put them into forced labor camps digging out Stalin's Canal. Almost all died in the gulag. Overall about 25% of the workforce died. 15% of the workforce was released. The remaining 60% were forced into ongoing suffering in new gulag camps or prisons.

Meanwhile the 8th Division had attacked from Tsinjarvi northwards to take the town of Paatene on the south west shore of Lake Seesjarvi, and from thence along the south shore of Lake Seesjarvi to the Maaselka peninsula north of Karhumaki. Here they took the Murmansk railway stations of Maaselka and Krivi.

On December 8th Mannerheim stopped any further advance. The Finnish forces set up defensive fortifications and settled into two years of trench warfare. In the first few months the Russian army attempted several major assaults to take back Karhumaki and the Maaselka Peninsula but these were turned back.

Uncle Kauko

Uncle Kauko, being in the 5th Company of the 1st Divisions' II Battalion was in the heart of the attack towards Petroksoi and Karhumaki.

On September 1st Uncle Kauko and the II battalion was about 30 kilometers north east of Hiisijarvi at Nuosjarvi. There they were loaded on trucks and driven to Sammajarvi, arriving at 05:00 on the September 3rd. The battalions' objective now became to push eastwards and help take Petroskoi.

From Sammajarvi they advanced along the railroad and road towards Petroksoi – 60 kilometers away. The route was defended by Russian defensive lines, tanks, artillery and bombing. The II battalion took part in continuing battles in the Saamajarvi – Kutsima area. During this advance Uncle Kauko was promoted to Corporal on September 26th.

On October 1st, the division took Petroskoi.

" Our companies pushed into the city at 04:30 and raised a Finnish flag on top of the Karjalan regions capitol building. "

The unit did not rest – moving back into the action after midnight – the objective being to take Karhumaki.

- On October 2nd after eating at 02:00 the battalion moved at 04:00 to the battle ground. During the day both the Finnish and Russian artillery were active.

A particularly heavy artillery and howitzer barrage made a direct hit on the regiments' field hospital (JSp). Pastor Lieutenant Honkala was killed. Lieutenant Doctor Nepponstrom was wounded. Under Serjeant Raatikainen was seriously wounded and died – likewise trooper Kuhmala.

- The next day- the 4th – the battalion was in a severe fight at Kenjakki. Three of the 5th companies' men were wounded including 2nd Lieutenant Peltola. The battle is noted in Uncle Kauko's military record.

- From the 4th to the 7th the unit advanced about 7 kilometers northwards each day. On the 6th the men cleared out a small motti.

- On the 7th the battalion was ordered to advance to the village of Motori , arriving at 16:00 on the 8th . The bridge had been mined by the Russians, but was cleared by the pioneers.

- The 9th brought the first snow. It also brought heavy Russian bombing. Five of the battalion were killed and 5 wounded.

- On the 10th the battalion cleared out Russians surrounded in a motti at the cost of 1 killed and 4 wounded. 35 Russians were killed and 20 captured.

- On the 11th the Finnish airforce, for a change, was unusually active.

- On the 12th while the Finnish forces were holding a victory parade in Petroskoi, the Russian air force was bombing the II Battalions' supply column.

- On the 13th the battalion moved to the Paljarvi shore.

- On the 14th they crossed an inlet across Suunjoki River towards the village of Suununsuu. The day

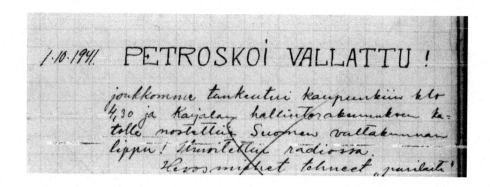

brought heavy Russian bombing and howitzer fire. The village of Suunjoki caught fire. The enemy was forced to retreat. Soldiers Laino and Metsberg were killed.

- From the 15th to the 19th they moved short distances each day, arriving at Juustijarvi on the evening of the 17th. The advance was interspersed with periodic Russian bombing runs and motti skirmishes.

- They advanced from the Juustjarvi road junction on the 19th towards Mantyselka. In Mantyselka on the 22nd Uncle Kauko's company was embroiled in a major battle.

20.10.41 At 10:00 the II and III battalion moved out of the village of Juustijarvi towards Karhumaki. About 4 kilometers past Juustijarvi there were Russian defensive lines. After a couple of hours firefight, the Russians retreated and at 17:15 we continued marching onwards. We bivouacked for the night on the northern side of the village of Tasojarvi.

21.10.41 At 13:40 the IInd and IIIrd battalions advanced towards Suurselka. Just 4 kilometers east of Torasjarvi there were prepared Russian defenses which the Russians abandoned after a short firefight. We bypassed the defenses to Suurselka watching the village of Torasjarvi burning. We slept the night near Suurselka village.

22.10.41 At 08:00 the 5th and 6th companies and half of the 7th company supported by artillery and howitzer fire attacked towards the village of Mantyselka. We reached the first enemy placements but the resistance was exceptionally fierce. We gave the order to retreat back to our start stations.

The Russian bombarded us with their artillery and howitzers...

23.10.41 We reinforced our positions. Artillery and tank fire from both sides.

24.10.41 In the morning at 8:00 we began an enormous howitzer and canon barrage, followed by an assault on Mantyselka. After a blanket of smoke was laid down the III battalion and half of our battalion started attacking . The advance into the village progressed very well and by 10:00 we had taken Mantyselka

- Uncle Toivo's battalion remained in the Mantyselka area for a week. All was quiet, except on the 25th and 26th, which brought artillery and howitzer fire all day from both sides. But there was no concern about an enemy attack – indeed on the 30th the mobile Lotta canteen arrived at the battalion encampment.

- On October 31st the battalion was on the move towards Karhumaki again. Over the next 2 weeks they battled through the Russian defenses on the road. The battalion was involved in battles at Kontivaara and at the Tsopina road junction. The Mantyselka and Tsopina battles are noted in Uncle Kauko's military records

31.10.41 At 06:00 the battalion moved out from Mantyselka arriving at 07:30 at the Kumsa village. It was filled with armaments that the Russians had left when Er P21 and JR26 took the village.

We stopped about 5 kilometers before the Kontiovaara village, pitched our tents, and ate. At that moment JR25 was attacking the village of Kontiovaara. At

18:00 it took the village and our battalion got orders to take up forward positions.

We moved out at 19:00. The 5th company and a machine gun squad set up positions in the east side of the village while the rest of the battalion set up in the village and on its' western side.

A few Russian patrols were on the move but otherwise it was quiet.

1.11.41 At 07:00 the 6th and 7th companies moved out to set up positions for 2 kilometers about 1 ½ kilometers south of the road near Tsopina. Around 09:00 they got attacked by the enemy.

At the same time the 5th company attacked the Russians from the north side of the road making a 200 meter wide break through the Russian fortifications. The enemy counter attacked with a battalion strong force, taking back their positions and forcing us to draw back to our original positions.

Concurrently the 6th and 7th had been successful in making some advance, but with the fierce Russian counter attack they as well had to retreat.

2.11.41 The 1st and 3rd battalions moved out from their positions attacking from the north side of the road. But like the day before the Russians launched a fierce counter attack. The 1st battalion retreated leaving the 3rd battalion to prepare defenses on the north side of the road.

A heavy Russian artillery barrage was directed towards our battalion.

3.11.41 The previous night at 1:30 Er P21 conquered the village of Tsopina. (The Er P21 battalion received an exceptional commendation from Marshall Mannerheim himself). The Russians started to draw back east along the road to Karhumaki.

- For the next three days the 5th company was in the midst of fighting around the village of Tsopina.

- After the fighting the battalion remained in Tsopina from November 6th to the 10th. The days were uneventful except for sporadic Russian artillery fire. The battalion sent out a couple of patrols – the 5th company sent one north towards Seesjarvi on November 8th.

    Uncle Kauko was probably not on that patrol as on November 8th he was awarded a Freedom Medal 2nd class (VM 2) for bravery.

- At 8:45 on the 11th the battalion started eastwards. From Tsopina it was only 15 kilometers to Karhumaki – but 15 kilometers heavily defended by the Russians. The road wound through bottleneck isthmuses defended by fortifications and Russian tanks.

- The battalion immediately became involved in fighting at Paduk just 5 kilometers down the road. The town had been taken by JR25 and JR26 - but the 35th had to stop major counter attacks from November 13th to the 17th.

- On Nov 19th the 2nd battalion received 55 much needed replacements.

By the end of November the battalion was on the outskirts of Karhumaki. While battles occurred in the outskirts of Karhumaki for several days, the attack on the town itself started at 04:30 on the 5th with the 1st Division, the 4th Division, the Os Lagus panzer brigade, and JR45 from the 8th Division. Karhumaki was captured in the evening of the 5th but fighting continued through to the 7th . Karhumaki

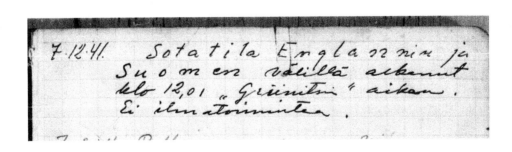

was one of the few towns where fighting continued from house to house along the streets.

Uncle Kauko's 2nd battalion did not enter the town itself. They fought with Russian forces north of the town and east of the Murmansk railroad from December 4th through the 6th – the fighting continuing amid bombing, company strength attacks and counter attacks, and patrols by both the enemy and our forces.

After the Finnish forces took Karhumaki on the 5th, England formally declared war against Finland at 12:01 Greenwich time on December 7th, 1941.

The battalion continued east towards Stalins Canal north of Poventsa engaging in patrols and skirmishes.

- On December 7th the 1 JPr took Poventsa. The next day the Russian forces exploded the locks. A huge wave of water rushed through the town. Only a few Finnish soldiers were killed and some tanks lost. On December 24th the Finns withdrew to the east side of Poventsa river.

- Uncle Kauko's unit was in Poventsa at some point, as the Poventsa battle is listed in his military record.

- On December 10th the unit was at the Kirvu station about 30 kilometers north of Poventsa. The station was at a junction of the Murmansk Railway and a spur line east to Stalin's Canal.

- At the end of December the 5th Company of JR35 was south of Kirvu at the Malu station north of Karhumaki.

The regiment set up fortifications and settled into 2 ½ years of trench warfare.

Uncle Vilho

At the beginning of October, 1941, Uncle Vilho and the 8th Division were transferred from the Karjala isthmus to the area north and east of Lake Ladoga to take part in the Maaselka campaign with the II Army Corps. Thus Vilho was actually in ancient Russia, as this area had never been part of Finland.

The 8th Division together with the Kuusari Brigade were tasked with:

- Taking Porajarvi,
- Then the Soutjarvi – Jankajari Tsinjarvi area, prior to,
- Capturing Paatene, and finally
- Cutting the Murmansk railroad north of Karhumaki

As well as the Russian opposition, the division had to deal with wilderness terrain and adverse weather conditions. The division took Paatene on October 19th, then moved along the south shore of Seesjarvi to the Maaselka station (40 kilometres north of Karhumaki) on November 21st, and the Kirvu station the following day.

Uncle Vilho was a leader of the divisional food supply depot / column. Being with the Divisional supply column he was thankfully only subject to bombing by the Russian planes and occasional artillery barrages. The divisional supply depot was generally about 10 to 20 kilometres behind infantry. They received supplies from the army corps depot or else directly from facilities in Finland, and forwarded them to the regiments. Each regiment had one supply column. When possible the supplies came via rail from Finland.

- The 8th Division started their move to the Maaselka front on September 30th.
- They moved via rail from the southern Kannas (From Kovisto ?) to Suojarvi near Kolla and from thence east via the Suojarvi - Petroksoi railroad. Units disembarked at Veskelys, Jessoila (South of Saamajarvi) and Suojoki. The move was complete by October 11th.

- From there the 8th Division attacked 100 kilometers north to take Paatene at the south west end of Lake Seesjarvi.
- The attack started on Ocober 12th. The 4th Regiment and Brigade Kuus took Porajarvi on October 14th. The Russians retreated, burning the village and destroying the bridges behind them.
- JR4 and Brigade Kuus took Paatene on October 19th. The Division units were still at Kostamus 15 kilometres south of Porajarvi. The Division had difficulty following its' troops as the road to Paatene was a muddy quagmire. Volume 3 of the Jatkosota Historia notes:

"The Division because of the poor road could not follow behind JR4 to Paatene. There, provision of food supplies was impossible without fixing the road. Even though the pioneers built a corduroy road it could not support two way traffic. Companies from JR24, Er P21 and KTR 11 were commandeered for several days to build the road under the direction of the pioneer captain.

As well as lack of proper transportation, lack of provisions limited movement. Division supply had been difficult for some time. JR4 only had 2 days worth of food supplies. In summer shoes, the horses had sank, but in them they had nonetheless travelled 200 kilometers from the Suojarvi –Petroksoi railroad.

Indeed in the village of Selki 20 kilomtres south of Paatene, JR 4 had to commandeer grain and food stuffs from the returning villagers.

The Division head quarters units along with Uncle Vilho and the food supply column arrived in Paatene on 0ctober 22nd.

- After capturing Paatene some of the units continued northwards on the west side of Seesjarvi to link with Colonel Raappana's 14th Division. This placed all of Karjala from the Syvari River at the south ends of Lake Ladoga and Lake Onega, to AlaKurtti near Salla in Lapland, in Finnish hands.
- On November 6th the 8th Division began their attack on Karhumäki in support of the VII AK.

The Division advanced along the southern end of Seesjarvi towards the Murmansk railway north of Karhumaki.

- The Finnish troops however did not move eastwards on the road adjoining Lake Seesjarvi as it was heavily defended. The Division's Sissi battalion identified a route through the wilderness south of the Lake Seesjarvi road. Sissi units were lightly equipped and trained to move through the wilderness.
- It was a different matter for regular infantry regiments with artillery and supply columns. The roads were merely paths that not even a horse and cart could get through. They struggled through the November sleet and snow in single file. The horses were now either pack horses or else harnessed behind one another pulling sinking artillery guns pushed from behind by floundering soldiers. Although the weather and the roads were bad, there were no enemy forces.
- The Finnish forces doubled back to the Russian enclave at Listephoja on the road south of Seesjarvi encircling them in a motti. Most of the Russian forces escaped across the ice on Lake Seesjarvi. The Finnish forces were able to capture some

armaments but most of the trucks had been burnt by the Russians before they escaped.

• During the advance Uncle Vilho's divisional supply unit did not follow the infantry units. The divisional supply depot remained at the village of Karjalan Maaselka 25 kilometres west of the Maaselka Station.

By Christmas the war settled into trench warfare. The 8th Division manned the trenchs between Seesjarvi and Maaselka Station. In January and February the Russian forces launched several major attacks but they were repulsed.

Afterwards the front was quiet. But that was of no consequence to Uncle Vilho's unit. The 8th Division was transferred south to the Syvari River front in March 1942.

PART V

On the Home Front

PART V

On the Home Front

On The Homefront

Life on the home front from June 1941 to Christmas 1941 changed for mother and my sisters, and for Sirkka and her folks.

Mother and my sisters moved to Kelloselka in Lapland to join dad.

The change for Sirkka and her family was much more momentous. Her father Erkki died of cancer. Afterwards she, her mother, her brother Martti, and Grandpa Juho were able to return back to the beloved homestead in Kavantsaari. Her younger siblings and grandmother remained in Finland, moving to stay with Aunt Hilda and Aunt Margit.

Kavantsaari and Kelloselka

CHAPTER 13

Kavantsaari and Kelloselka

Life on the home front from June 1941 to December 1941 was full of tension and hope. Tension and worry about the fate of the men. Hope that beloved Karjala would be freed again.

Mother and My Sisters at Kelloselka

Mother and my sisters Terttu and Tellervo moved to Lapland in the summer of 1941 to be with father.

They arrived in Kelloselka in September soon after the German and Finnish forces had recaptured Salla and advanced to the old border beyond Alakurtti. They joined father at his workplace while he managed the work crews building the 80 kilometer rail link from Kelloselka to Kemijarvi.

Kelloselka was near the border 15 kilometers east of Salla. Salla had originally been part of Finland but by the Winter War peace terms it became part of Russia. Today a town called Salla exists 16 kilometers west of Kelloselka. Finding Salla west of Kelloselka on todays' maps confused me somewhat until I checked old maps. The old maps had Salla east of Kelloselka. The current town was built after the Continuation War and named Salla in memory of the town that was lost to Russia.

Kelloselka was a small village in the Finnish wilderness. One small road led west from Kelloselka to Kemijarvi and east to Salla and Rutsi on the Murmansk line. Dad and my family lived in a meager cottage in Kelloselka. The village

consisted of wood frame cabins sporadically placed on both sides of a small dirt road. (photo on previous page) . The conditions were not the best. The two girls next door died of tuberculosis but Terttu and Tellervo were not affected. (Tellervo says she has always had a little non infectious trace of TB).

It was very, very cold outside during the winter – occasionally -52 C.

Dad went out at night in Kelloselka, riding the track in his rail way hand car, searching for any Russians partisans who might be sabotaging the track. While being on the Finnish / German controlled side of the front, Russian guerilla groups often struck the area in order to cut the German supply rail and road route from Kemijarvi.

Mother was very apprehensive whenever he went out. It was dangerous. Indeed some people in the village itself were dragged out of their own homes and killed by Russian infiltrators.

My sister Tellervo remembers;

That they did have some good occasions though, particularly when mom and dad came back from picking goose berries. Tellervo says that she ate so many of them, that she almost got sick.

On other occasions she remembers visiting the Saami (Laplanders) and watching as they milked their reindeer.

Sirkka and the Kavantsaari Home Folk

Sirkka, her mother Aunt Saima, her brothers Martti and George, her sister Irja and grampa and gramma continued to live together at the Jaakola place in Sukula. Her father Uncle Erkki had been called up but returned soon - diagnosed with terminal cancer.

Then in early summer when the Jatkosota started, dad was called up to the reserves as were the other men. A month later he was let go due to illness.

Dad did horse work for the home owner. Slowly his health weakened. In the fall gramma, gramps and mother had to bring in the fall harvest, and I had to nurse father. I remember bringing pieces of ice from the home owner's ice cellar which dad sucked on in his fever to help him from throwing up.

Once mother sent me shopping as the doctor had ordered eggs with alcohol. Normal food did travel through dads' system.

In the first shop they did not have it, nor in the second shop. Only when I told my story, as much as a 11 year old could, that during this time a hen had come and laid 2 eggs under the store counter. The egg purchase suddenly happened and a happy Sirkka peddled home on her fathers bicycle.

Gramps and dad together had a horse which needed to be shoed. In dads illness gramps had asked for money for horse nails. Dad said take even the shirt off the back of this wretch once I have died. And so it more or less happened.

By the beginning of September the Finnish forces had advanced to the Old Finnish Border. Uncle Erkki had hoped to spend his last days on the Kavantsaari homestead. But as Sirkka recounts:

Karjala was recaptured and dad hopefully waited to go home. Close the return home was. We had received approval, but God wanted dad in heaven. He called dad to his heavenly home on October 3ʳᵈ , 1941.

Directly after dad died gramma and my brother George went for the winter to Aunt Margits place

in Oripaa, Uncle Kauko being in the war. Aunt Hilda and Uncle Aatu took little Irja to their place in Vaajakoski.

In November of 1941, after having laid Uncle Erkki to rest, Aunt Saima and her two oldest children - Martti and Sirkka - returned to the farm. Martti would have been thirteen, and Sirkka eleven. Gramps waited in order to get a railway car in which to bring back the cattle.

They took a train to Antrea as the rail road to Kavantsaari had still not been repaired. From thence they took an army lorry to Kavantsaari.

From there they walked the short distance to the farm. To cross the Syvalahti River close to the farm, they had to use an army pontoon bridge as the original bridge had been destroyed -destroyed probably on August 23, 1941 by JR26 and Kevyt Os 1 as they advanced through Kavantsaari.

I looked for the stream when I was in Kavantsaari in 2012 and 2016. Now it is hard to notice any water. All there is is a culvert and a small rivlet choked in weeds.

Sirkka says:

"It felt so wonderful to be back. One can not picture the joy we felt when we arrived on our home yard – rollicking like calves let loose on spring pasture. We had to inspect all the outlying buildings.

The buildings were still intact and everything was much as it had been when they left. However there was no metal left. All the ovens and even the door hinges and knobs were gone. As well there was no electricity. Another large oven had been built downstairs by the Russians as a bakery. When we warmed it up huge smoke bellowed inside from between the tiles.

When night fell we became a bit anxious in the dark house and countryside. It was great when Uncle Arvo showed up during a couple day leave from the army with a big bag of candles he had found in Viipuri.

Grandfather arrived about 3 or 4 weeks later (He would have been 64), with the horses and the remaining 3 cows.

Mother and Uncle Arvo (home on leave for a day) went to Antera to meet gramps and help drive the cattle back to the farm.

My brother Martti and I stayed behind. Martti disappeared to visit the Iivonen neighbors. As night approached, the sun disappeared. An 11 year old girl all alone, I was scared. Thankfully I finally heard the sound of cattle and the folks approaching. And indeed even brother Martti suddenly appeared. I was happy that everyone had arrived.

Even the cattle were happy to be back, immediately going to their correct stalls in the barn."

Even though Finland was winning the war, they had to be wary of the Russian forces. The Russian air force continued to periodically bomb Finland. Sirkka remembers their first sauna being interrupted.

We had to heat the water outside in a big 20 litre kettle, as the iron water basin in the sauna had been taken by the Russians. It was evening and we had just got the fire burning brightly under the kettle when we heard the sound of a Russian bomber approaching from the east. We hastily smothered the fire and ran away until it passed overhead. But being good Finns, we shortly thereafter started up the fire again, and soon enjoyed our first sauna back at home.

Christmas soon came. And although war was still underway, and her father had died, Sirkka remembers:

That Christmas was one of my happiest.

Mother and gramps baked Christmas breads and I received a gift from Aunt Margit containing cloth for a dress.

And we were once more home !!

Trench Warfare

Trench Warfare – January 1942 – June 1944

All the battle fronts had settled into trench warfare by January 1942. This continued until the June 1944 assault by Russia.

On the Kannas, four divisions manned the defensive lines 20 kilometers north of Leningrad. These defensive positions were set up only 5 to 10 kilometers south of the Old Finnish Border.

Opposite them Russia positioned three divisions and a fortification brigade.

The four Finnish divisions were placed under the control of the I AK of Colonel Makinenen and II AK of Major General T Laatikainen. Starting from Lake Ladoga in the east the stretch to the Gulf of Finland was manned by: the 15th Division (Colonel N. Hersalo) and the 10th Division (Colonel J. Sihvo) of IAK; the 2nd Division (Major General A. Martola) and the 18th Division (Major General Pajuri) of the IIAK.

In our family:

- Uncle Aatu only served for 2 weeks with JR48 before being de-mobilized home

- Uncle Arvo continued serving with company 3 of Pion P 14. His unit de mined Viipuri and built fortifications and mine fields throughout the south west kannas.

- Uncle Toivo's asema sota however was not quiet. He manned the front lines trenches in Riihio and Ohta with JR28, JR49 and JR7.

In the Lapland theatre the front lines were on the Murmansk Front and at Vermijoki on the Salla front. Father was here overseeing the building of the Salla to Kemijarvi railroad.

In the Karjala/Ladoga theatre the trenches were set up on the Maaselka Front between Seesjarvi and Karhumaki; and, on the Aanus Front, on the south side of the Syvari River from Lake Onega to Lake Ladoga.Uncle Kauko served on the Maaselka front while Uncle Vilho served by the Syvari River.

Terror and Tedium on the Front

Terror and Tedium on the Front

On the Kannas Finland set up defensive fortifications across the Isthmus from Lake Ladoga to the Gulf of Finland about 5 to 10 kilometers south of The Old Finnish Border. In many cases they just augmented existing Russian fortifications. The front line consisted of fortified bunkers in no man's line, pill boxes, defensive trenchs, mine fields, barbed wire barriers, and tank barriers.

The Central and Western Kannas area from Riihio west to the Gulf where Uncles Toivo, Aatu and Arvo served, was divided into the Riihio, Ohta, Vaskisavota, Valkeasaari, Rajajoki, and Coastal sectors.

Uncle Aatu

For Uncle Aatu the asema sota was definitely quiet. He was demobilized on January 16, 1942 and returned home. As the war had settled into a trench warfare holding pattern, the army no longer needed 39 year old soldiers.

He returned home to his wife Hilda and daughters Anna Liisa and Maija in Vajakoski near Jyvaskyla. But even then he remained involved – ending up constructing fortifications for the Finnish munitions factory in Kanavuori.

Uncle Toivo

Uncle Toivo ended up in the Riihio and Ohta sectors in the trenches 30 kilometers north of Leningrad. He served there with JR28, JR49 and JR7.

Ending up on these sectors was equivalent of drawing the short straw. The Russian army shelled the trenches and bunkers continuously, sent patrols to obtain intelligence and prisoners, and occasionally launched full attacks.

- At the end of October 1941 Uncle Toivo was moved from Kevyt Os 7 to the 10th company of JR7.
- Two and a half months later on January 15th, 1942 he was transferred to the 2nd company of JR28.
- Four months later on the 24th of May he was moved to the 10th company of JR49; and,
- Five months later on October 10th 1942 he was with the 10th company of JR7 again.
- He stayed with JR7 for two years until the end of the war, although he was transferred from the 10th Company to the 9th Company a year later on October 16th 1943.

Changing Units

The movement from unit to unit was caused by the army realigning its forces after the summer assault. Older soldiers were disbanded home, and as the trench warfare required fewer soldiers, individual units were disbanded or consolidated. As well, divisional commanders changed and regimental alignment changed.

Not much changed for the soldiers though. All the units had been located close to one another on the Leningrad front and were part of the 2nd Division. Indeed during the period from October 1941 to October 1942 while Uncle Toivo is listed as serving with JR7, JR28 and JR49, he actually was with JR49. His battalion was seconded "temporally" to JR49 when he was with JR7 and JR28.

Battalion III/JR7 10th Company 27.10.41 – 15.1.42

On October 27th 1941 Uncle Toivo's 2nd Company of Kevyt Os 7 became the 10th Company of JR7. Kevyt Osasto 7 itself only remained active until March 31, 1942. At that point the whole unit was decommissioned. Kevyt Os 7's commander Major Gunnar Boisman seems to have retired at the same time.

While now with the JR7, Uncle Toivo's battalion was soon seconded to JR49 and spent the period up to January 15th on the front lines in the Lehto area of the Riihio sector.

Battalion I/JR28 2nd Company: 15.1.42 -24.5.42

On January 15th 1942 the 2nd Division units were once again shuffled. Uncle Toivo's 3rd battalion became the 1st battalion of the 28th Regiment (JR28) commanded by Lieutenant Colonel T Kotilianen. In mid February Major Ilmari Inomaa was placed in command of the battalion.

However two months later on March 28th 1942 the 1st battalion was once more seconded to JR49s' command (Colonel Eino Jarvinen). The 1st battalion took over the eastern border of the Riihio sector again (Harju sub sector). Patrols, skirmishes, sharp shooting and shelling continued - by both the Russians and the Finns.

On May 7th 1942 the battalion was returned to JR28 again. In June 1942 the JR49th commander Colonel Jarvinen thanked the 1st Battalion for its work with JR49 during the last 5 months.

I/JR28 has from the beginning admirably fulfilled its responsibilities in the front line trenches, withstanding numerous artillery barrages and enemy attacks as well as successfully completing a number of important reconnaissance forays behind the enemy lines. Throughout this long period, covering five months, the battalion has commendably handled both orders to hold firm, and to take action.

I thank the battalion for its loyalty and tenacity during this time. I wish to especially thank the battalion commander Major Inomaa, my old comrade in arms from the last war, and Captain Lehtea who in many situations ensured the success of the battalion, and in doing so sacrificed his own inspirational life.

Wishing the battalion, now upon its dissolution nothing but the every best, especially as it applies to ensuring that Russia is laid low.

JR49 Commander

Lieutenant Colonel E.I. Jarvinen

Battalion III/JR49 10th Company: 24.5.42 to 10.10.42:
Colonel Jarvinen must have been quite attached to the unit as a couple of days later it formally became the III battalion of JR49. The 2nd Company became the 10th Company.

Once more Uncle Toivo was in the Harju portion of the Riihio sector, unless his unit was on well deserved reserve in Seisjarvi.

On May 12th 1942 Major General Hannu E. Hannuksela, the highly regarded commander of the 2nd Division, died of a heart attack. He was replaced by Major General A. E. Martola.

The III Battalion continued to man the Harju portion of the Riihio sector. Attacks, skirmishes and shelling continued. Not all activity was onerous. Concerts and athletic competitions also occurred.

On July 19th 1942 the regiment was reinforced with 488 thirty one to thirty three year old reserves to replenish the demobilized older soldiers and casualties.

Battalion III/JR7th 10th Company: 10.10.42 to 1.11.43:
On October 10th 1942 the units were shuffled again. Uncle Toivo's battalion left JR49 and moved to JR7. Uncle Toivo continued with the 10th company. He remained with the 7th Regiment until the end of the war although he was transferred from the 10th to the 9th Company on November 1st 1943

Dissent in the Ranks

The soldiers of the 7th Regiment followed orders. They were courageous and were regarded as one of the best regiments in the army.

But they were not entirely without their own opinions, even though in the military soldiers have no voice, and are expected to follow orders without question. These opinions were handled in different ways dependent on who was the commander of Uncle Toivo's regiment.

Colonel Jarvinen, the commander of JR49, wrote a short history of his regiment and provided his perspective on war and the Finnish soldier.

" One can only appreciate our armies conscript forces fighting ability and spirit upon special inspection. As is well known, our too short peacetime military training, could not make soldiers of our men - to use an old fashioned phrase, "to be like a true Prussian soldier". They learned the essentials, but regarding posture, military behavior, and obedience, they remained the same "ruffians" that they had been before they started their service.

It is due to this, that people, particularly foreigners, who do not understand the Finnish people and their unique character, look at the Finnish soldiers with a slightly pitying smile. They cannot believe that such an unmilitary soldier can do anything.

But outward appearances deceive. Underneath the unsightly rumpled uniforms there lies an abundance of gold, perhaps more than that in any other countries soldiers.

The officer's job is to understand this gold properly. If he has the skill to do so one cannot envision greater happiness then to be allowed to lead these men, to be their faithful friend, to be their brother. Then one does not need harshness, senior officer hearings at headquarters, nor disciplining. Such an officer who has earned a Finnish soldiers respect and trust, will get their way almost without asking. The mere indication of the intent or wish of such an officer will result in the soldiers fulfilling it.

It is clear that in such a relationship between a superior and subordinates, service to one another - by both sides - is a prerequisite. With it even the most difficult tasks and situations can be easily straightened out and performed. In JR49 this philosophy was our cornerstone.

If an officers' influence over his company is based on rigid, formal enforcement, a not ideal relationship may result. Subordinates will obey because they are forced to obey, but they will complete their orders mechanically and only half heartedly.

One can blame difficult battles, where to the subordinates' basic nature a foolish leader always loses something, even though he can by force get his orders followed through. The Finnish soldiers' sense of honor and sense of justice will not tolerate this. He is not a machine which indiscriminately completes anything, he is a thinking human being, who willingly completes the requests of respected superiors, but reacts very critically to the orders of those superiors who have not succeeded in getting their confidence.

Colonel Jarvinen was faced with demand from the older cadre of his regiment during the spring of 1942.

His seasoned older soldiers asked to be given leave to go home. (In other battalions most of the older soldiers had already been disbanded).

They received leave.

Colonel Jarvinen was able to provide a solution which was militarily acceptable. He recognized that the major driving factor was the soldiers need to go home to do the spring planting. So in granting the leave he highlighted the need to support the home front. He recognized the importance of seeing the soldiers' perspective versus just applying military rigor.

Colonel Armas Kemppi who was the commander of JR7 from the start of the war until January 1943 faced a somewhat similar situation during late summer 1941. After the successful assault down the Kannas many of the soldiers did not want to proceed beyond the Old Finnish Border. One older serjeant was particularly vocal. He did not want to proceed any further as Finland now had its' beloved Karjala back. The officers of course could not have any soldiers questioning orders. As the old serjeant was one of the most respected and most courageous members of the regiment, the regiment commander Colonel Armas Kemppi decided that the only thing to do was to transfer him and some others to another unit. And it was done. And coincidentally Mannerheim stopped the advance towards

Leningrad after they were a mere ten kilometers over The Old Finnish Border.

Lieutenant Colonel Ehrnroot who took over command of the regiment took a different approach. In spring 1944 (spring planting time once more) a group of NCO's from the 3rd battalion presented a petition to the senior officers. They had been promised leave but it had been revoked even though at that point hostilities were months away.

The battalions' well regarded commanding officer Major Inomaa was receptive to their views but could not convince the group to withdraw their petition. He took the petition to the regiment commander Ehnroot. Ehnroot gathered them together and read them the riot act. He broke all the NCOs to the rank of private and lectured them, saying that,

"It was a shameful act that would forever taint them and the only way they could clear their reputation was for one honorable NCO in the group to sacrifice himself in the next battle. He ended it by quoting an ancient military saying that, "Only blood can wash away this shame."

The battalion commander Major Inomaa, whom Lieutenant Colonel Jarvinen of JR49 had praised along with the battalions' men, was replaced.

The battalion after the reprimand was only a pale shadow of the outstanding attack battalion it had once been. They worked to rule and avoided unneedy sacrifices. But in the final stand for Finland at Ayrapaa/Vuosalmi when Finlands' life was at stake they once more were ready to make the supreme sacrifice.

Why Colonel Ehrnrooth took a military rigor approach is not known. He does have a reputation as a successful regiment leader, undoubtedly well earned, but also one burnished through post war book publications, publicity and continued army service for several decades. There were many outstanding regiments. As Serjeant Eeri Hyrkko of JR35 recently commented:

"Our regiments contribution has been overlooked as no one in the regiment undertook to write about it".

JR35 was the regiment which took Petroksoi and Karhumaki and stopped the Russian assault at Ihantala.

Perhaps Colonel Ehrnrooth just made a major mistake on a bad day. Certainly it would be difficult to lead a battalion whose NCOs you had just demoted and whoser blood earned honor and that of their brothers-in-arms you had sullied.

While the officers give the orders and lead, it is the serjeants the men follow. The NCOs and men stand together shoulder to shoulder both in life and death. They share the same bunk houses, bunkers and machine gun posts. The officers live in their own buildings and "Generals die at home in their beds". After the war very few members of the JR7 s' 3rd battalion came to regimental reunions (apparently only 12%). I never heard Uncle Toivo provide any glowing references nor reminisce about regimental gatherings.

The matter at question had not been desertion; rather it was a formally submitted petition regarding promised leave.

Deserters were subject to execution. Vaino Linna in his book The Unkown Soldier describes vividly an instance of unwarranted execution against the sauna wall. Fortunately executions were not frequent. Only 62 soldiers were executed according to the official Jatkosota records. Different standards for desertion were however applied to officers. Colonel Kemppi, and in particular Major Backman, who ordered the abandonment of Viipuri against specific orders, were not executed. After a military tribunal hearing, Colonel Kemppi received a prison sentence of 25 days and Major Backman eight months.

Concerning Medals for Bravery

Interestingly the Mannerheim cross, the ultimate Finnish award for valour was not always an award for bravery. When I was in Finland I visited the Askaisten Ritaripuisto near Mannerheim's ancestral estate near my cousins' Nousiainen home. It had markers for all 197 recepients of the Mannerheim Cross. The vast majority were for officers. Of the 197 Mannerheim crosses awarded during the Jatkosota only 25 (12 ½ %) were awarded to soldiers, and 40 (20%) to NCOs. Given the Finnish soldiers reputation for bravery and self sacrifice, one cannot believe that the soldiers who made up 80% of the armed forces were less brave then the 5% officers. The 5% officers received 67% of the Mannerheim crosses. Upon researching the Mannerheim Cross, I found that while it is given for bravery for the enlisted man, it is also an acknowledgement for senior

officers running a successful campaign. The Mannerheim Cross was awarded,

> *"... to soldiers for extraordinary bravery, for the achievement of extraordinarily important combat objectives, or for especially well conducted operations."*

This is a strange combination – bravery and good management.

This is unlike the military awards of western countries. These focus only on valour in combat. The British Commonwealth Victoria Cross is

> *" ... for most conspicious bravery, or some daring or pre-eminent act of valour or self sacrifice, or extreme devotion to duty in the presence of the enemy.".*

The United States Medal of Honour is awarded

> *"...for conspicuous gallantry and intrepidity at risk of life and beyond the call of duty during combat".*

Certainly there were other awards for valour for Finnish soldiers, specifically the VM medal 1st and 2nd class. But a soldiers' valour did not warrant the same esteem as that of a successful campaign run by an officer.

Uncle Toivo received two military medals for valour (VM2) and multiple campaign medals and ribbons. No one in the family has ever seen them. Indeed Uncle Toivo's Talvisota medal is still listed as awaiting pick up. To Uncle Toivo war was nothing to be remembered nor celebrated. The acknowledgement of ones' brothers-in-arms sufficed.

Life in the trenches was dangerous and uncomfortable. JR 49s casualties during the trench warfare were 150 killed and 700 wounded out of regimental complement of 3,000 plus. Close to one in every three soldiers was a casualty. (I have not found a number for the JR7 casualties during the asema sota).

Trench warfare was dangerous.The major hazard was the enemy, but disease as well was a concern. One of every twelve soldiers who died during the war, died of disease. At the beginning of November 1943 Uncle Toivo was placed under the care of the 23rd Medical Company. But a week and a half later they had to send him to the 13th Army Hospital in Viipuri. He had typhus, but recovered, joining his regiment 3 weeks later.

Trench Stories

Uncle Toivo recovered to return and continue serving in the trenches. During the period he was with JR7 in 1943 and 1944, he served in the Ohta sector just west of the Riihio sector. Here was the dangerous Pola bunker.

The 9th Companies sotapaivakirja for March 17, 1944 provides a sample of what Uncle Toivo experienced on that day in the front line trenches:

> 02:15 *Noticed 30 men in snow camouflage uniforms with sleds at the Russian barriers on the Russian side of the battle field. Our own canon and howitzer fire drove them back. At the same time the Russians fired 25 canon shells, five 82 mm shells and 20 three inch howitzer shells at Bunker 3. During this time 104 shells of various calibers also landed behind our lines*

> 08:30 *11 howitzer shells (6") fired at Pollo.*

> 09:30-10:00 *27 howitzer (3") shells fired at Bunker 3; 12 howitzer (4. 5") shells and 5 (3") fired at Bunker 2; additional 5 howitzer shells fired at Bunker 3*

> 14:30- 15:30 *6 shells (6") fired at Bunker 2*

> 18:20 *Fierce artillery barrage started with howitzer and canon fire aimed at Bunker 2 plus some at Bunker 3, Bunker 1, and our artillery position. All together 700 heavy and 200 light howitzer shells, plus 600 various caliber canon shells were fired at us by the Russians.*

> *A 50-60 man Russian force attacked Bunker 3 between positions 3-5. One to three Russians got to our actual trenches but retreated quickly. 2nd Lieutenant Gustafson, Corporal Takkinen and soldiers Skaffari and Hartikainen distinguished themselves in the battle.*

> *Ten Russians were killed. Our own casualties were 1 soldier killed - Soldier Koski - and 3 wounded (Soldier Oranen wounded seriously on the jaw, soldier Pesonen on his back and forearm, and Corporal Toivonen on the ear and the back of the head).*

> *Soldiers Hanninen and Pullianinen fled from the battlefield and are being held.*

> 19:30 *Battle at an end. Later heard rustling from the front field as the Russians appeared to be going about their evacuation. Two Russian bodies were left in the no mans' land between the barbed wire barriers and our trenches, and one in front of the bunker.*

Additional attacks took place on the 16th, 21st and 25th. Russian forays continued every couple of days – and artillery barrages every day - for the rest of March.

The sotapaivakirja provides a cut and dry summary of the day. The recount of a veteran from Uncle Toivo's regiment, in the book A Frozen Hell, provides an illustration of what his life was like when it was his turn to be in the Pola bunker (The bunkers were heavily armed and strongly fortified concrete and steel dugouts in front of the trenches in "no mans land"):

> *In the Ohta sector of the 7th Infantry Regiment there was a base called Pola. Its' forward guard post was located opposite the hated and dangerous Ojanen bunker, just a bit over a hundred meters from it. The sturdy bunker's dark embrasure looked frightening. Its machine gun wiped across the Ohta plain causing us casualties almost every day.*

> *Our base's forward position was an old Soviet machine gun bunker. It was turned into a shelter by walling up the old door which was now facing the enemy and by opening a new entrance on the other side. The bunker's entrance was so low that you had to crawl in. The door was just a piece of canvas. The stove chimney was tilted so that it could be pushed through the door opening. There was hardly any draft. You often had to have a cloth in front of your mouth to be able to breathe. There were plenty of lice in the bunker. When you spread your sweater on the snow it looked like every loop of the wool had a louse.*

> *The winter of 1941-42 in Pola was one of the worst winters of my life. We had to melt water from the snow dirtied by grenades. The connecting trenches*

filled with snow when there was a flurry, so there was a lot of shoveling to do. It was difficult to get clean snow. The grenade contaminated snow made one sick.

Getting clean snow became the fateful task of private Herman. He went to get snow to boil water for coffee. Our guard Väinö saw when Herman got wounded. Vaino shouted to us: "Herman got hurt". We ran to him. He was lying on his stomach and groaning: "nothing doing, nothing doing". Foam came out of his mouth when he tried to speak to us. We carried him to the bunker and bandaged him. The bullet had scratched the back of his head and entered through the shoulders. I used the field telephone to call for medics who came soon with their stretchers. "Hey, let's go", Herman said when they took him. The same evening our company commander, Captain Aaro called and said that Herman had died on the operating table of the field hospital.

Our post had firepower. It included a 45 mm anti-tank gun, mortar, light machine gun, submachine guns, piled-up charges, hand grenades and Molotov cocktails. For observation we had a telescope fitted in an armored dome.

North of the base was a bend of the Ohajoki River which the enemy patrols used when they attempted to get into our positions, although the no-man's-land had barbed wire entanglements and mines. Sometimes we were almost surprised by the enemy even though we were alert all the time.

Throughout this period of trench warfare both sides tried periodic reconnaissance skirmishes to capture prisoners or disable bunkers. Uncle Toivo served as a scout on various reconnaissance patrols. The following recount, also from A Frozen Hell, of one large raid provides a flavor of the combat:

Captain Kiiskinen was ordered to organize a recon mission to the enemy side. For the purpose, a Combat Unit of 200 men was formed, consisting of three platoons, a command group, a signals group, a sapper squad, two flame-thrower squads, artillery and mortar fire-control groups, and medics.

Their task was to capture and destroy the enemy base located south of the Suur-Harvasuo swamp, north of Sevastopol and east of the so-called Inkiläinen forest, take prisoners and obtain intelligence material.

On the morning of the raid, the Suur-Harvasuo swamp crackled under the men's feet in the morning frost. Three artillery battalions, mortar company and direct-fire artillery sent salvos to the enemy bunker line.

The combat group spent a total of 50 minutes in enemy positions. They cold-bloodedly cleared the trenches in an area of about 400 by 500 meters. In that area they destroyed 11 dugouts, 12 covered pillboxes and two storage huts. The enemy lost an estimated 35 men. And most importantly: two prisoners were taken.

The Finns also had to pay a price. Some men of the recon patrol fell already in the first dashes to the enemy trench. The worst losses were suffered when the patrol withdrew. At one point the smoke screen vanished, enabling the enemy to fire more accurately.

Some of the losses were a result of troops not following orders. Although told to avoid the Inkiläinen forest during withdrawal, one squad did not follow this advice, taking a shortcut through the forest, only to be caught under fire from enemy mortars. About ten men got wounded then. All of the dead and wounded were brought back.

Uncle Arvo on the Kannas and in Viipuri

After the summer assault Uncle Arvo returned to the 3rd company of Pion P 14. Activity during the trench warfare period primarily involved building fortifications and laying mine fields, and even building houses.

In early 1942 he was in combat situations. On February 2, 1942 his company moved to the Rajajoki front lines to build fortifications and lay mine fields. While the pioneers did not engage in any skirmishes, laying the mine fields was dangerous work. One company pioneer was killed by a Russian marksman. During this period they also set mine fields in the ice off the coast by Rajajoki (and also during the following winter.) His military record records his time at Rajajoki from February 15th to March 22nd of 1942 as a battle.

The rest of the two and a quarter years from March 1942 until the June 1944 was generally uneventful.

- On March 22, 1942, Company 3 returned to Viipuri to do various sundry jobs and to receive additional training.

- On April 19th, 1942 they went back to work on the road from Kivena to Karvala.
- On April 29th they returned to Viipuri to clear further mine fields in the area.
- In June '42 the unit moved to a new base in the Palli schoolhouse. They built various houses through out the summer. One of the programs the army carried out was to build homes for the Karjalainens whose homes had been destroyed during the Talvi sota and the summer assault.

- On August 8th '42 they moved south to Perkjarvi to lay mine fields.

- On December 12th 1942, they returned to Viipuri, remaining for 2 ½ months doing varied construction work.
- At the end of February 1943 they moved to south of Lappeenranta to build houses for the army command. During this period they also returned to set mines in the frozen ice on the Rajajoki coast.

- Throughout the next year they were aligned with the 2nd Division (Uncle Toivo's division) doing various construction, mining and road work through out the Karjalan Kannas south of Viipuri.

- On November 11, 1943 Company 3 returned to Viipuri.

On March 25th, 1944 Uncle Arvo transferred to PionP 14 head quarters units' Jääkäri platoon - a move which placed him in the middle of the conflict when the Russians attacked that June.

Uncle Vilho on the Maaselka Isthmus and Syvari

Uncle Vilho was on the Maaselka Isthmus in the initial months of 1942. During this period the Russians conducted numerous attacks in an endeavor to break the Finnish defensive line before settling down to the relatively uneventful trench warfare (other then for periodic skirmishes as narrated in the Unkown Soldier)

Vilho was awarded the Vapauden Medali first class for bravery on December 29, 1941. While not the ultimate Mannerheim risti, it was awarded far less frequently than the VM second class medal.

As he was with the division supply unit well behind the front lines he would not have been rewarded it for combat. He probably received the medal for saving a local Lotta unit from a fire. As George and Sirkka recount:

> *"The Lottas cabin caught fire, trapping them inside. Vilho rushed to the scene. Unable to get in, he broke the window and pulled them out. During the process he himself got burned. "*

The Lottas were welcome additions on the front.

Uncle Vilho did not remain with the 8th Division supply unit. On March 14, 1942 he went to infantry school. On the 22nd after a weeks training he then joined the the 8th Company of the 45th Regiment of Division 8 in their Maaselka Isthmus trenches between the Maaselka and Krivi

stations. Thankfully he arrived after the major Russian attacks against the lines of January and February 1942.

He only had to remain in those trenches two months. In May of 1942 the 8th Division of Major General C. Winell moved 250 kilometers south to the Syvari front to replace the German 163rd Division. They took over the front lines from the shore of Lake Ladoga east to Seekenjarvi/ Gorka. The German 163rd Division moved back to the German Army on the south east side of Leningrad.

The 8th Division remained on the front lines until June 12,1943, at which point they were placed on reserve. A year later on May 26, 1944, they returned to the front lines but this time taking over the 17th Divisions position at the Syvari bridgehead half way between Lake Ladoga and Lake Onega.

Uncle Kauko on the Maaselka Isthmus

Uncle Kauko's army service changed after 1941. He changed from being front line soldier to a battalion head quarters support worker. He remained on the Maaselka isthmus.

From March 7 ,1942 to October 1st 1942 he was a driver with JR35 2nd battalion's head quarters unit. At that point the 35th regiment was located on the west side of Stalin's Canal by Poventsa.

On October 1st 1942, he went home to south western Finland – unfortunately not on leave. He was in Army Hospital 5 (5. SotaS) for five weeks until the 27th of October. Army Hospital 5 was in Turku close to his home in Oripaa. I do not know what he was in for. I am sure his wife Aunt Margit was able to visit - but certainly not for a while - as he was in isolation. He must have had some contagious disease. The conditions on the front with dead and decaying bodies of both men and horses, combined with extreme weather and unsantiary conditions taxed everyone's health. When he became ill, he was located by Stalin's Canal a historically disease prone area.

One of the few items that Uncle Kauko mentioned to his sons was that during 1941 assault to Petroksoi and Karhumaki:

As we marched and fought, we noticed that wherever we went packs of small rats always showed up. They of course were following to feast on the dead horses ... and men.

When he returned from the hospital, he was moved to the 1st battalion head quarters unit as a clerical assistant. At that point the 35th regiment was serving south of Seesjarvi near the Maaselka railway station – the same area as Uncle Vilho's 8th Division had attacked through in the fall of 1941.

A year later on the 22nd of October 1943 things got disagreeable. At that point there was a change in the command of the 35th regiment. He was moved to serve in prison camp 31 (SVL 31). Prison Camp 31 was in Karhumaki. It was one of Stalins' old prison camps. I am sure it was not a pleasant place.

After three months, on January 29, 1944, he moved to the II AK headquarters unit, located near Karhumaki, serving as a forestry unit leader.

He remained on the Maaselka Isthmus until the June 1944 Russian assault.

Father in Lapland

In the winter and summer of 1942, father continued to ride the rails at night from Kelloselka, protecting the railway from Russian insurgents. During the day he managed the completion of the construction of the railway track from Kelloselka to Kemijarvi.

In early winter 1943 he moved to Kemijarvi to build the Kemijarvi railway bridge.

PART VII

Hopeful Years
On The Home Front

Hopeful Years On The Homefront

The period from January 1942 to June 1944 was a hopeful one on the home front. While concern for their men folk on the front remained paramount, life at home was encouraging.

Sirkka, her mother, her brother Martti and grandfather settled into life back on the Kavantsaari homestead. Soon her other siblings, grandmother, and Aunt Margit returned to the farm as well.

Mother and father and my sisters remained in Lapland. At the start of 1943 they moved from Kelloselka to Kemijarvi as father was building the bridge over the Kemijoki River.

Grandmother Valencia moved back to Viipuri.

CHAPTER 15

The Kavantsaari Home

CHAPTER 15

The Kavantsaari Home

My cousin Sirkka in her memoirs describes life once more in Kavantsaari.

Aunt Alina and cousin Olavi came the first of the new year 1942. Life began to feel homelike.

Mother went to Aunt Hilda's home in Vaajakoski and brought Irja home.

As well dad's body was disinterred and reburied in Karjala beside his grandmother, as he wished.

In spring 1942 mother went and brought George home. At the same time grams came home from Oitti. George says that he had been keen on coming back with the earlier group but had fallen ill with scarlet fever, and had to wait.

Farm work started

Mother set aside a bag of potatoes to germinate– so we got early potatoes right after Mid Summer Eve.

The uncles did the spring planting with seeds that gramps had buried in a container in the ground in 1940 when he left home. Old settlers were wise – particularly gramps.

Mother was given a cow. A pig was also growing and mother went to buy a lamb and hens, and the house started to fill up.

Martti had learned during the evakko trip from Eino Jaakkola how to trap beaver. When he noticed beaver

tracks he started to trap beaver. With the monies he bought us furniture etc. He was the man of the house. He also went to the grist mill and saw mill doing a man's work as a 13 year old.

While work comprised a large part of the week, there was school and fun as well.

Martti and I went to school even though there wasn't a permanent teacher. Thesleff taught history and his wife music, and Kerttu Rahkonen sports.

In the Thesleff yard there were a few soldiers, just like at the police station. They organized ski races for us children. I remember when I went with Maija Iivosen and Veikko to soldier organized evening skis. Everything was fun. We came home across the ice, arriving at Iivosens. Then I had to walk alone through the forest. The wind howled in the trees. It seemed like enemies were behind each tree. I walked with big steps towards home taking my best spurt at the sauna corner. Thankfully the door wasn't locked. Even mother was worried. Oh, youth and imagination.

Martti often went out skiing in the back country. Once he made an unsettling discovery on top of a hill. It was sunny and he rubbed his skiis back and forth to get rid of the clinging snow. And as the snow got moved around he realized he was standing on top of a dead body – a sad remnant from the Talvisota, or indeed, the Jatkosota. A Russian soldier

? A Finnish soldier ? killed during the August 1941 assault down the Kannas ?

From 1942 to 1944, Aunt Saima along with her children, grandfather, grandmother and Uncle Kauko's wife Margit operated the farm. Often grandfather's cousin Matti helped. Aunt Tyyne occasionally also came to help. Cousin George mentioned that:

> *I was very helpful around the farm, particularly herding the cows.*
>
> *The cows were periodically pastured on Vuotsaari Island in the middle of the lake. It was not too far to the island but rather then swim all the way, I usually grabbed onto a cows tail, and got towed back to land. That is, until grandpa found out ...*

The men came home on leave whenever possible to help with the planting, harvesting and plowing. Uncle Arvo (opposite) was the most help. He came home often as he was located in, or near Viipuri. During the "trench warfare period" his units work was less crucial.

While Uncle Toivo as well was on the Kannas, he was not able to get leave as often as he was in the trenches with his rifle at Ohta –protecting Finland. Uncle Kauko, although he now owned the farm, was in the army far away in Karhumaki and could only come back periodically. Uncle Vilho as well was located a considerable distance away by the Syvari River.

The photo at the start of this chapter shows the expanded farm family in 1942/43. Starting from the left, they are: grandma, Aunt Alina, Uncle Toivo (home on leave), Aunt Margit, George, Sirkka, Aunt Tyyne (visiting), Martti, Irja, and Aunt Saima.

All however was not family happiness.

> *In the spring of 1943 Aunt Margit and cousin Raimo came from their home in Oripaa to Kavantsaari.*
>
> *Aunt Alina and Olavi left, moving to the nearby Rinta Hovi near Kavantsaari village.*
>
> *We had to move to the basement.*
>
> *Earlier in the summer of 1941 when father was dying of cancer, my father, his brother Kauko, and Gramps held closed door meetings. In those meetings mother*

> *was not invited. The meetings were about the sale of the farm. They tried to take the shirt off our back - and succeeded. In those meetings the agreement was that the farm would go to Uncle Kauko. (By custom the farm went to the oldest son and Uncle Armas who was the next son in line was living in Canada, and did not want it). We would get 2 hectares of the property and a small cottage. This was despite the fact that for some years we had already been paying for the farm and working the land. The agreement which dad had made with gramps was made without mothers' knowledge. The doors were closed.*
>
> *Knowledge of sale only came in 1943 when we were asked to leave. Erkki was good only as long as he lived. Children were then strangers.*
>
> *We were advised to go live in a dilapidated small shack, which many years before had been used by gramps cousin. But so terrible was the homesite that mother herself said; "Do you take me for a fool?" She went to the local magistrate who told mother:*

> > *"They must build you the cottage that was promised. Don't move anywhere. Your and your childrens home is there until what your man agreed to has been built."*

> *So we stayed, despite gramps and Uncle Kauko's orders. During the entire process Aunt Margit had*

been wonderful. She did not want us to be thrown out of the house.

So life went on together. Mother, Martti, and Sirkka, worked the farm together with Gramps, gramma, and Aunt Margit.

Mother as well got a cow - little Herta. Then I as well learned to milk. As it happened, the rich milk cow Unelma did not let Aunt Margit and Gramma milk her, kicking them away. Uncle Kauko came to exchange cows. I cried for a couple of days and asked mother not to exchange them. Uncle agreed to add a calf on top of the deal. The shining calf was beautiful and the deal was finalized. I believe in that deal I won, or at least someone had to back down.

The farm was a large one for those days, so the family periodically needed additional help.

Russian Prisoners of War were available to help for the payment of a nominal sum to the government. Grandpa got several to come and work on the farm during the summers of 1943 and 1944. At one point when they were constructing a few out buildings, there were four or five. The prisoners came at the beginning of the day and returned to their prison camp at the end of the day. Later there were only two. They stayed all week, returning to their prison camp on the week end.

They were very happy to be working on the farm as they also got extra to eat - Aunt Margit fed them on the veranda. And, I am sure the difference between a fenced in prison yard and country fields was a miracle for them. They even went to sauna. At first they were concerned about this hot new inferno but they got to like it. And obviously they needed it. George Öhman remembers that at first when they began to truly perspire, they smelled strongly of cabbage (Borscht was a staple Russian food).

One of the prisoners, Nikki became a favorite of grandpas. When Nikki first came his hands were cut and bleeding - and infected. Gramps made a concoction of nivea and home made lanoline. He lathered it on the hands and put wool mitts on them. The hands cleared up. (Gramps was the area folk medicine expert).

Nikki was from Crimea near Odessa on the Black Sea. Nikki was apparently a bright and forthright man. Gramps and he had similar attitudes and views on life. Grandpa and he sometimes sat together on the steps smoking cigarettes and conversing in Russian. Nikki himself started to learn Finnish – Enough to do some basic conversing, but not well enough for the Öhman kids not to tease him about it.

The Russian prisoners of war left when the battles started again. When they left, they had tears in their eyes. Everyone said they would visit each other after the war over. We don't know what happened to them after.

The story reflects the common soldiers' perspective on the war. Yes, fight when one must, but otherwise both sides were human beings.

It also reflects the humanity and kindness of grandpa. Gramps while not the most compassionate person, understood their pain having been a prisoner of war himself.

Mom & Dad in Lapland

CHAPTER 16

Mom & Dad in Lapland

Father and mother and my sisters Terttu and Tellervo continued living in Kelloselka through 1942.

My sister Tuula was born when they were living in Kelloselka. Tuula however was actually born in Turku on March 22nd, 1942. Certainly giving birth in Kelloselka would have been risky. Father was still spending nights riding along the rails protecting the railroad from Russian guerillas. Hospital facilities and doctors did not exist in Kelloselka. Mother would have had to go from Kelloselka to Kemijarvi for Tuula's birth. As the hospital / medical facilities in Kemijarvi were poor and as mom would have had to travel anyway, mother went to Turku for Tuula's birth.

I don't know why mother went to Turku as opposed to Oulu. Perhaps it was because dad had connections in Turku and it had the best facilities. But most probably it was because her mother was living nearby. In the March 1942, mother's mother was living at Aunt Margits in Oripaa close to Turku.

Mother said that it was a long tiring ride sitting on the hard railway car seats. I myself, as a youth in my prime, have ridden across Northern Ontario sitting on basic passenger train seats. To do an even longer journey sitting on hardwood seats while in the last weeks of pregnancy ...

But all went well, and mother returned to Lapland with a little bundle of joy - my sister Tuula.

In 1943 dad and the family moved to Kemijarvi so that dad could oversee the building of a major bridge over the Kemijoki River.

Kemijarvi was larger than Kelloselka with stores and schools. A German army encampment was also located here.

During those years, sister Tellervo recounts that she almost got killed (She would have been around 5).

Terttu and I went into the truck yards out of curiosity. Of course we were not supposed to go there. A truck came hurtling by and Terttu jumped to the side grabbing me. My coat got caught under the huge wheels. I received a sound spanking from the German soldier, but otherwise escaped unscathed.

The German troops missed their families. As Tellervo relates:

The German barracks were quite close to our home, so of course Terttu and I went there. Mom always warned us to stay away from the barracks. We didn't pay any heed. I recall very clearly how the soldiers took us on their knees, showed us their children's pictures, hugged us and then finally gave us candy. We didn't care for all the hugging etc., only the candy. We had no candy in our stores.

While it was cold in the winter, there was 24 hours of sunshine during the summer. Terttu and Tellervo enjoyed the bright nights – finding it hard to go to bed.

Terttu remembers being sent by mom to get milk from the store.

Just like dad in his early years in Viipuri, I lined up in the milk queue to get the milk allotment. I was always pleased when I was able to get milk and bring it home.

Terttu, at that time, also started school. Although she was a bit young for school she was able to go (In Finland you had to be 7 years old before you started school). She was keen on going as all her neighborhood friends were going.

Dad was pleased with the bridge he built over the Kemijoki (Photo at the start of this Chapter), proudly taking Terttu and Tellervo for a tour of it. In the summer of 2012 I visited Kemijarvi. I was struck by the bridge over the Kemijoki. It had been rebuilt after it was destroyed by the Germans when they retreated from Lapland. The bridge looked almost exactly the same as the one that dad had built !!

During the time in Kemijarvi, Tuula got gravely ill. The German doctor – Erich - stationed there, was very kind and was able to cure her. Dad and he became good friends.

I have a Christmas post card that Erich the doctor sent to dad after he returned to Germany. The card is dated December 20, 1943 and mentions that a small packet would be following. Terttu especially remembers receiving the packet as it included chocolate among other things. Inside the card Erich enclosed a picture of himself and the words:

Frohliche Wehnacthen und Gluckliches Nuejahr
Wunscht dir lieber Kaarlo,Sowie familie,
Dein Deutsche freund
Erich
Theo und Fritz wunschen dir des gleich
Ein kleines packhen folgt
Merry Christmas and Happy New Year
Wishing you dear Kaarlo, as well as the family,
Your German friend
Eric
Theo and Fritz wish you the same.
A small gift is to follow

Sadly Erich was killed in Berlin during the last months of the war.

Dad was also friends with other German troops. He received a card from four of them from Kelloselka (photo

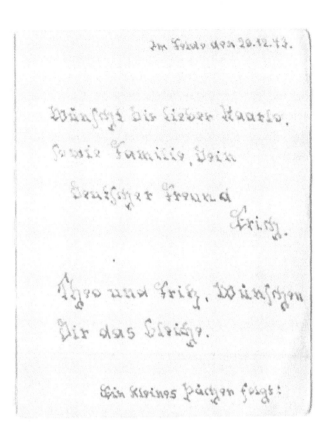

nexy page). The writing in Gothic script on the back of the photo reads:" Zum Andenken an deine guten Freunde"

"From Kelloselka 27.5.43 -
In remembrance from your good friends
Fritz Ewald Erich Gerbert "

The card and story show that the majority of Germans were caring and considerate people just like elsewhere in the world. One cannot condone the terrible persecution of 6,000,000 Jews and 4,000,000 minorities by the Nazis. However the Allied forces bombed and annihilated German

civilians – flattening whole cities with no remorse. The victors – the English, Americans and Russians wrote the post war story. The Nazi regime was a monstrous one beyond a doubt, and the German people were accountable for allowing it to happen. However, the populace and the soldiers were not the monsters Western media has portrayed them as.

Mom and dad got along well with the Germans until the end of the war; mom perhaps not quite as well as dad. Before they left mother broke all the preserves and jams she had made to ensure that the Germans did not get them.

CHAPTER 17

Grandmother Valencia
And
Viipuri during the War

CHAPTER 17

Grandmother Valencia and Viipuri during the War

Grandmother Valencia Tuira went back home to Viipuri.

After the liberation of Viipuri on August 29, 1941, Uncle Arvo and his fellow pioneers started to clear the cities of explosives – unexploded bombs and shells – and mines set by the Russian forces before abandoning the city – both conventional mines and Sakkijarvi Polka radio mines.

Viipuri had been destroyed by the Russians during the Winter War bombings. When they retreated at the end of August 1941 they destroyed it further, blowing up the railway station and burning much of mid town Viipuri. From the March 1940 Winter War Peace until to the end of August 1941 the city had lain in lonely waste. The only inhabitants were the Russian occupying forces, their support groups, government officials and a few civilians. All the 87,000 original inhabitants of Viipuri had fled..

Juha Lankinen's article Elamaa Viipurissa 1941-1944 in the book Kannaksen Suurhyokkays 1944, provides a good summary of Viipuri in the 1941 to 1944 years. Much of the information I include in this chapter draws on that article.

The city was in ruins. Of the 6,200 buildings in the city only 510 had escaped damage. 3,800 of the buildings were beyond repair. Much of the southern and south eastern part of the town had been totally laid to waste. Among the buildings destroyed was grandmother Valencia's house. It was located near the St Petersburg road between the railway station and the Ristimaki cemetery. The railway station was of course a prime bombing target, and the Ristimaki cemetery the time honoured attack route into Viipuri.

Many of the ancient Viipuri building, although damaged, escaped demolition - among them the Viipuri Linna, the Pyroea Torni, the Aaltonen City Library, the Taidemuseo, the water tower, hospitals and many schools and civic buildings.

The Peter Paul Church, the Orthodox Church only suffered slight damage. The Maaseurakunta Church was destroyed but the medieval Raati Torni beside it only lost its' belfry. The ancient monastery/Lutheran Church was devastated but its'Clock Tower survived. The main Lutheran Tuomiokirkko Church however was gone. A bomb destroyed the church nave during the Winter War. While the rest of the church remained standing in the year between the end of the Winter War and the start of the Continuation War the Russians took the entire church down brick by brick. Nothing was left.

The Viipuri Linna and the Pyorea Torni only suffered some holes in their roofs. Prior to leaving the city in 1941 the Russian forces had planted some explosives in Viipuri Linna but thankfully Uncle Arvo's Pioneer battalion found and removed them. The Pyroea Torni while only suffering roof damage was no longer a restaurant and club. It had been turned into a book repository. The Russians had thrown all the Finnish books in the city into the tower. But the Pyroea Torni having served many functions from knights' residence to grainery through its' 500 years probably thought naught of its' new role.

The Finnish forces quickly set about putting protective covers over the most important buildings, succeeding in protecting 60 buildings from the winter snows.

Repairs were quickly started on the three hospitals and other key buildings and on rebuilding the bridges into the city. The first passenger train arrived on September 24, 1941 – less than a month after the city was retaken. Russian street and building signs were quickly replaced by Finnish ones. Work was quickly undertaken to identify habitable buildings and to draw up permits to allow rental of units not in use.

On September 23, 1941 the first commercial enterprise opened – a barber shop, followed in the next days by a fruit market and general stores. By the end of 1941, a 100 businesses were open. The traditional Viipuri businesses such as SOK, Hackman, and Starckjohann reopened. Part of the Market Hall was renovated sufficiently to accomodate 40 shops.

The city came to life. People began to progressively return. In 1941 the army allowed 4,500 inhabitants to return. By the beginning of 1942, Viipuri had 9,700 people. And on February 13, 1942 the first new Viipurilainen (a baby girl) was born in the Women's hospital. By the time they had to retreat in haste once more in June 1944, 35,000 of the cities inhabitants had returned. – over 40% - and even more if the military contingent was included. An amazing number given that war was still raging 100 kilometers away and all able bodied men in the family were serving on the front.

I assume grandmother came sometime in 1942. While she undoubtly came via train, the station stop in Viipuri would have looked different. Before the Russians forces retreated in August 1941 they detonated a huge explosion in the train station leveling the architecturally reknowned Eliel Saarinen designed Viipuri railway station. Saarinen designed a sister station in Helsinki. In 2013 the BBC chose the Helsinki station as one of the world's most beautiful railway stations. Nothing was left of theViipuri railway station except two of the rock bears that had guarded the main entrance.

Grandmother would have been 56 when she returned all by herself. She had neither home nor job to return to. She would have known that her house did not exist any more. Nonetheless it must have been heartbreaking to only see charred remains. I wonder if she searched through them in the hopes of finding a momento of the past. But perhaps she did not look having already lived through the experience during the Finnish Civil War. Grandmother no longer had a source of income – neither a large house to rent out nor general store to run. She got accommodation in one of the larger apartment buildings and got a job doing sewing. And got on with living in Viipuri – her city!

By summer 1942 electricty and water were fully restored, and phone lines repaired (1,800 phones by 1944). The Linna and Papula bridges were rebuilt and the roads restored. Parks, paths, and market squares were cleaned and repaired by 2,000 Russian POWs along with women and boy volunteers.

Spring 1942 brought the reopening the Pyroea Torni market, although initial offerings were limited. By the fall there was fish and berries, along with some vegetables. Of course food was brought into the city from elsewhere in Finland. Everything however was rationed. This resulted in both a triving black market and trips to the countryside to pick and buy food. I wonder if grandmother Valencia went out to the Kavantsaari farm to get milk, fish, vegetables or berries. Restaurants reopened among them the restaurant in the Knut Posse Hotel. The Knut Posse Hotel is still in operation today.

Culture and sports returned in the summer of 1942. The open air sports stadium by Patterimaki was repaired, and soon hosted athletics and soccer. Live theatre reopened in the library club hall, the first performance on February 2, 1942 featuring the war themed "Jaakarin morsain". Later the theatre performances were held in a 350 seat hall in the enhanced Tyovaenopisto – Workers school building. The Viipuri Men's Choir and the Viipuri horn ensemble came back to life.

On January 28, 1942 the Kansan Tyo newspaper published the first paper, with the other Viipuri newspapers following soon after. A radio station opened – domiciled in Pyorea Torni. Along with some local programs one was able to get the YLE Finnish broadcasts as well as European news prepared by the Finnish Armed Forces. One could also pick up the BBC Finnish broadcast signals; and of course Russia's Finnish language "Moskovan Tiltun" propaganda.

Public schools reopened in January 1942 for 465 students. By the fall there were 1,600 students. Four high schools and trade schools reopened. The Viipuri Music School returned from Lahti.

In 1942 transportation was provided by eight taxis and one horse cab. In May 1943 street cars began to run again.

The city was becoming fully operational. Indeed the city fathers already in October 1941 had begun to plan for a long and prosperous future. They enlisted Viipuri's former city planner and architect Otto Meurman to develop a new city plan. The plan, completed in March 1943, was designed to support 200,000 people in 30 years - 1975.

But that was not to be. The Russians started their assault up the Kannas on June 9, 1944. On the 16th of June hundreds of army lorries arrived to take away personal and public effects.

A directive was given that all civilians must leave the city by noon on June 18th. On the afternoon of the 18th the Russians bombed Viipuri. At 16:45 on the 20th the Finnish flag was lowered from Viipuri Linna. At 16:55 the Linna bridge was blown up. At 17:30 the Russian flag went up.

Today Viipuri has a population of 79,900, a bit less than the population originally in 1939.

PART VIII

The Russian Assault Summer 1944

The Russian Assault Summer 1944

In June of the summer of 1941 the Russians began a massive attack to conquer Finland. The key attack came through the Kannas although attacks were launched on the other fronts as well.

On the Kannas they broke through the defensive lines at Valkeasaari on June 10th . The Finnish army retreated to the VT Line and from thence on June 15th north to the VKT Line.

- Viipuri fell on June 20th
- The VKT line held at Noskua from June 20th to June 28th
- The battle of Tali-Ihantala raged from June 25th to July 10th

- The battle of Ayrapaa/Vuosalmi took place from June 21st to July 17th ,and,
- The Viipuri Bay battle from June 30th to July 10th

On the Ladoga Karjala theatre the Finnish forces retreated from the Syvari River and the Maaselka Isthmus to the U Line near the 1940 border.

In Lapland the Russian army did not launch an attack. The German and Finnish forces remained in their asema sota positions just over The Old Finnish Border.

Although the Finnish forces had to retreat to Viipuri – and lost Viipuri, they were able to stop the Russian advance.

The Russian forces were not able to penetrate into current day Finland.

CHAPTER 18

On the Ladoga Front
and the Railroad

CHAPTER 18

On the Ladoga Front and the Railroad

In the Ladoga theatre the Russians started their attack in Ladoga Karjala two weeks after the start of their main attack on the Kannas.

On the Lapland front it was quiet. Russia did not launch an attack there. When the summer assault started father had already left Lapland to manage the railway between Kouvola and Riihimaki.

The Syvari & Maaselka Fronts

Finland had significant resources in the Ladoga theatre; over 130,000 soldiers. Shortly after the attack on the Kannas, Mannerheim determined that more troops were desparately needed on the Kannas. On June 10th when the Russian forces broke through the Finnish lines at Valkeasaari on the Kannas, he transferred half of the forces to the Kannas – the 4th, 6th, 11th and 17th Divisions and the 20th Brigade.

The Finnish Karjalainen Army began an orderly retreat to The Old Finnish Border. Mannerheim ordered them to conduct a methodical fighting retreat, delaying the Russians without incurring too many casualties. Mannerheim also ordered the Finnish forces not to conduct a scorched earth retreat, rather leave Eastern Karjala intact except for vital military targets.

The Russians began their attack on the Maaselka front on June 20th. On the Syvari front the attack commenced on June 21st.

On the Syvari front the VI AK "The Anus Group" under Major General Talvela had around 48,000 troops (The 5th, 8th, and 7th Divisions and the 15th Brigade). The Russian 7th Army of Krutokov had around 150,000 men, 340 tanks, 1600 artillery guns and 600 planes.

On the Syvari front the Finnish forces started to retreat to the PSS Line (Pisi-Saarmaki-Sammatus about 30 kilometres north of the Syvari River) on June 19th.

The Russians attacked across the Syvari River on June 21st. During the night of June 23rd the Russian naval forces landed behind the Finnish forces and severed the lakeside railway and road route north. The Finnish forces were however able to retreat north on secondary supply roads. By June 27th the Finnish forces had retreated to the Vitele - Jessoila line. The line stretched 60 kilometres from Vitele by Lake Ladoga just south of The Old Finnish Border, to Jessoila in the interior by Lake Saamajarvi on the Suojarvi - Petroksoi railroad and road.

Concurrent with the withdrawal from Syvari, on June 28th the Finnish forces withdrew from Petroksoi.

On July 7th the Finns retreated to the U Line – a reasonably fortified line stretching from Pitkaranta at the north end of Lake Ladoga to Loimala half way between The Old Finnish Border and the 1940 peace border. The Russians launched numerous major attacks but the Finnish defenses held. By the beginning of August the U Line settled into the trenches.

On the Maaselka front the Russians launched an offensive as well.

The II AK Finnish force commanded by Major General Einar Makinen consisted of about 20,000 men – Uncle Kauko's 1st Division, and the 21st Brigade (and later the Aanisjarvi Coastal Brigade). The Russian 32nd Army of Gorelenko committed 45,000 troops. One division of these was deployed north to face Rappanen's 14th Division.

With half their forces sent to the Kannas, the Finnish II AK lost Maaselka station on June 20th to a Russian attack.

The II AK retreated to Karhumaki. On the 23rd the Russian forces broke through here as well. The Russians forces did not press their attack and the Finnish forces were able to retreat along the southern side of Seesjarvi. They withdrew further west and south to the Jankajarvi –Lintujarvi Line reaching it on July 5th . At this point part of the force was moved further south from Lintujarvi to the Jessoila area to help the Aanus Group of Major General Talvela. By July 9th the IIAK forces had withdrawn back to the northern end of the U Line at Ilomansti (The Finnish side the 1940 border)

A major battle waged from July 9th to the 15th in Loimala-Suojarvi- Porajarvi. Fighting continued until August 9th without the Russian forces making a major break through.

Thereafter the entire theatre settled into trench warfare.

Both the Russian and Finnish sides suffered heavy casualties during the Lake Ladoga attack.

Both Uncle Kauko and Uncle Vilho were in the theatre. Uncle Vilho unfortunately became one of the Finnish casualties.

Uncle Vilho on the Syvari

In June 1944, Russia started its' attack on the Finnish lines.

The initial battle was the Syvarin Sillanpaa asema battle (Syvarin bridgehead station). This battle is listed in Vilho's records.

The Finnish army successfully retreated across the Syvari River abandoning their defensive trench lines south of the Syvari River without the Russians noticing. Thus when the Russians began their artillery bombardment and attack only a small contingent of Finns was there. Over the next four weeks the majority of the Finnish force retreated successfully to the U Line at the north end of Lake Ladoga.

Uncle Vilho's war however ended at the start of the Syvarin Sillanpaa asema battle. He was seriously wounded on June 12, 1944 before the major Russian attack.

He was in the army hospital for 4 months from June 6, 1944 to October 1944. According to Uncle Arvo, the mine

he was placing in no mans land went off prematurely in his hand. Cousin George Öhman recounted that:

> *"After the mine exploded, Vilho, bloody and stunned, dragged himself back to the Finnish lines with his one good arm. The Finnish soldiers almost shot him as he crawled back, but he kept shouting in Finnish – "Not Russian ! Don't shoot !!".*
>
> *He was put in a horse wagon to be taken to the hospital tent but the bouncing hurt so much that he got out and ran alongside to the aid tent. "*

From there he was transferred to the army hospital – first on June 6, 1944 to Army Hospital 66, and then on July 4, 1944 to Army Hospital 30. The only noticeable part of the injury was that Vilho lost two of his fingers. However, obviously if he was in the hospital for 4 months, the injury was more extensive then the loss of his fingers. Indeed, his daughter Pirjo said that, *"In the early days the doctors were worried that he would lose his whole arm."*

On a positive note, according to cousin Sirkka, Vilho met his wife Kirsti in the Jyvaskyla army hospital. Vilho and Kirsti remained married for over 50 years.

On a general note, medical units were a key part of the Finnish forces, given that a third of the soldiers were either killed or wounded (And many more in the actual fighting force).

Each company had a medical unit which did initial triaging and critical surgery. The main bandaging station, with 10 medics and 2 ambulances was located at the battalion HQ. The regiment HQ had no facilities - only the head doctor and a dentist. The division head quarters had a field hospital and an ambulance platoon. Further army hospitals were located within Finland, away from the front.

The medical staff was required to take care of wounded Russian prisoners as well as their own soldiers, as one of the medical veterans recounts in the Koskimaa's Tyrjän Rymentii book:

"During one of the major battles during the 1941 attack, many Finnish soldiers were wounded. The farm yard was full of stretchers with wounded soldiers. The Finnish soldiers tried to suffer in silence but from the side of the yard there was unending dreadful screaming. When the Finnish soldiers found out that it was coming from wounded Russians, they said, "Shoot them". To this the doctor replied; "One must treat all wounded the same way, but, if their screaming is bothering you so much, we can go treat the Russian soldiers first if you wish." The Finnish wounded muttered back, "Let them scream then".

Uncle Kauko and Retreat from Maaselka

At the end of 1943 Uncle Kauko had been transferred from the the 35th Regiment to the 31st Prison Camp administration for several months and then to the IIAK Headquarters as a forestry unit leader.

On the 16th of June he was a unit foreman with Firewood Factory 5 of the II AK. The II AK headquarters was located at Semsjarvi about 30 kilometres south of Seesjarvi and 50 kilometres west of Karhumaki.

The battles commenced on June 20th at Maaselka station with a Russian attack. From June 20th to July 9th Uncle Kauko retreated with the IIAK to Ilomantsi on the U Line. The retreat was generally orderly with only periodic fighting. I wonder what Firewood Factory 5 was doing during this period. I would think splitting wood was low on the task list. I am sure Uncle Kauko thought of the fall 1941 assault as they traversed through some of the same terrain they had fought through three years earlier.

After the battles had ceased in mid August and settled into trench warfare I assume forestry work began again.

Father and the Lapland Front

The Russians did not launch an attack on the Lapland Front.

However as a condition of the peace of September 1944, Russia required the Finns to drive the Germans out of Northern Finland. This Finland reluctantly did. The German troops burnt all of Lapland including Rovaniemi as they retreated. This included the big Kemijarvi bridge that dad had just built.

Mother and dad had left Kemijarvi after the bridge was built, before the Lapland war started. In late 1943 dad and the family returned to Kausala (near Iitti) in Southern Finland. He was responsible for the railway track between Riihimaki and Kouvola. This track section was the primary rail route from Viipuri to Helsinki and Turku.

I do not recall any specific stories from dad or others regarding this period. Father said in his memoirs which ended in 1935 that "There are many stories from the war years but that is for another time." Unfortunately that other time never came.

One story which dad recounted may have occurred at Kausala.

An unexploded bomb got stuck between two railway cars. The people in the area urged him to defuse it. Dad had both defused bombs successfully before, and had seen his compatriots blown to bits. He declined as it was extremely dangerous to defuse and was not an immediate danger to anyone.

The train engineer told the gathered civilians; "Let him be. We have called for the demolition experts. He has risked his life often enough already. Life is worth more than property."

Retreat on the Kannas
Uncle Arvo

CHAPTER 19

Retreat on the Kannas
Uncle Arvo

In June of the summer of 1941 the Russians began a massive attack to conquer Finland. The key attack came through the Kannas although attacks were launched on the other fronts as well.

The assault was launched on June 9th three days after the Allied landing in Normandy under the overall direction of General Leonard Govorov, the commander of the Leningrad Front.

The Russians had a massive numerical advantage over the Finnish forces. The Russian 23rd Army of Lieutenant General Alexander Tsherepanov had 260,000 men, 630 tanks, and over a 1,000 bombers and fighter planes.

The Finns by contrast had 44,000 men plus 32,000 immediate reserves. As importantly as having 4:1 superiority in manpower; the Russians had 5:1 superiority in tanks; 20:1 in artillery; and 15: 1 in air power.

As well as having greater numbers and improved weaponry, the Russians had revised their strategy and tactics.

The Finnish defense was led by the commander of the Army of the Isthmus Lieutenant General Karl Oesch. The eastern sector of the Kannas by Lake Ladoga was protected by the IIIAK of General Siilasvuo. The section north of the Gulf of Finland was under the VAK of Svensson. The key central section was held by the IVAK of the old campaigner Lieutenant General T Laatikainen. It was against this key 65 kilometer wide section of the Kannas, stretching from the Gulf of Finland to the Vuoksi River, that the main Russian attack was launched.

The Finnish army had three defensive lines (Map on next page):

- The Asemasota front lines just over The Old Finnish Border where the Finnish forces had stopped. In other words the trench warfare line consisting of sectors: Coastal; Rajajoki; Valkeasaari; Vaskisavotta; Ohta; and Riihio.
- The VT Line - Vammelsuu,Taipale, just 20 kilometers back; and
- The VKT Line – Viipuri, Kupparsaari, Taipale, about 60 kilometers back from the VKT line

The Russian objective was to take Viipuri and then move north to Lappeenranta and Imatra by June 28th and thence move east across unprotected Finland to Helsinki. Russia allocated its' total attention to the conquest of Finland stopping all activity on other fronts for two weeks. The intent was to roll over Finland and then move to attack Berlin.

Russian Attack on the Asemasota Front Line

On June 9th three days after Normandy, the Russians' launched a gargantuan plane and artillery bombardment across the entire Finnish front – against the front line fortifications, and the supply depots and head quarters in the rear. There was about 100 artillery pieces per mile. On the Valkeasaari sector there were 400. The bombardment

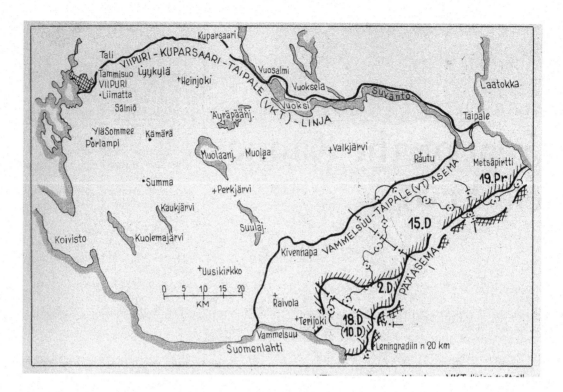

was made across the entire front in order to disguise the planned primary attack point. The sound of the barrage could be heard in Helsinki.

Minefields and bunkers were blown up, trenches caved in, and communications lines to regimental and divisional posts cut off.

For some reason the attack caught the Finnish high command by surprise. The men at the front knew all too well what was coming. But as is often the norm, the high command is distant from reality and does not give credence to front line forces.

The primary attack was through Valkeasaari. It was an area all too familiar to my uncles. Uncle Toivo's Kevyt Os 7 and Uncle Arvo's Osasto Kanerva had captured it in August 1941. The Valkeasaari sector was where Uncle Aatu had manned the trenches in the months before he was disbanded. His old 10th Division comrades still defended it.

The Russian forces fired all night and through the next morning. On June 10th the Russians fired 354,000 shells into the Rajajoki – Valkeasaari sectors. The Finnish 10th Division only fired 3,700 shells – 1% of Russia's total.

The soldiers were left to stop the Russian tanks and troops from shattered defensive fortifications. The Finnish troops did not have any portable anti-tank weapons. They only received Panzerfaust and Panzerschreck anti-tank guns the day of the attack. These they used to the best of their ability to shoot at the advancing tank behemoths. Having received no training they figured out how to shoot the guns as they unpacked them.

Soon the Russians broke through Valkeasaari. Without reinforcements or artillery support, the battered 10th Division soldiers fled for their lives. While the other sectors held, they too retreated - mostly after Mannerheim ordered a withdrawal to the VT line at 14:30 on June 11th.

During June 10th the attack was so fierce and the confusion so great that Lieutenant General Laatikainen in his IVAK headquarters 30 kilometers behind the front lines, had to send Finnish reconnaissance planes out to determine where his divisions and regiments were.

On the 11th the 3,100 strong Finnish 1st Jaakari Brigade of Colonel Puroma was ordered to counterattack and recapture Uusi Alakyla north of Valkeasaari. While they did slow the Russian attack they had to retreat quickly. As they did they were unable to blow up the bridge on the main road north.

The 1st Jaakari Brigade would be key counter attack units in the Tali-Inhantala and the Vuosalmi battles as well as during the initial Valkeasaari breakthrough. The 1st Brigade suffered 800 casualties in the counter attack and the subsequent rear guard action retreating back to the VT line. Prior to the Russian '44 summer attack, during the Finnish fall 1941 assault into Russian Karjala, they had played key roles in the overall assault and the capture of Syvari, Petroksoi, Karhumaki and Poventsa. Elite soldiers - I wonder what their outlook on life was as they were continuously placed in life threatening situations.

Retreat to the VT line

The VT Line stretched from Vammelsuu through Kuuterselka, to Kivennapa, Siiranmaki and thence east to Taipale. Generally it was only 20 kilometers behind the Asemasota front lines. This was too narrow a gap. The Russians did not have to move their heavy artillery guns, and the infantry and tanks could cover the distance in a couple of hours – thus leaving the Finnish forces insufficient time to regroup and get their reserves in place.

While the Russians only suffered 10% losses, this given the size of their force, was 10,000 a day.

While a noticeable portion of the 10th Division Finnish forces fled, major defensive battles took place at Kuuterselka and Siiranmaki.

In the June 11th to 15th battle at Kuuterselka the Russian forces broke through the VT line. Counter attacks by 1st Jaeger Brigade were almost successful but they were ultimately unable to recapture the line.

At Siiranmaki the Finnish forces stopped the Russian assault in a four day battle from June 13th to June 16th. Uncle Toivo and JR7 were there.

Retreat to the VKT Line

On June 15th Mannerheim ordered a retreat to the VKT line – but also ordered the Finnish forces to fight a delaying action and inflict as many casualties as possible on the Russian forces.

General Siilasvou's IIIAK withdrew to the VKT line portion stretching from Taipale at Lake Ladoga to Ayrapaa / Vuosalmi on the eastern bank of the Vuoksi River. General Siilasvou's forces consisted of the 19th Brigade and the 15th Division.

The western side of the Vuoksi River was defended by the IV AK. The 10th Division, the 3rd Division, the 18th Division, the 2nd Division, the Cavalry Brigades, the RTR2 shore brigade, and the Panzer Division retreated up the Isthmus. Reinforcements for the 1V AK began to arrive from the Maaselka and Syvari fronts.

- The 4th Division of Major General Autti arrived on the 14th of June from the Maaselka Isthmus and took up positions beside the 10th Division.
- On June 19th the 20th Infantry Brigade of Colonel Kemppi arrived from the Syvari River to hold Viipuri.
- On June 20th the 17th Division of Major General Sundman arrived from the Syvari River and set up west of the Saima Canal.
- On June 27th the 11th Division of Major General Heiskanan arrived from the Syvari.
- And on June 28th Major General E Vihma's 6th Division arrived from the Maaselka Isthmus. Both the 11th and 6th Divisions set up in Tali-Ihantala.

The 10th Division had been so shattered by the brunt of the Russian attack on Valkeasaari that it ceased being an active division after June 20th.

The situation was dire. Mannerheim's order on the 19th June was clear:

> *"By the morning of June 20th at the latest take your defensive positions on the VKT Line and defend them to your death."*

The IV AK positioned itself on the VDT Line with:

- Major General Pajari's 3rd Division at Kuparsaari;
- Major General Autti's 4th Division on the eastern side of Tali-Ihantala;
- In Tali-Ihantala: Major General Paalu's 18th Division, Major General Lagus' Panzer Division, Major General Heiskanen's 11th Division, and Major General Vihma's 6th Division
- Colonel Kemppi's 20th Brigade at Viipuri;
- Colonel Haantera's 3rd Brigade initially north east of Viipuri and later beside the Saima Canal; and ,
- Major General Sundmans' 17th Division on the west side of the Saima Canal.

Uncle Arvo
From Perkjarve to Ihantala

Uncle Arvo and his Pioneer Battalion 14, were in the depths of the Finnish defense of the western side of the Kannas.

After the Russian attack started on June 9th '44, Arvo's unit moved back up the Isthmus northwards from St. Petersburg setting mine fields and tank barriers as the Finnish army retreated.

On June 10th he was at Uusikirkko with the 10th Division; on the 14th at Suulajarvi with the Jaakari Brigade; and on the 15th at Kyyrola with the 4th Division.

On June 16th they were involved in a battle at Perkjarvi with the Panzer Division. The book "PionP 14", includes an article by Lieutenant Kaarlo Mietteinen recounting his memories of leading the Pion P14 Jääkäri platoon at Perkjarve and Ihantala. It includes several references to Uncle Arvo. My translation of the article follows:

On June 16th the IV Corps Pioneer commander Lieutenant Colonel Oinonen requested PionP 14 to build tank defenses and mines at Perkjarve. Captain Vartiainen the commander of PionP 14 dispatched Lieutenant Nyberg's Company 1 to build the defenses. My Jääkärijoukku went to Perkjarve as well as commander Vartiainen. Vartianinen had a lorry with additional munitions and equipment. At Perkjarve Captain Vartiainen handed me a map and told me to take my unit up Lountajoki Road and hold any attacking Russian forces until reinforcements arrived from Eastern Karjala. We left Captain Vartiainen, the lorry and the additional ammunition at the Perkjarve station

....

The enemy attacked Company 1 as they were setting up the tank defenses. They started to withdraw under a fierce Russians attack. We didn't have time to dig any fox holes, so each of my men picked the best looking tree they could find to shelter behind.

In a short time Nyberg and his company appeared pursued by three tanks and a large number of Russian infantrymen. The tanks blockaded the road intersection, the tanks and infantrymen firing at the scattering Pioneers. We tried to throw them back but with no success. The firepower of the Russian tanks and soldiers was so overwhelming that our job of pushing them back was left at merely having tried.

The Russian tanks and infantry fired with such fury at us that the mortar shells were exploding the trees around us. Arvo Äyräntö, our courier/messenger, was on the ground under one of the exploding trees when its' top fell off. The tree top fell on top of him, but luckily he was not hurt. It almost went poorly for me. I did not shelter myself well from the enemy. I was behind a tree but standing quite high. Around me, the bullets were making holes in the trees and chips were flying everywhere. The courier (Arvo) saw this and shouted for me to get down. That time I was saved by my courier.

...

In the end we got north of Perkjarve going along the bush beside the rail road which at that moment the Russians were not blanketing with artillery fire (It was close to 19:30). From here I asked our courier Arvo Äyräntö to find Captain Vartiainen in the Perkjarve station area and ask for new orders. I assigned a pioneer whose name I forget, to go with Äyräntö. His job was to bring munitions back to the company and to give moral support to the courier. During the lull in artillery barrage, I talked it over with the boys, about why our own army artillery had stopped firing. Our anti aircraft defense observation post where our fire directors were had been shot down. We also talked about our own groups' encounter. We felt we took care of it quite well given the circumstances. It could have been a lot worse.

After a while our courier and his munitions carrier returned. They said they could not find Captain Vartiainen, nor his truck. They recounted that there too there was concentrated artillery fire affecting the road south easterly from Perkjarve [the road swung around after several kilometers northward to Viipuri], leaving the traffic tangled in a confused grid lock of vehicles and equipment making that part of the road almost impassable.

Having heard this news, I had a short discussion with my boys and decided at this point to take our Jääkärijoukku through the woods along the other side of the track. From the map I could see a cart track that skirted the north side of Perkjarve and took us to the western shore of Lake Muolaa. From there we could go ahead along the west shore of Lake Muolaa and take the road at the north end at the village of Hotakka. The road would take us directly to Viipuri.

We started out in the planned direction. The bicycle transport was to wait somewhere at the north end of Perkjarve [Perkjarve was a lake as well as a village] for the on foot infantrymen. The distance was 3 kilometers. Even this track had been travelled a lot by the army. Field kitchens and other military equipment were abandoned on the sides of the trail. The Russian artillery bombarded the route but with little success. The marshy ground cushioned the shells impact making it almost harmless unless there was a direct hit. At the end of the trail there was some type of cabin. When all the men caught up, we had a short rest.

After the end of the trail, the land turned swampy so bicycles would have been of little help. When we wandered into Hotakka, by fate I met my own logistics man who was there waiting for us. From him we learned that in the house beside the road there were enough bikes for the whole unit, and that we were to bicycle through the night to Viipuri, about 30 kilometers distance. The night time passed away quickly, although fatigue weighed on everyone's legs.

On the morning of June 17, 1944, I went to meet with the commander of PionP 14, Captain Vartiainen. I wanted to clear up the Perkjarve defensive action but Vartiainen was still sleeping and woke up when I came in and was in a bad mood. When I reported our actions, he muttered that now was not the time to clarify matters. Rather he ordered me to leave on bicycle and travel to the Juustila canal. There I was to organize a means for the battalion to pass over the canal. This was equivalent to the worst possible work.

When we departed on our bicycles, we had not gone a kilometer when we had to protect ourselves from an aircraft bombing run. We survived without injury by diving for cover. Otherwise the work went well.

We arrived back at Markulinna [Markunlinna is just on the northern outskirts of Viipuri. It was the historical location of an army training school and firing range]. I went to report on the outcome of our work. Then it was illuminated that the battalion had a new commander – Captain P Halonen. The company had to first move to Lavola and, then worst of all, to the Palli school by the Juustila canal. Here at the Mustala lock, the battalion built a heavy barge for transporting tanks.

The company constructed needed defensive works without let up – work on the locks and on the tank obstructions in Portihoika and Ihantala. Lieutenant Veiho Touminen who led the building of the tank defenses was killed by an enemy bullet on June 29, 1944 at Portihoika.

After Lieutenant Tuominen fell, the tank defense squad became part of the Jääkarijouku and I had to become familiar with the Portihoika and Ihantala front line defenses [Uncle Arvo who was part of his Jääkari unit was already familiar with area as it was part of his Kavantsaari home area].

The Fall of Viipuri

CHAPTER 20

The Fall of Viipuri

On June 20, 1944 the Russian forces captured Viipuri in one day. The fall of Viipuri is considered one of the few black marks in Finland's military history.

Viipuri was defended by the 5,133 strong 20 Pr led by Colonel Kemppi. Colonel Kemppi was a renowned battlefield officer. He had earned his reputation at Tapiale during the Winter War, and during the summer of 1941 leading his regiment, JR7, through furious fighting down the Kannas. His brigade however was relatively inexperienced and had seen little fighting.

Viipuri fell in 10 hours. Only 19 Finnish troops died. 101 were wounded and 419 deserted - quite a change from the sacrifices of the rest of the Finnish forces.

I remember my cousin Sirkka recounting that:

> Two Finnish soldiers from Helsinki stayed overnight on our farm in June 1944 a couple of days before the start of the battles. They were related to our family in some way. They were on leave and were enjoying the Karjala countryside. I again met one of them in Lauritsala when we were fleeing Karjala. He was by himself. He said his comrade had been killed on the bridge in Viipuri.

Sirkka recounted this story before I became familiar with the defense of Viipuri. It struck me as odd at that point that the soldier was not with his unit. Now it seems that he was one of the deserters...

The reasons for the fall of the city have been a subject of analysis and debate for years.

I was only intending to allocate a half page to the fall of Viipuri. But as I briefly researched it, the familiar place names of my beloved father's home town, and my own enchanting visits started to call to me. So I read every book available on the subject. The Jatkosota Pikku Jattalainen provided analysis and four magazines provided good articles: the Ilta Sanomat - Viipurin Katkerat Viimeiset Tunnit (22.5.2014 edition) and Viipuri - (03.05.2012 edition); Kansa Taisteli # 5, 1979 and # 11, 1982. The book Veitsen Teralla provided some more detail. Not to be put off I resorted to the Jatkosodan Historia, the official six volume history of the Jatkosota written by the Finnish armed forces. All the sources differed somewhat. So I accessed the Sotapaivakirjat for each of Pr 20s units. This provided a bit more clarification but Sotapaivakirjat by definition are brief.

Finally I was able to obtain two books dedicated to the fall of Viipuri – one by Captain Uuno Tarkki (Taistelu Viipurista 20.6.1944); and one (Viipurin Viimeinen Paiva) by Captain Jantti. Jantti's book written in 1964 provided a good recounting and analysis. The book by Captain Tarkki, who actually fought at Viipuri with the 1st battalion of 20.Pr, finally provided a first person picture of the day and a clear analysis of the causes of the loss of Viipuri. He published the book in 1996 after he had retired from the army and was no longer constrained by army confidentiality requirements.

Colonel Kemppi and Major Backman (The commander of the 2nd battalion where the Russian breakthrough occurred) were court marshalled and made the scapegoats of the loss. While they did share some of the blame, the cause of the catastrophe (As Mannerheim called it) was multifaceted. Indeed with the benefit of historical hindsight it seems that the main cause of the loss can be laid at the feet of the commander of the Army of the Kannas General Karl Oesch and the commander of the IVAK Lieutenant General Tavetti Laatikainen. Neither of them saw defense of Viipuri as a priority. Their half hearted efforts - quite different from Russia's fanatic and successful protection of Leningrad, Moscow, and Stalingrad - were in response to Marshall Mannerheim's adamant directive that Viipuri must not be lost.

I am providing a summary of that sad event in the rest of this chapter. I know my information may have anomalies in it, given that it is sourced from multiple sources. But even the transcripts different parties gave in the court marshall concerning that chaotic day contained errors as Captain Tarkki points out. In any such cases I defer to Captain Tarkki's book.

The Defense of Viipuri

Since the break through of the main old border line on June 11th, the Finnish forces had been retreating continuously up the Kannas towards the VKT (Viipuri – Kuparsaari – Taipale) defensive line. The Russian forces broke through the Finnish defenses at Sainio, 15 kilometers south of Viipuri on the night of June 19 – 20. The IVAK units – PsD, and JR25 bypassed Viipuri retreating around the east side of Viipuri. JR58 retreated back along the Kovisto Road and then directly through Viipuri (Some of the PsD forces also retreated through Viipuri).

This left the defense of Viipuri to the 20th Brigade of Colonel Armas Kemppi. The 20th Pr had been located on the Syvari front through 1943 – 1944, north of Lotinpelto near the western end of the Syvari River. The period was quiet. While they protected the line the soldiers had never had to fight a battle. Indeed they were engaged in fortification work and saw little front line trench duty. While untested, they were led by a highly regarded, seasoned and brave commander - Colonel Kemppi. His officers however were not well suited for battle. Indeed Kemppi had been planning

to make replacements in anticipation of battle. However events overtook him before he could do so.

The movement of the 20th Pr to Viipuri was an indication of the chaos and uncertainty that the Russian assault had created in the Finnish High Command.

- On June 10th Mannerheim ordered the brigade to the Maaselka Isthmus north of Karhumaki to replace units moving to the Kannas. Indeed the 2nd battalion actually arrived in Karhumaki.
- On June 12th the order changed. The brigade was to stop the move to the Maaselka Isthmus and move with the greatest of haste to the Rautu area on the eastern Kannas.
- On the 15th the destination was changed to Viipuri. Due to congestion and bombing of the railway lines it took them several days to reach the Kannas.
- The brigade units progressively reached Viipuri through the 18th and 19th.

The 4th battalion reached Kavantsaari on the morning of the 17th.

Our family was still on the farm when the battalion arrived. I am sure cousin Martti observed the activities as he was working in the Kavantsaari saw mill.

They then marched 20 kilometers to Viipuri arriving in Viipuri on the morning of the 18th. While the battalion arrived in the city in good form, not all the men arrived. Some men deserted to pine cone collection units en route. (*Two of them might have been the Helsinki boys who overnighted at our Kavantsaari home before continuing on to Viipuri*). The town was quiet although it had been bombed a couple days before. While the military police had poured 18,000 bottles of booze into the sea, drunks and vandals still caroused in many places. One young country boy soldier recounted that although the city was bombed out and in disarray with drunks and thieves, it was nonetheless charming.

The other infantry battalions arrived on the 19th at either the Tammisuo or Tali station.

The 20th brigade had 5,133 men. They had a heavy artillery battery, a light artillery battery, a mortar company, an anti tank gun company, a pioneer company and a

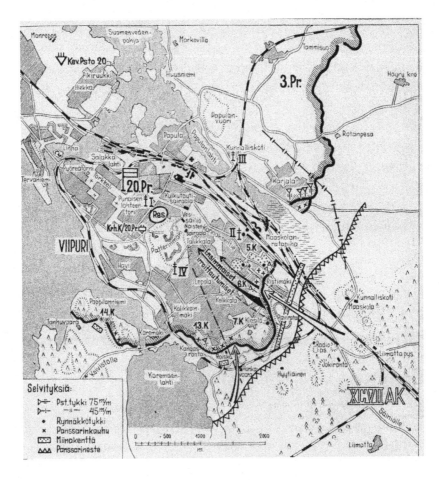

communications company. As well they were supported by a small tank company which had five assault gun tanks.

The attacking Russian force consisted of seven tank reinforced infantry divisions (Around 60,000 men), plus extensive artillery and air support. The Russian CVIII AK consisting of 4 divisions attacked from the south west along the Kovisto road. The 3 division Russian XCVII AK attacked from Sainio 10 kilometers south of Viipuri along the main road to Leningrad. The CXAK with 2 divisions was on reserve. Not all the Russian forces took part in the attack on Viipuri – some moved to the east of Viipuri to attack through Tali-Ihantala. But Stalin made clear that taking Viipuri was a key objective. He knew that capturing Viipuri would be a major propaganda victory; and, that it would not only be a tactical blow against the Finnish army, but also, most importantly, a psychological shock to the Finnish nation.

The Finnish front line ran for 6 kilometers from the Maaskola railyards just north of Ristimaki, south to Karemaenlahti Bay. As well a defensive line existed across the inlet in Pappilanniemi. The south end protected the important road south to Kovisto. The north end protected the main Kannastie road and the rail connection to Leningrad.

The front lines were 1 to 2 kilometers beyond Patterimaki – the old hilltop fortified by Czar Alexander II in the 1860s. Patterimaki of course is in the middle of town. Why the defenses were not drawn at Patterimaki from Laaninvankila toVesisailio, to Patterimaki, and to Havin is a quandry. At least Patterimaki should have been set up as the back defensive line as it had been during the Winter War. The terrain was highly suitable for fortification and effectively enveloped the main part of Viipuri.

The defensive line that was set up was not comparable to the VKT, VT and Old Border defensive lines – particularly in the Ristimaki area. The trenches were only a meter deep. They were not connected to one another. There were no barbed wire barricades. There were no bunkers, pill boxes, shrapnel shelters nor reinforced firing stations. Panzer tank stone barriers were in place about 300 to 600 meters from the front lines. Between the tank barriers and front lines there were mine fields. The Finnish Kannas Army had been deficit in not setting up better defenses for the Viipuri portion of the VKT line earlier. It was quite evident that Russia would make capturing Viipuri a priority.

Communications connections to the battalions via phone were unreliable. Only the artillery had radio connections. Connections to IV AK were only by radio. There was a phone connection to IVAK via military GHQ in Mikkeli but this connection was strictly for use in crisis.

The map on the next page shows Kemppi's positioning of his units:

- The 3rd Battalion, commanded by Lieutenant Colonel T Sorri, in Karjala town in Papula behind the railway station. The battalion headquarters was in the Old Folks Home in Maaskola. As well the 1st company of the 5th Fortification battalion - 1. /Lin. P5 - was located with them.

- The 3rd battalion had arrived the morning of the 19th at the Tali station, 5 kilometers from Viipuri. By mid day they were in their positions.

- Lieutenant Colonel Sorri at age 40 was a seasoned battlefield commander. The battalion had been well trained and prepared for battle by its' prior commander, Mannerheim Cross holder, Colonel Viiri.

- The 2nd Battalion, commanded by Major Kurt Backman, was on the key 2 ½ kilometer stretch from the Maaskola rail yards through Ristimaki, and Kiesala to Roisko. This portion of the line was a historical attack route, and one which suited tanks. The line, from north to south, was defended by the 5th company (Captain Laakso), the 6th company (Captain Aspola), and the 7th company (Captain Pohjola).

- The battalion did not have any weapons with which to stop the heavy Russian Klim and T-34 tanks
  - Lieutenant Sippelli's Er Ps K assault gun tank company was located with them, but the company only had five assault gun tanks. These were the weakest tanks in the Panzer Division

– altered Christie BT42s - no match for the Russian Klim and T-34 .

- The battalion had three 45 mm anti-tank guns. These were too light to destroy the heavy Russian tanks.

- A 75 mm anti-tank artillery gun that was to be positioned with the battalion never arrived. This was unfortunate as this canon was capable of stopping even the heavy Russian tanks.

- The battalion also received 4 Panzerschrecks and a large number of Panzerfaust anti-tank guns. The Panzerfaust "Panssarinyrki" was a soldier portable single shot recoilless anti tank gun. It only had a distance of 30 meters but was very explosive once it penetrated the armor. It required a bit of training in order for it to be shot effectively.

- The Panzerschreck "Panssarikauhu" was a soldier portable anti tank rocket launcher (bazooka). It had a distance of 150 meters and could penetrate heavier armor. While effective, the 20 Pr soldiers unfortunately did not have a chance to be properly trained in their use...and they never used them.

The 2nd Battalion had arrived at Tammisuo on the morning of the 19th and marched the 3 kilometers to their positions in Viipuri.
Major Backmann, who was 40, did not have any battlefield experience and had only been at the front for one year. While well meaning, he had a speech impediment, a fondness for alcohol, and a nervous disposition.

- The 4th Battalion, commanded by Major Viljo Kirma set up on the south side of Patterimaki by Viipuri Gulf near the road leading south west towards Kovisto on the Gulf. Its' 14th company was located across the inlet in Papilanniemi.

- They had one 45mm anti tank gun plus 6 Panzerfausts and 20 Panzerschrecks.

- They arrived in Viipuri at 08:00. After marching from Kavantsaari they immediately started setting

- up mine fields upon arriving as there were none on their front.

- Major Kirma who had been a home front Suojeluskunta administrator, did not have battle-field experience. Reassuring and popular, at 47 he was lame, somewhat hard of hearing, and seriously short sighted.

- The 1st Battalion, commanded by Kaptain A Malinen, was placed on reserve by the city hospital on the east end of Patterimaki near the water tower, a kilometer from the Red Square and a kilometer from Ristimaki.

- The 1st Battalion had arrived at Tammisuo at 03:00 on the 19th and were soon in Viipuri.

- Kaptain Malinen, age 30, had served with the VIAK Headquarters throughout the war – and not a day on the front lines. He did not have any rapport with his soldiers.

- Colonel Kemppi set up his own command post in the bank building at the Torkkeli Street and Punaisenlahti Street corner of the Red Square. He had arrived on the 18th .

- The light artillery battery - Kevyt Psto 20 - of Major I Forsblom - set up at Monrepos four kilometers from Viipuri Linna. They had pre WWI model 76 mm canons (76 K 02) which could carry for 8 kilometers.

- The heavy artillery battery - Rask Psto 40 - of Major T Ollila, set up even further back at Herttuala near Tienharra. It arrived on the evening of the 19th . They had 152 mm model 152 H 37 howitzers canons which carried for 16 kilometers.

- The mortar company - Krh.K- of Kaptain U Tohanen set up on the town side of the western end of Patterimaki. It had arrived in Tali at 10:30 on the 19th . It had two batteries, each with three 120 mm mortars.

- In addition each battalion had three of its' own mobile soldier moveable light 81mm mortars.

- The 19th anti tank company - 19.Tyk.K – arrived at 13:00 on the 19th in Tali. They had two 75 mm guns 75 k/40 and received two more by 10:00 on the 20th. The guns were fully capable of disabling even the heavy T-34, and the Klim Voroshilov tanks (The Klim only from the side). Two guns went to the IIIrd battalion and one was loaned to the neighbouring 3rd Brigade. This left only one gun in Viipuri. It was at the 20th Brigade headquarters awaiting dispatch. Effectively Viipuri did not have any operational anti tank guns.

- The company commander was Captain E Kantola.

- The Pioneer Company of Captain E Korhonen arrived at Tali at 17:50 on the 19th and set up in Pyorea Torni.

- Kaptain E Kurjenrauma the supply commander arrived on the 17th but his men did not arrive until 4 am on the 20th on the last train. They set up in Rappitilla behind Tienharra.

Munitions

A huge problem with the defense of Viipuri was the lack of ammunition.

- Heavy artillery shells ran out at 10:00-11:00
- Light artillery shells were replenished and did not run out until 16:42
- Heavy mortar shells ran out at 09:00
- Light howitzer and anti-tank shells ran out at 13:00
- Rifle and machine gun ammunition was inadequate. The 6th Company was in danger of running out of ammunition at 13:00. More arrived but not before the 6th Company had withdrawn for their posts.

The brigade had arrived with only ½ an infantry ammunition ration. A full infantry ration (per weapon) is 45 rifle bullets, 350 tommy gun bullets, 600 light machine gun bullets, and 1,200 machine gun bullets.

The artillery companies arrived with almost a full ration. The light artillery company had 1,800 shells, the equivalent of a days' ration. The heavy artillery unit had less then a full ration – 400 shells versus 480. A full ration is for a normal battle day.

The Mortar Company had only 9 to10 shells per 120 mm mortar. The battalion based light 81mm mortars had 80 shells for each mortar gun.

The Viipiuri battle required far, far more then a normal days ammunition ration.

The brigade had had sufficient rations at Syvari but was told to only take a ½ ration as they would be replenished at the Jessoila railway station. There were no munitions at Jessoila.

The provision of all munitions was the responsibility of the brigades' artillery commander Lieutenant Colonel P. Arra. He recognized that they badly needed munitions. The Brigades attempt to be replenished is a sad tale of IVAK intransigence and lack of response.

- On the 18th shortly after arriving Lieutenant Colonel Arra asked IVAK artillery Colonel Sippola for additional ammunition for three days. Colonel Sippola agreed to supply enough for one days heavy fighting. But nothing happened.

- On the evening of 19th IVAK said they should get one days supply from the IV AK Munitions store-house at Rautakorpi just north of Tienharra. Colonel Kemppi thought that was not enough and told Arra to request more as well as informing him that there was a munitions storehouse in Kavantsaari at the IVAK Headquarters as well as at Rautakorpi.

- Arra told Lieutenant Heikel to go get the promised ammunition. Lieutenant Heikel went to the Rautakorpi storehouse arriving at 24:00 on the 19th. Heikel was not given anything.He phoned the IVAK head quarters and was told that no munitions had been promised and to check in in the morning.

- Heikel returned to Viipuri. He did not inform Lieutenant Colonel Arra. He took six trucks and drove back to Rautakorpi. There he got into an argument with the storehouse commander,Captain

Rautumaa, regarding approval paperwork– to the point where both pulled out their pistols. Apparently Captain Rautumaa finally did agree to the replenishment.

- The loading of the munitions took some time as 30 to 40 trucks were waiting in front of them and the storehouse was in the process of moving. The trucks were not loaded until the morning of the 20th. The light artillery shells as well as the heavy artillery shells arrived before the fall of Viipuri. Catastrophically the heavy artillery shells were of no use as they were for the wrong model 152 H howitzer.

- When no ammunition had been received by the morning of June 20th, Major Nurmi, the 20th Brigade head of Operations and Weaponry, drove to Rautakorpi and got 100,000 bullets. He was able to distribute them to the 2nd and 4th battalions – but not until 13:30 after the 6th Company had retreated in panic and despair.

- During this time the heavy artillery and light artillery tried to source their own shells. Captain O Karttusen of the heavy artillery battery got 60 shells from the Pulsa fire station.

- Captain O Pyykko of the light artillery drove with their own vehicles to Pulsa and Rautakorpi and got a 1,000 shells. The light artillery had sufficient shells until 16:32, although they used the shells they got with discretion as their fire signal officers had withdrawn, and the position of the Finnish forces was not known.

- The mortar company and the anti tank company ran out of shells shortly after mid day. Heavy 121 mm mortar shells had run out almost immediately at 09:00. The remaining shells ran out at 13:00. They did not get any more. Lieutenant Heikel had tried to get some heavy mortar shells on the 20th from Rautakorpi but none were left. They were told to get some from Nurmi station but there were none there either.

- Some mortar shells arrived in Rautukorpi on the evening of the 20th and were sent to Viipuri in two trucks. The trucks never arrived and would have been too late anyway.

The fact that the 20 Pr did not have sufficient ammunition was a key factor in the fall of Viipuri:

- To the infantryman the prospect of runing out of bullets was catastrophic. As one 6th Company soldier replied when an officer ordered him to return to his station: *"There is no such law that states we must stand in the way of death without ammunition "*.
- The inability of the heavy artillery to support their infantry in even a modest manner was disastrous. The heavy artillery was the only deterrent to the Russian tanks. The infantry had received some anti-tank panzerfaust and panzerschreck guns but had not been taught how to use them. The one anti-tank 75 mm gun never did get into action. The five light Finnish tanks were no match for the heavy Russian tanks and retired early.
- Added to this even the light artillery and mortar units could not support the infantry, having run out of shells.

The Attack - Tuesday, June 20, 1944

03:00:

The Russian forces massed at Liimatta 2 kilometers south of the front lines at 3 am. I am sure mother and father could never have imaged such a sight when they lived in Liimatta before the Talvi Sota. Some 20 Pr reconnaissance units investigated but were quickly forced back by the Russian tanks.

04:30

The first Russian reconnaissance units arrived at the front lines.

06:00

Some Russian artillery fire started. Movement was detected south of the front line. The Finnish artillery fired some barrages. Sadly it was the remnants of JR58 that were retreating whose movement had been detected. Many were

killed by friendly fire. The remainder streamed unorganized through the 20th Brigades' lines.

09:00

Heavier Russian bombing and artillery barrages commenced, continuing through the morning.

10:00

The phone lines to 2nd battalion from the brigade headquarters were cut. This resulted in 20 minute delays before a messenger could bring information from the front line to Colonel Kemppi.

11:00

The Russians bombed for the second time and launched a heavy artillery barrage. They attacked the 2nd battalion at Ristimaki with 4 battalions and over 40 tanks. They launched a smaller attack against the 4th battalion near Papulanniemi with 2 battalions and some tanks. The Finnish forces stopped both the Papulanniemi and Ristimaki attacks before noon.

During this time the German Group Kuhlmey Stuka planes did a dive bombing run over the massed Russian tanks destroying a number of them. This was the only air force support the 20th Brigade received. The 20th Brigade did not have any anti-aircraft support. The anti-aircraft unit that had been located in Viipuri withdrew at 06:05 on the morning of the 20th.

12.00 - 13:00

The Russians aimed the brunt of their attack on the 6th Company sector south west of Ristimaki. They attacked with heavy tanks supported by infantry. The tanks broke through the stone tank barriers and over the mine fields past the race track.

The race track attack route into Viipuri had also been used during the Finnish Civil War. The tanks were a far cry from the horse carts of the Civil War ...

The mine field and tank barriers had already been significantly diminished by earlier bombing runs and the artillery barrages. The five Er Ps K Christie BT 42 assault tanks could not stop the attack. They pulled back for repair. Soon only one was operational. The Panzerfaust and Panzerschreck anti guns also were not inflicting major damage on the tanks. Not only was the Russian heavy tank armor very thick, the Panzerfaust guns effectiveness was reduced as the soldiers loaded them improperly due to inadequate training.

There was no Finnish artillery support as the gun batteries had no shells. After mid day there was not even anti tank gun and heavy mortar support. They ran out of shells shortly after 12:00.

The infantry, already with limited ammunition, were left to stop the Russian tanks and infantry with their own devices. They held back the attack until around 12:40 when several tanks broke through the mine fields towards the 6th company lines.

Confusion and panic took hold. A 6th Company 2nd platoon soldier shouted, *"Permission to withdraw has been given."*. In the confusion of the battle the platoon commander 2nd Lieutenant Casternin believed it and ordered a retreat. When he realized this was not true, he gave a new order to stand and fight, but it was too late. The company was in full retreat. Soon some other units joined in the flight.

13:00 – 14:00

At 13:00, for the first time in several hours, the heavy artillery fired the few emergency shells it had left. The light artillery kept firing until 16:30.

Shortly before the main attack, Major Kurt Backman, the commander of the 1st battalion had moved his command post further back. This set a bad precedent as well as placing him in a location where he was not near the rapidly unfolding attack. Major Backman started to stammer and flounder. Not a reassuring example of confidence and bravery to settle the panicking men. The men continued their flight, saying *"There is no such a law that we must stand in the way of death without ammunition "*.

Major Backman tried to contact his 5th and 7th companies and his neighboring battalions without success. As he did not want to be captured in a motti, he ordered an organized withdrawal, but it turned into full flight. He was able to gather a platoon together at the Infectious Disease Hospital 300 meters behind the front lines. But while he went to give the remaining assault tank directions, the men fled.

At 13:50 a perspiring, flustered Major Backman came into Kemppi's command post. He was so incoherent that it took several strong shots of cognac before he was able talk and be understood.

At 13:55 Kemppi sent a message to IV AK;

> *" Break through at Ristimaki. Counter attack underway. Artillery shells at an end. Request that shells be sent quickly."*

Ten minutes before at 13:40, Kemppi had already ordered Captain Uuno Tarkki's 1st Battalion strike force to counter attack. He directed another group under Kaptain Suutarinen which included 3rd battalion reserves, to take Ristimaki. They arrived at 15:45 and fanned out over the empty positions. The lines had not yet been manned by the Russians. Another group, Osasto Laiho, did not get to their Lehto destinations before the Russian break through. In both cases, it appears it took them two hours to reach destinations only ½ hour away.

Kemppi as well had ordered the 1st battalions' commander Kaptain Malinen and Lieutenant Korpisalo along with additional 3rd battalion reserves to counter attack from the north side by the Ristimaki cemetery in an endeavor to *"Take back the positions at whatever cost."* As there was no artillery support the counter attack failed. Some of the soldiers in the unit disappeared. Lieutenant Korpisalo and his platoon held the Russians back with their sub machine guns. When their ammunition ran out and only two of his platoon remained unwounded, he started taking back his wounded to safety. Lieutenant Korpisalo himself was wounded in the withdrawal. 1st Battalion commander Kaptain Malinen was killed during the battle. The last sight of him was cambering onto a Russian armored vehicle.

16:00

The Russians managed to break through a narrow seam at Ristimaki with a couple of heavy tanks.

After 16:00, the Russians widened the breech and soon over 20 heavy tanks started to roll towards Talikkala and the water tower. Soon over 50 tanks were rolling towards the centre of town – from the 4th battalions' sector as well as the 1st battalions sector.

4th Battalion

The Russians were attacking on the 4th Battalion's front as well. The 4th's commander Major Viljo Kirma was a quiet, well regarded, popular commander.

Colonel Kemppi ordered Kirma's battalion to counter attack. Kirma thought the situation was impossible and argued with Kemppi to withdraw. His last words to Kemppi were, *"The enemy is at the house corner"*. In the ensuing street fighting Kirma got separated from his men. Soldiers said that they saw him alive for the last time firing his pistol at an approaching Russian motor cycle. The Russian riding in the motorcycle side car shot him dead with his sub machine gun.

His 15th company (Lieutenant Heikki Erasen) continued to fight on as well. A large number of the company was encircled as they retreated. They hid in the Viipuri Library but soon surrendered to the Russians. One of the Finnish soldiers had been wounded. The Russian officer took him around the corner and killed him with a pistol shot. The rest of the soldiers were imprisoned – first in the old Perkjarvi prison, then in a Leningrad collective barn, next in Volvova in Inkerimaa, and finally Tserepovets south of Lake Onega. Not all the prisoners lived. One of the 15th company prisoners who returned in 1944 said he only skin and bones when he returned. Half of the 3,400 Finnish soldiers who were imprisoned never got back.

The Russians did not take wounded soldiers prisoner. (The Finnish forces were much better but not blameless). The 20 Pr 1st aid station was in the Women's Hospital. The two doctors Otto Salonen and Eino Varjola had the walking wounded helped back. They determined that the badly wounded could not be evacuated. They gave them morphine to quiet them down and took away their weapons so that it wouldn't be a provocation to the Russians. The Russians had no intention to take Finnish prisoners. They burst in firing and shot everyone dead. One of the wounded survived to become a prisoner. He survived because he faked being dead when the Russians burst in.

Kemppi

Kemmpi during this period continued to try to get assistance from IV AK. At 13:50 he sent a message to IV AK requesting:

"Permission to withdraw to the Terviniemi – Heikka - Pikiruukki line (Ahh, centered by the old mid 1730s

Tzarina Anna battlements directly across the bridge from Viipuri Linna).

No reply was received from the IV AK 's command post in Lappenranta. He sent another one twenty minutes later: *"Requesting fresh reinforcements.*

The first reply from IV AK came two hours later at 17:42. The only message was to

" Hold the lines on the eastern side of Viipuri at any cost."

Even if it had been possible it was too late. The full brigade had retreated almost an hour earlier.

Kaptain Tarkki's battle group had ended up on the Patterimaki battlements before having to retreat. They ran into Kemppi on the street corner. Kemppi asked Tarkki to show him where his soldiers were, saying that Patterimaki would have been a good spot to counter attack from. However when a soldier who came across them asked where the next defense position was, Kemppi replied;

" Go straight to the Tornio River".

The Tornio River is on the border between Finland and Sweden in Northern Finland. It is close to where my ancient ancestor watched as a boy as the Swedish troops retreated from Finland after losing Finland to Russia in 1809.

At 16:30 Russian tanks arrived in Red Square just outside Kemppi's post. Kemppi was despondent and did not want to move but was convinced by his adjutant to leave. They reached Viipuri Linna.

At 16:45 Kemppi requested that the Finnish flag be taken down from the tower. 15th company's 2nd Lieutenant Makinen ran up the two hundred and thirty nine tower steps and took down the flag. The Russian tanks fired at him, but without success as they could not lift the angle of their tank canons high enough to hit the top of the tower.

At 16:50 the Pioneer company blew up the Viipuri Linna bridge upon Kemppi's order. Two hours earlier he had ordered the Pioneer and Communications companies to take up positions by Pyorea Torni in an endeavor to stop the retreat of his forces. At that point he had also ordered the Pioneer company to mine the bridge.

At 18:00 on June 20th the Russian flag appeared on top of Viipuri Linna.

Viipuri was lost - forever.

Aftermath

The amount of casualties the 20th Brigade suffered continues to be debated – it varies from 120 to 162 killed, lost and wounded. Among the killed were Major Viljo Kirma the commander of the 4th Battalion, Captain Amos Malinen the commander of the 1st Battalion, and Captain Suutarinen of the 1st Battalion.

The 20th Brigade was transferred over to the command of Lieutenant Colonel Soralla. Colonel Kemppi and Major Backman were placed in prison in Hame. A military tribunal found Colonel Kemppi,

> Guilty of not informing the IV AK head quarters of the situation in time.

He received a sentence of 25 days, but more importantly he lost his hard earned honor. He died four years later in 1949 of sorrow.

Major Backman was found,

> Guilty of not defending despite being commanded to do so.

Major Backman was sentenced to 8 months hard labour but committed suicide before serving time.

Responsibilty

Many reasons have been put forward for the fall of Viipuri.

Certainly it was not just the fault of Colonel Kemppi and Major Backman. It was the shared fault of army headquarters, the officers, the soldiers, and the artillery coverage.

1.) The trigger for the fall of the city was the panicked flight of the 6th Company soldiers from their positions. Yes it was the fault of the 20 Pr officers and the soldiers. Finnish forces had fought more bravely and successfully in similar desperate situations – but only once before defending a city. With some exceptions, neither the 20th Brigade soldiers nor officers had any battle experience. They were untested in battle and panicked.

And they were not alone. The Finnish Army of the Isthmus fell apart under the weight of the overwhelming Russian tanks, the six fold superiority in numbers of the Russian forces, and its endless artillery and air power. The Finnish forces did not begin sacrificing themselves for the Fatherland until the Ihantala and Ayrapaa/Vuosalmi battles when the imminent specter of the Russian troops entering central Finland became a stark reality. This plus the addition of inventive Finnish artillery tactics, German air cover, and the availability of German anti-tank weaponry blunted the unstoppable Russian tanks.

As Captain Tarkki comments in his book regarding the panicked flight of the 6th Company soldiers (and officers):

> The troops should have been very inspired in order to be able to face an unequal and unhopeful battle. Undoubtedly the mens' courage and attitude would have risen if Mannerheims' passioned entreaty to the Finnish army to protect Viipuri and Finland, and Colonel Kemppi's communiqué of the challenge, criticality and honor of helping their brothers in arms stop the Russian attack up the Kannas, had reached the men, as they should have.

> Spirits sank when 50 tanks massed in front of their positions. A soldier left with only an open sight rifle felt oneself helpless.

> The anti tank weapons had not made a difference, neither the new type nor the old. Even the availability

*of bullets for ones rifles and machine guns began
to disappear.*

*Neither the artillery nor the mortars had provided
help. Heavy reinforcing artillery fire would have
raised ones spirits. The six inch shells would have
made great tracks in the Russian panzer formations.*

*Somehow it felt unsafe when even the officers
weren't bold.*

*The panzer turned. A mighty tank rumbling. Panic
rose in the air. Fear of death took a stronger grip on
the defenders. Beside it strode panic. It was stronger
then duty. It caused the defenders to flee.*

2.) It was caused by the lack of infantry ammunition and artillery, mortar and anti-tank canon shells as outlined in the Munitions section.

3.) The Finnish army command – GHQ, the Karelian Army of General Oesch, and particularly the IVAK of General Laatikainen were at fault. Although none of the Generals were allocated any blame, the blame was certainly theirs – incompetence, and even more damming, indifference

- The army command did not order the proper fortification of Viipuri during the long Asemasota years. This should have included proper communications capability and a back defense line as well as proper fortification of the front line.
- The overall Karjalian Isthmus command and GHQ was not supportive. Knowing the size of the Russian assault they nonetheless only sent an untried brigade of 5,133 men to defend Finland's second most important city - Viipuri. Indeed after changing their mind several times, they did not get the brigade to Viipuri until the day before the attack. Lieutenant General Karl Oesch is quoted as saying that they were sufficiently provisioned and that many other units had been able to overcome the enemy with only limited men and weaponry. Several years after the end of the war he admitted that both the manpower and artillery and armored support should have been much greater.

- Even more damming, Major General Lagus commander of the Panzer Division recommended on June 16th that Viipuri should be abandoned. Initially Oesch rejected the recommendation stating that Mannerheim wanted Viipuri held. Upon further pressure from Lagus he agreed to Lagus raising the issue with Lieutenant General Airo, Mannerheim's GHQ head of staff. Airo as well rejected the recommendation again quoting Mannerheim. When forced to send a tank unit to Viipuri, Major General Lagus sent five of his least effective tanks.
- The responsiveness of Lieutenant General Laatikainen and the IV AK was negligent. They did not reply to Colonel Kemppi's communications, send reinforcements, nor provide ammunition.
- As Captain Tarkki comments:

*Viipuri belonged to IVAK's responsibility, and to
it, it had allocated the 20th Pr. The IVAK should
have responded to the defense of the VDT line and
the protection of Viipuri as the Commander-in-
Chiefs order directed - with total support and
committment... It comes to mind that during the
1941 conquest of Viipuri Lieutenant General
Laatikainen worked without rest for 3 days. Now
during the summer of 1944 he was not interested in
defending Viipuri.*

Captain Tarkki ends his book written 50 years after the fall of Viipuri with the comments that:

*In the thoughts of his brothers in arms, Colonel
Armas Kemppi rests under the sod an honoured man.*

*Likewise the 2nd Battalion men honored their
commander Backman. He had created a good
spirit in the battalion before. They understood
that he was limited by his psychological and
physical shortcomings.*

*It is time to declare that the military honor of the 20th
Brigades' men is restored.*

Let time as well heal their psychological wounds.

*The men could not change the impossible to
the possible.*

The defense of Viipuri could have been possible if Viipuri had been important to the Finnish military command. It was not treasured and sacrificed for like Leningrad, Moscow, Stalingrad, London, and Berlin. Lieutenant General Oesch is quoted as saying: " *The loss of Viipuri was just a beauty error. It made little difference to stopping the Russian assault.*" But certainly Viipuri was important to Marshall Mannerheim. When Marshall Mannerheim heard that Viipuri had been lost his cheeks flared red with anger. The loss of Viipuri made a critical difference in the peace negotiations. It was not just a cosmetic error.

If the Army Corps Generals and senior officers involved had been Karelians (none were) I believe that that the story of the defense of Viipuri would have been different. Indeed if the 20 Pr had consisted of sons of Karjala and Viipuri as opposed to mostly men from Helsinki and Central Finland, it would have greatly helped.

Then Viipuri would not have been a dispensible, slightly exotic, frontier city. It would have been home and hearth – worth sacrificing everything for.

Ahh, the loss of Viipuri still remains bitter and controversial.

Uncle Toivo and the Battles
of
Siiranmaki and Ayrapaa /Vuosalmi

CHAPTER 21

The Battles of Siiranmaki and Ayrapaa / Vuosalmi and Uncle Toivo

During the Russian Summer Assault of 1944 on the Kannas, the second part of Russian attack was north from the Ohta and Riihio sectors to Ayrapaa/Vuosalmi.

The assault lasted from June 9th to July 17th, 1944.

It pitted Martola's 2nd Division consisting primarily of JR7 and JR49, against Anisimov's 98th Rifle Corps of 3 divisions – Colonel George Isakov's 281st Rifle Division, Major General Alexander Yakusov's 381st Rifle Division, and Major General Jacob Panitskins 92nd Rifle Division. On July 9th the Russian forces were by reinforced by a fresh army corps – Major General Kozatsek's three division strong 115th Rifle Corps. On July 11th Martola's 2nd Division was reinforced by Lagus's Panzer Division.

Uncle Toivo was in JR7. I did not need any books to determine where he and his regiment was during the 1944 assault. I just looked at the battles listed in his military record:

1. Multalamaki: June 11
2. Siiranmaki: June 13-16
3. Punnus: June 17
4. Pasuri: June 18
5. Salmenkaita: June 18
6. Valkjarvi: June 19
7. Ayrapaa June 20 – July 10
8. Vuosalmi July 11 – July 29

The division retreated from their Ohta/ Riihio front lines to Siiranmaki where they fought a desperate holding battle for 4 days from June 13th to June 16th.

They continued to retreat back to Ayrapaa fighting battles at Punnus: June 17; Pasuri: June 18; Salmenkaita: June 18, and Valkjarvi: June 19

They arrived in Ayrapaa on June 19th, 1944 weary and depleted, pursued by Anisimov's 98th Rifle Corps.

They did not have a chance to rest. The battle of Ayrapaa/ Vuosalmi, one of the largest battles of the entire war, started the next day.

The Battle of Ayrapaa / Vuosalmi took place from June 21st to July 17th. The objective of the Russian forces was to

cross the Vuoksi River, and proceed northwards to Antera and from thence into the heart of Finland. The battle took greater importance after July 7th after the Russians were unable to break through at Tali-Ihantala.

At its' peak the battle pitted a Finnish force of about 20,000 against a Russian force of 60,000. The Russian forces had a large tank contingent of 150 tanks – the Finns about 30 in the 3rd phase of the battle when the Lagus Panzer Division arrived. The artillery on both sides was very active. The Finnish artillery fired over 122,000 rounds of ordnance, the same amount as at Tali-Ihantala. The Russians of course fired far more. Russian air cover was heavy throughout the battle. The Finnish air force together with German Detachment Khulmey was able to provide some support after July 9th.

Finnish casualties were high – over 6,000 - of whom 1,100 were killed or missing. Russian casualties were about 15,000 – 3,300 killed or missing.

After the battle both sides settled into trench warfare.

The Finnish forces were successful in stopping the Russian 23rd Army and Russia's entry into Finland.

The Battle of Siiranmaki and the Fighting Retreat to Ayrapaa

On June 9th 1944 the Russian 98th Army Corps launched its' attack against the 2nd Division defensive lines at Ohta and Riihio.

The Finnish forces withdrew to the VT line arriving at Siiranmaki on June 12th.

The Finnish forces withdrew from their trenches on June 10th, fighting smaller battles at Multala and Hartonen until arriving at Siiranmaki on the 12th. At Siiranmaki JR7 and JR49 fought a fierce and successful defensive battle from June 14th to June 16th before being ordered by Army command to withdraw at 23:00 on June 16th. During the three day battle the 2nd Division suffered a 1,000 casualties.

The entries from the 9th Companies and the III Battalions sotapaivakirjas provide a view into the battle. The entry for June 9th is from the 9th Company journal. The entries after that are primarily from the III Battalion journal. Any 9th Company entries are indented. Battalion head quarters being located behind the battle lines had time for recording. The Companies only had time to fight for their lives.

Indeed from June 13th to July 5th there are no entires in the 9th Companies journal. The company was in continuous fighting, suffering heavy casualties including the loss of all their officers – either killed or wounded. The only entry in the 9th Company journal reads:

> 13.6.44 to 5.7.44
>
> Fierce battle in Siiranmaki. Russian artillery unceasing and tank groups large. Own casualties quite heavy. Got age group 1925 replacements. And came to Punnus village where we fought for a day. Withdrew through Pasuri countryside and Pollakkala and from there to Vuoksi River and Mustsaari and Vasikkasaari Islands. We dug in defensive positions here.

On June 9th at the beginning of the assault, the 9th Company journal is quite detailed ...for the last time.

Friday, 9.6.44 (Day 1)

00:40-01:00 Couple of howitzer shells fired at Bunker 3

01:00 – 3:00 Sound of tractors behind Russian lines at Oja

03:00-05:00 Four 82mm shells hit Bunker 1

05:30-7:00 Russians fired howitzers quite fiercely at Bunkers 1 and 2 – about 500 shells. Soldier Siitari, killed and soldier Hartainen seriously wounded at Bunker 2. All day the Russians shelled our positions quite fiercely.

16:30-19:30 Russians shelled Bunkers 1 and 2 and the back country heavily. Russians fired about 6,000 howitzer shells in total.

Russians attacked Bunker 1, getting into the trenches at position 4. The Russians tried to pull back soldier Kalle. They got hold of him. He fought to the end and fell. The Russians dragged him with them to the nearest barriers. Under Serjeant Luomaharra, Corporal Takkinen and soldier Lehto killed 6 Russians between the trenches and the barbed wire barriers and a couple further back. Russian fighter planes supported the attack, strafing and bombing the sector.

During the fight at Bunker 2, Corporal Lahikainen, and soldier Hietala were wounded on the hands by shrapnel, soldier Mintsanen wounded on the face by shrapnel and soldier Niskanen on the hand by a bullet.

In addition at Polla 2 soldiers were wounded by howitzer fire, one seriously and one lightly. At Bunker 1 soldier Sortola was wounded on the face by shrapnel and soldier Virtano on the back by shrapnel.

Saturday 10.6.44 (Day 2)

17:00 Regiment order to withdraw

21:00 Withdrew from trenches 9th Company on right and 10th Company on left - ½ at a time

> *9th Company Sotapaivakirja: 10.6.44*
>
> *05:30 Russians started to gather in front of Pola and 9th Company Bunkers 1 and 3. Artillery fire was brisk all day.*

24:00 *9th Company crossed Rajajoki and arrived in Termola.*

Sunday 11.6.44 (Day 3)

01:00 *9th Company arrived at Hartonen on whose south side set up stations, Jaarkari platoon as well. Enemy moving on Tonteri Road towards Hartonen.*

03:40 *Jaakari platoon and Regimental Pioneer Company led by Lieutenant Voitti sent to the road south of Hartonen in front of 9th Company positions*

14:40 *In contact with Russians around mid day from the direction of the Hartonen Road. Enemy moving along the road with the protection of tanks. Our anti tank squads with Panzerfaust destroyed two T-34 tanks (Private Liukkonan of 12th Company). In the bitter fight Lieutenant Hietanan of 9th Company fell and 2nd Lieutenant Vasarla of 12th Company. Enemy attack was fierce and the artillery fire intense. The enemy threw new tanks into the assault. Own infantry retreated about 1 kilometer to Uusikyla where we set up new positions.*

With additional help of Battalion Custer, started a counter attack. Pushed stations to the edge of the forest on the northern edge of Hartonen and held them until received order to withdraw. During this time the enemy and tanks moved between the houses firing at our infantry.

9th Company Sotapaivakirja: 11.6.44

07:30 *9th Company in Hartonen.*

Dug positions and awaited Russian advance – Russians attacked supported by tanks. Destroyed 3 tanks.

9th Company withdrew in the evening to edge of forest and set up new stations. Lieutenant Hietanen killed in Hartonen. Russians crossed over quite fiercely. Made 3 unsuccessful counter attacks. Lieutenant Tirronen wounded in the hand.

18:30 *After enemy artillery barrage 10th Company withdrew from Multala in the evening withdrawing to Seppala. Then got order to return immediately to Multala. Then got order to return nonetheless to Seppala and to remain there under command of Er P12.*

Regimental messenger brought order to withdraw. I Battalion and Heimo withdrew from the left side of the Hartonen Road crossing. Aided I Battalion and Heimo Battalion 3 to withdraw, then withdrew our IIIrd Battalion. 12th Company was placed to protect our withdrawal

Monday 12.6.44 (Day 4)

02:00 *Enemy did not follow us*

05:40 *Commanders talked with the officers in Kekrola. Enemy on south side of Seppala. Our battalion manned Ronnunkyla beside Er P12. Battalion orders were to take possession and man positions south of the village – 9th Company on left, and 11th Company on the right.*

We attacked through the open receiving heavy enemy infantry fire. At the moment the enemy was advancing towards the village and got into a fire fight with us and Er P12. We pushed the enemy to the forest on the south edge of the village. The village was now in our possession – We made contact with our own companies in Ronnunkyla. Enemy tried a counter attack against our weaker positions. Stopped with artillery fire and infantry fire and patrols banished.

9th Company Sotapaivakirja: 12.6.44

2:30 *9th Company withdrew towards Kekrola. Set up beside JR6's line a bit before Hartonen at the Kekrola cross roads. Came to outskirts of Seppala village and set up positions.*

7:00 *9th Company 2nd Lieutenant Gustaffson and soldier Halonen killed by bullets.*

8:10 *Under Serjeant Naveri and private Joensuu, and Corporal Rasanen wounded – all from shrapnel.*

12:00 *Defense of Ronnunkyla transferred to ErP12 battalion. Moving out 10th Company back to battalion command.*

13:40 - *Command post moved from south side of Seppala to Ronnunkyla.*

One company of III/JR49 seconded to us as our reserve. Placed our mortar company and our 13th Company under II Battalions'command.

Enemy continued attacking our positions with increased furiousity - 11th Company forced out of their positions in Seppala. Jaakari platoon counter attacked. Enemy moving actively in the forest. 9th Company drew their stations back a bit.

19:30 – *Enemy started fierce artillery barrage directed and towards Konnu. Enemy infantry supported by tanks attacked.*

20:00 Battalion Commander heard via radio that some of own forces were still in Kekrola defensive stations and were told to withdraw immediately. Also sent order to Er P12 on our right side to withdraw. The road on the north side of Polla swamp was manned by III JR49 and was the first defense position. 10th Company set up another defensive position with 2 machine guns at the Halttila Road junction. Battalion ordered to pull back north of Halttila, Saarenmaa, Siiranmaki to Vuotta. Move quickly as enemy is pursuing rapidly.

24:00 Battalion moved to Vottaa as regiment reserve.

Tuesday 13.6.44 (Day 5)

14:00 Regimental order to move 9th Company to Siiranmaki front lines as reserve for I Battalion. Bit later platoons of 12th Company, the Mortar Company and 10th Company to front lines as enemy attacking I Battalion positions fiercely.

19:00 12th Company sent as well. In reserve - Jaakari platoon and Communications platoon.

24:00 9th, 10th and 12th Companies back to reserve.

Wednesday 14.6.1944 (Day 6)

08:00 Fierce enemy attack against front lines and our rear. Dispatched greeting patrol to between 1st and 2nd Regiments and our battalions command post.

10:00 Entire battalion seconded to 1st battalion and moved to same front line.

Jaakari Company left to counter attack at Palomaki.

Exceptionally heavy enemy air cover, tanks, and extra harsh artillery fire. Entire battalion fell apart on the entire sector as we threw a company or a part of one toward a critical point. Casualties throughout the day were very exceptionally large. Captain Sirkkanen got wounded on the nose from shrapnel. Lieutenant Takala who had been ordered to command 9th Company was wounded lightly.

The men started to show symptoms of fatigue. Many left their stations on their own authority while others joined the "forest brigade" returning back several days later. Others were missing in action: didn't know whether they had been killed or where they had disappeared.

The enemy used exceptionally heavy tanks in the assault - KV Is. During the day we destroyed 6 with panzerfaust or with antitank canons. Despite this the Russians got a foot hold in the Siiranmaki trenches and infiltrated a lot of men into them.

We made several counter attacks and were able to stop their breakthrough spreading.

At the end taking back the trenches was hindered by the fact that the defensive positions were in a straight line all the way across the Siiranmaki hilltop. Rolling up the trench continuously was hence impossible.

All through the night the enemy gave harsh artillery fire on the positions and with a couple of tank breakthroughs moved to the slopes of Siiranmaki.

At 24:00 it quietened. The majority of the battalions' men stayed the night with other companies here and there mixed up with defensive positions. Some smaller squads returned in the morning night to Vuotta.

Thursday 15.6.44 (Day 7)

Enemy artillery fire continued unceasingly heavy. In the morning the enemy bombarded nonstop for 2 hours at the middle of our defenses and at our rear all the way to Vuotta. The enemy planes flew constantly overhead bombing and strafing. (On June 15th the Finnish LeR4 planes bombed the Russian forces – for the first and last time).

Around 15:00 after the air alert, the last scattered reserves were sent to the front line. The enemy tried to widen their gains at the Siiranmaki bridge. The enemy companies pushed to within throwing distance, but then were forced to take retreat.

Tired and startled from the fierce artillery fire, men started to move back from their stations. We reorganized all retreating men possible and returned them to their stations. Enemy artillery fire was unprecedentedly severe.

The number killed and wounded during the day was unusually large. Kaptain Ruuskanen, commander of 10th Company was deathly wounded during an artillery exchange. Both his legs were broken. Lieutenant Reunanen of 10th Company was wounded in the face with shrapnel. Lieutenant Pietarinen the commander of 11th Company fell.

As it now looked threatening that the main Siiranmaki defensive lines would be lost, we set up a closing - cut off line at Kyolmaoja. Another battalion and JR49 launched a counter attack to take back the main Siiranmaki defenses.

We took back almost all our positions by 21:00, only 150 meters of the trenches were not recaptured. Between the main line and the cut off line, some Russians and a few KV tanks were left. Set up a patrol to sweep these up.

We brought up Panzerfaust with passenger cars to the front. And we set these up to destroy tanks still moving between the lines. The situation now looked stabilized. Enemy artillery fire stopped. The night was relatively peaceful.

Our own battalion is now totally scattered. For a couple of days various companies have been seconded to I Battalion. The majority of our casualties have been caused by this.

Smaller groups are needed - to be gathered together as necessary and thrown in case by case where the need is the greatest.

Friday 16.6.44 (Day 8)

9th, 10th and 11th Companies do not have a single officer left. They have been either killed or wounded.

9th Company on roads' right side. Lieutenant Vaino and Lieutenant Hakala's companies strengthened with Panzerfaust and 2 machine guns

23:00 Started to withdraw from front lines – to Vuotta and onwards

> For the period from 17.6.44 to 4.7.44, I have not included the battalions entire recordings. Rather I have added those portions that pertain to Company 9 or reflect a major event.

Saturday 17.6.44 (Day 9)

14:50 Arrived Lamminpaa countryside – reorganized - Lieutenant Voitti placed in command of 9th Company. Lieutenant Voitti during the Siiranmaki battle had commanded a company with II/JR49.He was back with the battalion now.

On Punnusjoki line – III Battalion on left line but only manned by 11th Company.

Bivouacked in Lamminpaa countryside. Had the bandaging station (JSP) and munitions depot (AJp) beside us.

Sunday 18.6.44 (Day 10)

05:50 Regiment order to move immediately to Punnusjarvi and man the defensive position with 2 companies and 4 machine guns

06:00 Replacements arrive -5 officers and 2 men

08:30 9th Company manned the Pasurinkangus – U line. Company strengthened with 4 machine guns and an antitank gun.

11:45 Sounds of gun fire exchanges from 9th Company positions.

12:35 Reconnaissance patrol returned to 9th Companies sector.

On the Pasuri Road the Company got into a firefight with the enemy, who supported by tanks, had been trying to move west. They were successful in striking two of the tanks with their anti tank gun, and the enemy had drawn back. The 9th Companies' younger men (19 year old replacements who had arrived that day at Puunus) also drew back about 1 ½ kilometers, moving to the Er P6 lines.

13:05 Reconnaissance patrol returned from Lahdenpohja.

13:45 Got the news of Lieutenant Voittis' situation through radio contact with the company on the left side of the sector .

14:10 Serjeant Nykasens' patrol returned. The patrol got into a firefight with the enemy.

14:15 Gave one platoon of the 11th Company to the 10th Company to strengthen them.

14:27 Pioneers exploded the railway bridge west of the Korpioja station

15:00 Got radio contact with Lieutenant Voitti.

The 9th Company had received a startling send off from enemy tanks. As they did not have any Panzerfaust antitank guns left, the Company commander (Voitti) had drawn his men back to Er P6's line. Fight group Tk 38 was given the task of destroying the tanks.

17:00 Enemy attacked west with a battalion strength unit along the Jutikkala-Sarkola Road. Irrespective of fierce artillery fire they gained a foot hold by the train station pushing the 10th Company back.

18:00 On reserve 11th Company sent to man 10th Company lines. Gun exchanges sounded long through the night and the enemy harassed us steadily with light canon fire and howitzer barrages.

Monday 19.6.44 (Day 11)

01:30 Received order to withdraw. Our men were to be withdrawn and Er P6 and Raja JP2 were to replace us.

02:30 Began withdrawal as ordered, the platoons marched to the Punnus train station along the Salmenkalta road on the west side of the Lehmisuo swamp northwards towards Pollakkala village.

06:00 Arrived at Pollakkala village. ....

08:10 2nd Divisions commander arrived at the battalion command post. Explained yesterdays' encounters at the Korpioja station and in the Pansuri countryside. Battalion placed directly under 2nd Divisions' command.

11:00 Order arrived with a Division messenger to immediately leave Pollakkala village and march over the Vuoksi River along the pontoon bridge to Vuosalmi Village.

12:40 Departed from Pollakkala.

15:00 Command group arrived at Vuosalmi Village.

15:17 Radio contact with JR7s headquarters

Quickly set up our defensive sector – right border from Vuosalmi Village south to Niemela and the Vuoksi River -left border Hovi to Ruissaari.

9th Company manned Mustasaari and Vasikkasaari.

11th Company manned the sector from Liette meadows to Ruissaari island.

We only had 5 machine guns left (The rest had had to be destroyed during our retreat or else had to be left for the Russians). Three were allocated to 9th Company and 2 to 11th Company. Later we got more machine guns. In addition we set up one 75 mm artillery gun on Vasikkasaari.

The 9th Company was now settled in awaiting the next onslaught.

I wonder if one of the few stories I heard about Uncle Toivo occurred during that long, bitter, fighting withdrawal from Ohta to Ayrapaa. Uncle Toivo said that:

> *Once he was told to dig foxhole. While he was head down in the foxhole he was talking with his friend who was standing by the foxhole smoking a cigarette.*

Suddenly an artillery shell landed with a huge explosion. There was a splatter of blood. When he looked up again there was nothing left of his friend except his boots beside the foxhole – with his feet still in them.

The Battle of Ayrapaa- Vuosalmi

The Ayrapaa/Vuosalmi Battle went through 3 phases:

1. Initial smaller battles for two weeks from June 20th to July 3rd, wherein the Finnish 2nd Division held the western shore of the Vuoksi River at Ayrapaa;

2. The major battle of Ayrapaa from July 4th to July 9th wherein the Russian 98th Rifle Corps forced the 2nd Division to abandon Ayrapaa and cross to the eastern side of the Vuoksi River;

3. The Vuosalmi battle on the eastern shore of the Vuoksi from July 10th to July 17th wherein the Finnish forces reinforced by the Panzer Division and air cover contained the combined Russian forces of the new 115th Rifle Corps and the remnants of the 98th Rifle Corps to a 6 kilometer wide and 3 kilometer deep landing zone on the eastern shore of the Vuoksi River.

The 2nd Division reached Ayrapaa on June 19th - the III Battalion of JR7 arriving at 15:00 on the 19th .

The 2nd Division at this point consisted of JR7, JR49, ErP12, and HeimoP 3 - the ranks all weary and depleted after 11 days of non stop fighting and marching.

Most of the force was ordered to hold the 7 kilometer long ridge on the western side of the Vuoksi River. Some units crossed to the eastern side of the Vuoksi.

JR49 was set up to protect the northern portion of the ridge at Kyla-Paakkola while JR7 was positioned on the southern Harju sector at the Ayrapaa church and the main bridgehead over the Vuoksi River. JR7s' 1st and 2nd Battalions were on the Harju sector on the west side of the Vuoksi while the 3rd Battalion was set up on the east side of the Vuoksi River.

The 9th Company of JR7 was set up in the middle of the Vuoksi River - Uncle Toivo and his company were dispatched to defend Mustasaari and Vasikkasaari. Uncle Arvo recounted that his brother Toivo:

Barely survived the battle on Vasikkasaari. In the last minutes Toivo and his squad had to retreat in haste swimming across the river in a hail of bullets. According to Uncle Arvo, Toivo said that :

"He only survived because the Russians were such poor shots."

And that did happen on July 10th.

The Russians probed the area for two weeks, launching several attacks but were turned back by heavy and accurate Finnish artillery fire. Throughout the weeks Russian artillery fire and air bombing continued.

- On July 4th the Russian 98th Army Corps launched a full assault. The 381st Division attacked at Ayrapaa and the 281st Division at Kyla-Paakkola. The 92nd Division was in reserve.

- On the 4th , Lieutenant Colonel Ehrnrooth asked for permission for JR7 to withdraw from Ayrapaa, but IIIAK Lieutenant General Siilasvuo after initially agreeing, rescinded his approval and told the regiment to hold the Ayrapaa bridgehead. Ehrnooth asked again on July 6 and was again denied.

- The Finnish 2nd Division held out at Ayrapaa and Kyla-Paakola until they were forced to withdraw across the river on July 9th. The five day battle resulted in 3,000 Finnish casualties, almost all to JR7 and JR49. Russian casualties were 5,300 – of whom over 1,000 were killed – the leading Russian attack regiment shrank from 3,000 men to 150.

- Late on July 9 the newly arrived Russian 115th Rifle Corps successfully crossed the Vuoksi under cover of a smoke screen and heavy artillery and air support. They created a small bridgehead on the eastern shore. The majority of the Russian forces moved over. On July 10th Uncle Toivo's unit had to withdraw from Vasikkasaari.

- On July 11th the Lagus Armored Panzer Division (PsD) with its' tanks and Jaeger Brigade arrived from Ihantala to reinforce the Vuosalmi line. Detachment Khlumey's Stuka dive bombers as well arrived along with Finnish fighter planes and bombers. Attacks and counter attacks and artillery exchanges continued until July 17th. The Finnish forces managed to contain the Russian forces to a 6 kilometer wide and 3 kilometer deep landing zone. The Russians launched a final heavy artillery barrage on July 18 before the front settled into trench warfare.

The battle diary of June 19th to July 17th of Uncle Toivo's JR7 III Battalion provides a flavor of the battle. Uncle Toivo's 9th Company also had a diary from July 3rd to July 17th but the entries were short – a reflection of the extreme difficulty of surviving those days. The two short paragraphs are indented in.

For the period from June 20th to July 3rd , I have only included extracts of the more pertinent entries in the III Battalions diary.

Thursday 22.6.44

07:00 Found the battalions doctor, Lieutenant Castren in the brushes near the battalion bandaging site where he had shot himself dead with his pistol.

Saturday 24.6.44

Submitted a recommendation that Lieutenant Voitti be awarded the Mannerheim Cross 2nd grade. (He was not awarded it). xxx

Thursday 29.6.44

Lieutenant Lappalainen back from school, assigned as 9th Company platoon leader.

Saturday 1.7.44

All day heavy artillery fire on Vasikkasaari

Sunday 2.7.44

Two new officers arrive from officer school. Lieutenant Toivonen placed in command of a 9th Company platoon.

Monday 3.7.44

11:00 Own artillery fire set the raft boards stored at Pollakkala's sawmill afire. Huge billows of fire and smoke rose into the sky.

13:50 Nine Russian planes flew over from east to west strafing the church hill and dropping 3 incendiary bombs on Vasikkasaari. Several small fires flared up but were put out quickly.

At night the Russians fired 3 phosphorous shells at Vasikkasaari.

Tuesday 4.7.44

02:00 Five enemy boats rowed towards Ruokosaari from Pollakkala. Our own artillery fired hitting one boat.

04:00 Enemy started an attack against Harju sector. Artillery exceptionally heavy. Enemy planes – 4 to5 planes in formation – flew over 8 different times, bombing and strafing the sector. In the sector over 2,100 various types of shells and 120 bombs landed.

06:15 Regiment commanders order: Battalions' Jaakari platoon and 10th Company to be seconded to II Battalion for usage in counter attack against the middle sub sector of the Harju sector. They left immediately. Enemy aircraft badly harassed us above the Vuoksi River.

09:05 One patrol sent out with one company from the 15th Divisions right side. Sector quiet. The patrol recounted that they got hold of a Russian raft with 7 camouflaged men.

14:00-16:00 10 boats full of men left Ruokosaari. 6 boats and 7 men went back.

16:30 One boat with 2 Russians went from Ruokosaari to Pollakkala.

1 officer and 6 men killed and 2 officers and 14 men wounded (5 severely) in the sector by airplane bombing and strafing. One horse killed and 3 wounded.

Jaakari platoon which had been sent to counter attack Harju took back several bunkers. Russians left 1 captain and 30 men killed as well as 3 machine guns. Companies commander 2nd Lieutenant Hatakka was wounded lightly on the shoulder by shrapnel. Wounded as well were Under Serjeant Ekman and Ala-Risku. Good fighter Corporal Risku fell.

Battalion Mortar company fired in front of the neighboring sector during the battle providing shell cover – altogether 587 shells. Enemy artillery fired exceptionally heavy barrages and planes bombed. Got a direct hit on our artillery bunker from which we had luckily withdrawn our shells. No casualties resulted from the direct hit.

17:00 Enemy started new attack at the same spot as during the night. Artillery fire was not as heavy. Only about 250 various types of shells landed. In addition planes bombed and strafed.

Wednesday 5.7.44

01:00 Enemy attacked the Harju sector for the 3rd time. The enemy artillery fire was now much closer. Own artillery fired 104 shells as cutoff and cover in front of Harju sector. The Jaakari platoon and 10th Company are in the front of Harju sector. Er P25 moved from Harju sector. The Jaakari platoon and 10th Company got permission to return to their own battalion

15:00 Jaakari platoon returned.

14:30 2nd platoon of the 11th Company returned from the bridge head.

18:00 During the exchange the enemy launched a new attack against Harju sector. The returning units crossing over the Vuoksi inevitably took too long as there were not enough boats. Some men tried to swim over the Vuoski. As the Russian artillery fire was heavy several boats got direct hits and sank. Some swimmers drowned in the water from the weight of their gear. Only part of 10th Company succeeded in returning – the majority got left on the bridgehead.

19:10 10th Company ordered to move full company back to the bridge head.

16:00 – 7 enemy T34 tanks at the edge of the houses, firing at the transfer spot over to Vasikkasaari and on to the battalion command spot. Own artillery drove them away.

21:00 Enemy started a smoke screen from the Pollakkola shore plus additional smoke from the north west all the way to the Suokkaa house where the road to Valkjarvi could not be seen. Men were added to the sector with guards positioned all the way to Vesiraja. The smoke lessened by half by the evening and with a southeast wind through the night became quite light.

Thursday 6.7.44

02:35 Enemy got into more trenches, and got in 2 places all the way to the shore. The Regiment commander via phone told Major Olantera regrettably that Captain Rassina's request to withdraw from the bridgehead was denied.

03:35 New order from regiment command to be sent to Captain Raissina - the Kirkomaki-Kauppisenlampi- Harula

area must be kept, as the whole bridgehead defensive station will be cleared of the enemy by the army corps.

Throughout the long day we heard the sound of battle from the Harju sector. Our own counter attack from Wahlbecks direction was proceeding slowly but surely.

10th Company ordered to the bridgehead

14:15 One platoon of 11th Co ordered to reinforce bridgehead

Throughout the long day the enemy harassed the Vasikkasaari transfer point with artillery fire, making it difficult to cross over. Shrapnel wrecked boats so that they became leaky, others sank entirely. Howitzer shells landed on Taaemmaksi, and heavier shells to the rear area. Our own planes bombed the Russian stations. The enemy planes bombed the rear area with exceptionally heavy bombs.

23:45- 00:15 Enemy load speaker echoed on the Vuoksi southern shore. The Russian captives of JR7 interviewed said their forces were doing well.

Friday 7.7.44

09:30 Own fighter planes bombed the bridgehead breakthrough site.

13:00 Enemy started to attack towards Kirkomaki-Harjula

The bridgehead protection commander Major Kuusinen of ErP25 appeared at our battalion command post. He had fled leaving his position when the Russians had gone thru the Hovimaki countryside to the shore. The Kirkkomaki companies had been left in the bag. Part had surrendered, part at the last minute got over the Vuoksi.

The bridgehead defenses now disintegrated on the west side of the Vuoksi River. Now Mustassari and Vasikasaari became the battles' burning point.

The Russians had heavily shelled the Vasikkasaari cross over point and north eastern shore all day. Cross over was impossibly difficult.

15 Russian boats rowed from the Pollakkala shore to Ruokosaari and more were coming.

Saturday 8.7.44

00:05 Started an unbelievably heavy artillery fire at Vasikkasaari and at the Liette meadows

02:00 Enemy artillery fire diminshed a little.

Notice from Lieutenant Voitti via radio: a small number – about a company - of Russians had got hold of Vasikkasaari southern end. Request artillery fire between Vasikkasaari and Ruokkasaari.

02:15 Dispatched Jaakari platoon to launch a counter attack on Vasikkasaari.

02:51 Notice from Vasikkasaari: Own counter attack fully underway . Russians arose on the shore at their own mined location, stepping on many of their own mines. Counter attack continues.

06:10 Own fighters and dive bombers bombing opposite the enemy shore, one bomb dropped on our side, otherwise went well.

10:00-12:30 Regiment commander inspection of the Lower sector on the Eastern bank of Vuoksi.

12:05 Exceptionally heavy enemy howitzer barrage at Vasikkasaari.

12:25- 13:45 Notice from Vasikkasaari that every 15 minutes Russian boats were rowing to Ruokkosaari.

In between shelling a couple of Russian boats tried to reach Vasikkasaari shore but were rebuffed. Three Russians were seen swimming back to Ruokkosaari.

14:52 On Ruokkosaari north western side 20 Russians digging.

18:30 Started a counter attack against Vasikkasaari south-east shore led by Lieutenant Jokisen along with Jaakari platoon and 11th Company 2nd platoon. Made an opening in the fields where the men moved thru and onto the enemy. The enemy nonetheless made an immediate counter attack from the left onto the back of its own forces, whereupon we had to pull back. Lieutenant Joikinen fell and 9 men were wounded.

At the same time the enemy with a couple of boats made a landing on Mustasaari. It was stopped, the enemy losing 10 casualties. Our own forces fired and tackled the Russians in the reed beds.

22:00 Lieutenant ? and 2nd Lieutenant Ryynanen arrived at the battalion headquarters from the home front. The afore-mentioned was placed in command of the 11th Company and 2nd Lieutenant Ryyanen to lead the Jaakari platoon.

The lively activity of the Russians continued on Ruokkosaari for the whole evening.

20:00 ½ of the 11th Company was sent to Vasikkasaari.

22:00 Order for 10th Company to leave their current stations at Niemela house to the 2nd platoon of 6th Company, and go to Vasikkasaari

Company 9 Sotapaivkirja: 6-8.7.44

Russian started a heavy artillery barrage against the island. And attacked Vaasikasaari and were successful in reaching the shore of the island. Aerial bombing was harsh. Russians progressively gained a larger foothold on the island.

Sunday 9.7.44

05:45 -06:10 Often 10 enemy planes bombed the islands and occasionally the whole sector.

Russians had crossed over secretly from the Ayrapaa sawmill. Noticed many boats glistening in the water. At the same time boats had been pushed into the water by Lammasniemi and the church.

06:48 Notice by radio from Vasikkasaari: Russians found on the north shore of Vasikkasaari. Senior Serjeant Koljonen withdrawing his squad from the north side of the island.

Requested help from the regiment for a counter attack on the Lower sector. At 06:55 sent one company from II Battalion which with the 10th Company pushed the enemy to the Niemila – Juva line

Phone connection to Regiment cut.

07:00 Unable to contact Regiment with radio for an hour.

07:10 Contact with Regiment via II Battalion phone route.

Russians attacking Vasikkasaari from the south east and north and at the same time trying to gain Mustasaari.

10:33 Counter attack platoon under 2nd Lieutenant Antoni to move along the shore of Liette meadows to the west to the old howitzer firing station area, where the Russians are to be cleared out, and join with our own forces in the area of the Juvo house.

10:35 Radio contact with Lieutenant Voitti: Russians wading into the southeastern shore of Vasikkasaari.

11:30 Fierce fight on Vasikkasaari against the Russian advances. Killed many of them but more keep coming.

Got one captive but in bringing him back he fell. From him we nonetheless had found that there were 3 divisions attacking us.

11:30 Sent 10 men to Vasikkasaari, and with them, ammunition

12:00 Own bombers bombing the Church, the ridge and Ruokkosaari. Unbelievable fire and dust clouds flew into the air.

12:30 Notice from Vasikkasaari: 2ⁿᵈ Lieutenant Antoni arrived at Vasikkasaari; No enemy found on the northern part of island.

13:26 Notice from Vasikkasaari: Entire strength of island at this moment is 45 men. Help requested.

Entire remains of 10ᵗʰ Company have already been ordered to move to the island – likewise, the remains of 11ᵗʰ Company have received an order to move to the island.

The left Lower Sector opposite the island was left in the care of another battalion. After, in the evening, Group Sudblads' men were located along the entire shore.

20:30 Brought captives to Battalion Headquarters whom the 10ᵗʰ Company men had captured at the Niemela house area during the counter attack.

23:50 Russians setting smoke screen behind the shore road . A lot of smoke is covering a wide area. The wind is from the south east and is blowing the smoke towards Mustasaari and Vasikkasaari. By 21:10 the whole island was hidden by smoke. Able to see 50 meters at the most.

Russians attacking Vasikkasaari continuously, but the attacks have been repulsed. Russians are incurring large casualties

Monday 10.7.44

Regimental Headquarters informed that according to intercepted radio signals, a Russian attack should begin at 12:00 or at 13:00 at the latest.

12:45 All of Ruokkosaari hidden by smoke.

13:00 Enemy (10ᵗʰ Division of 115ᵗʰ AK) begins fierce attack at southeastern Vasikkasaari from the bridge head area. Our few men could not keep their own. The Russians got through in a short time to the actual island command post. Lieutenant Voitti was able to send a short radio message that the Russians have made a break through. At the same time said he was going to organize a counter attack. After this we heard nothing more.

14:50 Lieutenant Voitti with some men arrived at battalion headquarters from the island.

They had to leave the island as quickly as possible by whatever means they could. There was no possibility to save the members of 1ˢᵗ platoon on Mustasaari, Serjeant Kapin's squad, or the artillery fire director. Moving from Mustasaari and Vasikkasaari in the day light was impossible as the Russians could fire on the island from all directions. All of the Mustasaari force and the parts of the Vasikkasaari force who for whatever

reason - were wounded or did not know how to swim - were left as Russian captives. Likewise all the equipment was left on the island.

After this the entire battalion gathered at the barracks area at Orvankyla. Only the Mortar Company was seconded the next day to Group Sundbuld.

At Orvakyla the companies were able to rest and clean themselves and get new clothes. 32 replacements were received.

Company 9 Sotapaivakirja: 9.7 – 10.7.44

Russians improved their positions and we had to withdraw completely from the island, some by swimming or by boat. Several men were left on Mustasaari and Vasikkasaari among them Lieutenant Lappalainen and Senior Sergeant Kippia plus others.

In the evening we arrived at Orvakyla, where we bivouacked.

When we arrived in the village the Battalion Commander immediately addressed us - in which he praised and reproached us. Our strength was small, only around 50 men.

The 32 day campaign of fierce battles and fighting retreats had come to an end. Finland had survived but less than 25% of Uncle Toivo's 9ᵗʰ Company soldiers had.

The remainder of July was uneventful (relatively speaking) as highlights from the remainder of their company journal indicates:

10.7.44 Got re-equipped. Cleaned our guns and at the end of the day had a sauna and rested.

11.7.44 Training and cleanup. 28 replacements, 1904 age group - 40 year olds ! In the evening moved to the edge of the village to live in tents.

12.7.44 24 replacements, 1925 age group -19 year olds ! Also 2 new officers – Lieutenant Tuomola and Lieutenant Janhunen. Lieutenant Tuomola was placed in command of 9th Company.

13.7.44 Organized company affairs; Regiment commander review and distribution of medals; Started to march to the front lines; Arrived at 22:15 at Hiidenkankalla where we bivouacked in tents and shrapnel shelters.

14.7.44 Field work and housing improvement; No action – wounded returning.

18.7.44 Marched to Ayrapaa-Orvankyla road and set up fox holes about 8 kilometers from Ayrapaa.

19.7.44 Seven replacements, age group 1902 – 42 year olds !!

20.7.44 More wounded returning from hospital.

21.7.44 Under Serjeant Myntti, Staff Serjeant Parkkonen and deserter Private Lahtinen sentenced to 5 ¼ years.

30-31.44 Russian artillery fire and patrols. A lot of men wounded by shrapnel.

9th Company Sotapaivakirja ends

While the 9th Company was sent back to the lines and suffered further casualties later in July, those losses were minimal compared to their losses from June 9th to July 10th. The company had been at full strength on June 9th – 140 plus men, and had replaced many during the 32 day campaign. So the Company had lost over 100% of its' strength – indeed already by the last day of the Battle of Siiranmaki the Battalion had lost all their company officers.

The 9th Company had participated in two of the largest battles during the Continuation War – Siiranmaki and Ayrapaa/Vuosalmi. They had sacrificed all and played a key part in stopping Russia's assault and had helped save Finland. Yes, some of them had fled, and a few had deserted.

I wonder what Uncle Toivo, a grizzled veteran of the entire Winter War and the Continuation War, thought of the new 19 year old and 40 plus year old replacements. And even more of the officers fresh out of school who were now supposedly to lead them. And like all Finnish soldiers, I don't think he thought highly of the senior officers who fed them as cannon fodder from their safe posts behind the front lines – but then – *"Generals die at home in their beds"*.

But I was surprised by the phrase in the 9th Companies sotapaivakirja when after the valiant, physically and mentally exhausted remnants of the company struggled into battalion headquarters, the battalion commander "kiitti ja moitti them " (praised and criticized). I even went to the lengths of asking my cousin whether I had got the meaning correct. The reply was:

Hei again Kalle:

I thought about "kiitti ja moitti ", so -

Finns are independent and stubborn people. In difficult positions we do not obey orders if we think we know a better way to resolve problems. So a wise commander says kiitos and formally moitti- because of disciplinary reasons. As simple as that !

We Finns are strange people! You have been for too long in Canada!!! :-)

The Battle of Ihantala
&
Our Kavantsaari Home

CHAPTER 22

The Battle of Ihantala & Our Kavantsaari Home

The battle of Ihantala occurred in our church village just seven kilometers from our farm.

It was part of the Tali-Ihantala battle where the Russian's attacked past the eastern edge of Viipuri north through Tali to Ihantala.

The Tali- Ihantala battle was the largest battle ever in the Nordic countries. The battle involved 50,000 Finnish and 150,000 Russian soldiers. At Ihantala the Finnish forces stopped the Russian advance into Finland and saved the country. The Russians knew that if they won, they could sweep into Finland unhindered. The Finnish forces knew that losing would mean the loss of their country.

Thanks to the "sisu" of its' soldiers at Ihantala, Finland is celebrating its' 100th anniversary this year.

To quote the PBS documentary Fire and Ice:

This was the largest battle ever fought in the Nordic region of the world and was the key moment of the war for Finland. The battle began on June 25, with the Soviet forces attacking the Finnish 3rd Brigade stationed between Suomenvedenpohja and Lake Kärstilänjärvi.

The losses on both sides of this opening stage of the battle were horrific and were to set the tone for the entire battle. The fighting in the Tali-Ihantala region was as fierce as that seen on any front in World War II.

The battle was contained within an area of only 10 square kilometers, but this area was filled with troops, tanks, artillery, and the sky above had hundreds of planes engaged in the fighting.

From June 25 until July 9 the Finnish and Soviet forces battled for the key positions, with both Armies doing their best to break the backs of their opponents. By July 9 the Soviet advance had been stopped and was unable to regroup and advance further.

The Russians broke through Tali on June 25th and advanced forward to Portinhoikka, and from thence to Ihantala. Another smaller arm of the Russian force swung further westwards towards Juustila and the Saima Canal.

The battle at Ihantala itself commenced in full force on July 1st, although some Russian forces were already a kilometer south of Ihantala on June 25th. It continued without let up until July 10th.

Forces

The Tali – Ihantala battle pitted 50,000 Finnish soldiers and 4,000 German troops, commanded by Lieutenant General T Laatikainen of the IV Army Corps, against a 150,000 strong Russian force. The Finnish infantry was supported by a strong artillery force (21 batteries), a tank division (43 "tanks"), and 66 planes. As well the Finnish forces were augmented by 4,000 German troops and a German fighter/ bomber detachment.

- At the start of the battle on the 25th Finland had 2 infantry divisions at Tali-Ihantala – the 18th and the 4th ; and Lagus' Panzer Division . These were reinforced by the 11th Division on June 27th,and on July 1st by the 35th Regiment of the 6th Division.

- The Lagus Panzer Division consisted of a tank brigade (Osasto Bjorkman), and a Jaakari brigade (JPr 1) as well as field artillery. They had 23 tanks and 20 assault gun tanks. (Assault guns were similar to tanks but with light armour and often without turrets. They had a large gun and were used to support infantry assaults as opposed to tank to tank battles. Often they also had an anti tank gun).

- The divisions' tanks and particularly the Jaakari infantry were in the forefront of the counter attacks against the Russian forces from June 25th to July 1st. The Jaakari infantry fought with the 18th and 11th Divisions. The tank task force of Osasto Bjorkman supported the 4th Division on the north east side of Tali – Ihantala.

- The Panzer Division however did not take part in the battle of Ihantala. They were dispatched to help the Finnish forces at the battle of Ayrapaa / Vuosalmi. At Ihantala only Russian tanks were to be seen – and far too many of them.

- Germany also allocated forces to the battle – an Infantry Division, an assault Gun Battalion, and a fighter plane detachment.

- The 4,000 German soldiers consisted of the German 122nd Infantry Division, and the 304th Assault Gun Battalion. The 122nd Infantry Division saw limited action while the German 304th Assault Gun Battalion only engaged briefly before it moved to Vuosalmi with the Finnish Panzer Division. It had 26 assault gun tanks.

- The German fighter plane detachment, however, was an important addition. The 80 Stuka and Focke Wulf fighter/ bombers of Lufwaffe Gefechtsverband Kuhlmey played a key role in the battle. As well as downing Russian planes, the Stuka dive bombers were instrumental in destroying tanks. Together with the Finnish 4th Air Regiment (Le R4) they flew 1,020 flights and dropped 765 tons of explosives (Two thirds by the Luffwaffe). The German forces lost 33 planes, and the Finns 12. Although the German and Finnish air wings were only together for a month they developed a strong camaraderie based on mutual respect and understanding.

- The Russian forces at Tali Ihantala were 150,000 strong. When the battle reached its' peak the Russian 108th AK (Lt General Michael Tikonov), 109th AK (Lieutenant General I. Alfyorov), 110th AK (Major General Afansi Gryaznov) and the 30th Guards Rifle Corps (Lieutenant General Nicholas Simonyak) were engaged. They were part of the 21st Army of Colonel General D.N. Gusvev.

- The infantry soldiers were supported by a large armoured division, artillery brigades, and a large air force of bombers and fighter planes. The Russians had 280 tanks and 80 assault gun "tanks", of which they lost 215. They had so many artillery and howitzer batteries that no one has itemized them. Of the 1500 planes of the Russian 13th Air Army on the Kannas some 800 bombers and fighter planes saw action at Tali Ihantala. Huge 200 foot bomb craters can still be seen today at Ihantala. 415 of the Russian planes were downed.

- The Russian bombers pounded the Finnish forces daily. While the Russian forces dominated the skies the Finnish and German fighter planes downed 270 Russian planes during the Kannas assault and a significant number of the tanks. During the Tali Ihantala Battle the German Luftwaffe downed 30 Russian planes. Additional Russian planes were downed by artillery and 115 by Finnish anti aircraft fire – a total of 416 planes.

- The battle was a firestorm of constant explosions from bombs, artillery shells, tanks projectiles, and dive bombers runs. The Finnish artillery had 21 batteries with approximately 180 guns. The Finnish artillery was exceptionally effective as they invented a means of coordinating the simultaneous fire of multiple batteries against one target.

- On July 3rd the Finnish artillery fired over 11,000 shells – the Russians an estimated 15,000 shells – all in an area of less than 10 square kilometers. At the start of an attack on July 3rd, the Russian artillery fired 4,000 shells in 2 minutes using 250 guns.

- Over the duration of the battle the Finnish army fired 87,000 shells and used 2,600,000 kilograms of explosives – The Russians undoubtedly at least double that amount.

Battle Sequence

Before the battle started the Finnish IV AK had 3 divisions in the sector from Kavantsaari to Juustila – the 4th Division near Kavantsaari; the 18th Division in the centre at Ihantala; and the 17th Division and the 3rd Brigade by Juustila and the Saima Canal. The 3rd Division of Pajari was protecting the west bank of the Vuoksi River 20 kilometers away. That area however was not involved in the Tali-Ihantala battle.

Opposing them south of Tali was the 109th AK of Lieutenant General Alfyorov; and, south of Juustila, divisions of the 108th AK of Lieutenant General Tikhonov.

- On June 25th the Russian forces of 109AK and 30 KaAK, 5 divisions strong, attacked Tali. They overran the defenses of the 18th and 4th Divisions and moved to Portinhoikka, and momentarily reached Juustila.

- On June 26th the Lagus Panzer Division arrived. Its' Jaakari Brigade and one of its' tank battalions counter attacked together with the 4th and 18th Divisions, taking some of the ground back. However part of a Russian division was able to advance to Kaatera just a few kilometers south of Ihantala.

- On June 27th, joined by the newly arrived 11th Division of Colonel Hesikanen, the Jaakari Brigade was able to recapture Portinhoikka and push east to Kuusela and Aniskela. JR6 and JR48 of the 18th Division remained in the fray. JR48 was positioned at Ihantala.

- The 4th Division augmented by the armoured group of Osasto Bjorkman started to push towards Kuusela/Anoselka from the east. On the 27th the

Russian forces were being squeezed even though Russia now had 7 divisions in the battle.

- At Juustila the 3rd Brigade held off newly arrived Russian 108th AK forces.

- On June 28th the attack against the Russians continued see sawing back and forth - the Russians losing ground in some areas but able once again to make a narrow advance to Vakkila and Kaatera south of Ihantala. JR12 of the 6th Division arrived attacking aggressively south from Ihantala.

- On June 29th although a Panzer tank company finally joined the fight, the Russian forces started to slowly push back. Now the Russian forces comprised 11 divisions.

- On June 30th and July 1st the Russian forces broke through. The Finnish 35th Regiment of the 6th Division arrived from the Maaselka front (Uncle Kauko's old regiment).

- General Lagus' armoured division withdrew from the western front, the loss of the Jaakari Brigade leaving a particularly large hole.

- On the 4th Division sector, the Osasto Bjorkman tank brigade withdrew. The 4th Division infantry withdrew to south of Kaipola – just a couple of kilometres from our Kavantsaari farm.

- The 6th Division was now protecting the entire defensive line from Ihantala to just east of Juustila. JR50 of the 11th Division and JR6 of the 18th Division remained on the battleground.

- Of note the 3rd Brigade, although now pushed back to a peninsula south of the Saima Canal lakes, continued to hold out against 4 Russian divisions.

- From July 1st to July 10th, JR25 of the 4th Division continued to hold Kaipola.

- One division, the newly arrived 6th Division regiments JR35 and JR12, held the main Russian assault at bay on a 3 kilometer line from Ihantala to Tahtela.

- Through the majority of the battle, the third battalion of JR35 and the second battalion of JR12 were stationed on the Ihantala hilltop. The third battalion of JR12 was on the east side of the road by the old church. The other battalions were spread out over 3 kilometers west from the Ihantala hilltop to Tahtela:

- I/JR35 at Pyorakangas,
- I/JR12 at Vakkila, and
- II/ JR35 at Tahtela – Marjamaki.

There were no bunkers, concrete pill boxes nor defensive trenches. The only defenses were those provided by nature – bush, rocky hills, huge boulders, lakes, rivers, and swamps.

The last defensive lines were on the Ihantala church hill. Here the Finnish soldiers dug fox holes in the ground and sheltered behind boulders. The situation was so dire that trenches had to be dug through the grave yard – the grave yard where great grandmother Rakas Mummo Tiainen rested and Uncle Erkki had been buried two years earlier.

- The Pioneers played an important role in the battle – setting up rudimentary defenses, building mine fields, and blowing up bridges and roads in front of the advancing Russian forces.
- As well they played anti tank combat roles. On the 28th/29th vanguard Russian armoured columns were able to make a break through to Kaateri / Vakkila south of Ihantala. The defending Finnish JR48 and JR6 regiments had been decimated. When all seemed lost Lieutenant Colonel Inkinen of JR6 gathered groups of Pioneer anti-tank destroyer teams and the assault tanks in the area, and forced the Russian vanguard back to the Portinhoikka area. Units of the Pion P14 pioneer battalion were part of the assault. Lieutenant Veiho Touminen of Pion P14 was killed at Portinhiokka on the 29th.
- The Ihantala hill top is approached from Viipuri across an open field. A stream cuts across the meadow. A bridge spans the river.
- On June 30th with the Russian infantry and tanks approaching, a Finnish Pioneer squad tried to blow up the bridge but were killed. On the next day, July 1st, the Finnish artillery tried desparately to blow it up. After many attempts they were able to hit the

bridge twice but the shells did not explode. With only a few shells left, the gun battery was finally able to blow it up with a direct hit. With the hit they also destroyed three Russian heavy tanks.

- The river is really only big stream, and should have not been a deterent to the tanks. Fortunately the stream has large swampy banks. The area is quaymire. Several Russsian tanks tried to cross but sank into the mud. Certainly a Russian combat engineering company could have built a bridge, but that would have been impossible given the relentless Finnish artillery fire.
- So the Russian tanks could not advance to the Ihantala hill top, thus adding another factor to the miraculous Ihantala defense.
- On the 30th a strong assault by Russian tanks almost broke through along the road. The Finnish artillery batteries were able to concentrate their salvos and stopped the advance. During 1944 the Finnish artillery headquarters team of the legendary artillery commander Lieutenant General V. P. Nenonen, were able to develop a technique which allowed it to coordinate and concentrate the fire of multiple batteries. This revolutionary technical break through was a major help through out the battle.
- The following day - on July 1st just 2 minutes before the Russian attack the entire air force of LeR4 and

81 planes of Kuhley Detachment hit the Russian forces - a significant deterrent to the Russian attack.

- Over the next eight days the 6th Division infantry held out - greatly assisted by their artillery and the Finnish and German air force – and the sisu of the infantry man in the fox hole.

The attack stopped on July 10th – the Finnish resistence had been too fierce and the Russian losses too great. Russia transferred its' attention to capturing Berlin and supporting the Allied invasion. Overcoming the little Finnish lion was too time consunimg and costly.

The Cost

The Finnish forces suffered 8,800 casualties (1,350 dead, 1,100 missing and 6,350 wounded). On the deadliest day at Ihantala itself – July 2nd - the Finnish IV AK suffered 800 casualties.

JR12 and JR35 had been responsible for holding Ihantala.

When I was in Nouisianen visting with my Uncle Toivo's cousins (Uncle Toivo settled there after the war), I received the commemorative Nousiasisten Sotaveteraaninen book from my cousins. I notice that 31 soldiers from Nousianinen fought with JR35 at Ihantala. One was killed and four were wounded in the battle.

I also have the veterans' books for Simo and Kemijarvi. Ninety eight soldiers from Simo, my witch ancestral home fought at Ihantala. The small Simo parish seems to have had a strong warrior strain. It fielded 731 soldiers. Thirty percent of them were either NCOs (159) or Officers (56). The officers included a Colonel, a Major and three Captains. Close to 10% of the force made the ultimate sacrifice for Finland's freedom.

The home parish for JR12 was Kemijarvi, where father was. When I was in Kemijarvi in 2012, I purchased the veterans' book – Isamaan Vapauden Puolesta (For the Freedom of our Fatherland). Reviewing it now I see that 44 Kemijarvi soldiers fell at Ihantala. Half of the deaths record the date of death as being during the Ihantala battle, but do not specify Ihantala, only noting "jaannyt kentalle -left on the battlefield". Their bodies had either been blown to bits or left on the Russian side of the lines. The fallen were of all ranks - soldiers, corporals, serjeants, lieutenants; and, even a Lieutenant Colonel - Eero Leppanen the commander of JR12's second battalion.

During much of the Jatkosota, few senior officers were killed. Ihantala was different. Among the fallen were Majors, Colonels and even a General. Major General Einar Vihma the commander of the 6th Division died at the Ihantala front lines on August 5th. He was revered by his men as a true front line officer – not one who led from behind from a safe head quarters location. Among the stories attributed to him is that during the heat of the battle he drove up to his mens' positions in his black military Buick personally delivering and handing out Panzerfaust anti-tank guns that had just been received.

For the Finnish soldiers at Ihantala there is a simple plaque on a large boulder on the Ihantala hill top (photo at the start of this chapter). There is also a sankari hauta for the sons of Ihantala (photo earlier in this chapter). Two Ihantala brothers who died for their country were Arvo (almost 21) and Viljo Iivonen (age 22). They were killed within a week of one another in August – Arvo on 17.8.44 and Viljo on 12.8.44. I asked cousin Sirkka if she knew them. Sirkka said:

They were neighbours of ours from across the field.

I remember how thrilled I was when the handsome Arvo danced with me at a party when I was a young girl.

Stm. *Arvo Ahti Olavi Iivonen*
s. 30. 8. -23. † 17. 8. -44.
Kavantjärvi.

Over 5,000 Russians died, and 15,000 were wounded during the Tali-Ihantala battle.

There is a monument for the Russian dead – located at Portinhoikka. When I was driving from Viipuri to Ihantala and Kavantsaari in 2012 and in 2016, I stopped both times at the memorial. It is large and impressive, yet unpretentious.

On the walls of the memorial there are bronze plaques with the names of all the Russian dead. A few plaques were blank or partially filled. I asked our guide and driver Valeri why. He said they had been left blank so that the names of the soldiers whose bodies were discovered after the monument was built could be added. Even today a few are being found.

Veterans' Remembrances

A JR35 Veteran from Nousiainen

In his later years Eeri Hyrkko of Nousiainen who served in the 11th company of JR35 during the Ihantala Battle provided a first hand account of the battle. He was an under serjeant - the leader of an anti tank squad. He was 21 years old when he was in the Ihantala battle.

"On June 18th we were in Maaselka. We got orders to that we were moving out and that we should only pack the essentials and to send the rest home. We knew what that portended. And move out we did. The next day we started the 240 kilometer march to the Suojarvi railway station. There we were quickly loaded onto the train. It went non stop to Jaaski where we got off the train and marched to Ihantala.

Throughout the entire time, howitzer shells exploded continuously. I remember getting a feeling that, "I won't get out of this alive. It's not possible". We had no way of knowing when it would end.

At night the artillery fire and bombing was weaker but still continuous. The rest of the time it was a continuous wall of sound, so intense that we couldn't determine individual explosions.

My company, the 11th, were stationed on the Ihantala church hill. We threw back all the enemy attacks. The Russians were never able to reach our trenches.

For five days we had no sleep. Of course we periodically dozed off but only for some seconds before the explosion of a howitzer shell nearby woke us up. No sleep was possible. As a group leader, at night when it was a bit quieter I walked among my men, waking anyone who had dropped off. One could not help

it as sleep overtook the mind. We were on duty for five days before we were relieved. After five days without any sleep our eyes felt like they had sticks stuck in them. They were all red from no sleep. But young men can withstand a lot when the situation is truly desperate.

Why were we able to stop the Russians ? Of course there was the strong artillery and Stuka support. Everything worked well - communications and provisioning -all that was excellent. But often what is forgotten in the media accounts is the infantry soldier in the foxhole. For example in the Ake Lindman film Tali-Ihnatala 1944 -they are not shown.

There came a realization to all of us that if we withdrew from here then Finland would perish. There arose in everyone a determination that:

"From here we will not leave – and leave we did not".

There was a Serjeant, Serjeant Uuni from Viiipuri, who went from man to man saying; "Rest easy, we will hold". He made a large mark upon the unit as he provided all of us with confidence. He travelled through the whole company. He undertook it upon himself to do so. And that was his most important life task as he fell later in August.

By mid July things got quieter. We just waited for what would happen next, above all the arrival of peace. And I've often said that,

"When peace came it was as great an event as my wedding, or the birth of my children. The coming of peace is one the most important events in my life. I am thankful that I survived, and survived unwounded."

JR35 was Uncle Kauko's original unit. When it was transferred from the Maaselka front to Ihantala to reinforce the IV AK complement Uncle Kauko was with the II AK Headquaters Unit. As such he was still on the Ladoga front.

My cousin Arto, who lives in Nousianen knew Eeri Hyrkko. A masseuse, he gave Eeri and other veterans free massages in appreciation of their service. Arto said most of them never shared their experiences – the war was far too traumatic and personal.

Perhaps Eeri was one of the ones who did. He was proud of his regiment and made himself available to speak about it quoting that: *"Our regiment's contribution has been overlooked as no one in the regiment undertook to write about it."* As I am sure is the case for many other units.

Uncle Arvo

Uncle Arvo was there (3rd from left in photo below). Fortunately his unit played primarily a defense fortification and support role. Lieutenant Kaarlo Mietteinen, the leader of the Pioneer Jaakari platoon to which Uncle Arvo belonged, records in the Pion P14 book that:

The P 14 battalion constructed needed defensive works without let up – work on the locks and tank obstructions in Portihoika and Ihantala. Lieutenant Veiho Touminen, who led the building of the tank defenses, was killed by an enemy bullet on June 29, 1944 at Portinhoikka.

After Lieutenant Tuominen fell, the tank defense squad became part of the Jääkarijouku and I had to become familiar with the Portinhoikka and Ihantala front line defenses [Uncle Arvo of course was already familiar with area as it was part of his Kavantsaari home area].

In early July we were stationed north of Ihantala. Our Jääkarijouku of 32 men was ordered to stop any advancing Russian tanks with our Panzerfaust tank guns. We had heard that there could be about 40 Russian tanks. They never appeared which is probably why we are still alive to tell these tales.

Unlike great grandmother "Rakas Mummo" and Uncle Erkki whose graves in the Ihantala cemetery were blown to bits, Uncle Arvo survived. He is in the front row 3rd from the left in the photo on the previous page of the Jaakarijoukkue

Jääkärijoukkue / Pion P 14 (Miettinen) kesällä 1944.

squad from the Pion P 14 book. Now my cousin Sirkka and I were not quite sure whether that was Arvo. I showed the photo to my wife and my younger son Mike. Without prompting they said, "Gee he looks a lot like Doug" –our other son. So yes, it is Arvo.

After the Battle - An Ihantala Son Returns Home

Heimo Vakkilainen, a young soldier recounted his return to his home village on September 19, 1944.

"After the peace was declared, I got approval for day leave to go visit my home. After riding my bike over many kilometers, turns, and detours, I arrived at the Ihantala hill. The sight was disheartening. The giant pines on the Ihantala hilltop were now just broken tree trunks. The road was full of huge bomb and shell craters. The road side was full of wreckage from the battle. Here and there, were burnt out tanks. All the houses and buildings on the Ihantala hilltop were mere torched and ruined remnants of the battle.

At the hilltop cross roads there was an officers' guard post manned by a lieutenant, 2nd lieutenant, and sergeant. I asked for permission to go visit the sankari hauta. There my brother Niilo Vakkilainen and my brother in law Keijo Kekki were buried. The reply was curt: "Not one step forwards from here, the ground is full of mines and unexploded shells." I looked down from the Ihantala hill top towards a Russian campfire beside the Pekari Brook bridge, close to the old milk pick up stand. The Russians were cooking something.

I started towards our home – the guards warning me harshly that I should be careful where I stepped.

The trees in our yard had been shot to smithereens, large pits were everywhere. Depressing - dispiriting. The riddled burnt, metal roof leaned on the ruins of our house. Only a small corner remained of our new barn. A ghastly battle trench cut across the field towards Lake Ihantala and the boat slip, from whence one could get to the Hoviniemi point. After taking

in the scene for a short sad while, I returned back to Ihantala hill top.

It was a cloudy fall day and night was already drawing near. My bike did not have a lamp which I could use to light my way back to my companies encampment. I started back on the same route, but stopped one more time near the Aspisen home. There it was - the small path which ran from the Imatra road along the edge of our fields to the Antrea road. I left my bike beside the road and walked along by my battle pitted home fields. When I had been home on leave in May I had disced the fields and planted them with wheat. In the parts of the field that had survived the maelstrom of the battle, the wheat waved ripe and beckoning - waiting to be harvested - an opportunity that I would never have.

I went into a daze... suddenly I awoke, startled ... it wasn't raining, but somehow the corners of eyes were wet.

I returned to my bike and hurried back to my companies Kanaoja bivouac. There I learned that the older soldiers were to be disbanded home, while us younger troops were being sent north. We were to push the Germans out of Finland."

My "Return"

For me, my visit to Ihantala was almost as emotional as my return to Kavantsaari.

Now, seven decades later, everything was green and quiet. But nothing was left of our families' old church village. The scars of war had almost disappeared- but were still evident. Nothing was left of the old church except the church steps. The sankari hauta right beside the church was nicely enclosed and had an inscription on a big boulder – but there were no crosses or granite markers on the graves of Ihantalas' sons. The grave yard across the road where my Uncle Erkki and great grandmother were buried, and where the soldiers had dug trenches through graves, was a soft carpet of green – but no monuments nor crosses indicated who had been buried where...

Knowing the history of the battle, I could not help but be moved as I stood on the hilltop by the Finnish Memorial Boulder looking across the fields towards Viipuri Road– reminded further of the reality of it by a rusted helmet, artillery shell cases, and schrapnel resting by the boulder.

My cousin pointed down to the river from the hill top, saying to me: "There is the stream where the Russian attack stalled. One of the veterans from Nousiainen whom I have been treating told me to look for it. He was there that day and remembers all too well the terror of the moment."

The stream looked small, and the grassy banks benign. But huge it was for Finland.

Our Kavantsaari Home

Our Kavantsaari home was six kilometers from the Ihantala church yard. The Ihantala church was our families' church.

Kavantsaari village was 3 kilometers away. The Thesleff manor served as the headquarters for Lieutenant General Laatikainen and the IV AK during the battle.

Our fields were manned by Er P1 who moved in as soon as our family left. Er P1 was from Kristiinankaupunki - childhood home of my fathers' grandmother Maria Hellmann. She had been buried in the Viipuri Swedish German cemetery – undoubtedly now pitted from Russian bombs and artillery shells.

By July 6th the Russian 72nd Division (12,000 men) was on the western side of Pyrosaari just south of Kaipola. Defending the location was critical because if the Russian were able to break through they would reach Kavantsaari and the railroad and road north. As well they would be in a position to attack Ihantala from the rear.

By July 10th , JR5 of the 4th Division was on our farm. They dug in fortifications on the western edge of the farm by the small grassy Kapiolalahti lake.

JR25 of the 4th Division was on the other side of grassy lake just south of Kaipola village. The 22nd Finnish heavy artillery battery was positioned there. It had four 105 K/29 canons (14.4 km) and eight 152 H/38 (12 km) howitzers. The guns were pointed west, towards the Russian 168th Division across the small inlet.

Quite different from when Uncle Erkki was shooting ducks for dinner as they winged back from Kaipola – now it was death that was winging over the inlet.

There was a first aid site (JSP) at our farm. During the battle that started ten days after our family left, the first aid station was in full use. Hopefully not as fully utilized as the one a JR 35 antitank man at the Ihantala battle commented about:

I was in the JSP one evening as I was hit in the head with some shrapnel. It was a tough spot. The pastor greeted the dying on one side while the doctors treated the wounded on the other side.

Cousin Sirkka commented that:

The brother of one of our friends was at the first aid tent near the farm during the battle of Ihantala. He says he saw a lean black dog running around – barking at intruders. It was our dog.

When we fled the farm on June 20th the Kavantsaari road was full of Finnish tanks and trucks moving through towards their battle locations. Martti's beloved one year old dog Halli got scared by all the noise and escaped back to the farm.

It was my brother Marttis regret all his life that he had not been able to save his darling pet.

PART IX

The Home Front during The Summer of '44

The Home Front During Summer '44

The summer assault of 1944 was a difficult time for the family on the home front.

At that point mother and father had left Lapland and were in Kausala near Kouvola in south central Finland. Father was responsible for the railway track from Kouvala to Riihimaki.

For Cousin Sirkka, it was a traumatic time. Once more she and all the family had to leave the Kavantsaari home. Once more they were on the refugee trail.

For three weeks they travelled on foot and horse cart driving the cattle before them to Siuro, leaving Karjala forever.

Together
at
A New Railway Posting

CHAPTER 23

Together at a New Railway Posting

In November 1943 dad and the family returned to Kausala in Southern Finland. He was responsible for the railway track between Riihimaki and Kouvola (a 140 kilomtre stretch). Kouvola was the junction of the main tracks from Central / Western Finland and northern Finland to Viipuri and the east. The western Riihimaki end was the junction of the track to Helsinki and further west to Tampere and Turku.

The track was a critical supply route to the front. As such it was subject to Russian bombing runs, and required frequent repair. Anti-aircraft placements were positioned at major locations and an armored anti-aircraft car was added to some of the trains. I wonder if dad once more commanded a panzer car like he did in the Winter War.

The family stayed in Kausala until after my brother George was born there on September 5, 1944. Kausala was two stops west of Kouvola – about 20 kilometres.

They lived in the village. My sister Tellervo said *there was a large farm nearby whose owner was very friendly. I went there often and always ended up getting food treats. Indeed the farmer often gave me bread and milk to take home. Food was rationed due to the war, so any additional food was appreciated.*

Dad, as mentioned, was maintaining the rail road:

Once when he was pumping down the track with his veloped – 3 wheeled hand pumped railway car - with Terttu and Tellervo they almost got run over by a train. At the last minute they jumped off the veloped and he was able to throw the veloped off the track

(Dad was a very powerful man but in this case I think a rush of adrenalin helped). Dad knew all the train schedules but this time a train was coming from both directions on the double track.

The one on their track was a special train bringing back the fallen soldiers' bodies from the front. Tellervo to this day remembers the bodies stacked up like cordwood on the railway cars.

Grandmother Valencia Tuira

Fathers mother Grandmother Valencia Tuira had moved back to Viipuri some months after Viipuri was liberated. During the Continuation War 260,000 or 70% of the displaced population came back to Karjala – including both sides of our family – the Öhmans and grandmother Tuira.

In the case of Viipuri, starting in October 1941, 28,000 of Viipuri's population progressively returned to resettle and rebuild the city. Viipuri was in ruins.

My sister Terttu recalls visiting grandma there. Terttu, being the oldest, was able to travel a bit. Grandmother lived in a concrete apartment building as her former home had been destroyed. During the Talvisota, Viipuri was almost leveled - nearly 12,000 bombs along with 150,000 rounds of heavy artillery rained down on that lovely, late medieval city

In June 1944 everyone had to flee Viipuri when Russia started to advance on Viipuri. Dad said his mother was glad to escape alive. Grandmother was able to get a train back to central Finland. Of course she could only bring back a few suitcases. What little she had accumulated in the interim years was left behind. She once more settled in Hameenlahti near her younger son Yrjo.

Aunt Hilda

Aunt Hilda and Uncle Aatu had not gone back to Viipuri and were living in Jyvaskyla. When the attack occured cousin Anna Liisa recounts that:

> I was on a summer student trip in Ahvenamaa (The island archipelgo between Finland and Sweden). Although we heard of the attack we did not shorten our stay in Ahvenamaa.

CHAPTER 24

Leaving Our Kavantsaari Home Forever

Leaving our Kavantsaari Home Forever

Grandfather and grandmother; Aunt Saima and her children Martti, Sirkka, George and Irja; and Aunt Margit had settled into the family Kavantsaari home.

They were enjoying the sweet Karjala spring, but not without trepidation.

During 1944 the prospect of impending attacks by Russian forces was never far away. Gramps did not think they should build too permanently nor get too comfortable.

" I think the Russians will be chasing us out of here again soon enough. But don't tell anyone outside the family that I said that."

In 1943 and '44 the Russians had conducted reconnaissance work:

In the winter of 1942-43 someone landed with a parachute at our shore. Aunt Alina, Martti and George found it under the hay in the hay loft when they went to bring hay back to the barn. They could see the tracks of a man going across the lake. He had walked away towards Vuotsaari and Tali.

George said:

"My mother used part of the parachute to make a nice back pack for me to carry my school books in."

Another time a stranger came to the door asking a lot of questions. Although he spoke good Finnish, this was unusual. He was undoubtedly a spy looking for

information in preparation for the Russian assault on Tali- Ihantala.

In the early summer of 1944 the reconnaissance got a little more personal. A small Russian plane strafed the field where we were working. Aunt Margit hid behind a hay stack. Afterwards Grandma laughed, saying:

"You didn't really think the hay would stop the bullets, did you ?"

When the Russian assault started on June 9th 1944 Uncle Kauko was on spring planting leave from his unit on the Maaselka Isthmus. Uncle Kauko was in Kavantsaari at the mill with Martti when he received a sudden notice that he had to return to his unit. He told Martti to run back to the farm and bring back his army rifle. When Martti returned Kauko was already gone. I assume that the train arrived and he had to go.

It being summer, Martti, Sirkka and George, slept in the attic. George remembers hearing the artillery as the Russians advanced towards Viipuri. He commented that his mother called to them, saying: *"Come sleep down stairs. You shouldn't have to hear the war."*

Cousin Sirkka recounts:

It was the beginning of the new flight. Just then I had gone to fathers' grave in Ihantala to plant flowers. A week later I wanted to go and water the flowers but mother wouldn't let me go. After a couple of days we had to leave for the unknown.

The day before we left my 12 year old brother George nonetheless went to Ihantala to retrieve a wagon we had left there. George told me that:

> *I knew we had to have the other wagon. So I put the harness in my lap and rode one of the horses to Ihantala to bring back our wagon. When I got close, the soldiers told me "Go back, the Russians are only a few kilometers away." I continued on anyway, got the wagon from by the church, hitched up the horse to the wagon, and drove back to the farm."*

The last night when we were still home, soldiers came from the front to rest. They quietly crept into the down stairs chamber. We did not hear anything. When mother opened the door in the morning the soldiers were just leaving and apologized. Dark truths lay ahead.

The next day we left the farm in a real hurry. It was the Monday before Mid Summer just before Viipuri fell (Monday was June 19). The Harkonen neighbors left the day before on Sunday.

Grandmother, and Aunt Alina, with her babies Olavi and Anneli [Anneli died as a child], had gotten a ride in an army lorry to Lauritsala the day before we left.

The caravan started to move from our home yard, 3 horses with wagons, lambs, cows and calves.

Leaving, Grandfather drove one horse and cart, my younger sister Irja and cousin Raimo sitting with him. Although it was the Sunday sulky, the pigs were in crates in the back riding like gentlemen; my brothers' Martti and George drove the wagon George had recovered from Ihantala (occasionally Martti drove his bicycle); and gramps' cousin Matti drove a third big rubber wheeled wagon. George said:

> *"My horse was a handful – a 3 year old black stallion. I remember when he saw some mares nearby. I barely held him back from chasing them – wagon and all. I pulled on the reins so hard that I had bloody wrists as I had wrapped the reins around them."*

My mother, Aunt Margit, myself, and the hired girls herded the cattle and sheep.

We had only gone about 100 yards when gramps disappeared into the bushes with a knife and the 2 lambs. He reappeared without the lambs saying sadly they could never be able to keep up with us over the long journey.

After a couple of days walking the calves as well were killed as they as well were slowing down the evacuation and would not survive on their own, so they too had to be killed. One of the calves was my beloved gleaming Lemmike.

We left by going a short distance towards Kavantsaari before turning north – Gramps knew the best way to get to Lauritsala (near Lappeenranta).

The Kavantsaari road was full of Finnish tanks and trucks moving through towards their battle locations.

On the roads towards Lauritsala there was a big sandy hill on which every one was getting stuck trying to go up, as the wagons sank up to their axels in the sand. The soldiers helped pull wagons up with a tractor. George remembers that:

> *"I cut a willow switch, got on the wagon and whipped and yee hawed my stallion up the hill. We flew up, scattering soldiers and people left and right"*

I remember when we arrived at night fall at Nuijamaa. As we milked the cows, we watched Viipuri burning on the horizon. We continued our walking in the dusk and stayed overnight on the floor of someones house - on that trip there were many such nights.

At mid summer we arrived in Lauritsala. There we met Gramma, Aunt Alina Olavi and Anneli who had arrived uneventfully several days before in the back of the military lorry truck.

> *All of our lips were cracked. We got salve from the pharmacy.*

We stayed in Lauritsala for Mid Summers Eve. It rained so much that my cardboard bottom shoe soles fell apart. Thereafter I had to walk in my bare feet the rest of way to central Finland.

Gramma, Aunt Alina, Olavi and Anneli sailed away on Lake Saima. They took Raimo with them as he was too young to travel with the cattle.

After grandmother and her group sailed off, we started padding ahead, walking onwards with the cattle and horses west to Kouvola. We were only allowed to move in small groups as opposed to long lines in order not to provide a big target for Russian bombers and planes.

I remember when we passed by the Konnu prison camp. There the prisoners joined the refugee flock transporting the prisons cattle. (and it was odd that one of the prisoners ended up in the same house in Siiro.)

At Lauritsala we met one of the two Helsinki soldiers who had been at our place in Kavantsaari before our departure. He said that his friend fell on the Viipuri Linna bridge.

I guess this world has always been a bit askew when one weighs ones fortunes. Sometimes I wonder at the current life style as one doesn't know what one should eat, or put on, and the mattress is so poor that one can't get a good sleep.

There on the refugee trip we had what we could get. Usually it was milk and bread – a couple of times pea soup or stew. Gramps had a separator in his wagon with which we got cream and so we got to paint between the bread slices. There was no morning coffee or apple juice to serve. At one spot Mother and Aunt Margit went and baked bread in a small cottage (The kindly homeowner allowed us to use their oven). We slept outdoors and occasionally indoors in some kind householders home. It was a luxury if we got into a hay loft to sleep. I remember one exceptionally difficult three day period. We slept under the stars.

One day we had to stop to fix a wheel. We youngsters watched the cows as they grazed in the field beside where we had stopped. The owner of the farm

came out with a gun and told us to leave. Grandpa appeared and he backed down. He however disappeared to get the local sheriff. We fixed the wheel and left before anyone returned.

After 2 weeks of travelling we arrived at Selaanpaa. – north of Kouvola . We waited three days for space on a train to take us to Tampere. While we waited, at night we slept in the stations' hay loft. We cooked potatoes over an open fire.

Finally the cattle cars arrived. The women got in the baggage cars and the men and boys in open cars with the cattle and pigs. The trip continued westwards.

The cows were packed in so tight only one could lie down at a time. When the train stopped, everyone jumped out to feed and water the cattle – getting pails of water from ditch, and scything any available grass. It rained a lot that June.

Grandpa did not come with us on the train. Rather he took the horses overland to Kausala – Kaarlo and Martta's home (my folks). His cousin Matti continued with horse and wagon all the way to Hameenkyroon.

We arrived at Riihimaki. Mother said she was going into the station to see if she could get something to eat or drink in the restaurant but she soon returned.

In the railway yard there was a mortuary car carrying the bodies of the dead soldiers back from the front. The door was partly open and blood was running out onto the platform.

It is a wonder that no greater illnesses arose. It was not possible to wash. And there was no soap or other hygiene products.

The next stop was Hameenlinna. Aunt Margit thought that since we were again standing here that she would go to find Aunt Elina (her sister who lived in Hameenlinna) and see if she wanted to come and get some milk. When they returned to the station, our train had left and Aunt Margit was left off the train, and Aunt Elina left without milk.

Our train stopped for the next time in Toijalla. Aunt Margit met us there. She had taken a passenger train and was riding happily in a 2nd class car – speeding past our slow moving refugee train.

The journey continued. I remember as the morning sun broke at 4:00 am when we arrived in Tampere. We did not know then that Tampere would be the new Viipuri for us.

In Tampere we were shunted further west.

On a beautiful July evening we arrived in Siiro. There, ourselves, and our cattle were unloaded. - a long, trying, three week adventure was ended. Our journey should have rightly continued on to Hameenkyro. But mother did not want to go further so we were left to consider what to do.

There once more Mother and Aunt Margit puzzled about how to find food for the animals. Even that issue was resolved once the cows got into the Linnanvuori forest and milk was sold.

We slept on the ground in a factory store room underneath the chairs. George and Martti went to sleep in the workers building where there was sleeping quarters.

In Siiro mother cooked the first potatoes on the stove of Manta Gronstan's small cottage. There is certainly truth to the saying the smaller the house, the wider open the door is.

In Siiro we also got pea soup and bone soup. God took care of us. We were able to rent a room. I remember I first slept on a bare plank.

I went with Aunt Margit to the Hameenkyro church to look for our goods (The cargo had continued on to its' specified address). We puffed along Kyro Lake on a steamer for a whole day. In the evening light we picked up our knap sacks and Aunt Margit organized a ride for the rest of our goods onto the boat. The next morning the trip back to Siiro started. By nightfall we were back home.

The goods had endured all sorts of weather, rain, and pounding; but, nonetheless mothers' linens were in good shape. We heard of Gramma and Aunt Alinas' whereabouts. They had ended their trip in a place called Antolla on the Samia Lake waters near Sulkula.

Somehow or another we managed to live there afterwards.

Many people helped, some didn't.

And generally, "The smaller the house, the bigger the welcome."

PART X

Peace

PÄÄMAJA   22. 9. 1944.

YLIPÄÄLLIKÖN
PÄIVÄKÄSKY
N:o 132.

Suomen armeijan sotilaat!

Sota, johon kansamme joutui kolme vuotta sitten ja jossa siltä on vaadittu mitä raskaimpia uhrauksia, on päättynyt 19. p:nä syyskuuta 1944 solmittuun välirauhaan. Katkerien kokemusten jälkeen käsitämme, että tulevan elämämme edellytyksenä on saavuttaa pysyväiset luottamukselliset suhteet kaikkiin naapurikansoihimme.

Sota on Suomen kansaa luvanut koetellut. Mutta rakkautemme isiemme maahan, itsenäisyyteemme ja vapauteemme ei ole koskaan tuntenut uhrauksien rajaa.

Kiitän Teitä urhoolliset sotilaat. Te olette kokeneet paljon ja kestäneet paljon. Te olette empimättä olleet valmiit uhraamaan kaikkenne isänmaan eteen ja kestämään vaikeimmatkin koettelemukset. Miehekkään uskollisina isänmaan asialle Te sankarillisella urheudella ja uhrimielellä suorititte kovia taisteluja ja nurkumatta kestitte vuosikausiksi pitkittyneen sodan ankarat ponnistukset. Te taistelitte puutteellisin asein ja vaatimattomin varustein voimakasta ja urhoollista vastustajaa vastaan.

Suomen armeijan komentajat, upseerit, aliupseerit ja miehet! Teitä seuraa isänmaanne ikuinen kiitos ja ylipäällikkönne, vanhan soturin tinkimätön tunnustus.

Lausun myös hartaan kiitokseni Suomen naiselle, joka uskollisesti, itseään säästämättä on velvollisuutensa täyttänyt.

Kotirintama on vaatinut koko kansan äärimmäisiä ponnistuksia kaikilla työn ja elämän aloilla. Lannistumattomin voimin se on tehtävänsä suorittanut.

Liikuttunein ja kiitollisin mielin ajattelen haavoittuneita ja varsinkin invaliidejamme, joista monet koko elämänsä ajan joutuvat kantamaan raskasta kuormaa.

Hartain mielin muistelen sankarivainajiamme, joiden valkeat ristit kirkkojemme kummuilla kertovat niistä, jotka antoivat suurimman uhrin.

Isänmaan nöyrä kiitos keventäköön leskien ja orpojen taakkaa.

Sotilaani! Vaikeat ajat ovat vielä edessämme. Välirauhasopimus on allekirjoitettu, sen ehdot on täytettävä. Tilanne Lapissa on tällä hetkellä vielä selvittämättä, ja joukoiltamme vaaditaan yhä samaa velvollisuudentuntoa ja päättäväisyyttä, mitä ne koko sodan aikana ovat osoittaneet.

Tietoisina siitä, että olette täyttäneet velvollisuutenne, palaatte Te vähitellen kotiinne rauhan työsaroille. Olen vakuuttunut, että tartutte näihin toimiinne samalla tarmolla, antaumuksella ja itsekurilla, jonka olen oppinut Teissä tuntemaan sotapoluillanne ja jota Teissä aina olen ihaillut. Vakaa pyrkimyksemme olkoon rauhan toimin kohottaa maamme uuteen koko kansaamme kohdistuvaan kukoistukseen vilpittömissä ja ystävällisissä suhteissa naapurimaihimme.

Jumala Suomea suojelkoon!

Puolustusvoimain ylipäällikkö
Suomen Marsalkka *Mannerheim.*

PART X

Peace

Finland since late 1943 had recognized that it was doubtful that Germany could win the war. Without Germany's might Finlands' prospect of winning its' war against Russia was minimal.

It began overtures with Russia regarding a peace in 1943. These did not proceed far.

Then Russia attacked Finland in the summer of 1944. After initial battle ground defeats, Finland stopped the Russian advance at the heroic battles of Tali-Ihantala and Ayrapaa/Vuosalmi. Russia had demolished Karjala but its troops were never able to set foot in the rest of Finland.

On August 1st Finnish President Ryti resigned so that peace could be negotiated and Mannerheim was appointed President.

On September 4th Russia and Finland agreed to a ceasefire.

In the Interim Peace signed on September 19th Finland retained its independence. But it lost Karjala once more; was ordered to pay $300,000,000 in war reparations to Russia; and to force the German army out Lapland.

CHAPTER 25

A Bitter Peace

CHAPTER 24

A Bitter Peace

It had become evident for some time to Finland that Germany would not win the war, and that as a result Finland had no possibilty of winnng.

Discussions regarding peace had already been underway for some time through Russia's diplomat in Sweden Alexandra Kollontai - the very same person who had been the informal contact during the Winter War.

When Russia began its' attack on Finland again on June 9th Finland was badly in need of military materiel and grain from German. President Risto Ryti gave his personal guarantee to Hitler that Finland would not sue for peace "while he was governing Finland". Hitler provided badly needly grain, weapons, a division of troops, some tanks and an airforce fighter detachment. The German airforce detachment and the supply of German anti-tank Panzerfaust and Panzer guns were particularly useful in Finland's ability to stop the Russian summer 1944 assault.

As a pre-requisite for formal peace discussions on July 27th Russia demanded that the current Finnish government resign. Russia was at a minimum prepared to guarantee Finland would remain independent.

On August 1st, President Risto Ryti resigned. Mannerheim was named President of Finland.

Discussions continued until Russia put forward its' terms on August 27th. While these discussions were underway, Germany endeavored to convince Finland to remain in the Axis alliance. Mannerheim refused. Mannerheim respected Germany's capabilities and support, but had never been friendly with Germany - from the Finnish Civil War through the Winter and Continuation Wars. His desire had always been that Finland should be in control its' own military forces and country.

Ever chivalrous, he did however write a letter of regret and thanks to Hitler:

> Our German brothers-in-arms will remain forever in our hearts. The Germans in Finland were certainly not representatives of foreign despotism, but rather were helpers and brothers-in-arms. But even in such cases foreigners are placed in difficult positions requiring constant tact. I assure you that during the past years nothing whatsoever happened that could have induced us to consider the German troops intruders or oppressors. I believe the attitude of the German Army in northern Finland towards the local population and authorities will enter our history as a unique example of a correct and cordial relationship...
>
> I deem it my duty to lead my people out of the war. I cannot and will not turn the arms which you have so liberally supplied us against Germans. I harbour the hope that you, even if you disapprove of my attitude, will wish and endeavour like myself and all other Finns to terminate our former relations without increasing the gravity of the situation.

On September 2nd, in a closed session, the Finnish Parliament agreed in principle to the harsh peace terms presented by Russia.

On September 4th, 1944 ceasefire took place at 07:00 Helsinki time. The Russian forces continued to nonetheless fire for another day after they received the orders to cease fighting. The Finnish forces did not retaliate. However unlike the Romanians they did not withdraw, rather remaining in their positions. Russia earlier in the summer had agreed to a similar armistice with Romania. The Romanian soldiers had ceased fighting leaving their trenches only to be taken captive. The Russian forces then moved forward and completed the conquest of the now undefended country.

On September 7th a Finnish delegation under Foreign Minister Carl Enckell went to Moscow to negotiate the final peace agreement. Negotiations continued for a week. On September 14th Russia added additional conditions – the most onerous of which was Finland pay war compensation of $300,000,000. The Finnish government had no alternative but to sign the agreement (albeit an interim one as the Allies wanted to be signatories of the final agreement).

There were 23 points to the peace agreement signed on September 19, 1944 by Finland, Russia and England, of which the most important were:

- Finland must once more surrender the land lost (beloved Karjala) during the Winter War to Russia;
- Finland in addition must surrender Petsamo and part of the Salla area;
- Finland must lease the military port of Porkalla to Russia for fifty years. This placed Helsinki within the range of Russia's big artillery guns;
- The Finnish armed forces must immediately pull back behind the 1940 border;
- Finland must force the German armed forces out of Lapland with two weeks;
- Finnish army forces must to be reduced to the peace time level within two months;
- The airfields in the south and south west, and all the naval yards must be decommissioned;
- Finland must pay war compensation of 300,000,000 dollars to Russia. This is to be paid in materials and goods within six years;

In his radio broadcast at 22:00 on September 19th 1944 announcing the bitter peace terms, Finnish Prime Minister Ernst von Borni ended the broadcast with:

Citizens !!

In the news of the peace, Finland could not have dared to expect the joy and relief which would be customary after so many heavy years of war.

While worry about the future of our fatherland has gnawed at the breast of soldier and civilian alike, the stark reality, whose features are today in front of our face, is more galling then many could have believed possible.

Especially to YOU, the front line soldiers, who have shouldered the heaviest load through these years.

We are not the first Finnish generation who has asked; "Has it been for nothing, the struggles and suffering, for nothing all the sacrifices ? "

Not for the first time have Finlands' skies been gloomy. Even more harshly has God tried our earlier generations, and nonetheless the Finnish people have survived.

Our fatherland today does not need complaining about our troubles. Rather it needs men and women who even now believe in the future of our country and the victory of humanity.

Let us therefore not let todays heavy news depress us excessively, rather let us remember the eternal truth:

'Even though we are tested, God has not abandoned us'.

Mannerheim in his address on September 22nd to his army as Field Marshall, thanked his soldiers and country, and urged them to now address themselves to rebuilding Finland.

Mannerheim's Order of the Day of September 22, 1944

Soldiers of Finlands' army !!

The war which our nation was forced into three years ago and which required the heaviest sacrifices, ended on September 19th in the Interim Peace Agreement. After our bitter trials we understand that the coming life in front of us depends on trustworthy relations with all our neighbours.

War has always tried Finland's people heavily. But building our fatherland, our independence, and our freedom, has never known a limit to sacrifice.

I thank YOU, valiant soldiers. You have experienced much, and endured much. You have without hesitation been prepared to sacrifice all for your country and to bear the most difficult trials. With manly loyalty to our fatherland, you have with heroic bravery and sacrifice, made it through heavy battles and endured without complaint many years of wars harsh battering. You have fought unceasingly with inadequate weaponry and limited materials against a fierce and powerful opponent.

Finlands armies' commanders, officers, NCOs, and men ! To you will follow our fatherlands everlasting thanks, and an old warriors' unstinting admiration.

I also offer my heartfelt thanks to Finlands' women, who faithfully and without limit fulfilled their duty.

On the homefront it has called for the entire nations noblest efforts in all areas of work and life. With tireless strength, the homefront has completed its' tasks.

With an emotive and grateful mind, I think of the wounded, and especially the invalided, many of whom are forced to carry a heavy burden for their entire life.

I remember those brothers in arms whose white crosses on church mounds speak of those who made the ultimate sacrifice.

On behalf of the nation, I offer our humble thanks to the widows and orphans.

Soldiers ! Difficult times are still in front of us. The interim peace has been agreed and its terms must be met. The situation in Lapland at the moment is yet unfinished, and requires from you still the same duty, dedication and preserverance as you demonstrated throughtout the entire war.

Aware in the knowledge that you have fulfilled your duty, return to build a peaceful home. I am convinced that you will complete this work with the same energy, devotion and self discipline as I have known from you on the path of war, and which I have always admired in you. Our unwavering goal is to work with peaceful means to get the entire nation flourishing anew - living in sincere and friendly relations with our neighbours.

God protect Finland !

Mannerheim, after President Risto Ryti had stepped down, was now President of Finland as well as Field Marshall.

Baron Carl Gustaf Mannerheim (born 1867, died 1951) had an eventful life. Born on the Mannerheim estate to Count Carl Robert Mannerheim and his wife Helene von Julien, the daughter of a wealthy industrialist, he dedicated himself to a life of military and political leadership. He:

- Attended military school at the Hamina Cadet Academy in Finland and the Nicholas Cavalry School in St Petersburg;
- Served in Czar Nicholas IIs Imperial Chevalier Guard;
- Fought as a Cavalry Colonel in the Russo-Japanese War;
- Journeyed across Asia to Peking on horse back on a reconnaissance mission on behalf of the Czar;
- Was Lieutenant General of a Russian Cavalry Division on the Poland front in WW I;
- Served as the Commander-In-Chief of the Finnish White military force during the Finnish Civil War;
- Acted as Regent of Finland from 1918 to 1919;
- Served as President of Finlands' Red Cross;
- Served as Chairman of the Bank of Finland;
- Commanded the Finnish armed forces during the Winter War;

- Was Field Marshall and Commander-In-Chief of the Finnish armed forces during the Continuation War;
- Served as President of Finland from 1944 to 1946

While many people were responsible for Finland's success during the Winter and Continuation Wars, it is acknowledged that Finland would not have succeeded either militarily nor politically without Mannerheim's leadership.

He gained many admirers throughout the world.

Even Stalin respected and admired Marshall Mannerheim. Stalin is quoted as saying to a Finnish delegation to Moscow in 1947, that:

"The Finns owe much to their old Marshal.

Due to him, Finland was not occupied."

Mannerheim was, and still is, a legend in Finland.

The Lapland War

The Lapland War

The Lapland War started on September 19, 1944. As part of the terms of the peace agreement with Russia, Finland was to force the German Army out of Lapland.

Both Finland and Germany wanted a peaceful withdrawal. The withdrawal moved too slowly. After Russia threatened to invade Lapland and remove the Germans themselves, the withdrawal broke out into actual fighting.

A Finnish force landed successfully in Tornio on October 1st pushing back the German forces. The German army now launched a scorched earth campaign burning and mining Lapland as they retreated.

By late November the German Army had retreated to the Norwegian border at Kilpsijarvi and Kargasniemi – Utsjoki.

While there were some smaller battles, neither Finnish nor German casualties during the war were heavy. It however left a legacy of demolished villages, towns and cities and a heavily mined countryside.

Uncle Arvo participated in the Lapland war – being a Pioneer his expertise was needed to dismantle the mines.

100,000 Finns (most of the population) evacuated Lapland in advance of the war.

My ancestral homes of Oulu and Simo, while under German command, did not need to be evacuated.

In Simo however my distant cousin Elvi (11 years old then) did wage a war of her own against the Germans.

CHAPTER 26

The Lapland War
Uncle Arvo
&
Our Ancestral Witch Home

The Lapland War - Uncle Arvo - & Our Ancestral Witch Home

The Lapland war lasted from Oct 1, 1944 to April 1945. Casualties were limited on both sides. While the war started as a peaceful coordinated withdrawal between the Germans and the Finns, fighting heated up at the insistence of the Russians.

There was only one major battle - the successful Finnish invasion of Tornio from the sea. After this, the Germans adopted a scorched earth withdrawal, burning and destroying the city of Rovaniemi and other towns including part of the city of Oulu. They also destroyed all the bridges and heavily mined the roads during their retreat – including the very bridge that dad built.

By the time the last German troops were expelled in April 1945, the Finnish army only consisted of raw recruits. Thus, this portion of the war became known as the Children's Crusade.

The German devastation of Lapland caused hard feelings with the Finns, replacing the prior attitude of the Germans just being fellow soldiers. 100,000 Finns were temporarily displaced as a result of the scorched earth campaign.

The Military Campaign

The formal September 17th Peace Agreement required Finland to push the 220,000 strong 22nd German Mountain Army out of Lapland within two weeks.

When the armistice took place on September 4th, the German army was located north of Oulujoki River (north of Kajaani). The two main fronts were still Murmansk and Salla. In addition to the front line troops, German reserves were located in Oulu and in Hyrynsalmi (half way between Suomussalmi and Kajaani). The German headquarters was in Rovaniemi. Colonel General Lothar Rendulic was in command. The previous well regarded commander Lieutenant Colonel Eduard Dietl had been killed in mysterious circumstances in an air crash over the Alps in June 1944.

When the armistice was signed Finland had three battalion strength units north of Oulujoki River: Os Pennanen in Lapland and two other battalions near Suomussalmi. The two southern battalions moved south to Oulujoki. In the far north Os Pennanen moved to Kemi – Kariharra.

The Finns and the Germans were on good terms. Finland wanted to keep Lapland from being devastated. The Germans wanted to withdraw to Norway without losses. Russia however was adamant in its demand that the Finns push the German army out of Finland.

As the Simo veterans book comments:

It felt a bit unbelievable. To now fight against your comrades in arms whom you had fought and died with side by side. But it had to be done as Finland's life depended on it.

The Germans and the Finns arranged an unofficial secret agreement. The Germans would withdraw expeditiously as per their preplanned withdrawal "Operation Birke ". No fighting was to occur. The Germans would withdraw and the Finnish forces would occupy their positions after they were vacated. It was agreed that the Germans were allowed to destroy the bridges as they withdrew.

The "Phoney War" started well but soon disintegrated.

The first conflict occurred outside of Lapland on September 15th when German forces attempted to take Suursaari Island in the Gulf of Finland near Kotka. The island was a strategic gateway. The Germans wanted to secure it in order to be able to maintain the blockade of the Russian Baltic fleet. The Finnish force successfully rebuffed the attack.

As they withdrew in Lapland, the Germans began to plant mines on roads and in dwellings as well as on the bridges, but thankfully they withdrew from Oulu without inflicting major damage.

Finland had positioned forces south of the Oulujoki River. On September 19th the Finnish forces began to advance after the German army.

- By September 20th Lagus's Panzer Brigade was in Oulu, followed by the 3rd and 11th Divisions. On September 24th the 15th Brigade started towards Kemi. Russia however was unhappy with the slow progress and threatened to advance into Lapland and extradite the German Army themselves. (The Russians did launch an attack on Petsamo in October 7th but were beaten back by the German Army).

- On September 27th Mannerheim placed all the Finnish Lapland forces under the command of Lieutenant General Siilasvuo. This III AK comprised three divisions – the 6th, 3rd and 11th - plus the 15th

Brigade, a Border Guard brigade, Lagus' Panzer Brigade, and Os Pennanen.

- The "Phoney War" ended with the first combat of the Lapland War taking place at Pudasjarvi on September 28th.

- The war truly began on October 1st when the 11th Regiment under Lieutenant Colonel Halsti succeeded in making a surprise landing in Tornio. Battles began as the German forces retreated to Kemi and then north. While the Tornio landfall defused the threat of Russian invasion, it incensed German Colonel General Lothar Rendulic who ordered a scorched earth withdrawal from Lapland.

The Finnish III AK launched a three pronged attack.

1. In the east from Loiksa north to Kemijarvi and from thence to Sodankyla, Ivalo, and to the far northern border with Norway at Kargisniemi and Utsjoki.

2. Through the middle from Pudasjarvi (north of Kajaani) to Rovaniemi. From there part of the force swang north east to join the assault towards Sodankyla; and part north west to Kaukonen and Muonio.

3. In the west the attack forged north from Tornio by the Swedish border to Yli Tornio, Kolari, Muonio. From there the assault followed the German forces north west to Kilpisjarvi on the Norwegian border.

The German forces retreated waging a scorched earth policy as they withdrew. Larger battles were fought at Rovaniemi, Kemi, YliTornio, Muonio, Sodankyla. The largest number of Finnish casualties occurred at Ylimaa-Ranua south of Rovaniemi where 295 Finnish soldiers of the 2nd and 3rd Jaakari battalions of PsD / JPr were killed.

1. Kemijarvi was taken on October 2nd and Pelkosniemi on October 24th. Markajarvi on the border by mother and fathers hamlet of Kelloselka was taken on October 23rd. Taking Markajarvi was more a matter of protecting it from Russian occupation rather then forcing any Germans out.

2. Rovaniemi was taken on October 15th, Kaukonen on October 25th, Sodankyla on October 19th, and Ivalo on November 5th.

3. Kemi was taken on October 7th, Ylitornio October 13th, and Muonio on October 25th

On November 24th the German army was at the Norwegian border at Kilpsijarvi; and on November 21st in the far north at Kargasniemi – Utsjoki.

The Finnish army settled into trench warfare at these positions, but basically the Lapland War was over at the beginning of December, 1944.

This was fortuitous as per the terms of the Peace Agreement, the Finnish army had to be at its' peacetime level by the beginning of December. Only soldiers with less then two years service or who had been born in 1924-25, were allowed to remain in the army. The veteran Finnish forces had begun to demobilize in advance of the end of November, leaving the conflict to the young 18 to 21 year old soldiers. Thus due to this, and the minor nature of the battles, the Lapland War became known as the Childrens' Crusade.

Skirmishes did continue through to April 1945. Officially, at 13:30 on April 27, 1945 all German forces had been forced out of Finland.

While all the German forces had been forced out, the Finnish pioneer units kept clearing mines for another six months until the fall of 1945.

Finland at the height of the war had 75,000 troops in Lapland. Germany had 220,000.

The Finnish army suffered 4,081 casualties – (774 killed and 262 lost, 141 imprisoned and 2,904 wounded). The Germans suffered 4,255 casualties. (950 killed, 2,000 wounded, and 1,305 imprisoned). By the terms of the peace agreement Finland had to turn the prisoners over to Russia.

Almost all (100,000) of Lapland's population had fled. 56,417 went to Sweden while 47,468 went to "southern" Finland. Included in the exodus were 47,000 cattle.

50 percent of Lapland was destroyed during Germany's scorched earth withdrawal. 14,779 buildings were destroyed, as well as all the roads and bridges,.

The southern part of "Lapland", including Simo and Oulu, was neither evacuated nor demolished.

Nor was the spirit of the Lapland people and the independence of Finland.

Uncle Arvo's Campaign

Uncle Arvo served in the Lapland War. On September 9th, instead of being disbanded at the end of the Jatkosota, Pion P14 was ordered to Lappi (northern Finland) primarily working in Kemi and Rovanniemi. There during the Lapland War, they disarmed mines, cleared mine fields, disarmed aircraft bombs, and rebuilt bridges and roads. They remained in Lappi until mid November, near the end of the conflict.

Uncle Arvo remained with the Jaakaari Unit of the battalion.

The battalions' sotapaiva kirja and the Pion P14 book encapsulated the battalions' service.

• On September 29th, 1944 they left the Pioneer Head Quarters in Koria near Kouvola.

• By October 8th they had arrived at Ristijarvi north of Kaajani.

• On October 10 they were Kuivaniemi just 10 kilometers south of Simo.

• There they rebuilt the bridge over the Simo River that the reteating German forces had blown up.

• On October 15th they were in Kemi preparing for the Finnish forces cross over of the Kemi River.

• By October 22nd the full battalion had arrived in Rovaniemi. Part of the battalion was with Os Halsti on the west side of Rovaniemi, and part with Os Loimu.

- During the first day while they were clearing a mine field, Lieutenant Kosiken and Corporal Niitymaki were killed when a large mine they were defusing blew up. Pioneer Johannala was severely injured and died later of his wounds.

- They battalion remained in Rovaniemi until November 1st disarming mine fields and building a bridge over Ounas River.

- After the beginning of November they returned back to Tornio. One company went north to Muonio for a brief period. As well some pioneers went to Kemijarvi.

- By November 18th the entire battalion was at the Ii railway station between Simo and Oulu. They loaded themselves and their weaponry and materials unto railway cars. Their train left at 12:30 arriving in Koria near Kovola at 07:30 the next day.

- Arriving was a cause for some celebration. The battalion headquarters received a phone call at 13:45 that a few pioneers were persistently bothering some members of the local "control commission". A patrol was sent out to bring them home.

- On November 23rd 1944 Pion P14 was disbanded.

Uncle Arvo's war was finally over – a war that had started for him five years earlier in December 1939.

Uncle Arvo went to join his parents in Central Finland ... There was no Kavantsaari / Viipuri home to go back to.

Our Ancestral Witch Home

Simo was my Fathers' ancient ancestral witch home.

There was a German unit in Simo. During the German retreat from Lapland they blew up the bridges in Simo.

I have visited Simo several times. The last time I was there I was able to make contact with my delightful distant cousin Elvi. She still owns the old Ruikka "witch" home. I had a lovely visit with her there. Over dinner she recounted many stories about Simo and the home.

The home is beside the old main road from Oulu to Tornio. During the war many German soldiers were located in the village. Some barracked in the houses. They got along fine with one another until the Lapland War ignited. The soldiers were ordered to blow up the bridge near them. (It was not the bridge over the Simo River that Uncle Arvo rebuilt. It was a smaller one over the Sinikoski River).

Elvi is now a very spry 84 year old. Her eyes sparkled as she recounted:

The German soldiers came and told us that they had to blow up the bridge about 200 yards from our

house. They said that we should take the windows out as the explosion would otherwise blow them out. This we did, as well as leaving before the assigned time they gave for blowing up the bridge. It did most certainly generate a fierce compression wave of destruction. It even broke the oven in our house.

The Germans had wired up the bridge well in advance. Elvi's eyes sparkled as she said she and her older sister thought this should not happen. Their two brothers were serving in the front lines (photos opposite). They had to do their part. She and her sister decided to sabotage the explosion. The two of them put safety pins on the detonation wire. The

German soldiers found the problem – fixed it – and blew up the bridge.

The soldiers remained in the area for a couple of more days. They gave their nearby neighbours a hard time for trying to blow up the bridge. Elvi and her sister of course had not told anyone what they had done. And who would suspect two sweet young girls of such a thing. Elvi said that they kept it a secret for a long time. They did not tell their neighbours that they had done it until twenty years ago.

Patriotism comes in many forms.

The photo below shows Elvi standing in front of the "old Ruikka witch home".

After the War

After the War

After the war Finland settled into a precarious peace.

World War II would continue in Europe for another nine months , and in the Pacific for another year.

In the World War II period (which encompassed the Winter War, the Continuation War and the Lapland War) Finland lost 95,000 (killed) of a population of 3.7 million (2.6%). About 1/3 of the Finnish soldiers were wounded or killed. Finland's casualties during the wars were larger then any of the other World War II combatants relative to population other then Germany, Russia, and Japan.

The political leaders of Finland were tried for war crimes by Russia - among them President Ryti - but not Marshall Mannerheim.

Resettlement of the Karjala Finns and payment of the war reparations placed a strain on Finlands' economy. Finlands' social fabric embraced the challenge of building a new economy, and Finland slowly rejuvenated.

Our family, miraculousy lost nothing other then our precious Karjala home. All the men returned alive after 5 years of fighting.

The family settled in Finland, but slowly all members other then Uncle Toivo and cousin Martti left to start a new life in Amerika.

In 1951 my father and mother bundled up all five of us and left for Kanada.

The World and Finland

Yalta Conference February 1, 1945 – Nat'l Archives USA

CHAPTER 27

The World and Finland

After the Continuation War ended on September 19, 1944 between Finland and Russia, World War II continued between the Axis and Allied powers.

WW II Ends

WWII ended in Europe with the unconditional surrender of Germany on May 8, 1945. It ended in the Pacific with the surrender of Japan on August 15, 1945.

The terms of the European peace were formalized in the Paris Peace Treaty of February 10, 1947. This included the original terms of the Interim Peace Treaty between Finland, Russia and Britain. The terms of the Paris Peace Treaty were decided by Britain, the United States, and the Soviet Union (France was also a signatory but had minimal influence).

The Soviet Union led by Josef Stalin was the most influential member of the group. Both Britain and the United States were represented by leaders without experience with World War II. In Britain Clement Attlee had replaced Winston Churchill. In the United States Harry Truman had replaced Franklin Roosevelt.

As a result of this Russia was in a favorable position to expand into Europe. Russia annexed Estonia, Latvia and Lithuania and half of Poland directly into the Soviet Union. Bulgaria, Romania, Albania, Hungary, Czechoslovakia, Poland and Eastern Germanny became satellite states of the Soviet Union.

The war had been costly for Finland, but she retained her independence.

Casualties

The cost to Finland had been heavy in casualties, loss of territory, and reparations.

During the Continuation War and Lapland Wars, the Finnish military suffered major casualties, but significantly less than Russia did.

Finland suffered 208,000 casualties during the Continuation and Lapland Wars. 58,000 soldiers were killed, and 148,000 wounded. Navy and Air force casualties were minimal – 4,700 in the Navy and 554 in the Air Force. Of the total casualties 4.9% of the casualties were officers, 16.2 % NCOs and 78.8% soldiers.

The casualties in Uncle Kauko's 1st division were 9,400; and in Uncle Vilho's 8th division 7,300. I do not know what the casualty number was for Uncle Arvo's combat engineering battalion Pion P14.

But the casualty number for Uncle Toivo's 2nd division was 17,200 – more then the number of men in the division; and 42% more then the division with the next highest number of casualties. Small wonder that Uncle Arvo said Toivo was in the worst fighting of the war...And even more so he was a front line rifleman. Here the casualties were the highest ...

Russia's casualties on the Finland front are estimated at 820,000 of which 270,000 were killed and 550,000 wounded.

Germany's casualties in Finland were 84,000 - almost all suffered in Lapland / Northern Finland in battles against Russia. 23,000 Germans were killed and 61,000 wounded.

Finland's casualties during the wars were larger then any of the other World War II combatants relative to population other then Germany, Russia, and Japan. Finland lost 2.6% of her population relative to her population. 5.5 million German soldiers were killed, or about 6.3% relative to her population. Russia lost 11.4 million soldiers or about 6.3% of her population. – Japan 2.9% of her population. None of the other WWII combatants lost more then 1% of the population. Canada lost .4% and the USA .3%. The UK only lost .8% and France .5%.

The figures for the Allied Powers surprised me. The deaths for the United Kingdom and France were surprisingly low, and those for the United States even lower then those of Canada.

Civilian deaths were minimal. In the case of both Germany and Russia millions of civilians died due to military causes - over 3 million in Germany and 10 million in Russia. In addition in Russia millions more died due to disease and famine. Finland only suffered 2,000 civilian deaths. The war however resulted in 30,000 widows and 50,000 orphans.

The figures put into perspective the truism that:

> *"The victor writes the story".*

Needless to say the sacrifices of the Allied forces were sad - every life is precious. But if one were only to believe the post war Western media stories, as opposed to the actual figures, the WWII losses of the United Kingdom were horrendous, and the United States solely by itself saved the world.

Economy and Resettlement

The Paris Peace Treaties of 1947 confirmed the loss of Karjala. While all 400,000 inhabitants of Karjala had fled during the Winter War, 280,000 had returned after Finland reclaimed Karjala in the summer of 1941. Now they all left again.

After the war, Karelia was entirely devoid of people. It was slowly repopulated by Russia with people from all over Russia. Thus Karelia no longer has any Finnish population. The fact that the entire population of Karelia left is a testament not only to the nationalism of the Finns, but also to terror of the Stalin regime.

All the people from Karjala had to settle in Finland as best they could. The Finnish government supported the resettlement by allocating land in proportion to ones former property, or providing partial monetary compensation. The land that was provided was usually wilderness. The money was only a token amount. But most Karelians were able to build homes and farms nonetheless.

During the conflict itself, people were expected to put up the evacuees. While this was not welcomed by all the non Karelians, it exhibited that Finland had a truly patriotic government and people. Being a Finn truly meant that you were your countryman's keeper. But according to cousin Pekka:

> *"Unfortunately it was not that easy. There was forced taking over of private land for the refugees all over the country. Some resisted this fiercely, seeing the Karelian refugees as "Russians". However, the local police all over the country was given authority to shoot anyone opposing the resettlement of the fellow Finns."*

The resettlement of the Karjalaiset placed a severe strain on Finland's economy.

Added to this was the devastation of Lapland during the Lapland War and some destruction of Finland by the Russian bombers - and of course the war reparations.

The peace treaty specified that Finland pay the equivalent of $300,000,000 USA in gold to Russia within 6 years. In real terms this was almost double the figure as the $300,000,000 was at the 1938 exchange rate of gold to the dollar. Finlands' annual payment was equivalent to 15-16% of the Gross National Product – blood money. But Finland worked urgently to pay Russia on time. To not pay Russia in the post war period was an invitation for Russia to annex Finland. The Finns joshed wryly that:

The East took our men, the Germans took our women, and the Swedes took our children. But at least we are left with our war debt.

By September 1952 Finland had paid its' war reparations – the only country to pay its' WW II reparations in full.

The Allied powers did not aid Finland. There was no Marshall Plan for Finland. Russia forbade the United States from providing Finland any assistance.

Finland paid its' reparations in products that Russia requested as opposed to in money. The majority of the products consisted of ships and engineering products. As such it was instrumental in building a modern technology based economy.

While its' industry was healthy, post war life in Finland was strained – rationing and scarcity prevailed. The monies and products went to Russia.

War Trials

After the peace a Soviet Allied Control Commission arrived in Finland on October 5th, 1945. Its' role was to monitor the explusion of the German forces and and ensure repayment of the reparations. But another major role was to monitor and control the Finnish populance and politics. It ordered the disbandment of the Finnish patriot organizations the Suojeluskunta and Lotta Svard. It strongly encouraged political orientation towards Russia. The existing Finnish secret police cadre was replaced with communists and Soviet sympathizers. The newly staffed organization carried out arbitrary arrests and fostered citizen terror.

While the Soviet Allied Control Commission had British members, it in effect was a Russian organization.

Finland did continue on its' daily way as an independent country, enduring the Soviet interference with typical Finnish stoicism and iron resilience. Despite the upper echelon Russian presence there was no doubt about Finlands' will to remain an independent country and its' capability to fight forever.

On August 8, 1945 the Treaty of London defined three types of crimes, war crimes, crimes against peace, and crimes against humanity. While Finland was not guilty of any of these, it became evident that Finland couldn't be the only country fighting on the German side where leaders wouldn't be convicted. Thus the Soviet Allied Control Commission added a new definition to war crimes to convict political leaders who - "definitely influenced Finland in getting into a war with Russia and the United Kingdom in 1941, or prevented peace during the Continuation War." Those prosecuted were limited to the highest political leadership. Russia ensured that the Finnish Parilament passed a retroactive law to this effect on September 11, 1945.

Unlike other nations that were declared guilty, Finland was allowed to conduct the trials in Finland under Finnish law with Finnish judges. A special court sat from November 1945 to May 1946. It was comprised of the presidents of the Supreme Court of Finland and the Supreme Administrative Court of Finland, 12 Members of Parliament, and a University professor. The Soviet Allied Commission strongly influenced the court and the outcome.

The court placed eight Finnish political leaders on trial.

1. Risto Ryti ,the President of Finland was sentenced to ten years imprisonment
2. Jukka Rangell, Finland's 25th Prime Minister was sentenced to six years
3. Edwin Linomies, Finland's 28th Prime Minister was sentenced to 5 ½ years
4. Vaimo Tanner,Minister of Foreign Affairs (Winter War) & Minister of Finance (Continuation War) was sentenced to 5 ½ years
5. Toivo Kivimaki, the Finnish ambassador to Nazi Germany was sentenced to 5 years
6. Henrik Ramsay, Minister of Foreign Affairs was sentenced to 2 ½ years
7. Antti Kukkonen, Minister of Education was sentenced to 2 years
8. Tyko Reinokka, Deputy Minister of Finance was sentenced to 2 years

Mannerheim was not placed on trial. He was untouchable - too revered in Finland and too respected throughout the world.

The Finnish people considered the proceedings a Kangaroo court. No mention was of course made of Russia's invasion of Finland in 1939, nor of Russia's bombing of Finland in June 1941 as causes for the wars. One month after the end of the trial the Finnish judge in charge of the trial,Onni Petays, shot himself to death.

After the Paris Peace Treaty was ratified in the Soviet Union on August 29, 1947, the Allied Control Commission left Finland on September 26, 1947. Soon thereafter the Finnish President Passikivi paroled the prisoners before they had served their prison terms.

On May 19, 1949 Paasikivi pardoned Ryti. Ryti's health collapsed during the imprisonment and he remained an invalid until his death in 1956.

I by chance came across an interesting analysis of Risto Ryti byLord Mervyn King the former Governor of the Bank of England. He chose Risto Ryti as his Great Life for the BBC radio series Great Lives (Episode 8, January 30, 2015). Lord King knew Ryti for several decades before the war. In his radio broadcast he explained why he chose Risto Ryti.

Ryti was tried for war crimes by Russia in 1945 after peace was signed. He was found guilty and sentenced to 10 years hard labor.

In 1944 Ryti knew he had to choose between two devils in order for the country to survive. He knew that the war was lost but he needed temporary military support to delay the Russian offensive of 1944 long enough to cause the Russians to want to negotiate a cease fire with Finland. In order to do so he wrote a letter to Hitler pledging Finland's allegiance to Nazi Germany. He signed it personally and stated that "it would be force as long as there was any Finnish government chosen by me. "

Germany provided air and armor support and with this helped Finland stop Russia. Peace negotiations began with Russia and were signed in September 1944, almost a year before Germany's May 7, 1945 surrender.

Ryti then resigned in August 1944 after the Russian assault on Finland was stopped. Mannerheim took over as President. Mannerheim wrote Hitler saying;

" We both know that things are going badly. If Germany loses the war there will always be a

Germany. But if Finland loses this war that is the end of Finland."

Mannerheim negotiated a peace with Russia. It included the loss of Karjala and harsh terms but Finland survived.

Finland had to rewrite its' criminal code to allow the trail proceeding as Finland had not committed any war crimes. The Finns felt shame but could do nothing. Ryti was convicted and sentenced to 10 years imprisonment.

Ryti declined in prison despite reasonable conditions, and continued in poor health until his death in 1956.

He was an anglophone although he was cut off from England during war. Before becoming President of Finland he had been an economist, finance minister, and governor of the Bank of Finland. During the 1920s and 1930s he had worked closely with Britain - developing an excellent relationship with the Bank of England. Indeed in 1934 he was knighted by King George V for his work fostering Anglo-Finnish relations.

To Lord Mervyn King, Risto Ryti's was a great life as:

What was great about him was that he recognized the importance of looking at the big picture , understanding the true nature of the choices he faced, realizing that any choice was going to be unpleasant and unpalatable, but doing what he could to preserve the independence of his country.

I think his life shows that on almost all the big occasions he made the right choice, even though that involved an immense personal sacrifice.

Finland and Family

Akseli Gallen-Kallela: Sammon Taonta

CHAPTER 28

Finland and Family

Dispersal

After the war we settled in Kotka. Mothers' siblings (except for Armas and Ester in Amerika) settled in other locations through out Finland.

- Aunt Hilda, Uncle Aatu and family remained in Vajakoski near Jyvaskyla in central Finland.
- Aunt Tyyne stayed briefly in Finland before leaving for the USA in 1946.
- Uncle Kauko, Aunt Margit and family settled in Oripaa between Tampere and Turku.
- Uncle Toivo, Aunt Alina and family, as well settled in Oripaa. When Uncle Kauko moved to nearby Loimaa for a better job, Toivo got his previous job in Oripaa.
- Uncle Vilho married Kirsti Ilola. He met her before the war in Jyvaskyla. When he was in the Jyvaskyla army hospital, they met once more and got married after he was discharged. They settled in the Jyvaskyla area.
- Uncle Arvo married Anni Karra and settled near Hameenliina.

- Aunt Saima, Martti, Sirkka, George and Irja and her family remained in Siuro near Tampere.

Grandpa stayed with us after the war. Periodically he would travel through Finland to visit his wife Hilda and to stay with his other sons and daughters. Grandmother Hilda Öhman lived with her sons in Oripaa. Due to the lack of space (Grandpa lived in our sauna no less) there wasn't sufficient room nor food for both grandparents in one normal home. This was common in Finland after the war.

Grandfather died at our place in October, 1946 – just a year after the war ended. He died of lip cancer at the age of 69. Mother visited him daily in the hospital. She was distraught that she was not at his bed side when he passed away, having just left to come home.

Grandmother lived with Uncle Kauko until he and his family left for Canada in 1952. Grandmother then stayed with Uncle Arvo until they as well left for Canada. She then moved in to live with Uncle Toivo until Uncle Toivo and Aunt Alina put Alina's mother in an old folks home. No longer feeling comfortable there, she moved in with cousin Martti in Siuros. She died there after a few months and was buried in Oripaa.

Mother and Father

Our family lived in Kotka from 1945 until we left for Canada in 1951.

I was born in Kotka in November, 1947.

Dad was the engineer responsible for the rail road in that area (Kouvala- Kotka- Hamina). This included building a major railroad bridge into Kotka. I guess the old one was destroyed by Russian bombing during the war. Terttu says that dad often went into Kotka for meetings as well as travelling elsewhere in Finland.

In Kotka father continued to go out of his way to protect the railroads. In 1947 father received a commendation and a reward of 500 markka from the Finnish Railway (a significant amount in those days). It was awarded by the Chairman of the Finnish Railway for his actions in saving a train derailment in the Hovinsaari railway yards. He removed a boulder from the tracks just as a train was arriving. It had been placed there by a mentally unstable man. Dad managed to catch and hold the man until he was able to pass him on to the authorities. In the commendation there is a reference to two incidents – one on June 29, 1947 and one on July 13, 1947. I guess dad did not catch the man the first time.

Father was a well regarded man in Kotka. He had an amazing number of highly placed friends – most from his Viipuri days. After the war he got jobs for both Uncle Kauko and Uncle Toivo as well as for grandfather.

We had a modest house beside the tracks in Hovinsaari. It was owned by the rail road.

My sisters Terttu and Tellevo remember Kotka as a nice place.

Both Terttu and Tellervo went into Kotka to a private school. For some reason dad, and particularly Grandmother Tuira, felt that a private school was needed. Dad (and mother) were always supportive of all of us getting the very best education. Tuula went to the local public school. George just roamed around as he was too young to go to school. I didn't go much farther than the yard as I was only 3 then.

For many years after the war there was a shortage of food and materials in Finland as all the goods were going to Russia to pay war reparations and thus there was little left at home.

The USA Red Cross was very helpful during the lean years after the war, providing food and clothing.

Tellervo remembers getting coats from the Red Cross, and of mother lining up for a long time in the Red Cross queue shortly after I was born to get blankets and clothes for me, as mother had none. She was very happy when she got some.

Packages also came from relatives and friends in Canada and the USA. Aunt Ester used to send huge Christmas packages, containing clothes and food. Cousin Helen says she remembers watching her mother as she prepared the packages for Finland. The food included rice and dried fruit. Tellervo recounts that Mother made great pudding out of this which Tellervo really enjoyed. The clothes were often cousin Helen hand me downs. In one of the family portraits Tuula is wearing Helen's nice dress – and it looked fine. The problem was that the dress had the name "Helen" stitched across the front.

As material was hard to get after the war, Terttu remembers that she and Tellervo, to their dismay, were often dressed in the same fabrics. Mother sewed up outfits for the two of them from the only cloth she was able to get.

Sirkka and the Kavantsaari Folk

Aunt Saima and her children Martti, Sirkka, George and Irja had a difficult time. Aunt Saima with the help of Martti and Sirkka managed to house and feed the family. Sirkka recounts:

After the war life felt a bit odd and mirthless at first. Those mud flowers were on hearts window.

Nonetheless school started in the fall and I got friends and so the ice began to thaw from my heart.

I went to rippikoulu with Martti in 1945. Youth began.

In 1944 mother got a job in a basket factory. The next summer I got a job there as well. It was my first full time job. I was a grown woman.

Nonetheless the same fall I went to work in Tampere. Afterwards I had several jobs before settling in Hameenlinna. I had a good friend for life, a good job and met my prince. But that as well slipped through my fingers. For that I can only blame myself.

Martti went to house painting school and there was a lot of work. Later he got married and settled near Tampere. George as well started to earn his keep. He went to work at Nokia. It was night work and George decided to go to Canada. Bravely he learned the language, while going to work during the day and to the trade school at night.

I have happy memories from my Siuro and Hameenlinna times - and from the golden years in Karjala.

I have many memories of the war years - many heavy dreams which I saw after the wars, in the wilderness hurrying and afraid of the refugee departure.

Everyone to Amerika

CHAPTER 29

Everyone to Amerika

While the family settled successfully in Finland, ancestral Karjala was no more. As well everyone had to start from nothing again. House, home and friends had disappeared.

Unencumbered by belongings, in due course almost all the family moved to America – first coming to Canada. Some thereafter moved to the United States.

All settled and did well.

The only members of the family who remained in Finland were

- My Uncle Yrjo. He settled into a job with the railway in Hameenlinna. Even he came to Canada for a brief spell, working as a book keeper before returning to Finland.

- Uncle Toivo and Aunt Alina and their family. They as well came to Canada for a couple of years before returning to Nousiainen in Finland. Their three oldest children remained in Canada.

- Cousin Martti. He settled near Tampere, married and had a family.

The rest of the family came to Canada, including Aunt Saima, and cousins George and Irja. The last to leave Finland was Sirkka in 1958, as she says:

> And in 1958 Uncle Arvo came for a skiing competition in Finland and got Sirkka all excited about coming to Canada. I got a visa and on June 8 1958 found myself in Toronto.

Life in Amerika was not easy but everyone managed and ultimately all did well.

Voyage to Kanada

My own family came to Canada in July 1951.

Life in Finland for us in Kotka was reasonable given the post war shortages. Father had a good job with quite good pay.

It was because of myself that we left for Canada. I was quite sickly as a child suffering from respiratory aliments. Kotka had heavy air pollution caused by its pulp and paper mill and a garment factory. Father attempted several times to get a transfer to another city but was turned down by the railway management. In 1951 Uncle Armas said that there was a window of opportunity to immigrate to Canada - a good life and lots of fresh air. He was prepared to sponsor us. Mother having lived in Canada in 1929/1930 thought it was a good idea. Father wanted his children to have the best opportunities. Ever the courageous adventurer he said yes.

Dad went to Canadian embassy located in Stockholm to apply for immigration to Canada. There was no consulate in Finland. The immigration official was concerned that there were too many of us. "You have 5 children. How are you going to support them ?". Dad said that Uncle Armas, who was sponsoring us, had a farm. Father as well got a good reference from the Kotka police chief who was a friend of dads – and, who happened to be the local passport official.

According to Tellervo, we almost never got to leave as we had to pass a medical. The doctor visited us and examined everyone, listening with his stethoscope and tapping here and there. Tellervo was inquisitively standing right by the doctor, watching him work. Everyone was healthy except for myself. He was not going to sign a health certificate for me. Somehow dad was able to sweet talk the doctor into signing my form. Dad must have been a great convincer to get the doctor to OK everyone.

Once dad got the final approval, he went to Stockholm and picked up the papers. The visa in Dad's passport is marked as approved by the Helsinki British Legation visa section on June 14, 1951.

I remember him arriving home from Stockholm in the middle of the night. I was sick, and it was dark, but I woke up and marveled at the fruit he brought back - especially the grapes and cherries.

Before we left, we were not sure whether we would have enough money.

The cost of admittance to Canada had already come as a bit of a shock. Mother thought it was $80. In fact it was $800. Language is always a tricky business.

They arranged an indirect trip via ship as opposed to plane - one with many connections, in order to get the most economical passage. Mother and dad auctioned all their belongings to raise money to supplement the monies they already had. Dad's work colleagues helped as well. They very generously paid for the passage of one of the girls.

So my parents now in their early 40s and with five children left for Canada.

It was long trip from Kotka Finland via train, ferry, and boat to Cansfield, Canada (Uncle Armas's farm near Dunnville). There were many, many connections:

1.) We left Kotka via train for Helsinki. In Helsinki we stayed at grandmother's apartment (Must have been cozy. There was little room, and grandmother was distraught that she was losing her granddaughters forever . Grandma never paid much attention to George and myself).

2.) From Helsinki we went to Turku. The passport has a stamp showing us leaving Finland on June 25, 1951.

3.) From Helsinki we took the ferry to Stockholm, entering Stockholm June 26, 1951. The passport is stamped with:

Canada Immigrant – Destined to Canfield Ontario

Stockholm, Sweden

June 26, 1951

Visa – Canadian Consulate

According to Tellervo we stayed overnight in Stockholm in a big room in a boarding house.

4.) From Stockholm we took a train to Malmo, Sweden, exiting on June 27, 1951.

I was impressed by a group of young Swedish Cadets picking up their gear and exiting singing a rousing "up and at them chorus". Mom commented, "That's the spirit. We too should remain upbeat and confident. "

5.) From there, we took a boat / ferry to Kobenhavn, Denmark (Copenhagen) arriving on June 28, 1951 – via boat.

In Copenhagen we went to a restaurant where dad ordered steak for everyone. It was very expensive. Almost no one ate their steak, as it was too raw. Probably it was cooked medium. But for a Finn, that is raw. At home every piece of meat mom ever cooked was very well done – a Finnish tradition.

6.) We exited Esbjerg on June 28, 1951 bound for England. We took a ferry across the North Channel to Harwick just north of London.

Tellervo recounts that the trip was very, very stormy and she and everyone else except for George and myself were sea sick.

7.) We entered Harwick, UK on June 29, 1951 and caught a train from London to Plymouth.

The whole group (There were several other families from Finland that were also travelling to Canada) had some problems in getting to London and finding the right train and platform. Mother with her 2 years of English exposure in Canada was able to get all of us to the right place. The London train station, with it hustle and bustle, and steam generating locomotives, was quite dirty. Mother, a cleanliness fanatic, was distressed.

8.) We exited Plymouth, England - June 30, 1951 - bound for Canada on the SS Europa. SS Europa was a passenger ship going from Europe, France, and the UK, to Canada and New York.

Per Terttu,

> " It was a German ship with German crew. I often served as a German interpreter for others. It was exciting being on the boat as it had good sized rooms, room to run on the decks, and good food. (I guess Terttu had learned German during the 3 years she was in Kemijarvi and Kelloselka.)

Tellervo remembers that there were two shifts for food. Tellervo went by herself once because she was so hungry. She commented that the steward was disappointed when she would not eat the egg she had asked for. It was too soft. I guess Tellervo couldn't have been that hungry after all.

The weather was generally ok. I remember over cast skies and whales in the distance.

On the ship, and generally throughout the trip, mom took care of me while dad took care of George. George always escaped with his friends – once coming back with pine tar on his pants – according to George this was at the railroad station in Halifax. He says he almost got run over by a train in the process. He had slipped away unnoticed to do some exploring. While mom was distraught, it must have seemed normal for dad given his own childhood escapades.

9.) We arrived in Canada at Halifax harbor on July 6, 1951. There were war ships still in the harbor

We were whisked through immigration without any incidents.

Mom stepped out and bought bread and butter for the trip. Per Tellervo, mom was excited as the bread was sliced. Mom, once we got to Canada, did the translating.

We quickly and easily went from Pier 21 immigration to the train.

10.) The train trip from Halifax to Toronto through Montreal was long and hot.

While travelling between Halifax and Montreal, dad lost his engineering ring prying open a window to get air. Father said it was a portent that his engineering days were over – and so it turned out.

Dad was impressed by the band playing in Montreal station, greeting the train.

11.) When we arrived at Union Station in Toronto, we had to transfer to another train to go to Cansfield. The agent said there was no such place or train. Dad showed the ticket that had been given in Finland. (Perhaps it had been written Ganboro or Canberra.)

While we waited in the station we got free coffee and cake.

All of a sudden the agent came running back, "I have found it. Hurry, follow me". We got on the train – barely.

12.) We arrived in Cansfield and got off the train. Cansfield consisted of a stop in the middle of a field with nothing but a drop off for the mail bag. No one was there.

Shortly the mail lady arrived in her truck. She bundled us into the cab and into the back, and took us to her store in the centre of the town – or rather hamlet. There were only 5 or 6 houses. As is the case with small communities, she had heard that we were coming. She phoned Uncle Armas. He had gotten the dates wrong. While we waited, the post mistress gave us kids ice cream cones. When Armas came, we loaded the mail truck with our luggage again, got into uncles car, and away we went to Uncle Armas and Aunt Kerttu's place.

The trip was over. After three weeks of the unkown, we had arrived safely in CANADA with kids and luggage intact.

Terttu and I found a very sweet old newspaper clipping in dad's papers. It was from a local paper. Verbatim it reads:

"Mr. and Mrs. A. Öhman entertained a number of friends and relatives on Saturday evening to a surprise party in honor of the former's sister and brother-in-law, Mr. and Mrs. Feuira and family who recently arrived from Katka, Finland, and at present are making their home with the Öhman's. *To the Feuiras we extend a hearty welcome"*

There were many kind people in Canada.

While father was fluent in Finnish and Swedish and had a passable understanding of German and Russian, he did not speak English. So like many other immigrants, then and now, he could not find work in his old profession. He went to work in the lumber jack camps in Northern Ontario.

Life in Canada was not easy for them. As mother said, it was quite a change for dad to go from being an engineer walking around with his hands behind his back managing people to working as a lumberjack. Mother occasionally fretted about the circumstances. But I never heard father complain about his lot in life.

While we did not have much money we always had a loving home, clothes on our back, wonderful food, and the traditional Karjala joy in life. Father ensured we had the best education. While we were poor, I never felt second class.

Mother talked occasionally about the wonderful days in Karjala. Father hardly ever mentioned Karjala or Viipuri.

My brother, my sisters and I have done well in Canada. We are all fully and proudly Canadian.

For me, while I am proud of my Finnish heritage, it is Karjala that for some reason keeps calling.

CANBORO

Mr. and Mrs. A. Ohman entertained a number of friends and relatives on Saturday evening to a surprise party in honour of the former's sister and brother-in-law, Mr. and Mrs. Feuira and family who recently arrived from Katka, Finland, and at present are making their home with the Ohman's. To the Feuiras we extend a hearty welcome.

Returning "Home" to Karjala

Returning "Home" to Karjala

Well here it is June 2016 and I am going back to Viipuri !

This time I am going with second cousins Anna and Elina and Elina's husband Veikko. Both Anna and Elina are Karjalaiset. Their grandfather was my great uncle Hjlamar Hellman who had owned the Hellman bakery in Viipuri.

And this time I took the Allegro express train from Helsinki to Viipuri. Hopefully not a four hour inquisition at the border like last time I drove with cousins Arto and Reima.

The train whizzed down the tracks quickly and comfortably towards Viipuri. As we passed the border a moose raised its' head from a wildernesss lily pad – oblivious to borders made by man.

Within 15 minutes we pulled up at the Viipuri station. A few of us got out – most were continuing on to St Petersburg. There were a few police on the platform. I got the feeling that I was indeed in a foreign country. We moved quickly to a short customs queue. With a bit of trepidation I handed my passport through the wicket to the dour customs agent. She looked at my passport and for just a moment a broad smile formed on her face – ahh, from Canada. Forms sake being important, she immediately frowned and perused my passport. Then stamp, stamp, and I was through.

I was in Viipuri again !!

The railway station wasn't busy but there were guards with tommy guns and a metallic scanner at the exit of the railway station. Terrorism knows no bounds.

We walked to our hotel – Hotel Druzbah – on Salakalahti looking across the inlet to the castle and the old city. There was some confusion at checkin but the hotel turned out to be friendly and excellent. We had to leave our passport with the hotel for the night like before. Standard procedure - I remember doing it in Austria many years before. But I still felt a bit uneasy.

Off to the Pyroea Torni and a tour of Viipuri Linna and its' museum before turning in. I arranged a car and guide to take us to Kavantsaari the next day.

The weather was beautiful, sunny and warm.

Valerie our guide and driver met us at the hotel the next morning. His mother had been Finnish and he spoke better Finnish then I did. He was a former border guard. As we passed out of Viipuri he just said a few words to the guard at the checkpoint on the road heading north and the barrier was raised and we proceeded ahead. When I had been there in 2012 the guard post hadn't been manned.

Soon we approached Ihantala. This time I knew when we had reached the Ihantala village. We pulled into the Ihantala Battle Memorial. Valerie drove on past it. He knew where the Ihantala cemetery was. We got out after driving only a couple of hundred yards. There it was – a big boulder with inscription on it – and an empty green expanse among the pines – and the bones of Uncle Erkki and Great Grandmother "Rakas Mummo" somewhere. I was the first person to return since cousin Sirkka had laid some flowers at her fathers' grave a week before departing Karjala forever. I felt I was in a special place – and I was.

I paid my respects and we left but stopped at the Ihantala Battle monument – just a large boulder with some words chiseled into it. But it was here that Finland had preserved its' independence. I picked up a rusted bullet. After a few moments of contemplation we departed.

We went across the road to the ruined church steps and the sankari cemetery. The church where cousin George had come to collect the wagon before starting on the long heart breaking trek from Kavantsaari to Siuro.

We continued on into Kavantsaari village. This time we actually went to the old Theslett estate. The barn was still there along with some decrepit houses. People were still living there but the collective farm did not appear to be operational. And there was nothing that indicated that for 500 years it had been the country home of the rulers of Viipuri and Karjala. There were some people walking from the nearby Kavantsaari village dressed quite smartly. As it turned out it was the Russian independence weekend.

But my main objective was to walk on the old homestead.

I told Valerie where I thought the homedstead was. Valerie found a small road and drove right up to the property on a small hilltop surrounded by overgrown fields ! I jumped out leaving my second cousins. There was the boulder where mother and fathers picture had been taken. And there – that line of rocks and mortar must surely be the foundation of the house. Some old cherry trees still tried to blossom. Across the fields about a kilometer away the lake simmered in the distance. I wandered about the hill top exploring. It was soon time to go. Before leaving I picked up a small rock from the house foundation.

Valeri said, next time you should bring a picnic lunch and some champagne and spend some time soaking in the memories.

As we drove back I asked Valerie to stop at the Russian memorial at Portinhoikka. We did and looked at the thousands of names inscribed on the monument. Valerie explained the various plaques and smaller monuments – and why a few plaques were blank. They were to provide space for soldiers whose remains were even today being found and identified via their dog tags.

On into Viipuri - and past Viipuri - to the Red Civil War monument on the road to St Petersburg south of Viipuri. Although the Red soldiers had been buried at Papula or executed at Ristimaki and Heikka, the White Finns had not allowed a memorial to the Reds to be placed in Viipuri.

And then a stop at the Ristimaki cemetery to pay respects to my grandfather Georg Tuira just like before. This time I knew that there would be no grave marker to find. I paid my respects but I did not have any flowers to leave. I must do better next time. My second cousins looked for their grandfather Hjlamar's grave. Although they found the spot there were no grave stones any more.

On to the Water Tower and to Pattermaki. As we briefly toured Tsar Alexander II's fortifications I told Valerie that it

had been my father and his brothers' boyhood playground. He laughed saying it had been his as well.

The following morning we visited the Monrepos, Terraniemi, Heikka side of Viipuri on the Hamina Road: Tsarina Anna's fortifications - the original 1712 war memorial - Peter the Greats' statue on the hill where the Finnish lion had growled until 1940. The Ullberg designed civic building was still fully functional - but surrounded now only by big old decaying buildings.

The day continued with a tour of the Taidemuseum and the just renovated Alvar Aalto Viipuri Library. A nice dinner at the Kamelot – but far less relaxed then the last time we had been there. It was very busy. It was Russian independence week end ! Ahh one should remember these things.

Second cousin Anna convinced me to have a Viipurin rinkeli. As I mentioned in the first volume of my book it is a hard baked pastry in the form of a pretzel infused with spices. The rinkeli was brought to Viipuri by the Franciscan monks in 1500. Until the 1900s it was so expensive that it was only reserved for nobility. Tsar Alexander III had a standing weekly order for Viipurin rinkeli. I was surprised when I bit into it expecting a taste similar to an unsalted pretzel. But it wasn't. It was delicious with a subtle and a unique intemingling of spices.

We left the next afternoon – but not before a final tour of, and lunch in the Pyroea Torni. It was a comfortable and uneventful train trip back to Helsinki. Mind you I again was a little skittish as we left. What if the train did not arrive ? My visa was only good to the end of the day – and then what ? the tommy gun touting guards looked a bit intimidating....

Yes Viipuri was definitely still part of Russia.

But it was most definitely still part of me.

Yes there were many derelect buildings. As my fellow travelers and many visiting Finns have scoffed: "Tut tut look at that – terrible - You would never see that in Finland." To which I responded yes if we were in Helsinki all the buildings would have been torn down long ago and replaced with modern stark towers. There would be no old mediaeval town. So neglect has saved the city.

Derelect but charming, old and worn. Frozen in time and in peoples' memories. A city that had been at the cross roads of east and west for a millennium, blood soaked and battered, but with a special mysticism and humanity.

Viipuri Linna still stood there beckoning me to come hear the stories it could tell. The Pyroea Torni – hustling and bustling, ringing with laughter. The Raate Torni and the Clock Tower –-the Orthodox cathedral and the Swedish Lutheran Church - the sad empty space where the Tuomio Church had stood. Faith and religion - from medieval monks to Finnish modernity. Uuno Ullberg's Taide Museum and Alvar Alto's library. Modern architectural gems sprinkled among medieval towers and Jungen mansions – a strange but surprisingly complementary juxtaposition. The Torkelli Park and Punasian Lahti Square –statues of a bronze moose and a boy and a bear cub - places for people. All enveloped by the waters of the Viipuri Gulf. Guarded seemingly forever by Viipuri Linna.

Yes Viipuri and Karjala had always been in the path of war. But it had always been a font of civilization, culture, joy and fellowship among men.

When I return I hope I will be able to contact our guide Valerie again – and have that picnic in mother's Kavantsaari field of dreams – and a coffee and a rinkeli in fathers' Viipuri. And listen as Valerie tells me about his Viipuri.

As one old lady said, "Karjala will return to its days of glory be it 200 years from now". There is something special in the air there that transforms people.

APPENDICES

APPENDIX A

Bibliography

APPENDIX A

Bibliography

1. The Kalevala- Elias Lönnrot translated by Francis Peabody Magoun Jr; Harvard University Press 1963
2. Ancient Powers of the Baltic Sea: Matti Klinge; Aspasia books, Beaverton, On. Canada, 2007, original 1983
3. 9000 Vuotta Suomen Esihistoriaa: Matti Huurre; Otava, Helsinki,1979
4. Maamme Kirja: Topelius, Zacharias, 1875
5. Suomen Suvun Tiet - Eero Kuussaari; F. Tilgamann Oy; Helsinki, 1935
6. Suomen Sota 1808-1809 - Reima Luoto, Heikki Talvitie, Pekka Visuri; Fenix Kustannus Oy, Espoo 2008
7. Under the Northern Star, Vols I, II, III –Väinö Linna translated by Richard Impola; Aspasia Books Beaverton, Canada 1959-2002
8. Nummijuutarit - Aleksis Kivi: R.J. Gummerus, Jyvaskyla 1923
9. A Brief History of Finland – Matti Klinge; Otava, Helsinki, 1981
10. A History of Finland – Eino Jutikkala & Kauko Pirinen, translated by Paul Sjöblom; Espoo 1962
11. Suomen Historia; Jalmari Jaakola; WSOY Helsinki Porvoo, 1956
12. Pohjois-Pohjanmaa ja Lapin Historia; Armas Luukko; Osakeytiö Liiton Kirjapaino, 1954
13. Simonkylan Vanhojen Talojen Historiaa: Henrik Tariina, 1999-2000, Pahniklan Museo, Simo
14. Suomen Tasavallan Presidentit- Matti Kuusi et al; WSOY, Porvoo, 1952
15.
16. Karjalan Kuvat: Hannes Sihvo, Matti Ruotsalainen ; WSOY Porvoo 1986
17. Rakas Entinen Karjala – Olavi Paavolainen et al; WSOY Porvoo, 1947
18. Antrea; Antrean ja Vuoksenrannan Kuntien Muistojulkaisu-Seppo Simonen;Helsinki, 1951
19. Kotiseutumme Antrea – Antti Henttonen et al; Helsinki 1995
20. Ihantala, Rauhan ja Sodan Aikana – Teuvo Kuparin et al; Pieksämäki, 1991
21.
22. Viipurin Kirja; Aarno Tuurna, Koskinen,Koivu, Valtuo Sisalahetysseuran Raamattutalon Kirjapaino, Pieksamaki 1958
23. Aikamatka Viipuriin – Pekka Kantanen & Mikko Mäntyniemi; Kuopio 2010
24. Ikuinen Viipuri; Ajankuvia Seitsemältä Vuosisdalta – Matti Klinge et al; Otava, Helsinki, 1993
25. Viipuri: Muistoja Kaipuuni Kaupungista – Kalevi Tilli; WSOY, 1985
26. Viipurilainen Kertoo Viipurilaiselle - Pentti Rousku; Jväskylä, 1989
27. Rajatapauksia Vanhan Viipurin ja Karjalan Kulttuurimusitoja: Sven Hirn; Otava, Helsinki, 1964
28. Kultainen Rinkeli – Katri Veltheim; Helsinki 1985

29. Viipurilainen Kertoo... - Sirkka Rapola; Otava, Helsinki, 1946
30. Viipuri 1918; Teemu Keskisarja; Bookwell Oy 2013
31. Sissällissodan Pikku Jättiläinen: Pertti Haapala ja Tuomas Hoppuö, WSOY
32.
33. Talvisodan Historia – Volumes 1-4: Lieutenant Colonel Antti Juutilainen, Sotahistorian Tomisto ; WSOY, Porvoo 1977
34. Jatkosodan Historia – Volumes 1-6: Colonel Matti Lappalainen, Sotahistorian Tomisto ; WSOY, Porvoo 1988
35. Talvisodan Pikku Jättiläinen – Jari Leskinen & Antti Juutilainen; WSOY, Porvoo 1999
36. Jatkosodan Pikku Jättiläinen – Jari Leskinen & Antti Juutilainen; WSOY, Porvoo 2005
37. Suomi Suursodassa Finland I Storkriget – Olavi Autila; Jväskylä, 1988
38. Suomen Kohtalon Ratkaisut Talvisota ja Jatkosoat 1939-1944: Matti Koskimaa; Docendo Oy, Jyvaskyla, 2013
39. Finland at War 1939-45 – Philip Jowet & Brent Snodgrass; Osprey Publishing, Oxford, U.K.; 2006
40. Finnish Aces of World War 2: Stenman, Kari, Styling Mark; Osprey Publishing, Oxford, UK, 1998
41. Kollaa Kestää – E. Pololampi; WSOY Porvoo, 1940
42. Kempin Rykmentti: Kimmo Sorko & Erkki Seppanen; Menerva Kustannus Oy, 2005
43. Patterinpäällikönä Talvisodassa: Viho Pösö; Arvi A Karisto Oy, Häameenlinna 1982
44. A Frozen Hell, The Russo Finnish War of 1939-1940 – William R. Trotter; Algonquin Books, Chapel Hill, 2000
45. The Winter War: The Soviet Attack on Finland 1939-1940: Eloise Engle & Lauri Paananen; Stackpole Books, Mechanicsburg ,Pa, USA
46. The Winter War/Talvisota: Antti Tuuri; Aspasia Books, Beaverton On Canada , 1984/2003
47.
48. Pion P 14: IV AK:n Pioneeripataljoona 1941-1944 – Eero Vankka; Helsinki, 1999
49. Siiranmäen Miehet; Aake Jermo; Otava, Helsinki, 1977
50. Unknown Soldier – Väinö Linna; WSOY Porvoo, 1954
51. Panssarijuna Suomessa: Jouni Sillanmäki; Gummerus Kirjapaino Oy, Jyväskylä, 2009
52. Tyrjän Rykmentti - Matti Koskimaa; WSOY Porvoo, 1996
53. Veitsen Terällä - Matti Koskimaa; WSOY Porvoo, 1993
54. Panssari Sotaa 1941-1944 – Reino Lehväslaiho WSOY Porvoo, 1958
55. Kannaksen Suurhyokkays 1944 Venalaisen: Ilya Mostsanski; Helsinkin-kirjat Oy, 2010
56. Viipurin Viimeinen Paiva, Kesalla 1944: Lauri Jantti; WSOY, Porvo, 1964
57. Taistelu Viipurisata 20.6.1944: Uuno Tarkki: Gummerus Kirjapaino Oy, Jyvaskyla, 1996
58. Sotilaiden Aanet: Paavo Rintala; Weikin Goos Oy, Helsinki, 1966
59.
60. Nousiaisten Sotaveteraanien Matrikkeli Vols I & II - Volmar Tammi et al; Uusikaupunki, 1999
61. Isänmaan Vapauden Puolesta 1939-1945, Kemijarven Veteraanmatrikkeli Vols 1 & II; Kemijarvi 1998
62. Simo ja Simolaiset Vaaran Vuosina 1914-1945: Pekka Vilmi et al; Pohjolan Sanomat Oy, Kemi, 1986
63. Oulu ja Oululaiset Sodissa: Oulun kaupungin veteraanikirjatoimikunta; Painotalo Suomenmaa, Oulu 2002
64.
65. Suomen Marsalkka C.G. Mannerheim - Veijo Meri; WSOY, Porvoo 1988
66. Mannerheim, Tuttu ja Tuntemation - Martti Sinermaa et al; Helsinki, 1997
67. The Memoirs of Marshal Mannerheim translated by Count Eric Lewenhaupt; E.F. Dutton & Co,New York 1954
68. Kruschev Remembers - Edward Crankshaw; Little Brown & Co., 1970
69.
70. The Lapp King's Daughter – Stina Katchadourian; California, 2010

71. Siirtokarjalaiset 1941-44: Johannes Virolainen; Otava, Helsinki, 1989

Magazines and Papers:

1. Ilta- Sanomat Special Edition: Naisten Sota; 2011-01
2. Ilta- Sanomat Special Edition: Viipurin – Sellainen ol' Viipuri; 2012-23
3. Ilta- Sanomat Special Edition: Viipurin Muistot;2013-11
4. Ilta- Sanomat Special Edition: Karjala; 2013-26
5. Ilta- Sanomat Special Edition: 1918 – Kun Kansa Jakauti; 2014-02
6. Ilta- Sanomat Special Edition: Lottat; 2015-02
7. Ilta- Sanomat Special Edition: Evakot; 2016-02
8. Ilta- Sanomat Special Edition: Suurhyokkays; 2014-27
9. Suomen Sotilaan Historia: Jatkosota; 2016-32
10. Suomen Sotilas: Talvisodan Ihme, 31.1.2010
11. Seura:Tavisodan Ihme, 26.11.2009
12. Kansa Taisteli : Issues from 1957 to 1983
13. Places of Memory in the Red Vyborg Of 1918; Outi Fingerroos PhD, Docent; Department of History and Ethnology; University of Jyväskylä
14. Helsinki Sanomat 29.1.2008 International edition- After 90 years, the Finnish Civil War Remains a Sensitive Subject: by Teija Sutinen
15. The Tribes of Finland: Regional Characterizations Of The Finnish People; Irina Kyllönen, Spring 2004 (US) , FAST-FIN-1 (TRENAK1) Finnish Institutions Research Paper, FAST Area Studies Program Department of Translation Studies, University of Tampere

Original Manuscripts

1. Finnish National Archives Sotapäivä Kirjas:

  I. Talvisota; 1. Prikaati
  II. Talvisota;1. Prikatti, Pataljoona I
  III. Talvisota: 1_Prikaati_2_komppania
  IV. 1_Prikaati_Esikunta
  V. 1_Prikaati_I_pataljoona_Viestiosasto
  VI. Erillinen_pataljoona_4
  VII. Erillinen_pataljoona_4_1_komppania
  VIII. Erillinen_pataljoona_4_3_komppania
  IX. Erillinen_pataljoona_4_ Konekiväärikomppania_11
  X. Erillinen_patteristo_4_2_patteri
  XI. Erillinen_patteristo_4_Esikuntapatteri
  XII. Jatkosota; 1_Divisioona
  XIII. Jatkosota; Kevyt Osato 7
  XIV. Jatkosota; Kevyt Osato 7, Kompannia 2
  XV. Jatkosota; Kevyt Prikaati Tiiainen
  XVI. Jatkosota; 2. Divisiiona
  XVII. Jatkosota; Jalkaväkirykmentti 7
  XVIII. Jatkosota; Jalkaväkirykmentti 7, Pataljoona II
  XIX. Jalkaväkirykmentti_7_III_pataljoona
  XX. Jatkosota; Jalkaväkirykmentti 7, Kompannia 9
  XXI. Jatkosota; Jalkaväkirykmentti 28, Patajoona I
  XXII. Jatkosota; Jalkaväkirykmentti 48
  XXIII. Jatkosota; Jalkaväkirykmentti 49, Esikunta
  XXIV. Jatkosota; Jalkaväkirykmentti 49
  XXV. Jatkosota; 1. Divisiiona
  XXVI. Jatkosota; Jalkaväkirykmentti 35, Pataljoona II
  XXVII. Jatkosota; 8. Divisiiona
  XXVIII. Jatkosota Jalkaväkirykmentti 45, Pataljoona II
  XXIX. Jatkosota; Jalkaväkirykmentti 45, Kompannia 8
  XXX. Jatkosota; Pionccripataljoon 14
  XXXI. Jatkosota;20.Prikaati
  XXXII. Jatkosota; 20.Prikaati.I pataljoona and II, III, and IV

XXXIII. Jatkosota; 20.Prikaati.1.Kompania and 3, 4, 5, 6, 7, 8, 9, 10, 11, 12, 13, and 14

XXXIV. Jatkosota; 20. Prikaati. Pioneerikomppanaia

XXXV. Jatkosota; 20.Prikaati.Tykistokomentaja

XXXVI. Jatkosota; 20.Prikaati. Kranaatinheitinkompannia

XXXVII. Jatkosota; 20.Raskas psto

1. Juho Öhman, Valtiorikosoikeuden; Suomen Kansalliskirjasto 1918: Official Civil War Records for Crimes Against the State

2. Lieutenant Kaarlo Miettienen's memoirs of Uncle Arvo's Pioneer platoon in Pion P14 book

3. Finnish Labour Archives. The Commission of Finnish Labour Tradition (TA, TMT). Oral History of the Civil War 1918 in Vyborg.

4. The People's Archives (KA: 6B). Memoirs and interviews of the Civil War 1918.

5. Finnish Literature Society. Folklore archives (SKS, KRA). Oral history of the Civil War 1918.

6. Viipuri brouchure 1933: Viipuri City Council

My Families' Papers and Oral History

1. Father's memoirs on his youth in Viipuri
2. Veikko's papers of the Hellman Viipuri bakery
3. Cousin Sirkka's memoirs
4. Uncle Erkki's Talvisota letters home
5. Mother's stories of her Kavantsaari home and the wars
6. Father's stories of Viipuri and the wars
7. The reminisces of Cousin Sirkka on Kavantsaari and the war years
8. Cousin George's anecdotes on Kavantsaari and the war years
9. Cousin Anna Liisa's anecdotes on Kavantsaari and Viipuri
10. Uncle Yrjo's stories and ancestry research
11. The reminisces of my older sisters Terttu and Tellervo
12. Brother George's reminisces
13. The stories of my second cousins Eeva and Elina

APPENDIX B

Acknowledgements

APPENDIX B

Acknowledgements

The photos and images in the book are:

- personal family photos, and
- military photos courtesy of the Finnish Army (SA Kuva)
- public domain images

I wish to particularly thank the Finnish Sota arkisto for the SA Kuva and maps

The Public domain images from historical Finnish artists are for:

Book I

- Suomen Suvun Tiet - Eero Kuussaari; Helsinki, 1935 – illustrator E. Tanttu:
  - Seppa - pg 45
  - Iso Viha - pg 62
  - Tseremissien "Valkoista Kansaa" - pg 101
  - Vapauden Tiella - pg 83

- Akseli Gallen- Kallela
  - Hiiden Hirvi- Kalevala - page 50
  - Kullervon Sotaanlahto –Kalevala: 1901 pg 56
  - Kalevala - page 68
- Albert Edelfelt,
  - Silmapouli Karjalainen 1879 – pg 41
  - Porilaisten Marssi 1892 - pg 65
- Artist Unknown in Aleksis Kivi book, Nummijuutarit: R.J. Gummerus, Jyvaskyla 1923 - pg 45
- Werner Astrom
  - Lehma savu - pg 99

Book II

- Albert Edelfelt, Poltettu Kyla, 1879 - pg1
- Oma Tuppa, Suomen homestead settlement certificate pg 244

Book III

- Akseli Gallen-Kallea : Sammon Taonta - Kalevala" 1893 - pg 447

Rulers of Karjala

Swedish Monarchs

Emperors of Russia

The Grand Dukes of Finland

Commanders of the Fiefdom of Viipuri & Karjala

The Swedish Governor Generals of Finland

Tsars of Russia and Karjala

Tsars of the Grand Duchy of Finland

Bolshevik Rulers of Russia

Presidents of Finland

Owners of the Kavantsaari Estate

Rulers of Karjala

Swedish Monarchs

Swedish Monarchs

c.990 Erik VII the Victorious

993 - 1001 Erik VIII Arsaell

995 - 1021/22 Olof III Skoetkonung

1021/22 - 50/1 Anund Jacob

1050/1 - 60 Emund (the Old)

1060 - 1066 Stenkil

1066 - 1084 Halsten

1080 - 1110 Inge I (the Eldar)

1110 - 1118 Philipp

1118 - 1125 Inge II (the younger)

c.1130 Ragnvald

1135 - 1156 Sverker I (the eldar)

1158 - 1160 Erik IX the Holy

1160 - 1167 Carl VII Sverkersson

1167 - 1196 Knut Eriksson

1196 - 1208 Sverker II (the Younger)

1208 - 1216 Erik X Knutsson (Christianity to Finland)

1216 - 1222 Johan I Sverkersson

1222 - 1229 Erikk XI

1229 - 1234 Knut Lange

1234 - 1249 Erik XI

1250 - 1266 Birger Jarl (Regent)

1250 - 1278 Waldemar Birgersson

1278 - 1290 Magnus I BirgerssonLadulas

1290 - 1319 Birger Magnusson (Founding of Viipuri Linna)

1319 - 1362 Magnus II

1357 - 1359 Erik XII

1362 - 1363 Hakon Magnusson

1364 - 1388 Albrecht of Mecklenburg

1388 - 1412 Margarete

1396 - 1439 Erik XIII (of Pommerania)

1440 - 1448 Christoph (of Bavaria)

1448 - 1453 Carl VIII Knutsson (Commader of Viipuri Linna)

1454 - 1464 Christian I

1464 - 1465 Carl VIII Knutsson

1467 - 1470 Carl VIII Knutsson

1470 - 1471 Christian I

1470 - 1495 StenSture the Older (Regent) (Commander of Viipuri Linna)

1497 - 1501 Hans II

1501 - 1503 StenSture the Older (Regent)

1504 - 1511 Svante Nilsson Sture (Regent)

1512 - 1520 Sten Svantesson (StenSture the Younger) (Regent)

1520 - 1523 Christian II

Vasa Dynasty

1523 - 1560 Gustaf I Wasa (Regent from 1521 –
(Converts to Lutheranism. Eliminates feudal estates)
1560 - 1568 Erik XIV
1568 - 1592 Hans III
1592 - 1599 Sigismund III (Vasa)
1599 - 1611 Carl IX
1611 - 1632 Gustaf II Adolf
1632 - 1654 Christina

Wittelsbach Dynasty (Pfalzisks)

1654 - 1660 Carl X Gustaf
1660 - 1697 Carl XI
1697 - 1718 Carl XII (Charles XII – Charles the
Warrior King)
1719 - 1720 Ulrike Eleonore

Brabant Dynasty (Hessen)

1720 - 1751 Frederik I

Holsten-Gottorp Dynasty

1751 - 1771 Adolf Frederik (Adolphus)
1772 - 1792 Gustaf III
1792 - 1809 Gustaf IV Adolf (Last Finnish monarch)
1809 - 1818 Carl XIII (regent 2-4 months)

Bernadotte Dynasty

1818 - 1844 Carl XIV
1844 - 1859 Oscar I
1859 - 1872 Carl XV
1872 - 1907 Oscar II
1907 - 1950 Gustaf V (during Talvi and Jatko sotas)
1950 - 1973 Gustav VI Adolf

Emperors of Russia

Princes of Novgorod

- Rurik 862-879
- Oleg of Novgorod 882-912

Grand Princes of Kiev

- Igor I: 913- 94
- Saint Olga of Kiev 945-962
- Sviatoslav I the Great - 962- 972
- Yaropolk I : 972-980
- Saint Vladimir I the Great 972-101
- Sviatopolk the Accursed :1015 – 1019
- Yaroslav I the Wise: 1019-105
- Iziaslav I : 1054-107
- Sviatoslav II: 1073-1076
- Vsevolod I : 1078-1093
- Sviatopolk II : 1093-111
- Vladimr II: 1113-1125
- Mstislav the Great : 1125-1132
- Yaropolk II : 1132-1139
- Vsevolod II : 1139-1146
- Numerous
- In 1169 Vladimir troops took Kiev

Grand Princes of Vladimir

- Saint Andrei I: 1157-1174
- Several
- Vsevolod III the Big Nest: 1176-1212
- Yuri II: 1212-1216
- Konstantin of Rostov: 1216-1218
- Yuri II : 1218-1238
- Yaroslav II : 1238-1246
- Viatoslav II: 1246-1249
- Andrey II: 1249-1252
- Saint Alexander I Nevsky: 1252-1263
- Yaroslav III: 1264-1271
- Vasily of Kostroma : 1272-1277
- Dmitry of Pereslavl: 1277- 1293
- Andrey III: 1293-1304

- Saint Michael of Tver: 1304-1318
- Yuri Iii of Moscow : 1318-1322
- Dmitry I the Terrible Eyes: 1322-1326
- Alexander of Tver: 1326-1328
- After 1328 the title of the Grand Princes of Vladimir was assigned to the Princes of Moscow.

Grand Princes of Moscow

- Ivan I of Moscow: – 1328-1340
- Simeon the Proud: 1340-1353
- Ivan II the Handsome: 1353-1359
- Saint Dmitry Donskoy: 1359-1389
- Vasily I: 1389-1425
- Vasily II the Blind: 1425-1462
- Ivan III the Great: 1462-1505
- Vasily III: 1505-1533

Tsars of Russia

House of Rurik

- Ivan IV the Terrible: 1533-1547
- Feodor I: 1584-1598
- House of Godunov
- Boris I: 1598-1605
- False Dmitry I, II, III: 1605-1612

House of Shuysky

- Vasiliy IV: 1606-1610
- Seven Boyars

House of Vasa (Poland)

- Vladislav I: 1610-1634

House of Romanov

- Michael I : 1613-1645 (Moscow)
- Alexis I the Quietest: 1645-1676
- Feodor III: 1676-1682
- Sophia (regent): 1682-1689
- Ivan V jointly with Peter : 1682-1696

Emperors of all Russia

(Also Grand Princes of Finland from 1809 to 1917; and Kings of Poland from 1815 to 1916)

- Peter I the Great: (born Moscow) 1682-1721
- Catherine I (born Sweden): 1725-1727
- Peter II (St. Petersburg): 1727-1730
- Anna (Moscow): 1730-1740
- Ivan VI (child -disputed): St Petersburg: 1740-1741
- Elizabeth (Moscow): 1741-1762
- Peter III (Germany): 1762
- Catherine II the Great: (Prussia): 1762-1796
- Paul I (St Petersburg): 1796-1801
- Alexander I the Blessed (St Petersburg): 1801- 1825
- Nicholas I (St Petersburg) 1825-1855
- Alexander II the Liberator (Moscow) 1855- 1881
- Alexander III the Peacemaker (St Petersburg) : 1881 -1894
- Saint Nicholas II (St Petersburg) :1894-1917

Tsars of Russia and Karjala
(1715 -1809)

- Peter I the Great: 1682-1721
- Catherine I : 1725-1727
- Peter II : 1727-1730

- Anna : 1730-1740
- Ivan VI (child -disputed):: 1740-1741
- Elizabeth : 1741-1762
- Peter III : 1762
- Catherine II the Great: : 1762-1796
- Paul I : 1796-1801
- Alexander I the Blessed : 1801- 1825

Tsars of the Grand Duchy of Finland
(1809 – 1917)

- Alexander I the Blessed : 1801- 1825
- Nicholas I 1825-1855
- Alexander II the Liberator 1855- 1881
- Alexander III the Peacemaker : 1881 -1894
- Saint Nicholas II :1894-1917

Bolshevik Rulers of Russia
(1922 – 1964)

- Vladimir Lenin 1922-1924
- Alexei Rykov 1924-1926
- Joseph Stalin 1926-1953
- Georgy Malakov 1953-1955
- Nikita Krushchev 1955-1964

Grand Dukes of Finland
(13th to 16th century)

Between the 13th and 16th centuries the Swedish monarchs granted feudal title to Finland to their relatives. Finland basically became an independent principality / duchy ruled by the Duke of Finland. The most noted of these was Prince John 1556-1563 who settled in Turku and established a renaissance court there. Later in 1581 as King John III, he assumed the subsidiary title Grand Prince of Finland and Karelia. "Karelia" was soon dropped from the title and assumed part of Finland.

1. Benedict Duke of Finland 1284-1291 (also Bishop of Linkoping)
2. Prince Waldemar Duke of Finland 1302-1318 (also 1310-1318 of Uppland and Oland)
3. Christina , Duchess of Finland 1302-1305 the consort of Prince Waldemar
4. Princess Ingeborg Duchess of Finland 1312-1353 the second consort of Prince Waldemar
5. Benedict Duke of Finland 1353-1357 (also of Halland)
6. Ex King Carl Lord of Finland 1465-1467, then (again) King Carl II (VIII) of Sweden
7. Prince John Duke of Finland 1556-1563, later King John III of Sweden
8. Princess Catherine Duchess of Finland 1562-1563 , consort of Prince John, later Queen of Sweden
9. Prince John Duke of Finland 1589-1607 (also of East Gothland 1606-1618)
10. Crown Prince Gustav Adolph Grand Duke of Finland 1607-1611 (also Duke of Sodermanland, Estonia and Vastmanland, then King Gustav II Adolph of Sweden

The Swedish Governor Generals of Finland
(1623 - 1808)

The Swedish Kings from 1521 (King Gustaf I of Vaasa) until 1809 when King Gustav IV lost Finland to Russia, were also the Grand Prince of Finland

After the final abolition of the Duchy of Finland and related feudal privileges in the late 16th century, the King of Sweden, while also the Grand Prince of Finland, usually granted rule of most or all of Finland to a specially appointed Governor-General. The Governor General took care of the matters more or less according to his own best judgement. Best known of these officials is Count Per Brahe.

1. Nils Bielke (1623–1631)
2. Gabriel Oxenstierna (1631–1634)
3. Per Brahe (1637–40, 1648–54)
4. Gustav Evertsson Horn (1657–1658)
5. Herman Fleming (1664–1669)
6. Henrik von Rehbinder (1672-1680)
7. Carl Nieroth (1710-1712)
8. Gustaf Fredrik von Rosen (1747–1752)

Commanders of the Fiefdom of Viipuri & Karjala
(1293 – 1534)

The Swedish commanders of the castle wielded a formidable military and political power. During the 13th-15th century the province of Viipuri was almost an independent entity. During these times commanders pursued their own foreign and economic policies with interests of the province in mind and quite often with no regard whatsoever to the wishes of government in Stockholm.

As well as being responsible for holding the south eastern border of Sweden the fiefholders were also responsible for holding the northern border. In 1470s, they established another castle, OlaviLinna, over 100 kilometers north of Vyborg. Through the Middle Ages, that fortress remained under the command of Vyborg.

Under Swedish rule, Vyborg was closely associated with the noble family of Bååt, originally from Småland. The late-medieval commanders and fief holders of Vyborg were (almost always) descended from or married to the Bååt Family. Iin practice they functioned as Margraves (though not having this as their formal title), having feudal privileges and keeping all the crown's incomes from the fief to use for the defense of the realm's eastern border.

The founder of Viipuri Castle in 1293 and Karjala's first ruler was Torgils Knutsson.

In 1320, Lord Peter Jonsson (Haak) purchased the castle and its dominions from the Swedish crown. Thus began a 200 year "dynasty".

- 1320 - 1338 (or later): Peter Jonsson (In 1336 he was also Governor of all Finland)
- 1340 Dan Niklasson
- c 1348: Gerhard Skytte
- 1357 – 1364: Nils Turesson Bielke, kingdom's Lord High Justicar, son-in-law of Peter Jonsson's brother
- 1360s: Nils' heirs
- 1370 : King Albrckt
- 1371 – 1386: Bo Jonsson Grip (Also Governor of all Finland), Lord High Justiciar
- 1386 – 1399: Karl, Charles Ulysson, kingdom's Lord High Constable, stepson of a niece of Peter Jonsson
- 1403 – 1417: Tord Bonde, Lord High Constable, distant cousin of Peter Jonsson
- 1417 – 1442: Kristiern Krister Nilsson Vaasa, Lord High Justiciar, brother-in-law of Tord Bonde
- 1440 – 1448: Karl, Charles Knutsson, Lord of Fogelvik (b. 1408 - d. 1470), Lord High Constable, grandson of Charles Ulvsson and of TordBonde. Became King of Sweden in 1448
- 1457 – 1481: Erik Akselsson Tott (b. c.1420 - d. 1487), great-grandson of Tord Bonde, son of a first cousin of Charles Knutsson – Built the medieval walls around Viipuri
- 1481: Lars, Laurens Axelsen Thott, brother of previous commander Erik Tott
- 1483: Ivar, Iver Axelsen Thott, Overlord of Gotland, brother of previous, son-in-law of Charles Knutsson
- 1483 – 1495: StenSture the Elder, Kingdom's Regent, nephew of Charles Knutsson, great grandson of Charles Ulvsson, grandson of Charles Knutsson
- 1495 – 1496 : Knut,Knut Posse (d. 1500)
- 1497 – 1501: again Sten Sture the Elder (b. 1440 - d. 1503), between his terms as Regent of Sweden
- 1499 - May 1511: Erik Turesson Bielke (d. 1511), great-great-grandnephew of Nils Turesson
- 1511 – 1513: Gunilla Johansdotter Bese, widow of Eric Bielke, her predecessor
- 1513 – 1520: Tony Eriksson Tott, son-in-law of the two previous, great-nephew of Erik Akselsson, Laurens and Ivar of Gotland
- 1525 – 1534: Johan Count of Hoya and Bruchhausen (d. 1535), son-in-law of StenSture's nephew, brother-in-law of the reigning king Gustav I.

In 1534, Gustav I of Sweden, Sten Sture's grandnephew, abolished the independent fief.

When the next commander of Viipuri castle, Lord Nicholas Grabbe , took command (1534–45), he did not receive the feudal privileges held by earlier commanders.

Presidents of Finland
(From Finland's independence in 1917 to 1982)

- Kaarlo Stahlberg 1919-1925
- Lauri Relander 1925-1931
- Pehr Svinhufvud 1931-1937
- Kyosti Kallio 1937-1940
- Risto Ryti 194-1944

- Carl Gustaf Mannerheim 1944-1946
- Juho Passikivi 1946-1950
- Urho Kekkonen 1956-1982
- Carl Gustaf Mannerheim: Regent 1918-1919

Owners of the Kavantsaari Estate
(1500 to 1944)

In Kavantjarvi there were two fiefdom land holdings by 1500 – Saviniemi and Kavantsaari.

1.) The smaller land holding, Saviniemi, changed hands by marriage and trade/sale from:

- the Mjohundin family
- to the Stalarmin family
- to the Stubbelle, and, later
- to the Boijelle family.

About 1655 it was combined into the larger Kavantsaari estate owned by Taube/Rehbinder

2.) The main Kanvantsaari estate came into existence during the reign of Kustaa Vaasa of Sweden.

1. During King Kustaa Vasa's (Kustaa I) reign (1523-1560) it was owned by Maunu Niilonpoika Stiernfors the Steward of Viipurin Linna.
2. Mauno in 1555 had a disagreement with the king and was called back to Sweden and the land reverted to the Crown.
3. In 1562 King Erik XIV bestowed it to Bertil Goraninpoika Mjohundi who was also the Steward of Viipurin Linna.
4. Next it was bestowed on the Sklam family. They abandoned it, and it reverted to the Crown.

5. Queen Kriistina of Sweden (1632-1654) granted it to Lieutenant Colonel Bernard Taubelle. The grant included all Kavantjarvi and the Ahvola woods. It had 12 tenant farms. The lands were granted tax free forever for the nobility to enjoy (ralssitalo)
6. Around 1655 Henrik Rehbinder bought the lands. Rehbinder was Governor General of Finland from 1672 to1680 and Taubelle's brother in law. Rehbinder as well arranged a deal with Boijen to exchange his Hame land for the Boijen Saviniemi holdings, ending up owning both Kavantsaari fiefdoms. The additional land had ten crofters.
7. Upon Rehbinders death - his and Taubens heirs were unable to retain the holding and it reverted to the Swedish crown.
8. In 1710 after the loss of Karjala to Russia in 1710 it became the property of the Russian crown
9. For some years it served as the Colonel's headquarters/ administrative centre
10. In 1726 Katharine the Great granted the estate to Major General Ivan Schuwaloff the commander of Viipuri. The estate remained with the Schuwaloff family until 1803

11. In 1803 it was bought by the Olchi merchant family of Viipuri

12. In 1846 the estate was bought by Count Carl Gustaf Mannerhiem the President of the Court of Appeals

13. Soon thereafter in 1848, Mannerheim sold it to the Governor of Viipuri, Major General Alexander Thesleff (wife Eugenia (Jenny) Amalie Thesleff). It remained with the Thesleff family until Finland lost Karjala to Russia in 1944.

14. During the time of Olchin – Mannerheim – Thesleff, 25 crofts were established in Kavantsaari – 11 of the crofts were from the original Saviniemi hovi

15. Jenny Thesleff managed the estate after her husband Alexander died in 1856 until 1871 when Nikolaj came of age. Jenny and Major General Alexander Thesleff had 4 children:

   a. Alexander [1846-1905] – owned Jusstila sawmill

   b. Olga [1849-1911] & Berndt Aminoff

   c. Petter [1851 - 1915] – My probable great grandfather

   d. Nikolaj [1851-1909]

16. Nikolaj [1851-1909] & Mathlida Iversen [1862-1939]

   a. Jenny [1889-1935]

   b. Leo Alexander [1887 - ?]

   c. Nikolai Julius [1891-1959]

   d. Kurt [1895-19136]

17. Nikolai Julius [b. 1891 d. 1959 Janakkala Finland] & Agnes Julie Marie Reinberg [1895-1944]

18. No children

Timelines

Finland and Karjala's Timeline

Karjala/Viipuri/Kavantsaari Timeline

Finland's War with Russia during WWII

A Timeline of Finland and Karjala's History Prehistory to WW II

Pre History:

- 8,000 to 6,500 B.C. – Askola culture (late Holocene)
- 6,500 to 4,000 B.C. – Suomusjarvi culture (early Neolithic)
- 4,000 to 2,500 B.C. – Comb Ware culture
- 2,500 to 2,000 B.C. – Battle Axe, Bell Becker cultures & Asbestos Ceramics
- 2,000 to 1,500 B.C. – Kiukaisten & Asbestos Ceramics
- 1,500 to 500 B.C. – Bronze Age
- 500 B.C. to 600 A.D. – Roman Iron Age
- 600 A.D. to 800 A.D. - Merovingian Age (Clovis to Charlemagne)

Swedish Karjala:

Viking Forays (780-1050 A.D.)
The Swedish-Novgorodian Wars: 1150-1323

- The First Crusade -1155
- 1155 - Bishop Henry arrives in Nousiainen to convert Finnish pagans to Roman Catholicism
- Second Crusade – 1250-1293
- Third Crusade 1293-1323
- 1293 - Torgils Knuttsson establishes Viipuri Castle (ViipurinLinna)
- 1323 – The Treaty of Pähkinnäsaari/ Noteborg: Finland, Karjala and Viipuri officially became Swedish territory. At that point no northern boundary was set as the area north of Savonlinna was inhabited only by nomadic Saami.

The Russo-Swedish War: 1495-1497:

- The Russo – Swedish War ended in 1497 without any major territory changes.
- 1523 - King Gustaf Vaasa of Sweden converts to Lutheranism and begins purge of Roman Catholics and lingering pagans
- 1534 King Gustaf Vaasa takes fiefdoms, including Viipuri and Karjala back to the crown.

The Livonian War: 1554-1595

- The Treaty of Täyssinä (Kakisalmi) of 1595, as well as providing Livonia to Sweden, expanded Finland north to Murmansk by the Barents Sea.

The Ingrian War (Inkerinsota): 1610-1617

- The Treaty of Stolbovo of 1617 ended the war, adding Ingria (the area just south west of St Petersburg) and the west coast of Lake Ladoga (Kexholm/Käkisalmi) to Karjala.

The Ruptuuri War (Ruptuurisota)- Sweden's Second Northern War: 1650- 1658

- The Treaty of Kardis, signed in 1658 maintained the territorial accords of the Treaty of Stolbovo of 1617. Religious boundaries however changed. Karjala's Orthodox Christians fled to Russia, rather than being forced to convert to Lutheranism.

Karjala Under the Tsars

The Great Northern War (The Great Hate): 1700-1721

- The Treaty of Nystad / Uusikaupunki of 1721:Viipuri and Karjala became part of Russia, known as Old Finland. The borders of modern day Finland reflect those drawn up in the Treaty of Nystad / Uusikaupunki. Sweden also lost its' territories in Ingria, Estonia and Latvia.
  - Peter I the Great: 1682-1721
  - Catherine I: 1725-1727
  - Peter II : 1727-1730
  - Anna : 1730-1740
  - Ivan VI : 1740-1741

The Second Northern War (The Lesser Hate): 1740-1743

- The Treaty of Turku (Abo) of 1743. The border was moved 65 kilometers further west to the Kymi River – providing Russia with control of the stretch from Kotka to Savonlinna. This placed the old fortresses of Hamina and Olavinlinna in Russia.
  - Elizabeth : 1741-1762
  - Peter III : 1762
  - Catherine II the Great: : 1762-1796
  - Paul I : 1796-1801

The Suomen Sota (Finland's War): 1808-1809

- Treaty of Hamina – September 1809: Sweden ceded Finland to Russia thereby ending over 600 years of Swedish rule of Finland. Finland became a Grand Duchy of Russia, reporting directly to the Tsar. Karjala became part of the Grand Duchy of Finland

Finland & Karjala under the Tsars:

- Alexander I : 1801- 1825
- Nicholas I 1825-1855

- Alexander II : 1855- 1881
- Alexander III : 1881 -1894
- Nicholas II :1894-1917

The Finnish Civil War

- December 6, 1917: Finland's Declaration of Independence
- January 26, 1918: Civil War begins
- Feb 3, 1918: Whites defeat Reds in Oulu
- February 5,1918 Ahvola Karjala front set up between Reds and Whites and battles continue for next 2 1/2 months
- April 4, 1918: German division lands in Hango
- April 5, 1918: Whites defeat Reds at Raudu in Karjala
- April 6, 1918: Whites under Mannerheim defeat Reds in Tampere. 11,000 reds imprisoned
- April 13, 1918: Germans defeat Reds in Helsinki. 6,000 Reds imprisoned
- April 2x, 1918: Red forces withdraw from Ahvola Karjala front to reinforce Viipuri
- April 29, 1918 : Whites defeat Reds in Viipuri. 10,000 Reds imprisoned
- May 1, 1918: 20,000 Reds placed in prison camps in Fellman Fields in Lahti
- May 5, 1918: Final Reds surrender at Kymenlaakso. 12,000 imprisioned
- May 15, 1918: Grandfather Juho Öhman arrested by the Whites and placed in prison camp
- August 2, 1918: Grandfather Juho Öhman released from Viipuri prison camp by State Crimes Tribunal

The Sunshine Years: 1918- 1939

- July 17, 1919: Finland adopts democratic constitution with a President elected for 6 years by an electoral college, a Prime Minister chosen by the President. A 200 member single chamber parliament elected thru universal suffrage to 4 year term to which Prime Minister and cabinet are held accountable

- October 14, 1920 Russia and Finland sign Treaty of Tartu officially recognizing Finland and agreeing on the borders

- January 1932: Russia and Finland negotiate non aggression pact valid until 1944

Karjala/Viipuri/Kavantsaari Timeline

- The area where Vyborg is located used to be a trading center on the Vuoksi River's western branch, which has dried up. The area was inhabited by the Karelians
- 1278 – Russian Prince Jaroslav conducts military foray into Karjala
- 1293 – ViipurinLinna established by Torkkeli Knuutinpoika – during the so-called "Third Swedish Crusade". The Roman Catholic bishop visits.
- 1306 - Torkkeli Knuutinpoika executed in Stockholm
- 1323 – Pahkinasaaren Rauha / Treaty of Noteborg – Sweden, Russia and the Hanseatic League sign Pahkinansaaren peace. Vyborg becomes part of Sweden.

- 1403 – Viipuri receives town status and rights from King Erik XIII
- 1411 and 1464 - Russian conducts raids into Karjala
- 1470 – Kaarle Knuutinpoika Bonde dies as King of Sweden. From 1442 to 1448 he commanded Viipuri Castle. He returned to Stockholm to become King of Sweden and Norway.
- 1474 – Russia continues to raid Karjala. Viipuri builds town wall and medieval walls. Olavi Linna construction begins in Savo Finland
- 1489 and 1495 - Further Russian raids
- 1495 - Knut Possen's big explosion in ViipurinLinna drove Russian attacking force from city
- 1496-1499 – During the Russo-Swedish War Viipuri withstood a prolonged siege by Daniil Shchenya

- 1520 - Governor of Viipuri, Rolof Matinpoika writes that the inhabitants are 'poor but well behaved people'

- 1523 - Lutheran religion endorsed by King Kuusta Vaasa
- 1554 – Viipuri becomes a Catholic dioceses
- 1555 - Russ attacked Viipuri again and were driven back by an army of Karelians at Kivennalla
- 1557 – Mikael Agricola dies and is buried in Viipuri
- *1566 - Kavantsaari estate established*
- 1570 – Long 25 year war between Russia and Sweden ends with Tayssinan peace in 1595
- 1572 - Russians burn and raid
- 1586-87 - Famine ' God grant that the poor people stay alive until we get grain in the spring/'
- 1594 – Swedish King Kaarle IX makes commoners tax free so they could fight Russians – promising worthy horses and good swords
- 1595 - Kakisalmi peace

- 1600 – 3 fireballs destroy almost all of the city
- 1605 - Church tax initiated
- 1617 – Stolbavan Peace reduces the military importance of Viipuri. Kakisalmi and Inkerinmaa become part of Sweden
- 1618- Forces raised for various Swedish Wars
- 1656 - Ruptuuri war. Karjalas Orthodox Christians flee to Russia. Lutheranism becomes the established
- 1700 – Great Northern War begins with Kaarle XII of Sweden attacking Poland
- 1710 – Viipuri surrenders to Peter the Greats forces.
- In early spring a 7500 man army came over Kronstadt to Viipuri. Viipuri had a 4,000 man defensive force and although Sweden had thousands of soldiers it did not send any.

- In late spring more artillery was more and ships were brought and Peter the Great himself arrived. Viipuri surrendered.
- 1713-1721 – The Great Hate with Russia and Sweden pillaging and burning Finland
- 1721 – Great Northern war ended by Uudenkaupingin Peace/ Treaty of Nystsadt. Viipuri and Karjala becomes part of Russia, known as Old Finland
- *1726 – Catherine I grants Kavantsaari to Ivan Schuvaloff, Governor of Viipuri*
- 1741 – The Lesser Hate /Hattujen War ends in 1743 with Sweden surrendering more of Karjala to Russia with the Turun peace
- 1790 - On July 4, one of the largest naval battles in history, the Battle of Vyborg Bay, was fought in the Vyborg Bay
- The Russo-Swedish War of 1788-1790 started by the new King Gustav III of Sweden ended in the Treaty of Varala with neither side gaining territory, although the Swedish army achieved victories
- After the war Russia began to strengthen the defences in Old Finland. General Alexander Suvorov was tasked in 1791 by the Empress of Russia, Catherine II, to create a strong fortification system for Viipuri.

- 1808 – Suomen Sota /Finland's War between Russia and Sweden ends with Finland being ceded to Russia in 1809 with the Treaty of Hamina
- 1812 – Finland becomes a Russian Grand Duchy under Alexander I. Viipuri and Karjala is joined with Finland

- *1837 - Karl Gustav Mannerheim buys the Kavantsaari estate*
- 1839 – Viipuri receives own court of appeal jurisdiction
- *1848 – Major General Alexander Adam Thesleff buys Kavantsaari estate*
- 1856 – Saimaa canal opened. This benefited the local economy as it opened the vast waterways of the Karelian Isthmus, Ladoga Karelia and South-Eastern Finland to the sea.
- *1856 - Jenny Thesleff opens school for Kavantsaari children*
- 1857 – Last marks of the old Kannaksen waterway disappears
- 1860 - Good road now from Viipuri to Kavantsaari, Antrea, Kirvu, Sortavala
- 1862 - Kavantsaari switched to Antrea parish from Viipurin Maaseurakunta
- 1866 - Home stills banned
- 1867 - Famine year
- 1870 – Viipuri has population of 13,466. Rail road between St. Petersburg and Finland completed
- 1892 - Rail road from Viipuri to Antrea and Imatra opened
- 1901 - Strike in Kavantsaari at granite works
- 1906 - Strike at Thesleffs estate due to some torppas being evicted
- 1909 – Kavantsaari coop founded
- 1909 - Marttas founded
- 1918 – Civil war starts with skirmishes in Viipuri

Finland's War with Russia during WWII

The Winter War: 1939-1940

- August 24, 1934: Russia and Germany sign Molotov Ribbentrop mutual non aggression pact. Finland is assigned to Russia's sphere of influence
  - September 1, 1939: Germany invades Poland
  - September 3,1939: WW II begins. UK, France, Canada (Sept 10) , Australia (Sept 3), New Zealand (Sept 3), and South Africa (Sept 6) declare war against Germany
  - September 17 1939 Russia invades Poland
  - WW II begins
- October 11 -12, 1939: Finnish delegation receives demands for concessions in Kremlin
- October 14, 1939: Finnish counter proposal
- October 31, 1939: Molotov demands further concessions from Finland
- November 3, 1939: Finns make final counter offer
- November 13, 1939: Negotiations broken off. Stalin orders plans for immediate offensive versus Finland
- November 26, 1939: Russia shells own village of Manilia and accuses Finland of doing it
- November 27, 1939: Finland denies shelling and produces eye witnesses confirming it. Russia denounces existing non aggression pact which was valid until 1944
- November 29, 1939: Russia breaks relations with Finland
- November 30, 1939: Russia begins bombing and shelling Finland. War begins
- December 1. 1940: Russia proclaims puppet Finnish Government led by former Finnish Red O Kuusinen
- December 3, 1939: Finland makes eloquent but futile appeal to United Nations to intervene
- December 3-6, 1939: Finns draw back in good order to main Mannerheim Line
- December 7, 1939: Russia's failed attacks against Mannerheim Line begin

- December 14, 1939: Russia expelled from League of Nations
- December 23, 1939: Finnish ill considered counter offensive
- December 29, 1939: Successful Finnish counter attack north of Lake Ladoga versus Soviet 8th army
- January 7, 1940: Soviet General Timosenko appointed commander of Russian forces
- January 8, 1940: Spectacular Finnish victory at Suomussalmi encircling and destroying 2 Russian divisions
- February 1, 1940: Russian start artillery and bombing offensive on the Kannas
- February 5, 1940: Britain and France agree to intervene in Scandinavia to help Finns but primarily to seize control of Norwegian ports and Swedish iron ore
- February 11, 1940: Initial breakthrough of the Mannerheim Line at Lahde. First major break through February 13th
- February 12, 1940: Finnish cabinet authorizes government to seek peace terms
- February 15, 1940: Finns withdraw to Intermediate Line
- February 29, 1940: Russian forces try to break out of mottis at East Lemetti. One division succeeds and one is annihilated
- March 1-5, 1940: Fighting at Back Line and around Viipuri
- March 5, 1940: Finnish delegation goes to Moscow
- March 5-13, 1940: Furious fighting on Viipuri Gulf and around Viipuri. Finns thwart major Russian break through
- March 13, 1940: Peace at 11:00 – noon Moscow time

The Continuation War: 1941-1944

- March 30, 1941: Russia forbids the formation of a Scandinavian Defense Union between Finland, Sweden, Norway and Denmark
-
  - April 6, 1940: WW II: Germany invades Denmark and Norway
  - May 10, 1940: WWII: Winston Churchill becomes Prime Minister of England
  - June 4, 1940: WWII: Dunkirk: British forces evacuate Europe
  - June 22, 1940: WWII : France surrenders
  -
- June 17, 1940: Russian military forces annex Lithuania, Latvia and Estonia
- June 29, 1940: Finland signs a trade agreement with Germany
- July 8, 1940: Sweden agrees to allows German troops to pass through
  - July 10, 1940: WWII; Battle of Britain begins
- August 15, 1940: Vaino Linna, Finnish Minister of Supply forced to resign by Russia
- September 12, 1940: Finland agrees to passage of German troops through Finland to Norway
- September 26, 1940: Germany begins arms shipments to Finland
- September 27, 1940: WWII; Germany, Italy and Japan sign Tripartite pact
- November 12, 1940: Germany influences Russia to not invade Finland
- December 19, 1940: Finnish president Kallio dies. Risto Ryti becomes President of Finland
- May 31, 1941: Finland asks Germany to guarantee its independence, help restore its' 1939 borders, and provide food and weapons.
- June 7, 1941: German forces move to Lapland from Norway
- June 10, 1941: German S.S.Nord forces arrive in Rovaniemi
- June 12, 1941: German 169th Infantry Division disembarks in Tornio

- June 18, 1941: All Finnish reserves called up: Uncles Erkki, Kauko, Toivo, Vilho, and Arvo leave for the army
- June 22, 1941: WWII; Germany launches Operation Barbarossa attack on Russia
- June 25, 1941: Russia bombs Finland
- June 25, 1941: In the evening Finnish Parliament declares war against Russia. Jatkosota begins

Lapland / Northern Finland 1941

- June 29, 1941: Germany begins Operation Platinfuchs attack against Murmansk
- July 1, 1941: German Murmansk attack stalls at Kalastajasaarento and Litsajoki River
- July 6, 1941: German Kantalahti station attack captures Salla.
- July 11, 1941: Finnish 3rd Division Louhi station attack reaches Sohjana River
- July 28, 1941: German Kantalahti attack stalls at Kairala Narrows
- July 31, 1941: Finnish 3rd Division Louhi attack reaches Kietstinki
- September 17, 1941: Finnish 14th Division Sorokka station attack stopped Ontajoki River by Mannerheim 40 kilometers short of the Murmansk Railway
- September 19, 1941: German Kantalahti attack stopped just over Old Finnish Border 75 kilometers short of Murmansk railway
- October 26, 1941: Finnish 14th Division links up with 8th Division west of Seesjarvi
- November 17, 1941: Finnish 3rd Division and German SS Nord Louhi attack stopped at Nauvaara 50 kilometers short of the Murmansk Railway

Finnish Kannas Assault 1941

- June 29, 1941: Kevyt Os 7 attack on Enso stopped on first day by Russian forces. JR 7 attack likewise stopped at

- July 31, 1941: Finnish IIAK starts attack down the eastern side of the Kannas
- August 17, 1941: JR27 of Finnish IIAK takes western side of the Vuoksi River at Hopesalmi north of Ayrapaa
- August 1941: Finnish IIAK start to cross over the Vuoksi River at Ayrapaa/ Vuosalmi
- August 1941: II AK begins attack down centre of the Kannas towards Leningrad
- August 21, 1941: Finnish IVAK begins attack down western side of Kannas
- August 29, 1941: Finnish IVAK liberate Viipuri
- August 31, 1941: Finnish forces on the Kannas advance over The Old Finnish Border from Lake Ladoga to Gulf of Finland.
- September 9, 1941: Mannerheim stops Finnish advance north of Leningrad. War on the Kannas settles into trench warfare for 2 ½ years

Finnish Ladoga – Stalin's Canal - Old Russia Assault 1941

- July 10, 1941: The Karjalian Army attacks towards south and east from north of Lake Ladoga
- July 24, 1941: The Karjalian Army advances to the Old Finnish Border at Vitele/ Tuulos River by east shore of Lake Ladoga
- August 15, 1941 The Karjalian Army takes Sortavala
- September 13, 1941: Finnish capture Syvari Bridgehead and cross Syvari River
- September 30, 1941: 8th division transferred out to Maaselka Front from south of Viipuri
- October 1, 1941; Uncle Kauko and Finnish forces capture Petroksoi
- October 19, 1941: 8th Division takes Paatane
- November 6, 1941: 8th Division begins attack towards Karhumaki on south shore of Seesjarvi
- December 5, 1941; Uncle Kauko and Finnish forces capture Karhumaki
- December 6, 1941; Finnish forces capture Poventsa
- December 7, 1941; Mannerheim stops further advance against Russia and war settles into trench warfare on the Maaselka front and the Syvari River.

- December 1941: JR45 of 8th Division take Maaselka Station on Murmansk Railway
- December 10, 1941: JR35 of 1st Division at Kirvu Station of Murmansk Railway
- December 8, 1941; England declares war against Finland but does no initiate any military action against Finland. The United States advises Finland not to advance further against Russia but never declares war against Finland.
- December 8, 1941; WWII, After Japan attacks Pearl Harbor on June 7th, the United States and England declare war against Japan
- December 11,1941; WWII; United States declares war against Germany
- December 1941 – June 9, 1944: trench warfare on all Finnish fronts
- June 4, 1942; Hitler visits Mannerheim in Finland to honor Mannerheim's 75th birthday
- November 3, 1942; Finnish cabinet forbids deportation of Jewish refugees
- February 2, 1943; WWII, German forces surrender Stalingrad
- July 10, 1943: WWII, Allied forces land in Sicily
- October 13, 1943; WWII, Italy surrenders and declares war against Germany
- November 28- December, 1943: WWII, Stalin, Churchill and Roosevelt meet at Tehran Conference. Closer relations result but no major decisions
- February 14, 1944: WWII, Hitler lifts siege of Leningrad
- June 6, 1944: WWII - Allied forces land in Normandy

Russian Summer 1944 Attack

- June 9, 1944: Russian forces begin assault on the Kannas
- June 12, 1944: Uncle Vilho wounded in withdrawal at Syvari Bridgehead
- June 16-18, 1944: Uncle Arvo at battle at Perkjarve during withdrawal up the western Kannas
- June 21– July 7, 1944 Vi ak retreats from syvarii and petroksoi to u line

- June 20 – July 9; Uncle Kauko and IIAK retreats from Karhumaki to U Line at Ilomantsi
- June 12-16, 1944: Uncle Toivo at Battle of Siiranmaki
- June 20, 1944: Viipuri falls to the Russian forces
- June 25 – July 9, 1944 : Battle of Tali-Ihantala
- July 4- 17, 1944 : Battle of Ayrapaa-Vuoslami
- July 10, 1944: Uncle Toivo forced to swim across the Vuoksi River as his company retreats from Vasikkasaari during the Battle of Ayrapaa-Vuosalmi
- July 3 – 10, 1944: Finnish forces stop Russian Viipuri Gulf assault
- September 5, 1944: Ceasefire between Finland and Russia begins
- September 19, 1944: Finland signs peace agreement with Russia
- May 8, 1945: WWII – Germany surrenders
- August 10, 1945: WWII- Japan surrenders
- September 12, 1945: President Mannerheim resigns for health reasons at the age of 80. Juho Passikivi becomes President of Finland.

The Lapland War: 1944

- June 23, 1944: Colonel-General Eduard Dietl, German Commander of the Lapland Front throughout the war, dics in an odd plane crash over the Alps. Replaced by Colonel-General Lothar Rendulic
- September 15, 1944: Lapland War begins. German begins gentlemanly withdrawal
- October 1, 1944: Finnish 11th Regiment lands in Tornio. Phoney War ends. Germany undertakes scorched earth withdrawal
- October 15, 1944: Rovaniemi taken by Finnish forces
- November 21, 1944: Finnish forces at Kargasniemi-Utsjoki in far north Lapland
- November 24, 1944: Finnish forces take Kilpsijarvi by the Norwegian border. War settles into trench war at Norwegian border. Lapland War effectively ended although formal end not until April 25, 1945
- April 27, 1944: Lapland War declared over

My Karjala Family

My Karjala Family

Father, Mother & Us Children

Kaarlo Tuira:

Born 1908 in Viipuri; lived through the Civil War; enjoyed a lively boyhood in Viipuri; educated as an artist and civil engineer; married mother in 1935; in the Civil Guard during the Talvisota as a commander of a panzer train car, and commander of a portion of Finnish railroad; in the Jatkosota built part of the Kemijarvi to Kelloselka railway and patrolled the railroad at night; immigrated with the family to Canada in 1951. Died in Canada.

Wrote memoirs of early Viipuri years.

Martta (Öhman) Tuira:

Born 1907 in Kavantsaari. Died in Canada. Grew up on the farm in Kavantsaari. Emigrated to Canada but returned to marry dad in 1935. Barely survived when their Viipuri home was demolished by a bomb during the Talvisota. Fled to Finland. During the Jatkosota lived in Kelloselka and Kemijarvi with the children as dad was building the railroad.

Us Children:

- **Terttu**: born 1936 in Viipuri .
- Recounted various memories of Viipuri and the war years
- **Tellervo**: born in Viipuri in 1937.
- Recounted memories of living at Great Aunt Brita's during the Talvisota and of Lapland during the Continuation War
- **Tuula**: born 1942 in Turku / Kemijarvi
- **George**: born 1944 in Iitti
- **Kaarlo** (myself): born 1947 in Kotka

Father's Family – The Tuiras

Grandfather Georg Tuira

Born in Oulu in 1879. Moved to Viipuri in 1906. Owned machine shop. Died in Viipuri in 1923. Buried in Viipuri Ristimaki cemetery.

Married Valencia Hellman who lived across the street in Oulu, but not until 1907 when they were in Viipuri.

Two children: Kaarlo Tuira and Yrjö Tuira

Grandmother Valencia Hellman

Valencia Hellman: born Oulu; died in Helsinki in 1966. Married Georg Tuira in 1907 in Viipuri. Home burnt by the Whites in the Civil War. Home bombed by the Russians in the Talvisota. Fled Viipuri for Finland returning during the Jatkosota only to flee again in 1944.

Dad's brother : Yrjö

Born in Viipuri, died 2003 in Hameeenlinna.

In the Civil Guard during the Talviosta and Jatkosota, operating the railroad and serving with an anti aircraft unit.

Inspiration for my interest in history and genealogy

Grandfather Georg's ancestors

- Great Grandfather Karl Tuira: born and died in Oulu
- Great Grandmother Johanna Äström: born and died in Oulu

Their Children

- Jaako Aleksander and Martta
- Worked with his brothers in St Petersburg. Settled in St Petersburg but fled back to Finland during the Civil War / Bolshevik Revolution

- His wife Martta's brother was a senior Red leader during the Civil War who escaped to St Petersburg
  - 4 children: Teuvo, Terttu, Marie Onerva, and
  - Iiris Sinikka
  - 2nd cousins – Pekka and Leeni
- Frans Axel and family
- Georg (my grandfather)
- Brita Helena
- Mother and my sisters stayed at her home in Kuopio during the Talvisota
- Eino Urho

Early Ruicka ancestors of Simo:

- Landowners in Simo from 1540 to 1825.
- Peter the Greats troops pillaged and plundered our village in 1714 during the Great Hate.
- Sweden's troops marched by our front steps in 1809 when they retreated to Sweden in 1810 at the end of the Suomen Sota with Russia.
- Great, great grandfather moved to Oulu in 1825, bought the Tuira farm and took the Tuira name
- Olli and Bridgetta Ruicka :
- Wealthy influential landowners. Burnt at the stake in Simo in 1560 as witches by the King Gustav of Sweden and the Lutheran bishop

Grandmother Valencia's ancestors

- Great Grandfather Henrik Hellman born 1837 in Kovijoki, died in 1898 Oulu.
- Ancestors home was the site of the Battle of Juthas during the Suomen Sota
- Sailor and ombudsman.

- Great Grandmother Maria Christina Carren: born Kristiinankaupunki died Viipuri.
- Home was shelled by the British navy during the Crimean War. Buried in the Swedish German cemetery in Viipuri

Their Children:

- Hjalmar & Anna
- Hjalmar moved to Viipuri around 1908. Larger than life character.
- Owned the Hellman Bakery in Viipuri. Died in the Poyrea Torni Viipuri market
  - 4 children: Anna, Tyyne, and
  - Veikko
  - Dad's cousin & boyhood friend. Wrote the Hellman Bakery memoirs
    - My 2nd cousin Elina
  - Vieno
    - My 2nd cousin Eeva

- Constance & Jonne Starck
- Grandmother Valencia's older sister and friend. Her husband Jonne co owned the machine shop with my grandfather Georg. Imprisoned as a Red in the Suomenlinna concentration camp in Helsinki during the Finnish Civil War
  - Valter: Dad's boyhood friend
  - Risto: Dads' boyhood friend
  - Bridget:

- Georg and Maija
- Saved from execution by the Whites during the Civil War by his brother Hjalmar
  - 4 children: Sylvia, Yrjo, Uno, Kalevi

- Grandmother Valencia

- Jarl

Mother's Family - The Öhmans

Hyvaa Mummo was born in 1848 in Joutseno Karjala, about fifty kilometers north of Viipuri.

Lived and worked on the Kavaantsaari farm for 12 years after her husband died. Died in Kavantsaari in 1924 when mother was 17

Grandmother Hilda Maria Tiainen

Born out of wedlock in 1879 in Saaminki Karjala, died 1954 in Oripaa Finland. Her father was probably Petter Thesleff

Married Juho Öhman

Raised the family of ten children on the farm in Kavantsaari

Fled the farm with the womenfolk in December 1939 at the start of the Talvisota

Returned in December 1941 during the Jatkosota

Fled once more in to central Finland in June 1944 when Karjala was lost to Russia

Great Grandmother (Rakas mummo) Henrika Tiainen

Born in Saaminki Karjala in 1854; died on the farm in Kavantsaari in 1921 when mother was 14. Buried in the Ihantala cemetery.

One of her ancestors Colonel Anders Munck led the Karjala Cavalry Regiment during the Ingrian War

Great Grandfather ??

Probably Petter Thesleff, the son of Major General Alexander Thesleff who owned the Kavantsaari estate

Grandfather Juho Öhman

Born in Jääski Karjala in 1877; died in Kotka Finland in 1946

Married Hilda Maria Tiainen

Established the family farm in Kavantsaari in 1903, operating it and raising a family until Karjala lost to Russia

Arrested and imprisoned in the Viipuri concentration camp as a Red by the Whites during the Civil War

Fled to Central Finland with the cattle herd in June 1939 at the end of the Talvisota

Returned during the Jatkosota and fled once more in June 1944 when Karjala lost to Russia

Great Grandfather Erkki Öhman

Erkki Öhman – born Viitasaari Finland, lived in Karjala, died Viipuri

Hired farm hand, city labourer

Great Grandmother Maria (Esikonen) Öhman

The Öhman Children

Hilda Maria:

Born in 1900 in Viipuri; Married Atu (Adolf) Leskinen; Died in 196x in New Jersey USA

Arrested by the Whites during the Civil War, narrowly escaping being executed

Lived in Viipuri

Fled to Central Finland with her children and the Öhman womenfolk in December 1939

Moved to Jyvaskyla Finland after the Talvisota, remaining there until moving to the USA in the 1960s

Aatu, her husband served as a messenger with the 3rd company of the 4th independent infantry battalion (3.Er P4) during the Talvisota; and with the 48th infantry regiment (JR48) in the Jatkosota

Two daughters Anna Liisa and Maija

Anna Liisa

Recounted many memories of the war years. Now lives in the USA

Erkki:

Born 1902 in Viipuri; died in 1941 in Forsaa ;buried in Ihantala cemetery

Took over Kavantsaari farm

Served as a food supply driver in the Talvisota with 4th independent artillery battalion (Er.Psto4)

Married **Saima** Kaukinen born 1908 in Muolaa Karjala in 1929

Wrote letters home to his family during the Talvisota

Their Children

Martti

Grew up on the Kavantsaari farm

11 years old when fled during the Talvisota

15 when left at the end of the Jatkosota

Sirkka

Grew up on the Kavantsaari farm

9 years old when fled during the Talvisota

13 when left at the end of the Jatkosota

Wrote memoirs of her childhood and war years

Yrjö (George)

5 years old when fled from the farm in December 1939

9 at the end of the Jatkosota

Irja

3 at the start of the Talvisota

7 at the end of the Jatkosota

Armas

Born 1905 in Syvalahti near Kavantsaari. Left for Amerika in 1928

Ester

Born 1906 in Kavantsaari. Left for Amerika in 1928

Martta (mom – born 1907 in Kavantsaari)

Tyyne

Born in 1910 in Kavantsaari

Kauko

Born 1912 in Kavantsaari

Served in the Talvisota as a driver with the 4th construction battalion (Rak.P4) on the IV army corps Ladoga front

In the Jatkosota a light machine gunner, driver, clerk, and prison guard with the 35th infantry regiment (JR35) on the Ladoga front. Married Margit. One son Roy (Raimo) during the Jatkosota

Toivo

Born 1914 in Kavantsaari

Served in the Talvisota as a rifleman with the 1st infantry brigade (1.Pr). Fought on the Kannas

In the Jatkosota he was a light machine gunner with the 7th light brigade (Kev.Os.7) and the 7th and 28th infantry regiments (JR7 and JR28). Fought on the Kannas

Married to Alina. One child Olavi during the Jatkosota

Vilho

Born in 1917 in Kavantsaari

In the Talvisota was a medic with the 21st Anti- Aircraft battery in Antrea (I/21 Kev it.ptri)

In the Jatkosota was a supply column leader with the 8th Division and infantry man with the 45th infantry regiment (JR45)

Arvo

Born 1919 in Kavantsaari

Combat engineer (Pioneer) in the Talvisota with the (3./Pion Koul); in the Jatkosota with the Combat Engineering Battalions 4, 2, and 14 (Pion. P4 – 2- 14) and in the Lapland War with the 14th combat battalion (Pion P 14)

APPENDIX F

MAPS

The medieval walled town of Viipuri in 1500

My Families Finland

Finland and my ancestral homes

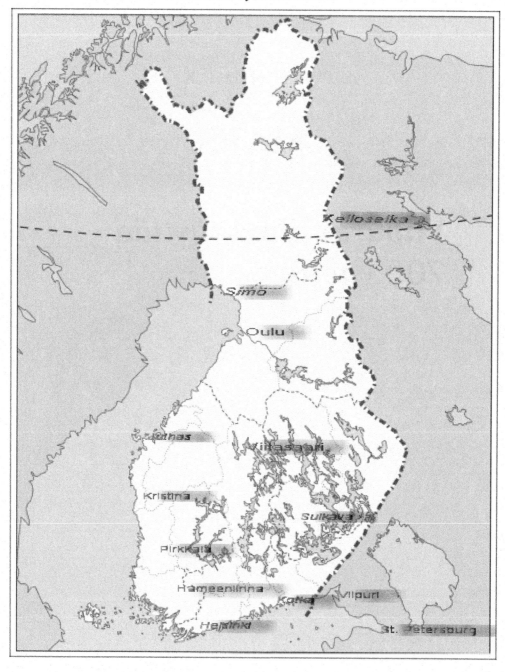

Viipuri

Viipuri in 1700 – a walled fortified town

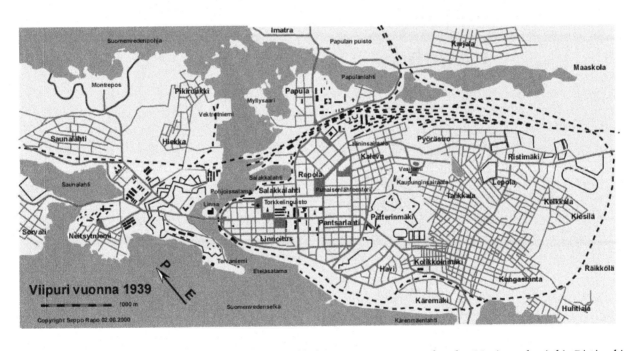

Viipuri in 1939. Our home was in near Pyorasuo. Grandfather Georg & great grandmother Maria are buried in Ristimaki

Karjala

Finland during the Civil War

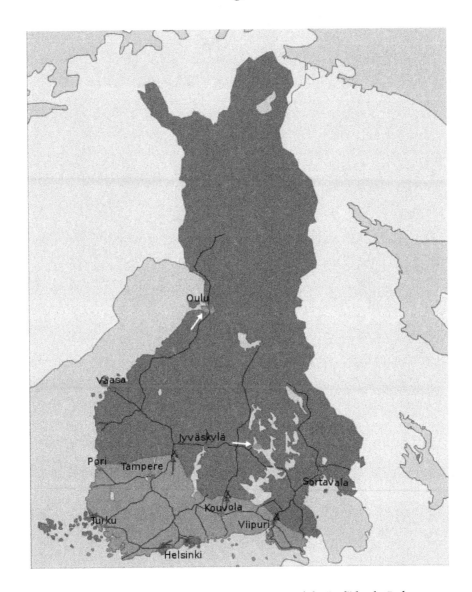

The blue area was controlled by the Whites and the "red" by the Reds

Talvisota Theatres

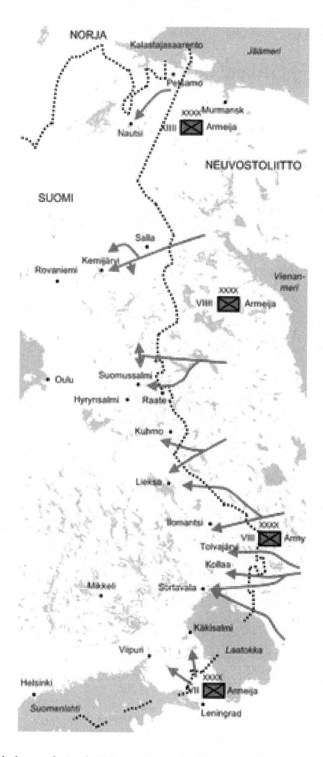

The battle theatres during the Talvisota showing the Russian attack.. All were in Karjala

Finnish Army on the Kannas

November 30, 1939

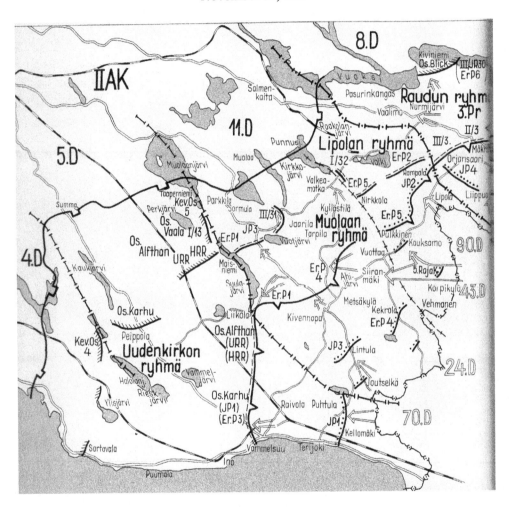

Positions of the Finnish Army Corps and Divisions at the start of the Talvisota. Note the location of the Lipola Delaying unit of Uncle Erkki and the Muolaa Delaying Unit of Uncle Atu – and Lipola and Kekrola on the Russian border where they located when fighting broke out November 30, 1939

Karjala

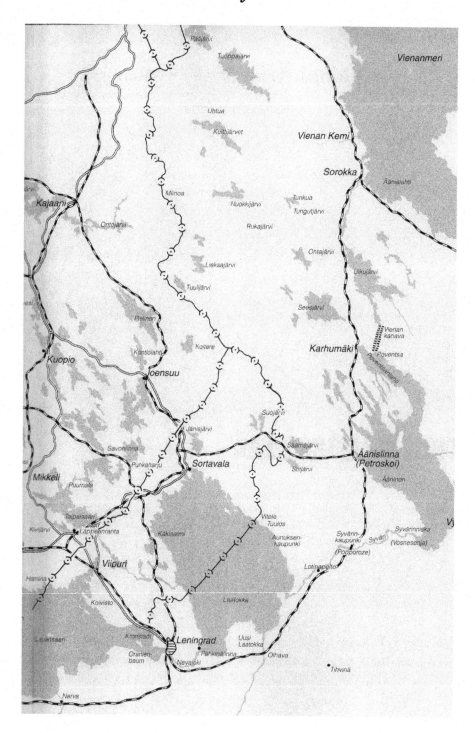

During the Jatkosota Uncles Arvo, Toivo and Aatu fought between Viipuri and Leningrad; Uncles Kauko and Vilho from Sortavala to Petroksoi and north of Karhumaki. In 1943 moved south to the Syvari River

The Karjala Kannas

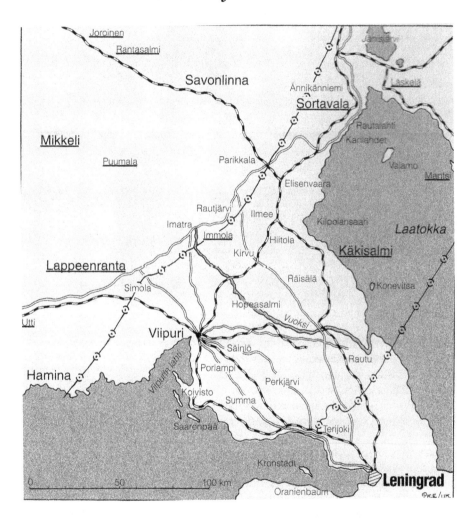

Kannas Defensive Lines

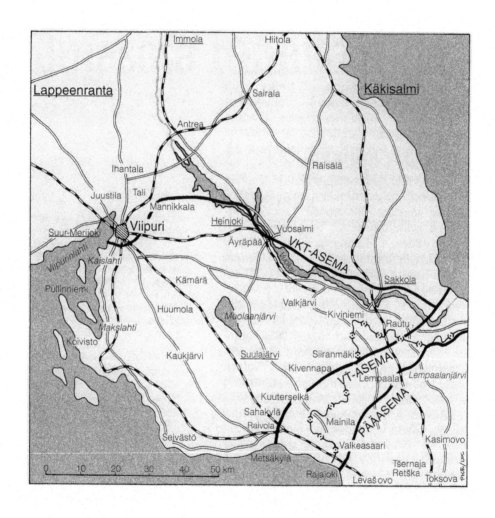

The Western Kannas

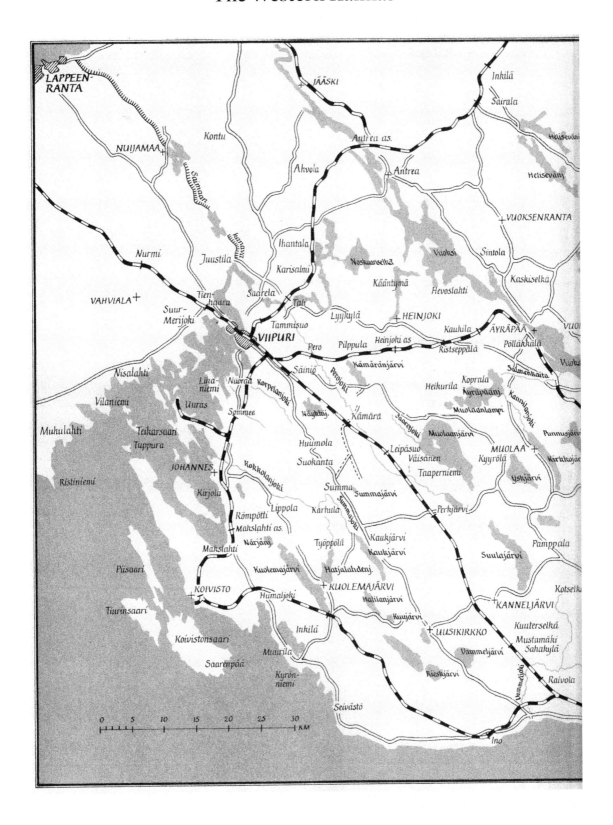

The Eastern Kannas

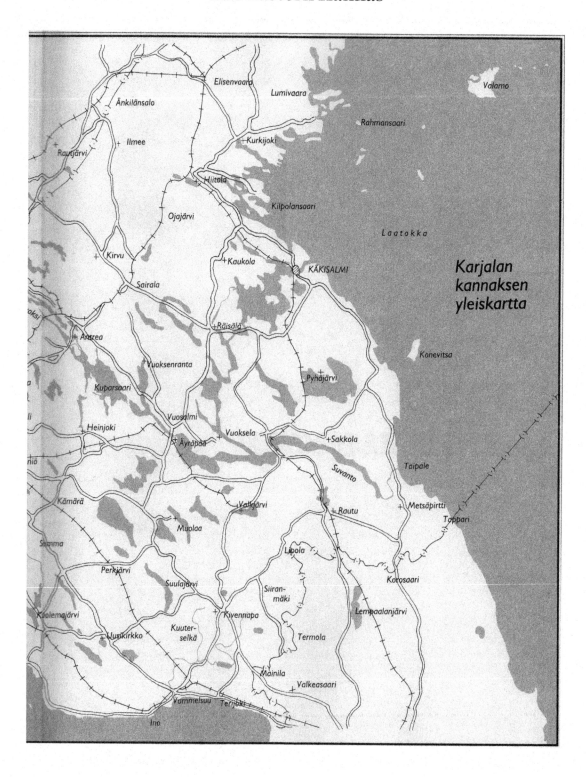

Ladoga & Old Russia

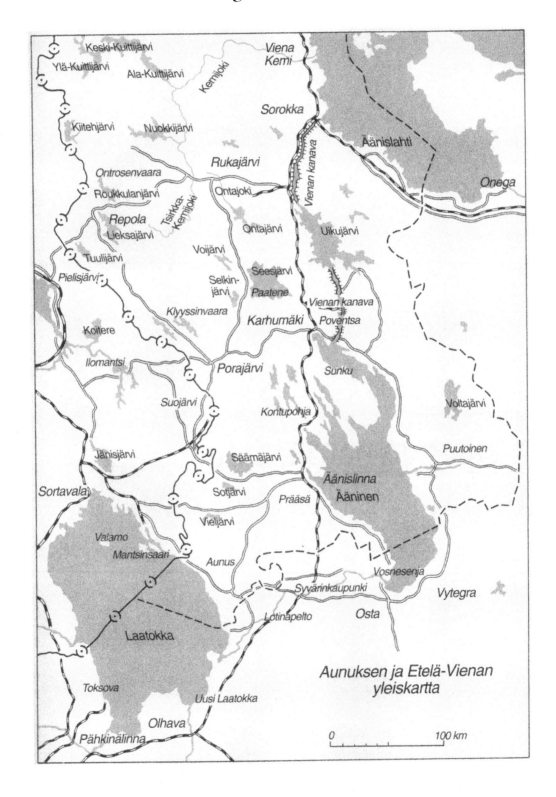

Keski-Kuittijärvi
Ylä-Kuittijärvi
Ala-Kuittijärvi
Viena
Kemi
Kemijoki
Kiitehjärvi
Nuokkijärvi
Sorokka
Äänislahti
Ontrosenvaara
Rukajärvi
Onega
Roukkulanjärvi
Ontajoki
Vienan kanava
Repola
Tsirkka-Kemijoki
Ontajärvi
Uikujärvi
Lieksajärvi
Voijärvi
Tuulijärvi
Selkin-
järvi
Seesjärvi
Pielisjärvi
Paatene
Klyyssinvaara
Vienan kanava
Koitere
Karhumäki
Poventsa
Ilomantsi
Porajärvi
Sunku
Suojärvi
Voltajärvi
Kontupohja
Puutoinen
Jänisjärvi
Säämäjärvi
Äänislinna
Ääninen
Sortavala
Sotjärvi
Prääsä
Valamo
Vieljärvi
Mantsinsaari
Aunus
Vosnesenja
Syvärinkaupunki
Vytegra
Lotinapelto
Osta
Laatokka
Aunuksen ja Etelä-Vienan
yleiskartta
Toksova
Uusi Laatokka
Olhava
0   100 km
Pähkinälinna

Murmansk

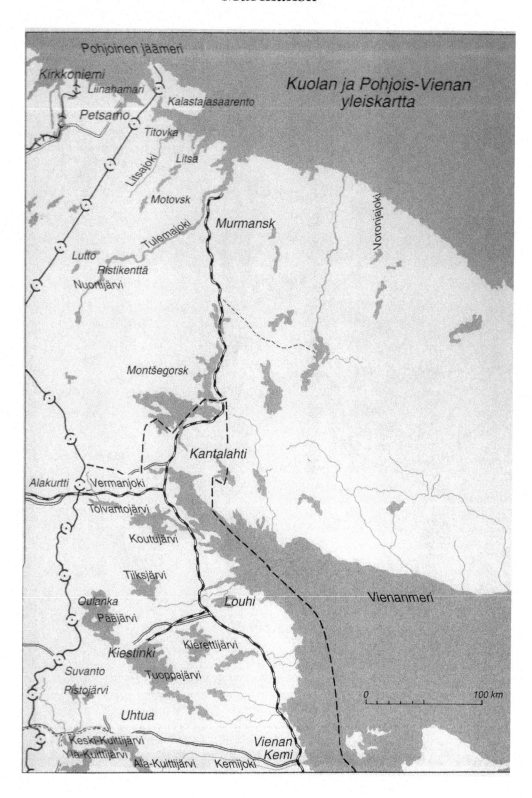

Pohjoinen jäämeri

Kirkkoniemi
Liinahamari
Kalastajasaarento
Petsamo
Titovka
Litsa
Litsajoki
Motovsk
Tulemajoki
Murmansk
Lutto
Ristikenttä
Nuortijärvi

Kuolan ja Pohjois-Vienan
yleiskartta

Voronjajoki

Montšegorsk

Kantalahti

Alakurtti
Vermanjoki
Tolvantojärvi
Koutujärvi
Tiiksjärvi
Oulanka
Pääjärvi
Louhi
Vienanmeri
Kiestinki
Kierettijärvi
Suvanto
Tuoppajärvi
Pistojärvi
Uhtua
Keski-Kuittijärvi
Ylä-Kuittijärvi
Ala-Kuittijärvi
Kemijoki
Vienan Kemi

0   100 km

Karjala Railway Map before the War

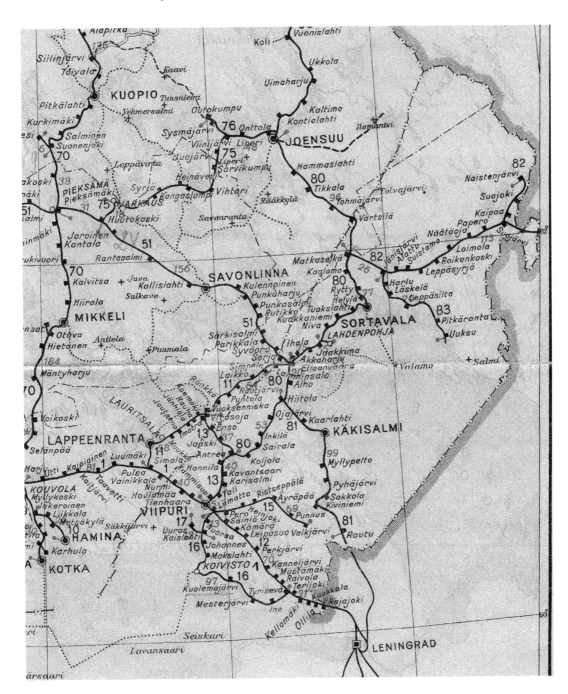

My father's railway map of the Kannas and surroundings

The Viipuri Battle

June 20, 1944 2

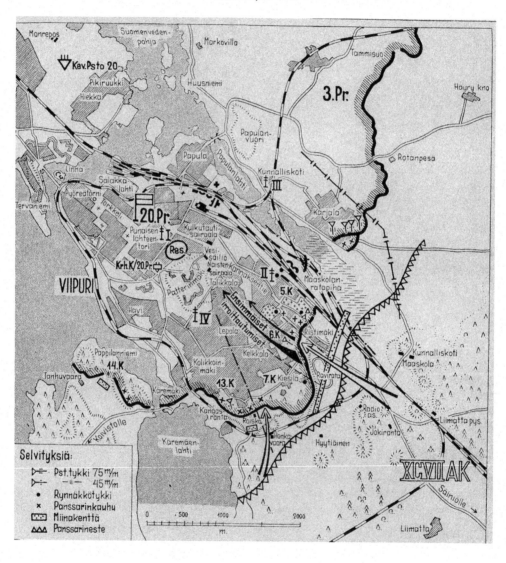

Lapland War

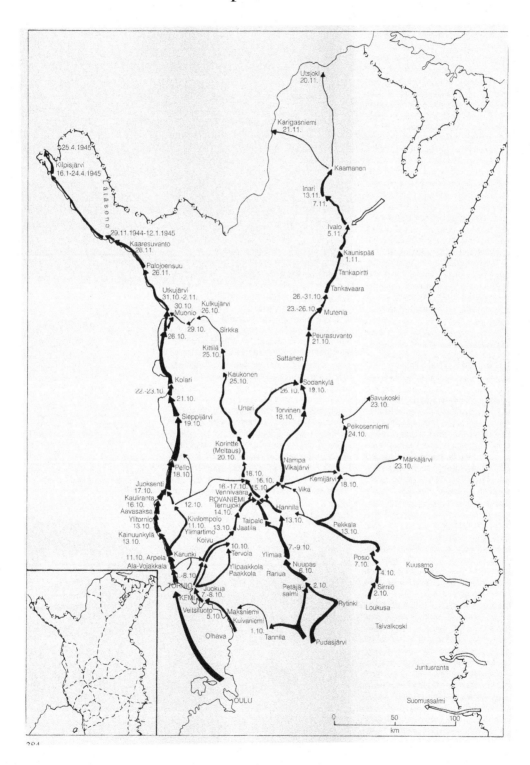

Utsjoki
20.11.

Karigasniemi
21.11.

Kaamanen

Inari
13.11.
7.11.

25.4.1945

Kilpisjärvi
16.1-24.4.1945

Ivalo
5.11.

Kaunispää
1.11.

29.11.1944-12.1.1945

Kaaresuvanto
28.11.

Palojoensuu
26.11.

Tankapirtti

Tankavaara

26.-31.10.

Utkujärvi
31.10.-2.11.
30.10   Kulkujärvi
Muonio   26.10.

23.-26.10.   Mutenia

26.10.

29.10.   Sirkka

Peurasuvanto
21.10.

Kittilä
25.10.

Sattanen

Kaukonen
25.10.

Savukoski
23.10.

Kolari

Sodankylä
19.10.

22.-23.10.

26.10.

21.10.

Unari   Torvinen
18.10.

Pelkosenniemi
24.10.

Sieppijärvi
19.10.

Korintte
(Meltaus)
20.10.

Nampa
Vikajärvi

Märkäjärvi
23.10.

Pello
18.10.

18.10.
16.-17.10. 16.10.
Vennivaara 15.10.

Kemijärvi
18.10.

Vika

Juoksenti
17.10.

Kauliranta
16.10.
Aavasaksa
Ylitornio
13.10.

ROVANIEMI
Ternujoki
14.10.

Hannila

12.10.

Kivilompolo
11.10.   Taipale
Yimartimo   Jaatila
13.10.

13.10.

Pekkala
13.10.

Kainuunkylä
13.10.

Koivu

10.10.
Tervola

Ylimaa

7.-9.10.

Posio
7.10.

Kuusamo

11.10. Arpela   Karunki
Ala-Vojakkala

Ylipaakkola
Paakkola

Nuupas
6.10.

Ranua

4.10.

1.-8.10.

TORNIO   Juokua
KEMI   7.-8.10.

Petäjä-
salmi

2.10.

Sirniö
2.10.

Veitsiluoto   Maksniemi
5.10.   Kuivaniemi

Rytinki   Loukusa

Taivalkoski

Olhava   1.10.   Tannila

Pudasjärvi

Juntusranta

OULU

Suomussalmi

0   50   100

km

About the Author

Karl Armas Tuira

Karl came to storytelling late in life after a global career as a high tech manager. Born in Kotka Finland he immigrated to Canada in 1951. His father was from the city of Viipuri in Karjala, and his mother from the nearby Kavantsaari countryside. His roots trace back 500 years in Karjala and Finland.

After earning his BA and MBA he held senior positions with high tech companies and management consultancies in Canada, the USA, Australia, and Europe. During his 40 year business career he conducted many studies and wrote many reports. He learned to make sure he got the facts correct and to write simply and to the point.

After retiring he wrote four family history books – one for each of the ancestral lines of his children.

Always interested in history, he became impassioned by the history of Karjala, the part of Finland that was lost to Russia in WW II. As there were no books in English (and very few in Finnish) on Karjala, he decided to write and publish a book on the subject. After over five years of research and writing the result is this book – The Karjala Story: Revolution, War, Wonder –the recounting of the history of Karjala from Prehistory to WW II as seen through the eyes of his family.

Karl now spends his time with wife and dog, enjoying gardening, sports and his grandchildren...and wondering whether to write again or learn to become a master BBQ chef and putter in the flower garden.

CPSIA information can be obtained
at www.ICGtesting.com
Printed in the USA
BVOW09s1625190318
510798BV00010B/189/P